# Muslim Friday Prayer

*A Collection of 100 Khutbahs
& Fiqh of Jumu'ah*

**BOOK POWER PUBLISHING**

**Muslim Friday Prayer: A Collection of 100 *Khutbahs* & *Fiqh* of *Jumu'ah***

Published by Book Power Publishing, a division of Niyah Press

www.bookpowerpublishing.com

Book Power books may be purchased for educational, business or sales promotional use.

For more information, email support@bookpowerpublishing.com

You may also contact the author directly at muslimfridayprayer@gmail.com

ISBN: 978-1-945873-22-5

*Islam / Religion / Spirituality*

# Muslim Friday Prayer

*A Collection of 100 Khutbahs*
*& Fiqh of Jumu'ah*

## DR. MUNAWAR HAQUE

**BOOK POWER**

DETROIT, MICHIGAN

*Dedicated in Humble Gratitude to the Caring Community of the
American Muslim Diversity Association (AMDA)*

# ADVANCE PRAISE
# FOR MUSLIM FRIDAY PRAYER

*"The author has carefully compiled a beautiful collection of 100 Friday sermons delivered by him over the past decade or so. The topics cover diverse subjects that are both educational and inspirational. Each sermon is a reminder for reflection and draws upon timeless truths from the Qur'an and the Sunnah - the two primary sources of Islam. Expressed very clearly, the message conveyed in each sermon is completely intelligible and easily understood. This book is a valuable resource for khateebs, especially those who opt to give khutbahs voluntarily and are hard pressed with time because of their regular occupations.*

*Additionally, the book also discusses the fiqh (rulings) of Friday prayer in clear and plain language. This section of the book will be helpful and useful to anyone seeking answers to questions related to different rulings of the Friday prayer.*

*This is an excellent work of reference and source of knowledge for students of Islam, and will be especially beneficial to all those who are engaged in delivering Friday sermons at mosques, colleges and universities, state and federal correctional facilities, and corporate offices.*

*I have personally benefitted from the author's sermons in my prison ministry work in state correctional facilities, and whole-heartedly recommend this book to the community. InshaAllah, it will be a valuable addition to the library of any student of Islam. May Allah Almighty reward Dr. Munawar Haque for his sincere efforts, ameen."*

**Dr. Amanullah Dada, Adjunct Professor, Lawrence Technological University, Southfield, MI; Principal, AMDA Academy, Sterling Heights, MI**

*"Comprehensive and inspirational are two words that describe the book under review. The author has skillfully discussed the essential rulings of Friday prayers and compiled one hundred of his sermons given over the years. The topics ordered alphabetically cover many areas of Muslim life, are non-controversial, and are bound to answer the questions arising in the most curious minds. The book is an excellent resource for khateebs and all others who want to know about essential topics in Muslim life. The book also offers an opportunity for personal reflections. Written in a lucid style, the beautiful collection of khutbahs is lovely, making the message conveyed easy to understand and retain. I highly recommend this book for all."*

**Dr. Amber Haque, Professor of Clinical Psychology, Doha Institute for Graduate Studies, Doha, Qatar**

*"All praise belongs to Allah Subhanahu Wa-Tala. He is the All-Wise and All-Knowing. Allah SWT sent down His divine revelations through His sincere messengers. I bear witness that there is no God except Allah, alone and without partner; to Him belongs the dominion and all praise, and He SWT has power over everything. And I bear witness that Muhammad, peace be upon him, is His messenger.*

*I have known Dr. Munawar Haque as an Imam, scholar of Islam, and a close friend. He has earned his Ph.D. degree in Islamic Studies with a specialization in Islamic Theology and Comparative Religion from the International Islamic University Malaysia (IIUM). As a professor there, he taught courses on Islamic Worldview, Islamic Jurisprudence and Ethics. Masha'Allah he is a well-rounded imam and scholar. He is also a very good person with a sweet personality.*

*He has committed a great deal of time and effort to prepare these excellent Khutbahs. The book is a thorough collection of what Muslims need to know about a wide range of subjects. It is an excellent read for all, particularly, Muslim youth. These one hundred Khutbahs discuss a variety of essential topics that are vital to a Muslim's daily life.*

*Early Muslims understood Islam theoretically and practically. That is why their lives reflected Islam through their every action. We need to do that as well. Non-Muslims do not read the Quran, but they read our characters and behaviors. Islam can be presented to the world as a successful way of life based on our manifestation of it as Muslims.*

*These Khutbahs will allow us to do this and would be great to study in our weekly gatherings or group discussions. We will undoubtedly learn a lot from them.*

*May Allah SWT reward Dr. Munawar in this world and the hereafter."*

**Ramzi Mohammad, Professor at Wayne State University, Member of International Scientific Signs of Quran, Author of "A Muslim's True Life Purpose"**

*"Assalaamu Alaykum, it is an honor and privilege for me to know Dr. Munawar Haque and to write a review on his book "Muslim Friday Prayer: A Collection of 100 Khutbahs & Fiqh of Jum'uah". After reading the book I find it very well researched with references from the Quran and hadeeth of our Prophet Muhammad SWS and clarification of the fiqh requirements from the four different major sunni madahib. The book begins by describing the fiqh of Jum'uah and other occasions where Khutbas are given. It covers different aspects of Friday prayers including its virtues and what is required before, during, and after the prayers. This comprehensive approach will enhance our understanding of the Jum'uah Prayers and worship benefiting every Muslim. This book is also an excellent guide for young Muslim leaders who want to learn how to give effective Khutbas. I think this book is a must in all Muslim homes, Masjid libraries, and especially with youth groups and MSA chapters.*

*I also find it to be very methodically described, covering all aspects of Jum'uah and other Khutbahs, followed by 100 well thought and designed Khutbahs."*

**Khalid Iqbal, Secretary of the Imams Council of Michigan, Founder of Rahmaa Institute**

*"Dr. Haque's work is great to use as a tool for trainers to train new imams on how to capture the attention of audiences at Friday ceremonies."*

**Imam Radwan Mardini of American Muslim Center**

*"Muslim Friday Prayer: A Collection of 100 Khutbahs & Fiqh of Jumu'ah" by Dr. Munawar Haque combines both important and essential information regarding to the juristic rulings of Jumu'ah Prayer and a rich variety of khutbahs with messages important for every Muslim. The khutbahs presented are well prepared and written from an analytic perspective both using the primary sources of Islam and contemporary social/scientific/psychological findings that help any audience to engage.*

*The themes presented throughout Dr. Haque's khutbahs are deeply rooted in the eternal message of the Qur'an and the Sunnah of Prophet Muhammad (SAW). Each is a beautiful reflection of the caring heart of a Muslim scholar who seeks to carry on the Prophet's legacy of conveying messages of hope, mercy, compassion, reconciliation and redemption for contemporary Muslim individuals, especially those struggling to find the true path.*

*Reading and reflecting on Dr. Haque's khutbahs, I have felt these messages can have a profound and deep effect on any Muslim on how to be inspired and transformed from a state of spiritual darkness to a state of guidance, peace and happiness through the light of the Loving and Merciful Lord and example of His Messenger (SAW). I believe that Dr. Haque's book will be a valuable resource for any imam, chaplain or khatib to be inspired and to inspire their respected congregation."*

**Mustafa Boz, Prison Chaplain**

# CONTENTS

## FIQH OF THE JUMU'AH PRAYER

# TRANSCRIPTS OF *KHUTBAHS*

# ABBREVIATIONS

The following abbreviations are used to represent common phrases recommended to be pronounced after the mention of the names of important individuals in Islam.

It is recommended to say out the phrase in your head when reading the names and these phrases. Think of these abbreviations as reminders.

(SWT)     *subhaanahu wa ta'aala*
"He is glorified and exalted"
Said after mentioning the name of Allah

(SAS)     *salla Allahu 'alayhi wa sallam*
"Peace and blessings of Allah be upon him"
Said after the name of the Prophet Muhammad

(AS)     *'alayhi as-salaam*
"Upon him be peace"
Said after the name of a prophet who came before the Prophet Muhammad

(RAA)     *radia Allahu 'anhu / 'anha*
"May Allah be pleased with him/her"
Said after the name of a companion of the Prophet

(RA)     *rahimahu Allah*
"May Allah have mercy on him"
Said after the name of a scholar from Islamic history

# PUBLISHER'S NOTE

The Muslim Friday prayer is a central part of Muslim identity worldwide and especially paramount to understanding the experience and identity of Muslims in the United States where it represents the primary regular community gathering.

The weekly *Jumu'ah* is a place of spiritual growth as well as community growth. By including Islamic reminders with the *fiqh* (rulings) of *Jumu'ah*, Dr. Haque simultaneously educates and inspires.

Dr. Haque has compiled a beautiful reference for students of Islam, *khateebs*, and speakers. It is also a rich resource for social scientists seeking to understand aspects of the Muslim experience in the U.S. Here we see a snapshot of what was discussed over a period of 7-9 years in one of the largest *masjids* in the state of Michigan, revealing the current events, social trends, and community concerns that were important to highlight each week.

As I read these *khutbahs*, I consider the fact that each of them was delivered live, in front of hundreds of people. People sat side by side listening to the exact same message, at the exact same time, with the exact same social circumstances happening around them. I reflected on what might have been their moments of attention or inspiration? How was the message received? Was it internalized and acted upon? Was it received with indifference? Did it light a small spark of awareness or questioning that the listeners carried with them for months or even years later?

The preservation and sharing of knowledge and the experiences of our elders has always been a cornerstone of Islam. We are excited to bring this volume forward to continue the written legacy of Dr. Haque and to inspire future generations by passing on these timeless messages of spirituality and community unity.

**Zarinah El-Amin**
Chief Spiritual Officer
Book Power Publishing

# ACKNOWLEDGEMENTS

All praises and thanks belong to Allah (SWT) for completion of this humble work. Peace and blessings of Allah (SWT) be upon the Prophet Muhammad (SAS) who duly conveyed the message of Islam to all of humanity.

First, I must express my special thanks and heartfelt gratitude to Imam Mustapha Elturk, Ameer of the Islamic Organization of North America (IONA), for graciously accepting to write the foreword of this book despite his many responsibilities. I had the privilege of working with him at IONA in the city of Warren, Michigan, and I was blessed to deliver my very first *khutbah* at the IONA *masjid* in 2011.

I wholeheartedly thank my son, Dr. Yousuf Haque, for providing insight into the rulings of the different schools of thought and the need to appreciate and respect all authoritative opinions. He also translated the invocations and supplications in the appendices which were generously provided to me by Sheikh Ahmed Suwaid, to whom I am also most grateful.

I am also thankful to Dr. Muhammad Azim and Dr. Ekramul Khan for going through the portion of the manuscript that covered the *fiqh* of the *Jumu'ah* Prayer and for making useful suggestions. Dr. Amanullah Dada, principal of AMDA's Sunday school and a prison ministry stalwart, was a constant source of inspiration to me throughout my journey from the time the thought of writing the book came to me until its publication.

My wife, Nasreen, has been very supportive as usual. She is very helpful and always a source of hope and inspiration in all my undertakings. The love of my children and the innocent smiles of my grandchildren cheered me up and rejuvenated me when I felt tired.

This book is intended to serve as an inspiration and a guide to believers on their journey toward Allah (SWT). I am deeply grateful to the people who made this book a reality: my family and friends who were my pillars through every step of this book's development; the publisher, Book Power Publishing, in particular Sr. Zarinah El-Amin; the editorial team, particularly the lead editor, Sr. Jennifer Crooker; the cover designer, Br. Ali Al-Katib; and the marketing and launch team, led by Sr. Nabila Ikram, for helping to bring this book to the reader.

Last, but not least, I would like to express immense gratitude to the Board of the American Muslim Diversity Association (AMDA) for wholeheartedly supporting the project, and the AMDA community for being the primary source of inspiration for the writing of this book. May Allah accept my own intentions and the intentions of all involved, named and unnamed. *Ameen.*

I pray that Allah (SWT) blesses this work and that the community will find it helpful and beneficial. I ask everyone who benefits from this book to please make *du'a`* for me and everyone who helped to make this book possible.

# FOREWORD

The Friday sermon (*khutbatal-Jumu'ah*) is an essential part of the life of a believer. Allah (SWT) has commanded in the Qur'an,

يَا أَيُّهَا الَّذِينَ آمَنُوا إِذَا نُودِيَ لِلصَّلَاةِ مِنْ يَوْمِ الْجُمُعَةِ فَاسْعَوْا إِلَى ذِكْرِ اللَّهِ وَذَرُوا الْبَيْعَ ذَلِكُمْ خَيْرٌ لَكُمْ إِنْ كُنْتُمْ تَعْلَمُونَ ۝

*O you who believe, when the call for the Jumu'ah (congregational) prayer is made, hasten to the remembrance of Allah and leave off your business. This is better for you, if you only knew. (al-Jumu'ah, 62:9)*

In addition to the many virtues of Friday and the congregational prayer, the sins of the believers are wiped out. The Prophet (SAS) said, "The five daily prayers and the time from one *Jumu'ah* to the next are an expiation for whatever sins come in between them, so long as one does not commit a major sin." Believers attend the Friday sermon to be reminded and admonished through the verses of the Qur'an and the sayings of the Prophet Muhammad (SAS).

Sermons are a unique form of address, and the content and delivery are equally important. I had the privilege to work with Dr. Munawar Haque at the Islamic Organization of North America (IONA) where he delivered *khutbahs* at the *masjid*. His background in Islamic theology and comparative religion has helped Dr. Haque convey messages effectively. His methodical approach keeps the listener focused, and he consistently researches his sermons and includes verses from the Qur'an and traditions of the Prophet (SAS) that are relevant to each subject. He addresses a variety of subjects including social and moral issues, as well as problems facing the Muslim community and ways to overcome such challenges. His sermons exhort congregants towards goodness and warn them from all types of evil. Dr. Haque engages congregants and invites them to think and reflect, then act and become better Muslims.

Dr. Haque's book, Muslim Friday Prayer: A Collection of 100 *Khutbahs* & *Fiqh* of *Jumu'ah*, makes a great addition to anyone's library. The book includes a collection of his sermons along with a chapter on the *fiqh* of *Jumu'ah* prayer, which is a very valuable section every Muslim should become familiar with to enhance his/her worship and gain maximum rewards. Dr. Haque covers every aspect of the Friday congregational prayer, including the virtues of the *Jumu'ah* prayer along with the etiquettes and rules of what to do before, during, and after it. I find it to be very useful and helpful.

May Allah (SWT) accept Dr. Haque's contribution toward knowledge and reward him for his efforts and hard work, *ameen*.

**Mustapha Elturk**
Ameer
Islamic Organization of North America, IONA
28630 Ryan Rd.
Warren, MI 48092

# PREFACE

All praises and thanks are for Allah (SWT), the Lord of the Worlds. May His blessings be upon the Prophet Muhammad (SAS), his family, his companions, and all those who follow them in righteousness until the Day of Judgment.

There are many books that contain a collection of Friday *khutbahs* (sermons), and there are many other books that discuss the rulings and procedures of the *Jumu'ah* (Friday) prayer. A humble attempt has been made in this book to combine a collection of *khutbahs* with the essential *fiqh* (rulings) of the *Jumu'ah* prayer that Muslims need to know. *Fiqh* is often described as the human understanding of the divine Islamic law as revealed in the Qur'an and the Sunnah. It is also applied to denote understanding, comprehension, and profound knowledge.

The chapter on the *fiqh* of the prayer helps the reader to know and comprehend the significance, virtues, rulings, and etiquettes related to the *Jumu'ah* prayer. The text of the "Sermon of Necessity" (*Khutbat al-Haja*), which the Prophet (SAS) used to recite at the beginning of the *Jumu'ah khutbah* has been incorporated. This is followed by a collection of transcripts of one hundred of my own *khutbahs*.

These *khutbahs* were delivered at the American Muslim Diversity Association (AMDA), a *masjid* (mosque) and Islamic center in Sterling Heights, Michigan where I have been serving as the imam and head of religious activities since 2014. The *khutbahs* discuss a wide range of subjects, covering the various dimensions of Islamic faith and practice, including moral and social issues as well as problems faced by the Muslim community and ways to face them. They exhort us to become the embodiment of the true message of Islam, and to think, live, and strive as good Muslims.

I have also included information and instructions for beginners on how to conduct the *Jumu'ah* prayer. Examples of traditional introduction and conclusion statements for the first and second *khutbahs*, such as the exhortation to have *taqwa* (God-consciousness),and the *Salawat al-Ibrahimiyya* (Salutations on Ibrahim) are given in Appendix 1. General *du'a`s* for the Muslim community *and du'a`s* for Muslims in adversity are given in Appendix 2. A few general *du'a`s* from the Qur`an and the Prophetic traditions have been compiled in Appendix 3. These have been translated into English for readers not well acquainted with classical Arabic.

The collection of *khutbahs* in these books can be used by *khateebs* (khutbah-givers), and other speakers as talking points for their presentations, not only for *Jumu'ah* prayer but for any occasion. Student and youth groups can also use them for group discussions and personal reflections.

May the Lord of the Worlds forgive my mistakes and make me consciously realize the enormity of the Day when every soul shall be individually summoned before Him to give an account of its stay on the earth. May He accept this humble effort with His Divine Grace. May peace and blessings of Allah be upon His last Prophet Muhammad, his family, companions, and all those who follow them in righteousness until the Day of Judgment.

**Munawar Haque**
Imam and Head of Religious Activities
American Muslim Diversity Association (AMDA)
44760 Ryan Road, Sterling Heights, MI 48314

# INTRODUCTION

The *Jumu'ah* prayer has a very special significance for Muslims: It is the weekly congregational prayer service where Muslims worship their Lord as one community. The word *Jumu'ah* is derived from the letters *jeem-meem-'ayn* in Arabic which mean "to gather." Muslims gather on this day every week, and Allah (SWT) has commanded the believers to gather for His worship. This congregational worship strengthens the bonds of brotherhood and rejuvenates *iman* (faith).

The five daily obligatory prayers are usually offered in congregation in every *masjid* in a locality but if one misses the congregation, these prayers can be offered individually. The *Jumu'ah* prayer, however, can be offered *only* in congregation. This provides an opportunity for all the people in the area to come together every Friday to listen to the *khutbah* (sermon) and pray together as the Prophet Muhammad (SAS) taught.

While migrating from Mecca to Medina in the year 622 CE, the Prophet (SAS) led the first Friday prayer (*Salat al-Jumu'ah*) at the settlement of Bani Salim ibn 'Awf on his way from Quba to Medina. Since then, *Jumu'ah* has remained a key Islamic institution.

The Prophet (SAS) used the Friday *khutbah* to convey his message to the people, to awaken their faith and inspire them to good deeds and a life lived in the service of Allah (SWT) and His creation. His Friday sermons were brief, to the point, and full of light and guidance. Generally, Muslims in the West try to maintain the original spirit and role of the Friday congregation. Every *salah* is Allah's remembrance for Allah says in the Qur`an,

$$وَأَقِمِ الصَّلَاةَ لِذِكْرِي ۝$$

*And establish prayer (salah) for my remembrance. (Ta Ha, 20:14)*

The *Jumu'ah* prayer, however, is unique. The prayer is preceded by the *khutbah*. The purpose of the *khutbah* of *Jumu'ah* is reminder and reflection. It represents a built-in arrangement for the education of the Muslims through which the battery of faith is regularly recharged, and the Islamic life strengthened. It educates the people about the teachings of Islam, awakens their moral consciousness, increases their understanding of the way of life (what we call the *deen*) of Islam, reflects upon the situation of the Muslims, and shares their concerns, aspirations, and obligations toward each other and toward humanity at large. It also provides the members of every community an opportunity to get together, meet and know each other, and become more integrated. The feeling of brotherhood and of oneness of the *ummah* (the worldwide Muslim community) is strengthened.

*Jumu'ah* also represents an example of the excellence of the Islamic culture. This is a day for special prayers and remembrance of Allah. When the call for prayer is made, all business and worldly activities have to be stopped until the prayer is over. Listening to the *khutbah* is obligatory, and an inseparable part of the congregational prayer. After the prayer, people are free to go back to their business and other activities. For Muslims, *Jumu'ah* is a working day, not an obligatory "day off" as in other religions. Allah says in *Surat al-Jumu'ah*,

فَإِذَا قُضِيَتِ الصَّلَاةُ فَانْتَشِرُوا فِي الْأَرْضِ وَابْتَغُوا مِنْ فَضْلِ اللَّهِ وَاذْكُرُوا اللَّهَ كَثِيرًا لَعَلَّكُمْ تُفْلِحُونَ ۞

*When the prayer is finished, spread through the earth and seek Allah's bounty and remember Allah much so that hopefully you will be successful. (al-Jumu'ah, 62:10)*

*Jumu'ah* is the symbol of Islam's distinct approach to life and the way problems should be faced. Allah's *dhikr* (remembrance) is the guiding light. It disciplines the community to respond to the call to prayer, fulfill the obligation of collective *dhikr*, then re-enter the business of life with full consciousness of what is good and what is wrong. This is the model for the entire life of a Muslim and an Islamic society. If our mundane life is permeated with the spirit of Allah's remembrance, it becomes an act of *'ibada* (worship). Islam does not divide life into separate parts of this-worldly and other-worldly, or religious and secular, rather it makes them one integrated whole.

# *Fiqh* of the *Jumu'ah* Prayer

# THE VIRTUES OF *JUMU'AH*

Many traditions have been narrated from the Prophet (SAS) which explain the virtues of the day of *Jumu'ah*.

"The best day on which the sun rises is *Jumu'ah*. It was on this day that Adam (AS) was created, the day on which he was granted entry into paradise, the day when he was taken out from it, and the day on which the Day of Judgment will take place." (Ahmad, Tirmidhi) The day Adam (AS) was removed from paradise is also significant because that became the cause for man's existence in this world, which itself is a great blessing.

"There is a time during the day of *Jumu'ah* in which if one asks anything of Allah, it is granted to him unless what one asks for is unlawful." (Bukhari, Muslim)

"*Jumu'ah* is the best of all days and the most virtuous in the sight of Allah. It has more greatness than 'Eid al-Fitr and 'Eid al-Adha." (Bukhari)

"The five daily prayers, and from one *Jumu'ah* to the next, are an expiation for whatever sins come in between, so long as one does not commit any major sin."(Muslim)

"Allah led those who came before us away from Friday. The Jews had Saturday, and the Christians had Sunday. Then Allah brought us, and Allah guided us to Friday. So there is Friday, Saturday, and Sunday, and thus they will follow us on the Day of Resurrection. We are the last of the people of this world, but we will be the first on the Day of Resurrection, and we will be dealt with before all others." (Muslim)

"The person who has a bath on Friday, puts on the best available clothes, applies perfume if available, and comes for the prayer, and takes his place quietly without disturbing the people, then offers the prayer that Allah has destined for him, and sits in perfect silence and peace from the time the imam takes his place until the completion of the prayer, this will expiate his sins committed between this Friday and the previous Friday." (Abu Dawud)

"The night before Friday is a white (lustrous) night and the day of Friday is a bright day." (Miskhat, Bayhaqi)

"There is no Muslim who dies on the day of Friday or the night of Friday, but Allah will protect him from the trial of the grave." (Ahmad, Tirmidhi)

It is narrated that once Ibn 'Abbas (RAA) was reciting the following verse:

الْيَوْمَ أَكْمَلْتُ لَكُمْ دِينَكُمْ وَأَتْمَمْتُ عَلَيْكُمْ نِعْمَتِي وَرَضِيتُ لَكُمُ الْإِسْلَامَ دِينًا ○

*Today I have perfected your religion for you, completed My blessing upon you, and chosen for you Islam as the acceptable system of faith and worship. (al-Ma`ida, 5:3)*

A Jewish man was sitting near him. On hearing this verse being recited he remarked, "If this verse was revealed to us, we would have celebrated that day as a day of 'Eid." Ibn 'Abbas replied, "This verse was revealed on two 'Eids" (meaning on the day of *Jumu'ah* and the day of 'Arafa.)

1

# OBJECTIVES OF THE *JUMU'AH* PRAYER

One of the main objectives of the *Jumu'ah* prayer is to provide a weekly reminder to the believers. At the beginning of *Surat al-Jumu'ah*, Allah (SWT) speaks about sending the Prophet (SAS) to recite His revelations to the people and to purify them and to teach them the Book and wisdom:

هُوَ الَّذِي بَعَثَ فِي الْأُمِّيِّينَ رَسُولًا مِنْهُمْ يَتْلُو عَلَيْهِمْ آيَاتِهِ وَيُزَكِّيهِمْ وَيُعَلِّمُهُمُ الْكِتَابَ وَالْحِكْمَةَ وَإِنْ كَانُوا مِنْ قَبْلُ لَفِي ضَلَالٍ مُبِينٍ ○

*It is He who raised a messenger from among the unlettered people to recite His Signs to them and purify them and teach them the Book and Wisdom, even though before that they were clearly misguided. (al-Jumu'ah, 62:2)*

This reminder helps the individual and the community preserve their religion and identity. Muslims are in constant need of renewing the strength of their faith. It is for this reason that the *khutbah* should instill the essentials of faith within the congregation. Another objective is to give hope and encouragement to Muslims by emphasizing Allah's love and mercy and the need to be mindful of Him at all times, to seek His forgiveness, and to constantly turn to Him in repentance. Fostering brotherhood among Muslims is an objective of every congregational prayer but this is actualized to a greater degree in the *Jumu'ah* prayer.

# CONSEQUENCE OF NEGLECTING THE *JUMU'AH* PRAYER

We must never be neglectful of the *Jumu'ah* prayer. There are grave consequences for the one who neglects it. The Prophet (SAS) said, "The *Jumu'ah* prayer is obligatory on every Muslim who believes in Allah and the Last Day; the one who ignores it on account of sport or fun, or trade and business, will be ignored by Allah, and Allah is Self-Sufficient and Glorious." (Daraqutni) He also said, "People must cease neglecting *Jumu'ah* prayer or else Allah will put a seal over their hearts and they will truly be among the negligent."(Muslim) Ibn 'Abbas (RAA) narrates that the Messenger of Allah (SAS) said, "The person who leaves out *Jumu'ah* prayer without a valid reason is written down as a hypocrite in a book that is absolutely protected from any changes and modifications." (Mishkat) In other words, he will be labeled as a hypocrite forever. However, if he repents, or Allah forgives him solely out of His mercy, then this is another matter.

# DIFFERENCES OF OPINION AND
# FOLLOWING SCHOOLS OF *FIQH*

When seeking to learn the rulings and rituals of Islam, Muslims frequently refer to "the *fiqh* of" the issue at hand such as "the *fiqh* of *salah*" or "the *fiqh* of fasting." The word *fiqh* means the system of legal rulings described by Islamic scholars throughout history. Muslims have always understood that there is room for disagreement in matters of these laws, and that multiple opinions may coexist as long as the person issuing the opinion is educated and authorized to derive rulings from the Qur`an and the Sunnah.

It is important to understand that even the *sahaba* (companions of the Prophet) differed in some rulings, as did the generations after them. The *shari'a* (Islamic law system) is characterized by its practicality, and it takes people's concerns into account and it does not overlook people's immediate needs and compelling situations. Islam is not oblivious to the realities of life or to differing human abilities to face them.

Today, Sunni Muslims recognize four rigorously preserved and transmitted *madhhabs* or "schools of thought" based on the methodology established by a particular founder, for whom each school is named. These are: Imam Abu Haneefa (the Hanafi school), Imam Malik (the Maliki school), Al-Imam Ash-Shafi'i (the Shafi'i school), and Imam Ahmad ibn Hanbal (the Hanbali school). These schools all share most principles in common, with minor differences on how to solve problems that arise when analyzing evidence from the texts of the Qur`an and Sunnah, or making rulings on concerns that are not to be found in a particular clear text. Contemporary scholars continue the methodologies of these schools to address new issues faced by Muslim communities all over the world.

Most Muslims are not aware of the school of *fiqh* they practice, and many people are actually following the school that is most dominant in the area of the Muslim world they live in or from which they originate. Many Muslims also tend to follow a mixture of *fiqh* opinions, drawn from their cultural background, the *fiqh* preferred and taught by the leaders in their *masjid* or community, internet websites they have consulted for answers, and even urban legends. Sometimes Muslims follow "rules" that are not rules of *fiqh* at all, but misunderstandings about Islam and cultural practices. This is why it is important for Muslims to study and learn the basics of their *deen* and to constantly engage in seeking knowledge and seeking to determine if a practice or belief is based on the Qur`an and Sunnah.

*The various schools of fiqh are valid interpretations of the shari'a (Islamic legal system) but they are not binding interpretations.* Islamic scholars generally recommend that Muslims should try to follow rulings that satisfy the requirements of all schools, in order to avoid falling into areas of disagreement. They also recommend that one's practice and learning focus primarily on a single school: This way people can learn a method and put it into practice in a systematic and consistent way, with a disciplined mindset, willing to apply rulings whether easy or not so easy.

However, scholars have also recognized that differences are a mercy, and that there are circumstances such as undue hardship when authoritative opinions from schools other than one's own may be followed. Some opinions regarding *Jumu'ah* can be considered more precautionary, in the sense that most schools agree on them. Other authoritative positions may also be followed and cannot be condemned, even if they are unfamiliar to followers of other schools. Sometimes it may also be advisable to follow certain rules in order to avoid disputes and maintain harmony in the community.

One should consult traditionally trained scholars to understand the details of other opinions and when they may be followed. The following sections will cover the most commonly applied opinions and practices in the West but there may be other valid opinions being followed in some places.

## THE OBLIGATION OF THE *JUMU'AH* PRAYER

In *Surat al-Jumu'ah* Allah (SWT) states,

يَا أَيُّهَا الَّذِينَ آمَنُوا إِذَا نُودِيَ لِلصَّلَاةِ مِن يَوْمِ الْجُمُعَةِ فَاسْعَوْا إِلَى ذِكْرِ اللَّهِ وَذَرُوا الْبَيْعَ ذَٰلِكُمْ خَيْرٌ لَّكُمْ إِن كُنتُمْ تَعْلَمُونَ ◯

*O you who believe! When the call to prayer is made on Jumu'ah, hasten toward the remembrance of Allah and leave all transactions—that is best for you, if only you knew. (al-Jumu'ah, 62:9)*

According to Shaykh As-Sayyid Sabiq in the book *Fiqh us-Sunnah*, "The *Jumu'ah* prayer is an obligation upon every free, adult, sane, resident Muslim who has the ability to attend the prayer and does not have a valid excuse to miss it." It is not an obligation upon a woman, a child, a sick person, a slave, or a traveler. The person who is sick and faces hardship if he goes to the *masjid* is excused if he fears that his sickness will be increased, or his recovery delayed. This also includes the person who is a caretaker to someone who is sick especially if the sick person cannot manage in the absence of the caretaker.

Ibn 'Abbas reports that the Prophet (SAS) said, "Whoever hears the call for the salah and does not respond to it (by coming to the salah), there will be no prayer for him unless he has an excuse." The people inquired, "O Messenger of Allah, what is a (valid) excuse?" He answered, "Fear or illness." (Abu Dawud) It is also advisable for people to not attend *Jumu'ah* if they have a contagious disease that could infect and harm others.

During the COVID-19 crisis, the *Fiqh* Council of North America, along with most other Muslim legal bodies and organizations, recommended the suspension of Salat al-Jumu'ah in order to protect the community from spreading contagious disease.

The exemption from *Jumu'ah* prayer for the traveler is based on the fact that the Prophet (SAS) traveled and did not perform the *Salat al-Jumu'ah* but only prayed the *Dhuhr* and *'Asr* together during the time of *Dhuhr*. The caliphs after him and others also did the same. A traveler can still attend the Friday prayer and receive the reward for attending. In the Hanafi school, travel on Friday isn't disliked, and it is considered permissible to embark on travel any time before the Friday prayer begins, but in the Shafi'i school, one must travel before *fajr* to be exempt from attending the Friday prayer.

## THE TIME OF THE *JUMU'AH* PRAYER

The time of the *Jumu'ah* prayer is the same as that of *Dhuhr*, the midday prayer. Imam Ahmad and Imam Muslim record in their hadeeth collections that Salama ibn al-Akwa' said, "We would pray *Salat al-Jumu'ah* with the Prophet (SAS) when the sun had passed its meridian, and when we returned from the *salah*, we would be following our shadow." (Ahmad and Muslim) According to As-Sayyid Sabiq in *Fiqh us-Sunnah*, "[Al-Imam] ash-Shafi'i said, 'The Prophet (SAS), Abu Bakr, 'Umar, and 'Uthman and the imams after them all prayed the *Jumu'ah* when the sun had passed its zenith.'"

However, there is an opinion in the Hanbali school that allows the *Jumu'ah* prayer to be offered anytime in the morning, like the 'Eid prayer. Some people apply this ruling in times of need. In countries where space in the *masjid* is limited, and the window of time for *Dhuhr* prayer is short (such as in the Northern Hemisphere), one can follow this opinion and hold *Salat al-Jumu'ah* before the time for *Dhuhr*.

There is a general consensus among the scholars that it is also permissible to delay *Jumu'ah* prayer until close to the time for *'Asr*, in such a way that the *Jumu'ah* prayer ends just before the time for *'Asr* begins. The scholars differ on beginning of *'Asr* time, so this time can also differ slightly. The majority of schools say that the time enters when the shadow of an object is equal to the length of the object, whereas the Hanafi school holds that the time of *'Asr* enters when the shadow of an object is equal to *twice* the length of the object. The Hanafi position would allow one to extend the time for *Jumu'ah* prayer based on the later *'Asr* time.

# PLACES WHERE *JUMU'AH* PRAYER CAN BE PERFORMED

According to As-Sayyid Sabiq in *Fiqh us-Sunnah*, "It is valid to perform the *Salat al-Jumu'ah* in any country, city, *masjid*, any building in a city, or in any space in a city as it also is valid to have it performed in more than one place... 'Umar wrote the following to the people of Bahrain, 'Offer the *Jumu'ah salah* wherever you may be.'"

As long as one prays in a place that is *tahir* (clean and ritually pure), then the prayer is valid. It is not obligatory for the prayer to be valid that one covers the floor, unless one knows that impurity exists in the place of prayer. Of course, it is more hygienic and precautious to remove shoes, cover the floor with prayer rugs, sheets, blankets, and so on, and this is what is commonly practiced.

If one prays in a room with images of animate beings, or one with statues, then many scholars would consider this to be disliked, so it should be avoided, though the prayer would still be valid. Multi-faith rooms that do not have images or statues would therefore be acceptable. If there is no alternative that is easily available, it would be advisable to cover the images or statutes. One should strictly avoid praying toward the images or statues.

# HOLDING MULTIPLE *JUMU'AH* PRAYERS IN ONE *MASJID*

The traditional opinion of all schools is to have one *Jumu'ah* prayer offered in the *masjid*. A contemporary opinion frequently practiced in the West states that multiple *Jumu'ah* prayers can be offered at the same *masjid*. This arises out of the need to accommodate many attendees in limited spaces. If there is an empty space outside the *masjid* that can be used for prayer or there are alternatives that allow all Muslims to pray at the same time, it is better. Otherwise, there is no restriction on performing the prayer twice or more times in the same *masjid*.

It is preferable that the person who delivers the *khutbah* also leads the prayer. However, it is permissible for someone else to lead the prayer. Jamaal al-Din Zarabozo writes in his book *The Friday Prayer*, "Ibn Qudamah states that the *sunnah* is for the same person who gave the *khutbah* to also lead the prayer. This was the practice of the Prophet (SAS) as well as that of his successors. Only if there is some viable excuse to do otherwise, is it considered acceptable for another person to lead the prayer."

According to Dr. 'Abdul-Fattah Idrees, "It is also preferable that each *Jumu'ah* prayer has its own imam. If this is not possible, then it is acceptable to have the same imam for the two prayers. His first prayer will be obligatory while the second will be *nafl* (supererogatory or voluntary). Some of the companions used to do the same. They used to attend the prayer with the Prophet (SAS) and then leave to their people to lead them in prayer."

## EID AND *JUMU'AH* OCCURRING ON THE SAME DAY

If 'Eid falls on a Friday, most of the schools state the *Salat al-Jumu'ah* is obligatory. The Hanbali school has a position that when 'Eid occurs on Friday, and if one has performed the 'Eid prayer, then one has the option of not performing *Salat al-Jumu'ah*, though if one does, this would be praiseworthy. In *Fiqh us-Sunnah*, As-Sayyid Sabiq writes that the Prophet (SAS) "gave an exemption concerning the *Jumu'ah*, saying: 'Whoever wishes to pray it may pray it.'" For this reason it is considered better for the *masjid* to organize *Salat al-Jumu'ah* for those who wish to attend, or for those who missed *Salat al-'Eid*.

## PREPARING FOR THE *JUMU'AH* PRAYER

Taking a *ghusl* (ritual bath/shower) on the day of *Jumu'ah* is from the Prophet's *sunnah* and recommended for anyone attending *Jumu'ah* prayer. This is encouraged by the Prophet (SAS) in numerous traditions. He (SAS) said, "Taking a bath on Friday is compulsory for every male Muslim who has attained the age of puberty and (also) the cleaning of his teeth with *miswak*, and the using of perfume if it is available." (Bukhari, Muslim) He (SAS) also said, "When any one of you intends to come for *Jumu'ah* prayer, he should take a bath." (Muslim) There are numerous similar authentic narrations from the Prophet (SAS) instructing the believers to perform a *ghusl* and clean the teeth prior to attending *Salat al-Jumu'ah*.

It is also recommended to clip one's nails, apply some perfume (for men), and brush the teeth or use the *miswak* (tooth stick made from the *arak* tree). The Prophet (SAS) has emphasized the importance of attention to one's oral hygiene, especially during prayers. The scholars have also emphasized the need for oral hygiene when we recite the Qur'an, as it is the words of Allah. There is a hadeeth that says, "The *miswak* cleanses and purifies the mouth and pleases the Lord." (al-Nisa'i and others) Hence, we have to give due consideration to others when attending the *masjid* and ensure to purify ourselves of foul odors, which may result from eating raw garlic or onions, or from smoking. The general principle is to avoid odors that disturb others in their worship.

# DRESSING WELL ON THE DAY OF *JUMU'AH*

While praying in general, men are required to be covered at the bare minimum between the navel and knees, and all parts of a woman are required to be covered other than the face and hands. (The Hanafi school allows the feet to remain uncovered.) Clothing should not be so thin that an average glance would be able to discern the color of one's skin beneath the clothing.

The parts that are covered are referred to as *'awra*. The schools differ regarding the validity of the prayer if part of the *'awra* becomes uncovered. The Shafi'i school is the strictest, maintaining that if the *'awra* is not immediately covered the prayer is invalidated. The Hanafi school holds that the prayer is only invalidated if more than a quarter of a limb is uncovered for the duration it takes to utter three repetitions of *Subhan Allah*. In all cases, being lax about covering properly would be sinful, even if according to some schools the prayer remains legally valid.

The day of *Jumu'ah* is a day for dressing as nicely as possible. The Prophet (SAS) advised that we should dress well on the day of *Jumu'ah* and put on our finest clothing when he said, "Every Muslim should have *a ghusl* on Friday and wear his best clothing, and if he has perfume, he should use it." (Bukhari, Muslim, Ahmad)

Allah (SWT) says in the Qur`an,

$$\text{يَا بَنِي أَدَمَ خُذُوا زِينَتَكُمْ عِنْدَ كُلِّ مَسْجِدٍ} \bigcirc$$

*O Children of Adam! Take your adornment at every time and place of prayer. (al-A'raf, 7:31)*

The word *zeena* (adornment) in this verse refers to full and proper dress. While performing prayer people are required not only to cover the private parts of their body, but also to wear a garment that both covers and gives one a decent appearance. The emphasis on praying in a proper and decent dress is to oppose the idea held by some peoples throughout history that people should worship God either nude or semi-naked, or with a shabby and unkempt appearance. These people believe that nudity or shabby dress is an act of humility in front of God. In Islam, people should be free from all kinds of nudity and indecency, and instead they should wear good and clean clothing during worship. We commonly think about doing this on the day of 'Eid, but *Jumu'ah* is also considered a day of 'Eid for Muslims.

The Prophet (SAS) used to love white clothing and he encouraged wearing white clothing to the *Jumu'ah* prayer. 'Abdullah ibn 'Abbas (RAA) relates that the Messenger of Allah (SAS) said, "Wear white clothes, because they are the best of your clothes and shroud your dead in it." (*Bulugh al-Maram*)

# NUMBER OF PEOPLE THAT MAKE UP A CONGREGATION FOR THE *JUMU'AH* PRAYER

*Salat al-Jumu'ah* is inherently a group and community prayer that is not performed alone. The scholars differ on how many people are required for *Jumu'ah*. The more precautionary position of the Shafi'i school states that at least forty men who are *mustawtineen* (people whose homes are in the area, not travelers or temporary residents) are required to be present for the *Jumu'ah khutbah* and *salah*. The Hanafi school holds that at least three men, whether residents or travelers, besides the *imam* are required. As the *Jumu'ah* prayer is not obligatory on women and children, they do not count toward the required the number of attendees.

# COMING EARLY FOR THE *JUMU'AH* PRAYER

Another thing we should try to do on the day of *Jumu'ah* is to go early for prayers and be at the *masjid* before the imam arrives to deliver his *khutbah*. There are Prophetic traditions that speak about higher rewards for persons who go early for the Friday prayer. Abu Hurayra (RAA) reports that the Prophet (SAS) said, "Whoever makes *ghusl* on *Jumu'ah* like the *ghusl* one makes due to *janaba* (major ritual impurity that necessitates *ghusl*), and then goes to the prayer in the first hour (meaning early), it is as if he sacrificed a camel. If he goes in the second hour, it is as if he sacrificed a cow. If he goes in the third hour, it is as if he sacrificed a horned ram. If he goes in the fourth hour, it is as if he sacrificed a hen. And if he goes in the fifth hour, it is as if he offered (something like) an egg. When the imam comes out, the angels come to listen to the *khutbah*." (Bukhari, Muslim)

Those who come late to *Jumu'ah* prayers because of laziness or without a good reason should take heed of the Qur'anic statement in which Allah (SWT) reprimands the hypocrites for showing laziness toward their *salah*.

إِنَّ الْمُنَافِقِينَ يُخَادِعُونَ اللَّهَ وَهُوَ خَادِعُهُمْ وَإِذَا قَامُوا إِلَى الصَّلَاةِ قَامُوا كُسَالَى يُرَاءُونَ النَّاسَ وَلَا يَذْكُرُونَ اللَّهَ إِلَّا قَلِيلًا ◯

*The hypocrites try to deceive Allah but it is He who causes them to be deceived. When they get up to pray, they get up lazily, showing off to people, and only remembering Allah a very little. (an-Nisa`, 4:142)*

This was the attitude of the hypocrites at the time of the Prophet (SAS). Now what we observe is a somewhat similar phenomenon. Even today, some of our brothers wait until the imam is about to finish his *khutbah*, then they come in only to catch the two *rak'as* of *Salat al-Jumu'ah*. We should be very careful about punctuality when attending the Friday prayer service and remember and make an effort to seek the benefits of listening to the *khutbah*.

## WHAT HAPPENS IF ONE ARRIVES LATE FOR THE *JUMU'AH* PRAYER

Someone who misses one or more *rak'as* of the *Jumu'ah* prayer will have to make up some *rak'as*. According to the Hanafi school, as long as the worshipper joins the imam in the *tashahhud* prior to the *salaams*, he has validly joined the *Jumu'ah* prayer, and should complete the *rak'as* he missed (whether one or two) after the imam's *salaams*.

However, the other schools say the worshipper has validly joined the *Jumu'ah* prayer only if has prayed at least one full *rak'a* with the imam—that is, only if he has caught the *Jumu'ah* prayer prior to the imam rising from the second *ruku'*. Hence, if the worshipper misses the second *ruku'*, he has not validly entered the *Jumu'ah* prayer, and he must complete four *rak'as* of *Dhuhr* after the imam's *salaams*.

If the *Jumu'ah* prayer is being prayed prior to the entrance of *Dhuhr* (following the Hanbali school), then if the worshiper misses the second *ruku'*, he cannot make up the prayer as *Dhuhr*, since the time of *Dhuhr* has not entered. He must make up the prayer as two *rak'as* of *nafl* and attend another *Jumu'ah* prayer. If he cannot, he prays *Dhuhr* after its time has entered.

## PRAYERS OFFERED BEFORE AND AFTER THE *JUMU'AH* PRAYER

It is praiseworthy to offer *sunnah* and *nafl* prayers in the *masjid* prior to the commencement of the *khutbah*. Once the *khutbah* commences, one should not initiate any prayers. The only exception to this is offering two *rak'as* of the *tahiyyat al-masjid* (prayer of greeting the *masjid*), which according to the Shafi'i and Hanbali schools, is recommended. *Tahiyyat al-masjid* during the *khutbah* is not offered according to the Hanafis and Malikis. They have their proofs, but that is beyond the scope of the book. If the *Jumu'ah* prayer is being held in a place that is not a dedicated *masjid*, the *tahiyyat al-masjid* prayer is not offered.

There are some differences of opinion about the type and number of prayers to offer prior to the *khutbah*. The Hanbali school holds that there are no specific *sunnah* prayers prior to the *Jumu'ah*. The Hanafi school and the Shafi'i schools hold that the *sunnah* prayers prior to the *Jumu'ah* are like the *sunnah* prayers prior to *Dhuhr* in terms of number.

The schools agree that there are *sunnah* prayers after *Jumu'ah*, though there is disagreement about the number—whether it is two, four, or six, and how many of these are considered to be emphasized versus not emphasized. The reasons for the differences are a longer discussion than this book allows for, so believers are encouraged to consult their local imams or scholars they trust for more information about which opinion they would like to practice.

## ETIQUETTE FOR THE CONGREGATION

There are certain manners and obligations the congregation needs to observe when attending the *Jumu'ah* gathering. If we are not mindful of these things, we will lose the blessings and goodness of the *Jumu'ah* prayer and the reward may even be nullified.

When entering the *masjid*, it is considered disliked to push one's way through the congregation after the *khutbah* has started. It is also disliked that one walks between sitting people or tries to sit between people unless there is an empty spot to fill. If a person needs to get up and leave, for example to use the washroom and renew his wudu`, this is permissible, but he should be mindful of the people and avoid disturbing them as much as possible.

It is also an obligation for the congregation to remain silent during the *khutbah*. It is permissible to engage in conversation before the *khutbah* starts, but *laghw* (vain talk) should be avoided. The Prophet (SAS) said, "Whoever takes a bath on Friday, purifies himself as much as he can, then uses his (hair) oil or perfumes himself with the scent of his house, then proceeds (to the prayer) and does not separate two persons sitting together, then prays as much as (Allah has) written for him and then remains silent while the imam is delivering the *khutbah*, his sins in between the present and the last Friday would be forgiven." (Bukhari) He (SAS) also warned against speaking during the *khutbah*, even to tell another talking person to be quiet, saying, "If you (even) ask your companion to be quiet on Friday while the imam is delivering the sermon, you have in fact spoken *laghw* (vain talk)." (Muslim) Another form of *laghw* during the *khutbah* is fiddling or picking at things as if to relieve boredom. The Prophet (SAS) said about this topic, "Whoever touches the pebbles has engaged in *laghw* (frivolous behavior)." (Ibn Maja).In fact, *laghw* refers to "that which is not given any consideration, whether speech or other than speech."

When people are leaving the *masjid* after the congregational prayers, it can seem difficult to avoid passing in front of a person who is still praying, however this should be avoided as much as possible, as the Prophet (SAS) said, "If the one who passes in front of a person who is praying knew what (a burden of sin) he bears, it would be better for him to stand for forty rather than pass in front of him." (Abu Dawud) Abu'l-Nadar – one of the narrators – said, "I do not know whether he said forty days or months or years. (Bukhari, Muslim) If one passes, one should give the worshipper at least enough space to perform his *sujud* (prostrations). The place of *sujud* is considered the *sutra* (screen/cover) for someone who has not explicitly set up a *sutra*. A *sutra* is an object used by a person performing *salah* as a barrier between himself and one passing in front of him. The place of *sujud* is considered the *sutra* for someone who has not explicitly set up a *sutra*.

## THE OBLIGATION OF LISTENING TO THE *KHUTBAH*

The *khutbah* is an integral part of the *Jumu'ah* prayer. This is based on the verse:

يَا أَيُّهَا الَّذِينَ آمَنُوا إِذَا نُودِيَ لِلصَّلَاةِ مِن يَوْمِ الْجُمُعَةِ فَاسْعَوْا إِلَىٰ ذِكْرِ اللَّهِ وَذَرُوا الْبَيْعَ ذَٰلِكُمْ خَيْرٌ لَّكُمْ إِن كُنتُمْ تَعْلَمُونَ ◯

*O you who believe! When the call to prayer is made on Jumu'ah, hasten toward the remembrance of Allah and leave all transactions—that is best for you, if only you knew. (al-Jumu'ah, 62:9)*

Here the word "remembrance" means the *khutbah*, according to one of the opinions in *tafseer* (meanings of the Qur`an).

In addition, the Prophet (SAS) always delivered a *khutbah* before the two *rak'at* of the *Salat al-Jumu'ah*. One who attends the minimum required amount of *Salat al-Jumu'ah* counts this as a replacement for *Dhuhr* prayer. Scholars are of the opinion that the *khutbah* replaces two of the *rak'at* of *Dhuhr* prayer. If a person misses the *Jumu'ah* prayer altogether, they pray *Dhuhr* prayer instead. Although the schools agree that one who misses the *khutbah* and prays at a minimum one *rak'a* of *Salat al-Jumu'ah* has still met the obligation of *Jumu'ah* and does not need to pray *Dhuhr*, it is still sinful to deliberately miss the *khutbah*. Much of the blessing of attending the *Salat al-Jumu'ah* comes from hearing the remembrance of Allah as contained in the *khutbah*.

## SPECIAL SITUATIONS

As with all other prayers, ritual purity is one of the conditions of one's *Salat al-Jumu'ah* being valid. So one must have a valid wudu` during the *khutbah* and the prayer. If one loses their wudu` they should leave the prayer area to go and renew their wudu`. Their attendance at *Salat al-Jumu'ah* will still be valid as long as one catches the end of the prayer itself. The same applies for one who comes late to the prayer. Ibn 'Umar reports that the Prophet (SAS) said, "Whoever catches only one *rak'a* of the *salah* and then adds to it the other one, his prayer will be complete." (an-Nasa`i, Ibn Maja, Daraqutni)

If one starts to feel sleepy during the *khutbah*, it is recommended to get up and move to a different spot in the *masjid*. Ibn 'Umar reports that the Prophet (SAS) said: "If one of you becomes sleepy while he is in the *masjid*, he should move from his place to another place." (Ahmad, Abu Dawud, Tirmidhi)

# HOW TO MAKE THE *ADHAN* AND *IQAMA* FOR THE *JUMU'AH* PRAYER

There are two *adhans* and an *iqama*. The first *adhan* is called after the time for *Dhuhr* prayer enters, the second when the imam has ascended the *minbar* (pulpit) to deliver the *khutbah*. The *iqama* is called when *Salat al-Jumu'ah* is about to commence.

In the time of the Prophet (SAS) and the first two caliphs Abu Bakr (RAA) and 'Umar (RAA), there was a single *adhan* for *Jumu'ah*, followed by the *khutbah*, and then the *iqama* and then the *salat al-Jumu'ah*. The *adhan* used to be pronounced when the imam sat on the pulpit. According to As-Sayyid Sabiq in *Fiqh us-Sunnah*, "Later, 'Uthman (RAA), the third caliph, introduced an additional *adhan* which would be given earlier in the marketplace rather than the *masjid*, in order to make it easier for people to start preparing for *Jumu'ah*, since the Muslim population had increased significantly by then. Since then, the practice has continued in much of the Muslim world, even if it was not a consensus."

It is a *sunnah* to respond to the mu`addhin (*adhan*-giver) repeating what he says after him in a soft voice. Allah's Messenger (SAS) said,

مَنْ قَالَ حِينَ يَسْمَعُ النِّدَاءَ اللَّهُمَّ رَبَّ هَذِهِ الدَّعْوَةِ التَّامَّةِ وَالصَّلاَةِ الْقَائِمَةِ آتِ مُحَمَّدًا الْوَسِيلَةَ وَالْفَضِيلَةَ وَابْعَثْهُ مَقَامًا مَحْمُودًا الَّذِي وَعَدْتَهُ، حَلَّتْ لَهُ شَفَاعَتِي يَوْمَ الْقِيَامَةِ

*"Whoever after listening to the adhan says, 'O Allah! Lord of this perfect call and of the regular prayer which is going to be established, give Muhammad the right of intercession and illustriousness, and resurrect him to the best and the highest place in*

*paradise that You promised him, then my intercession for him will be allowed on the Day of Resurrection.'" (Muslim)*

One should not miss out on this *sunnah* by initiating *nafl* (voluntary) prayers while the *adhan* is being called.

Once the *mu'addhin* completes the *adhan*, both he and the congregants send blessings upon the Prophet (SAS), and recite the *du'a'* after the *adhan*. 'Abdullah ibn 'Amr ibn al-'Aas reported that the Prophet (SAS) said,

إِذَا سَمِعْتُمُ الْمُؤَذِّنَ فَقُولُوا مِثْلَ مَا يَقُولُ ثُمَّ صَلُّوا عَلَيَّ فَإِنَّهُ مَنْ صَلَّى عَلَيَّ صَلاَةً صَلَّى اللَّهُ عَلَيْهِ بِهَا عَشْرًا ثُمَّ سَلُوا اللَّهَ لِيَ الْوَسِيلَةَ فَإِنَّهَا مَنْزِلَةٌ فِي الْجَنَّةِ لاَ تَنْبَغِي إِلاَّ لِعَبْدٍ مِنْ عِبَادِ اللَّهِ وَأَرْجُو أَنْ أَكُونَ أَنَا هُوَ فَمَنْ سَأَلَ لِيَ الْوَسِيلَةَ حَلَّتْ لَهُ الشَّفَاعَةُ

*"When you hear the mu'addhin, repeat what he says, then invoke a blessing on me, for everyone who invokes a blessing on me will receive ten blessings from Allah; then beg from Allah al-waseela for me, which is a rank in paradise fitting for only one of Allah's servants, and I hope that I may be that one. If anyone who asks that I be given the waseela, he will be assured of my intercession." (Sahih Muslim)*

Between the first and second *adhan* people offer *nafl* prayers, or engage in *du'a'*, *dhikr*, or recitation of the Qur'an.

After the *khateeb* ascends the pulpit and is seated, the *mu'addhin* calls the second *adhan*, and, as before, those present respond to the *mu'addhin*, and after the *adhan* everyone sends blessings upon the Prophet (SAS) and recites the *du'a'* after the *adhan*. Then the *khateeb* delivers the *khutbah* in two parts, as outlined below. After the *khutbah* has been delivered and the prayer is about to commence, the *mu'addhin* calls the *iqama*.

## *KHUTBAH* PROCEDURE

Here, the basic procedure for the *khutbah* that one would generally follow is outlined, without encumbering the reader with details about what is obligatory versus recommended. Such distinctions can be found elsewhere.

The *khateeb* gives *salaams* to the people near the *minbar* (pulpit) before ascending it, then ascends the *minbar*, faces the congregation, greets them again with *salaams*, and then sits. Thereafter, the *mu'addhin* delivers the second *adhan*, standing near the *khateeb*.

The *khateeb* then rises and commences the first *khutbah* with (1) praising Allah, (2) sending blessings and greetings upon the Prophet (SAS), and (3) exhorting people to *taqwa*, all in Arabic. (Texts and translations for these speeches are found in Appendix 1.)

It is from the *sunnah* of the Prophet (SAS) to begin the *khutbah* with a speech known as the *khutbat al-haja* or "sermon of necessity." At the very beginning of his sermon, the *khateeb* should say the following words in Arabic, preferably with its translation in English, if the sermon is to be in English.

This is not the only permissible version that can be used, but it is popular and in accordance with the *sunnah*. Here is the text:

إِنَّ الْحَمْدَ لِلَّهِ نَحْمَدُهُ وَنَسْتَعِينُهُ وَنَسْتَغْفِرُهُ وَنَعُوذُ بِاللَّهِ مِنْ شُرُورِ أَنْفُسِنَا وَمِنْ سَيِّئَاتِ أَعْمَالِنَا ، مَنْ يَهْدِهِ اللَّهُ فَلَا مُضِلَّ لَهُ ، وَمَنْ يُضْلِلْ فَلَا هَادِيَ لَهُ ، وَأَشْهَدُ أَنْ لَا إِلَهَ إِلَّا اللَّهُ وَحْدَه لَا شَرِيكَ لَهُ وَأَشْهَدُ أَنَّ مُحَمَّداً عَبْدُهُ وَرَسُوْلُه

*"All praises are due to Allah. We praise Him, we seek His help and we ask for His forgiveness. We seek refuge in Allah from the evil in our souls and from our sinful deeds. Whoever Allah guides, no one can misguide. And whoever Allah leaves astray, no one can guide. I bear witness that there is no one worthy of worship except Allah. He is One, having no partner. And I bear witness that Muhammad (SAS) is His servant and messenger."*

Then one recites the verses from the Qur`an:

يَا أَيُّهَا الَّذِينَ آمَنُواْ اتَّقُواْ اللَّهَ حَقَّ تُقَاتِهِ وَلاَ تَمُوتُنَّ إِلاَّ وَأَنتُم مُّسْلِمُونَ ⬭

*O you who believe, be conscious of Allah with all the consciousness that is due to Him and do not die except as Muslims. (Aal 'Imran, 3:102)*

يَا أَيُّهَا النَّاسُ اتَّقُوا رَبَّكُمُ الَّذِي خَلَقَكُم مِّن نَّفْسٍ وَاحِدَةٍ وَخَلَقَ مِنْهَا زَوْجَهَا وَبَثَّ مِنْهُمَا رِجَالًا كَثِيرًا وَنِسَاءً وَاتَّقُوا اللَّهَ الَّذِي تَسَاءَلُونَ بِهِ وَالْأَرْحَامَ إِنَّ اللَّهَ كَانَ عَلَيْكُمْ رَقِيبًا ⬭

*O people, be conscious of your Lord, who created you from a single soul, and from it created its mate, and from the pair of them spread countless men and women far and wide; be mindful of Allah, in whose name you make requests of one another. Beware of severing the ties of kinship. Allah is always watching over you. (an-Nisa`, 4:1)*

يَا أَيُّهَا الَّذِينَ آمَنُوا اتَّقُوا اللَّهَ وَقُولُوا قَوْلًا سَدِيدًايُصْلِحْ لَكُمْ أَعْمَالَكُمْ وَيَغْفِرْ لَكُمْ ذُنُوبَكُمْ وَمَن يُطِعِ اللَّهَ وَرَسُولَهُ فَقَدْ فَازَ فَوْزًا عَظِيمًا ⬭

*O you who believe, be conscious of Allah, and speak the right words. He will put your actions right for you and forgive you your wrong deeds. Whoever obeys Allah and His Messenger has certainly achieved a great success. (al-Ahzab, 33:70-71)*

The formats of the introductory speeches may be different from one *khateeb* to another. However, it is essential to praise, thank, and glorify Allah (SWT) and invoke peace and blessings upon the Prophet (SAS) in both parts of the *khutbah*.

A few examples of the introductory speeches given in the first and second *khutbahs* are mentioned in Appendix 1.

Next, the *khateeb* addresses the congregation in the language the people understand (usually English in the West), exhorting them to piety, and citing verses from the Qur`an and giving references of hadeeth to support his statements.

He sits briefly after the first *khutbah* and takes this opportunity to make a *du'a`* in a soft voice. Then the *khateeb* stands for the second *khutbah*, once again commencing in Arabic with praising Allah, sending blessings and greetings upon the Prophet (SAS), and exhorting people to *taqwa*. (See Appendix 1.) Thereafter, he offers his final remarks and concludes with making *du'a`* that Allah forgive, guide, and aid the Muslims, ensuring that at least some portion of the *du'a`* is made in Arabic. Many people also take this opportunity to make *du'a`* for specific needs in the community.

## THE LANGUAGE OF THE *KHUTBAH*

There exist differences among the scholars regarding the validity of delivering the *khutbah* in the local language. Most contemporary scholars in the West have opted for following the opinion that the main talk of the *khutbah* can be in the local language, and this opinion is consistent with a number of classical works in both the Hanafi and Shafi'i school. Many Hanafi imams in the West adhere to the position that the language of the *khutbah* be Arabic and accommodate this by having a non-Arabic talk prior to the *khutbah*, followed by a brief Arabic *khutbah*.

However, according to later Shafi'i authorities, the essential elements of the *khutbah*, such as praising Allah and sending blessings on the Prophet (SAS), and enjoining *taqwa*, must be in Arabic, but the main talk can be in the local language. Most imams tend to follow this approach, and this ruling has also been expressed by many international *fiqh* committees in different countries.

## GOALS OF THE CONTENT OF THE *KHUTBAH* OF *JUMU'AH*

Islam teaches that humanity is by definition forgetful, which obliges all Muslims to remind each other of its principles. The *khutbah*'s very function is to remind, because the Qur`an says, "reminding benefits the believers."(*adh-Dhariyat*, 51:55)

The content of the *khutbah* should be limited to one main subject or topic, which should be defined and made known to the congregation. As the time for *khutbah* is very limited in the West, it is essential that we do not exceed this time. It is also *Sunnah* of the Prophet that he kept his *khutbah*s short and relevant to the state of the community. Therefore, the *khutbah* should be brief and should be delivered within a 25-30 minute time frame.

The idea of surrendering to Allah is stressed in almost all *khutbah*s, the main purpose being to improve the congregation's relationship to Allah and His *deen*. It should encourage them to reconnect with Allah and to become more devoted to Him. The best way for the *khateeb* to do this is to put forth his ideas with references to the Quran, Sunnah, Islamic heritage, and history. The *khutbah* should remind people of the eternal truths of Islam while also discussing the topic with its relevance to today's Muslim community.

The message of the Friday *khutbah* should reflect its name, *Jumu'ah*, which means "to bring together." The *Jumu'ah* prayer is meant to gather all Muslims and unite their hearts in mutual love and piety. Therefore, any topic that might cause division among Muslims should be avoided and any topic that might lead to the unity of Muslims should be encouraged. Topics that are divisive or highlighting disagreements among Muslims in practices or beliefs, with a view to show superiority of one group over the other or singling out a particular cultural or religious group are all unacceptable. Issues on which we may disagree are very few and minor. There is so much to say on those issues on which we all agree.

Some issues that we may feel are important, but which are also controversial require a different forum for discussion where the audience can participate to air their views and ask questions of the speakers. The Friday *khutbah* is not the right forum to raise controversial issues where people may feel uncomfortable and forced to listen but unable to speak. The creation of such a situation is neither good for the imam nor for the congregation.

The focus should be on humanitarian or moral concerns. Events and stories are narrated in the Qur`an for their morals and to take lessons from them. Muslim social problems are to be addressed positively without hurting anyone by pointing fingers, but rather by using generality and examples from the *Seerah* (the life of the Prophet) in dealing with similar problems. Rather than putting down any group of people, supplication should be made for the misguided to be guided. Political issues or events if at all discussed, should only be for the purpose of educating the Muslims and raising their level of awareness, and should be evaluated in accordance with the guiding principles of the Qur`an and Sunnah that offer solution to such or similar issues or events. One should avoid disparaging governments or politicians whether local or foreign.

Mosques in North America usually represent a wide range of ethnic backgrounds and cultures. In addition, the Friday prayer is attended by men and women, seniors and children, and also sometimes by visitors who are not Muslim. It can be very challenging to deliver a message to a widely mixed congregation that tends to have different experiences. The selection of topic and the choice of words have therefore to be kept in mind. Giving good advice means preserving people's dignity when giving advice. It means inspiring a positive and balanced approach and a respect for the listeners' intelligence.

The *khateeb* must also give special consideration to women. Their role as mother and educator of the coming generations deserves special emphasis and attention. Care should be taken to address both genders, even if the female attendees are not visible to the *khateeb*.

It is of utmost importance that the *khateeb's* ideas are organized during the *khutbah* so as to provide a clear message to the attendees. The topic should be clearly introduced and then supported by presenting relevant verses of the Qur`an, hadeeth and stories. The *khateeb* must do his best to use only sound hadeeths and verified stories and information in his *khutbah*. In addition, he should highlight the lessons and wisdoms to be taken from the divine teachings.

He should then conclude by connecting the passages quoted to a practical way of implementation for the attendees, so that the *khutbah* does not remain abstract and theoretical; rather worshippers should be able to realize that the lessons mentioned are relevant to their lives. Toward the end of the *khutbah*, it is a good practice to summarize the message conveyed one more time. The congregation should be urged to apply in their daily lives what they have heard and not to make them feel that this is a routine thing needed to be delivered and forgotten after the prayer.

The ultimate objective of the *khutbah* is to give Muslims hope and encouragement. *Khutbahs* should be spiritually uplifting and inspiring, giving people the drive to improve themselves. Emphasis should be on forgiveness and chance for repentance rather than on fear and punishment. The Friday prayer should bring people together, physically and spiritually. Members of the congregation should leave the service feeling inspired and encouraged rather than depressed and angered. Occasionally, choosing a topic that is especially spiritually uplifting and heart-soothing is recommended.

## PRACTICAL ADVICE FOR THE *KHATEEB*

It is natural to feel nervousness when one is new to delivering a *khutbah*. Remember that this is a door for you to serve Allah's servants, and to seek His pleasure. Allah teaches in stages, and in time, you will learn in stages as well. Four general pieces of advice in this regard are:

1.  Rectify your intention and turn to Allah by making a *du'a`*. One example of this would be to say *a'oodhu bi-llahi min ash-shaytani ar-rajeem, bismillahi*

*ar-rahman ar-raheem* or another example would be to say *la ilaha illa anta subhanaka inni kuntu min adh-dhalimeen.*

2. Choose a topic that interests you, or one that you are passionate or personally convinced about—this is an easy way to make your *khutbah* genuine, reduce nervousness, and engage listeners.

3. Prepare your talk so that it is structured well, and, if needed, rehearse.

4. Keep the *khutbah* short and simple. The *khutbah*s of the Prophet (SAS) were short and focused on an idea that the congregation could easily remember.

# OTHER RECOMMENDED ACTS OF WORSHIP ON FRIDAYS

## *SENDING BLESSINGS ON THE PROPHET (SAS)*

Sending blessings upon the Prophet (SAS)is recommended on all days and on Fridays in particular. The Prophet (SAS) said, "Of your best days is Friday. On that day Adam was created, and on it his (soul) was taken, and on it is the blowing (of the trumpet), and on it is the swoon. Therefore, increase in sending your blessings (*salawat*) upon me, for your blessings upon me are presented to me." (Abu Dawud)

The Qur`an and Sunnah have emphasized the importance of sending blessings upon the Prophet (SAS) in many ways: (1) Allah commands us in the Qur`an to send blessings upon him, (2) the Prophet (SAS) himself has asked us to do this in many traditions, (3) *iman* (faith) is perfected when our love for the Prophet (SAS) is greater than our love for any other human being, and sending blessings upon him is an expression of our love, (4) we are told in some authentic hadeeths that when we greet him with *salaams*, he returns our greetings, (5) when we send blessings upon him, Allah blesses us tenfold, (6) when we do so abundantly our worries are alleviated and our sins forgiven, and (7) those closest to him on the Day of Judgment will be those who were most abundant in sending blessings upon him.

One can choose to send blessings using a relatively short phrase, such as, *Allahumma salli 'ala sayyidina Muhammad*, or one can choose to send blessings upon him by reciting the *Salawat al-Ibrahimiyya* or other versions.

It is the Prophet (SAS) who brought guidance to us. He guided us from darkness to light. He purified our hearts by the grace of Allah (SWT). In gratitude and appreciation for the great blessing we received through him from Allah (SWT), it is obligatory upon us to keep invoking Allah's blessing upon him, especially on the day and night of *Jumu'ah*.

## *RECITING SURAT AL-KAHF*

Numerous hadiths exist on the virtue of reciting *Surat al-Kahf* on Friday, indicating that those who recite *Surat al-Kahf* on Friday shall have a special light that extends until the next Friday. Some scholars mention that given that the Day of Resurrection shall be on Friday, there is wisdom in reciting *Surat al-Kahf* on Friday, as this reminds one of the portents and terrors associated with the Day of Resurrection. Further, Allah (SWT) narrates to us different stories in this *surah* relating to different trials that we encounter during our earthly existence.

## SPECIAL TIME FOR MAKING *DU'A'*

One should also be keen to make *du'a'* on Friday, seeking to have one's *du'a'* coincide with the special moment of acceptance that, according to the *sunnah*, has been placed on this day. Two main opinions exist regarding the timing of this special moment of acceptance: It lies somewhere between either (1) the time the imam sits on the pulpit and the conclusion of the Friday prayer, or (2) between *'Asr* and *Maghrib* on Friday. One can join between both opinions, implementing the first by saying *ameen* to the *du'a'* of the imam during the *khutbah*, and by making *du'a'* while the imam is seated between the two *khutbahs*, and in the final sitting during the prayer; and implementing the second by dedicating some time to make *du'a'* between *'Asr* and *Maghrib* on Friday.

# Transcripts of *Khutbahs*

# • 1 •

# ALLAH IS OUR *RABB* (LORD)

The topic of today's *khutbah* is based on verses thirty through thirty-two of *Surat Fussilat*. These blessed verses talk about the special people who say that Allah is their *Rabb* (Lord) and then they remain firm on what they say.

إِنَّ الَّذِينَ قَالُوا رَبُّنَا اللَّهُ ثُمَّ اسْتَقَامُوا تَتَنَزَّلُ عَلَيْهِمُ الْمَلَائِكَةُ أَلَّا تَخَافُوا وَلَا تَحْزَنُوا وَأَبْشِرُوا بِالْجَنَّةِ الَّتِي كُنْتُمْ تُوعَدُونَ ○

*The ones who say, Allah is our Rabb, and then remain steadfast, the angels will descend on them, saying, Have no fear and do not grieve. Rejoice in the good news of the Garden that you have been promised. (Fussilat, 41:30)*

The word *Rabb* is very profound. It means provider, sustainer, protector, benefactor, owner, and master. If Allah is accepted as one's *Rabb*, as He should be, then He is to be obeyed totally. There is no question of complying with some commandments of Allah and not complying with others or considering some parts of these commandments to be practicable and others to be impracticable. To consider some commandments of Allah as impracticable is not to trust in the knowledge and wisdom of Allah. Whatever comes from Him is out of His absolute knowledge and wisdom, every divine command is to be accepted and obeyed. Allah says in the Qur`an,

يَا أَيُّهَا الَّذِينَ آمَنُوا ادْخُلُوا فِي السِّلْمِ كَافَّةً ○
*O you who believe! Enter Islam totally. (al-Baqara, 2:208)*

At the same time, there has to be complete *tawakkul* (reliance) on Allah. *Tawakkul* means putting in one's best efforts, leaving no stone unturned, and then putting one's trust in Allah and not in one's own efforts or means. Whatever the outcome, it comes about only with the approval and decree of Allah and not otherwise. It is reported that one day Prophet Muhammad (SAS) noticed a Bedouin leaving his camel without tying it. He asked the Bedouin, "Why don't you tie down your camel?" The Bedouin answered, "I put my trust in Allah." The Prophet (SAS) then said, "Tie your camel first, then put your trust in Allah."

The true believers remain steadfast on the affirmation that Allah is indeed their *Rabb*. They stick to what they claim. They demonstrate it in their thinking, feelings, actions, and behavior. According to a hadeeth, a companion by the name of Abi 'Amrah

Sufyan bin 'Abdullah (RAA) said to the Prophet (SAS), "O Messenger of Allah, tell me something of Islam which I can ask of no one but you." The Prophet (SAS) replied, "Say I believe in Allah, and then be steadfast."

To declare "I believe in Allah" is easy, but to hold on to it and earnestly live by it is not that easy. It takes no effort or energy to utter the few simple words of la ilaha illa Allah (there is no god but Allah) but to be firm on it, to stick to it, and to stand up for it is not easy at all. Claiming Allah to be one's *Rabb* means that one should not have any complaint about Allah's decisions and should accept them with complete calmness. Sometimes, the things we go through by the will of Allah may even be unpleasant, but whatever comes from Allah is going to benefit us in the long run. Nothing befalls a person without His permission. Allah says in the Qur'an,

$$مَا أَصَابَ مِن مُّصِيبَةٍ إِلَّا بِإِذْنِ اللَّهِ وَمَن يُؤْمِن بِاللَّهِ يَهْدِ قَلْبَهُ وَاللَّهُ بِكُلِّ شَيْءٍ عَلِيمٌ ○$$

*No misfortune occurs except by Allah's permission. Whoever has belief (iman) in Allah, He will guide his heart. Allah has knowledge of all things. (at-Taghabun, 64:11)*

A true righteous believer who says, "Our *Rabb* is Allah" and remains firm on it has attained the level of *ihsan* (excellence in faith), which is the highest state of *iman* (belief). When there is real *iman*, there is no fear. This is because true believers understand that nothing happens without Allah's permission. Nothing can harm them unless He wills it. And if any harm comes, it is only with His permission, and is therefore acceptable to them, as He is their *Rabb*, their Lord. His decision, however unpleasant it may seem, has to be for some ultimate good. The prick of an injection is painful but beneficial. Surgical amputation of a limb is a loss, but it saves one's life. Hence the friends of Allah have no fear and are not grieved even if a calamity befalls them. In *Surat at-Tawba*, the believers are told to say to the hypocrites:

$$قُل لَّن يُصِيبَنَا إِلَّا مَا كَتَبَ اللَّهُ لَنَا هُوَ مَوْلَانَا وَعَلَى اللَّهِ فَلْيَتَوَكَّلِ الْمُؤْمِنُونَ ○$$

*Say, nothing can happen to us except what Allah has ordained for us. He is Our Master. It is in Allah that the believers should put their trust. (at-Tawba, 9:51)*

What happens to the believers who say that their *Rabb* is Allah, stick to what they say, and lead their lives accordingly?

$$○ تَتَنَزَّلُ عَلَيْهِمُ الْمَلَائِكَةُ$$

*Angels descend upon them. (Fussilat, 41:30)*

There is a general consensus that angels descend upon believers when they are about to die and move from this world to the next world. The angels come from the invisible world to welcome the souls of these believers and escort them honorably to that world. Imagine this: You are on your death bed, and while everyone is crying around you, angels descend upon you tell you that you have nothing to fear and nothing to be sad about. They give you the glad tidings of *jannah* (paradise). What more can a Muslim strive for? That is the reward of taking Allah as one's *Rabb* and then staying firm on it.

Do angels descend upon virtuous believers only when they are about to die, or do the angels also descend upon them in this life? The Qur'an speaks about angels descending to help and support believers in their fight against the forces of evil. For example, the angels descended upon them in the Battle of Badr. We also learn this through a hadeeth that says: "Any group of people that assembles in one of the Houses of Allah to study the Qur'an, tranquility will descend upon them, mercy will engulf them, angels will surround them and Allah will make mention of them to those in His proximity (i.e., the angels)." And what do the angels say to these righteous believers?

نَحْنُ أَوْلِيَاؤُكُمْ فِي الْحَيَاةِ الدُّنْيَا وَفِي الْآخِرَةِ وَلَكُمْ فِيهَا مَا تَشْتَهِي أَنْفُسُكُمْ وَلَكُمْ فِيهَا مَا تَدَّعُونَ ⦿ نُزُلًا مِنْ غَفُورٍ رَحِيمٍ ⦿

*We are your companions in this life and in the hereafter. Therein you shall have all that your souls desire, and therein you shall have all that you ask for. (Fussilat, 41:31-32)*

We should know that Allah has created man and has placed in him the desire for worldly things and satisfying his desires. This is ingrained in human nature. Allah says,

زُيِّنَ لِلنَّاسِ حُبُّ الشَّهَوَاتِ مِنَ النِّسَاءِ وَالْبَنِينَ وَالْقَنَاطِيرِ الْمُقَنْطَرَةِ مِنَ الذَّهَبِ وَالْفِضَّةِ وَالْخَيْلِ الْمُسَوَّمَةِ وَالْأَنْعَامِ وَالْحَرْثِ ذَلِكَ مَتَاعُ الْحَيَاةِ الدُّنْيَا وَاللَّهُ عِنْدَهُ حُسْنُ الْمَآبِ ⦿

*The satisfaction of worldly desires through women, children, heaped-up treasures of gold and silver, pedigreed horses, cattle, and land, is attractive to people. All this is the provision of the worldly life; but the most excellent abode is with Allah. (Aal 'Imran, 3:14)*

At the same time, the wrong and the right path have also been clearly indicated:

وَهَدَيْنَاهُ النَّجْدَيْنِ ⦿

*And We showed him the two paths [of good and evil]. (al-Balad, 90:10)*

Having been endowed with free will, man is solely responsible for the moral choices he makes. A true believer, despite his natural inclination to satisfy his worldly desires, does so only through *halal* (lawful) means, and checks himself from indulging in anything that is *haram* (unlawful), however tempting or attractive it may be. When one leads a pious and righteous life in this world, he is promised paradise. In paradise he will be able to satisfy all his desires to the maximum, and he will have whatever he asks for of things that he likes. When all their desires are fulfilled, the last and final desire of the people of paradise will be to have a direct sight of their Lord, with no covering between Him and them.

The people of paradise are the guests of Allah. No one knows what Allah will actually give to them. We learn through a hadeeth that the Messenger of Allah (SAS) said, "Allah, the Exalted, has said, 'I have prepared for my righteous slaves what no eye has seen, no ear has heard, and the mind of no man has conceived.'" Furthermore, Allah says in the Qur`an,

$$\text{فَلَا تَعْلَمُ نَفْسٌ مَّا أُخْفِيَ لَهُم مِّن قُرَّةِ أَعْيُنٍ جَزَاءً بِمَا كَانُوا يَعْمَلُونَ}$$

*No soul knows what joy is kept hidden in store for them as a reward for their labors.*
(as-Sajda, 32:17)

May Allah make us also among the inhabitants of that abode of eternal bliss. *Allahumma ameen.*

# •  2  •

# ALLAH NEVER BREAKS HIS PROMISE

The topic of today's *khutbah* is: "Allah never breaks His Promise." In other words, Allah never fails to fulfill His promise.

$$\text{رَبَّنَا إِنَّكَ جَامِعُ النَّاسِ لِيَوْمٍ لَّا رَيْبَ فِيهِ إِنَّ اللَّهَ لَا يُخْلِفُ الْمِيعَادَ}$$

*Our Lord, You will gather all people on the Day in which there is no doubt: Surely Allah never breaks His promise. (Aal 'Imran, 3:9)*

$$\text{وَعْدَ اللَّهِ حَقًّا وَهُوَ الْعَزِيزُ الْحَكِيمُ}$$

The promise of Allah is true, and He is exalted in Power, Wise. (Luqman, 31:9)

$$\text{يَا أَيُّهَا النَّاسُ إِنَّ وَعْدَ اللَّهِ حَقٌّ فَلَا تَغُرَّنَّكُمُ الْحَيَاةُ الدُّنْيَا وَلَا يَغُرَّنَّكُم بِاللَّهِ الْغَرُورُ}$$

*O mankind! Allah's promise is true. So do not let the life of the world deceive you, nor let the Deceiver deceive you about Allah. (Fatir, 35:5)*

$$\text{وَعْدَ اللَّهِ لَا يُخْلِفُ اللَّهُ الْمِيعَادَ}$$

*This is Allah's promise: Allah never fails in His promise. (az-Zumar, 39:20)*

All these verses in the Qur`an tell us that that when Allah promises something, He means it and that thing will come to pass. Fulfilling promises is a great virtue. We like and respect people who fulfill their promises. Allah also promises many good things to the righteous believers. They know that Allah's promise never fails. Let us reflect upon some of the many promises that Allah has made to his believing servants.

One of the promises Allah makes is:

$$لَئِن شَكَرْتُمْ لَأَزِيدَنَّكُمْ ﴿ ﴾$$

*If you are thankful, I will certainly give you more. (Ibraheem, 14:7)*

Do we thank Allah enough? Do we think about all the free gifts of life: The air we breathe, the water we drink, the food we eat, the faculties of hearing, seeing, and thinking; the muscles and limbs that we use to do any act, and the list goes on. We should thank Allah with our tongues, with our hearts, with our minds, and through our actions by using His blessings for good purposes, and by worshiping and obeying Him. If we do this, we're surely going to get more. This is Allah's promise and He does not break His promise.

Another promise Allah makes is:

$$مَنْ عَمِلَ صَالِحًا مِنْ ذَكَرٍ أَوْ أُنْثَى وَهُوَ مُؤْمِنٌ فَلَنُحْيِيَنَّهُ حَيَاةً طَيِّبَةً وَلَنَجْزِيَنَّهُمْ أَجْرَهُمْ بِأَحْسَنِ مَا كَانُوا يَعْمَلُونَ ﴿ ﴾$$

*Whoever does good, whether male or female, and is a believer, We will surely bless them with a good life, and We will certainly reward them according to the best of their deeds. (an-Nahl, 16:97)*

This verse corrects the idea that those who adopt a just, honest, and pious life will somehow be losers in this world. Instead, Allah explains that righteous attitudes and actions not only lead to a happy life in the hereafter, but they also guarantee a pure and happy life in this world. It is a fact that those who are sincerely righteous, honest, and fair enjoy a much better quality of life. The confidence, honor, and respect that they enjoy because of their good character is not enjoyed by those who employ illegal, unfair, and immoral ways to achieve success in this world. Further, the rank of the righteous believers in the hereafter shall be determined according to their best deeds. In other words, if a person has done both small and great deeds, he will be awarded that high rank which he would merit according to his greatest virtues. Ibn Taymiyya (RA) said, "If the kings knew the happiness and pleasure that we feel in our hearts, they would come and try to take it away from us with the tips of their swords."

Allah also promises that He responds to those who call upon Him.

وَقَالَ رَبُّكُمُ ادْعُونِي أَسْتَجِبْ لَكُمْ ○

*And your Lord said: Call on me. I will respond to you. (al-Ghafir, 40:60)*

The Qur`an also tells us about the extraordinary importance of praying to Allah for all our needs.

وَإِذَا سَأَلَكَ عِبَادِي عَنِّي فَإِنِّي قَرِيبٌ أُجِيبُ دَعْوَةَ الدَّاعِ إِذَا دَعَانِ فَلْيَسْتَجِيبُوا لِي وَلْيُؤْمِنُوا بِي لَعَلَّهُمْ يَرْشُدُونَ ○

*When My servants ask you about Me, say that I am near. I respond to the call of one who calls, whenever he calls to Me: let them, then, respond to Me, and believe in Me, so that they may be rightly guided. (al-Baqara, 2:186)*

We should make *du'a`* with great hope and conviction. The Prophet (SAS) tells us, "Pray to Allah with the conviction that you will be answered and know that Allah does not answer a supplication that comes from a careless and inattentive heart." In another hadeeth he (SAS) tells us, "Any Muslim who makes a *du'a`*, provided the *du'a`* contains nothing which is sinful or which involves breaking family ties, Allah will give one of three things: He will quickly grant him what he asked for, or save the reward for him for the hereafter, or turn away from him a similar hardship." This means that the hardship would have hit him in the absence of that *du'a`*. Another promise that Allah makes in the Qur`an is:

فَاذْكُرُونِي أَذْكُرْكُمْ وَاشْكُرُوا لِي وَلَا تَكْفُرُونِ ○

*So remember Me; I shall remember you. And thank Me, and never be ungrateful. (al-Baqara, 2:152)*

How can we remember Allah throughout the day without withdrawing from the routine of our daily life? How can we make sure that our personal life, family life, professional life, and all other activities continue in full swing while filling every moment with the remembrance of Allah? This is something that appears to be very difficult, but al-hamduli-llah, it is something that can be accomplished if we want. Each one of us should say to himself or herself: I am in Allah's presence, and He is watching me. He is with me wherever I am.

وَهُوَ مَعَكُمْ أَيْنَ مَا كُنتُمْ وَاللَّهُ بِمَا تَعْمَلُونَ بَصِيرٌ ○

*And He is with you wherever you are; He sees all that you do. (al-Hadeed, 57:4)*

When the Prophet Muhammad (SAS) was asked by a companion about the best method of purifying himself, he replied, "You should always remember that Allah is with you wherever you are." He also said, "Be mindful of Allah, and Allah will protect you. Be mindful of Allah, and you will find Him before you."

Allah also promises that He accepts repentance of those who sincerely repent and turn to him.

أَلَمْ يَعْلَمُوا أَنَّ اللَّهَ هُوَ يَقْبَلُ التَّوْبَةَ عَنْ عِبَادِهِ وَيَأْخُذُ الصَّدَقَاتِ وَأَنَّ اللَّهَ هُوَ التَّوَّابُ الرَّحِيمُ ◯

*Do they not know that Allah alone accepts the repentance of His servants and receives their charity, and that Allah alone is the Acceptor of Repentance, Most Merciful? (at-Tawba, 9:104)*

One of the beautiful names of Allah is "at-Tawwab," which means "The Accepter of Repentance." Allah accepts repentance of those who sincerely repent and turn to him. The name "at-Tawwab" gives the sense of "oft-returning," which means that Allah accepts a person's repentance again and again. We commit sins and make mistakes. We then repent and He accepts our repentance. Then we again commit sins and make mistakes and we repent. And He again accepts our repentance. He keeps on giving us opportunities to repent and mend our ways.

One of the most beautiful things about repentance and turning to Allah and doing good deeds is that Allah not only wipes the sins away, but also replaces them with good deeds.

مَنْ تَابَ وَآمَنَ وَعَمِلَ عَمَلًا صَالِحًا فَأُولَئِكَ يُبَدِّلُ اللَّهُ سَيِّئَاتِهِمْ حَسَنَاتٍ وَكَانَ اللَّهُ غَفُورًا رَحِيمًا ◯

*Those who repent, believe, and do good deeds, Allah will change the evil deeds of such people into good ones. He is most forgiving, most merciful. (al-Furqan, 25:70)*

According to a hadeeth, the Prophet (SAS) said, "The one who repents from sin is like one who did not sin." This means that if a person commits a sin, sincerely repents, gives it up, regrets having done it, prays for forgiveness, and does not go back to it, Allah will accept his repentance and treat him like one who did not sin. Allah makes another promise by saying,

وَالَّذِينَ آمَنُوا وَعَمِلُوا الصَّالِحَاتِ سَنُدْخِلُهُمْ جَنَّاتٍ تَجْرِي مِنْ تَحْتِهَا الْأَنْهَارُ خَالِدِينَ فِيهَا أَبَدًا وَعْدَ اللَّهِ حَقًّا وَمَنْ أَصْدَقُ مِنَ اللَّهِ قِيلًا ◯

*And those who believe and do good, We will soon admit them into gardens under which rivers flow, to stay there forever. Allah's promise is true. And whose word is more truthful than Allah's? (an-Nisa`, 4:122)*

Allah guarantees paradise to those who believe and do good deeds. Paradise is the eternal abode we should all be striving for in this world. Our deeds in this world should bring us closer to Allah and closer to attaining jannah. If they are not bringing us closer to Allah, then we need to reevaluate our lives, purify our intentions, make a concerted effort to refrain from sins, and seek Allah's forgiveness and His mercy. Let us place our trust in Allah and have full faith in His promises and see how our life changes for the better.

وَتَوَكَّلْ عَلَى اللَّهِ وَكَفَى بِاللَّهِ وَكِيلًا ◯

*And put your trust in Allah. Allah is sufficient as a Trustee. (an-Nisa`, 4:81)*

Brothers and sisters! There is a promise that Allah (SWT) makes when He says,

إِنَّ الَّذِينَ آمَنُوا وَعَمِلُوا الصَّالِحَاتِ إِنَّا لَا نُضِيعُ أَجْرَ مَنْ أَحْسَنَ عَمَلًا ◯

*As for those who believe and perform good deeds: We do not let the reward of anyone who does a good deed go to waste. (al-Kahf, 18:30)*

Allah promises us that our good deeds will never be wasted. Every single righteous deed will be rewarded, in this world and in the hereafter. In this world, the reward may not be in the form we wanted, but it will be in the form that is best for us, because Allah loves us. The reward in the hereafter will be far better and far beyond our imagination. True righteous believers always pray to Allah to make them worthy of the promises that He has made to them. They cry out:

رَبَّنَا وَآتِنَا مَا وَعَدْتَنَا عَلَى رُسُلِكَ وَلَا تُخْزِنَا يَوْمَ الْقِيَامَةِ إِنَّكَ لَا تُخْلِفُ الْمِيعَادَ ◯

*Our Lord! Grant us what You have promised to us through Your messengers, and do not humiliate us on the Day of Resurrection. Surely You never fail to fulfill Your promise. (Aal ‘Imran, 3:194)*

Such people do not doubt the fact that Allah will fulfill His promises. What they do doubt is whether they will be counted among those for whom those promises were made. Hence, they pray to Allah to make them worthy of His promised rewards.

These are some of the many promises of Allah Almighty to His believing servants which we can benefit from by following our faith and religious responsibilities submissively.

# • 3 •

# ARE WE PRACTICING MUSLIMS?

Are we practicing Muslims? We pray five times a day. We fast in the month of Ramadan. We pay our *zakat*. We have performed the hajj or intend to do so. We participate in Islamic activities. We are contributing members of Islamic organizations. We practice *dhikr* (remembrance of Allah). We donate to charities. After doing all this, should we consider ourselves as practicing Muslims?

These days, the term "practicing Muslim" is usually understood to mean a person who practices the "five pillars" of Islam. The emphasis seems to be more on the observance of rituals in order to be called a practicing Muslim or Muslima. But is it enough that we are simply physically practicing these rituals? What about the importance of our aims and objectives? How are we to ensure that our objectives are being met or that we are, at the very least, moving in the right direction?

In the Muslim community there are two categories of people. One group consists of people focused on the rituals of Islam. They never miss prayers, they fast frequently, they do 'umrah and hajj, they are very conscious of their Islamic dress, and they read the Qur`an. Unfortunately, however, some of them do not have a pleasant character. They don't care for their neighbors, have no sympathy for their colleagues and employees, and at times they are even rude, mean, and stingy with their family members. In short, they often display bad manners and ethics.

And then there are those who have all the humanitarian qualities: Forever helpful, cheerful and kind, generous and polite, honest and hardworking. But they do not practice the rituals. They do not believe in praying or fasting. They would rather give the money in charity than spend it on going to hajj. They will eat, drink, and dress the way they feel like because they are not concerned about following Islamic teachings.

Yet both these groups are Muslims. Actually, we have compartmentalized Islam into separate components, and as a consequence, our efforts are not producing the results we would expect. Yet, if we study the Qur`an carefully, then it will become quite obvious that a people who are satisfied with their state of indignity, dependence, hopelessness and insecurity are a people experiencing Allah's wrath.

We need to recognize that compassion and mercy, engagement with others, and genuine self-sacrifice are key aspects to our faith for a reason. Allah promises that He will give us power and dignity in this world in return for our faith and good deeds.

وَعَدَ اللَّهُ الَّذِينَ آمَنُوا مِنْكُمْ وَعَمِلُوا الصَّالِحَاتِ لَيَسْتَخْلِفَنَّهُمْ فِي الْأَرْضِ كَمَا اسْتَخْلَفَ الَّذِينَ مِنْ قَبْلِهِمْ

وَلَيُمَكِّنَنَّ لَهُمْ دِينَهُمُ الَّذِي ارْتَضَى لَهُمْ وَلَيُبَدِّلَنَّهُمْ مِنْ بَعْدِ خَوْفِهِمْ أَمْنًا ◯

*Allah has promised those of you who believe and do good that He will certainly make them successors in the land, as He did with those before them; and will surely establish for them their faith which He has chosen for them and will indeed change their fear into security. (an-Nur, 24:55)*

And we also read in *Surat an-Nahl,*

مَنْ عَمِلَ صَالِحًا مِنْ ذَكَرٍ أَوْ أُنْثَى وَهُوَ مُؤْمِنٌ فَلَنُحْيِيَنَّهُ حَيَاةً طَيِّبَةً وَلَنَجْزِيَنَّهُمْ أَجْرَهُمْ بِأَحْسَنِ مَا كَانُوا يَعْمَلُونَ ◯

*Whoever does good, whether male or female, and is a believer, We will surely bless them with a good life, and We will certainly reward them according to the best of their deeds. (an-Nahl, 16:97)*

In many Muslim societies it is common to practice the five pillars of Islam, but we still don't experience the same quality of society enjoyed by the Prophet (SAS) and his companions. Let's explore some reasons why this might be the case. Remember the Prophet's saying, "He is not a believer whose stomach is filled while the neighbor to his side goes hungry."

A man asked the Prophet (SAS), "Which Islam is best?" The Prophet (SAS) said, "Feed the hungry and greet with peace those you know and those you do not know."

The Qur'an covers all aspects of life and offers us insight into how to live. That means Islam is a system of life. Other religions address only the personal relationship between the individual and God. Islam, on the other hand, addresses both personal and societal aspects of life. To this end, Islam considers every believer to be an extremely important individual, whose every action and struggle will have an effect on the society at large.

If one's religious practice has not resulted in dignity, self-respect, power, and independence, then a reassessment is necessary. If we look to the time of our Prophet (SAS) and attend to the programs and plans of Muslims in those days, will we not find that the very same pillars of faith that transformed that society are not producing the desired results for us today?

On sincere reflection, we will come to know that our practice of those very same pillars seems to have taken us nowhere. Not only should we then refrain from self-acclaim in pronouncing ourselves to be practicing Muslims, but more importantly we must spend time in self-examination and reflection in regard to correcting our errors, and then seek to rebuild and establish a society truly worthy of the name, "practicing Muslims." We are given the book of guidance that shows us how. We need only attend to the message given.

An important note here is that we should avoid making sweeping statements and passing judgments about people as to whether or not they are practicing Muslims. Only Allah knows each one of us inside out. He alone can read our hearts. He also knows if we're sincerely sorry for our mistakes. Even the Muslim who appears to be non-practicing on the outside may have a deep love for Allah within.

So rather than us categorizing Muslims into practicing and non-practicing, we should look into the Qur`an, which has clearly categorized Muslims into three different categories. We read in the Qur`an in *Surat Fatir*,

$$ ثُمَّ أَوْرَثْنَا الْكِتَابَ الَّذِينَ اصْطَفَيْنَا مِنْ عِبَادِنَا فَمِنْهُمْ ظَالِمٌ لِنَفْسِهِ وَمِنْهُمْ مُقْتَصِدٌ وَمِنْهُمْ سَابِقٌ بِالْخَيْرَاتِ بِإِذْنِ اللَّهِ ذَلِكَ هُوَ الْفَضْلُ الْكَبِيرُ $$

*Then We have given the Book for inheritance to those We have chosen from Our servants. Some of them wrong themselves, some follow a middle course, and some are foremost in good deeds by Allah's Will. That is the greatest bounty. (Fatir, 35:32)*

Thus, the Qur`an divides the Muslims into three categories:

(1) Those that wrong themselves or are unjust to themselves: They are those who believe sincerely and honestly that the Qur`an is the Book of Allah and Muhammad (SAS) the Messenger of Allah, but in everyday life they do not fully follow the Book of Allah and the Sunnah of His Messenger (SAS). They are believers but sinful, wrongdoers but not rebellious. They are weak of faith but not hypocritical or unbelieving at heart. Therefore, although they are unjust to themselves, they have been included among the chosen servants of God and among the heirs of the Book. This category is most numerous among the Muslims. (2) Those following a middle course: They are the people who fulfill their obligations to some extent but not fully. They are obedient as well as going astray. They have not left their *nafs* (self) altogether free but try as best as they can to turn it to God's obedience. However, at times they give it undue freedom and become involved in sin. Thus, their life becomes a combination of both good and evil actions. They are less numerous than the first category of Muslims. (3) Those excelling in good deeds: They are the people of the first rank among the heirs to the Book, and they are the ones who are doing full justice to the inheritance. They are in the forefront in following and adhering to the Qur`an and the Sunnah by conveying the message of God to His servants, offering sacrifices for the sake of the true faith, and doing every pious and good work. They are not the ones who would commit a sin deliberately, but if they happened to commit a sin by mistake, they would be filled with shame as soon as they became conscious of it. They are less numerous than the people of the first two groups.

Imam Ibn Katheer (RA) has explained these three kinds by saying that "the one who wrongs himself" means a person who falls short in fulfilling some obligatory duties, and goes on to commit some of what is forbidden as well. And the one who follows the middle course is a person who fulfills all legally binding obligations and avoids everything forbidden, but on occasion leaves out what has been recommended and falls into what is blameworthy. And excellent is the one who goes ahead of everyone in good deeds, fulfills all obligatory and recommended duties, avoids everything declared forbidden or reprehensible, and even goes further to leave what is allowed to him because of his devotion to acts of worship or because of some doubt in its lawfulness.

Now, it is up to each one of us to see which category we fall into according to the categorization given by the Qur`an. And the ultimate judgment lies with Allah (SWT).

For believers, the goal of a blissful existence both in this life and the hereafter must be pursued with good actions, expressed in terms of what is truly human and humane in the world in which we live. May Allah give us *tawfeeq* for this and may He bless each one of us. *Ameen!*

<br>

## • 4 •

# ARE WE MUSLIMS BY CHANCE OR BY CHOICE?

Are we Muslims by chance or by choice? If someone asks, "Are you a Muslim?" the immediate answer will be, "Yes I am." But what if someone asks, "Why are you a Muslim?" This will make you stop answering that question immediately and will make you start to think. For most of us the answer might be, "It's because I was born and raised in a Muslim family." But is that the correct answer? What if we hadn't been born into a Muslim family? Would we still be a Muslim?

Each person, as we know, is born into circumstances which are not of their own choosing. The religion of his family or the ideology of the state is thrust upon him from the very beginning of his existence in this world. By the time he reaches his teens, he is usually fully brainwashed into believing that the beliefs of his particular family or society are the correct beliefs. Generally, he becomes a Jew, Christian, Muslim, Hindu, Sikh, Buddhist, or follower of any other religion or creed because of being born and raised in a family of that faith or creed.

When some people mature and are exposed to other belief systems, however, they begin to question the validity of their own beliefs. The seekers of truth often reach a point of confusion upon realizing that each and every religion, sect, ideology, and philosophy claims to be the one and only correct way for mankind.

Indeed, they all encourage people to do good deeds, so which one is right? They cannot all be right since each claims all others to be wrong. Like every religion, Islam claims to be the one and only true way to God. In this respect it is no different from other systems. We must keep in mind that we can only determine the true path by putting aside the emotions and prejudices which often blind us to reality. Then and only then will we be able to use our God-given intelligence and make a rational and correct decision. The Prophet (SAS) said, "Every child is born in a state of *fitra*. Then his parents make him a Jew, a Christian, or a Zoroastrian..." *Fitra* is a natural belief in God and an inborn inclination to worship Him alone. This means that if the child were left alone, he would worship God in his own way, but all children are affected by the environment. So just as the child submits to the physical laws which Allah has imposed upon nature, in the same way his soul also submits naturally to the fact that Allah is his Lord and Creator. But if his parents try to make him follow a different path, the child is not strong enough in the early stages of his life to resist or oppose the will of his parents. In such cases, the religion which the child follows is one of custom and upbringing, and God does not hold him to account or punish him for his beliefs until he becomes old enough and mature enough to use his intellect.

Converting to Islam means transforming a person's religion to the primordial religion of Islam by choice. Islam has been the religion of all the prophets and messengers of Allah from Adam (AS), the first man on earth; to Muhammad (SAS), the last and final Messenger of Allah. Religious leaders and others are often more interested in converting persons from other religions to their religions, but not as interested in converting the persons of their own religion from "by chance" to "by choice." For now, let us focus on the Muslims: Usually, they are born into a Muslim family and hence have "Muslim names." They are Muslims "by chance," and do not feel the necessity to convert or to become Muslims "by choice." Why? Because they can enjoy all the privileges of Islam even if they do not fulfill the duties and responsibilities which Islam imposes upon them.

A Muslim "by chance" can marry a Muslim. He or she can hold the highest office in an Islamic organization and can even become the President or Prime Minister of a Muslim country without having to face any questions about his or her beliefs and practices of Islam. To become a Muslim "by choice" would mean to follow Islam in letter and spirit: by leaving the unlawful and submitting to Allah instead of one's whims and base desires. Hence, to continue living as a Muslim "by chance" is much easier than to become a Muslim "by choice" which is hard and demands sacrifice. In *Surat an-Nisa`*

Allah (SWT) admonishes the weak Muslims and the hypocrites to believe:

يَا أَيُّهَا الَّذِينَ آمَنُوا آمِنُوا بِاللَّهِ وَرَسُولِهِ وَالْكِتَابِ الَّذِي نَزَّلَ عَلَى رَسُولِهِ وَالْكِتَابِ الَّذِي أَنْزَلَ مِنْ قَبْلُ وَمَنْ يَكْفُرْ بِاللَّهِ وَمَلَائِكَتِهِ وَكُتُبِهِ وَرُسُلِهِ وَالْيَوْمِ الْآخِرِ فَقَدْ ضَلَّ ضَلَالًا بَعِيدًا ◯

*O you who believe! Believe in Allah and His Messenger and in the scripture He sent down to His Messenger, as well as what He sent down before. He who denies Allah, His angels, His scriptures, His messengers and the Last Day has surely gone far astray.*
(an-Nisa`, 4:136)

To ask believers to believe might at first seem strange. But the fact is that "belief" here has two meanings. Firstly, a person "believes" because he was born and raised in a Muslim home. Therefore, by default, he joins the camp of the believers. Secondly, "belief" indicates true faith, which means a person's believing in the truth with full sincerity. It denotes one's sincere determination to mold his way of thinking, his likes and dislikes, his conduct and character, his friendship and enmity, and the direction of his efforts and striving, in compliance with the creed which he has resolved to embrace. In this verse of the Qur`an, the believers in the first sense of the term are being asked to change themselves into true believers, meaning "believers" in the second sense. The first group of believers may be categorized as Muslims "by chance" and the second as Muslims "by choice."

The next verse in the same *surah* tells us,

إِنَّ الَّذِينَ آمَنُوا ثُمَّ كَفَرُوا ثُمَّ آمَنُوا ثُمَّ كَفَرُوا ثُمَّ ازْدَادُوا كُفْرًا لَمْ يَكُنِ اللَّهُ لِيَغْفِرَ لَهُمْ وَلَا لِيَهْدِيَهُمْ سَبِيلًا ◯

*Those who believed, and then disbelieved, then believed, and again disbelieved, and then they became more intense in their disbelief, Allah will neither forgive them nor guide them to the right path. (an-Nisa`, 4:137)*

This refers to those Muslims who do not consider the question of faith as a serious matter but play with it as long as it suits their desires and fancies. One wave carries them to the fold of Islam and the next to that of disbelief. Allah will neither forgive such people nor guide them to the right path. Such Muslims "by chance" often behave like hypocrites. They are secular, liberal, and modern like their disbelieving friends in culture, in thoughts, and in their way of life.

Islam is a lifestyle and value system. Every aspect of life has a paradigm, a pattern, or a model for daily living. The paradigm of the self-destructive global civilization generally, and the secular modern Western civilization specifically, is to work only for material success in this world. This paradigm teaches that death is the end of all life, and therefore people will not be held accountable for their deeds. This is in sharp contrast to the Islamic worldview that considers man to be accountable for all his actions in this life because he will be judged by God Almighty in the next life. He will then be either among the people of paradise enjoying an eternal blissful life, or among the people of hellfire suffering from a painful punishment. May Allah admit us into paradise and keep us far away from the hellfire, ameen.

Brothers and sisters! *Al-hamduli-llah*, we are all Muslims. We claim to be Muslims. As Muslims, we believe in every word of the Qur`an. The Qur`an states:

إِنَّ الدِّينَ عِندَ اللَّهِ الْإِسْلَامُ ○

*The deen in the sight of Allah is Islam. (Aal 'Imran, 3:19)*

Allah (SWT) also says,

وَمَن يَبْتَغِ غَيْرَ الْإِسْلَامِ دِينًا فَلَن يُقْبَلَ مِنْهُ وَهُوَ فِي الْآخِرَةِ مِنَ الْخَاسِرِينَ ○

*If anyone desires anything other than Islam as a deen, it will not be accepted from him,*
*and in the hereafter, he will be among the losers. (Aal 'Imran, 3:85)*

What is our level of certainty (*yaqeen*) in Islam? Do we ever care to assess our *yaqeen* in the truthfulness of Islam? Are our hearts full of love for Allah (SWT) and the Prophet Muhammad (SAS)? Do we experience Allah in our daily lives, influencing everything around us? Are we conscious of Him with all the consciousness that is due to Him? When we hold His book in our hands, do we think of it as the speech of the One whose mercy is beyond our comprehension, the One that created us and therefore knows us better than we know our own selves? When we look at the nature around us and at our own bodies, do our hearts testify to the existence of the Creator of the heavens and the earth?

In this age of doubt, when atheism and agnosticism have become commonplace, and when media outlets have become saturated with attacks on Islam and Muslims, many of us can find it hard to achieve the highest levels of certainty. It is crucial that the basis of our Islam be an unshakable *yaqeen* in Allah, in His Messenger (SAS), in the Qur`an, and in the hereafter. If we have it, we will always want to act in a manner pleasing to Allah.

The central principle of Islam and its meaning is "the surrender of one's will to God." In order to actually submit to God's will, one must continually choose between right and wrong. Indeed, man is blessed by God with the power not only to distinguish between right and wrong but also to *choose* between right and wrong. This God-given power carries with it an important responsibility—that man is answerable to God for the choices he makes. It follows, then, that man should try his utmost to do good and avoid evil and to consciously live by the dictates of the divine teachings. Such a believer can be said to be a Muslim "by choice."

I will conclude by reminding myself and you to become Muslims "by choice."

يَا أَيُّهَا الَّذِينَ آمَنُوا ادْخُلُوا فِي السِّلْمِ كَافَّةً وَلَا تَتَّبِعُوا خُطُوَاتِ الشَّيْطَانِ إِنَّهُ لَكُمْ عَدُوٌّ مُبِينٌ ○

*O you who believe! Enter Islam totally. Do not follow in the footsteps of Shaytan. He is an outright enemy to you. (al-Baqara, 2:208)*

وَلَا تَهِنُوا وَلَا تَحْزَنُوا وَأَنتُمُ الْأَعْلَوْنَ إِن كُنتُم مُّؤْمِنِينَ ○

*Do not weaken or grieve: you shall have the upper hand, if you are true believers. (Aal 'Imran, 3:139)*

May Allah guide us and help us increase our level of *yaqeen*, and may our Islam be our *choice*, even if we are also Muslims "by chance." May we live on Islam and die on Islam, *ameen*.

<br>

# • 5 •

# BACKBITING *(GHEEBA)*

<br>

Today's *khutbah* is on the topic of *gheeba* or backbiting. It is one of the greatest sins and yet it is something we do day after day. The discussion shall revolve around addressing questions such as: What is meant by *gheeba*? How is *gheeba* defined? Why is *gheeba* so harmful? Why do people fall into the sin of *gheeba*? What are the exceptional circumstances under which *gheeba* is allowed? What should we do to avoid *gheeba*?

What is meant by *gheeba*? *Gheeba* is derived from the three letter Arabic root (*ghayn-yaa-baa*) meaning that which is unseen or absent. The words *ghaabahu* or *ightaabahu* mean, "He spoke evil of him in his absence." Allah says in the Qur'an,

يَا أَيُّهَا الَّذِينَ آمَنُوا اجْتَنِبُوا كَثِيرًا مِنَ الظَّنِّ إِنَّ بَعْضَ الظَّنِّ إِثْمٌ وَلَا تَجَسَّسُوا وَلَا يَغْتَب بَّعْضُكُم بَعْضًا أَيُحِبُّ أَحَدُكُمْ أَن يَأْكُلَ لَحْمَ أَخِيهِ مَيْتًا فَكَرِهْتُمُوهُ وَاتَّقُوا اللَّهَ إِنَّ اللَّهَ تَوَّابٌ رَّحِيمٌ ○

*O you who believe, avoid much suspicion. Indeed, some suspicion is a crime. And do not spy on one another and do not backbite one another. Would any of you like to eat the flesh of his dead brother? No, you would hate it. Fear God, God is ever forgiving and most merciful. (al-Hujurat 49:12)*

The Prophet (SAS) was sitting with his companions one day and one of them was speaking badly about someone who wasn't there. As the man got up to leave the Prophet (SAS) said to him, "Pick Your Teeth!" "But I haven't eaten anything," the man protested. "No," the Prophet (SAS) said, "you have eaten the flesh of your dead brother."

"How is *gheeba* defined? *Gheeba* has been clearly defined by the Prophet (SAS) so that we can identify it and keep away from it. In a hadeeth reported in Sahih Muslim, Abu Hurayra (RAA) narrated that the Prophet (SAS) said, "Do you know what is backbiting?" They (the companions) said, "Allah and His Messenger know best." Then the Prophet (SAS) said, "Backbiting implies your talking about your brother in a manner which he does not like." Someone then asked the Prophet (SAS), "What if what I say about my brother is true?" The Prophet (SAS) said, "If what you said about him is true then you would have backbitten him, and if it is not true, then you have slandered him." Therefore, it is clear that the act of *gheeba* is to talk about a person in such a manner that he would dislike it, even if it is true. It is one of the major sins in Islam.

Why is backbiting so harmful? Backbiting is harmful because it is a clear violation of the sanctity of a Muslim and the sanctity of his honor.

We can reflect upon just how much we lose every time we utter some bad words about another person. The Prophet (SAS) once asked his companions, "Do you know who is bankrupt?" They replied, "The person among us who is bankrupt is the one who possesses neither money nor provision." The Prophet (SAS) said, "The bankrupt of my *ummah* is he who comes on the Day of Resurrection with prayer, charity, and fasting to his credit. However, he had insulted this person, struck that person, and seized the wealth of another, on account of which his good deeds will be taken away from him. Then, if his good deeds are exhausted, the sins of those whom he wronged will be taken from them and foisted upon him and then he will be cast into the fire."

Brothers and sisters! We should know this hadeeth, understand it, and keep it mind in order to avoid being bankrupt and a loser on the Day of Judgment.

Why do people fall into the sin of *gheeba*? People fall into the sin of *gheeba* because they enjoy making fun of others and belittling others. Do they not realize that they do not just taunt and defame their brothers and sisters, but in the process, they actually abuse, insult, and offend Allah too? How? Mostly their *gheeba* involves the description of the person: their features, color, disabilities, shortcomings, lack of money, and other things they have no control over. It is Allah (SWT) who gave the form to everyone and everything He created. It is He who gives wealth or withholds wealth from whom He wishes. It is He who elevates some over others. Addressing the believers, Allah (SWT) says,

يَا أَيُّهَا الَّذِينَ آمَنُوا لَا يَسْخَرْ قَوْمٌ مِنْ قَوْمٍ عَسَى أَنْ يَكُونُوا خَيْرًا مِنْهُمْ وَلَا نِسَاءٌ مِنْ نِسَاءٍ عَسَى أَنْ يَكُنَّ خَيْرًا مِنْهُنَّ وَلَا تَلْمِزُوا أَنْفُسَكُمْ وَلَا تَنَابَزُوا بِالْأَلْقَابِ بِئْسَ الِاسْمُ الْفُسُوقُ بَعْدَ الْإِيمَانِ وَمَنْ لَمْ يَتُبْ فَأُولَئِكَ هُمُ الظَّالِمُونَ ◯

*O believers! Let no men laugh at other men who may perhaps be better than themselves; and let no woman laugh at another woman, who may perhaps be better than herself. Do not defame through sarcastic remarks about one another, nor call one another by*

*offensive nicknames. It is an evil thing to be called by a bad name after being a believer, and those who do not repent are the ones who are the wrongdoers. (al-Hujurat, 49:11)*

Another reason that people participate in backbiting is on account of the company they keep. They backbite people to please their peers and friends. Allah says, conveying to us the words of the inhabitants of hell,

$$وَكُنَّا نَخُوضُ مَعَ الْخَائِضِينَ ۝$$

*We used to gossip along with the gossipers. (al-Muddathir, 74:45)*

Having too much spare time can also cause a person to fall into backbiting, because it is easy for an idle mind to become busy with other people's honor and faults. To correct this, a person must spend his time in acts of obedience to Allah, worshipping, seeking knowledge, and teaching others.

Another reason is arrogance and lack of awareness of one's faults. Such people should think about their own faults and try to correct themselves and feel ashamed to criticize others when they have many faults themselves.

Another reason is hatred, enmity, and envy toward others. Ibn Taymiyya says, "Some people are inspired by envy to backbite, and in doing so, combine two ignoble traits: backbiting and envy."

Weakness of faith and impiety are also reasons which make a person speak thoughtlessly and carelessly and transgress against others when he speaks.

What are the exceptional circumstances under which *gheeba* is allowed?*

1. If the person is being oppressed: In this case you are allowed to talk about the person who oppresses so that the oppressed may take what is rightfully his. He should only talk out of necessity and only to the one who can assist the oppressed person in taking his right from the oppressor.

2. Requesting a *fatwa* (Islamic ruling): For example, you may say "my brother did such and such (recalling the event), what do I do?" It is permitted to recall the incident without mentioning the name of the person (this is better) so that a fatwa may be obtained.

3. When seeking marriage: If a man asked someone about a third person who has made a proposal for marriage, it is permitted for the one being asked to say what he knows about the one who has proposed. When talking about him (the one seeking marriage) the one who knows him should be honest about what he says, without diminishing the person's value or exaggerating his faults.

4. Cautioning people about bad/evil-doers: If a person propagates something that is forbidden or evil, or something which contains *shirk*, it is permitted to warn people about that person.

5. If a person openly commits evil, such as seizing people's wealth unlawfully, it is

permissible to speak of what he is doing.

6. For identification: if someone is known by a nickname such as the dim-sighted one, or the blind man or the one-eyed or the lame one, it is permissible to identify him as such, but it is wrong to mention that by way of belittling him. If it is possible to identify him in some other way, that is better.

What should be done to stop ourselves from committing *gheeba?* We can protect ourselves from speaking ill of others by cultivating our fear of Allah and our sense of shame before of our Lord. This can be achieved by reflecting often upon the verses of the Qur`an and the Sunnah of our Prophet (SAS) that speak about Allah's punishment, that encourage us to repent, and that warn us against evil deeds. Allah says,

$$أَمْ يَحْسَبُونَ أَنَّا لَا نَسْمَعُ سِرَّهُمْ وَنَجْوَاهُمْ بَلَى وَرُسُلُنَا لَدَيْهِمْ يَكْتُبُونَ ﴿﴾$$

*Or do they think that We do not hear their secrets and their private counsels? Indeed, we do, and our messengers are by them to record. (az-Zukhruf, 43:80)*

The Prophet (SAS) said, "Feel shame before Allah as you ought to feel shame before Him. So guard the head and what it contains, guard the stomach and what you put in it, and think upon death and returning to dust."

A beneficial remedy that can help us to rid ourselves of this evil habit is to reflect upon our own shortcomings and work to improve ourselves. If we preoccupy ourselves with our own faults, we will not find time to worry about the faults of others. We should fear that if we speak about someone else's shortcomings, then Allah might punish us by afflicting us with the same.

Keeping the company of righteous people and avoiding bad company helps us to avoid backbiting. The Prophet (SAS) said, "The likeness of a good companion and a bad companion is that of a person carrying musk and another who works the bellows. The person carrying musk might give you some of it or at the very least you will enjoy the pleasant scent. The person with the bellows will either burn your clothing or at least make you suffer from the bad smell."

A person who has a habit of backbiting others needs to make a firm and determined resolution to stop because it is one of the greatest sins and yet it is something we do day after day.

Let me remind you and myself first that one of the easiest ways to lose one's *hasanat* (good deeds) without realizing it is to backbite someone.

Let me conclude with an *ayah* of the Qur`an and a beautiful saying of our beloved Prophet (SAS), which if followed will ensure the protection of our tongue. Allah says in *Surat Qaf,*

$$مَا يَلْفِظُ مِنْ قَوْلٍ إِلاَّ لَدَيْهِ رَقِيبٌ عَتِيدٌ ﴿﴾$$

*Not a single word is uttered by one but there is a watcher near him, ready (to record). (Qaf, 50:18)*

And the Prophet (SAS) said, "Whoever believes in Allah and the Last Day let him either speak good or keep silent."

We seek Allah's forgiveness from the sin of *gheeba* and we seek His *tawfeeq* (divine assistance) to take out the sin of *gheeba* from our lives.

---

*Please refer to https://thekhalids.org/newsletter-archive/306-now-what-does-gheebah-mean

•  6  •

# THE *BARZAKH*

A human being is made up of a body and a soul intertwined. While the body and the soul are joined in the mother's womb before birth, they are separated from each other permanently at the time of death.

This phenomenon of the separation of the body and soul takes place daily during our sleep, when the soul is temporarily removed from the body even though we are not dead. We experience what is called "minor death" every day. We wake up after our sleep, and this phenomenon continues until our appointed time comes when we permanently depart from the present world to the world of the hereafter. Allah (SWT) says in the Qur`an,

اللَّهُ يَتَوَفَّى الْأَنْفُسَ حِينَ مَوْتِهَا وَالَّتِي لَمْ تَمُتْ فِي مَنَامِهَا فَيُمْسِكُ الَّتِي قَضَى عَلَيْهَا الْمَوْتَ وَيُرْسِلُ الْأُخْرَى إِلَى أَجَلٍ مُسَمًّى إِنَّ فِي ذَلِكَ لَآيَاتٍ لِقَوْمٍ يَتَفَكَّرُونَ ◯

*It is Allah who takes away the souls of people upon their death and the souls of the living during their sleep. He then keeps those for whom He had decreed death and restores the souls of others for an appointed term. There are certainly signs in this for those who reflect. (az-Zumar, 39:42)*

Taking the souls during sleep implies the suspension of the powers of feeling and consciousness, of understanding and will. We must realize that life and death are entirely in Allah's Hand. No one is guaranteed that he will certainly wake up in the morning when he goes to sleep at night. No one knows what disaster could befall him at any time, and whether the next moment would be a moment of life for him or of death. Whether one is asleep or awake, in the house or outside it, some unforeseen calamity, from inside his body or from outside, can suddenly cause his death. Thus, being so helpless, it is foolish for man to turn away from Allah (SWT) or become heedless of Him.

My *khutbah* today is on the topic of the *barzakh*. The literal meaning of the Arabic word *barzakh* is "barrier between two things." It is the intermediary period between the two worlds of the present world and the world of the hereafter. The *barzakh* starts with the extraction of the soul from the body and ends with the resurrection on the Day of Judgment. The state of the dead person in the world of the *barzakh* is similar to our experience of having pleasant dreams or nightmares while asleep.

The Qur`an describes the concept of the *barzakh* in relation to those who had been heedless during their worldly lives.

حَتَّى إِذَا جَاءَ أَحَدَهُمُ الْمَوْتُ قَالَ رَبِّ ارْجِعُونِ ۞ لَعَلِّي أَعْمَلُ صَالِحًا فِيمَا تَرَكْتُ كَلَّا إِنَّهَا كَلِمَةٌ هُوَ قَائِلُهَا وَمِنْ وَرَائِهِمْ بَرْزَخٌ إِلَى يَوْمِ يُبْعَثُونَ ۞

*Until death comes to one of them, he says: "My Lord, send me back," so that I may do good in that which I have left behind." No, it is but a word he is speaking. And there is a barrier (barzakh) to prevent them from going back until the Day they are all resurrected. (al-Mu`minoon, 23:99-100)*

What happens to a person when his soul is extracted? And what happens to him when he is buried in his grave? All this is from the knowledge of the unseen (*al-ghayb*) which we learn from the Qur`an and the Prophetic traditions. This knowledge is part of our faith.

During a wicked person's dying moments, he wishes that death were delayed so that if he were a non-believer, he would become a believer; or if he were a disobedient believer, he would repent from his sins. Our bodies return to the same source they came from—the earth. Our bodies will eventually decay, decompose, and return to dust while our spirits await the Day of Judgment.

وَلَيْسَتِ التَّوْبَةُ لِلَّذِينَ يَعْمَلُونَ السَّيِّئَاتِ حَتَّى إِذَا حَضَرَ أَحَدَهُمُ الْمَوْتُ قَالَ إِنِّي تُبْتُ الْآنَ وَلَا الَّذِينَ يَمُوتُونَ وَهُمْ كُفَّارٌ ۞

*Repentance is not for those who continue to do evil until death confronts them and then say, 'Now I repent,' nor of those who die disbelieving. (an-Nisa`, 4:18)*

So *iman* (faith) is not accepted from anyone at the time of death. Also, repentance is useless if the person has started to experience the throes of death. The Prophet (SAS) said, "Allah accepts repentance from a person as long as death does not reach his throat." As for the righteous believers, may Allah make us among them, Allah says,

إِنَّ الَّذِينَ قَالُوا رَبُّنَا اللَّهُ ثُمَّ اسْتَقَامُوا تَتَنَزَّلُ عَلَيْهِمُ الْمَلَائِكَةُ أَلَّا تَخَافُوا وَلَا تَحْزَنُوا وَأَبْشِرُوا بِالْجَنَّةِ الَّتِي كُنتُمْ تُوعَدُونَ ○

*Those who say, ´Our Lord is Allah, and then remain steadfast, the angels descend on them, saying: Do not fear and do not grieve but rejoice in the garden you have been promised. (Fussilat, 41:30)*

And thus, the angels convey the news to the departing souls: good news of paradise to the believers and disappointing news of punishment to the disbelievers. The believing souls will enjoy the comfort of their grave, anxious to be raised and admitted to their final abode that is beautiful beyond description. We learn from *a hadeeth qudsi* in which the Prophet (SAS) quotes Allah as saying, "I have prepared for My righteous servants what no eye has seen and no ear has heard, and no heart has conceived." The disbelieving souls, on the other hand, will be tormented in their grave.

While burying our dead, a Muslim remembers and recites the verse of the Qur`an which says,

مِنْهَا خَلَقْنَاكُمْ وَفِيهَا نُعِيدُكُمْ وَمِنْهَا نُخْرِجُكُمْ تَارَةً أُخْرَى ○

*From it (the earth) We created you, into it We shall return you, and from it We shall raise you once again. (Ta Ha, 20:55)*

One may wonder what happens to the spirit at the time of death. Allah tells us,

إِذَا جَاءَ أَحَدَكُمُ الْمَوْتُ تَوَفَّتْهُ رُسُلُنَا وَهُمْ لَا يُفَرِّطُونَ ○

*When death overtakes any of you, Our messengers take his soul. They never fail in their duty. (al-An'am, 6:61)*

The souls of the wicked will be harshly extracted while the souls of the righteous will come out gently. Taking an oath, Allah (SWT) says,

وَالنَّازِعَاتِ غَرْقًا ○ وَالنَّاشِطَاتِ نَشْطًا ○

*By the (angels) who forcefully pull out (the souls of the wicked); and by the (angels) who gently take out (the souls of the righteous). (an-Nazi'at, 79:1,2)*

We are told that at time of death the unseen world becomes visible.

لَقَدْ كُنتَ فِي غَفْلَةٍ مِنْ هَذَا فَكَشَفْنَا عَنكَ غِطَاءَكَ فَبَصَرُكَ الْيَوْمَ حَدِيدٌ ○

*Certainly you were heedless of this, but now We have removed from you your veil, so your sight today is sharp. (Qaf, 50:22)*

This phenomenon is similar to one who is asleep and dreaming. The dream ends upon waking up. Similarly, when the eyes close for good, one's dream-world ends, and the state of wakefulness begins. At that time one is able to recognize the realities of the hereafter. According to 'Ali ibn Abi Talib (RAA), "People are asleep; when they die, they will wake up."

No one has risen from the grave and shared their experience. The knowledge of the supernatural realm belongs only to Allah (SWT). Through revelation and inspiration, the Prophet Muhammad (SAS) brings the news of that domain to us. We have a complete account from the Prophet (SAS) regarding the journey of the spirit and the reality of the grave in a very long hadeeth, which it is difficult to narrate in a short *khutbah*. The overall message of the hadeeth, however, is that a good soul comes out of the body with ease, while an evil soul, which resists leaving the body, is taken out harshly by the Angel of death. The two types of souls are accordingly honored or dishonored in their respective journeys to the heavenly dimensions and back, when they are then questioned in the graves. There is a Prophetic *du'a*` that says:

$$اَللّٰهُمَّ حَاسِبْنِيْ حِسَا بًا يَّسِيْرًا$$

*"O Allah! Make my accounting easy."*

The grave or the *barzakh* is the first station in our journey toward eternal life. The Prophet (SAS) said, "Indeed, the grave is the first station of the stations of the hereafter. Hence, whoever is successful, then what comes after will be easy for him and whoever fails, there is only hardship ahead of him." According to another hadeeth the Prophet (SAS) said, "Whoever from among you dies is shown his final resting place morning and evening continually, whether he be a dweller of paradise or of hell. It is said to him: This is the place which you will enter when Allah will raise you back to life on the Day of Resurrection and will call you into His presence."

Referring to the fate of Pharaoh and his followers, Allah says in *Surat Ghafir*,

$$النَّارُ يُعْرَضُونَ عَلَيْهَا غُدُوًّا وَعَشِيًّا وَيَوْمَ تَقُومُ السَّاعَةُ أَدْخِلُوا آلَ فِرْعَوْنَ أَشَدَّ الْعَذَابِ$$

*They are exposed to the fire morning and evening, and on the Day when the Hour will be established, it will be said: Admit Pharaoh's people into the severest punishment.*
(*Ghafir*, 40:46)

This verse is an explicit proof of the torment of the *barzakh*, which has often been mentioned in the Sunnah as the torment of the grave. In clear words, Allah has mentioned two stages of the torment. The first stage is a lesser torment, which is being given now to Pharaoh and his people before the coming of the Day of Resurrection. They are presented before the fire of hell morning and evening, and the sight of hell strikes terror in their hearts. After this, when the Day of Resurrection comes, they will be given the real and greater punishment which is destined for them: They will be hurled into the same hell, which they have been made to witness since the time they were drowned. Likewise, the evil people will continue to witness their terrible end, from the hour of death until the Day of Resurrection. On the other hand, the righteous people are made to continually see the pleasant picture of the good end which Allah has destined for them.

The punishment in the grave is so real that the Prophet (SAS) himself sought refuge in Allah from the torment of the grave. He used to make a *du'a`* saying,

اللَّهُمَّ إِنِّي أَعُوذُ بِكَ مِنَ الْبُخْلِ وَأَعُوذُ بِكَ مِنَ الْجُبْنِ وَأَعُوذُ بِكَ أَنْ أُرَدَّ إِلَى أَرْذَلِ الْعُمُرِ وَأَعُوذُ بِكَ مِنْ فِتْنَةِ الدُّنْيَا وَأَعُوذُ بِكَ مِنْ عَذَابِ الْقَبْرِ ◯

*"O Allah, I seek Your protection from miserliness, I seek Your protection from cowardice, and I seek Your protection from being returned to an age of feeble-mindedness, I seek Your protection from the trials of this world and from the torment of the grave."*

Brothers and sisters! Do we ever think about the day we will die? Are we ready and prepared for our departure from this earth? There is no denying that fear of death is something natural that hangs around each one of us. Every day that passes by brings us closer to death, and every breath we take takes away a portion of our life. When the appointed time comes, we belong among the dead. As believers, if we trust in Allah, think positively of Allah, humble our hearts before Allah, and try our best to have *taqwa* of Allah, we will know that death is a return to the most generous and merciful Lord. The Prophet (SAS) tells, us, "None of you should die except hoping good from Allah." Therefore, we should never ever despair of Allah's mercy. Allah also says in the Qur`an,

قُلْ يَا عِبَادِيَ الَّذِينَ أَسْرَفُوا عَلَى أَنْفُسِهِمْ لَا تَقْنَطُوا مِنْ رَحْمَةِ اللَّهِ إِنَّ اللَّهَ يَغْفِرُ الذُّنُوبَ جَمِيعًا إِنَّهُ هُوَ الْغَفُورُ الرَّحِيمُ ◯

*Say: O My servants who transgressed against themselves, do not despair of Allah's mercy. For Allah forgives all sins. He is the Forgiver, the Merciful. (az-Zumar, 39:53)*

May Allah give us the realization that death can strike us suddenly; anywhere, anytime. May Allah not let our deaths be in a state of sin. May Allah take away the love of sins from our hearts and put the love of good deeds into our hearts. May Allah bless us with strong faith and good deeds that are acceptable to Him. May Allah make it easy for us to make sincere repentance before death overtakes us. May Allah make our last days to be the best days of our life, and our last deeds to be the best of our deeds.

O Allah! let the best day be the day we meet you. O Allah! Make us successful in this life, in the *barzakh*, and in the life of the hereafter. *Allahumma ameen.*

# • 7 •

# BELIEF IN THE HEREAFTER

The essence of any Friday *khutbah* is to remind ourselves of the divine teachings and commands, even if we already know them. We need to be reminded again and again because we are humans. The word for human in Arabic *is insaan* made up from the root letters *nuun-seen-yaa*, from which we have the word *nasiya* which means "to forget." Since we forget, we need to be reminded. If we understand this, then we can appreciate why God Almighty says in the Qur`an,

وَذَكِّرْ فَإِنَّ الذِّكْرَى تَنْفَعُ الْمُؤْمِنِينَ ○

*And remind, for indeed, the reminder benefits the believers. (adh-Dhariyat, 51:55)*

In today's *khutbah*, I intend to share with you some aspects of belief in the hereafter, called the *akhira*. Along with belief in God, His angels, His books, His messengers, and His divine decree, belief in the hereafter is one of the articles of the Islamic faith. It is impossible to discuss the teachings of Islam without referring to the great significance that the hereafter possesses, not only for man's final destination but also for his life in this world.

What does the hereafter signify? It signifies "the other and ultimate state of existence in the world to come and the life of everlasting duration." Death is a reality that awaits all human beings. The existence of a life after death in one form or another has engaged the imagination of humans since the earliest times. It is recognized by some and denied by others, but belief in the afterlife is common to many religions of the world. It exists in Judaism and Christianity with varying interpretations. Some ideas about an afterlife also exist in Hinduism, Buddhism, and among the peoples of the ancient world, such as the Zoroastrians, the Romans, the Egyptians, the Greeks, the Babylonians, and the ancient Chaldeans.

In the Islamic worldview, there is not only the life of this world but also the life of the world to come. In essence, time-space in the overall perspective of the Qur`an has a beginning and an end. The starting point is, of course, the creation of the world, which will culminate in or lead to exhaustion and disintegration. Since human beings are situated in this time-space dimension, they are equally subject to the same fate. The end of the world, however, is not a complete extinction or an ultimate end, but the beginning of a completely new state of existence with new laws and systems that entail eternity. Likewise, death is not the permanent end of humankind, but the passage into a new and eternal life. The Qur`an leaves no doubt that the alternatives for each individual on the Day of Judgment are two: The bliss of the heaven or the torment of the hell.

What is the Qur`an's argument about the hereafter? The Qur`an makes it clear and provides assurances that God can and will raise the dead and that such a resurrection is a binding promise and an integral part of all creations. Allah says in the Qur`an,

كَمَا بَدَأْنَا أَوَّلَ خَلْقٍ نُّعِيدُهُ ۚ وَعْدًا عَلَيْنَا ۚ

*We shall reproduce creation just as we produced it the first time: this is our binding promise. (al-Anbiya`, 21:104)*

Man is born to die and then be resurrected. Resurrection, or the final accounting, is an idea that disbelievers and materialists have always found very hard to accept. That is not to say that such people doubt the reality of death. Of course, they witness their family members and associates dying one after another before their very eyes. But they don't connect death and resurrection. To them, death is the dead end, the ultimate extinction of all beings. They deny resurrection, something that has been unambiguously assured by God Himself.

What is the necessity and wisdom of the hereafter? Despite all the protests against the probability and the possibility of the hereafter, the Qur`an considers it crucial for multiple fundamental reasons. It is the manifestation of divine justice. The quality of people's performance must be judged. Fairness cannot be ensured merely on the basis of what transpires in this life. The imperfection of worldly justice makes the quest for another life, where justice will be rendered, necessary. Some criminals and oppressive rulers may enjoy luxury until the end of their lives. They may escape the grasp of justice and never suffer the natural consequences of their deeds. On the other hand, other people might be righteous and lead a virtuous life but might not survive to reap the fruits of their labors. If the files of both groups of people were closed in this world, what would become of the infinite justice, wisdom, and mercy that God cherishes for His servants? Nobody who has the slightest notion of love and justice would consent to such a state of affairs.

It is also obvious that not all good and evil deeds are subject to final accounting in this worldly life. Certain crimes and evils are so extensive in their effects that they cannot be adequately punished in this world. Some individuals are directly involved in bloody massacres or genocides of innocent people. Even if they are punished for their crimes against humanity, the punishment involved would be unjust and grossly unequal. Similarly, certain virtues cannot be rewarded in a fitting and complete manner in this world. What reward can be given in this world to someone who has dedicated his entire life to the service of people just to seek God's pleasure? The basic idea underlying the Qur`an's teaching on the hereafter is that there will come a time when every human will squarely and starkly face his or her own doings and misdoings. That is why the Qur`an admonishes people by saying,

لَقَدْ كُنْتَ فِي غَفْلَةٍ مِنْ هَذَا فَكَشَفْنَا عَنْكَ غِطَاءَكَ فَبَصَرُكَ الْيَوْمَ حَدِيدٌ ○

*You were sunk in deep heedlessness of this [accounting], but now we have lifted the veil from you, so your sight today is sharp. (Qaf, 50:22)*

The hereafter is also the time when the intentions behind actions and aspirations are exposed. What were the means adopted to carry out these actions and for what ends? Philosophers often consider happiness as the ultimate end to which all our actions are directed. It is considered as the complete good in itself. But happiness in this life cannot be our ultimate goal because life is temporary. It passes away. For happiness to be real, it must be constant. However great or extensive one's happiness might be, it is exhaustible. Death ends it all. So the hereafter is better than this worldly life not only because of the quality of life therein, but also because of the permanence of such a life. The Qur`an simultaneously maintains both characteristics when it states:

وَالْآخِرَةُ خَيْرٌ وَأَبْقَى ○

*But the hereafter is better [in terms of the quality of that life] and more enduring [in terms of its duration]. (al-A'la, 87:17)*

In order to give our life and efforts a purpose there must be an ultimate end toward which human actions are directed; a time when the true meaning of our actions will be known and the true end of our aspirations will be disclosed. The hereafter fulfils this requirement.

The hereafter is also the time of conflict resolution. Disputes and conflicts must be finally resolved. Most human differences are caused by motivations of selfishness whether they are of individuals, groups, or nations. These motivations will be unveiled on that day. The Qur`an makes frequent reference to such conflicts and conflict resolution.

قُلْ لَا تُسْأَلُونَ عَمَّا أَجْرَمْنَا وَلَا نُسْأَلُ عَمَّا تَعْمَلُونَ قُلْ يَجْمَعُ بَيْنَنَا رَبُّنَا ثُمَّ يَفْتَحُ بَيْنَنَا بِالْحَقِّ وَهُوَ الْفَتَّاحُ الْعَلِيمُ ○

*Say: You will not be questioned about our sins, nor will we be questioned about what you do. Say: ʿOur Lord will bring us all together and then will judge between us with the truth. He is the Judge; the All-Knowing. (Saba`, 34:25-26)*

What are some of the benefits of belief in the hereafter? Belief in the hereafter has several benefits at different levels. There are individual benefits, social benefits, and civilizational benefits. At the individual level, it gives man a unique and valuable advantage with a greater choice that has an eternal implication. He knows that with his own hand, he can sow the seed of his future destiny, making a good life in the hereafter within his reach. In other words, belief in the hereafter lets one realise that his eternal abode, either in heaven or in hell, depends on his course of action in this worldly life.

Anyone who is concerned with his eternal welfare will immediately feel the burden of disobedience awaiting him once he allows himself to commit a sin. Whenever he commits a sin by mistake, he immediately repents and implores God for His forgiveness and mercy. His behavior is therefore shaped by truthfulness and sincerity. His drive for unrestrained enjoyment will be brought under control, and he will avoid the greedy, irrational, and undisciplined accumulation of wealth and power. Belief in the hereafter also provides a psychological benefit to an individual. It prevents man from fearing the passing difficulties of life and makes him accept them with calmness, and even transforms those difficulties into means of development and ascent toward lofty goals.

A society composed of individuals who believe in the hereafter and work for it has much to gain. It is known that in every society there is a mixture of virtue and vice, right and wrong. Many right actions are not properly appreciated and many wrong deeds are not noticed. Belief in the hereafter, when virtue will be compensated many times over, encourages those who do good deeds to persevere in their acts. Similarly, belief in the Supreme Tribunal of the hereafter, where every misdeed will be taken into account, will pacify the oppressed ones and prevent them from seeking revenge, potentially triggering chaos and perpetual war in society.

After belief in God, belief in the hereafter has the primary place in preserving social security and preventing the spread of corruption, crime, and violation of law. It is a force capable of taming the rebellious desires of the soul. That is because whoever holds this belief will obey ethical principles without hypocrisy or the need for external pressure. Anyone seriously concerned with his eternal abode will become accustomed to good conduct and society will be protected from wrongdoing.

Belief in the hereafter also has benefits for civilization. It is obvious that for the rise and growth of a civilization, there must be optimum utilization of physical, cultural, spiritual, and human resources. However, optimum utilization of mankind's potential and the natural resources of the earth are not sufficient to create a responsible civilization. Enamoured with his vast potential and tremendous material achievements, man can do many things—virtue and vice, commendable and abominable—simply because he can do them. This attitude will lead to irresponsible subjugation of nature, amounting to unsustainable development. However, belief in the hereafter where everyone will be accountable for his deeds and misdeeds will instill a sense of responsibility, which is a condition of sustainable development. Man will consequently choose the right course of action, pursuing only that which *should* be pursued and not just whatever that *can* be pursued.

Belief in the hereafter should be seen as a source of strength and not weakness, for responsible individuals, societies and civilizations.

To conclude, we may ask, "Is there anything to lose if one believes in the hereafter and works for it?" The answer is no! To invest one's thoughts and actions in the hereafter means to live a purposeful and responsible life in this world and to prepare for one's eternal happiness in the world to come. Belief in the hereafter is not a fairy tale born of "blind faith." Rather, it is rational and necessary if only to make sense of the existence of this worldly life.

The important lesson to be learned is to always keep in mind the reality of afterlife, and the ultimate consequence of one's actions and one's responsibility toward Allah (SWT) for what one does.

• 8 •

# BLESSINGS OF *BISMILLAH AR-RAHMAN AR-RAHEEM*

Brothers and sisters! In today's *khutbah*, I want to share some thoughts with you on the explanation of the Qur`anic expression, *bismillah ar-Rahman ar-Raheem*, which means "In the name of Allah, Most Gracious, Most Merciful." This phrase is so central to our everyday life that not a single day should pass by without uttering it.

One of the many practices taught by Islam is that its followers should begin their activities in the name of Allah. This principle, if consciously followed, will necessarily yield good results. One will be able to restrain oneself from evil, since the habit of pronouncing the name of Allah is bound to make one think when one is about to commit an evil act. How such an act can be reconciled with the uttering of Allah's name? Also, when a person begins something by pronouncing Allah's name, they will enjoy Allah's help and guidance. Allah will bless their efforts and protect them from the whispering and temptations of Satan, for whenever one turns to Allah, Allah turns to them as well. Saying *bismillah* is actually a prayer. By virtue of this prayer, a man seeks help from two great attributes of Allah: *ar-Rahman* and *ar-Raheem*. Both of these attributes secure for him the blessings and help of Allah. Anything done without this prayer certainly fails to reap these blessings.

It was a custom in the Age of Ignorance (*jahiliyya*) before the advent of Islam for people to begin everything they did with the names of their idols or gods. Therefore, the first verse of the Qur`an which Jibreel (AS) brought down to the Prophet (SAS) commanded him to begin the Qur`an with the name of Allah.

$$اقْرَأْ بِاسْمِ رَبِّكَ الَّذِي خَلَقَ ◯$$

*Recite: In the name of your Lord, who created. (al-'Alaq, 96:1)*

*Bismillah ar-Rahman ar-Raheem* appears in the Qur`an at the beginning of every surah except *Surat at-Tawba*. It also appears once within the text inverse thirty of *Surat an-Naml*. The famous *mufassir* (explainer of the Qur`an) Jalal ad-Deen as-Suyuti says that besides the Qur`an, all other divine books also begin with *bismillah*. A study of the Qur`an reveals that all revealed scriptures since ancient times have always mentioned the meaning of this expression in one form or another. For example, the followers of the prophet Nuh (AS), said something similar when boarding the ark.

$$وَقَالَ ارْكَبُوا فِيهَا بِسْمِ اللَّهِ مَجْرَاهَا وَمُرْسَاهَا إِنَّ رَبِّي لَغَفُورٌ رَحِيمٌ ◯$$

*He (Noah) said: Board it. In the name of Allah it shall sail and anchor. My Allah is most forgiving and merciful. (Hud, 11:41)*

Similarly, the prophet Sulayman (AS) began his letter to the Queen of Sheba with these blessed words.

$$إِنَّهُ مِن سُلَيْمَانَ وَإِنَّهُ بِسْمِ اللَّهِ الرَّحْمَنِ الرَّحِيمِ ◯$$

*It is from Solomon, and it says: In the name of Allah, Most Gracious, Most Merciful. (an-Naml, 27:30)*

By instructing man to begin everything with the name of Allah, Islam has given his whole life an orientation toward Allah so that he may, with each step he takes, renew his allegiance to his covenant with Him. Thus, all worldly activities of man, each movement and gesture, becomes transformed into an act of worship. How brief is this action which consumes neither time nor energy, and yet how immense is the gain!

There is a difference of opinion among scholars as to whether *bismillah ar-Rahman ar-Raheem* is an integral part of *Surat al-Fatiha* and all other surahs or not. According to Imam Abu Haneefa, it is not an integral part of any *surah*, except where it is found in the text of *Surat an-Naml*; rather it is in itself an independent verse of the Qur`an which has been revealed for placement at the beginning of every surah in order to separate and distinguish one surah from another. The other opinion is that *bismillah ar-Rahman ar-Raheem* is a part of *Surat al-Fatiha*. However, there is consensus of the majority of the scholars from early generations that *Surat al-Fatiha* contains seven verses.

The term *bismillah* is a combination of three words: *bi, ism*, and Allah. The particle *bi* carries meanings of "by," "in," "for," "with," "through," or "by means of," and points toward that which comes next. The next word in this phrase is *ism*, which means "a distinguishing mark of a thing" and points toward the very essence and underlying reality of something. "Allah" is the Arabic word for God. It is a personal name by which Allah calls Himself in the Qur`an. The word "Allah" does not allow for any plurality or gender. Allah is the real Existent—the Real Being who possesses the most beautiful names and attributes. Allah says in Surat *Ta Ha*,

اللَّهُ لَا إِلَهَ إِلَّا هُوَ لَهُ الْأَسْمَاءُ الْحُسْنَىٰ ۞

*Allah, there is no god but Him. The Most Beautiful Names are His. (Ta Ha, 20:8)*

The concept of the word "Allah" also existed in pre-Islamic times in Arabia. The people of Arabia practiced polytheism, yet they never equated any of their deities with Allah. They always acknowledged Him as the sole Creator of this world. They worshiped other deities only because they wrongly believed that these deities were close to Allah and could intercede for them. Their views are stated in the Qur`an.

مَا نَعْبُدُهُمْ إِلَّا لِيُقَرِّبُونَا إِلَى اللَّهِ زُلْفَىٰ ۞

*We worship them only that they may bring us nearer to Allah. (az-Zumar, 39:3)*

Two attributes of Allah are mentioned in bismillah ar-Rahman ar-Raheem. They are *ar-Rahman* and *ar-Raheem*. The roots of both these names of Allah are made up of the same root letters from which is derived the word rahma, which conveys the meaning of mercy and compassion, and a sense of loving tenderness and grace. The divine name ar-Rahman indicates a meaning of excessiveness and vastness of the attribute of mercy. No one else is more merciful than Allah. He shows mercy to every creature, even to those who do not believe in Him. It is Allah's attribute of being ar-Rahman that made Him create man, grant him the ability to speak, and teach him the Qur`an. As Allah says in Surat ar-Rahman,

الرَّحْمَٰنُ ۞ عَلَّمَ الْقُرْآنَ ۞ خَلَقَ الْإِنْسَانَ ۞ عَلَّمَهُ الْبَيَانَ ۞

*It is the Most Merciful. who taught the Qur`an; He created man and taught him speech? (ar-Rahman, 55:1-4)*

These blessed words remind man of the reality that one of the greatest favors of Allah upon them is that He has blessed them with the faculty of speech.

The aspect of mercy in the word *ar-Raheem* conveys a sense of permanence and continuity. Allah's blessings are not confined to this world only. Those who lead their lives according to the path prescribed by Him shall be blessed with eternal life and joy in the hereafter. A little consideration shows that Allah's mercy on His creation possesses both of these characteristics. The boundlessness and vastness, along with the enthusiasm and warmth of mercy expressed by the divine name of *ar-Rahman* are complemented by the permanence and continuity of mercy in the name of *ar-Raheem*. It is not that His attribute of *ar-Rahman* induced Him to create, and He later forgot to sustain His creation. Indeed, He is nourishing them and taking proper care of them because He is *ar-Raheem* as well. Whenever a person invokes His help, He hears his calls and accepts his prayers. As Allah says in *Surat al-Baqara*,

وَإِذَا سَأَلَكَ عِبَادِي عَنِّي فَإِنِّي قَرِيبٌ أُجِيبُ دَعْوَةَ الدَّاعِ إِذَا دَعَانِ ۞

*And when My servants ask you about Me, say that I am near. I respond to the call of one who calls, whenever he calls Me. (al-Baqara, 2:186)*

It should also be known that *ar-Rahman* is the exclusive attribute of Allah (SWT) and the word is employed only when one is referring to Him. It is not permissible to describe any created being as *ar-Rahman*, for there cannot possibly be anyone other than Allah whose mercy is all-embracing and all-inclusive. Just like the word "Allah," there is no dual or plural for the word *ar-Rahman*, because these words are exclusive to the One and Absolute Being. Allah says in the Qur`an,

قُلِ ادْعُوا اللَّهَ أَوِ ادْعُوا الرَّحْمَٰنَ أَيًّا مَّا تَدْعُوا فَلَهُ الْأَسْمَاءُ الْحُسْنَىٰ

*Invoke Allah or invoke ar-Rahman, by whatever name you invoke Him (it is the same), for to Him belong the Best Names. (al-Isra`, 17:110)*

The meaning of the word *ar-Raheem*, on the contrary, does not contain anything which it should be impossible to find in a created being, for a man may be perfectly merciful in his dealings with another man. So, the word *ar-Raheem* may justifiably be employed in the case of a human being. The Qur`an itself has used the word *raheem* in speaking of the Prophet Muhammad (SAS), in *Surat at-Tawba*.

لَقَدْ جَاءَكُمْ رَسُولٌ مِّنْ أَنفُسِكُمْ عَزِيزٌ عَلَيْهِ مَا عَنِتُّمْ حَرِيصٌ عَلَيْكُم بِالْمُؤْمِنِينَ رَءُوفٌ رَّحِيمٌ ۞

*A Messenger has come to you from among yourselves. Your suffering distresses him: he is deeply concerned for you and full of kindness and mercy toward the believer. (at-Tawba, 9:128)*

Brothers and sisters! The expression *bismillah ar-Rahman ar-Raheem* also testifies to the truth of a prediction that was made about the Prophet Muhammad (SAS) found in previous scriptures. According to this prediction, he would teach and instruct people "in the name of Allah." The book of Deuteronomy in the Hebrew Bible says, "I will raise up for them a prophet like you from among their brothers; I will put My words in his mouth, and he will tell them everything I command him. If anyone does not listen to My words that the prophet speaks in My name, I myself will call him to account."

Saying *bismillah* transforms the profane into the sacred. It transforms the *dunya* into the *deen*. A disbeliever eats and drinks just as a Muslim does but in saying *bismillah* as he begins to eat, the Muslim affirms that it was not in his power to obtain this morsel of food. It has passed through innumerable stages from the sowing of the seed to the reaping of the grain, and it required the labors of the wind, the rain, the sun, the heavens. the earth, and of numerous people. It is Allah alone who has granted him this morsel of food by making it go through all these stages. A disbeliever goes to sleep, wakes up, and goes about his day as much as a Muslim. But while going to sleep or waking up, the Muslim mentions the name of Allah, thus renewing his relationship with Him. His economic and worldly needs and activities then acquire the characteristic of the remembrance of Allah, and are counted as acts of worship. Brothers and sisters! Let's make it a point to bring *bismillah* more into our lives and to start all our tasks in the name of Allah by saying *bismillah ar-Rahman ar-Raheem* whenever we begin an activity.

## • 9 •

# CALLING TO ALLAH AND RESPONDING TO HIM

There is a verse in *Surat al-Baqara* in which Allah (SWT) addressing the Prophet (SAS) says,

وَإِذَا سَأَلَكَ عِبَادِي عَنِّي فَإِنِّي قَرِيبٌ أُجِيبُ دَعْوَةَ الدَّاعِ إِذَا دَعَانِ فَلْيَسْتَجِيبُوا لِي وَلْيُؤْمِنُوا بِي لَعَلَّهُمْ يَرْشُدُونَ ◯

*When My servants ask you about Me, say that I am near. I respond to the call of one who calls, whenever he calls to Me: let them, then, respond to Me, and believe in Me, so that they may be rightly guided. (al-Baqara, 2:186)*

What is meant by calling to Allah and responding to Him? This is the topic of my *khutbah* today. *Du'a`* (calling to Allah) means to invoke Allah for any help or need, whether it is for something of this world or the next. It is quite normal and justified in this worldly life to ask someone for something that one may need, but it is important that before we ask people, our first stop should be Allah. Based on our sincerity and intention, and His knowledge and wisdom, Allah will make things easy for us with or without a medium.

There is a hadeeth which the Prophet (SAS) says, "*Du'a`* is the essence of worship." According to another hadeeth, the Prophet (SAS) also said, "There is no Muslim who calls to Allah with words in which there is no sin or cutting of family ties but Allah will give him one of three things: He will answer his prayer soon, or He will store it up for him in the hereafter, or He will remove from him some harm or evil of an equivalent amount." The latter part of the *ayah* we just mentioned says,

$$\text{فَلْيَسْتَجِيبُوا لِي وَلْيُؤْمِنُوا بِي لَعَلَّهُمْ يَرْشُدُونَ} \bigcirc$$

*Let them, then, respond to Me, and believe in Me, so that they may be rightly guided.*

The *mufassiroon* (explainers of the Qur`an) interpret the meaning of, "let them then respond to Me" to mean "let them then obey Me." To be able to respond to Allah, one has to know what Allah wants from him. The best way to know what Allah wants from us is to read the Qur`an thoroughly and repeatedly, paying attention to each and every word. In present times, many people find this difficult to do because of their busy lifestyles and their time constraints.

This problem, however, can be overcome by benefiting from the advice of 'Abdullah ibn Mas'ud (RAA) who is reported to have said that special attention should be paid to the verses that begin with *yaa ayyuha an-naas* ("O people") and *yaa ayyuha alladheena aamanu* ("O you who believe") because Allah is addressing us directly in these verses, and therefore, we had better listen! By reading these verses, we can find out what Allah wants from us, and then we can respond to Him accordingly. In *Surat Aal 'Imran* we see one of the many examples of what Allah wants from us.

$$\text{يَا أَيُّهَا الَّذِينَ آمَنُوا اتَّقُوا اللَّهَ حَقَّ تُقَاتِهِ وَلَا تَمُوتُنَّ إِلَّا وَأَنْتُمْ مُسْلِمُونَ} \bigcirc \text{وَاعْتَصِمُوا بِحَبْلِ اللَّهِ جَمِيعًا وَلَا}$$
$$\text{تَفَرَّقُوا وَاذْكُرُوا نِعْمَةَ اللَّهِ عَلَيْكُمْ إِذْ كُنْتُمْ أَعْدَاءً فَأَلَّفَ بَيْنَ قُلُوبِكُمْ فَأَصْبَحْتُمْ بِنِعْمَتِهِ إِخْوَانًا وَكُنْتُمْ عَلَى شَفَا}$$
$$\text{حُفْرَةٍ مِنَ النَّارِ فَأَنْقَذَكُمْ مِنْهَا كَذَلِكَ يُبَيِّنُ اللَّهُ لَكُمْ آيَاتِهِ لَعَلَّكُمْ تَهْتَدُونَ} \bigcirc \text{وَلْتَكُنْ مِنْكُمْ أُمَّةٌ يَدْعُونَ إِلَى}$$
$$\text{الْخَيْرِ} \bigcirc \text{وَيَأْمُرُونَ بِالْمَعْرُوفِ وَيَنْهَوْنَ عَنِ الْمُنْكَرِ وَأُولَئِكَ هُمُ الْمُفْلِحُونَ} \bigcirc$$

*O you who believe, have taqwa of Allah with the taqwa due to Him and do not die except in a state of complete submission to Him. Hold fast to the rope of Allah and let nothing divide you. Remember the blessings He has bestowed upon you; you were enemies and then He united your hearts and by His grace you became brothers; you were on the brink of a pit of fire and He rescued you from it. Thus, Allah makes His signs clear to you, so that you may find guidance. Let there be a group among you who call others to good, and enjoin what is right, and forbid what is wrong: those who do this shall be successful. (Aal 'Imran, 3:102-104)*

At the individual level, Allah wants us to have *taqwa* which means that we become righteous and pious and remain conscious of Him. The first thing that needs to be done individually is to carry out the modes of worship such as *salah*, *zakat*, fasting, hajj, etc. Beyond that, there has to be total obedience of Allah and submission to Him, and there has to be total conviction while saying,

$$\bigcirc \ \text{إِيَّاكَ نَعْبُدُ وَإِيَّاكَ نَسْتَعِينُ}$$

*You alone we worship, and to You alone we turn for help. (al-Fatiha, 1:5)*

We should be worshipping only Allah and turning only toward Him for help. Unfortunately, there are Muslims who turn to dead saints, angels, palm readers, fortune tellers, and the like seeking their help or intercession.

We are also told to collectively hold fast to the Qur`an, and not to get divided. We are asked to remain united, as we are members of one single Muslim *ummah*. As a matter of fact, Muslims do remain divided on the basis of their race, nationality, language, and cultural backgrounds. To emphasize the importance of leaving behind all traces of tribalism and racism and to remain united, the Prophet (SAS) addressed a multitude of believers in his farewell sermon during hajj and he said, "All mankind is from Adam and Eve. An Arab has no superiority over a non-Arab nor a non-Arab has any superiority over an Arab. Also, a white person has no superiority over a black person nor does a black person have any superiority over a white person except by *taqwa* (piety). Learn that every Muslim is a brother to every Muslim and that the Muslims constitute one brotherhood."

There is no problem with being proud of one's cultural heritage, but that should not override one's faith. We are Muslims first, and then we are other identities. After all, differences of race and tribe among people have been made by Allah Himself so that people may recognize each other. This diversity among human beings is something to be celebrated, and not something that should cause enmity among them.

The *ummah* has to remain united under the banner of *la ilaha illa Allah*. Only then is it possible to collectively embark upon the real task: The task of calling people toward what is right and good and forbidding them from what is wrong and evil. A community or group has to rise from within the larger *ummah* to carry out this obligation. This would entail calling Muslims back to the Qur`an. Most Muslims, even though they may be praying and performing other acts of worship, have either strayed away from or are unaware of the Qur`anic commands and guidance pertaining to different spheres of life; whether moral, ethical, personal, social, economic, or political. The invitation to come back to the Qur`an is invitation to all that is good. As Allah (SWT) says,

$$\bigcirc \ \text{قُل بِفَضْلِ اللَّهِ وَبِرَحْمَتِهِ فَبِذَلِكَ فَلْيَفْرَحُوا هُوَ خَيْرٌ مِّمَّا يَجْمَعُونَ}$$

*Say: It is the blessing and mercy of Allah; so let them rejoice. It is better than all that they gather. (Yunus, 10:58)*

The "blessing and mercy of Allah" mentioned in this verse refers to the Qur`an, which is indeed better than all the wealth than one can accumulate.

The non-Muslims have to be called to Islam. This has been the call of all the prophets and messengers of Allah. The Qur`an describes how they all invited their people to the worship of One God:

يَا قَوْمِ اعْبُدُوا اللَّهَ مَا لَكُمْ مِنْ إِلَهٍ غَيْرُهُ ○

*O my people worship God; you have no other god but Him. (al-A'raf, 7:73)*

Before we go out to make *da'wa* to non-Muslims, the first and foremost people worthy of our *da'wa* are those who are close to us. This is the Prophetic methodology. The Prophet (SAS) began his *da'wa* with his own relatives and others who were very close to him. May Allah (SWT) give us a true understanding of His *deen* and make us live by it.

Brothers and sisters! As Muslims, we have a responsibility toward all our brothers and sisters in humanity. This is because Allah sent prophets and messengers specifically for each nation, tribe, and people. It was only Prophet Muhammad (SAS), the last and final messenger of Allah, who was sent for the entire humankind and for all times to come. Since the institution of prophethood ended with the Prophet Muhammad (SAS), the responsibility of guiding humanity now falls upon the Muslims.

Inviting people toward good is not enough unless it is complemented by forbidding them from evil. This is crucial because of the evil all around us. The *shayateen* (devils) among jinn and humankind are busy corrupting people's minds, thoughts, attitudes, and behavior. Social evils are rampant. There is a sharp decline in the standards of morals and universal values such as honesty, truthfulness, and trustworthiness among individuals as well as institutions. At the same time, bigotry, racism, and other vices are on the rise everywhere. Drinking, drugs, gambling, prostitution, and all types of blatantly obscene activities (*fawahish*) are contributing to the breakdown of families.

Muslims are duty-bound to fight *munkar* (evil). The Prophet (SAS) said, "He amongst you who sees something evil should change it with his hand; and if he does not have strength enough (to do it with his hand), then he should do it with his tongue, and if he does not have strength enough (to do it with his tongue), then he should (hate it) from his heart, and that is the least of faith."

The Qur`an repeatedly warns us that past nations who did not pay heed to Allah's prophets and messengers and kept committing major sins were utterly destroyed. Modern humanity is not going to be completely destroyed by divine punishment despite the evil, mischief, corruption, and transgressions of evil doers, because Allah says,

وَمَا كُنَّا مُعَذِّبِينَ حَتَّى نَبْعَثَ رَسُولًا ○

*We never punish until We have sent a Messenger. (al-Isra`, 17:15)*

There is no prophet or messenger to come after Muhammad (SAS). However, being the last *ummah*, we have been entrusted to try to change the condition of the people for the better, and this is not possible if we do not change ourselves from within. There is hardly an evil that is not found in the Muslim community. We have to keep in mind that unless we change ourselves, we cannot change the society at large. The Prophet (SAS) said, "By Him in Whose Hand my life is, you either enjoin good and forbid evil, or Allah will certainly soon send His punishment to you. Then you will make supplication and it will not be accepted."

Rather than shortchange our God-given obligations, we should live with a sense of urgency because once that day comes, there is no turning back. Allah instructs us in the Qur`an,

اسْتَجِيبُوا لِرَبِّكُمْ مِنْ قَبْلِ أَنْ يَأْتِيَ يَوْمٌ لَا مَرَدَّ لَهُ مِنَ اللَّهِ مَا لَكُمْ مِنْ مَلْجَأٍ يَوْمَئِذٍ وَمَا لَكُمْ مِنْ نَكِيرٍ ◯

*Respond to your Lord before a Day comes from Allah which cannot be turned back. On that Day you will have no refuge and no means of denial. (ash-Shura, 42:47)*

So calling to Allah has to be accompanied with responding to Him, which means obeying Him and submitting to Him. May Allah give us the *tawfeeq* to call Him and to respond to Him till we leave this world for our eternal abode. *Ameen!*


•  10  •

# CELEBRATING *MAWLID AL-NABI*


This is the month of *Rabi' al-Awwal*. It is the third month of the Islamic lunar calendar. Both the birth and the death of our beloved Prophet Muhammad (SAS) are reported to have taken place during this month. Let me share some thoughts with you on the issue of celebrating or commemorating the Prophet's birthday. I also wish to discuss some of his noble attributes that provide a model for us to follow.

There is always a debate in the Muslim community on whether to celebrate the Prophet's birthday or not. People are divided into different groups based on their understanding of the concept of innovation in matters of religion, or *bid'a*. One group condemns commemorating anything to do with the Prophet (SAS) as a bad innovation. Another group often sanctions all kinds of practices, including some border on *shirk*, under the pretext of expression of love of the Prophet (SAS).

It is best that we keep to the middle path. In the words of Imam Hasan Al-Basri (RA), "The Religion of Allah stands midway between extreme rigidity and extreme veneration." Rigidity implies being obsessed with the letter of the law to such an extent that one neglects the spirit. It is wrong to venerate or idolize the Prophet (SAS) in the manner that Christians idolize Jesus (peace be on him). We must shun both extremes.

We have room in Islam for expressing our genuine love and reverence toward the Messenger of Allah (SAS), and may commemorate events of his life as long as we stay clear of excesses. This can be done through writings, speeches, songs, documentaries, and other print and electronic media as long as this is done within the limits of the *shari'a*. We know from the *Seerah* that the companions celebrated the Prophet's arrival in Medina with singing. We also know that 'Umar ibn al-Khattab (RAA) commemorated the *hijra* by synchronizing it with the starting of the Islamic Calendar. He even considered the option of using the Prophet's date of birth or the Prophet's first missionary call to Islam for the start of the Islamic Calendar, but he turned down these proposals for practical reasons.

Some scholars, both past and present, have ruled that we cannot consider celebration of Prophet's birthday as a bad innovation simply because it was not practiced in the early times. They say that there is no harm in instituting new customs in areas other than the strictly prescribed acts of worship. Obvious benefits associated with celebration of *Mawlid an-Nabi* include inspiring new generations and educating people. So there is nothing wrong in commemorating the event of the Prophet's birth to express our love for the Prophet (SAS), and as a sign of our commitment to him and his teachings.

I take this opportunity to remind myself and you about some of the noble attributes of our beloved Prophet Muhammad (SAS). We learn these attributes from the Qur`an and the Prophet's *Seerah*. The uniqueness of Prophet (SAS) is that he was not only a great person in his own time, but he is great for all times, and for all people of any race, color, nationality, or geographical location. His example was good for the seventh century Arabs and it is good for the humanity living now at the beginning of this twenty-first century. He is an excellent example for rich and poor, for young and old, for rulers and ruled, and for people of all levels of education. Allah sent him as His Prophet for all humanity. Allah says in *Surat Saba*`,

$$\text{وَمَا أَرْسَلْنَاكَ إِلَّا كَافَّةً لِلنَّاسِ} \bigcirc$$

*And we have sent you to all people. (Saba`, 34:28)*

Over fourteen hundred years after his physical departure from the world, the number of those who love him has increased by hundreds of millions. But not many live according to his teachings. During his lifetime, the Prophet motivated a whole generation of people on the basis of the divine teachings and his noble character. However, against his teachings, the Muslim *ummah* is divided on sectarian lines. Every sect wants to own him and claims that it is following his path.

Where is the sense of loyalty to him? What happened to his teachings reminding us that the believers are one *ummah*? If one part of the *ummah* suffers, then the others feel the pain. Yet there are those who swear by his name who take pride in killing each other in his name! Various sects and parties of Muslims continue to kill each other. How do these people celebrate the Prophet (SAS) when they cannot even overcome their petty sectarianism? The Prophet (SAS) taught love, kindness and compassion to his people, and was seen to be the most loving, kind, and compassionate of all of them. Allah mentions his kind and gentle behavior in the Qur'an,

لَقَدْ جَاءَكُمْ رَسُولٌ مِنْ أَنْفُسِكُمْ عَزِيزٌ عَلَيْهِ مَا عَنِتُّمْ حَرِيصٌ عَلَيْكُمْ بِالْمُؤْمِنِينَ رَءُوفٌ رَحِيمٌ ○

*A Messenger has come to you from among yourselves. Your suffering distresses him: he is deeply concerned for you and full of kindness and mercy toward the believers.*
(at-Tawba, 9:128)

Allah (SWT) called him "a mercy to the worlds."

وَمَا أَرْسَلْنَاكَ إِلَّا رَحْمَةً لِلْعَالَمِينَ ○

*And We have not sent you except as a mercy to the worlds. (al-Anbiya`, 21:107)*

He was merciful to his family, followers, friends, and even enemies. He was merciful to young and old, to humans and to animals. Those who persecuted him in Mecca and killed his relatives and his followers were forgiven by him.

With the example of his personal life, the Prophet (SAS) encouraged a peaceful family life where love and compassion characterize the relationship between the spouses. Yet there are many Muslim women today who suffer from domestic violence. As the *ummah* of Prophet Muhammad (SAS), we must take stock of our actions and make sure that we work to adopt a model character within ourselves and our families.

The Prophet (SAS) stood up for the rights of the neglected and marginalized and showed the utmost respect to those who struggled with lower socioeconomic status. He was commissioned by Allah to instill respect for character, sincerity, and brotherhood. He worked to establish a culture where human resources would not be exploited by the powerful to serve their tribal and political interests. To identify with the concept of oneness of humanity, he visualized a world where people would rise above their sectarian and racial differences.

He wanted the bloodshed in the name of religion and tribalism to come to an end. He wanted people to accept the differences they inherited. He promoted the idea of free will and free inquiry in determining one's own course of life. He advocated pluralism and coexistence. His aim was simple: every human being has the capacity to discover his humanity and create a better world for all people to live a dignified life.

We should understand that his struggles and his teachings were not only meant to be marveled at and celebrated during public gatherings, but to be lived in everyday life. True respect for the Prophet (SAS) is only possible and meaningful when the principles that he stood for are lived by his followers. Otherwise, whatever we say and do will be nothing more than a ritual. The fact that the Prophet (SAS) was chosen by Allah to communicate His message for the last time to humanity should remind us of our responsibility to humanity.

Let us remember the Prophet (SAS) and celebrate his birthday by striving to build our characters based on his model, for Allah (SWT) says in the Qur`an,

لَقَدْ كَانَ لَكُمْ فِي رَسُولِ اللَّهِ أُسْوَةٌ حَسَنَةٌ لِمَنْ كَانَ يَرْجُو اللَّهَ وَالْيَوْمَ الْآخِرَ وَذَكَرَ اللَّهَ كَثِيرًا ◯

*The Messenger of God is an excellent model for those of you who put your hope in Allah and the Last Day and remember Him often. (al-Ahzab, 33:21)*

Our beloved Prophet Muhammad (SAS) was the beloved of God and an example among humans. May Allah (SWT) give us the *tawfeeq* to follow his example. *Allahummaameen.*

The Prophet (SAS) practiced what he preached. He followed and lived the Qur`an at every moment and in every detail of his life. His life was the reflection of Allah's words. In fact, when the Prophet's wife 'A`isha (RAA) was asked about his conduct, she replied, "His character was the Qur`an."

Addressing His beloved Prophet, Allah says in *Surat al-Qalam,*

وَإِنَّكَ لَعَلَى خُلُقٍ عَظِيمٍ ◯

*And you are surely on an exalted standard of character. (al-Qalam, 68:4)*

When we claim to love someone, we need to learn more about that person, and this is especially true about Prophet Muhammad (SAS). Loving the Prophet (SAS) also means that we are willing to give up our desires to follow his example and that we prefer him over everyone and everything else. In fact, Allah makes following the Prophet (SAS) a condition for loving Him, as He says in *Surat Aal 'Imran,*

قُلْ إِنْ كُنْتُمْ تُحِبُّونَ اللَّهَ فَاتَّبِعُونِي يُحْبِبْكُمُ اللَّهُ وَيَغْفِرْ لَكُمْ ذُنُوبَكُمْ وَاللَّهُ غَفُورٌ رَحِيمٌ ◯

*Say, If you love Allah, follow me, and Allah will love you and forgive you your sins; Allah is most forgiving, most merciful. (Aal 'Imran, 3:31)*

Let us invoke blessings upon the noblest and the greatest of all souls ever to be born until the end of times, for Allah (SWT) says,

إِنَّ اللَّهَ وَمَلَائِكَتَهُ يُصَلُّونَ عَلَى النَّبِيِّ يَا أَيُّهَا الَّذِينَ آمَنُوا صَلُّوا عَلَيْهِ وَسَلِّمُوا تَسْلِيمًا ◯

*Indeed, Allah and His angels bless the Prophet; O you who believe, invoke blessings on him and invoke peace upon him in a worthy manner. (al-Ahzab, 33:56)*

# • 11 •

# CHALLENGES AND OPPORTUNITIES FOR MUSLIMS IN AMERICA

How do we, as American Muslims, go about confronting the ever-growing challenges that we face in present-day America and how do we go about cashing in on the opportunities available to us? We must remind ourselves that Allah is in control and that He intervenes in history. Islamophobia, misinformation about Islam and Muslims, hate crimes against Muslims, racial discrimination, bigotry, and so on are a test of our trust in Allah and a test for all of us to see if we truly believe in His plan. Allah says in the Qur`an that His plan is far better than anyone else's plan.

وَيَمْكُرُونَ وَيَمْكُرُ اللَّهُ وَاللَّهُ خَيْرُ الْمَاكِرِينَ ○

*And they plan and God plans, but God is Best of the ones who plan. (al-Anfal, 8:30)*

We must remember that we must accept whatever befalls us, whether favorable or unfavorable, as part of Allah's plan. As Allah also says in the Qur`an,

قُلْ لَنْ يُصِيبَنَا إِلَّا مَا كَتَبَ اللَّهُ لَنَا هُوَ مَوْلَانَا وَعَلَى اللَّهِ فَلْيَتَوَكَّلِ الْمُؤْمِنُونَ ○

*Say: Nothing shall befall us except what Allah has willed for us. He alone is our Protector. It is in Allah that the believers should put their trust. (at-Tawba, 9:51)*

Moreover, Allah reminds us,

وَعَسَى أَنْ تَكْرَهُوا شَيْئًا وَهُوَ خَيْرٌ لَكُمْ وَعَسَى أَنْ تُحِبُّوا شَيْئًا وَهُوَ شَرٌّ لَكُمْ وَاللَّهُ يَعْلَمُ وَأَنْتُمْ لَا تَعْلَمُونَ ○

*And it may be that you dislike a thing and it may (turn out to) be good for you. And it may be that you like a thing and it may (turn out to) be evil for you. Allah knows and you don't know. (al-Baqara, 2:216)*

The current developments in America are not to be seen as holding a bleak future for the Muslim community, but as an opportunity that Allah has given us to increase our efforts to make Islam relevant to the challenges facing our country. We should not let the feelings of fear, pain, and anxieties obstruct us from doing good, establishing justice, and getting civically engaged. There is not room for despair. We have to work hard, be patient, and trust in Allah, who is sufficient for us. In the Qur`an, Allah describes the believers as saying in times of hardship:

$$حَسْبُنَا اللَّهُ وَنِعْمَ الْوَكِيلُ$$

*Allah is sufficient for us and the best of protectors. (Aal 'Imran, 3:173)*

The Prophet (SAS) once said to 'Abdullah ibn 'Abbas (RAA), "Young man, I will teach you some words. Be mindful of Allah, and He will take care of you. Be mindful of Him, and you shall find Him at your side. If you ask, ask of Allah. If you need help, seek it from Allah. Know that if the whole world were to gather together in order to help you; they would not be able to help you except if Allah had written so. And if the whole world were to gather together in order to harm you, they would not harm you except if Allah had written so."

So there is no need to panic. We need to move beyond the cycle of panicked reactions to a crisis and begin working more systematically to address issues concerning us and our fellow citizens.

A primary idea that has separated the United States of America from virtually every other nation in history is the concept of it being "a nation of laws, not a nation of men." A nation of laws means that laws, not people, rule. Everyone is to be governed by the same laws, regardless of their station—Whether it is the most common American citizen or members of Congress, high-ranking bureaucrats or the president of the United States; all must be held to the just laws of America. No one is, or can be allowed to be, above the law.

America is an exceptional nation in the history of the world because its Constitution is one of the best political documents ever written. Its founders said that God gives us rights by nature, and that government is not the author or source of our rights. Government is there to secure those rights. That's America: Freedom of religion, freedom of the press, freedom of association, and freedom of speech. The First Amendment is the heartbeat of the American Constitution and the American idea itself.

The majority of US residents are empathetic and compassionate people. Most US residents are hospitable, welcoming, and inclusive of diversity. They treat their neighbors with respect and decency. The exception to this pluralistic attitude and behavior is found in a dangerous fringe of racist supremacists. We have to attempt to mitigate the attractiveness of this fringe by working with people of conscience to develop a language of political discourse that creates space for those desiring to uphold the best of American values in real, deep, and clear ways.

Organizations that fight for civil rights, human rights, and justice have pointed out some of the challenges that Muslim Americans face today. Some of these are as follows:

1. People with anti-Muslim biases attempt to stop mosque construction with the misuse of zoning laws and other tactics.

2. Employers terminate, suspend, or act against an employee on the basis of the employee identifying with the Islamic faith.

3. Government agencies use secret lists to intimidate Muslims into doing things they don't want to do and are not legally required to do, such as becoming a spy.

4. Law enforcement agents use informants to mentally, financially or emotionally target vulnerable community members in an attempt to catch them agreeing to commit a criminal act, even though the target had no previous interest in such activities.

5. Immigration agents single out Muslims or immigrants with Muslim-sounding names to delay or deny status.

6. Federal law enforcement agencies maintain a list of names, mostly Muslim, and use this list to stop individuals from boarding flights, in effect preemptively convicting the individuals of the crime of being "suspiciously Muslim" and denying them due process.

Despite all this, the US Constitution is on the side of every American. Muslim Americans will continue to stand up for justice, freedom and liberty. Indeed, the history of the civil rights movement in the United States is a history of patience and perseverance, and to persevere, we will need to face these challenges together. We should never feel that we are somehow less American or feel shy about our faith or identity. Muslims have made so much progress in academics, sports, politics, media, and professional fields. We should not downplay how far we have come. We should never ever underestimate our potential. Allah (SWT) has provided us with ample opportunities to prove who we are. We have just to cash in on them.

Brothers and sisters! It is the diversity of our country that makes us strong. Just as we are feeling pain and anxiety, so are other minority groups. We must reach out to them and give them comfort. We are taught to be caretakers of the earth and we must also ensure we are taking care of one another. We are in the battle of ideas—not a physical battle—but one of fighting against racism and discrimination. We must rally to face the forces of hatred and bigotry head on, as a community, and we must do this through openness and dialogue.

Studies show that Muslims, like most other Americans, consider Jewish Americans to be a successful and well-respected community. However, that was not always the case in America. As Nazis were profiling Jews, registering them, detaining them, and sending them to concentration camps, a ship named *St. Louis* loaded with over nine hundred Jewish refugees reached America's shores in the year 1939. None of these Jewish refugees was allowed to enter US. Instead they were sent back to Europe. Research shows that half of them were killed by the Nazis after returning. What did Jewish-Americans do to turn around such strong bigotry and hate in less than a century?

Four major things helped bring about an extraordinary turnaround of the position of the Jewish community in America:

1. Media: The Jewish community mastered the art of communication to tell their own story by investing in media and public relations.
2. Politics: They empowered themselves by investing in politics.
3. Coalitions: They supported civil rights organizations, built coalitions with African Americans, as well as invested in better Christian-Jewish relationships.
4. Social Services: They served their neighbors by investing in human and social services.

These four areas are the same areas the American Muslim community must consider as it develops its plan for the future.

Today's America is far better than the place Jewish refugees on the *St. Louis* encountered in 1939, thanks to the civil rights movement. African Americans and other minorities substantially contributed to this movement before the rest of America joined them. It is our time to contribute and take America forward.

Brothers and sisters! We must work hard to make Islam relevant and a solution to the challenges our nation faces by making a moral commitment to oppose injustices that happen to any citizen regardless of race, ethnicity, gender, or political affiliation. We should show empathy, love, and compassion to one another in these tense times.

We need to continue to increase our outreach efforts to our neighbors, work colleagues, fellow students, and others. This does not mean that we go about trying to convert people. There is no compulsion or coercion in Islam. Our duty is only to convey. This means that we should be available for the questions anyone may have.

We have to be visible and present in any volunteer or community service opportunities in our local community. We have to participate in town hall meetings to share our concerns with the wider community. We have to conduct more open houses in our mosques. We have to reach out to other interfaith and minority groups to establish meaningful relationship and partnerships. But none of this can be achieved unless we realize that we are facing huge challenges which provide a tremendous opportunity for us to allocate our time and money to our priorities.

We hope that we will be the agents of positive change, improving our state of affairs, eradicating hate and fostering love in the hearts of our fellow Americans. Allah instructs us in the Qur'an,

ادْفَعْ بِالَّتِي هِيَ أَحْسَنُ فَإِذَا الَّذِي بَيْنَكَ وَبَيْنَهُ عَدَاوَةٌ كَأَنَّهُ وَلِيٌّ حَمِيمٌ ۝

*Repel evil with what is better; then you will see that one who was once your enemy has become your dearest friend. (Fussilat, 41:34)*

We have a job ahead of us, and that job is to do our utmost best to serve our Creator in our personal and public lives, and to follow in the footsteps of our Prophet (SAS) in all circumstances, until we leave this world. We must proceed with faith.

Let me conclude by saying that there is a higher plan and logic governing events. It is impossible for us to comprehend everything. But Allah in His infinite knowledge and mercy has all factors under consideration and is the best of planners. The coming days will reveal to us the realities of which we are currently ignorant. Do not despair, work hard, and be patient.

May Allah help, bless, and protect us all. May Allah bless this country and all of humanity, *ameen.*

•  12  •

# COMPASSION

"Islam" today means different things to different people. Seeing the magnitude of violence afflicting many Muslim societies, there are non-Muslims who ask, "Are Muslims capable of showing any compassion at all?" Given the media's representation of Islam and Muslims, coupled with some Muslims' un-Islamic behavior, and their desire to draw the attention of the world to their struggles, it is not surprising that people ask this question. There are many ethical concepts and values that have not been given much prominence in today's discourse on Islam. One such concept is compassion.

Let me first clarify that Muslim ethics is universal. The Prophet Muhammad (SAS) himself was sent as a mercy to all creatures. Allah says in *Surat al-Anbiya`,*

وَمَا أَرْسَلْنَاكَ إِلَّا رَحْمَةً لِلْعَالَمِينَ ۝

*We have only sent you as a mercy for the worlds (i.e. as a mercy for all creatures). (al-Anbiya`, 21:107)*

In today's *khutbah*, I want to share some thoughts with you on the concept of compassion in Islam. Muslims are encouraged to recite *bismillah ar-Rahman ar-Raheem* before they begin any act. This expression which means, "In the name of Allah the Most Compassionate, Most Merciful" is central to a Muslim's everyday life activities. Saying *bismillah* is actually a prayer. In this prayer, a believer seeks help from two great attributes of Allah: *ar-Rahman* and *ar-Raheem*.

Both of these names of Allah are made up of the same root letters, *raa-Haa-meem* and from this root the word *rahma* is derived. This word conveys the meaning of mercy and compassion; a sense of loving tenderness and grace, which stimulates in one the urge to show kindness to others. The name *ar-Rahman* indicates the meaning of excessiveness and vastness of the attribute of mercy. And the aspect of mercy in the name *ar-Raheem* conveys a sense of permanence and continuity.

Allah (SWT) as portrayed in the Qur'an is essentially a benevolent God. In fact, Allah's mercy is one of the grandest themes of the Qur'an. The frequent recitation of *bismillah ar-Rahmanar-Raheem* is also supposed to be a reminder for Muslims to embody the divine values of mercy and compassion within themselves.

When we look at some of the key verses in the Qur'an describing our beloved Prophet Muhammad (SAS), we notice that Allah (SWT) describes him as a compassionate person. We read in the Qur'an in *Surat at-Tawba*,

لَقَدْ جَاءَكُمْ رَسُولٌ مِنْ أَنْفُسِكُمْ عَزِيزٌ عَلَيْهِ مَا عَنِتُّمْ حَرِيصٌ عَلَيْكُمْ بِالْمُؤْمِنِينَ رَءُوفٌ رَحِيمٌ ◯

*There has come to you a Messenger from among yourselves. Your suffering distresses him: he is deeply concerned for your welfare and full of kindness and mercy toward the believers. (at-Tawba, 9:128)*

The Prophet Muhammad (SAS) would always feel the suffering of people and is praised by Allah (SWT) for his compassionate nature. The Prophet (SAS) himself encouraged us to be sympathetic to each other. He was reported to have said, "The believers in their mutual kindness, compassion and sympathy are just like one body. When one of the limbs suffers, the whole body responds to it with wakefulness and fever."

Allah describes believers as those who practice compassion that moves them to help others. He says in the Qur'an,

وَمَا أَدْرَاكَ مَا الْعَقَبَةُ ◯ فَكُّ رَقَبَةٍ ◯ أَوْ إِطْعَامٌ فِي يَوْمٍ ذِي مَسْغَبَةٍ ◯ يَتِيمًا ذَا مَقْرَبَةٍ ◯ أَوْ مِسْكِينًا

ذَا مَتْرَبَةٍ ◯ ثُمَّ كَانَ مِنَ الَّذِينَ آمَنُوا وَتَوَاصَوْا بِالصَّبْرِ وَتَوَاصَوْا بِالْمَرْحَمَةِ ◯

*And how would you know what is the difficult path? It is to free a slave, or to feed on a day of severe hunger an orphan of near relationship or a needy person in misery; and to be one of those who believe and urge one another to patience and compassion. (al-Balad, 90:12-17)*

The Prophet (SAS) is praised by Allah (SWT) for his compassionate nature toward his companions after the disaster at the Battle of Uhud, even though it was the disobedience of some of them that led to their near defeat. Allah says,

فَبِمَا رَحْمَةٍ مِنَ اللَّهِ لِنْتَ لَهُمْ وَلَوْ كُنْتَ فَظًّا غَلِيظَ الْقَلْبِ لَانْفَضُّوا مِنْ حَوْلِكَ فَاعْفُ عَنْهُمْ وَاسْتَغْفِرْ لَهُمْ وَشَاوِرْهُمْ فِي الْأَمْرِ فَإِذَا عَزَمْتَ فَتَوَكَّلْ عَلَى اللَّهِ إِنَّ اللَّهَ يُحِبُّ الْمُتَوَكِّلِينَ ◯

*It is a mercy from Allah that you were gentle with them. If you had been rough or hard of heart, they would have scattered from around you. So pardon them and ask forgiveness for them and consult with them about the matter. Then when you have reached a firm decision, put your trust in Allah. Allah loves those who put their trust in Him. (Aal 'Imran, 3:159)*

In compliance with the core principles of Islamic leadership, Muslim leaders should overlook mistakes and failures of their subordinates and view them as learning opportunities. They should ask Allah to forgive the lapses of their followers. They should also not exclude them from consultation but consult with them again in the future while putting their trust in Allah (SWT).

What is empathy? It is the ability to recognize, understand and share the feelings of others. It is like walking in someone else's shoes. There are numerous examples of the compassion and empathy of the Prophet (SAS) that we learn from the *seerah*, the Prophetic biography. One account of the Prophet's empathy in action is when he was sitting with his companions, and members of a miserable tribe approached them. They had no shoes and their skin was stuck to their bones because of hunger. The Prophet (SAS) became instantly moved upon seeing their condition. The color of his face changed. He had Bilal (RAA) give the call to prayer and gathered his companions. After praying, they took up a collection for the tribe, generously helping them.

There is also the famous hadeeth in which we learn about the Prophet's (SAS) empathy for mothers in the *masjid*. The Messenger of Allah (SAS) said, "I start prayer and I want to make it long, but then I hear an infant crying, so I make my prayer short, because I know the distress caused to the mother by its crying."

The Prophet's empathy and compassion was vast and inclusive to the point that even animals could find refuge in his kindness. Once, upon entering a garden, the Prophet (SAS) saw a camel that was just skin and bones. Upon seeing it, the Prophet (SAS) began crying, and then he put his hand on its head until it was comforted. He said to the owner of that camel, "Don't you fear Allah about this beast that Allah has given in your possession? It has complained to me that you keep it hungry and load it heavily which makes it tired."

It is important to note that compassion is an ethical concept that should be extended to all of humanity, as well as the natural world. In one narration, one of the companions by the name of Abu Musa al-Ash'ari (RAA) said to the Prophet (SAS), "You remind us so frequently concerning compassion even though we already think that we are compassionate toward one another." To this, the Prophet (SAS) replied, "But I mean compassion to all." The meaning here is to have compassion for humanity at large as well as to animals and all of Allah's creations.

May Allah (SWT) give us the *tawfeeq* to be kind and compassionate to one another, to our fellow brothers and sisters in humanity, and to all creatures.

There is a story of an old woman who tried her best to irritate the Prophet (SAS) by throwing garbage in his way every day. One day, when he walked out of his home, there was no garbage. This made the Prophet (SAS) inquire about the old woman and he came to know that she was sick. The Prophet (SAS) went to visit her and offered any assistance she might need. The old woman was greatly moved by this kindness and love of the Prophet (SAS). She understood that he was truly the Prophet of Allah and that Islam was the true religion. And she became a Muslim.

There is a hadeeth in which Abu Hurayra (RAA) narrates, "While we were sitting in the company of Allah's Messenger (SAS) a man approached and said, 'O Messenger of Allah! I'm ruined!' The Prophet said, 'What is the matter?' The man said, 'I had sexual relations with my wife while I was fasting in Ramadan.' Allah's Messenger then asked him, 'Can you find a slave whom you can free?' The man could not. The Prophet asked, 'Then, are you able to fast for two consecutive months?' The man said he could not. The Prophet asked, 'Then do you have the means to feed sixty poor people?' The man again said no. So the Prophet stopped and thought, and we waited like that until a large basket of dates was brought to him. He asked, 'Where is that questioner?' The man spoke up and said, 'Here I am.' The Prophet (SAS) said, 'Take this and give it out in charity.' The man then asked, 'Messenger of Allah, must I find someone poorer than myself to give it to? By Allah, there is no household in town poorer than my own.' The Prophet (SAS) laughed until we could see his teeth, and said, 'Go feed your family.'"

In this story, we learn how to exhibit empathy and compassion. The Prophet (SAS) did not criticize or humiliate the man during his admission of guilt. He understood that this man was deeply faithful, genuinely felt devastated for having sinned, and was repentant. He gently suggested various ways by which the man could make amends. He offered the man a way out of his dilemma and proceeded gradually so as to gauge the extent of the person's ability to recompense for what he had done. His manner of dealing with this man was likely to encourage others not to hold back should they sin or make any kind of mistake.

Brothers and sisters! Showing empathy and compassion will improve our relationships and develop our character as Muslims. When we show someone that we understand them, we bring instant comfort, relief, and peace to that person.

We should remember that even when the pagan Arabs reacted to the message of the Prophet (SAS) with extreme hatred, he showed love and kindness to them. If we are to honor the Prophet (SAS), it can only come about by adopting his sublime character. May Allah (SWT) give us the *tawfeeq* to make empathy and compassion a part of our being. *Allahumma ameen.*

## • 13 •

# CONSTANT AWARENESS OF ALLAH

How can we remember Allah throughout the day without withdrawing from the routine of our daily life? How can we make sure that our personal life, family life, professional life, and all other activities continue in full swing while filling every moment with the remembrance of Allah? This is something that appears to be very difficult, but al-hamduli-llah, it is something that can be accomplished if we want. We just have to be conscious about our different states of consciousness. My *khutbah* today is to remind myself and you about some of the states of consciousness that we must strive to develop by remembering certain things, absorbing them, and reminding ourselves about them.

Firstly, each one of us should say to himself or herself: I am in Allah's presence. He is watching me. When I am alone, He is the second and if I am with someone else, He is the third. This means that He is with me wherever I am. We read in the Qur`an in *Surat al-Hadeed*,

وَهُوَ مَعَكُمْ أَيْنَ مَا كُنْتُمْ وَاللَّهُ بِمَا تَعْمَلُونَ بَصِيرٌ ◯

*And He is with you wherever you are; He sees all that you do. (al-Hadeed, 57:4)*

And we read in Surat al-Mujadila,

مَا يَكُونُ مِنْ نَجْوَى ثَلَاثَةٍ إِلَّا هُوَ رَابِعُهُمْ وَلَا خَمْسَةٍ إِلَّا هُوَ سَادِسُهُمْ وَلَا أَدْنَى مِنْ ذَلِكَ وَلَا أَكْثَرَ إِلَّا هُوَ مَعَهُمْ
أَيْنَ مَا كَانُوا ◯

*No three people can meet secretly without Him being the fourth, nor five without Him being the sixth, nor less than that, nor more, without Him being there with them wherever they may be. (al-Mujadila, 58:7)*

On one hand, Allah is transcendent—beyond time, beyond space, beyond direct experience, existing outside the created world—and on the other hand He is closer to us than we can even imagine. Allah says in *Surat Qaf*,

وَلَقَدْ خَلَقْنَا الْإِنسَانَ وَنَعْلَمُ مَا تُوَسْوِسُ بِهِ نَفْسُهُ وَنَحْنُ أَقْرَبُ إِلَيْهِ مِنْ حَبْلِ الْوَرِيدِ ○

*We created man and we know what his soul whispers to him. We are nearer to him than his jugular vein. (Qaf, 50:16)*

He is watching everything we do and hearing everything we say. His knowledge is all-encompassing. We should remind ourselves of this reality as often as we can throughout the day, every time we begin a new task, and every time we speak. Indeed, our aim should be to imprint this on our hearts in such a way that this consciousness becomes our very breath. When the Prophet Muhammad (SAS) was asked by a companion about the best method of purifying himself, he replied, "You should always remember that Allah is with you wherever you are."

Secondly, we should say to ourselves: Everything we possess has been given to us by Allah. All the blessings we have, known and unknown, our very existence, our body, our provisions, and all our abilities and accomplishments are from Allah. Allah says in the Qur'an in *Surat an-Nahl*,

وَمَا بِكُم مِّن نِّعْمَةٍ فَمِنَ اللَّهِ ○

*Whatever blessing you have is from Allah. (an-Nahl, 16:53)*

And we read in *Surat Ibraheem*,

وَإِن تَعُدُّوا نِعْمَتَ اللَّهِ لَا تُحْصُوهَا ○

*And if you were to count God's blessings, you could never count them. (Ibraheem, 14:34)*

In all the *adhkar*, which are the supplications and the invocations that the Prophet (SAS) has taught us, there is a constant theme of *hamd*, which means praise and thanks, with gratefulness and gratitude to Allah. Many of these *adhkar* are simple to learn. We should learn as many of the *adhkar* as we can. Throughout the day, as we witness all that Allah has blessed us with, we should punctuate our day with these *adhkar*. If we feel that there is nothing else to thank Allah for, then we should thank Him for the life that He has given us. So long as there is life, there is hope.

If we ever feel short of things to be thankful for, we should recall the hadeeth in which the Prophet (SAS) says, "There are three hundred and sixty joints in the body and for each joint you must give a charity each day." The joints in the human body enable it to work and make all kinds of movements. If man's body did not have these joints, it would have been impossible for him to sit, stand, lie, move, or make use of the different organs of his body. Thus, every joint is a blessing for which one must express gratitude to Allah.

On one occasion the Prophet (SAS) said, "Charity is prescribed for each descendant of Adam every day the sun rises." He was then asked, "From what do we give charity every day?" The Prophet (SAS) answered, "The doors of charity are many...enjoining good, forbidding evil, removing harm from the road, listening to the aggrieved, leading the blind, guiding one to the object of his need, hurrying with the strength of one's legs to one in sorrow who is asking for help, and supporting the feeble with the strength of one's arms—all of these are charity prescribed for you." He also said, "Every good deed is charity. Even a smile in the face of others is charity."

Charity can be practiced by everyone no matter how poor he or she is. There is charity in glorifying Allah by saying *subhan Allah*. There is charity in praising and thanking Allah by saying *al-hamduli-llah*. There is charity in exalting and magnifying Allah by saying *Allahu akbar*. And there is charity in declaring Allah's oneness by saying *la ilaha illa Allah*.

Thirdly, we should know that nothing in this world can happen without Allah's permission. Everything lies in the hands of Allah. No harm can befall us, and no benefit can reach us except as Allah ordains. Allah says in the Qur`an,

وَإِن يَمْسَسْكَ اللَّهُ بِضُرٍّ فَلَا كَاشِفَ لَهُ إِلَّا هُوَ وَإِن يَمْسَسْكَ بِخَيْرٍ فَهُوَ عَلَىٰ كُلِّ شَيْءٍ قَدِيرٌ ○

*If Allah should let any harm touch you, no one could remove it except He; while if He should let some good touch you, know that He has the power to do all that He wills.*
(al-An'am, 6:17)

The Prophet Muhammad (SAS) would supplicate to Allah the Almighty after each prayer, saying, "O Allah, whatever you want to give me, no one can stop it from coming to me and whatever you want to prevent from coming to me, nobody can give to me." We should keep reminding ourselves throughout the day, especially as we expect things to happen or not to happen, that everything happens only as He commands, and by His permission.

Fourthly, one should say to oneself, "I am going to return to Allah one day and that day could be today." We do not know when we will leave this world. It may be that the coming morning is our last morning, or perhaps the coming evening is our last evening. Indeed, it may be that this hour is our last hour, or even that this moment is our last moment. Such an uncertainty does not, of course, justify a complete withdrawal from this life. What is required of us is to be always conscious of this uncertainty. This motivates us to spend every moment of our remaining life seriously, considering it as a gift from Allah and spending the resources He has blessed us with in a manner that pleases Him.

To help us attain this state of consciousness, we should recall and reflect upon the following Qur`anic verse as much as we can throughout the day:

$$\text{إِنَّا لِلَّهِ وَإِنَّا إِلَيْهِ رَاجِعُونَ} \; \bigcirc$$

*To Allah we belong, and to Him is our return. (al-Baqara 2:156)*

These are the four states of consciousness that can help us achieve a life completely devoted to the remembrance of Allah (SWT). May we be blessed with His conscious remembrance.

'Ali ibn Abi Talib (RAA) defined *taqwa* or consciousness of Allah as "fearing Allah, adhering to His commandments, being content with what He provides one with, and getting ready for the Day of Judgment."

We are here in this world on a journey; to be tested by Allah. We are returning back to Him. If we are conscious of this fact, then we should do whatever we can to go back to Allah in a state where He is pleased with us and we are pleased with Him, as He says in the Qur`an,

$$\text{رَضِيَ اللَّهُ عَنْهُمْ وَرَضُوا عَنْهُ ذَٰلِكَ لِمَنْ خَشِيَ رَبَّهُ} \; \bigcirc$$

*Allah is well pleased with them and they are well pleased with Him. Thus shall the God-fearing be rewarded. (al-Bayyina, 98:8)*

The companions of the Prophet (SAS) were so mindful of Allah that they became genuinely concerned when this verse of *Surat Aal 'Imran* was revealed.

$$\text{يَا أَيُّهَا الَّذِينَ آمَنُوا اتَّقُوا اللَّهَ حَقَّ تُقَاتِهِ وَلَا تَمُوتُنَّ إِلَّا وَأَنتُم مُّسْلِمُونَ} \; \bigcirc$$

*O you who believe, be conscious of Allah with all the consciousness that is due to Him, and do not die except as Muslims. (Aal 'Imran, 3:102)*

The *sahaba* expressed to the Prophet (SAS) their inability to abide by this divine command, saying that because of their worldly preoccupations, they simply could not be mindful of Allah all the time to a degree that He merited. In His infinite mercy Allah (SWT) revealed the verse:

$$\text{فَاتَّقُوا اللَّهَ مَا اسْتَطَعْتُمْ وَاسْمَعُوا وَأَطِيعُوا وَأَنفِقُوا خَيْرًا لِّأَنفُسِكُمْ} \; \bigcirc$$

*So be mindful of Allah as best as you can; and listen and obey; and spend in charity: it is for your own good. (at-Taghabun, 64:16)*

There is another verse in which Allah says,

$$\text{لَا يُكَلِّفُ اللَّهُ نَفْسًا إِلَّا وُسْعَهَا} \; \bigcirc$$

*Allah does not burden any soul with more than it can bear. (al-Baqara, 2:286)*

While such verses provide tremendous relief to the believers, they also imply that one's effort toward achieving righteousness, piety, and consciousness of Allah should be stretched to the utmost. Allah knows the potential and the capability of each one of us. Each one of us has to exert his or her best. As Allah says in *Surat Aal 'Imran*,

وَسَارِعُوا إِلَىٰ مَغْفِرَةٍ مِّن رَّبِّكُمْ وَجَنَّةٍ عَرْضُهَا السَّمَاوَاتُ وَالْأَرْضُ أُعِدَّتْ لِلْمُتَّقِينَ ۝

*Race with one another toward forgiveness from your Lord and toward a paradise the width of which spans the heavens and the earth. It has been prepared for the muttaqeen. (Aal 'Imran, 3:133)*

May Allah make us among them. *Allahumma ameen.*

• 14 •

# CONTRIBUTION OF MUSLIM SCHOLARS TO THE SCIENCES

As we know, Islam is a complete and comprehensive system of life, and not merely a religion describing the relations between man and his Creator. Therefore, far from discouraging a life of well-being in this world, Allah actually praises those who say,

رَبَّنَا آتِنَا فِي الدُّنْيَا حَسَنَةً وَفِي الْآخِرَةِ حَسَنَةً وَقِنَا عَذَابَ النَّارِ ۝

*Our Lord! Give us good in this world as well as good in the hereafter and protect us from the torment of fire. (al-Baqara, 2:201)*

It is this quest for well-being which urges man to study and learn in as perfect a manner as he can about all that exists in the universe, in order to profit by it, and to be grateful to Allah. As to the method of increasing knowledge, it is inspiring to note that the very first revelation that came to the Prophet Muhammad (SAS) was a command to read.

اقْرَأْ بِاسْمِ رَبِّكَ الَّذِي خَلَقَ ۝

*Read in the name on your Lord who created. (al-'Alaq, 96:1)*

The Qur`an has repeatedly urged Muslims to mediate over the creation of the universe, and to study how the heavens and earth have been made subservient to man. Therefore, there has never been a conflict between faith and reason in Islam This is why Muslims very quickly began a progressive and serious study of the sciences. They did not merely attain political and intellectual supremacy and establish empires, but they also surpassed all other nations in knowledge and intellectual endeavors. My *khutbah* today is about the contribution that Muslim scholars made to the sciences.

Muslims scholars did not limit their studies to religious sciences. They also studied chemistry, physics, astronomy, botany, mathematics, medicine, geography, history, and a host of other disciplines of the physical, natural, social, and human sciences. Some of these scholars have guided the world in the sciences for several centuries and left an indelible mark on the world of knowledge.

Islam deals not only with what man must do and must not do, but also with what he needs to know. The first part of the testimony of faith in Islam, *la ilaha illa Allah* ("There is no god but God") is a statement of knowledge concerning reality. Muslims look upon the various sciences as different bodies of evidence which point to the truth of this most fundamental statement. This statement is what is popularly known in Islam as the principle of *tawheed* (divine unity).

The scientific spirit of Muslim scientists and scholars flows, in fact, from their consciousness of *tawheed*. The origin and development of the scientific spirit in Islam differs from that of the West. Nothing better illustrates the religious origin of the scientific spirit in Islam than the fact that this spirit was first demonstrated in the religious sciences. Muslims did not begin to cultivate the natural sciences in earnest until the third century of the Islamic era or the ninth century of the Common Era. When they began, they were already in the possession of a scientific attitude and a scientific frame of mind, which they had inherited from the religious sciences.

Long before Francis Bacon introduced and popularized the experimental method into European science in the 13th century, empirical studies based on observation and experimentation were already widespread in the Muslim world. Such studies were carried out by Muslims on a far more extensive scale than had ever been attempted in all the previous civilizations. Numerous Muslim scientists were famous for their observational powers and experimental methods as displayed in their wide-ranging studies of the natural sciences.

Inspired by the teachings of the Holy Qur`an and the Sunnah of the Prophet (SAS), many Muslims investigated matter and drew their own inferences. They also carefully observed the motions of heavenly bodies and drew their own inferences which were often different from those of the early Greek thinkers, whose reasoning was mainly limited to speculative thought ("philosophy" or "metaphysics").

Muslims became the torchbearers of knowledge at a time when Europe was deeply sunk into ignorance. The factors that led to the intellectual revolution in Arabia were the Qur`an and the Sunnah—the divinely guided lifestyle of the Prophet (SAS). The Qur`an makes knowledge a condition for the attainment of *taqwa* (piety) and invites the Muslims to pray for the increase of knowledge.

رَبِّ زِدْنِي عِلْمًا ◯

*My Lord! Increase me in knowledge. (Ta Ha, 20:114)*

The Sunnah obliges Muslims to acquire knowledge from the cradle to the grave. In other words, acquisition of knowledge in Islam is a lifelong process. The Qur`an, in attaching special importance to promotion of knowledge, compares "wisdom" to abundant good.

وَمَنْ يُؤْتَ الْحِكْمَةَ فَقَدْ أُوتِيَ خَيْرًا كَثِيرًا وَمَا يَذَّكَّرُ إِلَّا أُولُو الْأَلْبَابِ ۝

*And whoever is given wisdom has been given abundant good, but only insightful people bear this in mind. (al-Baqara, 2:269)*

Reference to the vital significance of knowledge occurs on almost every page of the Qur`an. The word "knowledge" occurs at least eighty times in the Qur`an, and derivatives of the word occur about eight hundred times. Other attributes of the mind such as "understanding," "remembering," "thinking," "reasoning," etc., and their derivatives are also numerous.

يَرْفَعِ اللَّهُ الَّذِينَ آمَنُوا مِنْكُمْ وَالَّذِينَ أُوتُوا الْعِلْمَ دَرَجَاتٍ وَاللَّهُ بِمَا تَعْمَلُونَ خَبِيرٌ ۝

*Allah will raise in rank those of you who believe and who have been given knowledge. And Allah is well aware of what you do. (al-Mujadila, 58: 11)*

The Prophet (SAS) laid special stress on the acquisition of knowledge by saying, "The seeking of knowledge is obligatory upon every Muslim."Further highlighting the sanctity of knowledge, the Prophet (SAS) said, "He who goes out in search of knowledge, is in Allah's path till he returns." Knowledge was to be acquired from all possible sources. According to another hadeeth, the Prophet (SAS) said, "The word of wisdom is the lost property of the believer, so wherever he finds it he has a better right to it."

Speaking of the exalted position of the scholars, there is a hadeeth in which the Prophet (SAS) tells us that the learned ones are the heirs of the prophets. He also tells us that they leave knowledge as their inheritance, and the one who inherits it inherits a great fortune.

While it was the exhortation of the Qur`an and Prophetic traditions to seek knowledge that led the intellectual revolution in the Muslim world, the main factor that contributed to Europe's ignorance was the Church. The struggle between the Church and science started with the discovery made by Copernicus that the earth was not the center of the universe. He also discovered that the earth was not static but moving and that it moved around the sun; whereas the Church taught that the earth was the center of the universe, that it was static, and that the sun and the stars moved around it.

It is the Muslims who saved Europe from ignorance. This fact is acknowledged by many European thinkers. Sir James Jeans, a British physicist and astronomer of the 20<sup>th</sup> century writes in praise of al-Biruni, a Persian astronomer of the 10<sup>th</sup> century. Jeans writes that while the science of the Greeks was based upon speculation, al-Biruni established a method based on experience and experimentation. He is not the lonely supporter; others prominent scientists and philosophers have made similar praises of scientists and philosophers of the golden age of Islamic civilization.

Many of the works written by Muslim scientists were so significant that they were translated into Latin and remained major references in the universities of Europe until the sixteenth century, becoming a starting point for European research. In places such as Baghdad, Kufa, Basra, Cairo, and Cordova, great universities sprang up which acquired such worldwide fame that students from all parts of the world, particularly Europe, began to flock to these institutions in search of knowledge. Without the work of Muslim scientists, the Renaissance of the 13<sup>th</sup>-14<sup>th</sup> centuries in Western Europe would not have taken place and the modern Western civilization would have never emerged. May Allah increase us in knowledge!

Brothers and sisters! Logical thinking, mathematical analysis, observation, experimentation, and even rational interpretation of scriptures were all part of the scientific enterprise of early Muslim scientists. Science, therefore, became an extensive cultural undertaking that occupied the minds and energies of many of the leading intellectuals in medieval Muslim societies. Indeed, science was practiced on a scale unprecedented in earlier human history. Numerous scientific manuscripts, from various regions of the medieval Islamic world are scattered in modern libraries all over the globe. Until the rise of modern science, no other civilization engaged as many scientists, produced as many scientific books, or provided as varied and sustained support for scientific activity.

The Muslims continued their work in the service of science until great misfortunes afflicted their principal intellectual centers; Baghdad in the East, and Cordova-Granada in the West. These were occupied by barbarians, to the great misfortune of science, at a time when the printing press had not yet come into being. The burning of libraries with their hundreds of thousands of manuscripts led to tremendous and irreparable loss. What had been constructed in centuries was destroyed in days. Once a civilization declines due to such calamities, it takes several centuries as well as numerous resources before one can make up the losses.

The calamity that befell the *ummah* is not the only reason for its political and intellectual decline. There are other factors which make up the chemistry of the political domination and intellectual supremacy of a community over other communities of the world, such as intellectual ingenuity, creative academic pursuits, and applying reasoning to practical matters.

The failure of the Muslims to continue to advance the sciences which they initially developed is an unfortunate event for the whole of the human race. It warrants attention from all those genuinely interested in the problems of survival and revival of human culture and civilization. Both theoretically and practically, the ways to overcome the challenges that confront us an *ummah* include holding on to the Qur'an and Sunnah, employing the faculties of thinking and searching, and working hard.

May Allah (SWT) bless us with the true understanding of our *deen* in letter and spirit, and bless us with the *tawfeeq* to live by it, *ameen*.

• 15 •

# CULTIVATING LOVE FOR FELLOW MUSLIMS

There is a hadeeth in which the Prophet (SAS) says, "None of you [truly] believes until he loves for his brother that which he loves for himself." In another hadeeth he (SAS) tells us, "The servant does not reach the reality of faith until he loves for the people what he loves for himself of goodness." There is another hadeeth related to this topic in which the Prophet (SAS) says, "Whoever loves to be delivered from the hellfire and enter paradise should die with faith in Allah and the Last Day, and should treat the people the way he would love to be treated."

These Prophetic traditions lay down a significant principle for the behavior of people toward each other. As for Muslims, a true Islamic community is built upon love and compassion between its members. This can only arise when barriers to brotherhood are removed. These barriers can come from divisions based on race, ethnicity, color, and economic status. They can also arise from extreme affiliations to different schools of thought or religious groups, sects, or schools of thought. Other barriers that contribute to division between Muslims are diseases of the heart such as arrogance, jealousy, greed, selfishness, hatred, and so on.

We should not hold any hatred for Muslims in our hearts. It's a very sad thing to imagine that communities become polarized through following different scholars, and even within like-minded communities there are differences and quarrelling. When we deal with Muslims in the community, we should deal with them in the best possible manner. One of the ways to do this is to choose the best words in our conversation.

Good words minimize disputes and confrontations. Allah instructs in the Qur'an,

وَقُل لِّعِبَادِي يَقُولُوا الَّتِي هِيَ أَحْسَنُ إِنَّ الشَّيْطَانَ يَنزَغُ بَيْنَهُمْ إِنَّ الشَّيْطَانَ كَانَ لِلْإِنسَانِ عَدُوًّا مُّبِينًا ○

*And say to My servants that they should say what is best. Satan stirs up discord among them. Surely, Satan is an outright enemy to man. (al-Isra`, 17:53)*

وَقُولُوا لِلنَّاسِ حُسْنًا ○

*And speak kindly to people. (al-Baqara, 2:83).*

وَقُولُوا قَوْلًا سَدِيدًا ○

*And say what is right. (al-Ahzab, 33:70)*

A behavior that we should be watchful of is arrogance. Arrogance means having or showing an exaggerated opinion of one's own importance, merit, and ability, while looking down upon others and considering oneself to be better than others. The Prophet (SAS) tells us, "No one who has the weight of a seed of arrogance in his heart will enter paradise." Isn't it unfortunate that arrogance is rampant even among the Muslim lands in the form of racism and ethnic pride? As Muslims, we need to be humble.

Living by this hadeeth is the topic of today's *khutbah*. As Muslims, we should not be jealous of other Muslims. A jealous person does not like to see others happy, successful, and prosperous. One must realize that being jealous of others is actually a way of being displeased with Allah for his bounties upon that person. Allah in His infinite wisdom bestows what He wills upon who He wills. We have to be able to deal with the situation by being grateful for what He has given to us and being patient with what has not been given to us. It is not blameworthy for one to ask Allah to give him something similar to what has been given to another person, but it is blameworthy to wish for it to be taken away from that person. According to Prophetic traditions, there are only two cases or two categories of people that can be envied. The Prophet (SAS) says, "There is no envy but in two cases: a man whom Allah has given this Book (the Qur'an) and he stands to recite it by night and day, and a man whom Allah has given wealth and he spends it in charity by night and day." In another hadeeth the Prophet (SAS) says, "There is no envy but in two cases: a man whom Allah has given wealth and he spends it rightly, and a man whom Allah has given wisdom and he acts according to it and teaches with it." Scholars say that wisdom refers to knowledge of the Qur'an and the Sunnah.

It is only due to the blessing of Islam that we have attained whatever good that we enjoy ourselves. Thus we should wish the same for other Muslims. In fact, we should wish for them to be better than us, just as parents love their children and wish their children to be better than themselves. At the same time, we should also be constantly striving for our own self-improvement. It is not enough to merely wish for something which is good for other Muslims while we ourselves are deficient and not striving to be better Muslims ourselves.

One important concept that is emphasized from the teachings of the hadeeth about cultivating love for fellow Muslims is brotherhood. There are many Muslims in the world today, but unfortunately many of them, are weak in faith, except those upon whom Allah has bestowed His mercy. Many of these weak Muslims commit sins regularly and violate the principles of Islam. However, it is not appropriate to dissociate ourselves from them. This will be counterproductive. In fact, even people with the minimum level of *iman* (faith) should be regarded as brothers in Islam. If they were to commit sins, we should love for them to leave sinful acts. We should love them and care for them the way we love ourselves, so that they are guided toward the obedience of Allah (SWT).

One of the ways to do this is by giving *naseeha* (sincere advice) to them. Giving naseeha to the Muslims includes guiding them to what is best for them in this life and the hereafter; teaching them about their religion and other things that they may be ignorant about; helping them in times of need; providing what is beneficial for them; encouraging them with kindness and sincerity to do good, and forbidding them from doing evil. When we advise others, we should do it in a good way based on our love for them and not for personal reasons. When advising others, it is better to clearly mention that we are advising them because we love them and care for them. If an advice is specific to an individual, it should be done in private so as to avoid offending the person.

We also have to be merciful toward other Muslims. Showing mercy and respect to each other is among the many noble teachings of our deen. The Prophet (SAS) said, "He is not one of us who does not show mercy to our young ones and respect to our elderly." We should also be aware of the Prophetic saying, "Whoever harms others, Allah will harm him. Whoever is harsh with others, Allah will be harsh with him." In fact, we are taught by the Prophet (SAS) says to "remove harmful things from the path of the Muslims." In another hadeeth he also tells us, "The Muslim is one from whose tongue and hands the Muslims are safe." It is narrated that once a man asked, "O Messenger of Allah, what is Islam?" The Messenger of Allah (SAS) replied, "That you surrender your heart to Allah and that the Muslims are safe from your tongue and hand."

One of the first manifestations of piety after iman is to have kindness, sympathy, and mercy toward others. The Prophet (SAS) is recorded to have said in a hadeeth, "He who is deprived of kindness is deprived of good." There is another hadeeth in which he says, "Whoever relieves a believer from one of the hardships of this world, Allah will relieve him from one of the hardships of the Day of Judgment. And whoever eases a difficult circumstance (for the believer), Allah will make it easy for him in this life and the hereafter; and whoever covers a believer, Allah will cover him in this life and in the hereafter. Allah is at the assistance of the slave (of His) so long as the slave is at the assistance of his brother."

Brothers and sisters! The frequent recitation of bismillah ar-Rahman ar-Raheem before reciting a surah of the Qur`an, or before starting to do something, is also a reminder for Muslims to embody the divine values of love, mercy, and compassion within themselves. Pious believers have the right attitude. They love doing good to others not for worldly gains or praise, but for the sake of pleasing Allah (SWT). This notion is beautifully reflected in the verse of the Qur`an, which speaks of true believers as saying,

إِنَّمَا نُطْعِمُكُمْ لِوَجْهِ اللَّهِ لَا نُرِيدُ مِنْكُمْ جَزَاءً وَلَا شُكُورًا ۝

*We only feed you for the sake of Allah. We do not desire from you any reward or thanks.*
(al-Insan, 76:9-10)

Cultivating love among Muslims also calls for *shura* (mutual consultation) within the Muslim community. Describing some of the characteristics of believers, Allah says in the Qur`an,

وَالَّذِينَ اسْتَجَابُوا لِرَبِّهِمْ وَأَقَامُوا الصَّلَاةَ وَأَمْرُهُمْ شُورَى بَيْنَهُمْ وَمِمَّا رَزَقْنَاهُمْ يُنْفِقُونَ ۝

*And those who respond to their Lord, pray regularly, conduct their affairs by mutual consultation, and spend out of what We have provided them. (ash-Shura, 42:38)*

The Islamic way of life requires that the principle of *shura* should be used in every collective affair, big or small. If it is a domestic affair, the husband and the wife should act by mutual consultation, and when the children have grown up, they should also be consulted. If it is a matter concerning the whole family, the opinion of every adult member should be solicited. If it concerns a tribe or a fraternity or the population of a city, and it is not possible to consult all the people, the decision should be taken by a local council or committee, which should comprise the trustworthy representatives of the concerned people.

The hadeeth that is the topic of today's discussion can be practiced at many different levels and different ways. Through practicing this beautiful hadeeth, the seeds of love and brotherhood can be planted in our *ummah*, while we protect ourselves from contempt, pride, suspicion, selfishness, and other evils. When we show someone that we understand them, we bring instant comforting relief and peace to that person. This should be all the more within believers themselves.

May Allah guide us to what is best and grant unity to the Muslim *ummah*. May Allah bless each one of us with a desire to love for our brothers and sisters in faith and humanity what we love for ourselves, and may He bless us with physical, mental, and spiritual health, and sound hearts.

## • 16 •

# DA'WA

My dear brothers and sisters! In today's *khutbah*, I intend to share with you some thoughts on the concept of *da'wa* in Islam. *Da'wa* is an Arabic word which literally means "making an invitation." This term is often used to describe how Muslims share their faith and practice with others. *Da'wa* is an Islamic duty. Believers are instructed in the Qur`an to invite people to the way of their Lord. Allah says,

ادْعُ إِلَى سَبِيلِ رَبِّكَ بِالْحِكْمَةِ وَالْمَوْعِظَةِ الْحَسَنَةِ وَجَادِلْهُمْ بِالَّتِي هِيَ أَحْسَنُ إِنَّ رَبَّكَ هُوَ أَعْلَمُ بِمَنْ ضَلَّ عَنْ سَبِيلِهِ وَهُوَ أَعْلَمُ بِالْمُهْتَدِينَ ۝

*Invite people to the path of your Lord with wisdom and good advice and argue with them in the most courteous way, for your Lord knows best who strays from His path and knows best who is rightly guided. (an-Nahl, 16:125)*

Brothers and sisters! We must understand that while doing *da'wa*, it is not the responsibility or right of Muslims to attempt to forcibly convert others to Islam for Allah says,

لَا إِكْرَاهَ فِي الدِّينِ قَدْ تَبَيَّنَ الرُّشْدُ مِنَ الْغَيِّ ۝

*Let there be no compulsion in religion, for the truth stands out clearly from falsehood.*
*(al-Baqara, 2:256)*

We are to share with non-Muslims the universal message of all of Allah's prophets and messengers: the message of monotheism (*tawheed*) and its meaning and implications. We are to explain to them our faith in simple and effective ways. It is up to the invitee or listener to make his or her own choice.

Allah (SWT) has given us the ability to know what is good and what is evil. We instinctively like goodness and dislike evil. But this instinct is not sufficient to guide us in the all the many complex aspects of our life on this earth. Hence in His mercy,

Allah (SWT) has sent down messengers with clear guidance to help live our lives in peace and harmony. This is also necessary because we are accountable for our conduct to Allah (SWT) on the Day of Judgment. We could plead ignorance if we did not know what the right path was. Allah explains this in the Qur`an,

رُسُلًا مُبَشِّرِينَ وَمُنْذِرِينَ لِئَلَّا يَكُونَ لِلنَّاسِ عَلَى اللَّهِ حُجَّةٌ بَعْدَ الرُّسُلِ وَكَانَ اللَّهُ عَزِيزًا حَكِيمًا ۞

*They were messengers giving good news and warnings so humanity should have no excuse before Allah after (the coming of) the messengers. And Allah is Almighty, All-Wise. (an-Nisa`, 4:165)*

Each messenger was sent to his own people so that he would explain the message to them in their own language. But the prophethood of Muhammad (SAS) was twofold: He was sent down to the people of Arabia as well as to all humankind. Now that the institution of prophethood has come to an end, the responsibility for conveying the message of Allah to all humanity until the end of time rests on this *ummah*. Allah explains this in the Qur`an,

وَكَذَلِكَ جَعَلْنَاكُمْ أُمَّةً وَسَطًا لِتَكُونُوا شُهَدَاءَ عَلَى النَّاسِ وَيَكُونَ الرَّسُولُ عَلَيْكُمْ شَهِيدًا ۞

*Thus, We have made you an ummah justly balanced, so that you may act as witnesses for mankind, and the Messenger may be a witness for you. (al-Baqara, 2:143)*

We know that there will always be at least one group in this *ummah* that will stand firm on *deen* and convey the message of truth. Thus, *da'wa* is not just one of the many good deeds to be undertaken but it is actually the prime responsibility of this *ummah*.

كُنْتُمْ خَيْرَ أُمَّةٍ أُخْرِجَتْ لِلنَّاسِ تَأْمُرُونَ بِالْمَعْرُوفِ وَتَنْهَوْنَ عَنِ الْمُنْكَرِ وَتُؤْمِنُونَ بِاللَّهِ ۞

*You are the best of peoples, evolved for mankind, enjoining what is right and forbidding what is wrong and believing in Allah. (Aal 'Imran, 3:110)*

The process of *da'wa* involves the message, the one who gives the message, and the one who is given the message. In order to protect the message and its continuous propagation, Allah (SWT) has undertaken upon Himself to preserve the Qur`an from corruption. Allah says,

إِنَّا نَحْنُ نَزَّلْنَا الذِّكْرَ وَإِنَّا لَهُ لَحَافِظُونَ ۞

*Indeed, it is We who have sent down the Reminder, and indeed it is We who will preserve it. (al-Hijr, 15:9)*

The message is to submit to Allah, which means to become a Muslim. There is a difference between simply being a self-satisfied passive Muslim and becoming a true practicing Muslim. Becoming a Muslim has two implications: The first is to invite oneself to surrender to the will of Allah and the second is to invite the whole of society to live in submission to the will of Allah. These two processes continue simultaneously. Allah says,

وَمَنْ أَحْسَنُ قَوْلًا مِّمَّن دَعَا إِلَى اللَّهِ وَعَمِلَ صَالِحًا وَقَالَ إِنَّنِي مِنَ الْمُسْلِمِينَ ۝

*And whose words are better than someone who calls others to Allah, does good, and says, "I am truly one of those who submit? (Fussilat, 41:33)*

The best words that any human being can speak are words of guidance inviting people to the purpose of their creation—the worship of God. This being the case, the reward for giving *da'wa* must be tremendous. Thus, it is no surprise to find that the Prophet (SAS) addressed the great reward for this righteous pursuit when he said, "Whoever directs someone to do good will gain the same reward as the one who does good." He was also reported to have said, "Whoever calls to guidance will receive the same reward as the one who follows him without any decrease in the reward of (his follower)."

Who is the one who gives the message or the *da'iy*? Every Muslim is a *da'iy*. Some people say that if we ourselves are sinners how can we invite others to goodness? Some say that they are not learned enough to do *da'wa*. Remember the Prophet (SAS) said, "Convey from me even if it is one *ayah*." Consequently, virtually no Muslim is excused from giving some *da'wa*. While giving his sermon on occasion of the farewell pilgrimage, he said to his companions, "Let those who are present convey (the message) to those who are not present. It may be that some of those to whom it will be conveyed will understand it better than those who have actually heard it." Thus, we see from the lives of the companions that they conveyed this message to the farthest corners of the earth.

Who is the one to be invited to Islam? Everyone should be invited to Islam as everyone is a potential Muslim. As each individual is different, we have to know the psychology of those whom we invite or give *da'wa* to. It is essential that we respect their feelings and avoid hurting their feelings. We have to choose the proper time and place to present the message. If someone argues, we should not try to win the argument by humiliating him.

Brothers and sisters! We must realize that *da'wa* is a long and ongoing process. It needs lots of patience and perseverance. Even then it may not bring any result. Thus, people often give up in despair. But we should realize that our duty is only to convey the message and we cannot change people's hearts if they themselves do not want to change. It is only Allah who gives guidance to whom He wills. And His will is based on His absolute knowledge and wisdom. If we study the lives of the Prophets, we will see that many of them failed to change the hearts of their own families. The Prophet Nuh (AS) preached for nine-hundred fifty years yet even his wife and his son did not accept Islam. The father of the Prophet *Ibraheem* (AS), the wife of the Prophet Lut (AS), and

Abu Talib, the uncle of Prophet (SAS) did not accept Islam.

May Allah (SWT) give us the *tawfeeq* to understand the noble *deen* of Islam and may He bless each one of us, *ameen!*

Brothers and sisters! How do we go about giving *da'wa*? We have to be friendly, respectful, and gentle, and a living example of the truth and peace of Islam. It's always good to have a dialogue rather than a monologue. The discussion should be conducted rationally, in a civilized manner, and using decent language, so that the ideas of the other person may be reformed. Our aim should be to appeal to the addressee's heart, and to convey the truth to them. We do not want to be like a wrestler whose only object is to defeat his opponent. Allah instructs us in the Qur'an,

$$ وَلَا تُجَادِلُوٓا أَهْلَ الْكِتَٰبِ إِلَّا بِالَّتِى هِىَ أَحْسَنُ ۝ $$

*And do not argue with the people of the Scripture except in the best manner. (al-'Ankabut, 29:46)*

We also have to choose our time and place for *da'wa* carefully. We should find common ground; and speak a common language with our audience. Allah provides us an example in *Surat al-'Ankabut.*

$$ ءَامَنَّا بِالَّذِىٓ أُنزِلَ إِلَيْنَا وَأُنزِلَ إِلَيْكُمْ وَإِلَٰهُنَا وَإِلَٰهُكُمْ وَاحِدٌ وَنَحْنُ لَهُ مُسْلِمُونَ ۝ $$

*We believe in what was revealed to us and in what was revealed to you, and our God and your God is the same; to Him we surrender. (al-'Ankabut, 29:46)*

We should also try to clear up some of the common misconceptions about Islam. Islam is a widely misunderstood religion, and many of those misconceptions have become even more firmly entrenched in recent years. Those who are unfamiliar with the Islamic faith often have misunderstandings and misconceptions about Islam's teachings and practices. Some people believe that Muslims worship a moon-god. Many Christians don't know that Muslims don't believe in Jesus. Many people believe that Islam is oppressive to women, that Islam is a faith that promotes violence, and Islam is intolerant of other faiths. People mistakenly believe that the Qur'an was written by Muhammad (SAS) and copied from Christian and Jewish sources.

Also, if one does not know the correct answer to a question asked about Islam or Muslims, one should be humble and willing to say, "I don't know. I can find out for you and let you know." We should also try our best not to confuse between religious, cultural, and political issues. We should also provide follow-up and support for anyone who expresses interest in learning more.

*Da'wa* can be done individually or collectively depending on the circumstances. It is helpful to join a *da'wa* organization and support it with any skill that one may have through social media, print media, creating videos, writing articles, etc.

May Allah may make us realize our duty of conveying the message of Islam and give us the faith and courage so that we take up this task as is required of us. *Ameen!*

## • 17 •

# DEALING WITH HARDSHIPS

We find ourselves in the last few days of the blessed month of Ramadan. As we celebrate this great month together, and as we look forward to celebrating 'Eid al-Fitr, let us remember those members of our human family and of our Muslim family, whose 'Eid al-Fitr will be different from ours. As we celebrate, they mourn. While we plan for the festivities, they organize funerals. They are suffering from instability, persecution, oppression, injustice, and senseless war. People's houses are being blown apart. Innocent men, women, and children are being killed. And as believers, we feel it. We feel the pain and suffering of what's going on in Gaza. We feel the pain and suffering of refugees in war-torn Syria. We feel the suffering of those who are living under tyranny and oppression.

We feel pain, confusion, and anguish about what is going on with the *ummah*. We find ourselves in a dilemma: How do we as believers process and deal with these events taking place all around the world? We have a bit of a disconnect because *al-hamduli-llah*, we live here in this place of stability, comfort, and prosperity for the most part. But we see images that are hard to believe. How do we respond?

Brothers and sisters! Let me explain to you the three most of us generally respond, and why we should avoid responding in those ways.

The first response is one of despair. Being so far and so distinct from the place of conflict, we feel ourselves incapable of making any change with our hands. We can't stop the bleeding that's going on, so we give up hope. We feel hopeless and that we can't do anything. We find ourselves confused, not knowing what to do. This feeling of depression is understandable, but this is not the Islamic response.

Another response that we often find ourselves making is one of trying to ignore the situation. It's too overwhelming and too painful, so we choose to ignore the media and we don't read about what's going on or face the injustice in the world. We find ourselves avoiding the reality on the ground, and this is also not the Islamic way.

A third way we often respond is by being fanatic and hyper-focused on the issues to the point that we get overburdened. We find ourselves fanatically trying to engage with these issues and troubles and begin to consume every piece of news and follow every detail of what's going on in each of these conflicts around the world. My dear brothers and sisters; this is a very understandable response, but this too is not the Islamic response.

Let us remember that even with all the bad news around us, we also have good news at the same time. Despite the trials and tribulations facing the *ummah* and the human race, including the challenges we find ourselves in here in the US such as gun violence, domestic violence, and homelessness, we always have good news. That is a promise from Allah, for Allah says in the Qur`an,

لَا يُكَلِّفُ اللَّهُ نَفْسًا إِلَّا وُسْعَهَا ۝

*Allah does not charge a soul with more than it can bear. (al-Baqara, 2:286)*

So despite all of the hardship, pain, and suffering that is going on, Allah has equipped us with a capacity to bear them. It's part of our human nature to feel compassion for our fellow human beings and ask ourselves the question, "Why is this happening?" God has wisdom beyond our capacity to reach. His way of operating the world is beyond our comprehension. We don't always know why Allah allows certain things to unfold. But we do know this: He has given us the capacity to bear whatever He puts before us. We should ask questions such as: How do we respond to the challenges we face in a way that's most beautiful and pleasing to Allah? How do we respond to the brutality, inhumanity, and indignity that we inflict upon one another as human beings? How do we respond with a mannerism, a mindset, and a heart that is pleasing to our Creator, the One who has placed us in these circumstances and is telling us that we have the capacity to bear them?

Allah (SWT) offers us a promise; a contract; a covenant; an agreement that we can enter into with Him, to help us answer the question of how to respond to the hardships of life. Allah says in *Surat as-Saff*,

يَا أَيُّهَا الَّذِينَ آمَنُوا هَلْ أَدُلُّكُمْ عَلَى تِجَارَةٍ تُنْجِيكُمْ مِنْ عَذَابٍ أَلِيمٍ ۝ تُؤْمِنُونَ بِاللَّهِ وَرَسُولِهِ وَتُجَاهِدُونَ فِي سَبِيلِ اللَّهِ بِأَمْوَالِكُمْ وَأَنْفُسِكُمْ ذَلِكُمْ خَيْرٌ لَكُمْ إِنْ كُنْتُمْ تَعْلَمُونَ ۝ يَغْفِرْ لَكُمْ ذُنُوبَكُمْ وَيُدْخِلْكُمْ جَنَّاتٍ تَجْرِي مِنْ تَحْتِهَا الْأَنْهَارُ وَمَسَاكِنَ طَيِّبَةً فِي جَنَّاتِ عَدْنٍ ذَلِكَ الْفَوْزُ الْعَظِيمُ ۝

*O you who believe! Shall I lead you to a bargain that will save you from a painful punishment? You should believe in God and His Messenger and strive for Gods cause with your possessions and your lives. That will be better for you, if you only knew. and He will forgive you your sins and admit you into Gardens with rivers flowing under them. He will lodge you in fine dwellings in the Gardens of Eternity; that is indeed the supreme achievement. (as-Saff, 61:10-12)*

There is a bargain, a trade, a transaction that Allah (SWT) wants us to enter into with Him to be successful. That is to struggle with everything that we have: our whole self, our whole soul, our whole spirit. If we do this, He will forgive our sins, enter us into paradise, and give us victory. This is what we need.

What defines success? What will help us achieve success? As long as there is life on earth, there will be struggles. There will be struggles against one another. It is the nature of human beings. We have to strive and struggle against illness, we have to struggle economically, we have to struggle in our relationships, and we have to struggle against our lusts and desires. Success in absolute terms comes from responding to these difficult circumstances to the best of our ability in the way prescribed by God. On this day of *Jumu'ah*, on this day of fasting in this blessed month of Ramadan, let us call out to our Lord and ask Him to assist us and aid us in our response to these difficult circumstances that face the *ummah*.

Brothers and sisters! The good news is that as long as we make our best effort to do what is right, we are promised success and victory. If we struggle in God's path with our possessions, our money, and our whole being, and as long as we put in our best efforts, we have achieved success, even if we don't ultimately change our fate. Because we will ultimately stand before our Creator on that day when everyone will be concerned about one's own reckoning and accounting so much so that a nursing mother will abandon her child, and a brother will run away from his brother.

Our beloved Prophet Muhammad (SAS) outlined the political foundations and the social foundations of the new Muslim community in Medina. What were the first words that he uttered upon his arrival to Medina? Tirmidhi reported that the Prophet (SAS) said, "O people! Spread the greeting of peace, feed the poor, behave kindly to your relatives, offer prayer when others are asleep, and (thus) enter paradise in peace." Following this hadeeth in letter and spirit is a gateway to paradise, to ultimate success.

The first advice is to spread the greetings of peace among ourselves. We come from so many different backgrounds. We don't know each other. We don't understand each other. Peace is an activity, an action. We have to proactively establish peace. We have to make each other feel welcome. We have to greet each other, hug each other, love each other, and know each other. This is the foundation of a healthy community.

The second advice is to feed people who are hungry. The Prophet (SAS) arrived in a city full of economic injustice and we also see this situation here and everywhere in the world. There is a disparity between the "haves" and the "have nots." What is implied in the Prophetic advice is to bridge the gap, bring the people together, and address each other's needs. This is the second step in creating a coherent society.

The third advice is to behave kindly toward one's relatives and maintain family connections. The challenges we face are often of our own making. We create hostility between one another as brothers as sisters; as husbands and wives, as parents and children. We cut ties. Don't cut ties with one another. Maintaining healthy and harmonious family relationships is vital for a healthy community.

The fourth advice applies particularly during this month, and that is to offer prayers while others are asleep. This is to gain spiritual strength because making peace, sharing our wealth, and maintaining family ties all require an exertion of our spiritual energy. And after we spend it, we replenish our spiritual energy through our connection with Allah (SWT). And the best way to do that is through the remembrance of Allah in those moments when others are asleep.

Let us pray to Allah (SWT) for His forgiveness of our shortcomings and for His help in achieving a healthy community and in responding to the overwhelming hardships that we face in this world.

O Allah! Help our brothers and sisters who are facing instability, death, and destruction in Gaza and in all other areas of conflicts. O Allah! Grant *jannah* to those who have passed away from the atrocities inflicted upon them. O Allah! There are so many who have been injured from bombardments on a besieged population. O Allah! give them speedy recovery; give them endurance; give them deep faith. Help us to help them. O Allah! Help us to fulfill our responsibilities by educating ourselves of the circumstances; by serving as ambassadors of the marginalized. O Allah! Let us speak in their name to counter the negative media portrayals that we face about the conflicts around the world. Let us speak the truth. Let our voices represent those who are not heard. O Allah! Empower us to be of assistance to them. O Allah! Respond to our call and make us respond to Your call. *Allahumma ameen.*

• 18 •

# DISEASES OF THE HEARTS AND THEIR REMEDIES

The topic of today's *khutbah* is "Diseases of the Hearts and their Remedies." The human is made up of the body and the spirit, intertwined with each another. The spirit is the inner dimension of our being. The essential reality of the human lies in the spirit or *ar-rooh*, also referred to as *an-nafs* (the soul), *al-qalb* (the heart), or *al-'aql* (the intellect).

According to a hadeeth reported by both Bukhari and Muslim, the Prophet (SAS) said, "Indeed there is in the body a piece of flesh which if it is sound, then the whole body is sound, and if it is corrupt, then the whole body is corrupt. Indeed, it is the heart." The reference in this hadeeth is to the spiritual heart. Numerous times the Qur'an alludes to the spiritual heart. For instance, describing the Day of Judgment, Allah says,

$$يَوْمَ لَا يَنْفَعُ مَالٌ وَلَا بَنُونَ ۝ إِلَّا مَنْ أَتَى اللَّهَ بِقَلْبٍ سَلِيمٍ ۝$$

*It is the Day when neither wealth nor children can benefit anyone except one who comes to Allah with a sound heart. (ash-Shu'ara`, 26:88-89)*

And in *Surat Qaf*, we read,

$$مَنْ خَشِيَ الرَّحْمَنَ بِالْغَيْبِ وَجَاءَ بِقَلْبٍ مُنِيبٍ ۝ ادْخُلُوهَا بِسَلَامٍ ذَلِكَ يَوْمُ الْخُلُودِ ۝$$

*The one who feared the All-Merciful in the Unseen and came with a heart turned to devotion. So enter it in peace. This is the day of everlasting life. (Qaf, 50:33-34)*

In a hadeeth narrated by Abu Hurayra (RAA), Allah's Messenger (SAS) said, "Allah neither looks at your figures, nor at your outward appearance; He looks at your hearts and your deeds." Just as there are diseases of the physical heart, there are also diseases of the spiritual heart.

So brothers and sisters, it is extremely important for the spiritual heart to be sound. Spiritual health is as important as physical health, if not more. Physical health is important for a meaningful life and success in this world, but spiritual health is indispensable for success and salvation both in this world and in the hereafter.

In his book *Ihya` 'Uloom ad-Deen* (Revival of the Sciences of Religion), Imam al-Ghazali says that every organ of our body has a function; when it fails to perform its function, it is sick. The function of the soul or the spiritual heart is to know its Creator, to love Him, and to seek closeness to Him. If the heart fails in this function, then we must know that it is sick. It is important to know the ailments that make the heart weak and sick. In the language of the Qur'an it is not only the eyes that get blind; the hearts also become blind.

$$فَإِنَّهَا لَا تَعْمَى الْأَبْصَارُ وَلَكِنْ تَعْمَى الْقُلُوبُ الَّتِي فِي الصُّدُورِ ۝$$

*It is not their eyes which are blind but the hearts in their breasts which are blind. (al-Hajj 22:46)*

The Qur'an has spoken in many places about the sicknesses of the hearts. Referring to the sickness in the hearts of the hypocrites, Allah says in *Surat al-Baqara*,

$$فِي قُلُوبِهِمْ مَرَضٌ فَزَادَهُمُ اللَّهُ مَرَضًا وَلَهُمْ عَذَابٌ أَلِيمٌ بِمَا كَانُوا يَكْذِبُونَ ۝$$

*There is a sickness in their hearts and Allah has increased their sickness. They will have a painful punishment because they have been lying. (al-Baqara 2:10)*

And what will be their fate? Allah tells us,

$$إِنَّ الْمُنَافِقِينَ فِي الدَّرْكِ الْأَسْفَلِ مِنَ النَّارِ وَلَنْ تَجِدَ لَهُمْ نَصِيرًا ◯$$

*The hypocrites will be in the lowest depths of hell, and you will find no one to help them.*
*(an-Nisa` 4:145)*

Who is a hypocrite? In a hadeeth reported by both Bukhari and Muslim, the Prophet (SAS) teaches us that there are four qualities which if found in a person make him a pure hypocrite, and the one who has a portion of them has a portion of hypocrisy until he leaves them: (1) when given a trust, he betrays it, (2) when he speaks, he lies, (3) when he promises, he breaks it, and (4) when he quarrels, he behaves in an evil and insulting manner.

All these are the qualities of a sick heart. We have to be watchful to know if we knowingly or unknowingly, openly or secretly, intentionally or unintentionally, harbor any of these qualities. When the heart gets sick, it loses its desire and ability to do right and good deeds. This affects one's morals, manners, and general behavior. What are the major diseases that affect the heart? How do we take precautions to prevent them and what are the cures in case one is afflicted with these ailments? Some of the many diseases of the heart are: (1) arrogance (*takabbur*), (2) ostentation or showing off (*ar-riya'*), (3) jealousy (*hasad*), malice (*hiqd*) and deceit (*ghush*), (4) suspicion, (*soo` adh-dhann*), (5) anger (*ghadab*), (6) stinginess (*bukhl*), and (7) excessive love of money, position, power, and fame (*hubb ad-dunya*).

The diseases of the heart, if not treated, may even lead to major sins. In the Qur`an and the Sunnah and in the spiritual writings of Muslim scholars such as Imam al-Ghazali, Ibn Taymiyya, and Ibn al-Qayyim we find a lot of discussion about the treatment of these diseases. I will very briefly go over a few of these spiritual diseases.

Arrogance means having or showing an exaggerated opinion of one's own importance, merit, ability, etc. This is the first step to many evils. Besides, it is unjustified because all of our gifts are from Allah, as He says in the Qur`an,

$$وَمَا بِكُمْ مِنْ نِعْمَةٍ فَمِنَ اللَّهِ ◯$$

*Whatever blessing you have is from God. (an-Nahl 16:53)*

What did we have when we came into this world? Nothing! What will we have when we leave this world? Nothing except two pieces of cloth to enshroud our body! We have to keep reminding ourselves that we are the servants and slaves of Allah. We are totally dependent on Him for our existence. Allah (SWT) says in *Surat al-Insan,*

$$هَلْ أَتَى عَلَى الْإِنْسَانِ حِينٌ مِنَ الدَّهْرِ لَمْ يَكُنْ شَيْئًا مَذْكُورًا ◯$$

*Was there not a period of time when man was not a thing worth mentioning? (al-Insan, 76:1)*

So what justification is there for man to be arrogant when there was a period of time when he did not even exist and there will be a period of time when he will cease to exist? In *Surat al-Isra'* Allah admonishes man in the following words:

وَلَا تَمْشِ فِي الْأَرْضِ مَرَحًا إِنَّكَ لَنْ تَخْرِقَ الْأَرْضَ وَلَنْ تَبْلُغَ الْجِبَالَ طُولًا ۝

*And do not walk in the land arrogantly, for you cannot cut through the earth, nor will you reach the mountains in height. (al-Isra', 17:37)*

The best treatment of this disease is to cultivate humility and modesty. May Allah make us more humble.

Ostentation (*ar-riya'*) is a desire to show off and seek praise from others. It is referred to as the "hidden *shirk*." This disease of the heart is so hidden and so dangerous that the one who feels safe from it is usually the one who gets entrapped in it. There is a hadeeth in which the Prophet (SAS) says that just as the creeping of a black ant on a black rock on a pitch dark night is hidden and unnoticeable, so also is the disease of *ar-riya'* unnoticeable. An example of this could be someone who writes an article so that people say he is a scholar. The one who gives a lecture to impress the audience is showing off. Even the person who performs the *salah* becomes guilty of *ar-riya'* if his or her intention is to show off and impress others. This is why Allah tells us in *Surat al-Ma'oon*,

فَوَيْلٌ لِلْمُصَلِّينَ ۝ الَّذِينَ هُمْ عَنْ صَلَاتِهِمْ سَاهُونَ ۝ الَّذِينَ هُمْ يُرَاءُونَ ۝

*So woe to those who pray; who are unmindful of their prayer; those who show off. (al-Ma'oon, 107:4-6)*

The best cure for this disease is to check one's intention (*niyya*) before any action. Any action done should only be for the sake of Allah (SWT).

What about the disease of jealousy or *hasad*? A jealous person does not like to see others happy, successful, and prosperous. One must realize that being jealous of others is actually being displeased with Allah for his bounties upon that person. Allah in His infinite wisdom bestows what He wills upon whom He wills. We have to be able to deal with the situation by being grateful for what He has given us and being patient with what has not been given to us. It is not blameworthy for one to ask Allah to give him something similar to what has been given to another person, but it is blameworthy to ask for it to be taken away from that person. The Prophet (SAS) said, "Jealousy devours good deeds like fire devours wood." A person who is jealous hurts himself with the feelings of rage and frustration that consume his heart, and in this process, he destroys his hereafter in addition to eliminating his comfort and peace of mind. The disease

92

of jealousy is remedied by frequently praising the person against whom the jealousy is directed. Praise him no matter how difficult this may seem. Honor him and meet him with respect and humility. Another treatment is to compete with others in acts of goodness, and this should be an incentive to achieve more and do better.

Suspicion, in Arabic *soo' adh-dhann*, creates cynicism, distrust, and doubt, and it takes away hope and optimism. A suspicious person is usually inclined to think negatively about others. Suspicion may lead to making poor decisions and may even lead to violence. It is good to be cautious and careful, but it is also important to have a positive attitude. If we want to be trusted, we must trust others as well. Allah says in the Qur`an,

$$\text{يَا أَيُّهَا الَّذِينَ آمَنُوا اجْتَنِبُوا كَثِيرًا مِنَ الظَّنِّ إِنَّ بَعْضَ الظَّنِّ إِثْمٌ}$$

*O you who believe! Avoid much suspicion; verily some suspicion is a sin. (al-Hujurat, 49:12)*

Anger, or *ghadab*, is a natural human trait but if it is not properly controlled it becomes very destructive. In the Hadeeth the Prophet (SAS) calls anger "fire." The Prophet (SAS) is reported to have said that in a state of anger, one should change one's environment, one's position, and drink some water. He also advised the angry person to seek Allah's refuge from Shaytan by saying *a'oodhu bi l-lahi min ash-Shaytani ar-rajeem*. He also said, "The strong person is not the one who overcomes other people by his strength, but the strong person is the one who controls himself while in anger."

Stinginess, known as *bukhl*, is also a terrible disease. The Prophet (SAS) taught us to seek refuge in Allah from stinginess. It leads to an attitude of not caring for others. It holds people back from fulfilling their duties and recognizing the rights of others. Allah says in the Qur`an,

$$\text{وَمَنْ يَبْخَلْ فَإِنَّمَا يَبْخَلُ عَنْ نَفْسِهِ}$$

*And whoever is stingy is only being stingy to himself. (Muhammad, 47:38)*

This is because Allah (SWT) multiplies what we spend in His way and gives it back to us both in this world as well as putting it toward our homes in *jannah*. Thus, the miser is only miserly toward himself or herself.

Excessive love of money, position, power, and fame, what we call *hubb ad-dunya*, is another major disease of the heart. Do we not read in the Qur`an,

$$\text{أَلْهَاكُمُ التَّكَاثُرُ ○ حَتَّى زُرْتُمُ الْمَقَابِرَ ○}$$

*You are obsessed by greed for more and more; until you go down to your graves. (at-Takathur, 102:1-2)*

In a well-known hadeeth, the Prophet (SAS) said, "If a son of man had a valley full of gold, he would desire to have two. Nothing can fill his mouth except the earth (of the grave). Allah turns with mercy to him who turns to Him in repentance."

The cure for this disease is to keep reminding oneself that the temporary life of this world is a test and trial. The real and everlasting life is in the hereafter.

Brothers and sisters! Each and every one of us should know which spiritual diseases we possess and try our utmost to get rid of them. Spiritual health involves curing the diseases of the hearts. Remembrance of Allah is a cure for the hearts. Reflecting upon the Qur`an is a cure for the hearts. Leaving sins and doing righteous deeds is a cure for the hearts. Making sincere repentance to Allah is a cure for the hearts. Leaving bad company and being in the company of good people is a cure for the hearts. And last but not least, remembering that one day we have to leave this world is a cure for the hearts.

May Allah (SWT) bless us all with physical, mental, and spiritual health and sound hearts.

## • 19 •

# DIVINE DESTINY *(QADR)*

Brothers and sisters, the subject of today's *khutbah* is divine destiny, also called fate, predestination, or *qadr*. One of the articles of faith in Islam is to believe in the divine destiny. This is established from the Qur`an as well as the Sunnah. According to a well-known hadeeth called "the hadeeth of Jibreel," faith includes believing in Allah, His angels, His books, His messengers, the Last Day, and in divine destiny.

What is *qadr*? Very simply, it means that Allah knows, but we don't know. Since Allah knows, He causes everything to happen the way it's going to happen. *Qadr* can be understood at two levels: First, we believe that Allah (SWT) knows through His ultimate knowledge all the deeds that His creation will perform, even before their existence. Allah recorded all this knowledge in *al-Lawh al-Mahfoodh*, "the Preserved Tablet."

We believe it is the will of Allah that these deeds will occur regardless of whether they are good or bad. Second, we also have to know that Allah created us with free choice and the ability to do things. We can only do something if we are willing to do it and capable of doing it. Thus, regardless of the ultimate fate of our actions, we are responsible for the choices we make.

Many Muslims erroneously believe that the actions which they are going to do are caused by what has already been written in *al-Lawh al-Mahfoodh*. Please understand that what we do is not caused by what is written by Allah. Yes, Allah with His ultimate knowledge already knows as to what we are going to do. All that we do in our lives will match that which has already been written, but it is not a matter of causation. Allah is Just. So he will only reward or punish according to what we do. Hence, what we do is out of our own willingness and ability, and we are fully responsible for the choices we make.

For example, if we were to drive recklessly and that results in an accident where a person dies or gets injured, we simply cannot blame it on fate or predestination. This is abusing the concept of fate to justify our mistake. The incident did take place in accordance with what was already written down and known to Allah. Nevertheless, we are still responsible for the death or injury of someone because it is through our reckless action that this incident took place. That is why we have to bear the consequences of our actions, both in this world and in the hereafter. Even if we escape punishment in this world, we'll have to live our entire life with a sense of guilt.

If fate is used as an excuse, then many crimes will go unpunished. A thief can simply claim that he stole because it was predestined for him to steal. Likewise, a murderer can claim that he murdered someone because it was predestined for him to kill that person. Those who abuse the concept of destiny are those who fail to be responsible. They abuse destiny to justify their misdeeds. The same argument holds when it comes to religious obligations. We cannot blame divine destiny for committing sins or failing to do an obligatory act of worship, as some Muslims do. We have to know that we are responsible for the moral choices we make.

Divine destiny can be seen as an excuse in situations wherein someone exerts himself to do his best to fulfill an obligation, but due to an unavoidable circumstance he could not fulfill that obligation. In this case he may be excused. We can take an example of a student who studies hard for an exam. On the day of the exam, he falls sick and does poorly, or is unable to take the exam. This student can then say that it was the destiny and the will of Allah that this happened.

The occurrence of sickness is also a matter of fate. But we have been commanded by the Prophet (SAS) to look for a cure should we become sick. He said, "Seek treatment, O slaves of Allah! For Allah does not create any disease but He also creates with it the cure, except for old age." Therefore, finding a cure is also fate. Thus, one matter of qadr can be solved through another matter of qadr.

If something unfortunate happens to us, such as losing our job, we should not react by saying that this is *qadr* and take a defeatist attitude by doing nothing about it. We should take an optimistic approach and look for another job. The consequence of this will be another *qadr*. Hence, for any hardship that comes in our path, we must try to minimize it or overcome it. In one hadeeth, the Prophet (SAS) said, "Be keen for whatever is beneficial to you. Seek the assistance of Allah and do not give up (or do not be reckless)." This hadeeth implies that we must make the effort to do the right thing.

In a situation where a believer has no control over the blows of fate, such as the untimely death of a loved one in the prime of his or her youth, a baby born with a congenital deformity, or an unexpected and sudden accident or calamity, then the only recourse to relieve oneself from the sad and stressful condition is to submit to the divine destiny and strive to actualize a state of contentment with patience and dignity. Even from a purely worldly perspective, contentment is the greatest remedy for stress, as it brings about an enormous relief.

Brothers and sisters! Life on this earth has its sweetness and bitterness. The Prophet (SAS) highlighted this principle when he said, "Know that what does not afflict you could never have afflicted you, and what afflicts you would never have missed you." He then followed the statement with the remedy for afflictions: "And know that victory comes with patience, relief with affliction, and hardship with ease." As human beings, our life in this world is characterized by fluctuating conditions making us happy and sad. Life by its very nature is a test. It is neither meant to be paradise nor is it possible to be like the life in paradise. The only life that is without stress and without the blows of fate is the life in paradise. Allah says in the Qur'an,

وَمَا هَذِهِ الْحَيَاةُ الدُّنْيَا إِلاَّ لَهْوٌ وَلَعِبٌ وَإِنَّ الدَّارَ الآخِرَةَ لَهِيَ الْحَيَوَانُ لَوْ كَانُوا يَعْلَمُونَ ◯

*This worldly life is no more than play and amusement. But the hereafter is indeed the real life, if only they knew." (al-'Ankabut, 29:64)*

We should always remember that nothing exists except that it reflects Allah's infinite wisdom, for He has called Himself "The All-Wise" (al-Hakeem). There is always the big picture, a larger context that we are unable to perceive with our short-sightedness. Allah is fully aware of how things will unfold in the long run, and we must place our trust in Him, fully realizing that there is wisdom in His decisions.

In this regard, the Prophet (SAS) advised us to maintain a good opinion of our Lord, and in a hadeeth *qudsi* the Prophet (S) tells us that Allah says, "I am as My servant thinks I am." If we are convinced that Allah is looking out for our best interests when He decrees painful situations, and that He will replace what is lost with something much better for us in both this life and the next, then that is exactly how we will find Him.

In a very well-known hadeeth, the Prophet (SAS) said, "One of you may do the deeds of the people of paradise until there is nothing between him and it (paradise) but the length of a forearm, then the decree overtakes him and he does a deed of the people of hell and enters it. And one of you may do the deeds of the people of hell until there is nothing between him and it (hell) but the length of a forearm, then the decree overtakes him and he does a deed of the people of paradise, and enters it."

The explanation of this hadeeth according to Ibn al-Qayyim (RA) is that it applies to the one who does not do deeds with sincerity and faith; rather he does deeds of the people of paradise as it appears to people only. Ibn Rajab (RA) said that the words "as it appears to people" indicate that what is hidden may be different from what is apparent to people. He explains that it is a bad end because of a hidden problem in the person that people are not aware of, whether it is a bad deed and the like, and that hidden quality may lead to a bad end at death. Similarly, a man may do a deed of the people of hell, but inwardly he has some good quality, and that prevails at the end of his life, and leads to a good end for him.

May Allah bless each one of us with a good end, and may He bless each one of us with a deep understanding of the *deen*.

Brothers and sisters! There is a famous hadeeth in which the Prophet (SAS) says, "Actions are according to intentions, and everyone will get what was intended." Indeed, our actions are based on our intentions because we don't know the outcome of our actions. But Allah knows. He is going to make it happen in the grand scheme of things to come. We don't really have a clue about what really is going to happen tomorrow, and we may not even live to see tomorrow.

The person whose intention was to do something good already has his reward with Allah. This is because he had the intention to do that good act. The more we intend and desire to do good, the more goodness is recorded for us. The one who does good should not fear any injustice or unfairness from Allah. Allah will never cause the deeds of any doer of good to be lost, no matter how small, and He will never wrong any soul in the slightest. And the person who wanted to do evil with full intention of doing evil, and he actually did that evil, then this is what he will be punished for because he did the bad deed with his free will and intention.

*Al-hamduli-llah!* Islam is such a beautiful, balanced, and practical way of life. It appeals to the rational mind, and it gives us room to repent, to seek forgiveness, and to do good deeds so that we get back to the right path. Allah says in the Qur'an,

$$إِنَّ الْحَسَنَاتِ يُذْهِبْنَ السَّيِّئَاتِ ذَٰلِكَ ذِكْرَىٰ لِلذَّاكِرِينَ ۞$$

*Surely good deeds wipe out evil deeds. That is a reminder for those who remember.*
(Hud, 11:114)

The essence of Islam is to submit to the will of Allah, thereby achieving peace—peace with oneself, peace with God, and peace with God's creation. A Prophetic tradition teaches us to say:

$$۞ رَضِيْتُ بِاللهِ رَبّاً وَبِالْإِسْلامِ دِيْناً وَبِمُحَمَّدٍ صَلَّى اللهُ عَلَيْهِ وَسَلَّمَ رَسُوْلاً$$

*"I am pleased with Allah as my Lord, with Islam as my way of life (deen), and with*

May Allah make us among those who pronounce this statement and who believe in it, and that includes believing in all the articles of faith including divine destiny.


• 20 •

# EFFECTS OF SINS ON OUR LIVES


I want to share a reminder about the effects of sins on our lives. Human beings as individuals, groups, societies, and nations commit sins. We are passing through a time in history when the concept of virtue and vice seems to have become very blurred. This era of postmodernism through which we are passing denies the existence of any ultimate principles and claims that there is no absolute version of reality, no absolute truths. This philosophy weakens the strength of institutions and religions that deal with objective realities.

Muslims believe, and will continue to believe until the end of times, in the ultimate principles laid out in the Qur`an, the last and final revelation of Allah (SWT) to mankind. The Qur`an was explained and expounded on through the sayings and actions of the last and final Messenger of Allah (SWT) to mankind—Muhammad (SAS).

What is sin? The Prophet (SAS) said, "Sin is that which causes discomfort within your soul and which you dislike that people should come to know of it." This is an indicator to know whether an act is a sinful act or not. Basically, sin consists in transgressing the bounds set by Allah.

No harm comes to man immediately for the moral choices he makes. He thinks, therefore, that he can get away with what he does because he does not believe, does not care, or is not conscious about being rewarded or punished for his deeds in the hereafter. Allah warns us in the Qur`an,

كَلَّا إِنَّ الْإِنْسَانَ لَيَطْغَى ○ أَنْ رَآهُ اسْتَغْنَى ○

*No indeed, man exceeds all bounds; when he thinks he is self-sufficient. (al-'Alaq, 96:6-7)*

But the fact of the matter is that man has to return to his Lord.

إِنَّ إِلَىٰ رَبِّكَ الرُّجْعَىٰ ۝

*Truly, to your Lord is the return. (al-'Alaq, 96:8)*

Among the effects of sin is that it creates all kinds of evil in the land and sea. Allah says in the Qur'an,

ظَهَرَ الْفَسَادُ فِي الْبَرِّ وَالْبَحْرِ بِمَا كَسَبَتْ أَيْدِي النَّاسِ لِيُذِيقَهُم بَعْضَ الَّذِي عَمِلُوا لَعَلَّهُمْ يَرْجِعُونَ ۝

*Evil has spread on land and sea as a result of man's own doings, and He will make them taste the consequences of some of their own actions so that they may turn back.*
*(ar-Rum, 30:41)*

Allah shows the evil consequences of some of the acts of people in this world before the punishment of the hereafter so that they understand the reality, feel the error of their conjectures, and turn to the righteous belief.

Brothers and sisters! Allah commands people to do or not to do only that which will bring them benefit in this world and the next. Disobeying Allah's commands leads to sins. The effects of sins can be seen in the individuals and the society. Sins affect the heart and the body. 'Abdullah ibn 'Abbas (RAA) said, "Good deeds brighten the face, enlighten the heart, expand provision, strengthen the body, and cause love in the hearts of the creation. Evil deeds darken the face, darken the heart, weaken the body, restrict provision, and cause hatred in the hearts of the creation."

When sins become widespread in a society, its affairs become difficult and the members of that society find all gates of good and well-being closed in their faces.

My dear brothers and sisters! I advise myself and you to try our utmost to keep away from all sins both major and minor, and to beware of sin, for sin is bad news for the one who does it. The following is a list of some of the effects of sin, as described by Ibn al-Qayyim (RA) in his work *Al-Jawaab Al-Kaafi*.*

Being deprived of knowledge. Knowledge is light that Allah causes to reach the heart, and sin extinguishes that light. Al-Imam ash-Shafi'i (RA) said that he complained to his teacher about the weakness of his memory. So, his teacher ordered him to abandon disobedience, and informed him that knowledge was light, and that the light of Allah was not given to the disobedient.

Being deprived of provision. In the *Musnad* of Imam Ahmad, it is narrated that Thau'ban (RA) said, "The Messenger of Allah (SAS) said, 'A man is deprived of provision because of the sins that he commits.'"

A feeling of alienation comes between a person and his Lord, and between a person and other people. One of the righteous predecessors said, "Whenever I commit a sin, I see the impact of that in the behavior of my wife and my riding animal toward me." This is because Allah protects the believers who obey Him from the evils of this world and the hereafter. Allah says in the Qur'an,

$$\text{إِنَّ اللَّهَ يُدَافِعُ عَنِ الَّذِينَ آمَنُوا} \bigcirc$$

*Truly, Allah defends those who believe. (al-Hajj, 22:38)*

Things become difficult for him, so that he does not turn his attention toward any matter, but he finds the way blocked or he finds it difficult. By the same token, for the one who fears Allah, things are made easy for him. Allah says in the Qur`an,

$$\text{وَمَن يَتَّقِ اللَّهَ يَجْعَل لَّهُ مِنْ أَمْرِهِ يُسْرًا} \bigcirc$$

*And whoever fears Allah and keeps his duty to Him, He will make his matter easy for him. (at-Talaq, 65:4)*

The sinner will find darkness in his heart. Obedience is light and disobedience is darkness. The stronger the darkness grows, the greater becomes his confusion until he falls into innovation, misguidance, and other things that lead to doom without even realizing.

Deprivation of worship and obedience. If sin brought no punishment other than that it prevents a person from doing an act of worship, that would be bad enough, and because of the sin, he is cut off from many acts of worship. Al-Hasan al-Basri said, "Disobedience is a cause of the servant being held in contempt by his Lord. They became contemptible in (His sight) so they disobeyed Him. If they were honorable (in His sight) He would have protected them." Allah (SWT) says,

$$\text{وَمَن يُهِنِ اللَّهُ فَمَا لَهُ مِن مُّكْرِمٍ} \bigcirc$$

*And whoever Allah disgraces, none can honor him. (al-Hajj, 22-18)*

Sin breeds sin until it dominates a person and he cannot escape from it.

Sin weakens a person's willpower. It gradually strengthens his will to commit sin and weakens his will to repent until there is no will in his heart to repent at all.

He will become desensitized and will no longer find sin hateful, so it will become his habit, and he will not be bothered if people see him committing the sin or talk about him. This is the ultimate shamelessness in which he finds great pleasure, such that he feels proud of his sin and will speak of it to people who do not know that he has done it, saying, "O so and so, I did such and such." The disappearance of modesty is the disappearance of all that is good. The Prophet (SAS) said: "Modesty is good; all of it."

When there are many sins, they leave a mark on the heart of the person who commits them, so he becomes one of the negligent.

$$\text{كَلَّا بَلْ رَانَ عَلَىٰ قُلُوبِهِم مَّا كَانُوا يَكْسِبُونَ} \bigcirc$$

*No. In fact what they have been doing has rusted their hearts. (al-Mutaffifeen, 83:14)*
The explanation of this rust as given by the Prophet (SAS) is as follows: When a servant commits a sin, it marks a black stain on his heart. If he offers repentance, the stain is

washed off, but if he persists in wrongdoing, it spreads over the entire heart.

May Allah grant us the *tawfeeq* to use His blessings—our eyes, ears, tongue, stomach, private parts, hands, feet, health, wealth, well-being, rational faculty, and above all, our faith, for good purposes, by obeying Him, and not to use them for wrong purposes, by disobeying Him, *Ameen*.

Brothers and sisters! There is a verse in *Surat al-Anfal* where Allah says,

وَاتَّقُوا فِتْنَةً لَا تُصِيبَنَّ الَّذِينَ ظَلَمُوا مِنْكُمْ خَاصَّةً وَاعْلَمُوا أَنَّ اللَّهَ شَدِيدُ الْعِقَابِ ○

*And guard against the mischief that will not only bring punishment to the wrong-doers among you. Know well that Allah is severe in punishment. (al-Anfal, 8:25)*

This refers to those widespread social evils whose harmful and destructive effects are not confined only to those addicted to them, but which affect every single person in that society. For example, if filth is found at just a few places in a locality, it will possibly affect only those who have not kept themselves or their houses clean. However, if it becomes widespread and no one is concerned with removing filth and maintaining sanitary conditions, then everything including water and soil will become contaminated. As a result, if epidemics break out, they will not only afflict those who were responsible for spreading filth and who themselves lived in unsanitary conditions, but virtually all the residents of that locality.

What is true of unsanitary conditions in a physical sense also holds true for filth and uncleanliness in a moral sense. If immoral practices remain confined to a few people here and there but the overall moral concern of the society prevents those practices from becoming widespread and public, their harmful effects remain limited. But when the collective conscience of the society is weakened to a point whereby immoral practices are not suppressed, when people indulge in evils without any sense of shame and even go around boasting their immoral deeds, when good people adopt a passive attitude and are content with being righteous merely in their own lives and are unconcerned with or silent about collective evils, then the entire society invites its doom. Such a society then becomes the victim of a punishment that does not distinguish between the grain and the husk. It would afflict even those individuals who neither themselves committed evils nor were instrumental in spreading them and who might in fact have been righteous in their personal conduct.

The Prophet (SAS) said, "Whoever among you sees an evil action, let him change it with his hand, and if he cannot, then with his tongue, and if he cannot, then with his heart, and that is the weakest of faith." Therefore, rejecting evil with the heart is obligatory upon every single believer. This rejection inside the heart of the believer relieves him from the responsibility if he is incapable of removing the evil with his hand or tongue.

Dear brothers and sisters! Each one of us has committed some error or fallen into some sin in our lives. The Prophet (SAS) said, "All sons of Adam are sinners and the best of sinners are those who repent." Allah Almighty says in *Surat Aal 'Imran*,

$$وَالَّذِينَ إِذَا فَعَلُوا فَاحِشَةً أَوْ ظَلَمُوا أَنْفُسَهُمْ ذَكَرُوا اللَّهَ فَاسْتَغْفَرُوا لِذُنُوبِهِمْ وَمَنْ يَغْفِرُ الذُّنُوبَ إِلَّا اللَّهُ وَلَمْ يُصِرُّوا عَلَى مَا فَعَلُوا وَهُمْ يَعْلَمُونَ ۞$$

*And who, when they have committed an indecency or have wronged their souls, remember Allah and pray that their sins be forgiven for who but Allah can forgive sins? And they do not knowingly persist in their misdeeds. (Aal 'Imran, 3:135)*

Sincere *tawba* purifies our heart from the filth of sins. Repentance from all sins is obligatory on every adult Muslim. This is emphasized by Allah when He says,

$$وَتُوبُوا إِلَى اللَّهِ جَمِيعًا أَيُّهَا الْمُؤْمِنُونَ لَعَلَّكُمْ تُفْلِحُونَ ۞$$

*And repent to Allah, all of you believers that you may succeed. (an-Nur, 24:31)*

May Allah (SWT) grant us the *tawfeeq* to sincerely repent for our sins and to mend our wrongful ways. May He make us among those with whom He is pleased and who are pleased with Him. *Ameen.*

---

*Please refer to https://islamqa.info/en/answers/23425/sin-and-its-effects-on-the-one-who-commits-it

<br>

• 21 •

# ENJOINING GOOD AND FORBIDDING EVIL

The topic of today's *khutbah* is enjoining good and forbidding evil (*al-amr bil-ma'roof wa an-nahi 'an al-munkar*). The term *amr* means to invite, to encourage, to promote, to command, or to enforce. *Ma'roof* is anything that Islam orders one to do and is synonymous with virtue and goodness. So *al-amr bil-ma'roof* means to enjoin what is good. The term *nahi* means to discourage, to advise not to do, or to prevent from doing something. *Munkar* is anything that Islam forbids one to do, and is synonymous with sin, vice, or evil. So *an-nahi 'an al-munkar* means to forbid evil.

The practice of enjoining good and forbidding evil is the core of our religion and one of the most important Islamic duties. It is the mission of prophets, messengers, and the righteous. It is a sign of faith and a means to success. Allah says,

وَلْتَكُنْ مِنْكُمْ أُمَّةٌ يَدْعُونَ إِلَى الْخَيْرِ وَيَأْمُرُونَ بِالْمَعْرُوفِ وَيَنْهَوْنَ عَنِ الْمُنْكَرِ وَأُولَئِكَ هُمُ الْمُفْلِحُونَ ◯

*Let there be a group among you who call others to good, and enjoin what is right, and forbid what is wrong: those who do this shall be successful. (Aal 'Imran, 3:104)*

The Qur`an has characterized the real believers as those, who among other obligations, fulfil the responsibility of enjoining good and forbidding evil.

وَالْمُؤْمِنُونَ وَالْمُؤْمِنَاتُ بَعْضُهُمْ أَوْلِيَاءُ بَعْضٍ يَأْمُرُونَ بِالْمَعْرُوفِ وَيَنْهَوْنَ عَنِ الْمُنكَرِ ◯

*The believers, both men and women are friends to each other. They enjoin what is good and forbid what is evil. (at-Tawba, 9:71)*

On the other hand, the hypocrites are described as those who do the opposite by enjoining evil and forbidding good.

لْمُنَافِقُونَ وَالْمُنَافِقَاتُ بَعْضُهُم مِّن بَعْضٍ يَأْمُرُونَ بِالْمُنكَرِ وَيَنْهَوْنَ عَنِ الْمَعْرُوفِ ◯

*The hypocrites, both men and women, are all alike: they encourage what is evil, forbid what is good. (at-Tawba, 9:67)*

Any deviated and morally corrupt society is an example of ignoring these two principles. Neglect of the obligation of enjoining good and forbidding evil may result in becoming entrenched in falsehood, the spread of corruption, and prevalence of sin. This incurs the wrath of Allah and hastens the punishment of individuals and nations. Allah got angry with the Children of Israel because they failed as a society in this important duty. Allah says in the Qur`an,

كَانُوا لَا يَتَنَاهَوْنَ عَن مُّنكَرٍ فَعَلُوهُ لَبِئْسَ مَا كَانُوا يَفْعَلُونَ ◯

*They would not prevent one another from doing the wrong things they did. Evil indeed were their deeds. (al-Ma`ida, 5:79)*

When a community fails in its duty to command the good and forbid the evil, its supplications will cease to be accepted. The Prophet (SAS) said, "By the one in Whose hand is my soul, you must certainly command good and forbid evil, or else a punishment from Him would soon be sent upon you, after which you would call upon Him yet your *du'a*` would not be answered." Praising the *ummah* of the Prophet Muhammad (SAS), Allah says,

كُنتُمْ خَيْرَ أُمَّةٍ أُخْرِجَتْ لِلنَّاسِ تَأْمُرُونَ بِالْمَعْرُوفِ وَتَنْهَوْنَ عَنِ الْمُنكَرِ وَتُؤْمِنُونَ بِاللَّهِ ◯

*You are the best community ever raised for humanity—you encourage good, forbid*

*evil, and believe in Allah. (Aal 'Imran, 3:110)*

The practice of enjoining good and forbidding evil, therefore, is mandatory upon the whole *ummah*—rulers and subjects, men and women—each according to his or her circumstances and abilities. Those who consciously undertake this mission must be of good character and must understand the objectives of the *shari'a*. They must call people with wisdom and fair preaching and deal with them in a kind and gentle manner, so that Allah may guide those whom He wills at their hands.

ادْعُ إِلَى سَبِيلِ رَبِّكَ بِالْحِكْمَةِ وَالْمَوْعِظَةِ الْحَسَنَةِ وَجَادِلْهُمْ بِالَّتِي هِيَ أَحْسَنُ إِنَّ رَبَّكَ هُوَ أَعْلَمُ بِمَنْ ضَلَّ عَنْ سَبِيلِهِ وَهُوَ أَعْلَمُ بِالْمُهْتَدِينَ ◯

*Call people to the path of your Lord with wisdom and good advice, and reason with them, in the most courteous manner, for your Lord knows best who strays from His path and He knows best who is rightly guided. (an-Nahl, 16:125)*

The Prophet (SAS) said, "Whoever among you sees an evil action, let him change it with his hand, and if he cannot, then with his tongue, and if he cannot, then with his heart, and that is the weakest of faith." Therefore, rejecting evil with the heart is obligatory upon every single believer. This rejection in the heart of the believer relieves him from the responsibility if he is incapable of removing the evil with his hand or tongue.

The hand mentioned in this hadeeth is a symbol of power and authority. Whenever and wherever one is in power, one must try to prevent evil among those who are under his authority. The tongue is a symbol of words and can be used to admonish people and remind them of the evil consequences of their conduct. The admonishment may be done through verbal preaching or the print and electronic media. A true Muslim is not one who lives in isolation and cares only about himself but is one who endures the difficulties of living in an immoral society and tries his best to do something to change what he can change.

When believers are commanded to do something, they should be the quickest people to do it, and if they are forbidden to do something, they must be the ones who keep furthest away from it. Allah has issued a warning in *Surat as-Saff.*

يَا أَيُّهَا الَّذِينَ آمَنُوا لِمَ تَقُولُونَ مَا لَا تَفْعَلُونَ ◯ كَبُرَ مَقْتًا عِنْدَ اللَّهِ أَنْ تَقُولُوا مَا لَا تَفْعَلُونَ ◯

*O you who believe! Why do you say that which you do not do? It is most hateful to Allah that you say that which you do not do. (as-Saff, 61:2-3)*

No matter how righteous a person may be, he still needs sincere advice, guidance, and reminders in the light of the Qur`an and the Sunnah. It is part of our nature that we are fallible, forgetful, and follow our lusts and desires which usually lead to neglecting our duties or to committing evil. That is why we are always in need of being reminded to keep on the right way. Allah has commanded His Messenger (which is a command to us too) to keep preaching and reminding his companions.

$$وَذَكِّرْ فَإِنَّ الذِّكْرَىٰ تَنفَعُ الْمُؤْمِنِينَ ○$$

*And continue to remind for surely the reminder benefits the believers. (adh-Dhariyat, 51:55)*

May Allah make us among those who enjoin good and forbid evil, and who actually practice what we teach and preach.

Brothers and sisters! We are exhorted to carry on with the practice of enjoining good and forbidding evil at whatever level we can, even if we are faced with rejection. At least we will be discharging our duty. A total neglect of this practice would lead to the collapse of the religion, widespread corruption, and wickedness in the society. Some people may be able to safeguard themselves against wickedness and corruption, but when it becomes widespread in the society, our children can fall victim to it and we may not be able to protect them. Thus, when we combat evil, we are indirectly protecting ourselves and our families against all types of corruption.

Some people raise objections against the practice of enjoining good and forbidding evil. There are those who are against the notion itself and there are others who are against the way it is practiced by some people.

The first objection is that this is a type of interference in the personal affairs of others and against their personal freedom. To discuss this objection, it is fair to argue that there is no one in this world who recognizes absolute freedom. The idea of law itself is founded on the principle of restricting personal freedom. Law is merely a set of restrictions, limitations, and punishments. The only difference between different laws is the scope and limits of personal freedom.

Islam teaches that personal affairs are respected as long as they remain personal affairs. If a sin or evil which does not involve the rights of individuals or society is committed alone where no one can see it, certainly no one will interfere with it. It will be between the offender and Allah. But when one commits evil openly in front of others or violates the rights of others, even secretly, it would not be considered as a personal affair anymore. It would concern the society, affect its members, and challenge their moral responsibility. The worst situation is when the society accepts this evil as something usual and normal to the extent that even those who would like to prevent it from taking place will hesitate to rectify it and will be blamed if they do so. That is why Allah (SWT) condemns those who encourage the spread of evil and warns them of a severe punishment.

The second objection is that the practice of enjoining good and forbidding evil may amount to playing the role of the public authorities and taking the law into one's own hands. It is a well-established rule in Islamic teachings that no one is allowed to take the law into one's own hands. Doing so will create chaos and disorder in the society.

The only problem that might be faced when enjoining good and forbidding evil is about practices and things considered immoral and prohibited by Islam but considered legal under the laws of the country. In this situation, the blame should not fall on people who are enjoining good and forbidding evil as they are fulfilling their religious and moral duties. Rather, the blame should fall on the laws of the country as they run against the religious beliefs and the value system of the people.

The motivation to correct others should be out of sincere love and care for them. The Prophet (SAS) taught us that religion is *naseeha*. *Naseeha* means sincerity and sincere advice. He is reported to have said, "None of you truly believes until he loves for his brother what he loves for himself."

I will conclude by asking myself and you: Are we encouraging good and preventing evil? Are we taking part in the betterment of society and the world? Are we donating our time and money for the good of our community and humanity? Are we feeding the poor and taking care of the destitute? Are we reaching out to others to inform them through our words and actions about the values of Islam? Are we condemning Muslims when they perform evil acts? Are we preparing for tomorrow? If we are, *al-hamduli-llah!* And may Allah give us further *tawfeeq*. If we are not, then it is time to wake up. May Allah mend our ways, have mercy on us, and bless each one of us. *Ameen.*

• 22 •

# FAMILY INSTITUTION IN ISLAM

My *khutbah* today is on the subject of the family institution in Islam. Family, as we know, constitutes the foundation of a society. Its strength or weakness determines the strength or weakness of society. It is no secret that Western society as a whole is in a deep social crisis. This is primarily due to the breakdown of the family institution. This breakdown of Western families is proceeding at an alarming speed. It is estimated that every thirteen seconds someone somewhere files for divorce in the United States.

We live in an era in which the nature, function, and structure of the family have been thrown into question. Many, for example, would consider an unmarried couple, a single mother, and homosexual couples as equally legitimate expressions of the family unit. Islam takes a more conservative stand, arguing that the family is a divinely inspired institution, with marriage at its core.

An Islamic family begins with the families of each of the spouses. Marriage in Islam is a civil contract between two individuals – man and woman – with the backing of their respective families. As such, the two families with all their human, economic, and wisdom resources are at the service of the newly wedded couple. All these resources are available for the two spouses if there is any problem.

Marriage in Islam requires the consent of the two prospective spouses entering marriage and is signed and agreed upon and witnessed by guardians and elders of the spouses. This becomes a legal and binding document. It is a commitment of the spouses and their families to each other, and therefore, it increases the sense of responsibility among them and induces a spirit of sacrifice for each other. As a result, Muslim families are more stable as indicated by relatively lower divorce rates in Muslim-majority countries.

Because Islam considers marriage a very serious commitment, it has prescribed certain measures to make the marital bond as permanent as humanly possible. The parties must strive to meet the conditions of proper age, general compatibility, reasonable dowry, good will, free consent, unselfish guardianship, honorable intentions, and judicious discretion. When the parties enter a marital contract, the intention must be clear to make the bond permanent.

The courtship between a Muslim husband and wife starts after marriage, and not before marriage. This grows and becomes stronger with the passage of time. In the Western system, love and courtship start before marriage. Our understanding from the Qur`an and Sunnah is that people of the opposite gender should avoid situations, relationships, or actions that might lead to a violation of the principle that couples should abstain from sexual intimacy until after marriage. Living in the West, it is important to emphasize to our brothers and sisters in faith to stay chaste, to guard the elements of respect and shame within their God-given bodies, to consult with parents regarding selection of marriage partner, and to live in close contact with the extended family as much as possible.

Since people in Western societies tend to be individualistic, the essential ingredient of sacrifice for each other is generally missing. Therefore, marriages have a very fragile relationship and people stay married as long as it is convenient for them. Each person in the relationship insists on fulfilling his or her personal needs, and none is willing to give in. When problems develop along with declining morals, they seek comfort elsewhere which results in disloyalty, which has become very common. Finding a solution to marital problems takes time and instead of waiting and resolving the issues, most marriages end up in divorce courts.

In Islam, a woman – married or single – is seen as a person in her own right, and not merely an adjunct to another person. As such, she has full right of ownership and disposal of her own property and earnings, even after marriage. When she is married, she retains her family name, instead of adopting her husband's surname. The Prophet (SAS) said, "A believing man does not despise a believing woman. If he dislikes some behavior of hers, he finds satisfaction with another."

The Creator's perfect wisdom is that He has created both men and women from the same species, and He has created them both with the same matter. Yet the two have been created with different physical structures, different mental and psychological qualities, and different emotions and desires. There has been created such a wonderful harmony between the two that each is a perfect counterpart of the other. The physical and psychological demands of one squarely match with the physical and psychological demands of the other. Women and men do not compete with each other; they complement one another.

Islam assigns the family leadership role to men. Therefore, men are responsible for supporting all female relatives in addition to their own household. This is clear from the following verse in the Qur`an:

$$\text{الرِّجَالُ قَوَّامُونَ عَلَى النِّسَاءِ بِمَا فَضَّلَ اللَّهُ بَعْضَهُمْ عَلَى بَعْضٍ وَبِمَا أَنْفَقُوا مِنْ أَمْوَالِهِمْ} \bigcirc$$

*Men are the protectors and maintainers of women, because Allah has given the one more (strength) than the other, and because they support them from their means. (an-Nisa`, 4:34)*

What does the word *qawwam* mean? It means standing, being active, involved, being protective, constant source of support, providing security, maintainers, and caretakers. It does not mean having the upper hand. It also means that men must repeatedly evaluate if they are being fair to the women. Allah (SWT) has placed this responsibility on all men.

Also, note that the word *ar-Rijalu* means men; not just husbands, implying that men are responsible for women in their family which includes wife, mother, sister, daughter, or other dependent close female relatives. In the few words of this verse, Allah (SWT) is telling men to provide and protect their women and give them security. In a hadeeth, the Prophet (SAS) said, "Among the Muslims the most perfect, as regards to his faith is the one whose character is excellent, and the best of you are those who are best to their women."

Allah (SWT) has made women biologically and psychologically suited to concentrate on the home and family and all that is required to operate and develop this institution and its associated areas. This is a tremendous responsibility, which no one else can either take away from them or adequately attend to it. It is wisely said that the function of childbearing remains incomplete without its more crucial part of child-rearing and upbringing, education, orientation, character-building, and general initiation into religion and culture. It is because of this aspect that family care becomes a full-time job. No other institution or even number of institutions can take care of this function.

However, differences in roles or functions between men and women do not mean differences in their humanity nor that one is superior to the other. Allah (SWT) says in the Qur`an in several places on the equality of men and women. We read in *Surat an-Nisa`*,

وَمَنْ يَعْمَلْ مِنَ الصَّالِحَاتِ مِنْ ذَكَرٍ أَوْ أُنْثَى وَهُوَ مُؤْمِنٌ فَأُولَئِكَ يَدْخُلُونَ الْجَنَّةَ وَلَا يُظْلَمُونَ نَقِيرًا ⬤

*If any do deeds of righteousness - be they male or female - and have faith, they will enter heaven. And not the least injustice will be done to them. (an-Nisa`, 4:124)*

A question often raised surrounding married Muslim women is do Muslim women have to stay at home, or can they work? This depends on the family's culture and circumstances. It is not necessarily based on religion. Nothing in the Qur`an or Sunnah prohibits women from working. In fact, in most Muslim communities, numerous Muslim women work outside the home. However, while working outside the home, they must operate within the parameters set by Islam which includes maintaining their modesty and chastity at all times. Of course, men are also obligated and morally bound to maintain their modesty and chastity at all times. May Allah (SWT) give us a deep understanding of the noble *deen* of Islam.

Brothers and sisters! The Qur`an gives us an insight into the spousal relationship when it describes wives and husbands as being garments for one another.

هُنَّ لِبَاسٌ لَكُمْ وَأَنْتُمْ لِبَاسٌ لَهُنَّ ⬤

*They are like a garment for you, and you are like a garment for them. (al-Baqara, 2:187)*

Why would Allah (SWT) compare a husband and wife to a garment? Perhaps one compelling reason is that we wear our clothes very close to our bodies. Similarly, spouses should be held close to each other - emotionally, physically, and spiritually. Just as garments cover us and protect us, spouses must cover each other's shortcomings and protect each other from any harm.

When it comes to the subject of building a strong Muslim family, we must value the meaning of what it means to be a Muslim. The Prophet (SAS) said, "The Muslim is the one from whom other Muslims are safe from his hand and tongue." This brings us to the question: How does Islam view domestic violence and spousal abuse? Both domestic violence and spousal abuse violate the Islamic principle of respect for human dignity.

Statistics reveal that every nine seconds in the United States a woman is either assaulted or beaten. Around the world, at least one in every three women has been beaten, coerced into sex, or otherwise abused during her lifetime. Most often, the abuser is a member of her own family. Domestic violence is the leading cause of injury to women—more than car accidents, muggings, and rapes combined. Men who witnessed domestic violence as children are twice as likely to abuse their own wives than sons from a nonviolent household.

It should be a cause of great concern for us that among American Muslims, there are frequent reports of domestic violence and increased divorces. We must reform ourselves as well as teach others about the beauty of Islam. It is a vital role that we have to play for our own good, the good of our country where we live, and the wider humankind.

The Prophetic traditions are explicit in instructing believers not to mistreat women, and to treat them with kindness and dignity. The Prophet (SAS) did not abuse any of his wives or children. His biographies do not have a single record or incidence of him having hit a woman or even a child. He always condemned those who did. As for the children and elderly, he (SAS) said, "He who does not show mercy to our young ones and respect for our elders is not from us."

Man is ordained by God to extend his utmost help and kindness to his relatives, and to show them true feelings of love and care. It might be interesting to note that the word for "kinship" in Arabic is derived from an Arabic root word which means "mercy" (*rahm* and *rahma*). The extension of kind treatment to relatives is described by the Prophet (SAS) as a divine blessing of one's life and provisions. It is a sacred duty to be good to one's family even though they may not respond in a similar way. The duty is enjoined by Allah and should be observed for the sake Allah.

May Allah (SWT) enable us to follow His commandments and the teachings and example of our beloved Prophet Muhammad (SAS) so that we become the best husbands, the best wives, the best parents, and the best children, and being an example for the society to follow. May Allah bless us to live upon faith, die upon faith, and May He unite us in the heavenly abode with our loved ones and with the righteous ones.

رَبَّنَا هَبْ لَنَا مِنْ أَزْوَاجِنَا وَذُرِّيَّاتِنَا قُرَّةَ أَعْيُنٍ وَاجْعَلْنَا لِلْمُتَّقِينَ إِمَامًا ◯

*Our Lord! grant us joy in our wives and children and make us a model for the righteous.*
(al-Furqan, 25:74)

# FATHERHOOD FROM THE ISLAMIC PERSPECTIVE

In the United States there are two special days that are celebrated to honor parents – Mother's Day which is celebrated on the second Sunday of May and Father's Day which is celebrated on the third Sunday of June. Mother's Day is a day set aside to appreciate and honor mothers. Father's Day is a day set aside to appreciate and honor fathers.

Mothers endure the burden of pregnancy, tolerate the pain of childbirth, and sacrifice their own comfort to provide comfort to their children. Therefore, people naturally feel inclined to place the mother at the center of the process of raising children, but they unwittingly ignore the father's role. As a result, they often tend to focus on the father as a mere individual, not as someone who should and can play a central role within his family. It is important to note that the role of a father is highly recognized and valued within Islam. The Prophet (SAS) said, "The pleasure of the Lord is in the pleasure of one's father and the anger of the Lord is in the anger of one's father."

In today's *khutbah*, I'll be sharing some thoughts with you on the concept of fatherhood from the Islamic perspective. Islam, as we know, is a complete code of life and gives guidance with regard to every aspect of life. It outlines a complete code of family life, which is the foundation of every society. A clear guidance as to how family structure should be built is outlined in detail in Islam. Islam confers different roles for man and woman. As such, women do not compete with men rather men and women complement one another. So in addition to the mother, the role of the father is also very significant in a Muslim family.

A father is not just a breadwinner, but also a teacher, guide, mentor, and shepherd of the entire family. There is an overall culture within Muslim families to show respect to one's parents through gestures such as not addressing them by their names, not shouting or talking back to them, greeting them with respect, not smoking in front of them, trying to fulfill their requests and wishes to the best possible extent, and respecting their opinion because they are wiser and more experienced.

It is sad to see children in the Western world generally not show proper respect to their parents and teachers who rightfully deserve it. The fathers are mostly treated as mere breadwinners, responsible only for getting food on the table and meeting other family expenses. Working like machines, fathers often put in long hours at work and may even have to remain away from home in case their jobs require frequent traveling.

This work schedule of fathers has almost become a global phenomenon depriving them of their authority as guardians and shepherds of their families. This results in fathers delegating this responsibility to the mothers. It is difficult and rather impossible for mothers to handle and manage both of the main roles of homemakers and guardians.

The roles of mothers and fathers have been clearly outlined and assigned in a Prophetic tradition which states, "Every one of you is a shepherd and is responsible for his flock. The leader of people is a guardian and is responsible for his subjects. A man is the guardian of his family and he is responsible for them. A woman is the guardian of her husband's home and his children and she is responsible for them. The servant of a man is a guardian of the property of his master and he is responsible for it. No doubt, every one of you is a shepherd and is responsible for his flock."

Islam encourages us to show continuous kindness, respect, care, and concern toward fathers as it can often be difficult to keep a steady balance between working, taking care of a household, and fulfilling the many roles of a father. Abu Hurayra(RAA), one of the close companions of the Prophet (SAS), always encouraged other people to be kind and good to their parents. One day, he saw two men walking together and inquired of the younger one, "Who is this man to you?" to which the young man replied, "He is my father". Abu Hurairah advised him by saying, "Do not call him by his name, do not walk in front of him, and do not sit before your father does."

There is much emphasis taught in Islam on the intention behind any action. This being the case, a Muslim father must check his intentions and ask himself several questions such as: Why did I get married? Why do I want children? Is it because everyone around me is getting married and having children? I should get married because it is a recommended practice (*sunnah*) of the Prophet Muhammad (SAS). I should get married to safeguard myself from falling into the sin of engaging in premarital and extramarital relationships. I should get married to raise a righteous and pious family that is obedient to Allah and His messenger. I should get married to be able to have children who will follow in the footsteps of our beloved Prophet Muhammad (SAS) and who will be inspired by the Islamic lifestyle and virtues of our pious predecessors. It will be unjust if I were to restrict my role as a mere breadwinner and not give sufficient time to my children.

According to a recent research by the Pew Research Center, "About 6 in 10 dads say that they spend too little time with their kids." From an Islamic perspective, for fathers not to spend quality time with their children is unacceptable. This is because fathers are not only responsible for providing the living expenses for their children but are also responsible for taking care of their moral, ethical, and spiritual development. A father must promote Islamic morality by demonstrating to his children the values of truthfulness, kindness, keeping trusts, leniency, forbearance, generosity, hospitality, spreading greetings, charitable treatment, and fulfilling financial commitments. He must also teach his children to refrain from lying, betraying, harboring envy, hate or contempt toward others, cruelty, greed, and stinginess. He has to be a role model for his children. After all, the Prophet (SAS) was sent to perfect noble qualities and morals for he said: "Verily, I was sent for no other reason except to perfect the noble traits of character."

This responsibility of the father toward his children cannot be delegated totally to the mother, who while taking care of the children, is also pressured with the execution and management of the household chores. Without a doubt parenting is the joint responsibility of the mother and the father. It is observed, however, that the mother finds it more difficult than the father to control her college or university-going teenage sons and/or daughters. Discipline plays an important part in child-rearing because it helps the child to develop an understanding of right and wrong behavior. Effective discipline is one of the building blocks of child-rearing. It involves educating with a loving heart and being persistent about the consequences of right and wrong.

The father needs to sit with his children, eat with them, take them to the *masjid*, read Qur'an with them, ask them about their school and about their friends, and be conscious about imparting them with knowledge that is based on Islamic morals, values, and teachings. There is no benefit for a father if his child goes to the best institution of higher learning but is unable to recite the opening verses of the Qur'an. Also, success for a Muslim father is not dependent on his being financially rich or poor. A father who is rich financially but has children who are ignorant about Islam is in fact poor and is most likely to lose his children. A father who is poor financially but has children who are knowledgeable about Islam and who practice Islam in their daily lives is indeed rich. Virtuous children pray for their parents even after they have passed away, and thus become a source of perpetual charity (*sadaqa jariya*) for their parents.

What is the way forward for Muslim fathers? Oftentimes, they have poor relationships with their children. There is lack of dialogue, tenderness, and affection. We need to creatively tap into Islamic values for solutions because that is what Muslim families are most likely to be receptive to. The father is more than just an individual. He can play an important role, far beyond just being the financial protector. The Prophet Muhammad (SAS) himself was a role model as a father. When his own daughter would come to him, he would stand up out of respect for her and kiss her on her forehead. We have forgotten these aspects of the Prophetic example.

How a father lovingly teaches and counsels his son about good conduct and behavior is brought forth beautifully in the Qur'an in the story of the wise sage Luqman.

وَإِذْ قَالَ لُقْمَانُ لِابْنِهِ وَهُوَ يَعِظُهُ يَا بُنَيَّ لَا تُشْرِكْ بِاللَّهِ إِنَّ الشِّرْكَ لَظُلْمٌ عَظِيمٌ ۝

*And remember when Luqman said to his son, while advising him, "O my dear son! Never associate anything with Allah in worship, for associating others with Him is truly the worst of all wrongs. (Luqman, 31:13)*

The next advice Luqman gave to his son was to keep the prayers (*salah*) established, to enjoin others to whatever is good (*ma'roof*), and forbid others from whatever is evil (*munkar*).

يَا بُنَيَّ أَقِمِ الصَّلَاةَ وَأْمُرْ بِالْمَعْرُوفِ وَانْهَ عَنِ الْمُنْكَرِ وَاصْبِرْ عَلَى مَا أَصَابَكَ إِنَّ ذَلِكَ مِنْ عَزْمِ الْأُمُورِ ◯

*"O my dear son! Establish prayer, encourage what is good and forbid what is evil, and endure patiently whatever befalls you. Surely this is something which requires firm resolve. (Luqman, 31:17)*

Another gem of advice that Luqman gives to his loving son is:

وَلَا تُصَعِّرْ خَدَّكَ لِلنَّاسِ وَلَا تَمْشِ فِي الْأَرْضِ مَرَحًا إِنَّ اللَّهَ لَا يُحِبُّ كُلَّ مُخْتَالٍ فَخُورٍ ◯ وَاقْصِدْ فِي مَشْيِكَ وَاغْضُضْ مِنْ صَوْتِكَ إِنَّ أَنْكَرَ الْأَصْوَاتِ لَصَوْتُ الْحَمِيرِ ◯

*And do not turn your cheek away from people with scorn or pride and do not walk proudly and haughtily on the earth, for Allah does not like anyone who is self-conceited, and boastful. Be modest in your gait and keep your voice low. Indeed, the most unpleasant of all the voices is the braying of the ass. (Luqman, 31:18-19)*

Brothers and sisters! Grown up children have to be treated in a friendly way and made to feel responsible. Young boys and young girls have a tendency to be independent, oversensitive, and sometimes even rebellious. The father should diminish the sense of authority in his speech and actions and regard the child from a different perspective. The youth's ideas must be respected and never undermined or ridiculed. Thus, the child is given a chance to confide in him in case of troubles or decision-making.

There is a story that explains the best gift one can give to one's father to make him happy. A young man asked a scholar how he could make his father happy. He was expecting that the scholar will tell him to buy an expensive gift for his father, but instead the scholar surprised the young man and told him that the best gift he could give to his father was that he became an obedient and righteous child. That will make his father the happiest person on earth. The scholar said that if the children only knew how much parents suffered from the disobedience of their offspring, when they see them going astray, then their obedience to their parents was the best gift ever to give to them.

Let me conclude by saying that showing gratitude and dutifulness to parents should not be confined to one day out of the year because being dutiful to parents is not confined to a specific time. It is an obligation that should be observed all of the time. In Islam, every day is a Mother's Day and every day is a Father's Day.

وَاعْبُدُوا اللَّهَ وَلَا تُشْرِكُوا بِهِ شَيْئًا وَبِالْوَالِدَيْنِ إِحْسَانًا ◯

*Worship Allah and do not associate anything with Him. And be good to your parents.*
*(an-Nisa`, 4:36)*

وَقُل رَّبِّ ارْحَمْهُمَا كَمَا رَبَّيَانِي صَغِيرًا ⭕

*And pray, 'My Lord! Be merciful to them as they raised me when I was small. (al-Isra`,*
*17:24)*

•  24  •

# FEAR OF ALLAH AND HOPE IN ALLAH

In today's *khutbah*, I intend to speak on the topic of fear of Allah and hope in Allah. Let us try to understand what these two terms "fear" and "hope" mean when used with respect to our relationship with Allah (SWT).What are the degrees of fear? What are the degrees of hope? What is the best approach one should take with respect to fear of Allah and hope in Allah? How does one balance fear with hope? Allah (SWT) says in the Qur`an,

مَا فَرَّطْنَا فِي الْكِتَابِ مِنْ شَيْءٍ ⭕

*We have left out nothing in the Book. (al-An'am 6:38)*

Allah (SWT) in His infinite mercy has explained to us the issue of fear and hope along with how to call on Him and make *du'a`* to Him. In *Surat al-A'raf,* Allah says,

وَادْعُوهُ خَوْفًا وَطَمَعًا إِنَّ رَحْمَةَ اللَّهِ قَرِيبٌ مِّنَ الْمُحْسِنِينَ ⭕

*Call on Him with fear and hope. Allah's mercy is close to those who do good. (al-A'raf,*
*7:56)*

In this *ayah*, the two states of fear and hope are joined together in order that the slave of Allah is both fearful and hopeful of Him. And while describing the *mu`minoon* (the believers), Allah says in *Surat al-Isra`,*

وَيَرْجُونَ رَحْمَتَهُ وَيَخَافُونَ عَذَابَهُ إِنَّ عَذَابَ رَبِّكَ كَانَ مَحْذُورًا ⭕

*They hope for His mercy and fear His punishment. Surely, the punishment of your*
*Lord is to be feared. (al-Isra`, 17:57)*

Referring to the believers who get up from their beds late at night to perform their *tahajjud* (extra nighttime) prayers, Allah says in *Surat as-Sajda*,

$$\text{تَتَجَافَى جُنُوبُهُمْ عَنِ الْمَضَاجِعِ يَدْعُونَ رَبَّهُمْ خَوْفًا وَطَمَعًا}$$

*Their sides leave their beds to supplicate their Lord in fear and hope. (as-Sajda, 32:16)*

A *mu`min* (a believer) leads his life between fear and hope. The thing that necessitates fear is recognizing with awe, inspiration, and reverence the glory, grandeur, and the power of Allah on the one hand coupled with the knowledge of the severity of His punishment on the other. What necessitates hope is recognizing the mercy of Allah and the tremendous reward He has for us *in sha` Allah*. In *Surat al-Hijr*, Allah says,

$$\text{نَبِّئْ عِبَادِي أَنِّي أَنَا الْغَفُورُ الرَّحِيمُ ۞ وَأَنَّ عَذَابِي هُوَ الْعَذَابُ الْأَلِيمُ}$$

*Tell My slaves that I am the Ever-Forgiving, the Most Merciful, and that My punishment is a painful punishment. (al-Hijr, 15: 49-50)*

Fearing Allah means recognizing the generosity of Allah and hopes for mercy from Him, while also fearing His punishment. A hadeeth has been narrated in this sense, in which the Prophet (SAS) explains that if the fear and the hope of the *mu`min* were to be weighed, they would be generally found to be equal in weight. But it is preferred that throughout one's life, fear predominates somewhat so that it will lead us to do right action. Then, as one draws closer to the time of death, it is urged that hope predominates more so that you have great hope in the mercy and forgiveness of Allah at the time of death. In another hadeeth the Prophet (SAS) said, "Let none of you die without having a very good opinion of Allah." This means having high hope of the mercy of Allah and expecting the very best from Him. Allah says in the Qur`an,

$$\text{وَرَحْمَتِي وَسِعَتْ كُلَّ شَيْءٍ}$$

*My mercy encompasses (extends to) all things. (al-A'raf, 7:156)*

Imam Ja'far as-Sadiq is reported to have said, "Verily, one who has hope of something pursues it, and one who fears something flees from it." Talking about the true believers, the Qur`an says in *Surat al-Mu`minoon*,

$$\text{أُولَئِكَ يُسَارِعُونَ فِي الْخَيْرَاتِ وَهُمْ لَهَا سَابِقُونَ}$$

*They are the ones who race toward good things, and they will be the first to get them. (al-Mu`minoon, 23:61)*

We read in the same *surah* that these believers are filled with the fear of their Lord.

$$\text{إِنَّ الَّذِينَ هُمْ مِنْ خَشْيَةِ رَبِّهِمْ مُشْفِقُونَ}$$

*Those who are filled with the fear of their Lord. (al-Mu`minoon, 23:57)*

Such believers even avoid things and turn away from things which are frivolous like idle gossip and senseless talk.

$$وَالَّذِينَ هُمْ عَنِ اللَّغْوِ مُعْرِضُونَ \bigcirc$$

*And who keep themselves away from vain things. (al-Mu`minoon, 23:3)*

There are three degrees of fear. The first degree is weak fear. It has no real effect on either the inward or the outward. This fear might as well be nonexistent because it is of no benefit or use. The second degree is strong fear which wakes up the person from his heedlessness and carries him to become obedient and upright. It drives him from his neglectfulness and makes him go on the straight path. The third degree of fear is the severe, overpowering fear that reaches such a level that the believer loses hope in Allah. This is not permissible. It is impermissible to allow fear to reach such a degree. We read in *Surat az-Zumar,*

$$قُلْ يَا عِبَادِيَ الَّذِينَ أَسْرَفُوا عَلَى أَنْفُسِهِمْ لَا تَقْنَطُوا مِنْ رَحْمَةِ اللَّهِ إِنَّ اللَّهَ يَغْفِرُ الذُّنُوبَ جَمِيعًا إِنَّهُ هُوَ الْغَفُورُ الرَّحِيمُ \bigcirc$$

*Say: O My servants who transgressed against themselves, do not despair of God's mercy. For God forgives all sins. He is the Forgiving, the Merciful. (az-Zumar, 39:53)*

It is commonly known that the best of affairs is the middle of them. The best form of fear is not the weak form which has no effect on one's inward state or one's outward behavior, nor is it the one that is so strong that it makes one lose hope in Allah's mercy, but it is the fear that transforms one's life and makes one perform upright actions and abandon wrong actions.

People have three stations with respect to fear. The fear of ordinary people is the fear of wrong actions, and consequently the fear of the punishment of such wrong actions. Wrong actions can be active or passive. This means that wrong actions can be done by actively doing something that is prohibited, or they can be passive by leaving out something which is commanded.

There is a *mawqoof* hadeeth (a narration from a companion which is not ascribed to the Prophet (SAS) himself) in which Ibn Mas'ud (RAA) said, "A believer sees his wrong actions as if he were at the foot of the mountain which he fears will fall on top of him. The corrupt person sees his wrong actions as if they were a fly flying above his nose." The degree of fear for the ordinary Muslim is the fear of the wrong actions. The fear of the elite of the believers is the fear of the conclusion of their lives, of the final act of their lives, the final state they are in, and the condition of the spiritual heart when they die. There are many supplications in which the righteous people ask for a good end to their lives. The fear of the elite of the elite is the fear from what has been written down and decreed for one and for that reason, Ibn Mas'ud (RAA) used to recite a *du'a`* in the following words:

$$اللّٰهُمَّ إِنْ كُنْتَ كَتَبْتَنِي فِي أَهْلِ الشَّقَاءِ فَامْحِنِي وَأَثْبِتْنِي فِي أَهْلِ السَّعَادَةِ ○$$

*O Allah, if you have decreed me as one of the wretched, You erase it and write me as one*
*of the blessed.*

Brothers and sisters! Just as fear has three degrees, hope also has three degrees. The first is the hope for the mercy of Allah along with engaging in things which will earn the mercy of Allah, which means doing right actions and giving up disobedience. This is the praiseworthy type of hope. The second type of hope is the hope which accompanies wrong actions and disobedience. This type of hope is delusion and self-deception. It is wishful thinking (*umniyya*); just hoping that everything will work out all right and not working hard enough for it. This is the blameworthy type of hope. The third degree of hope is very strong which reaches to a degree of considering oneself safe. This is absolutely wrong. Allah says in *Surat al-A'raf*,

$$أَ أَمِنُوا مَكْرَ اللّٰهِ فَلَا يَأْمَنُ مَكْرَ اللّٰهِ إِلَّا الْقَوْمُ الْخَاسِرُونَ ○$$

*Do they feel secure against Allah's plan? Only the losers feel secure against Allah's*
*plan. (al-A'raf, 7:99)*

Just as the state of fear has three stations, the state of hope also has three stations. The majority of the people hope for the reward of Allah for doing right actions and for being one of the people of *iman*. The station of the elite is the hope for the good pleasure of Allah. This is contained in a beautiful *du'a`* which has been transmitted to us. The meaning of this *du'a`* is, "O Allah, I ask you for your good pleasure and the garden and whatever of words and deeds that will bring me closer to them and I seek refuge with You from Your displeasure and the fire and whatever of words and deeds bring me closer to them." And the degree of the elite of the elite is the hoping of meeting with Allah out of love for Him and longing for Him. Referring to this, we read in *Surat al-Kahf*,

$$قُلْ إِنَّمَا أَنَا بَشَرٌ مِثْلُكُمْ يُوحَى إِلَيَّ أَنَّمَا إِلَهُكُمْ إِلَهٌ وَاحِدٌ فَمَنْ كَانَ يَرْجُوا لِقَاءَ رَبِّهِ فَلْيَعْمَلْ عَمَلًا صَالِحًا وَلَا$$
$$يُشْرِكْ بِعِبَادَةِ رَبِّهِ أَحَدًا ○$$

*Say: I am only a human being like you who has received revelation. Your god is One*
*God. So let him who hopes to meet his Lord act rightly and not associate anyone in the*
*worship of his Lord. (al-Kahf, 18:110)*

*Iman* is between fear and hope. A believer lives between fear and hope. The correct and the approved kind of fear is that which acts as a barrier between the believer and the things forbidden by Allah. But if fear is unreasonably excessive, then the person will fall into despair and pessimism. On the other hand, the approved state of hope is that which compels one to do good deeds and this makes one optimistic and hopeful that they will be rewarded for it. It also includes making sincere repentance for sins committed and being hopeful of being forgiven. On the contrary, if one does not repent and continues to indulge in sins and excesses and is hopeful that he would be forgiven without mending his ways, then this is self-deception.

It is said that fear and hope are like the two wings of a bird. If they are well balanced, the flight will be balanced. But, when either or both wings are deficient, the bird cannot fly properly. It is advisable to strengthen the wing of fear during good times when heedlessness is feared, and to strengthen the wing of hope at times of calamity and when near death. May Allah (SWT) make us among the people of praiseworthy fear of Him and praiseworthy hope of Him.

• 25 •

# FINAL JOURNEY

Brothers and sisters! My *khutbah* today is about remembering and preparing for our final journey from this life to the next life in the hereafter.

كُلُّ نَفْسٍ ذَائِقَةُ الْمَوْتِ وَإِنَّمَا تُوَفَّوْنَ أُجُورَكُمْ يَوْمَ الْقِيَامَةِ ۞

*Every soul will taste death and you will be paid in full only on the Day of Resurrection.*
(Aal 'Imran, 3:185)

Such is the reality of death and what comes after it. Every one of us shall taste it whether poor or rich, healthy or sick, old or young, leader or led, and none of us can escape it, wherever we may be.

أَيْنَمَا تَكُونُوا يُدْرِكُكُمُ الْمَوْتُ وَلَوْ كُنْتُمْ فِي بُرُوجٍ مُشَيَّدَةٍ ۞

*Death will overtake you wherever you be, even in the mightiest of towers. (an-Nisa`,*
*4:78)*

A person may die in the prime of his or her youth. Death takes hold of a person at the appointed time. Such is the mystery of death. This being the case, are we ready and prepared for the death which is looming over each one of us?

And what is this worldly life? Philosophers and thinkers have always been grappling with this question. Rather than debate about their speculative thinking, it is best to know what Allah (SWT) Himself says about this worldly life.

اعْلَمُوا أَنَّمَا الْحَيَاةُ الدُّنْيَا لَعِبٌ وَلَهْوٌ وَزِينَةٌ وَتَفَاخُرٌ بَيْنَكُمْ وَتَكَاثُرٌ فِي الْأَمْوَالِ وَالْأَوْلَادِ ۝

*Bear in mind that the life of this world is just a game, a diversion, an attraction, a cause of boasting among you, of rivalry in wealth and children. (al-Hadeed, 57:20)*

People generally get so enchanted by the glamour of this materialistic world and the high standards of living it offers that they become forgetful and neglectful of death. Even though death is certain people tend to live as if they are going to live forever. Death and life are both creations of Allah (SWT) and have a purpose.

الَّذِي خَلَقَ الْمَوْتَ وَالْحَيَاةَ لِيَبْلُوَكُمْ أَيُّكُمْ أَحْسَنُ عَمَلًا ۝

*It is He who created death and life to test which of you is best in action. (al-Mulk, 67:2)*

In this worldly life, people are constantly put through all types of tests.

وَلَنَبْلُوَنَّكُم بِشَيْءٍ مِنَ الْخَوْفِ وَالْجُوعِ وَنَقْصٍ مِنَ الْأَمْوَالِ وَالْأَنْفُسِ وَالثَّمَرَاتِ وَبَشِّرِ الصَّابِرِينَ ۝

*We shall certainly test you with fear and hunger, and loss of property, lives, and crops. But give good news to those who are patient. (al-Baqara, 2:155)*

Believers are urged to be patient while facing these tests and trials.

الَّذِينَ إِذَا أَصَابَتْهُم مُّصِيبَةٌ قَالُوا إِنَّا لِلَّهِ وَإِنَّا إِلَيْهِ رَاجِعُونَ ۝

*Those who, when disaster strikes them, say, 'We belong to Allah and to Him we will return. (al-Baqara, 2:156)*

وَنَبْلُوكُم بِالشَّرِّ وَالْخَيْرِ فِتْنَةً وَإِلَيْنَا تُرْجَعُونَ ۝

*We test you all through the bad and the good, and to Us you will all return. (al-Anbiya`, 21:35)*

True righteous believers are really blessed. The Prophet (SAS) said, "Amazing is the affair of the believer for there is good in every matter of his and this is not the case with anyone except the believer; if he is happy, then he thanks Allah and thus there is good for him; and if he is afflicted with a calamity, then he shows patience and thus there is good for him."

What is the reality of death? When it comes, the spirit or *rooh* leaves the body. We learn through Prophetic traditions that a good soul comes out of the body with ease, while an evil soul, which resists leaving the body, is taken out harshly by the angel of death. The two types of souls are accordingly honored or dishonored in their respective journeys to the heavenly dimensions and back, when they are questioned in the graves. There is a Prophetic *du'a`* in which we are taught to say,

اَللّٰهُمَّ حَاسِبْنِيْ حِسَا بًا يَّسِيْرًا ◯

*O Allah! Make my accounting easy.*

During a wicked person's dying moments, he wishes that death were delayed so that if he were a nonbeliever, he would become a believer; or if he were a disobedient believer, he would repent from his sins.

حَتَّى إِذَا جَاءَ أَحَدَهُمُ الْمَوْتُ قَالَ رَبِّ ارْجِعُونِ ◯ لَعَلِّي أَعْمَلُ صَالِحًا فِيمَا تَرَكْتُ ◯

*When death comes to any of them, he says: My Lord, send me back; that I may act righteously in what I have left behind... (al-Mu`minoon, 23:99-100)*

وَلَيْسَتِ التَّوْبَةُ لِلَّذِينَ يَعْمَلُونَ السَّيِّئَاتِ حَتَّى إِذَا حَضَرَ أَحَدَهُمُ الْمَوْتُ قَالَ إِنِّي تُبْتُ الْآنَ وَلَا الَّذِينَ يَمُوتُونَ وَهُمْ كُفَّارٌ ◯

*Repentance is not for those who continue to do evil until death confronts them and then say, 'Now I repent,' nor of those who die disbelieving. (an-Nisa`, 4:18)*

So, *iman* or faith is not accepted from anyone at the time of death. Also, repentance is useless if the person has started to experience the throes of death. The Prophet (SAS) said, "Allah (SWT) accepts repentance from a person as long as death does not reach his throat." As for the righteous believers, may Allah make us among them, Allah says in the Qur`an,

إِنَّ الَّذِينَ قَالُوا رَبُّنَا اللَّهُ ثُمَّ اسْتَقَامُوا تَتَنَزَّلُ عَلَيْهِمُ الْمَلَائِكَةُ أَلَّا تَخَافُوا وَلَا تَحْزَنُوا وَأَبْشِرُوا بِالْجَنَّةِ الَّتِي كُنْتُمْ تُوعَدُونَ ◯

*Those who say, "Our Lord is Allah," and then remain steadfast, the angels descend on them, saying: "Do not fear and do not grieve but rejoice in the Garden you have been promised. (Fussilat, 41:30)*

May Allah make us among them, *ameen!*

Brothers and sisters! Man takes nothing with him in his grave. We learn through a hadeeth that the Prophet (SAS) said, "When a man dies, his deeds come to an end except for three things: perpetual charity (*sadaqa jariya*), knowledge which is beneficial, and a virtuous descendant who prays for him." Such admonitions remind us that we should hasten in doing good deeds before our time is up and our book of deeds gets closed forever. We should not be among those hypocrites who will cry to Allah (SWT) to give them more time to spend in His way and to be one of the righteous.

وَأَنْفِقُوا مِنْ مَا رَزَقْنَاكُمْ مِنْ قَبْلِ أَنْ يَأْتِيَ أَحَدَكُمُ الْمَوْتُ فَيَقُولَ رَبِّ لَوْلَا أَخَّرْتَنِي إِلَى أَجَلٍ قَرِيبٍ فَأَصَّدَّقَ وَأَكُنْ

مِنَ الصَّالِحِينَ ◯

*And spend out of what We have provided for you before death comes to one of you and he says: My Lord! If only You would postpone it for a little while, then I would give in charity and be among the righteous. (al-Munafiqoon, 63:10)*

We should strive to be among those about whom Allah (SWT) says,

وَالَّذِينَ آمَنُوا وَعَمِلُوا الصَّالِحَاتِ لَنُبَوِّئَنَّهُم مِّنَ الْجَنَّةِ غُرَفًا تَجْرِي مِن تَحْتِهَا الْأَنْهَارُ خَالِدِينَ فِيهَا نِعْمَ أَجْرُ الْعَامِلِينَ ◯ الَّذِينَ صَبَرُوا وَعَلَىٰ رَبِّهِمْ يَتَوَكَّلُونَ ◯

*We shall lodge forever those who believe and do good works in the mansions of paradise beside which rivers flow. How excellent is the reward of those who labor; and who are steadfast and put their trust in their Lord. (al-'Ankabut, 29:58-59)*

Deeds are very important, but the intentions behind those deeds are still more important. A good deed with bad intention carries no reward with Allah (SWT). An example of this is to do an act with the intention of showing off. We have to be very clear about our intentions. We have to take extra care to see that our deeds are done to seek the pleasure of Allah (SWT), and that nothing is done with an intention to deceive or show off. Man gets the reward of what he intends. This is very clearly explained through a hadeeth in which the Prophet (SAS) says,

إِنَّمَا الْأَعْمَالُ بِالنِّيَّاتِ وَإِنَّمَا لِامْرِئٍ مَا نَوَى ◯

*Actions are according to intentions, and every man shall have only what he intended....*

The condition of the heart is also to be kept in mind. We understand from the meaning of a hadeeth that hearts get rusted. When someone asked the Prophet (SAS), "What could cleanse the hearts again," he replied, "Frequent remembrance of death and recitation of the Qur'an." One of the descriptions of the Day of Judgment in the Qur'an is in *Surat ash-Shu'ara'*.

يَوْمَ لَا يَنفَعُ مَالٌ وَلَا بَنُونَ ◯ إِلَّا مَنْ أَتَى اللَّهَ بِقَلْبٍ سَلِيمٍ ◯

*The day when neither wealth nor children will benefit anyone; except for someone who comes to Allah with a sound heart. (ash-Shu'ara', 26:88-89)*

When people are completely immersed in the material world, believing that the world is all that exists and all that matters, and that they are not accountable for their actions, they cause the spiritual death of their hearts. May Allah save us from this situation, *ameen.*

O Allah! Give us the realization that death can strike us suddenly – anywhere and anytime. O Allah! Don't let our death be in a state of sin. O Allah! Take away the love of sins from our hearts and put the love of good deeds into our hearts. O Allah! Bless us with *iman*(faith), *yaqeen*(certainty), and deeds that are acceptable to you. O Allah! Bless us with sincere repentance before death overtakes us. O Allah! Let our last days be the best days of our life, and our last deeds the best of our deeds. And let the best day be the day we meet you. *Allahumma ameen.*

•   26   •

# FINDING TRUE HAPPINESS IN LIFE

In my *khutbah* today, I wish to share some thoughts with you on the subject of happiness. What is true happiness? Who is a happy person? How can we find happiness in our lives? Each one of us wants to feel happy. We all want to find inner peace within ourselves. It may not be wrong to say that the main motivating factor behind all our actions is the desire to feel happy.

However, the paths people take to find this happiness are different. There are those who believe that happiness will be found through material possessions, through wealth, through owning luxurious houses and cars. All their efforts are directed and focused toward increasing their assets in diverse forms—money, stocks, jewelry, silver, gold, precious stones, movable and immovable properties, and so on.

There are others who think that happiness will be found through fame and recognition. The most asked question on the mind of such people is "What can make me famous? How can society recognize me?" Celebrities, artists, actors, actresses, models, and others who go into music and singing with the intention to gain popularity and recognition may be said to be among such people.

Then there are people who believe that happiness is found through satisfying their sensual instincts and animal desires, even if these actions go against all dictates of ethics and morality. They turn to activities involving unlawful or disapproved gratification of sexual desires, watching obscene images, listening to lewd music, consuming alcohol and drugs, and indulging in games of chance like gambling and lottery.

And sadly enough, there are some who believe that happiness is a combination of all these factors. This is how we find "happiness." But in reality, when we look at the people who have spent their lives following these paths, and have attained great heights of richness, of fame, of power, and those who are most evil in terms of sensuality, we find that they are not happy in their personal lives. They have not achieved the happiness that the public may think they have achieved.

As a matter of fact, these sources of happiness become a curse for such people. They get enslaved and entrapped in the things they chase and cannot live normal lives any longer. They become so caught up with their activities in pursuit of this so-called "happiness" that they lose the real joys of life. They have no time for their family, and no time to be happy. The inner peace and tranquility (*sakeena*) are lost.

Their happiness, if any, is like a poisoned sweet. They enjoy it for a while, and then as soon as that enjoyment finishes, the sweet, outer layer dissolves and what is left is bitter poison that rots the heart. This is something which people experience in their daily lives. When they commit a sin, they enjoy it. That's why they committed it. If there was no pleasure, why would they commit it? But let them ask themselves. While during the act of sinning or as soon as the act of sinning is finished, do they feel proud of themselves? Do they feel good? Do they feel happy on the inside? No, they feel disgusted. They feel dirty on the inside.

All this shows us that the paths to "happiness" that mankind has chosen are not the ultimate paths to real happiness. What is then the path to real happiness? To understand this, we must first understand who we are and what we are made of. We all know that the human being is made of a body (*jasad*) and a soul (*rooh*). The body and soul put together form life as we know it.

The body is made of earth—clay. Since the body is made of earth, in order to feed the body, we need produce, and the nutrients that come from the earth. So, we eat and drink from the earth which is the source of our body. Many people, if not most, consider pleasure to have to do with the body only and so they seek pleasure through bodily experiences. They forget that what actually makes them human is the soul. What makes the human being above all other creatures is the intelligent soul given to them by Allah (SWT). And this soul, this *rooh*, where did it come from? Did it come from this earth? No! After fashioning Adam (AS) out of clay, Allah tells the angels,

$$وَنَفَخْتُ فِيهِ مِن رُّوحِي ۝$$

*And I have breathed into him from My Spirit. (al-Hijr, 15:29)*

This does not mean that there is any sort of divinity in man. It means, as the scholars say, that the *rooh* is a creation of Allah (SWT) which He blew into man. Allah says in the Qur`an,

$$وَيَسْأَلُونَكَ عَنِ الرُّوحِ قُلِ الرُّوحُ مِنْ أَمْرِ رَبِّي وَمَا أُوتِيتُم مِّنَ الْعِلْمِ إِلاَّ قَلِيلاً ۝$$

*They ask you: What is the rooh? Say: The rooh is by the command of my Lord, and you have only been given a little knowledge about it. (al-Isra`, 17:85)*

What is the food and nourishment for the soul that will make it healthy and happy? Remember it is the soul more than the body that makes us human. The body grows, dies, disintegrates, will be resurrected, and thus goes through different phases. The soul will always remain a soul. Being eternal and coming directly from Allah, it has to be nourished spiritually by establishing a conscious connection with its Creator—Allah (SWT). How do we establish a connection with Allah? By following His commands. And this is exactly what brings true happiness. Every act of ritual worship and every good deed feeds the soul and makes it happy. And even if the body is sick, weak, or dead, the soul remains peaceful and happy because it is alive and connected with its Creator and Master.

But, God forbid, if the soul becomes sick or weak by not being connected with its Maker, then no matter how well the body is fed, and no matter how healthy it is, the soul will be almost dead. At this stage, one does not feel any purpose of life, one does not enjoy living. Allah likens such a person who does not worship Him to one who is completely dead, saying,

مَن كَانَ مَيْتًا فَأَحْيَيْنَاهُ وَجَعَلْنَا لَهُ نُورًا يَمْشِي بِهِ فِي النَّاسِ كَمَن مَّثَلُهُ فِي الظُّلُمَاتِ لَيْسَ بِخَارِجٍ مِّنْهَا ○

*Can he who was dead, to whom We gave life, and a light whereby he could walk among people be like him who is in utter darkness from which he can never emerge? (al-An'am, 6:122)*

According to the scholars of *tafseer*, the explanation of the Qur`an, this *ayah* tells us that the person who does not worship Allah is spiritually dead, even though he is physically living. "We gave him life" implies bringing him into the sphere of connecting himself with Allah, giving him a reason to live, and a reason to feel happy.

Brothers and sisters, ultimate happiness comes from Allah. In order to get that happiness, we need to establish a connection with Him. Once we establish that connection, then possessions, wealth, fame, power, and status all become secondary. The world does not become our ultimate goal. And when the world ceases to be our ultimate goalwe are content with what we have. Our money, our wealth, our fame, our family, our health – if we have any or all of them –we thank Allah and say *al-hamduli-llah*(praise be to Allah). If we don't, we still thank Him and say *al-hamduli-llahi 'ala kulli haal* (praise be to Allah in every circumstance). We remain optimistic and hope for the best from Him. This is how we begin to feel really happy. May Allah make us taste true happiness. *Allahumma ameen.*

Brothers and sisters, let us ask ourselves a question, and answer it in our own minds. How do we feel on a day we offer our five obligatory prayers with full consciousness and in their proper times? How do we feel when we recite the Qur`an? How do we feel inwardly at the time of breaking the fast with *iftar* after a long day of fasting in Ramadan? How do we feel after performing 'umrah and hajj? We truly feel happy. Can all the money in the world purchase that happiness inside of us? No, it cannot.

We feel happy and satisfied because through these acts, we establish a connection with Allah. He becomes a part of our life. When our goal is to please Allah in whatever we do, we feel fulfilled because we are fulfilling the purpose of our creation which is to worship and obey Him. Allah says in the Qur`an,

وَمَا خَلَقْتُ الْجِنَّ وَالْإِنسَ إِلَّا لِيَعْبُدُونِ ○

*I did not create the Jinn and the humans except to serve Me. (adh-Dhariyat, 51:56)*

But when we neglect Allah, when we neglect the *deen*, what happens? No sinful pleasure-seeking activity brings true happiness. Rather, we feel bad, we feel disgusted. There is only sadness and regret. Our life gets wasted. Can all the money in the world get rid of the feeling that one gets after committing a sin; that feeling of guilt, that feeling of distancing oneself from Allah? No, it cannot. People, including Muslims, experience this feeling in their lives.

Each one of us has been given an appointed time to live. Our life is like ice that is melting. It is never too late. Let us wake up to the ultimate reality, to the realization that we are in transit, and our final journey is close at hand, closer than we can imagine. Allah says in *Surat al-Infitar*,

يَا أَيُّهَا الْإِنسَانُ مَا غَرَّكَ بِرَبِّكَ الْكَرِيمِ ○

*O man! What has deceived you about your generous Lord. (al-Infitar, 82:6)*

And He says in Surat al-Muddaththir,

فَمَا لَهُمْ عَنِ التَّذْكِرَةِ مُعْرِضِينَ ○

*What is the matter with them? Why do they turn away from the warning? (al-Muddaththir, 74:49)*

What's the problem? We know that sins increase our guilt, and ultimately make us unhappy. Worshipping and obeying Allah increase our happiness. Let us make an effort to diminish our sins. We are not angels. We are not perfect, but we have to strive toward perfection. We have to keep on repenting to Allah, turning to Him in sincere repentance. We have to continue strengthening our relationship with Allah. Let us challenge ourselves not to approach the major sins; otherwise they will destroy us. Let us begin to taste the sweetness of *iman*. Once we taste it, it will be more addictive than any other sweetness on this earth, and this will raise us higher and higher *in sha` Allah*. Let me conclude by quoting an *ayah* of the Qur`an that summarizes the entire *khutbah*.

$$\text{أَلَا بِذِكْرِ اللَّهِ تَطْمَئِنُّ الْقُلُوبُ} \bigcirc$$

*Truly it is in the remembrance of Allah that hearts find peace. (ar-Ra'd, 13:28)*

And with peace comes genuine happiness.

<br>

# • 27 •

# *FITNA*

<br>

In today's *khutbah*, I intend to speak on the concept of *fitna* in Islam. What do we mean by *fitna*? Is there any purpose or goal behind every *fitna* that keeps coming one after the other, whether we like it or not? How should we cope with *fitna* when confronted with it and make it work to our advantage?

The word *fitna* is derived from the Arabic root *faa-taa-nun* which means "to burn" or "to test" in order to separate the good from the bad. The word *fatanahu*, therefore, means "he burned it" or "he tested it." In Arabic, the classical name for the goldsmith is *fattan* meaning the one who causes *fitna*. What does he do? He melts the gold in order to separate its impurities so that what is left is pure.

The word *fitna* has many shades of meaning including temptation, trial, and affliction. We read in the Qur'an, in *Surat al-Baqara*, the story of two angels Hart and Marot who warned the people of Babylon not to use the knowledge taught by them for any evil purpose. But the evil people used that knowledge to sow discord and enmity between a man and his wife. The knowledge they gained from the two angels became a source of *fitna* for them. What did the angels say before passing on knowledge to anyone?

$$\text{إِنَّمَا نَحْنُ فِتْنَةٌ فَلَا تَكْفُرْ} \bigcirc$$

*We are but a test; so do not disbelieve. (al-Baqara, 2:102)*

*Fitna* also means attractiveness, and captivation. In Arabic the word *fatten* it used when it is said, "Wealth attracted people to it." The expression *fatanathu* means, "She captivated his heart." Some other meanings of *fitna* are that of persecution and oppression. There are still other meanings of *fitna* such as discord, sedition, riot, and civil strife. In this sense, Allah says in the Qur'an,

وَالْفِتْنَةُ أَشَدُّ مِنَ الْقَتْلِ ⬡

*And oppression (or persecution) is even worse than killing. (al-Baqara, 2:191)*

In Surat al-Buruj Allah says,

إِنَّ الَّذِينَ فَتَنُوا الْمُؤْمِنِينَ وَالْمُؤْمِنَاتِ ثُمَّ لَمْ يَتُوبُوا فَلَهُمْ عَذَابُ جَهَنَّمَ وَلَهُمْ عَذَابُ الْحَرِيقِ ⬡

*Indeed, those who persecute the faithful men and women, and then do not repent, for them there is the punishment of hell, and for them there is the punishment of burning.*
*(al-Buruj, 85:10)*

Is there any purpose or goal behind every *fitna* that we face? Yes, every *fitna* that we face has a reason, purpose, and goal behind it. If we understand this, we can understand the concept of *fitna* in Islam. Allah (SWT) inflicts us with *fitan* (plural of *fitna*) for a reason. There is wisdom and goal behind it. Allah says,

أَحَسِبَ النَّاسُ أَنْ يُتْرَكُوا أَنْ يَقُولُوا آمَنَّا وَهُمْ لَا يُفْتَنُونَ ⬡ وَلَقَدْ فَتَنَّا الَّذِينَ مِنْ قَبْلِهِمْ فَلَيَعْلَمَنَّ اللَّهُ الَّذِينَ صَدَقُوا وَلَيَعْلَمَنَّ الْكَاذِبِينَ ⬡

*Do people think they will not be tested because they say, "We have faith?" We tested those before them so that Allah would know the truthful and would know the liars.*
*(al-'Ankabut, 29:2-3)*

In *Surat Ta Ha* Allah (SWT) says to the Prophet Musa (AS),

فَنَجَّيْنَاكَ مِنَ الْغَمِّ وَفَتَنَّاكَ فُتُونًا ⬡

*We rescued you from trouble and tested you with many trials. (Ta Ha, 20:40)*

So what kind of *fitan* (trials) are people tried with? Brothers and sisters! We are tested both by way of evil things as well as good things. In *Surat al-Anbiya`* Allah says,

كُلُّ نَفْسٍ ذَائِقَةُ الْمَوْتِ وَنَبْلُوكُمْ بِالشَّرِّ وَالْخَيْرِ فِتْنَةً وَإِلَيْنَا تُرْجَعُونَ ⬡

*Every soul will taste death. We will test you with evil and good by way of trial, and it is to Us that you will return. (al-Anbiya`, 21:35)*

And in *Surat al-'Ankabut,* Allah says,

أَنْ يُتْرَكُوا أَنْ يَقُولُوا آمَنَّا وَهُمْ لَا يُفْتَنُونَ أَحَسِبَ النَّاسُ ⬡

*Do people think they will not be tested because they say, "We have faith?" (al-'Ankabut, 29:2)*

The word "people" here includes everyone. It includes all categories of people. You might even be tried and tested by your own self! One may be tested by one's parents, one's spouse, one's children, one's wealth, one's poverty, one's knowledge, one's ignorance, one's good health or one's sickness. One may be tested through prosperity and adversity. Allah says,

وَجَعَلْنَا بَعْضَكُم لِبَعْضٍ فِتْنَةً أَتَصْبِرُونَ وَكَانَ رَبُّكَ بَصِيرًا ○

*And We have made some of you as a trial for others to see if you will have patience. And your Lord is all-seeing. (al-Furqan, 25:20)*

The rich are a *fitna* for the poor and vice versa. The believers are a *fitna* for the disbelievers and vice versa. We are all *fitna* to one another in terms of our nationalities, our ethnicities, our languages and so on. If we look down upon other people as inferiors, we cause ourselves to be a *fitna* for them.

وَاتَّقُوا فِتْنَةً لَا تُصِيبَنَّ الَّذِينَ ظَلَمُوا مِنْكُمْ خَاصَّةً ○

*And beware of a test that will not only afflict those among you who do wrong. (al-Anfal, 8:25)*

We cannot get out of this general rule of *fitna*. We need to understand that being tested is an inescapable part of being in this world. It is our responsibility as Muslims to be prepared for the tests. Our job is to successfully pass the test. We must remember that no matter how difficult things become in our lives, Allah (SWT) is the Merciful and the Compassionate. Allah tells us in the Qur`an,

لَا يُكَلِّفُ اللَّهُ نَفْسًا إِلاَّ وُسْعَهَا ○

*Allah does not burden any soul with more than it can bear. (al-Baqara, 2:286)*

The Prophet (SAS) said, "A time will come when the nations (of the world) will surround you from every side, just as people invited to a feast gather around the main dish." Somebody asked, "O Messenger of Allah, will it be on account of our being few in number at that time?" The Prophet (SAS) replied, "No, but you will be scum (everywhere) like the scum of flood water. Feebleness will be in your hearts, and fear will be removed from the hearts of your enemies, on account of your love for the world, and your hatred of death."

The Muslim population of the world is huge. Yet our lives and our feelings do not count for much. It is other nations that are respected, revered, and feared. This hadeeth tells us that excessive love of this world makes us forget that we have to die and leave this world; that there is a hereafter; and that there is a day of judgment. This puts us in a position whereby our principles are compromised, and we are no longer a force to be reckoned with. Today, we are living in very tough times. What the Muslim *ummah* is currently facing is a chain of *fitan*. We face bigotry, negative stereotyping, malicious accusations, blasphemy, Islamophobia, and the list goes on. We are facing *fitan* as individuals, as a community, and as an *ummah*. When we realize that the purpose of *fitan* is to test us, what should we do?

We should remain firm to our *deen*. We should never hide our faith. We should never sacrifice Islam and never feel embarrassed or ashamed about who we are. We are Muslims and are proud of being Muslim. We should keep clinging to our *deen* and eventually we will pass over the *fitna* and emerge from it in a purified state.

We should turn to Allah (SWT) with full sincerity and strengthen our relationship with Him. The Prophet (SAS) commanded us to seek refuge with Allah (SWT) against all types of *fitan*. The Prophet (SAS) said, "When any one of you utters the last *tashahhud* (the last long prayer in our *salah* that starts with the phrase *at-tahiyyatu li-laah*) he must seek refuge with Allah from four trials by saying, 'O Allah! I seek refuge with You from the torment of hell, from the torment of the grave, from the trial of life and death, and from the evil of the trial of the Antichrist (*Dajjal*).'" The Prophet (SAS) also used to seek refuge with Allah from another set of trials by saying, "O Allah! I seek refuge with You from cowardice, and I seek refuge with You from being brought back to a bad stage of old life, and seek refuge with You from the afflictions of the world, and seek refuge with You from the punishments in the grave."

We should increase our worship of Allah (SWT). A *fitna* is meant to make us better and purify us. During times of *fitna*, we should increase our worship, our *nawafil* (supererogatory or extra) prayers, our *sadaqa* (charity), our recitation of the Qur'an, and we should race with one another in doing good deeds. In one hadeeth we read that the Prophet (SAS) informed us that a time will come when a person will go to sleep as a believer and wake up as a disbeliever, or wake up as a believer and go to sleep as a disbeliever. Why will this happen? The Prophet (SAS) warned us that a person will be willing to sell his own religion for the price of this world. May Allah (SWT) protect us from this situation.

We should study our religion and learn what Islam is all about. We should read the Qur'an, read the *seerah* of the Prophet (SAS), and learn the basic aspects of *fiqh* and worship, because knowledge thus gained will equip us to comprehend the *fitan* and respond to them appropriately. Have we ever thought about the amount of time we invest toward our secular studies and how little time we invest in learning about the *deen* of Islam? The Prophet (SAS) said, "The Hour (Last Day) will not be established until (religious) knowledge will be taken away (by the death of the people of knowledge), earthquakes will be very frequent, time will pass quickly, afflictions (*fitan*) will appear, murders will increase and money will overflow amongst you."

Once we have gained knowledge, we need to start teaching and preaching. The purpose of the candle is not to burn for itself but to light the way for others. Similarly, the purpose of the knowledge we possess is not to keep it enclosed in our chest but to spread it to other people. Every single one of us must become a *da'iy* (a caller to Islam), starting their *da'wa* with their family, their friends, and their acquaintances. We don't all have to become *'alims* and *muftis*, but everyone has the ability and responsibility to be a true representative of Islam. When Muslims start living as true Muslims by living up to the ideals of their own religion, the *da'wa* will then be done by their actions and by their character. This is one way to counter the *fitna*.

We should have patience, or *sabr*. Sometimes we may not see the result of what we do in our own lifetime. *Sabr* comes from an Arabic root which means "to restrain oneself." In the spiritual sense, it means to stop ourselves from losing hope and panicking, and to stop our tongues from complaining. It means that we act wisely and restrain ourselves from doing things that will cause more harm. Islam emphasizes patience and perseverance in times of adversity or calamity. Our life is not a bed of roses. It is a life of struggle. We continuously struggle to survive as well as to succeed. Throughout our everyday lives, we face many unpleasant events. Islam provides a powerful psychological leverage to deal with such occurrences. When we place our trust in Allah (SWT), we can face many obstacles and misfortunes with a unique mental strength not available to others. Such psychological state cannot be achieved overnight. But patience and perseverance can help us to achieve that goal.

Finally, the way to successfully emerge from trials and tribulations is given in the last verse of *Surat al-'Ankabut*.

وَالَّذِينَ جَاهَدُوا فِينَا لَنَهْدِيَنَّهُمْ سُبُلَنَا وَإِنَّ اللَّهَ لَمَعَ الْمُحْسِنِينَ ۝

*As for those who strive in our cause, We will guide them to our paths. For Allah is with the doers of good. (al-'Ankabut, 29:69)*

We seek refuge with Allah (SWT) from all types of *fitan*. We seek refuge with Him from all types of trials and tribulations both hidden and apparent. If it is destined that a *fitna* strikes us, then we ask Allah (SWT) to make us emerge from it successfully and to make it a source of seeking His pleasure and His closeness. *Ameen!*

•   28   •

# FORGIVENESS

The subject of today's *khutbah* is forgiveness. A man named Alexander Pope wisely said, "To err is human, to forgive is divine." Both parts of this statement are true. All people commit sins and make mistakes. God forgives them, and people are acting in a divine way when they forgive. Part of being human is that we make mistakes. Sometimes we make mistakes unintentionally, and other times we make mistakes and fall into sin intentionally. Islam speaks about two elements of forgiveness: Allah's all-encompassing mercy and forgiveness, and the need for human beings to forgive one another. We need both because we do wrong in our relationship with Allah (SWT) as well as in our relationships with one another.

Out of the many beautiful names and attributes of Allah (SWT), some of them are related to His divine mercy and forgiveness. One of them is *al-Ghafoor*, which means "The Most Forgiving." There are other names such as *al-Ghafir* and *al-Ghaffar* that are derived from the same Arabic root word *ghafara*, which means to cover or to hide, and from this root comes the meanings "to excuse," "to pardon," and "to forgive." Allah does all these things. The Prophet (SAS) was told to convey to all people the good news that Allah keeps forgiving and is most merciful.

نَبِّئْ عِبَادِي أَنِّي أَنَا الْغَفُورُ الرَّحِيمُ ○

*Tell My servants that I am indeed the Oft-Forgiving, Most Merciful. (al-Hijr, 15:49)*

Allah describes Himself in *Surat Ghafir,*

غَافِرِ الذَّنبِ وَقَابِلِ التَّوْبِ ○

*The Forgiver of sin and the Accepter of repentance. (Ghafir, 40:3)*

Allah also tells us that we must turn to Him to seek His forgiveness.

اسْتَغْفِرُوا رَبَّكُمْ إِنَّهُ كَانَ غَفَّارًا ○

*Ask forgiveness of your Lord. Indeed, He is ever forgiving. (Nuh, 71:10)*

In a Hadeeth *Qudsi* the Prophet (SAS) informs us that Allah (SWT) said, "When Allah decreed the creation, He wrote in His Book with Him on His Throne: 'My mercy prevails over My wrath.'"

One of the other names and attributes of Allah (SWT) is *Al-'Afuw*, which means "The Pardoner." This reflects another dimension of forgiveness. Literally, the word *'Afa* means "to pardon," "to forgive," "to pass over," and "to restore." Thus, in relation to Allah, it means that Allah will release us from the burden of punishment due to our sins and mistakes and restore our honor after we have dishonored ourselves by committing sins and making mistakes. Sometimes in the Qur'an both names, *'Afuw* and *Ghafoor*, come together.

فَأُولَٰئِكَ عَسَى اللَّهُ أَن يَعْفُوَ عَنْهُمْ وَكَانَ اللَّهُ عَفُوًّا غَفُورًا ○

*It may well be that Allah will pardon them. Allah is Ever-Pardoning, Ever-Forgiving.*
*(an-Nisa`, 4:99)*

Another excellent name is *at-Tawwab,* which means "The Accepter of Repentance." Allah accepts repentance of those who sincerely repent and turn to Him. The word *tawwab* gives the meaning of "oft-returning," which means that Allah accepts a person's repentance again and again. We commit sins and make mistakes. We then repent and He accepts our repentance. Then we again commit sins and make mistakes and we repent. And He again accepts our repentance. He keeps on giving us opportunities to repent and mend our ways. Allah reminds us in the Qur`an,

أَلَمْ يَعْلَمُوا أَنَّ اللَّهَ هُوَ يَقْبَلُ التَّوْبَةَ عَنْ عِبَادِهِ وَيَأْخُذُ الصَّدَقَاتِ وَأَنَّ اللَّهَ هُوَ التَّوَّابُ الرَّحِيمُ ۞

*Do they not know that Allah alone accepts the repentance of His servants and receives their charity, and that Allah alone is the Acceptor of Repentance, Most Merciful?*

(at-Tawba, 9:104)

One of the most beautiful things about repentance and turning to Allah and doing good deeds is that Allah not only wipes the sins off, but also replaces them with good deeds. Allah tells us in *Surat al-Furqan,*

مَنْ تَابَ وَآمَنَ وَعَمِلَ عَمَلًا صَالِحًا فَأُولَئِكَ يُبَدِّلُ اللَّهُ سَيِّئَاتِهِمْ حَسَنَاتٍ وَكَانَ اللَّهُ غَفُورًا رَحِيمًا ۞

*Those who repent, believe, and do good deeds, Allah will change the evil deeds of such people into good ones. He is most forgiving, most merciful. (al-Furqan, 25:70)*

The Prophet (SAS) also said, "The one who repents from sin is like one who did not sin." This means that if a person commits a sin, then repents sincerely from it, gives it up, regrets having done it, prays for forgiveness, and does not go back to it, Allah will accept his repentance and treat him like one who did not sin. The sincere repentance of Adam and Hawwa (AS) opened the doors for Allah's forgiveness to reach them. What did they both say?

رَبَّنَا ظَلَمْنَا أَنْفُسَنَا وَإِنْ لَمْ تَغْفِرْ لَنَا وَتَرْحَمْنَا لَنَكُونَنَّ مِنَ الْخَاسِرِينَ ۞

*Our Lord, we have wronged ourselves, and if You do not forgive us and have mercy upon us, we will surely be among the losers. (al-A'raf, 7:23)*

Allah (SWT) is also known by His beautiful name of *al-Haleem,* which means "The Most Forbearing." He is not quick to judge or punish but gives time to each one of us. He shows clemency and is most patient to see His servant return to Him.

وَاعْلَمُوا أَنَّ اللَّهَ غَفُورٌ حَلِيمٌ ۞

*And know that Allah is All-Forgiving, Most Forbearing. (al-Baqara, 2:235)*

There are two other names of Allah (SWT) by which He wants us to remember Him every time we take a step in our life. They appear in the phrase *bismillah ar-Rahman ar-Raheem*. The name *ar-Rahman* means "The Most Gracious" and the name *ar-Raheem* means "The Most Merciful." Our beloved Prophet Muhammad (SAS) is reported to have said that "no man's good deeds are enough to get him admitted into paradise, but it is only by the mercy of Allah that people will enter paradise." Our deeds are only the tools or the means to get close to Allah so that we can be hopeful of His mercy. Therefore, let us do our good deeds, let us have our correct faith, and let us perform our obligations as best as we can, but then leave the rest to Allah's mercy.

At times we find people questioning if Allah (SWT) will forgive them for the sins they have committed. Shaytan pushes them to believe that there is no hope for forgiveness for them. They get into a state of desperation and lose all hope in Allah's mercy. So, they never repent and seek forgiveness from Allah. But Allah says,

قُلْ يَا عِبَادِيَ الَّذِينَ أَسْرَفُوا عَلَى أَنْفُسِهِمْ لا تَقْنَطُوا مِنْ رَحْمَةِ اللَّهِ إِنَّ اللَّهَ يَغْفِرُ الذُّنُوبَ جَمِيعًا إِنَّهُ هُوَ الْغَفُورُ الرَّحِيمُ ○

*Say: O My servants who transgressed against themselves, do not despair of Allah's mercy. For Allah forgives all sins. He is the Forgiver, the Merciful. (az-Zumar, 39:53)*

Imagine the beauty of Allah's forgiveness that when non-Muslims enter into the fold of Islam, Allah forgives all their evil deeds but preserves all their good deeds that would be taken into account on the Day of Judgment. It is as if they were born again but carrying years of good deeds with them. The paths to forgiveness are many and all that is needed is our traveling on one of those paths. Having good character and conduct results in forgiveness, so if one is truthful and upright when they speak, they will be forgiven for their sins. Allah says in the Qur`an,

يَا أَيُّهَا الَّذِينَ آمَنُوا اتَّقُوا اللَّهَ وَقُولُوا قَوْلاً سَدِيدًايُصْلِحْ لَكُمْ أَعْمَالَكُمْ وَيَغْفِرْ لَكُمْ ذُنُوبَكُمْ وَمَن يُطِعِ اللَّهَ وَرَسُولَهُ فَقَدْ فَازَ فَوْزًا عَظِيمًا ○

*O you who believe, be conscious of Allah, and speak the right words. He will put your actions right for you and forgive you your wrong deeds. Whoever obeys Allah and His Messenger has certainly achieved a great success. (al-Ahzab, 33:70-71)*

We should not only seek Allah's forgiveness when we have sinned but should also seek it when we have not sinned. Our beloved Prophet Muhammad (SAS), despite being sinless, used to seek forgiveness from Allah every single day, and used to say, "O people seek forgiveness from Allah. Verily I seek forgiveness from Him one hundred times a day." Seeking forgiveness or making *istighfar* is an act of worship done by all prophets, messengers, and pious believers.

How often do we let days go by without seeking Allah's forgiveness even once? Allah wants to forgive us, and He wants us to feel His mercy in this life and in the hereafter. Unfortunately, much of what we learn and what we deliver to others is not the mercy, love, and forgiveness of Allah, but the anger of Allah and how we should fear Him. In order that we develop some appreciation of our relationship with Allah, listen to what He tells us in the Qur`an.

$$وَرَحْمَتِي وَسِعَتْ كُلَّ شَيْءٍ$$

*My mercy encompasses everything. (al-A'raf, 7:156)*

We need to realize that there is great mercy and forgiveness from Allah and all that is required of us is to ask for it through our words and actions. How often do we sit in our prayers seeking forgiveness? May Allah give us the *tawfeeq* to do so.

Brothers and sisters! While the concept of forgiveness in Islam lies in seeking the forgiveness of Allah (SWT), it also lies in being forgiving to one another. We must learn from the forgiving nature of Prophet Yusuf (AS) who looked upon his brothers and said,

$$قَالَ لَا تَثْرِيبَ عَلَيْكُمُ الْيَوْمَ يَغْفِرُ اللَّهُ لَكُمْ وَهُوَ أَرْحَمُ الرَّاحِمِينَ$$

*There is no blame on you today. May Allah forgive you! He is the Most Merciful of the merciful. (Yusuf, 12:92)*

Yusuf (AS) never spoke about the wrong that his brothers had committed against him. He was one of the most powerful men in the land and could have sought revenge, but he chose to forgive and leave us all an example to learn from. No matter how a high position of power we may be in, the characteristic of forgiving one another should always be within us.

The Prophet Muhammad (SAS) was someone whose patience and forgiving nature is an example for all of humanity. The wrongs that were committed against him were never held in his heart. Imagine that the man who assassinated the beloved uncle of the Prophet (SAS) Hamza ibn 'Abd al-Muttalib (RAA) was informed by the Prophet (SAS) himself, that Allah was ready to forgive him if he were to accept Islam. This was a time when the Prophet Muhammad (SAS) was crying over the loss of his martyred uncle after the Battle of Uhud. The pain that he must have felt cannot be put into words. Yet, the Prophet (SAS) remained forgiving. There are many stories of those who committed excesses against the noble Prophet (SAS) and were later embraced by him with open arms.

The need to be forgiving starts with our dealings with our own family members. Perfection belongs only to Allah (SWT). We are not perfect. There is no perfect family. We do not have perfect parents. We do not marry a perfect person. We do not have perfect children. Sometimes we have complaints from each other. Sometimes we disappoint each other. There is no healthy marriage or healthy family without the exercise of forgiveness. It is vital to our

emotional health and spiritual survival. Without forgiveness, the family becomes a ground of conflict. Without forgiveness, the family becomes ill. Whoever does not forgive does not have peace in their heart nor close association with Allah (SWT). Those who do not forgive are physically, emotionally, and spiritually ill.

Forgiveness is the remedy that heals. In order to achieve peace and harmony, we need to forgive one another and not hold grudges or feelings of resentment against one another because surely these ill feelings are chains that tie us down. The power of forgiveness needs to be earned through the power of forgiving and by never losing hope in Allah's mercy.

We must sincerely repent to Allah and seek His forgiveness for our sins, regardless whether they are major or minor, open or secret, intentional or unintentional. Indeed, He accepts sincere repentance. He is the Most Forgiving, the Most Merciful. May Allah have mercy on us above the earth, below the earth, and on the Day when our deeds will be shown to us. May He make us merciful and forgiving to one another. May He lead us to ways that make us qualify for His mercy and forgiveness. May He help us achieve all that is good and righteous. *Allahumma ameen.*

<br>

### • 29 •

# FREEDOM OF SPEECH AND EXPRESSION

We are all aware that on January 7, 2015, a terrorist attack in France resulted in the death of seventeen people including journalists of the French satirical weekly magazine *Charlie Hebdo*. This magazine had attracted attention for its depictions of the Prophet Muhammad (SAS) in a distasteful and offensive manner. However, the violent and senseless action of those individuals who killed civilians in the name of Islam left many people in a state of fear and anxiety. It has been rightly condemned worldwide by Muslims and non-Muslims alike.

I do not want to discuss the political intrigues and implications that surround this particular incident. I would, however, like to highlight two important points in my *khutbah* today. First, what does the Qur`an have to say regarding insults against our Prophet (SAS). Secondly, we will address the need to educate ourselves and others about the real meaning of free speech and expression.

On multiple occasions, Allah (SWT) tells us in the Qur`an how His prophets were insulted, how they were made fun of, how they were rejected by their own people. Allah wants us to remember that His prophets, even though they were the most honored and noble of Allah's creations, were people who faced the worst kinds of insults and ridicule. The Qur'an that honors the Prophet (SAS) also records the most hurtful words that were said to him. He was called a magician, an insane person, a fortune teller, a poet, and a liar. So many false accusations were made against the Prophet (SAS) and they are all recorded in the Qur'an.

If anybody should have been infuriated when the Prophet (SAS) was insulted, it should have been his companions whose implicit faith in Allah and true love for the Prophet are beyond comparison. How come they did not react in the way we do? They did not go out yelling and screaming in rage, killing those who insulted the Prophet? They understood that the Qur'an didn't just come to give them the love of the Prophet, but also to guide that love, and to teach them how to respond to the insults that were hurled at the Prophet (SAS) by the disbelievers. Allah (SWT) says to the Prophet (SAS) in the Qur'an,

$$\text{وَاصْبِرْ عَلَىٰ مَا يَقُولُونَ وَاهْجُرْهُمْ هَجْرًا جَمِيلًا}$$

*Be patient over what they say, and ignore them politely. (al-Muzzammil, 73:10)*

Where in the Qur'an is it justified to be angry over what the disbelievers say to the Prophet (SAS)? The one thing we should feel toward those who misunderstand Islam and make hateful speech toward Muslims is sorrow. We should feel sorrow for these people. They can't hurt the Prophet. They can't take away his honor. It was given to him by Allah (SWT). Nothing on earth can take it away. No writing, no speech, no cartoon, no film is going to take away the dignity of our Prophet (SAS). All these types of attempts to undermine the message of Islam and denigrate the Prophet (SAS) are futile. The enemies of Islam want Islam to be misrepresented. By reacting to accusations made against the Prophet (SAS) through violence and killing, we would only be misrepresenting Islam and Muslims. If we are to be angry at anything, it should be at our own selves because we do not comply with the teachings of the Qur'an on how to respond to insults. Allah says,

$$\text{ادْفَعْ بِالَّتِي هِيَ أَحْسَنُ السَّيِّئَةَ نَحْنُ أَعْلَمُ بِمَا يَصِفُونَ}$$

*Repel evil with that which is better. We are well-aware of the things they say. (al-Mu'minoon, 23:96)*

Some may argue that this was an early policy in Islam, during the Meccan period of the Prophet. He and his followers were supposed to be passive, but after their migration to Medina, battles were fought with the disbelievers. Now, the policy was to react by engaging in active resistance. But let's look at *Surat Aal 'Imran*, a *surah* revealed in the Medinan period. What does Allah tell the believers in this *Surah*?

وَلَتَسْمَعُنَّ مِنَ الَّذِينَ أُوتُوا الْكِتَابَ مِن قَبْلِكُمْ وَمِنَ الَّذِينَ أَشْرَكُوا أَذًى كَثِيرًا وَإِن تَصْبِرُوا وَتَتَّقُوا فَإِنَّ ذَٰلِكَ مِنْ عَزْمِ الْأُمُورِ ◯

*You shall surely hear many hurtful things from those who were given the Book before you and from those who set up partners with Allah, but if you endure with fortitude and restrain yourselves, that indeed is a matter of strong determination. (Aal 'Imran, 3:186)*

This, my brothers and sisters, is supposed to be the reaction of the Muslims. The more we react in the way the enemies of Islam want us to react, the more we will be encouraging others to pursue hateful speech and expression against Islam, Muslims, and our Prophet (SAS). We have to learn to respond in a civil manner, in the way the Qur`an and the legacy of our Prophet teach us. We must turn the current narrative surrounding Islamophobia into something positive. May Allah (SWT) give us the understanding and the *tawfeeq* to do so.

In contemporary times, it is under the cover and shelter of "freedom of speech and expression" that all distasteful, indecent, vulgar, offensive, and hateful materials are published in every kind of media. Having discussed the way to respond to accusations against the Prophet (SAS), we should at the same time be very clear about what free speech and expression imply.

We should understand that free speech is an ideological liberal position. It does not represent the default position. It is not a neutral position. It is not a universal position. Billions of people around the world are not liberals. It is basic human courtesy to respect others. To insult others means to treat them with disrespect. The onus is upon those who want to allow such behavior to prove why this immorality should be permitted. The idea of free speech and expression is flawed in theory and politicized in practice. For instance, when justifying one of the controversial anti-Islamic movies called *Innocence of Muslims* that insulted the Prophet (SAS) and touched on themes of pedophilia, womanizing, and homosexuality, the White House said, "We cannot and will not censor freedom of expression in this country." Then Secretary of State Hillary Clinton said, "Our country does have a long tradition of free expression...We do not stop individual citizens from expressing their views no matter how distasteful they may be." These sentiments have also been echoed by leaders in Europe and Australia.

But these statements are simply not true. Free speech does not exist in absolute form. There is no absolute freedom to insult. Even across the liberal West, we find defamation laws, sedition laws, professional standards, and journalistic standards of reporting about politicians and celebrities. Both in Germany and France, denial of the Holocaust is prohibited by law. In the United Kingdom, the Public Order Act makes "threatening, abusive, or insulting words" a criminal offense. In Australia, Commonwealth Criminal Code makes it an offense for a person to use a postal or similar service "in a way that reasonable persons would regard as being offensive."

The right to freedom of expression is recognized as a human right under Article 19 of the Universal Declaration of Human Rights, but the same Article goes on to say that the exercise of this right carries "special duties and responsibilities" and may "therefore be subject to certain restrictions" when necessary.

The fact of the matter is that the principle of free speech is wielded selectively as a political tool. Who decides about when and how to qualify free speech? The real question, then, is not about freedom. It's about power using the guise of freedom to extend and enforce its reach. Ultra-liberals may say here that they disagree with all these laws and cases and maintain absolute free speech for all—unqualified, *carte blanche*. But is such a position conducive to society? Would we accept a student insulting his teacher or a child his parent? Everyone teaches their children to respect others and not to insult others because insult begets insult. Is that the type of society we want for ourselves and for our children?

Some forget that even in the Western tradition, free speech was upheld as a most basic value for specific ends: to allow the profession of ideas, to allow inquiry into truths, and the ability to hold government to account. Do any of these noble ends—all of which are upheld in Islam – require the freedom to insult? Insulting other people's beliefs makes them more defensive and prepared to retaliate. That's human nature.

We should also know that secular liberalism has dominated both East and West, not by the strength of its values, but by the strength of its policies of aggression and domination. Unlike Christianity and Judaism, which crumbled under the force of secularism, Islam did not. Muslim lands were divided and colonized, conquered and exploited. The Islamic state—the Caliphate – was dismantled, but *al-hamduli-llah*, the Islamic mind remained. Insults are part of an effort to break this resistance and impose secular liberalism so that it can consolidate its victory forever.

Is the Western world really in a position to lecture others about violence or about values? The "free world" seeks to dominate and impose itself upon the rest of the world, destroying entire countries through war and invasion. More attention should be focused on the broader context in which the global Muslim reaction to insults comes. Critique of ideas or beliefs is always welcome. But mocking, denigrating, or provoking should not be acceptable in a civilized society. Insulting others is not an acceptable mode of interaction for mature, self-respecting people. Insults bring nothing to society except hate and divisiveness. Sacred beliefs and holy things such and God and His messengers, should be protected from insult. The Qur'an tells us,

$$\text{وَلَا تَسُبُّوا الَّذِينَ يَدْعُونَ مِنْ دُونِ اللَّهِ فَيَسُبُّوا اللَّهَ عَدْوًا بِغَيْرِ عِلْمٍ} \bigcirc$$

*Do not insult those they call upon besides Allah, lest they, in their ignorance and hostility insult Allah. (al-An'am, 6:108)*

Let me conclude by saying that when insults are hurled at God or any of His prophets, the Qur`an teaches us to restrain ourselves with endurance, fortitude, and to repel that evil with that which is better. At the same time, we must have an insight into the real meaning and implication of the right to free speech and expression. The exercise of this right carries special duties and responsibilities.

May Allah grant us the *tawfeeq* to use the precious gift of speech and expression with utmost care and caution. May He make us among those from whom others are safe. May He also keep us safe from the evil designs of others. *Ameen.*

• 30 •

# GETTING TO KNOW ALLAH

There is a well-known hadeeth *qudsi* that shows our relationship with Allah (SWT) and some of His divine attributes. What is a hadeeth *qudsi*? It is a hadeeth, which from the perspective of its meaning, is from Allah (SWT), and from the perspective of its wording, is from the Prophet Muhammad (SAS). The Prophet (SAS) would receive the meaning from Allah (SWT) by way of inspiration or dream, and then he would inform his community of this in his own words.

The hadeeth *qudsi* I want to talk about today is "On the authority of Abu Dharr al-Ghifari (RAA) from the Prophet (SAS) from his Lord, Who said,

"O My servants! I have forbidden oppression (*dhulm*) for Myself, and I have made it forbidden among you, so do not oppress one another. O My servants, all of you are astray except those whom I have guided, so seek guidance from Me and I shall guide you. O My servants, all of you are hungry except those whom I have fed, so seek food from Me and I shall feed you. O My servants, all of you are naked except those whom I have clothed, so seek clothing from Me and I shall clothe you. O My servants, you commit sins by day and by night, and I forgive all sins, so seek forgiveness from Me and I shall forgive you. O My servants, you can neither do Me any harm nor can you do Me any good. O My servants, if the first of you and the last of you, and the humans of you and the jinn of you, were all as pious as the most pious heart of any individual among you, then this would not increase My Kingdom in anything. O My servants, if the first of you and the last of you, and the humans of you and the jinn of you, were all as wicked as the most wicked heart of any individual among you, then this would not decrease My Kingdom in anything. O My servants, if the first of you and the last of you, and the humans of you and the jinn of you, were all to stand together in one place and ask of Me, and I were to give everyone what he requested, then that would not decrease what I possess, except what is decreased of the ocean when a needle is dipped into it. O My servants, it is but your deeds that I account for you, and then recompense you for. So, let him who finds good praise Allah, and let him who finds other than that blame no one but himself."

This hadeeth was related by Muslim, and it is found in the *Forty Hadeeth* collection of Imam an-Nawawi. It has very important lessons for us, some of which we will discuss in this *khutbah*.

Allah never does *dhulm* on anyone. This means that He never oppresses anyone, and He is never unjust to anyone. He never wrongs anyone. There are numerous verses in the Quran that allude to this.

$$وَلَا يَظْلِمُ رَبُّكَ أَحَدًا$$

*And Your Lord wrongs no one. (al-Kahf, 18:49)*

$$إِنَّ اللَّهَ لَا يَظْلِمُ مِثْقَالَ ذَرَّةٍ$$

*Surely Allah does not wrong anyone by as much as an atom's weight. (an-Nisa`, 4:40)*

$$وَمَا اللَّهُ يُرِيدُ ظُلْمًا لِّلْعِبَادِ$$

*Allah never wills any injustice for His creatures. (Ghafir, 40:31)*

$$وَمَا رَبُّكَ بِظَلَّامٍ لِّلْعَبِيدِ$$

*Your Lord is never unjust to His creatures. (Fussilat, 41:46)*

Allah forbids all forms of injustice. The first and the most extreme form of injustice is *shirk*, or associating partners with Allah. Allah says in the Qur`an,

$$إِنَّ الشِّرْكَ لَظُلْمٌ عَظِيمٌ$$

*Surely, associating partners with Allah is the greatest injustice. (Luqman, 31:13)*

The second form of injustice is being unjust toward oneself by committing sins, and the third form is to be unjust toward others by oppressing them. Injustice leads to Allah's displeasure and warrants His punishment. Thus, we are admonished never to be unjust. This hadeeth also teaches us that no one is guided unless he is guided by Allah. Those who sincerely seek guidance and work for it are guided. Allah turns their hearts to His obedience and worship. A Prophetic *du'a`* teaches us to say:

يَا مُقَلِّبَ الْقُلُوبِ ثَبِّتْ قُلُوبَنَا عَلَى دِينِكَ

*O, Turner of the hearts, keep our hearts firm on your religion.*

اللَّهُمَّ مُصَرِّفَ الْقُلُوبِ صَرِّفْ قُلُوبَنَا عَلَى طَاعَتِكَ

*O Allah, the Turner of the hearts, turn our hearts to your obedience.*

It is incumbent upon us to seek Allah's guidance and help. In *Surat al-Fatiha*, we recite:

اهْدِنَا الصِّرَاطَ الْمُسْتَقِيمَ ○

*Guide us to the Straight Path. (al-Fatiha, 1:6)*

Another thing we learn from this hadeeth is that sustenance and provisions are from Allah alone. He provides for all His creatures.

وَمَا مِن دَابَّةٍ فِي الْأَرْضِ إِلَّا عَلَى اللَّهِ رِزْقُهَا ○

*There is no creature on earth except that its provision is from Allah. (Hud, 11:6)*

In Surat al-Fatiha, Allah says,

الْحَمْدُ لِلَّهِ رَبِّ الْعَالَمِينَ ○

*Praise be to Allah, the Rabb of the entire universe. (al-Fatiha, 1:1)*

This means that Allah is the Lord and Master, the Sustainer, the Provider, the Supporter, the Nourisher, the Guardian, the Sovereign, and the Ruler of the universe. Therefore, we must worship Him alone, and seek help from Him alone. This is what we recite in *Surat al-Fatiha:*

إِيَّاكَ نَعْبُدُ وَإِيَّاكَ نَسْتَعِينُ ○

*You alone we worship. You alone we ask for help. (al-Fatiha, 1:5)*

The statement "all of you are hungry except those whom I have fed ... all of you are naked except those whom I have clothed" is a reminder of our poverty before Allah. It's a reminder of our inability to bring about good for ourselves and to ward off harm from ourselves, except by the help of Allah. When we see the traces of blessings upon ourselves, then we should be grateful to Allah. True gratefulness by the heart is manifested through sincere belief that all the blessings we have—the known and the unknown—our very existence, our life, our body, our physical appearance, and all our abilities and accomplishments are from Allah. Allah says in *Surat an-Nahl*

وَمَا بِكُم مِّن نِّعْمَةٍ فَمِنَ اللَّهِ ○

*Whatever blessing you have is from Allah. (al-Nahl, 16:53)*

Gratefulness by the body is shown by using one's limbs, organs, faculties, and abilities for the purpose for which they were created. Next, the hadeeth talks about seeking Allah's forgiveness. Brothers and sisters! Humans are inclined to sin, and none can forgive sins but Allah. So, we must seek Allah's forgiveness for our sins. The door of repentance is always open for all of us all the time. Islam is a practical religion. It acknowledges human weaknesses. We read in the Qur`an,

يُرِيدُ اللَّهُ أَن يُخَفِّفَ عَنكُمْ وَخُلِقَ الْإِنسَانُ ضَعِيفًا ۝

*Allah desires to lighten your burden, for man was created weak. (an-Nisa`, 4:28)*

Allah's saying "you commit sins by day and by night, and I forgive all sins" implies that no one who has committed a sin should despair of the mercy of Allah, no matter how great that sin may be. There is always room for sincere repentance, and for seeking forgiveness. Allah tells us in the Qur`an,

قُلْ يَا عِبَادِيَ الَّذِينَ أَسْرَفُوا عَلَىٰ أَنفُسِهِمْ لَا تَقْنَطُوا مِن رَّحْمَةِ اللَّهِ إِنَّ اللَّهَ يَغْفِرُ الذُّنُوبَ جَمِيعًا إِنَّهُ هُوَ الْغَفُورُ الرَّحِيمُ ۝

*Say: O My servants who transgressed against themselves, do not despair of Allah's mercy, for Allah forgives all sins. He is the Forgiver, the Merciful. (az-Zumar, 39:53)*

Seeking Allah's forgiveness(*istighfar*) is one of the ways of being blessed; of bringing *baraka* in our lives. With many people, there is no *baraka* in their lives because they do not do *istighfar* nor are they grateful to Allah. Remember what the prophet Nuh (AS) told his people about the manifold blessings of *istighfar*. He said,

اسْتَغْفِرُوا رَبَّكُمْ إِنَّهُ كَانَ غَفَّارًا يُرْسِلِ السَّمَاءَ عَلَيْكُم مِّدْرَارًا وَيُمْدِدْكُم بِأَمْوَالٍ وَبَنِينَ وَيَجْعَل لَّكُمْ جَنَّاتٍ وَيَجْعَل لَّكُمْ أَنْهَارًا ۝

*Ask forgiveness of your Lord: He is ever forgiving. He will send down abundant rain from the sky for you; He will give you wealth and children; He will provide you with gardens and rivers. (Nuh, 71:10-12)*

We read about the mercy of Allah in *Surat al-An'am*.

كَتَبَ عَلَىٰ نَفْسِهِ الرَّحْمَةَ ۝

*He has made mercy incumbent upon Himself. (al-An'am, 6:12)*

And according to another hadeeth *qudsi*, the Prophet (SAS) teaches us that Allah (SWT) said, "When Allah created the creation, He pledged upon Himself in His book which is with Him over His throne, certainly, My mercy overcomes My anger."

May Allah cover us with His mercy! *Ameen!*

As for the saying of Allah, "If the first of you and the last of you, and the humans of you and the jinn of you" until the end; it is an indication that even if all the humans and jinn became as pious as the most pious of them, that would not affect or increase the Kingdom of Allah in the least. And even if all the humans and jinn became as wicked as the most wicked of them, that would not affect or decrease the Kingdom of Allah in the least.

When Allah (SWT) says, "were all to stand together in one place," it is an exhortation to the creation to ask Allah in all affairs, and not to feel shy in asking Him, for verily that which is with Allah does not decrease, as His treasures are inexhaustible.

When He says, "except what is decreased of the ocean when a needle is dipped into it" this is a metaphor which means that what is with Allah does not diminish at all.

At the end of the hadeeth, it is stressed that everyone will be accountable for their deeds. Whoever finds a good record should be thankful to Allah and praise Him for that. Anyone who finds other than that should not blame anyone except himself. This is a clear statement that shows that we are responsible for our actions because of the freedom of choice – we do good or evil.

In conclusion, it may be said that this hadeeth shows us the proper relationship between mankind and Allah (SWT). It teaches us about many attributes of Allah such as how merciful, forgiving, and powerful He is. It stresses the prohibition of all forms of injustice and oppression. It encourages us to seek help, guidance, and forgiveness from Allah, and to rely solely on Him. It highlights Allah's infinite blessings and bounties, and our need to be His humble and obedient servants. Those who seek Allah's pleasure are truly successful. May Allah make us among them, *ameen*.

• 31 •

# GIFT OF SPEECH AND VALUE OF WORDS

All praise is for Allah (SWT) who has honored man and has created him in the best of forms. All praise is for Allah (SWT) who has blessed man with the ability to speak with his tongue. My dear brothers and sisters! My *khutbah* today is on the gift of speech and value of words. Allah says in the Qur`an,

الرَّحْمَنُ ○ عَلَّمَ الْقُرْآنَ ○ خَلَقَ الْإِنْسَانَ ○ عَلَّمَهُ الْبَيَانَ ○

*The Merciful, who taught the Qur`an. He created man and taught him speech. (ar-Rahman, 55:1-4)*

Allah (SWT) has taught man how to convey or clearly express his feelings and thoughts. Speech is the distinctive quality which distinguishes man from the animals and other earthly creatures. Try to imagine a world without the gift of speech where communication comprised of just grunts and groans, not words. Allah's guidance has come to us through the words of the Qur`an and the words of His Prophet Muhammad (SAS). Allah (SWT) compares a good word to a good tree in *Surat Ibraheem.*

أَلَمْ تَرَ كَيْفَ ضَرَبَ اللَّهُ مَثَلًا كَلِمَةً طَيِّبَةً كَشَجَرَةٍ طَيِّبَةٍ أَصْلُهَا ثَابِتٌ وَفَرْعُهَا فِي السَّمَاءِ ○ تُؤْتِي أُكُلَهَا كُلَّ حِينٍ بِإِذْنِ رَبِّهَا وَيَضْرِبُ اللَّهُ الْأَمْثَالَ لِلنَّاسِ لَعَلَّهُمْ يَتَذَكَّرُونَ ○

*Do you not see how Allah compares a good word to a good tree? Its root is firm, and its branches reach the sky, always yielding its fruit in every season by the Will of its Lord. This is how Allah sets forth parables for the people, so perhaps they will be mindful. (Ibraheem, 14:24-25)*

Though the expression *kalimatan tayyibatan* literally means "pure word," here it stands for "truthful saying" and "righteous creed." According to the Qur`an, this saying and creed are the acceptance of the doctrine of monotheism (*tawheed*), belief in the Prophethood, revelation, and in the life of the hereafter, for it declares these things to be the fundamental truths. The entire system of the universe hangs upon the reality contained in this pure word which the believer professes. This pure word is so fruitful that every person who bases his system of life on it gets benefit from it every moment for it helps to produce strength in character, purity in morals, and firmness in conduct.

وَمَثَلُ كَلِمَةٍ خَبِيثَةٍ كَشَجَرَةٍ خَبِيثَةٍ اجْتُثَّتْ مِن فَوْقِ الْأَرْضِ مَا لَهَا مِن قَرَارٍ ○

*And the parable of an evil word is that of an evil tree, uprooted from the earth, having no stability. (Ibraheem, 14:26)*

An "evil word" is the opposite of a "pure word." It may be applied to everything that is unreal and wrong but here it stands for any false creed that one might adopt as a basis of his system of life, irrespective of whether it be disbelief, atheism, agnosticism, polytheism, or any other "ism" that has not been brought by a Messenger. A false creed has no stability because it is against the law of nature. It could never have been allowed to develop if man had not been tested with freedom of choice. That is why when people endeavor to establish any system of life on earth that is against the law of nature, it is allowed to grow to a certain extent, but it produces nothing but harmful results as long as it lasts. And no sooner does it encounter adverse circumstances than it is thoroughly uprooted from the earth.

As for the use of our tongue, we should always have control over our speech and refrain from uttering words that are useless, harmful, or may have negative repercussions.

$$\text{مَا يَلْفِظُ مِنْ قَوْلٍ إِلاَّ لَدَيْهِ رَقِيبٌ عَتِيدٌ} \bigcirc$$

*Not a word does a person utter without having a vigilant observer ready to write it down. (Qaf, 50:18)*

Indeed, this is a frightening prospect. Throughout the day, we utter so many words without realizing how harmful they may be. We pass remarks about what we perceive to be people's negative traits. We use abusive language. We are responsible for every word we say especially when it may harm others by accusing them falsely, gossiping, backbiting, mocking, or telling lies. Even by uttering just one word such as "divorce," a man can destroy a coherent family.

Another careless word may infringe upon relations between friends, relatives, or loved ones. Marriage, divorce, financial transactions, and contracts all require verbal or written wordings. We hardly ever stop to think that the words we utter are being recorded and will be presented to us on the Day of Judgment. Truly, on the Day of Judgment, people will be questioned about their false claims and testimonies. Allah (SWT) says,

$$\text{سَتُكْتَبُ شَهَادَتُهُمْ وَيُسْأَلُونَ} \bigcirc$$

*We shall record their testimony, and they will be questioned. (az-Zukhruf, 43:19)*

Truly, anyone who recognizes the tremendous impact that words can bring would most definitely hold his tongue and reflect on whatever he says.

There are many Prophetic traditions on the issue of guarding and controlling one's tongue. According to a hadeeth, the Prophet (SAS) said, "The Muslim is the one from whose tongue and hand the Muslims are safe, and the emigrant (*muhajir*) is the one who abandons what Allah has forbidden." On another occasion he said, "Most of the sins of the children of Adam are on their tongues."

The Prophet (SAS) also said, "Most people will be thrown into hell facedown because of the transgressions of their tongues." And he also said, "Every morning all the limbs of a person plead with his tongue: 'Fear Allah for our sake, for our fate is tied to yours. If you follow the straight path so shall we. And if you go astray, so shall we.'" The Prophet (SAS) said, "Whosoever gives me a guarantee to safeguard what is between his jaws (meaning the tongue) and what is between his legs (meaning the private parts), I shall guarantee him paradise." We have to remember that on the Day of Judgment, our physical organs will stand as witnesses against us if we use them in the wrong way. Allah (SWT) says in the Qur'an,

$$يَوْمَ تَشْهَدُ عَلَيْهِمْ أَلْسِنَتُهُمْ وَأَيْدِيهِمْ وَأَرْجُلُهُم بِمَا كَانُوا يَعْمَلُونَ ۝$$

*On the Day when their own tongues, hands and feet shall bear witness against them about what they did. (an-Nur, 24:24)*

One of the hallmarks of righteous behavior is good speech. A person who stays mindful of Allah will want to refrain from sins of the tongue such as backbiting, slander, gossip, lying, swearing, cursing, and vain talk. Allah and His Messenger warn us in the Qur'an and Sunnah against these sins of the tongue. A true righteous believer is not supposed to taunt, curse, abuse, or talk indecently. Indeed, the one who is able to be responsible for whatever he says is the one who will be successful. By so doing, he will close doorways in the face of Satan and ruin his evil plans that are aimed at spreading conflict and disunity among people. Look how Allah (SWT) admonishes us to say what is best.

$$وَقُل لِّعِبَادِي يَقُولُوا الَّتِي هِيَ أَحْسَنُ إِنَّ الشَّيْطَانَ يَنزَغُ بَيْنَهُمْ إِنَّ الشَّيْطَانَ كَانَ لِلْإِنسَانِ عَدُوًّا مُّبِينًا ۝$$

*And say to My servants that they should always say what is best. Satan stirs up discord among them. Surely, Satan is an outright enemy to man. (al-Isra', 17:53)*

$$وَقُولُوا لِلنَّاسِ حُسْنًا ۝$$

*And speak kindly to people. (al-Baqara, 2:83)*

$$وَقُولُوا قَوْلًا سَدِيدًا ۝$$

*And say what is right. (al-Ahzab, 33:70)*

In our daily communication, we should say what is right and ensure that we choose the best and most kind words. The Prophet (SAS) emphasized the need to adopt a lenient and gentle approach when talking to one another. He also linked such behavior to the true belief in Allah, and the Day of Resurrection when he said, "Whoever believes in Allah and the Last Day should talk what is good or keep silent." Thus, we should be sensible and think about what we say and the possible consequences of our words before we speak. To this effect, one should choose the speech that is beneficial and more likeable to others. Otherwise, it is safer to remain silent.

In this context, one occasion when good words are especially encouraged is when talking to one's parents.

$$وَقَضَى رَبُّكَ أَلَّا تَعْبُدُوا إِلَّا إِيَّاهُ وَبِالْوَالِدَيْنِ إِحْسَانًا إِمَّا يَبْلُغَنَّ عِندَكَ الْكِبَرَ أَحَدُهُمَا أَوْ كِلَاهُمَا فَلَا تَقُل لَّهُمَا أُفٍّ وَلَا تَنْهَرْهُمَا وَقُل لَّهُمَا قَوْلًا كَرِيمًا ۝$$

*Your Lord has commanded that you should worship none but Him and show kindness to your parents. If either or both of them attain old age with you, say no word of contempt to them and do not rebuke them, but always speak gently to them. (al-Isra`, 17:23)*

The way a Muslim relates to others is also important when trying to mend relationships between people. In these situations, one should only say that which may lead to resolving the issue in hand and bringing peace of mind and soul to those in dispute. They should be God-conscious in all that they say. In return, the doorways of goodness will, by Allah's grace, be opened to them and their provisions of good deeds will increase. This is because speaking good is among the best acts of charity as emphasized by the Prophet (SAS) when he said, "A good word is charity."

Describing the believers, Allah says in the Qur`an,

وَالَّذِينَ هُمْ عَنِ اللَّغْوِ مُعْرِضُونَ ○

*Those who turn away from useless talk. (al-Mu`minoon, 23:3)*

They avoid *laghw* or whatever is vain and frivolous. *Laghw* is anything meaningless and vain, and things which are not conducive to achieving one's goal and purpose in life. If, by chance, they happen to come across such things, they keep away and avoid them.

وَإِذَا مَرُّوا بِاللَّغْوِ مَرُّوا كِرَامًا ○

*If they have to pass by what is useless, they pass by like dignified people. (al-Furqan, 25:72)*

It takes just a few words to encourage love for each other and strengthen unity, words that may earn us the reward of Allah and the pleasure of people. Likewise, it takes just a few words to spread animosity and division among people, earning us the wrath of Allah and the disrespect of people. Communication entails a big responsibility requiring every one of us to think and reflect on the far-reaching consequences before uttering any word. This is especially true for those who are engaged in activities that may spread or may impact people's life.

Brothers and sisters! Good words bring about all sorts of goodness. They are a means for solving problems, ending enmities, spreading peace, strengthening bonds and love among people, and fostering harmony in the community. And there are huge rewards for that in the hereafter. The Prophet (SAS) said, "Indeed in paradise there are chambers, whose outside can be seen from their inside, and their inside can be seen from their outside." A Bedouin stood and said, "Who are they for, O Messenger of Allah?" The Prophet (SAS) replied, "For those who speak well and feed others." That is, for those who address people gently and with kindness and avoid insulting them in any way. May Allah (SWT) make us among them, *ameen*.

My dear brothers and sisters! The degree of importance attributed to speech of an individual is directly related to the standing of that individual. For instance, what leaders say has great influence on others because leaders are regarded as examples among the people. Similarly, teachers carry the responsibility of instructing their students to be good in words and in deeds and to keep away from words and deeds that are evil and harmful.

The *khutbah* of *Jumu'ah* is a speech. It carries messages of goodness and righteousness intended to remind people of the great teachings and principles of Islam. It is a duty incumbent upon the *khateeb* to encourage all that is good and beneficial and forbid all that is evil and harmful. The practice of enjoining good and forbidding evil is at the core of our religion and one of the most important Islamic duties.

To conclude, I admonish myself and you to refrain from vain talk, to stop spreading rumors, to verify any news before jumping to conclusions, to stop all types of backbiting against one another, to speak softly and gently, to increase our knowledge of Islam, to learn and teach, to take the initiative of making *da'wa* for the love and pleasure of Allah, to keep busy in doing something good for yourselves and to others, and to keep watch over your mistakes and sins.

May Allah accept our repentance for the irresponsible use of our tongues, our eyes, our ears, our limbs, and our minds. May He make us among those from whom others are safe. *Ameen.*

· 32 ·

# GOD-CONSCIOUSNESS *(TAQWA)*

The topic of today's *khutbah* is *taqwa*. I will speak briefly on the meaning of *taqwa*, the attributes of the people of *taqwa*, the benefits of *taqwa*, and some of the ways to achieve *taqwa* in our lives.

*Taqwa* is one of the primary concepts in the Qur`an. It is derived from the Arabic root *waqa* made up of the three Arabic letters *waw-qaaf-yaa`* which carries meanings of "to be protected from that which is harmful." The Arabic word *wiqaya* means preventing or protecting something from that which may harm it. As a *shari'a* term, *taqwa* means to protect oneself from acts that are sinful by leaving what is unlawful or forbidden.

Allah the Almighty through His infinite knowledge, wisdom, and mercy has informed us through the final divine message revealed in the Qur`an and the guidance of the Prophet Muhammad (SAS), the final messenger, as to what is lawful and beneficial, and what is unlawful and harmful. Only Allah's laws and rules are perfect. Any man-made legal, moral, and ethical code, however sound and rational it may appear to be, will always be imperfect because of limitations, prejudices, and weaknesses of human beings. When Allah (SWT) prohibits acts it is because they are harmful to us. Those acts cannot become beneficial or permissible even if the whole world says otherwise.

Allah (SWT) does not desire any harm to befall His creatures. But we often bring harm upon ourselves. *Taqwa* is the protection from that harm. *Taqwa* is put into the heart of the believers to cause them to fear the punishment of Allah (SWT). The example of *taqwa* is like that of a thorny path. When you see a thorn, you keep away from it because of the fear of getting pricked by it. Similarly, when you see a sin, you keep away from it because of the fear of Allah.

The term *taqwa* has also to be understood in the context in which it is used in the Qur`an because it has different grades of meanings, some of which are: God-consciousness, righteousness, piety, and fear. A God-conscious person will always try to obey Allah (SWT) and seek His pleasure. He knows that by disobeying Allah (SWT), even if he escapes harm or punishment in this world, he will be punished in the hereafter, and the ultimate punishment is to fail in the hereafter, the consequence of which is hellfire. Addressing the believers, Allah says in the Qur`an,

يَا أَيُّهَا الَّذِينَ آمَنُوا قُوا أَنْفُسَكُمْ وَأَهْلِيكُمْ نَارًا ⬡

*O you who believe, save yourselves and your families from the Fire. (at-Tahreem, 66:6)*

Who are the people of *taqwa*, the *muttaqeen*? What are their attributes? What is so special about them? Let us see how Allah describes them in the Qur`an. Allah says in *Surat Aal 'Imran*,

وَسَارِعُوا إِلَى مَغْفِرَةٍ مِنْ رَبِّكُمْ وَجَنَّةٍ عَرْضُهَا السَّمَوَاتُ وَالْأَرْضُ أُعِدَّتْ لِلْمُتَّقِينَ ⬡

*Race with one another toward forgiveness from your Lord and toward a paradise the width of which spans the heavens and the earth. It has been prepared for the God-fearing. (Aal 'Imran, 3:133)*

So, the first thing a believer must realize is that he is weak and not free from sin. The person of *taqwa*, the *muttaqi*, is one who runs to seek Allah's forgiveness. The next *ayah* says,

الَّذِينَ يُنْفِقُونَ فِي السَّرَّاءِ وَالضَّرَّاءِ وَالْكَاظِمِينَ الْغَيْظَ وَالْعَافِينَ عَنِ النَّاسِ وَاللَّهُ يُحِبُّ الْمُحْسِنِينَ ⬡

*Those who spend (for Allah's sake) in prosperity and adversity, and those who control anger and forgive people. And Allah loves those who are good in their deeds. (Aal*

'Imran, 3:134)

"Spending" here implies not only spending of our wealth but also includes spending our time, our labor, our energy, our experience, our planning, and our priorities. So we have to ask ourselves how much we are spending from these things in the path of Allah and what priority does *deen* have in our lives.

The *muttaqeen* also control their anger and do not even show that they are angry. They forgive others out of love, and this is something very difficult, because people generally tend to be unforgiving and vengeful. If we can't control our anger over little things, how can we expect Allah not to get angry over our misdeeds? Allah says in the next verse in *Surat Aal 'Imran,*

وَالَّذِينَ إِذَا فَعَلُوا فَاحِشَةً أَوْ ظَلَمُوا أَنْفُسَهُمْ ذَكَرُوا اللَّهَ فَاسْتَغْفَرُوا لِذُنُوبِهِمْ وَمَنْ يَغْفِرُ الذُّنُوبَ إِلَّا اللَّهُ وَلَمْ يُصِرُّوا عَلَى مَا فَعَلُوا وَهُمْ يَعْلَمُونَ ۝

*And those who, when they commit an immorality or wrong themselves remember Allah and seek forgiveness for their sins - and who can forgive sins except Allah? - And [who] do not persist in what they have done while they know. (Aal 'Imran, 3:135)*

Here, "immorality" refers to all types of lewd, vulgar, and shameful deeds. A person wrongs himself when he commits sins because he puts himself in the path of harm. The person of *taqwa*—the *muttaqi*—as soon as he finds he has fallen into sin; he immediately remembers Allah (SWT) and asks for His forgiveness and his faith gives him hope. He abandons his wrong conduct and makes amends. He does not persist in doing anything wrong that he may have done.

Now let us reflect upon the qualities of the people of *taqwa* and see where we stand compared to them. Let us go through some of the verses of the Qur'an that mention the benefits and rewards for those who have *taqwa*.

ذَلِكَ الْكِتَابُ لَا رَيْبَ فِيهِ هُدًى لِّلْمُتَّقِينَ ۝

*This is the Book! There is no doubt in it; a guide to the muttaqeen. (al-Baqara, 2:2)*

وَاتَّقُوا اللَّهَ وَاعْلَمُوا أَنَّ اللَّهَ مَعَ الْمُتَّقِينَ ۝

*And have taqwa of Allah and know that Allah is with those who have taqwa. (al-Baqara, 2:194)*

وَاللَّهُ وَلِيُّ الْمُتَّقِينَ ۝

*Allah is the Protector of those who have taqwa. (al-Jathiya, 45:19)*

فَإِنَّ اللَّهَ يُحِبُّ الْمُتَّقِينَ ۝

*Allah loves those who have taqwa. (Aal'Imran, 3:76)*

وَمَنْ يَتَّقِ اللَّهَ يُكَفِّرْ عَنْهُ سَيِّئَاتِهِ وَيُعْظِمْ لَهُ أَجْرًا ۝

*Whoever has taqwa of Allah – He will erase his bad actions from him and greatly increase his reward. (at-Talaq, 65:5)*

وَمَنْ يَتَّقِ اللَّهَ يَجْعَلْ لَهُ مَخْرَجًا وَيَرْزُقْهُ مِنْ حَيْثُ لَا يَحْتَسِبُ ۝

*Whoever has taqwa of Allah — He will find a way out for him and provide for him from where he does not expect. (at-Talaq, 65:2-3)*

وَمَنْ يَتَّقِ اللَّهَ يَجْعَلْ لَهُ مِنْ أَمْرِهِ يُسْرًا ۝

*Whoever has taqwa of Allah — He will make matters easy for him. (at-Talaq, 65:4)*

إِنَّمَا يَتَقَبَّلُ اللَّهُ مِنَ الْمُتَّقِينَ ۝

*Allah only accepts from people who have taqwa. (al-Ma`ida, 5:27)*

إِنَّ الْمُتَّقِينَ فِي جَنَّاتٍ وَعُيُونٍ ۝

*The people with taqwa will be among gardens and springs. (adh-Dhariyat, 51:15)*

يَوْمَ نَحْشُرُ الْمُتَّقِينَ إِلَى الرَّحْمَنِ وَفْدًا ۝

*On that day, we will gather those who have taqwa as a delegation. (Maryam, 19:85)*

فَأَمَّا مَنْ أَعْطَى وَاتَّقَى ۝ وَصَدَّقَ بِالْحُسْنَى ۝ فَسَنُيَسِّرُهُ لِلْيُسْرَى ۝

*As for him who gives and has taqwa, and believes in the truth of the ultimate good, We will smooth his way toward ease. (al-Layl, 92:5-7)*

إِنَّ أَكْرَمَكُمْ عِنْدَ اللَّهِ أَتْقَاكُمْ ۝

*The noblest among you in Allah´s sight is the one with the most taqwa. (al-Hujurat, 49:13)*

وَاتَّقُوا اللَّهَ وَيُعَلِّمُكُمُ اللَّهُ ۝

*Have taqwa of Allah and Allah will give you knowledge. (al-Baqara, 2:282)*

May Allah make us of the people of *taqwa*, Ameen.

It is only Allah who knows the state or degree of *taqwa* of a person because the seat of *taqwa* is the heart. On one occasion, the Prophet (SAS) pointed his finger toward his heart and said, "*Taqwa* is here." And only Allah (SWT) knows what is in the heart of a person.

What are the ways to achieve *taqwa*? *Taqwa* is not something that can be achieved overnight. One has to consciously, persistently, and diligently work for it. Some of the means to achieve *taqwa* are:

We should remember Allah (SWT), and the best way of remembrance is through the Qur`an, which is also called the *dhikr* or "remembrance." In this sense, this would mean reading, understanding, and implementing the teachings of the Qur`an in our lives.

We should observe Allah's commandments and avoid His prohibitions.

We should repent for the sins of the past.

We should refrain from committing sins in the future.

We should be fearful of Allah whenever we think of committing a sin.

We should be hopeful of Allah's forgiveness.

We should guard our senses and ensure that what we see, hear, and say will not displease Allah.

We should remember death and know that the life of this *dunya* is only a passing phase where each one of us is being tested, both in prosperity and adversity.

Brothers and sisters! What better time could there be than this holy month of Ramadan to cultivate *taqwa* within us. The Qur`an tells us that the primary objective of fasting is to attain *taqwa*.

يَا أَيُّهَا الَّذِينَ آمَنُوا كُتِبَ عَلَيْكُمُ الصِّيَامُ كَمَا كُتِبَ عَلَى الَّذِينَ مِنْ قَبْلِكُمْ لَعَلَّكُمْ تَتَّقُونَ ⬡

*O you who believe, fasting is prescribed for you, as it was prescribed for those before*
*you, so that you may have taqwa. (al-Baqara, 2:183)*

May Allah turn our hearts toward *taqwa* and toward His obedience. May He guide us toward what is right and help us to resist what is wrong. May He make us among the *muttaqeen. Ameen.*

# • 33 •

# GRATITUDE TO ALLAH

In today's *khutbah*, I intend to share some thoughts with you on the subject of gratitude, or thankfulness and gratefulness to Allah (SWT). What is gratitude all about? What is its importance? What are its benefits? How to attain it? These are some of the issues that I will try to address in my *khutbah* today.

Gratitude is at the core of man's relationship with Allah (SWT). Gratitude helps us focus our minds on Allah, something that has unfortunately become so difficult today on account of life's attractions and distractions. Showing gratitude to Allah is an essential part of having faith in Him. This means that a person who is ungrateful to Allah has no true faith in his or her heart. Gratefulness to Allah may be expressed by the heart, by the tongue, or through good deeds and gestures. True gratefulness in the heart is manifested through sincere belief that all the blessings we have—our life, our body, our physical appearance, our abilities and accomplishments—are all from Allah. Allah says in the Qur`an,

وَمَا بِكُم مِّن نِّعْمَةٍ فَمِنَ اللَّهِ ◯

*Whatever blessing you have is from Allah. (an-Nahl, 16:53)*

Gratefulness or thankfulness by the body is shown by using one's limbs, organs, faculties, and abilities for the purposes for which they were created. It is reported that the Prophet Muhammad (SAS) used to pray at night until his feet became swollen, and when asked why he was doing this, when Allah had forgiven all his past and future wrong actions, his reply was, "Should I not be a grateful slave?" The Prophet (SAS) always thanked Allah and recommended his followers to do so. One of his favorite supplications is:

اللهم أعنّي على ذكرك و شكرك و حسن عبادتك ◯

*O Allah, help me remember You, to be grateful to You, and to worship You in an excellent manner.*

The more we thank Allah, the more He will grant us from His bounties, for He promises,

لَئِن شَكَرْتُمْ لَأَزِيدَنَّكُمْ ◯

*If you are thankful, I will give you more. (Ibraheem, 14:7)*

Yet, if we were to be ungrateful, Allah does not say outright that He will punish us, rather He leaves it open as if to remind us, "Look, My punishment is severe. That is all you need to know. So start becoming thankful for your own benefit."

وَلَئِن كَفَرْتُمْ إِنَّ عَذَابِي لَشَدِيدٌ ۝

*But if you are ungrateful, then know that My punishment is severe indeed. (Ibraheem, 14:7)*

The words *shakartum* and *kafartum* used in this *ayah* are derived from *shukr* meaning thankfulness, and *kufr* meaning thanklessness. The root *ka-fa-ra* means to cover something up, and that is why linguistically, a farmer in the Arabic language is also known as *kafir* because he covers up the seeds with the soil. In the religious sense, the *kafir* is one who is ungrateful because he covers up or conceals his *fitra*, the inborn *iman*, the faith that is embedded in the soul of every human being. Thus, he shows his ingratitude to Allah (SWT). *Shukr* and *kufr* are diametrically opposite to each other. This relationship between these two opposing concepts is highlighted elsewhere in the Qur'an where Allah pairs these two words together.

فَاذْكُرُونِي أَذْكُرْكُمْ وَاشْكُرُوا لِي وَلَا تَكْفُرُونِ ۝

*So remember Me; I will remember you. Be thankful to Me and do not be ungrateful. (al-Baqara, 2:152)*

Satan's ultimate goal is to make people into disbelievers by preventing them from being thankful to Allah. In a dialogue with Allah (SWT), Satan openly declared,

ثُمَّ لَآتِيَنَّهُم مِّنْ بَيْنِ أَيْدِيهِمْ وَمِنْ خَلْفِهِمْ وَعَنْ أَيْمَانِهِمْ وَعَنْ شَمَائِلِهِمْ وَلَا تَجِدُ أَكْثَرَهُمْ شَاكِرِينَ ۝

*Then I will surely come to them from before them and from behind them and from their right and from their left, and then You will find most of them ungrateful. (al-A'raf, 7:17)*

How important it is then to be grateful to Allah? The first and foremost step toward developing a feeling of gratitude and consciousness of Allah's boundless favors is to acknowledge and appreciate those favors. It is a general human weakness that if one is afflicted with a misfortune, they keep complaining about it to others. However, a person hardly speaks about the countless bounties that he or she enjoys. Allah declares in the Qur'an,

وَإِن تَعُدُّوا نِعْمَةَ اللَّهِ لَا تُحْصُوهَا إِنَّ اللَّهَ لَغَفُورٌ رَّحِيمٌ ۝

*If you tried to count God's blessings, you would never be able to calculate them. God is ever forgiving and most merciful. (an-Nahl, 16:18)*

A little reflection on the blessings we enjoy should be enough to make us realize that our lives would be miserable without them. Let me give you a very simple example. Do we truly thank Allah on coming out of the restroom after relieving ourselves? We often take things for granted. Just imagine the uneasiness one would feel, and the pain and agony one would undergo if one could not relieve oneself properly. That is why we are reminded through a Prophetic supplication to thank Allah every time we relieve ourselves by saying,

الْحَمْدُ لِلَّهِ الَّذِي أَذْهَبَ عَنِّي الْأَذَى وَعَافَانِي ◯

*All praise and thanks be to Allah who removed the difficulty and gave me ease.*

There are numerous Prophetic supplications for different occasions that teach us to thank Allah for His blessings. Although thankfulness is a religious act of great significance, few people truly do it. Allah says,

وَقَلِيلٌ مِّنْ عِبَادِيَ الشَّكُورُ ◯

*Few of my servants are truly thankful. (Saba`, 34:13)*

Also, we should avoid focusing on those who have been blessed with more than us, rather we should look more at those who have been given less than us, and there are so many. Those who fail to do this are always complaining about their problems and are never blessed with satisfaction or contentment. It is impossible for anyone to be in a state that is in all respects better than that of everyone else. There is always someone who has less or is tested more than we are.

Not recognizing Allah's blessings can prevent us from gaining His pleasure. We know that if Allah were to punish us for our negligence, He would be justified in doing so. We are informed by Allah (SWT) in the Qur`an,

وَلَوْ يُؤَاخِذُ اللَّهُ النَّاسَ بِمَا كَسَبُوا مَا تَرَكَ عَلَى ظَهْرِهَا مِنْ دَابَّةٍ وَلَكِنْ يُؤَخِّرُهُمْ إِلَى أَجَلٍ مُسَمًّى فَإِذَا جَاءَ أَجَلُهُمْ

فَإِنَّ اللَّهَ كَانَ بِعِبَادِهِ بَصِيرًا ◯

*If Allah were to take people to task for they have earned, He would not leave a single living creature on the surface of the earth; but He grants them respite until an appointed time; and when their appointed time comes, then they will know that Allah is indeed observant of all His servants. (Fatir, 35:45)*

But Allah provides us a way to escape that punishment by being thankful to Him. He says in *Surat an-Nisa`,*

مَا يَفْعَلُ اللَّهُ بِعَذَابِكُمْ إِنْ شَكَرْتُمْ وَآمَنْتُمْ وَكَانَ اللَّهُ شَاكِرًا عَلِيمًا ◯

*Why should Allah punish you if you are grateful to Him and believe in Him. Allah is all- appreciative; all-knowing. (an-Nisa`, 4:147)*

May Allah make us among those who sincerely praise Him and thank Him for all His blessings and favors.

Shaykh Sa'di Shirazi, a Persian poet of the 13th century, narrates a story in which he says that while he was traveling, he reached Damascus in a miserable condition. He did not have any money to buy new shoes to replace his old ones. It pained him that he was unable to buy a new pair of shoes. With these thoughts, he entered the mosque where he observed a person without feet. On seeing this, he immediately fell into prostration, thanking Allah profusely for having provided him with feet, even though he had no shoes.

This incident identifies the perspective with which we should look at things. Those with a feeling of gratitude observe numerous manifestations of Allah's favors, which then fill them with greater gratitude. However, there are others who are always complaining of what they do not have and are, therefore, unable to thank Allah for the many blessings He has bestowed upon them. Allah does not need our thanks and gratitude. It is in our benefit to be thankful.

وَمَنْ يَشْكُرْ فَإِنَّمَا يَشْكُرُ لِنَفْسِهِ وَمَنْ كَفَرَ فَإِنَّ اللَّهَ غَنِيٌّ حَمِيدٌ ۝

*He who is grateful, is grateful only for the good of his own soul. But if anyone is ungrateful, then surely Allah is self-sufficient and praiseworthy: (Luqman, 31:12)*

Gratitude helps us to slow down and to enjoy what we have rather than always waiting for the next wish to come true. Gratitude can help us recognize that we already have enough of what many people have long been yearning for. We must therefore tame our *nafs* to understand that if we can't find happiness in the blessings that we have today, then we won't be happy with what we get tomorrow. You see, gratitude is a sense of fulfillment that comes not from wanting more but rather from a sense of knowing that Allah has already blessed us with what we need.

Gratitude helps us recognize other people's favors to us. The Prophet (SAS) said, "He who does not thank people, does not thank Allah." Thus, he made it quite clear that expressing our gratitude to Allah by thanking Him also involves thanking people who do favors for us. There is another hadeeth in which the Prophet (SAS) says, "Whoever does you a favor, then reciprocate; and if you cannot find anything with which to reciprocate, then pray for him until you think that you have reciprocated him."

Gratitude also trains our minds to focus on the right things in life. When we let our minds look for problems, we see plenty of them. Instead, if we look away from problems and focus on possibilities and go for solutions, we will get those too. Therefore, let us use gratitude to motivate ourselves to find possibilities and solutions, and not focus on the negatives associated with problems.

Let me conclude by saying that having a sense of gratitude is a great blessing and those of us who work to grow that sense within ourselves not only seek Allah's pleasure but embody a sense of happiness, relieving us of many pressures and anxieties.

# 34

# GUARDING THE TONGUE

In my *khutbah* today, I wish to share some thoughts with you on Allah's amazing gift of the tongue that we humans have been endowed with. It is the gift of that fleshy muscular organ in our mouths used for articulating speech, among its many other functions. I will restrict my talk today only to the moral and ethical aspects of the tongue's function as an instrument and organ of speech, and how to best use it to please Allah rather than to displease Him.

Try to imagine a world without speech where communication is composed of just grunts and groans, not words. Without words, we are deprived of Allah's ultimate gift—divine guidance. Allah's guidance has come to us through the language of the Qur'an and the words of His Prophet (SAS). Keeping this in mind, we can begin to appreciate the blessings attached to our ability to speak.

It is the capacity to speak that allows us to communicate with our Creator through our prayers, supplications, repentance, and constant remembrance of Him. It allows us to recite the Qur'an, to communicate with each other, to give good advice, to soothe and comfort those in pain, to urge people to do good and forbid them from doing bad. It is through our ability to speak that we greet each other, thank each other, disseminate knowledge, and engage in *da'wa* activities.

We are responsible for what we look at, what we listen to, what we say, and what we do, for Allah has shown us the two paths of good and evil. Allah reminds us in the Qur'an,

أَلَمْ نَجْعَل لَّهُ عَيْنَيْنِ ۝ وَلِسَانًا وَشَفَتَيْنِ ۝ وَهَدَيْنَاهُ النَّجْدَيْنِ ۝

*Have We not given him two eyes, and a tongue, and a pair of lips, and shown him the two paths? (al-Balad, 90:8-10)*

However, just as one may become used to misusing one's eyes to look at things that are undesirable, and misusing one's ears to listen to things that are not right, one may also tend to misuse one's tongue to utter things that are blameworthy.

We lie, we criticize, we backbite, we use vulgar language, we exaggerate, we brag and boast, we falsely accuse others, we mimic, and we make fun of people. This kind of irresponsible speech sometimes has far-reaching consequences on the lives of others and can cause great harm and pain. Just as we will be held accountable for all our actions, big or small, so too we will be held accountable for each and every word that comes out of our mouths. There is a stern warning in the Qur'an regarding this.

مَا يَلْفِظُ مِنْ قَوْلٍ إِلاَّ لَدَيْهِ رَقِيبٌ عَتِيدٌ ۝

*Not a single word is uttered by anyone except that there is an observer near him, ready*
*(to record. (Qaf, 50:18)*

Indeed, this is a frightening prospect. During the course of the day, we say so many things without realizing how harmful they are. We pass remarks about people's looks, and about what we perceive to be people's negative traits. So-and-so is ugly, fat, stupid, lazy, worthless, and so on. We use abusive language. Worse still are the biting remarks some of us make without knowledge about Islam, about the Qur'an, about the prophets, and sometimes even about Allah, never stopping to think that it's all being recorded and will be presented to us on the Day of Resurrection. There are many Prophetic traditions on the issue of guarding and controlling one's tongue.

The Prophet (SAS) said, "Whosoever gives me a guarantee to safeguard what is between his jaws (meaning the tongue), and what is between his legs (meaning the private parts), I shall guarantee him paradise." We have to remember that on the Day of Judgment, our physical organs will stand as witnesses against us if we use them in the wrong way. As Allah says in *Surat an-Nur*,

يَوْمَ تَشْهَدُ عَلَيْهِمْ أَلْسِنَتُهُمْ وَأَيْدِيهِمْ وَأَرْجُلُهُم بِمَا كَانُوا يَعْمَلُونَ ۝

*On the Day when their own tongues, hands and feet shall bear witness against them*
*about what they did. (an-Nur, 24:24)*

According to a hadeeth, the Prophet (SAS) said, "Whoever believes in Allah and the Last Day, let him either speak good or keep silent." He also said, "The Muslim is the one from whose tongue and hand the Muslims are safe, and the emigrant (*muhajir*) is the one who abandons what Allah has forbidden." On another occasion he also said, "Most of the sins of the children of Adam are on their tongues."

It has been said that "Silence is wisdom, whereas few act according to it." It has also been said, "Speak only when your words are more beautiful than silence." One of the hallmarks of righteous behavior is good speech. A person who stays mindful of Allah will want to refrain from sins of the tongue such as backbiting, slander, gossip, lying, swearing, cursing, and vain talk. In the Qur'an and Sunnah Allah and His Messenger constantly warn us against these sins of the tongue.

Taking time to ask oneself the following questions will help avoid vain speech or idle talk: (1) "Will this saying of mine please Allah?" (2) "Will this saying of mine bring me closer to Allah?" and (3) "Does this saying reflect obedience to Allah?" If one is uncertain, he or she should keep quiet rather than risk saying something which contradicts Islamic belief or behavior. This doesn't mean that a person can't engage in casual conversation. Rather, it means that we should guard our speech and choose our words carefully.

The ultimate success for a Muslim is to be admitted into paradise. Good speech plays a role in earning that reward. *Surat al-Mu`minoon* begins with these words:

$$\text{قَدْ أَفْلَحَ الْمُؤْمِنُونَ ۝ الَّذِينَ هُمْ فِي صَلَاتِهِمْ خَاشِعُونَ ۝ وَالَّذِينَ هُمْ عَنِ اللَّغْوِ مُعْرِضُونَ ۝}$$

*Successful indeed are the believers; those who are humble in their prayers; Who avoid vain talk. (al-Mu`minoon, 23:1-3)*

Conversely, sins of the tongue can lead a Muslim to hell. The Prophet (SAS) said, "A man may be so close to paradise such that the distance between him and paradise is one arm's length and he speaks a word and he becomes distant from it further than Sana'a." (This means he goes very far away from paradise.) He also said, "The faith of a servant is not put right until his heart is put right, and his heart is not put right until his tongue is put right." This shows that the Prophet (SAS) has made the purification of faith conditional on the purification of the heart and the purification of the heart conditional on the purification of the tongue.

'Uqba ibn 'Amr reported, "I said: 'O Messenger of Allah, what action will save us?' The Messenger of Allah (SAS) said, 'Control your tongue, let your house be sufficient for you, and weep for your sins.'"

Brothers and sisters! How many of us weep over our sins? It is essential that we refrain from sins such as gossip, backbiting, slander, lying, and cursing. By remembering and fearing Allah, we will find it easier to choose our words carefully. May Allah give us the *tawfeeq* for this.

One tip for controlling the tongue is to think before speaking. The phrases "think before you speak" and "if you don't have something nice to say, don't say anything at all" seem to be worn out *clichés* and stereotyped expressions but they are not. They hold a lot of weight in the life of Muslims. We have become so accustomed to speaking without thinking that words just seem to fly out of our mouths before we know it. Take a few moments before you speak to evaluate whether what you are about to say is beneficial or necessary. When your thoughts wander to saying something unnecessary or possibly hurtful, turn your focus to doing *dhikr* or simply contemplating, rather than wasting time on unnecessary speech, which is not beneficial and could actually be harmful.

Also, as hard as it may be, if we do happen to say something that is hurtful to someone, simply apologize. This can have nothing but positive effects. Many of us have trouble apologizing to people and accepting our mistakes so saying "sorry" will humble us and ensure that we are more careful next time. Secondly, it can help improve our relationship with the other person because we are showing that we are aware of their feelings and that we care about them.

The company we keep also has a lot to do with controlling our tongues. If you are going to be with people, surround yourself with good company. It takes two to gossip. Most people who engage in backbiting and slandering will not do it all the time or with all people. In fact, they may have a select group of friends who share this habit. If you find that certain people make it easier for you to engage in this, stay clear of this crowd!

One way to atone for any slandering, lying, and backbiting is to identify those persons who you spoke about wrongly. Seek their forgiveness, and if this cannot be done for any reason, then at least mention them well and praise them in the same circles of people in which you had earlier spoken about them negatively.

If we evaluate the time we have spent talking and how much of that time was spent on productive talk versus unproductive talk, the results can be revealing. While some of us may have "the gift of the gab," meaning we can speak well, we should also train ourselves how not to speak. This can help us to reflect on exactly how useful silence is. Indeed, the Prophetic teachings tell us that we should remain silent, especially if we do not have anything good to say.

Last but not least, we should make it our habit to mention the name of Allah (SAS) in our conversations. Without this, there is little protection from falling into the traps of Satan and losing control of our tongues. We will be asked to account for every word we say. Let our speech not be the source of regret in the hereafter. Let us make our tongues moist with the remembrance of Allah (SWT).

My dear brothers and sisters! I advise myself first and all of us to refrain from vain talk, to stop spreading rumors, to verify any news before jumping to conclusions, to stop all types of backbiting against one another, to speak softly and gently, to increase our knowledge of Islam, to learn and teach, to take the initiative of making *da'wa* for the love and pleasure of Allah, to keep busy in doing something good for ourselves and for others, and to keep watch over our mistakes and sins.

May Allah accept our repentance for the irresponsible use of the precious gifts of our tongues, our eyes, our ears, our limbs, and our intellect. May He make us among those from whom others are safe. *Ameen!*

# 35

# GUIDANCE

Today's *khutbah* is on the topic of understanding guidance from the Islamic perspective. We as Muslims beg Allah to be guided to the straight path at least seventeen times a day due to the obligation of reciting *Surat al-Fatiha* in our five daily prayers. We are taught to say,

اهْدِنَا الصِّرَاطَ الْمُسْتَقِيمَ ۝

*Guide us to the straight path. (al-Fatiha, 1:6)*

Have we ever reflected upon the nature of this guidance and the straight path that we are supposed to be upon? In Arabic, the word *hidaya* means "guidance." The word *hadiyya*, or gift, also comes from the same root letters as the word for *hidaya*. Religious guidance is the greatest gift that a person can possess. It is also something that we do not control or own, rather it is bestowed upon us in an act of infinite mercy and grace by Allah (SWT). Guidance has several degrees.

The first degree of guidance is general, given to all creation, and it covers everything that is in the universe. By this guidance, the animals, plants, minerals and all other inanimate objects fulfill the purpose for which they are created. Thanks to this general guidance, everything in the universe is performing its allotted function with precision and efficiency. That is to say, Allah has given every created thing a particular nature and function and guided it in a way which should correspond to its station in the scheme of things. When Fir'awn asked Musa (AS) to tell him who his Lord was, Musa (AS) said,

رَبُّنَا الَّذِي أَعْطَى كُلَّ شَيْءٍ خَلْقَهُ ثُمَّ هَدَى ۝

*Our Lord is He who gives each thing its created form and then guides it. (Ta Ha, 20:50)*

Allah also makes it quite clear in the Qur'an that all forms of existence in the universe and every particle of dust possesses life, sensitivity, and even consciousness and understanding in its own way, and according to its own sphere of existence. In an *ayah* in *Surat al-Isra`* Allah informs us,

وَإِن مِّن شَيْءٍ إِلَّا يُسَبِّحُ بِحَمْدِهِ وَلَٰكِن لَّا تَفْقَهُونَ تَسْبِيحَهُمْ ۝

*There is not a single thing that does not celebrate His praise, though you do not understand their praise. (al-Isra`, 17:44)*

The second degree of guidance, unlike the first, is not general but particular. It is limited to those creatures which are considered to be rational, that is, endowed with the faculty of reason. These include the humans and jinn. This kind of guidance comes to every human being through prophets and revealed books. Some accept this guidance and become believers while others reject it and become disbelievers. This is the type of *hidaya*, or guidance referred to in *Surat al-Insan*, where Allah (SWT) says,

إِنَّا هَدَيْنَاهُ السَّبِيلَ إِمَّا شَاكِرًا وَإِمَّا كَفُورًا ۝

*We have guided him to the path, whether he be one who is thankful or ungrateful. (al-Insan, 76:3)*

The third degree of guidance is still more particular, being special to the true believers, to the God-fearing, and to the virtuous among people. Like the first degree, the third kind of guidance also descends directly to the individual from Allah, and it is called *tawfeeq*. This is Allah's grace which provides an individual with means and circumstances that make it easy, and even pleasant for him or her to accept and act upon divine guidance and makes it difficult to ignore or oppose it. The scope of the third degree of guidance is limitless. Increase in virtuous deeds brings with it an increase in divine guidance. Allah gives us the promise of this increase in the Qur`an.

وَالَّذِينَ اهْتَدَوْا زَادَهُمْ هُدًى وَآتَاهُمْ تَقْوَاهُمْ ۝

*And those who are guided, He increases their guidance, and grants them piety and protection from sinning. (Muhammad, 47:17)*

وَالَّذِينَ جَاهَدُوا فِينَا لَنَهْدِيَنَّهُمْ سُبُلَنَا وَإِنَّ اللَّهَ لَمَعَ الْمُحْسِنِينَ ۝

*As for those who strive in our cause, We will guide them to Our paths. For God is with those who do good. (al-'Ankabut, 29:69)*

It is in this field of progress that we see the prophets and their followers striving, seeking increase in divine guidance and help till their last breath. Allah tells us in the Qur`an that the Prophet Shu'ayb (AS) said,

وَمَا تَوْفِيقِي إِلَّا بِاللَّهِ ۝

*And my guidance (or success) can only come from Allah. (Hud, 11:88)*

Keeping in mind the three distinct degrees of guidance, one can easily see that guidance is a thing which everyone does possess in some way, and yet everyone still needs to achieve more advanced and higher stages of guidance. Hence, of all the prayers man can address to Allah, the most important is the prayer for guidance, which has been taught to us in the very first *surah* of the Qur`an. This prayer is as necessary for the greatest of prophets and men of Allah as it is for an ordinary Muslim.

To avoid any confusion, it is important to note that Allah sometimes speaks in the Qur`an of the type of divine guidance that is general and common to believers and nonbelievers along with all creatures, and sometimes He discusses the type of guidance that is particular and special to the God-fearing. On one hand, Allah reminds us that He does not grant guidance to the transgressors and the unrighteous and on the other hand, He declares that He guides all. The misunderstanding which may arise here is removed by knowledge of the degrees of guidance. The general guidance is given to all without any distinction, but the third and very special degree of guidance is not granted to those who rebel or refuse guidance.

The first and the third degrees of guidance pertain to a direct act of divine grace, and no prophet can have anything to do with it, for the function of the prophets is related only to the second degree—that is they are guides.

$$وَلِكُلِّ قَوْمٍ هَادٍ \bigcirc$$

*And for every people there is a guide. (ar-Ra'd)*

It is neither the function of a prophet nor is it in his power to provide *tawfeeq* to anyone, or to make it easy for anyone to accept guidance. Addressing the Prophet Muhammad (SAS), Allah says in *Surat al-Qasas,*

$$\bigcirc إِنَّكَ لَا تَهْدِي مَنْ أَحْبَبْتَ وَلَكِنَّ اللَّهَ يَهْدِي مَن يَشَاءُ وَهُوَ أَعْلَمُ بِالْمُهْتَدِينَ$$

*You cannot guide those you would like to but Allah guides those He wills. He has best knowledge of the guided. (al-Qasas, 28:56)*

Those of us who invite or guide others to Islam should be humbled and should internalize the fact that we have no real power over this matter, and that true guidance is the sole dominion of Allah, the "Turner of Hearts." This should not make us lose hope in the work we do, for our ultimate reward is with Allah. Rather it should increase our confidence in inviting others, knowing that the result is not dependent on our *da'wa* or speech, but it is in the hands of Allah, the One who can instantly change the hearts of the most wicked and tyrannical into the most pure and righteous. We ask Allah (SWT) to turn our hearts to His *deen* and to His obedience. We are taught by the Prophet (SAS) to say the following *du'a`:*

$$يَا مُقَلِّبَ الْقُلُوبِ ثَبِّتْ قُلُوبَنَا عَلَى دِينِكَ$$

*O, Turner of the hearts, keep our hearts firm on Your deen (religion).*

$$اللَّهُمَّ مُصَرِّفَ الْقُلُوبِ صَرِّفْ قُلُوبَنَا عَلَى طَاعَتِكَ$$

*O Allah, the Turner of the hearts, turn our hearts to your obedience.*

My dear respected brothers and sisters! We have a divine principle mentioned in *Surat an-Najm*, which is very clear and straightforward.

$$\text{لَيْسَ لِلْإِنسَانِ إِلَّا مَا سَعَىٰ} \bigcirc$$

*Man can have nothing but what he strives for. (an-Najm, 53:39)*

Applying this general rule, one must strive hard to qualify to become the recipient of the precious gift of guidance. It does not come to the one who does not want to be guided or who does not work hard enough to be guided. That is why the special degree of guidance is not granted to the unjust and the unrighteous.

In *Surat al-Fatiha* we are instructed by Allah to ask for guidance to the straight path, *as-sirat al-mustaqeem*. The path that we are asking to be guided to is the path of Islam itself. It is a straight path as it is a correct and firmly established way that is pure and protected from any crookedness or deviation from the truth. Islam is also easy as Allah (SWT) has said,

$$\text{يُرِيدُ اللَّهُ بِكُمُ الْيُسْرَ وَلَا يُرِيدُ بِكُمُ الْعُسْرَ} \bigcirc$$

*Allah desires ease for you; He does not desire difficulty for you. (al-Baqara, 2:185)*

The Prophet (SAS) said, "The *deen* is easy. Anyone who makes the *deen* too hard on himself will find that it becomes too much for him. So aim for what is right, follow a middle path, and head for the goal in the morning, evening, and some of the night, and you will reach the goal." Allah clearly says in the Qur`an,

$$\text{لَا يُكَلِّفُ اللَّهُ نَفْسًا إِلَّا وُسْعَهَا} \bigcirc$$

*Allah does not burden a soul beyond its capacity. (al-Baqara, 2:286)*

There will be challenges, temptations, and difficulties in living as a Muslim, but they are challenges that we ultimately have the capacity to bear. Everything in shari`a (Islamic law) benefits us or wards off harm from us. Islam, which is submission to the commands of Allah (SWT), is also a familiar and well-trodden path, the path of all the prophets and their followers. As Allah (SWT) says,

$$\text{وَمَن يُطِعِ اللَّهَ وَالرَّسُولَ فَأُولَٰئِكَ مَعَ الَّذِينَ أَنْعَمَ اللَّهُ عَلَيْهِم مِّنَ النَّبِيِّينَ وَالصِّدِّيقِينَ وَالشُّهَدَاءِ وَالصَّالِحِينَ وَحَسُنَ أُولَٰئِكَ رَفِيقًا} \bigcirc$$

*Whoever obeys Allah and the Messenger will be with those whom Allah has blessed: the Prophets and the truthful, the martyrs and the righteous. What excellent company such people are. (an-Nisa`, 4:69)*

The final and universal revelation of Islam is wide and spacious and accommodates all, regardless of color, race, or social status. And indeed, the path of Islam leads to the desired destination, which is Allah's pleasure gained by obeying Him. Allah tells us in the Qur`an,

فَأَمَّا الَّذِينَ آمَنُوا بِاللَّهِ وَاعْتَصَمُوا بِهِ فَسَيُدْخِلُهُمْ فِي رَحْمَةٍ مِّنْهُ وَفَضْلٍ وَيَهْدِيهِمْ إِلَيْهِ صِرَاطًا مُّسْتَقِيمًا ۝

*Allah will admit those who believe in Him and hold fast to Him into His mercy and favor; He will guide them toward Him on a straight path. (an-Nisa`, 4:175)*

The one who is guided in this life to the straight path will be guided to the straight path in the hereafter that leads to paradise. Paradise is the ultimate destination that each one of us desires, and Allah tells us in the Qur`an that while entering paradise the believers will say,

الْحَمْدُ لِلَّهِ الَّذِي هَدَانَا لِهَذَا وَمَا كُنَّا لِنَهْتَدِيَ لَوْلَا أَنْ هَدَانَا اللَّهُ ۝

*Praise be to Allah who has guided us to this! We would not have been guided, had Allah not guided us. (al-A'raf, 7:43)*

May Allah (SWT) make us among those who are truly guided, *Ameen.*


• 36 •

# HAJJ: TAKING LESSONS FROM THE PILGRIMAGE


My *khutbah* today is on the topic of taking lessons from hajj. *Al-hamduli-llah*, we are passing through the first ten days of the month of *Dhu al-Hijja* which is the 12th month of the Islamic calendar. These are the days when pilgrims make a journey to Mecca to perform hajj. These days are blessed for both pilgrims and non-pilgrims. Rewards of good deeds are multiplied in these days. The Prophet (SAS) said, "There are no days in which righteous deeds are more beloved to Allah than these ten days."

One of the reasons why these days are distinguished is due to this being the time in which all of our foundational acts of worship are collectively carried out: prayers, fasting, charity, and hajj are carried out in conjunction with one another at the same time. These acts are not carried out collectively in any other days. Just as the month of Ramadan is a period of attaining *taqwa* and God-consciousness throughout the

Islamic world, so also is hajj a time for revival of hearts and a time for reawakening of the Muslim *ummah*.

Hajj, which is one of the five pillars of Islam, has been part of our heritage for many hundreds of years. It is more effective and powerful than any other human gathering, and it serves as an example of the movement of Islam throughout the world. Islam is the most powerful movement in the world, motivating human beings in the name of Allah and making them into a brotherhood transcending race, color, and nationality. As long as the Ka'ba remains the center of the Islamic world, it will be impossible to end the life of this body of the Muslim *ummah*.

We usually think of journeys as being one of two kinds: those made for business and those made for pleasure. In both cases, we leave our homes and families and spend money on a journey to fulfill our worldly desires and to benefit ourselves. The journey is undertaken purely for our own sake. But the journey to perform hajj is quite different. This journey is not meant for any personal end. It is undertaken solely for Allah, and for fulfillment of the duty prescribed by Allah. The person going for hajj is prepared to incur great expenses on a journey that will bring no material rewards.

Let us reflect upon some of the many lessons that we could learn from hajj and the great benefits for Muslims, both individually and collectively, to be attained from it.

One important lesson to be derived from hajj is one of attaining *taqwa* or God-consciousness leading to righteousness and piety. While ordaining the rules and ethics of hajj, Allah says in *Surat al-Baqara*,

وَتَزَوَّدُوا فَإِنَّ خَيْرَ الزَّادِ التَّقْوَى وَاتَّقُونِ يَا أُولِي الْأَلْبَابِ ۝

*Provide well for yourselves: the best provision is to be mindful of Allah- always be mindful of Me, O people of intelligence. (al-Baqara, 2:197)*

Referring to the practice of sacrificing animals, Allah says in *Surat al-Hajj*,

لَنْ يَنَالَ اللَّهَ لُحُومُهَا وَلَا دِمَاؤُهَا وَلَكِنْ يَنَالُهُ التَّقْوَى مِنْكُمْ ۝

*Their flesh and blood do not reach Allah but what reaches Him is your taqwa. (al-Hajj, 22:37)*

In another verse of *Surat al-Hajj* Allah tells us that honoring the sacred rites ordained by Allah is an outgrowth of the piety of hearts.

وَمَنْ يُعَظِّمْ شَعَائِرَ اللَّهِ فَإِنَّهَا مِنْ تَقْوَى الْقُلُوبِ ۝

*As for those who honor Allah´s sacred rites; that comes from the taqwa in their hearts. (al-Hajj, 22:32)*

Ibraheem (AS) gave Muslims a great lesson by doing exactly what Allah ordered him to do. Once he passed the test, Allah showered His mercy upon him and made his great sacrifice a confirmed act of *sunnah* for Muslims until the Day of Judgment. This is a great lesson of love and sacrifice and comes only with piety of the heart.

Hence, to show their love and obedience to Allah, the people of *taqwa*, despite their natural human inclination to love money, keep away from practices involving usury, gambling, cheating, false oaths, and all types of injustices since they are ordered by Allah to refrain from such evil practices. Despite their other natural desires, they keep their gaze lowered, maintain their chastity, and guard their private parts, all because Allah has ordered them to do so. Therefore, one of the most important lessons of hajj is to cultivate within oneself the *taqwa* of Allah (SWT).

A second lesson is that of unity and brotherhood. Just visualize what it must be like to see people from countless communities and countries converging on one center from the east and from the west, from the north and from the south. Their faces are different, their colors are different, their languages are different, but on reaching a point near the center, all pilgrims replace their differently designed garments they are wearing for a simple uniform of the same design. This single, common uniform of *ihram* distinguishes them as the army of one single King. It becomes the symbol of obedience and submissiveness to the One Supreme Being.

Acquiring good morals is another lesson from hajj. Pilgrims are trained to be tolerant and patient. They have to restrain their anger, which could be aggravated by the extraordinary presence of the multitude of people all around them, by tiredness, and by the fatigue experienced while performing the rites of hajj. Pilgrims know that hajj is performed during a limited number of days and they do not want to nullify their hajj by giving free rein to their evil desires or by becoming intolerant and impatient. They learn to be generous, righteous, and merciful, and to favor other people over themselves. When they get used to enduring hardships and practicing good morals during the hajj days, they will hopefully maintain good morals for the rest of their lives.

Another lesson from hajj is to become accustomed to being in state of constant *dhikr* or the remembrance of Allah. This is because *tawaf, sa'iy, rami al-jamra, wuqoof al-'Arafa, udhiya,* and all other rites and rituals were legislated in order to remember Allah. When pilgrims remember Allah constantly while performing these acts of worship, they feel assured. They have peace of mind and heart, and they draw closer to Allah. All this leaves a mark on their hearts and helps them to get accustomed to remembering Allah even after hajj.

Yet another lesson is to get used to making *du'a* or supplication and to repent sincerely for one's sins and shortcomings. The hajj trip is a great opportunity for supplicating to Allah as pilgrims have many merits that make their supplications more likely to be answered. This is because pilgrims supplicate during honored days and at honored places. There are certain rites and rituals and certain times when *du'a* is more worthy of being answered. The hajj season makes the pilgrims get used to invoking Allah in the future as well.

Time management is also an important lesson that pilgrims learn from hajj. There is no time to be wasted during the limited period of hajj. Many rites, rituals, and activities have to be carried out meticulously with the optimum utilization of time. Every pilgrim strives sincerely toward perfect time management so that his or her hajj is accepted by Allah (SWT). Naturally, this is a lesson for life and not just for the four days of hajj. May Allah (SWT) give us the *tawfeeq* to put in practice these useful lessons in our daily lives.

My dear brothers and sisters! Being thankful and grateful to Allah (SWT) is another lesson that hajj offers. During hajj, a pilgrim sees many people who are physically challenged and some others who may even be completely incapacitated. He thanks Allah for granting him health. He also sees the poor and the needy. So, he thanks Allah for granting him wealth. He sees crowds of people sitting on the ground, sleeping in the tents, and remembers the spacious place where he lives, back home, and thanks Allah for this. He praises Allah for making him perform hajj and making it easy for him while many other Muslims long for hajj but cannot perform it. He also thanks Allah for making him a Muslim and this makes him adhere to Islam and to live Islam as a way of life.

The hajj also provides a vivid remembrance of the hereafter and particularly of the Day of Judgment. When a pilgrim sees crowds of people surging over each other at one place, humbling themselves to the Almighty, he too is humbled with the awe and love of Allah. He remembers the Day of Judgment when he will be called upon to give an account of his life on earth. He begins to avoid indulging in useless and time-wasting activities and starts preparing himself for the day he will meet His Lord.

Another lesson is a reminder that Shaytan (Satan) is a clear enemy to man. Allah (SWT) has ordered us to take him as an enemy and never to follow in his footsteps. People of understanding learn this lesson and realize the wisdom of *rami al-jamra* or stoning the devil, which is a symbolic rite of rejecting the Shaytan and his temptations. They apply this lesson when dealing with allies of Shaytan from among humans and jinn who want to prevent them from obeying Allah (SWT). They know that anyone who tries to sidetrack them from the way of Allah is a *shaytan* regardless of his appearance and behavior. They detest Shaytan, keep away from him, and seek Allah's refuge from him and his agents.

Let me conclude by saying that combined with prayer, fasting, and charity, and seen as a whole, we can see that hajj constitutes a preparation for the great task which Islam wants Muslims to do. This is why it has been made compulsory for all who have the money and the physical fitness for the journey to the Ka'ba. This ensures that, in every age, there are Muslims who have passed through this training.

Now that we have discussed some of the valuable lessons that can be derived from hajj, what is the reality on the ground? Every year, nearly three million pilgrims go to the center of Islam and come back after having had the privilege of performing hajj, but does that experience have the desired positive effect on all of them? Do the pilgrims who have returned home make any impact on their people and communities after their return from hajj? Unfortunately, many of them persist in their former undesirable habits and lifestyles that they had before performing hajj. Yet if hajj is performed as it is intended to be, it would change the lives of millions of Muslims, and attract thousands of non-Muslims to Islam.

May Allah (SWT) accept the hajj of all the *hujjaj*. May Allah accept their *tawaf*, their *sa'iy*, their sacrifice, their *salah*, and their *du'a`*. May Allah (SWT) forgive our sins and help us to turn to Him. *Allahumma ameen.*

•  37  •

# HOW TO SAVE OURSELVES
# FROM SATAN

The topic of today's *khutbah* is how to save ourselves from Satan. We are repeatedly told in the Qur`an that Satan deceives us, that he is our enemy, and that we should treat him as such. We are warned not to be deceived by him. First of all, Satan deceives us about Allah.

وَلَا يَغُرَّنَّكُم بِاللَّهِ الْغَرُورُ ○

*Do not let the Deceiver deceive you about Allah. (Fatir, 35:5)*

How does Satan deceive us about Allah? One of the ways he does that is to make some people believe that Allah does not exist at all. He involves other people in the misunderstanding that Allah, after having once created the world, has retired and has now practically nothing to do with the running of the universe. He misleads others into thinking that even though Allah runs the universe, He has taken no responsibility for providing guidance to creation. Therefore, revelation and prophethood are a mere deception. Satan gives false hope to some by emphasizing that since Allah is All-Forgiving and All-Merciful, He will forgive a person no matter what, even if they commit blatant sins on purpose without repentance. Satan makes some others believe that Allah has beloved ones, and if one remains attached and devoted to them, success and salvation are assured regardless of what the individual does themselves in life. We are warned in the Qur`an that Satan is our enemy.

إِنَّ الشَّيْطَانَ لَكُمْ عَدُوٌّ فَاتَّخِذُوهُ عَدُوًّا ۝

*Satan is your enemy so treat him as an enemy. (Fatir, 35:6)*

The way we save ourselves from the accursed Satan is not to follow in his footsteps, and to submit wholeheartedly to the will of Allah (SWT).

يَا أَيُّهَا الَّذِينَ آمَنُوا ادْخُلُوا فِي السِّلْمِ كَافَّةً وَلَا تَتَّبِعُوا خُطُوَاتِ الشَّيْطَانِ إِنَّهُ لَكُمْ عَدُوٌّ مُبِينٌ ۝

*O you who believe, enter wholeheartedly into Islam and do not follow in Satan's footsteps, for he is your sworn enemy. (al-Baqara, 2:208)*

We need to keep reminding ourselves about our Islamic way of life – *deen* – that embraces our individual as well as our collective lives.

وَذَكِّرْ فَإِنَّ الذِّكْرَىٰ تَنفَعُ الْمُؤْمِنِينَ ۝

*And remind, for indeed, the reminder benefits the believers. (adh-Dhariyat, 51:55)*

Every day, we experience many whisperings from Satan. Some lead us to sin and some lead us to abandon what we should be doing as Muslims. It is our duty to safeguard ourselves from these whisperings so that Satan does not mislead us. One of the effective ways to ignore whisperings of the Satan is to be aware of them, and then once we have recognized them, we actively work to ignore them. We should be quick to recognize the feelings that usually mean that Satan is whispering to us. Sometimes we have a feeling that we are being driven by our temptations to do bad deeds. Other times we experience feelings of laziness or procrastination that prevents us from doing good deeds. When we sense these feelings, we should actively ignore that whispering. It comes from Satan, and Satan has one desire: to make the believers go astray, make them confused, make their life miserable, and cause them distress to the extent that they distance themselves from the Islamic faith or leave Islam without realizing it. What is the Prophetic methodology to keep oneself protected from Satan? This is important to know as the Prophet (SAS) is our model. Allah (SWT) says in the Qur`an,

لَقَدْ كَانَ لَكُمْ فِي رَسُولِ اللَّهِ أُسْوَةٌ حَسَنَةٌ لِمَنْ كَانَ يَرْجُو اللَّهَ وَالْيَوْمَ الْآخِرَ وَذَكَرَ اللَّهَ كَثِيرًا ۝

*The Messenger of Allah is an excellent model for those of you who put your hope in Allah and the Last Day and remember Allah often. (al-Ahzab, 33:21)*

The Prophet (SAS) did not let a moment or an occasion pass by without invoking Allah (SWT). Thus, he began his day by supplicating to Allah at the time he woke up and invoked Allah before going to bed. In between morning and night, he supplicated to Allah on all possible occasions and situations as mundane as entering and exiting the home, before and after eating and drinking, visiting the marketplace, entering and exiting the mosque, putting on a garment and taking it off, visiting the toilet and coming out of it, making ablution (wudu`), visiting the sick, looking into the mirror, travelling to a place and returning from it, and so forth. He would make other supplications glorifying Allah, praising Allah, thanking Allah, and seeking His mercy, forgiveness, and refuge. These supplications for different occasions are found in various books of hadeeths and specific books of Prophetic supplications. It is highly recommended that we should memorize as many of these supplications as we can and make them a constant source of remembering and invoking Allah (SWT). Allah says in the Qur`an,

وَإِمَّا يَنزَغَنَّكَ مِنَ الشَّيْطَانِ نَزْغٌ فَاسْتَعِذْ بِاللَّهِ إِنَّهُ سَمِيعٌ عَلِيمٌ ○

*And if an evil whisper comes to you from Satan, then seek refuge with Allah. Verily, He is All-Hearer, All-Knower. (al-A'raf, 7:200)*

Saying *a'oodhu bi l-laahi min ash-shaytani ar-rajeem* which means "I seek the protection of Allah from Satan the accursed" is one of the best ways to repel the whispers of Satan. Whenever you find yourself thinking about doing something that you know is sinful or when you feel yourself getting angry, say this phrase and try to change your thoughts so that Satan will not have a hold over you. We read in *Surat al-Mu`minoon* that Allah tells us,

وَقُل رَّبِّ أَعُوذُ بِكَ مِنْ هَمَزَاتِ الشَّيَاطِينِ وَأَعُوذُ بِكَ رَبِّ أَن يَحْضُرُونِ ○

*And say, 'My Lord, I seek refuge in You from the temptations of the devils, and I seek refuge in You, my Lord, so they may not come near me. (al-Mu`minoon, 23:97-98)*

Another way to seek refuge from Satan is to recite the last two chapters of the Holy Qur`an—*Surat al-Falaq* and *Surat an-Nas*— by supplicating for Allah's protection from all evil. One of the tricks Satan uses with those who are obedient to Allah (SWT) is to sow discord among the Muslims, especially between friends who are righteous. The Prophet (SAS) said, "Satan has lost hope of being worshipped in the Arabian Peninsula, but he will sow seeds of discord among them." Imam An-Nawawi explains that this means that he has despaired of being worshipped by the people of the Arabian Peninsula, but he will strive to sow discord among them with arguments, disputes, wars, and tribulations.

Another of Satan's ploys is to make righteous company hateful to people and causes them to prefer harmful isolation. The Prophet (SAS) tells us, "There are no three men in a town or in the desert among whom prayer is not established, but the Satan has taken control of them, so you must adhere to the collective (*jama'a*) for the wolf only eats the sheep that wanders away on its own." Having good company, frequenting the *masjid* for congregational prayers, and avoiding debates among different factions of Muslims all help a person to keep himself protected from Satan's attacks.

We should do our best to be in the company of the righteous believers. They will motivate you to want to read the Qur'an, to go to the *masjid*, and to do righteous deeds. They will inspire you to do things that will keep the whispers of Satan away from you. Satan finds it easy to penetrate our minds through the company that we keep. For example, if you hang out with your friends in a place and they drink alcohol while you don't, there is bound to be someone who will try to persuade you into having some alcohol yourself. They may say things like, "It will help you relax." Know that Satan is whispering to you through whoever says this. The Prophet (SAS) said, "A man follows the religion of his friend so each one should consider whom he makes his friend." One of the best defenses against Satan and his whisperings is to have faith and trust in Allah (SWT) for we are informed in Surat an-Nahl,

$$\text{إِنَّهُ لَيْسَ لَهُ سُلْطَانٌ عَلَى الَّذِينَ آمَنُوا وَعَلَىٰ رَبِّهِمْ يَتَوَكَّلُونَ ۝}$$

*Truly he (Satan) has no power over those who believe and trust in their Lord. (an-Nahl, 16:99)*

The message, therefore, is clear. We must direct our attention not to what works in helping Satan in his goals, but to the *taqwa* or reverential fear of Allah (SWT) by doing what He wants us to do.

$$\text{وَمَنْ يَتَّقِ اللَّهَ يَجْعَلْ لَهُ مَخْرَجًا وَيَرْزُقْهُ مِنْ حَيْثُ لَا يَحْتَسِبُ ۝}$$

*Whoever has the taqwa of Allah, He will find a way for him to get out (of every difficulty). And will provide him from (sources) he never could imagine. (at-Talaq, 65:2-3)*

Another weapon used by Satan is to induce fear in the hearts of human beings. He tries to frighten the believers with apprehension of various consequences and difficulties in following the straight path.

$$\text{الشَّيْطَانُ يَعِدُكُمُ الْفَقْرَ وَيَأْمُرُكُمْ بِالْفَحْشَاءِ وَاللَّهُ يَعِدُكُمْ مَغْفِرَةً مِّنْهُ وَفَضْلًا وَاللَّهُ وَاسِعٌ عَلِيمٌ ۝}$$

*Satan promises you poverty and orders you to commit immoral acts. Allah promises you His forgiveness and abundance. Allah is bountiful and all-knowing. (al-Baqara, 2:268)*

Allah (SWT) warns us that one of Satan's tactics is to make us fear his friends, supporters, and followers.

إِنَّمَا ذَٰلِكُمُ الشَّيْطَانُ يُخَوِّفُ أَوْلِيَاءَهُ فَلَا تَخَافُوهُمْ وَخَافُونِ إِن كُنتُم مُّؤْمِنِينَ ◯

*It is Satan who urges you to fear his followers; do not fear them, but fear Me, if you are true believers. (Aal'Imran, 3:175)*

We should engage in *dhikr* or remembrance of Allah to ward off Satan's whisperings. Imam An-Nawawi said, "When the Satan hears *dhikr*, he slinks away, and *la ilaha illa Allah* ("there is no God but Allah") is the best of *dhikr*. The most effective remedy for warding off whisperings of Satan is to remember Allah a great deal." There are many *adhkar* that are found in the popular book *Fortress of the Muslim* (called *Hisn al-Muslim* in Arabic). May Allah (SWT) make us among those who are in constant remembrance of Him, *ameen*.

Brothers and sisters! The confidence Satan expressed in his ability to mislead people stems from his assurance that most people are ungrateful to Allah (SWT). What did Satan claim? As Allah tells us in the Qur`an, Satan said,

ثُمَّ لَآتِيَنَّهُم مِّن بَيْنِ أَيْدِيهِمْ وَمِنْ خَلْفِهِمْ وَعَنْ أَيْمَانِهِمْ وَعَن شَمَائِلِهِمْ وَلَا تَجِدُ أَكْثَرَهُمْ شَاكِرِينَ ◯

*I will approach them from their front, their back, their right, their left, and then You will find most of them ungrateful. (al-A'raf, 7:17)*

So, one of the antidotes against attacks from Satan is to be in a state of constant consciousness of Allah (SWT) and know that He is with us and He is watching us. And of course, we have to be grateful to Allah (SWT) for whatever blessings we have are from Him.

وَمَا بِكُم مِّن نِّعْمَةٍ فَمِنَ اللَّهِ ◯

*Whatever blessing you have is from Allah. (an-Nahl, 16:53)*

Satan also induces false confidence in a person, making him feel that he has reached perfection or that he is far better than others. This leads to arrogance, self-admiration, and distancing oneself from reality. As a result, the person starts viewing others with contempt. And we know that it was Satan's arrogance that drew the wrath and curse of Allah (SWT) upon him.

When we fall into our temptations to commit wrongdoing, we should remind ourselves that even Satan knows the truth, yet he is determined to make us earn Allah's anger. Let us remember that when the judgment has been passed on the Day of Judgment, Satan will simply say,

وَمَا كَانَ لِيَ عَلَيْكُم مِّن سُلْطَانٍ إِلَّا أَن دَعَوْتُكُمْ فَاسْتَجَبْتُمْ لِي فَلَا تَلُومُونِي وَلُومُوا أَنفُسَكُم ◯

*I did not have any authority over you. I only called you, and you responded to me. So do not blame me; blame yourselves. (Ibraheem, 14:22)*

The Qur`an and Sunnah tell us what we need to know about our enemy Satan, how to seek Allah's protection from him, and the deceptive ways in which he approaches man. Let us have utmost caution and try our best not to fall prey to his ploys and tricks. Man is weak. However, with strong determination, sincere repentance, constant remembrance of Allah (SWT), and the help of Allah, we can ward off Satan and his evil designs. May Allah (SWT) bless each one of us with the *tawfeeq* to do so. *Ameen!*

## • 38 •

# HOW TO STRENGTHEN ONE'S *IMAN*

In a previous *khutbah* on the topic of "*Iman* and its Implications," we discussed the meaning and implications of *iman*, or faith, and how important it is to keep assessing the level of our *iman*. In today's *khutbah*, I will share with you some of the symptoms of weak *iman*, some of the causes that lead to weakness of *iman*, and some of the ways to strengthen one's *iman*. The Prophet (SAS) taught us, "*Iman* wears out in the heart of any one of you just as clothes wear out, so ask Allah to renew the *iman* in your hearts."

Our *iman* is not always as sound and strong as we want it to be. From time to time, the level of our *iman* dwindles. If we feel our *iman* declining, then we should take measures to restore it. It is our responsibility to know what decreases our *iman* and how to avoid those things; and what increases our *iman* and how to embrace those things.

It is crucial that we keep a check on the state of our *iman*. Weakness of *iman* manifests itself in many ways such as:

Having no desire to perform the obligatory acts of worship
Having no desire to read the Qur`an, let alone getting moved by its verses
Finding difficulty in remembering Allah
Committing sins and not feeling any guilt
Not feeling bad when things are done against the *shari'a*
Not feeling any responsibility to promote Islam
Lack of concern about the situation of Muslims
Feeling jealous of others' blessings
Feeling pleased when things are not going well for others
Trying to find shortcuts by walking close to that which is disliked (*makrooh*)

Preaching to others to do good when not doing it oneself

Being mean and miserly and not wanting to part with wealth

There are many other symptoms of weak *iman*, and these are just a few.

One of the main causes for weakness of *iman* is being detached from the Qur'an, which means not reading it, not pondering upon its meanings, not memorizing it, not trying to implement it in our lives, and not conveying it to others. The Prophet (SAS) said, "People can never obtain closeness to Allah through anything better than what came from Him." By this the Prophet (SAS) means the Qur'an, which is the most reliable source of our *deen*. If there is no attachment to the Book of Allah, then how can there be attachment to Allah Himself? If this is the case with us, then we should not be wondering why our *iman* is weak. The Prophet (SAS) also said, "I have left two matters with you. As long as you hold onto them, you will not go the wrong way. They are the Book of Allah and the Sunnah of His Prophet."

In another hadeeth, the Prophet (SAS) said, "Indeed this Qur'an is a rope: one end of it is in the hand of Allah and the other end is in your hands. So hold firmly to it and you will never go astray, nor be destroyed after that." In *Surat Aal 'Imran* Allah tells us,

$$وَاعْتَصِمُوا بِحَبْلِ اللَّهِ جَمِيعًا وَلَا تَفَرَّقُوا ۚ$$

*And hold firmly to the rope of Allah, all of you, and do not be separated. (Aal 'Imran, 3:103)*

So, if we let go of that rope, then we lose our connection with the Book of Allah. The only way we know about Allah is through what He revealed to us about Himself, and that can only be found in His words in the Qur'an. Reading the words of Allah is very crucial. Can any *salah*, which is a means to connect with Allah, be valid without uttering the words of Allah? The closer we are to the Qur'an, the nearer we are to Allah, and the farther we are from it, the farther we are from Allah. If we don't pick up the Qur'an at least once a day, read a little something of it, and try to understand it, then we are on our way to losing our connection with Allah. If our hearts are not attached to Allah, it is not a surprise that we are disobedient. Without that attachment, we lose our consciousness of the all-pervading presence of Allah, and the reality of our accountability on the Day of Judgment.

We also have to cling to the Sunnah of the Prophet (SAS) who followed and lived the Qur'an at every moment, in every detail of his life. His life was the reflection of Allah's Words. In fact, when the Prophet's wife 'A'isha (RAA) was asked about his conduct, she replied, "His character was the Qur'an." Addressing His beloved Prophet, Allah says in *Surat al-Qalam*,

$$وَإِنَّكَ لَعَلَى خُلُقٍ عَظِيمٍ ۚ$$

*And you are surely on an exalted standard of character. (al-Qalam, 68:4)*

And in *Surat an-Nisa`* Allah says,

مَّن يُطِعِ الرَّسُولَ فَقَدْ أَطَاعَ اللَّهَ ۞

*He who obeys the Messenger obeys Allah. (An-Nisa`, 4:80)*

In *Surat Aal 'Imran* we are told that following the Prophet (SAS) is a condition for true love of Allah (SWT).

قُلْ إِن كُنتُمْ تُحِبُّونَ اللَّهَ فَاتَّبِعُونِي يُحْبِبْكُمُ اللَّهُ وَيَغْفِرْ لَكُمْ ذُنُوبَكُمْ وَاللَّهُ غَفُورٌ رَحِيمٌ ۞

*Say: If you love Allah, follow me, and Allah will love you and forgive you your sins;*
*Allah is most forgiving, most merciful. (Aal 'Imran, 3:31)*

Filling our hearts with the remembrance of Allah through His words and following the Sunnah of the Prophet (SAS) is the best way to strengthen our *iman*.

Another thing which causes weakness of *iman* is staying away from a faith-filled and *iman*-nourishing environments. This ultimately causes people to fall into sin and sinning without sincerely repenting is something that weakens *iman*. If you are sitting in the *masjid*, the House of Allah, how many times do you think of sinning? Perhaps never or very little. But the moment we are outside the *masjid*, we become active with society, other people, and the media. Many of us sin not because of willful disobedience but because we get pulled into the act unconsciously. It is no secret that certain social and other pressures tend to push us into committing sins that we normally would not commit. When in such situations, we suppress the voice of our conscience and then go with the flow. This is one of the reasons why the Prophet (SAS) warned us about keeping company that can take us away from the straight path. He said, "A man will follow the way of his close friends, so let each one of you look at who he takes as a close friend." Listen to what Allah says in the Qur`an about the person who, on the Day of Judgment, will express his sorrow and regret over taking some undesirable person as his friend.

يَا وَيْلَتَى لَيْتَنِي لَمْ أَتَّخِذْ فُلَانًا خَلِيلًا ۞ لَقَدْ أَضَلَّنِي عَنِ الذِّكْرِ بَعْدَ إِذْ جَاءَنِي وَكَانَ الشَّيْطَانُ لِلْإِنْسَانِ خَذُولًا ۞

*Woe to me! I wish I had not taken so-and-so as a friend! He led me astray from the Reminder after it came to me. Satan has always betrayed mankind. (al-Furqan, 25:28-29)*

Let us therefore ensure that if our social circles are directly or indirectly pushing us to commit sins or discouraging us from performing good deeds then we should disengage from such groups and people immediately because this will weaken our *iman*. When we silence our conscience in the face of social pressures, we also start to slowly regard many wrongs as rights and gradually lose our innate ability to assess right and wrong.

It's very important to create a faith-filled environment for ourselves even outside the *masjid*. At home, for example, the husband and wife should be reminding each other and their children about remembering Allah and thanking Him. The children are going to naturally repeat the behavior of the people who raised them.

We ask Allah (SWT) to turn our hearts to His *deen* and to His obedience. *Ameen!*

Brothers and sisters! An obsessive preoccupation with the *dunya* also causes weakness of *iman* and forgetfulness of the hereafter. The human heart is like a boat in the ocean of the *dunya*. The boat keeps sailing and sinks only if something allows the ocean's water to enter it. Similarly the heart that allows this world to enter and fill it will "sink" in this life. It becomes filled with our jobs, our gadgets, our social networking, fashion trends, marketing tools, money, power, status, and the list goes on. The heart that is owned by this life is a prisoner of the worst kind. The heart that is owned by any other master than the Master of masters—Allah (SWT)—is the weakest of all slaves.

Some of us may wrongly think that we can live our lives any way we like, and then at the time of death, we will just say *la ilaha illa Allah* and everything will be fine. But at the time of death, the tongue cannot speak except what the heart commands. Whatever is in the heart will come out. The bankrupt heart will have nothing but love of *dunya* to speak of on that day. If our heart is empty of Allah during our life, how can it be full of Allah during our death? If our heart is full of love of this life, love of status, love of wealth, love of the creation over the Creator, then that what will come on our tongue when we die. The heart is the seat of *iman*. Speaking about curing the diseases of the heart, and the heart, Ibn al-Qayyim al-Jawziyya (RA) said, "The keys to the life of the heart lie in reflecting upon the Qur`an, humbling oneself before Allah in secret, and leaving sins." He also said, "The heart will rest and feel relief if it is settled with Allah and it will worry and be anxious if it is settled with people." To increase our *iman*, we have to work for it just as we work for anything else. Allah says in *Surat an-Najm*,

$$\text{وَأَن لَّيْسَ لِلْإِنسَانِ إِلَّا مَا سَعَىٰ ۝}$$

*And that man shall have only that for which he strives. (an-Najm, 53:39)*

And He says in *Surat al-Baqara*,

$$\text{لَا يُكَلِّفُ اللَّهُ نَفْسًا إِلَّا وُسْعَهَا لَهَا مَا كَسَبَتْ وَعَلَيْهَا مَا اكْتَسَبَتْ ۝}$$

*Allah does not burden a soul beyond its capacity. It gets every good that it earns, and it suffers every ill that it earns. (al-Baqara, 2:286)*

Brothers and sisters! In conclusion, I remind myself and all of us that we must strive our utmost to treat the problem of our weak *iman*. Let us connect with the Qur`an and the Sunnah. Let us feel the greatness of Allah. Let us push ourselves to acts of righteousness and pray that they are accepted with the fear that they might not be accepted. Let us seek knowledge because knowledge builds certainty and certainty bring trust in Allah. Let us remember the day we will bid farewell to this life and the day we will stand before Allah. Let us humble ourselves to Allah and make *du'a'* to Him to make our hearts filled with *iman*.

# • 39 •

# HUMAN BEINGS ARE ONE FAMILY

The topic of today's *khutbah* is "Human Beings Are One Family." We often forget that all human beings come from the same source and from the same first human family. They are all children of Adam and Hawwa (AS) who were the first parents of all later generations to come till the end of time. Allah (SWT) says in the Qur'an,

يَا أَيُّهَا النَّاسُ إِنَّا خَلَقْنَاكُمْ مِنْ ذَكَرٍ وَأُنْثَى وَجَعَلْنَاكُمْ شُعُوبًا وَقَبَائِلَ لِتَعَارَفُوا إِنَّ أَكْرَمَكُمْ عِنْدَ اللَّهِ أَتْقَاكُمْ إِنَّ اللَّهَ عَلِيمٌ خَبِيرٌ ⬡

*O mankind! We created you from a single man and a single woman and made you nations and tribes so that you may know one another. The best among you in the sight of Allah is the one who is most mindful of Allah. Allah is All-knowing and All-Aware.*
(al-Hujurat, 49:13)

Being the offspring of the same parents, all humans share this earth. It does not belong to any particular person or any particular group of people. It belongs to the Creator of the heavens and the earth—Allah (SWT). Each and every human being has a right to be on this earth. The lines that we find dividing us are political lines. Countries and boarders were created for political reasons. Whether a person is a Muslim, Christian, Jew, Hindu, Sikh, Buddhist, or follower of any other religion, or even if one is an agnostic or an atheist, everyone has exactly the same right to inhabit the earth, provided he meets a few basic requirements of the land in which he wants to live.

No one has the right to physically harm or attack anyone because he chose to believe in something that is different from what you believe. If I have a problem with you, I don't have the right to harm you or kill you, nor do you have the right to do that to me. We must understand that we belong to the same Maker and come from the same family: the human family. Even those who don't believe that they were created by God Almighty still believe that the human species comes from the same source.

People may disagree with each other, but that disagreement must be with respect, and not by harming or killing those with whom we disagree. If I disagree with someone's ideology, I need to challenge it with respect, and not with hate. Bigotry, racism, and hate crimes have risen to an alarming degree, reminding us how quickly hate can transform into violence.

Sometimes we see immigrants of a particular race, ethnicity, or color decide that other immigrants who are not of their race, ethnicity, or color or those who immigrated later than them are less entitled to live in that country and to access the opportunities that it offers. They forget that they themselves were not originally from that place. The original people of New Zealand are the Maoris, the original people of Sri Lanka are the Sinhalese, the original people of the United States are the Native Americans, and the original people of Australia are the Aboriginal people. All other people living in these lands are immigrants. Therefore how does one group of immigrants have any right over another group of immigrants in the same country?

Remember, all of us have come from somewhere. Even in our so-called "native countries" our forefathers and ancestors might have also been from somewhere else. Adam (AS) was not from this part of the globe, but he was on this globe. So people cannot discriminate on the basis of their original homeland. We condemn the recent violent incidents and killings that have taken place on the basis of this discrimination and on the basis of religious discrimination. Terrorists comprise a very small fraction of the peace-loving mainstream population of any country. The crimes committed by terrorists, often in the name of their religion, are actually against the teachings of their religion. They become hateful and hurtful toward others because of negative stereotypes, malicious propaganda, and racist rhetoric of demagogues and politicians over a long period of time. This is why rhetoric against people of particular religions, colors, races, or ethnicities is so dangerous.

We don't need to insult or attack people while we are disagreeing with them. We must be respectful to each other. When Allah (SWT) speaks about discussing the differences between us and the People of the Book (meaning the Jews and the Christians) He says in *Surat al-'Ankabut,*

$$\text{وَلَا تُجَادِلُوا أَهْلَ الْكِتَابِ إِلَّا بِالَّتِي هِيَ أَحْسَنُ} \bigcirc$$

*And do not argue with the people of the Book except in the best manner. (al-'Ankabut, 29:46)*

In *Surat an-Nahl,* Allah (SWT) says,

$$\text{ادْعُ إِلَى سَبِيلِ رَبِّكَ بِالْحِكْمَةِ وَالْمَوْعِظَةِ الْحَسَنَةِ وَجَادِلْهُمْ بِالَّتِي هِيَ أَحْسَنُ ۝}$$

*Call to the way of your Lord with wisdom and kind advice and argue with them in the best manner. (an-Nahl, 16:125)*

Sometimes when we are talking or arguing with people, we are convinced that we are right, and they are convinced that they are right. So what do we do? Leave it to Allah. Never become so passionate that it leads you to violence, attacking people, or even killing them. The permission to give and take away life belongs only to Allah.

$$\text{هُوَ يُحْيِي وَيُمِيتُ وَإِلَيْهِ تُرْجَعُونَ ۝}$$

*It is He Who gives life and causes to die and to Him you will return. (Yunus, 10:56)*

If Allah had willed, he would not have created them in the first place, or He would have made all humans into a single community. As He says in the Qur`an,

$$\text{وَلَوْ شَاءَ اللَّهُ لَجَعَلَكُمْ أُمَّةً وَاحِدَةً وَلَكِنْ لِيَبْلُوَكُمْ فِي مَا آتَاكُمْ فَاسْتَبِقُوا الْخَيْرَاتِ إِلَى اللَّهِ مَرْجِعُكُمْ جَمِيعًا}$$
$$\text{فَيُنَبِّئُكُمْ بِمَا كُنْتُمْ فِيهِ تَخْتَلِفُونَ ۝}$$

*Had Allah willed, He would have made you a single community, but He wanted to test you regarding what has come to you. So compete with each other in doing good. Every one of you will return to Allah and He will inform you regarding the things about which you differed. (al-Ma`ida, 5:48)*

Muslims are people who respect life and the Muslim community is a moderate community. Allah even describes the Muslim community in the Qur`an.

$$\text{وَكَذَلِكَ جَعَلْنَاكُمْ أُمَّةً وَسَطًا ۝}$$

*And thus, We have made you a moderate community. (al-Baqara, 2:143)*

Do we have any problem with the people who live around us, work with us, or who happen to have a different faith than ours or no faith at all? No! Whatever our belief and practice, we are all part of the same human family. Acts of a few evil people do not justify generalizing their action to the entire people of their faith or nationality. Anyone claiming that Muslims and non-Muslims do not have a responsibility to coexist peacefully is expressing a deviant ideology.

The recent massacre of Muslims in New Zealand on a Friday when they had assembled to offer their *Jumu'ah* prayer; the suicide bombings in Sri Lankan churches on Easter, the holiest day of the Christian calendar; the shooting and killing of Jews inside a Pittsburgh synagogue; and other such incidents have made people worry about the safety of houses of worship and ask, "Who may be next?" All this is due to bigotry, racism, hate, and intolerance coupled with misinformation about various faith traditions.

The fact that these horrific evil acts have multiplied recently highlights the critical need for proper moral education rooted in belief in a Supreme Being. The awareness that God is watching should prevent anyone from unjustly taking away the life of another human being. We need to promote Islamic literacy and mutual respect, and counter prejudice and discrimination through education about Islam and Muslims. We should also learn about the people of other faith traditions and worldviews who make up our country. This has to be done within the framework this country's values of religious freedom and pluralism. The United States was founded on the concept of religious pluralism and presenting Islam in this context makes it easier for your audience to be open to learning about Islamic beliefs and practices. May Allah grant us a deep understanding of our *deen*. Ameen!

Brothers and sisters! Fear and intolerance seem to dominate the news with churches, synagogues, temples, and mosques increasingly being targeted. Considering the scale and proximity of violent acts directed at places of worship, and as the month of Ramadan approaches, mosques across the country are having conversations about where they are going to get more resources for security. Some mosques have applied for government grants for security cameras and guards. Others are holding fundraisers. They are trying to do everything they can to ensure the safety of all congregants. We at AMDA are also trying to do whatever we can with our humble means and meager effort. We are in desperate need of healing, and healing comes with love and forgiveness. It does not come with revenge and retaliation. It is peace that we all require, and it is peace that we should all aspire for. The Prophet (SAS) taught us a beautiful du'a` to ask Allah to grant us peacefulness.

اللَّهُمَّ أَنْتَ السَّلَامُ وَمِنْكَ السَّلَامُ، تَبَارَكْتَ يَا ذَا الْجَلَالِ وَالْإِكْرَامِ ○

*O Allah! You are peace, and peace comes from You. Blessed You are, O Possessor of Glory and Honor.*

And he also taught us to pray,

اللَّهُمَّ أَلِّفْ بَيْنَ قُلُوبِنَا وَأَصْلِحْ ذَاتَ بَيْنِنَا وَاهْدِنَا سُبُلَ السَّلَامِ وَنَجِّنَا مِنَ الظُّلُمَاتِ إِلَى النُّورِ وَجَنِّبْنَا الْفَوَاحِشَ مَا ظَهَرَ مِنْهَا وَمَا بَطَنَ وَبَارِكْ لَنَا فِي أَسْمَاعِنَا وَأَبْصَارِنَا وَقُلُوبِنَا وَأَزْوَاجِنَا وَذُرِّيَّاتِنَا وَتُبْ عَلَيْنَا إِنَّكَ أَنْتَ التَّوَّابُ الرَّحِيمُ وَاجْعَلْنَا شَاكِرِينَ لِنِعْمَتِكَ مُثْنِينَ بِهَا قَابِلِيهَا وَأَتِمَّهَا عَلَيْنَا ○

*O Allah, join our hearts, mend our social relationship, guide us to the path of peace, bring us from darkness to light, save us from obscenities, outward or inward, and bless our ears, our eyes, our hearts, our spouses, our children, and turn toward us; truly you are Oft-Returning, Most Merciful. Make us grateful for Your blessings and make us praise it, while accepting it and give it to us in full.*

# HUMAN HEART FROM THE ISLAMIC PERSPECTIVE

In today's *khutbah*, I intend to share some thoughts with you on the human heart from the Islamic perspective. In the Arabic language, the human heart is called *qalb*, which means heart, mind, and conscience all at once.

أَلَا بِذِكْرِ اللَّهِ تَطْمَئِنُّ الْقُلُوبُ ○

*Truly, it is in the remembrance of Allah that hearts find peace.* (ar-Ra'd, 13:28)

In the Qur'an, Allah (SWT) also refers to the heart as *sadr*, meaning "chest."

فَمَن يُرِدِ اللَّهُ أَن يَهْدِيَهُ يَشْرَحْ صَدْرَهُ لِلْإِسْلَامِ ○

*Whoever Allah wills to guide, He opens their heart to Islam.* (al-An'am, 6:125)

Sometimes the heart is referred to as *fu'ad* meaning "intellect."

إِنَّ السَّمْعَ وَالْبَصَرَ وَالْفُؤَادَ كُلُّ أُولَئِكَ كَانَ عَنْهُ مَسْئُولًا ○

*Indeed the ear, the eye, the heart, each will be questioned.* (al-Isra', 17:36)

All of this illustrates the centrality of the heart in Islam. There are also many sayings of the Prophet (SAS) mentioning the heart. For example, the Prophet (SAS) said, "Truly, Allah does not look at your outward forms and wealth, but rather at your heart and actions." This means that believers should focus on the reformation of their hearts in addition to accumulating good deeds. Pointing to his heart, the Prophet (SAS) said, "Consciousness and fear of Allah is here!" The Prophet (SAS) used to pray asking Allah to guide and rectify the heart in different ways.

يَا مُقَلِّبَ الْقُلُوبِ ثَبِّتْ قَلْبِي عَلَى دِينِكَ

*Oh Turner of hearts! Keep my heart firm upon Your religion.*

اللَّهُمَّ مُصَرِّفَ الْقُلُوبِ صَرِّفْ قُلُوبَنَا عَلَى طَاعَتِكَ

*O Allah, the Turner of hearts! Turn our hearts to Your obedience.*

Although we are taught in the Qur'an and Sunnah in many different ways about the spiritual heart, there are also references made by the Prophet (SAS) about the physical heart. For example, he said, "Truly, there is a piece of flesh in your body, which if sound, the whole body is healthy and if it is diseased, the whole body is diseased. Truly it is the heart!"

Another reference to the physical heart is the incident that occurred when the Prophet (SAS) was a child playing with other children. The Angel Jibreel came to him, opened his chest, removed his heart, and washed it with *Zamzam* water and then restored it back in its proper place.

In nearly every culture in the world, people use idioms and phrases that directly or indirectly allude to the heart. For example, we call certain types of people "warmhearted" because they are kind and merciful. And there are those who are "cold-hearted" because they are unsympathetic or even cruel. People with "large hearts" are generous. To "have a lot of heart" means to be particularly empathic, compassionate, or loving. The "downhearted" people are called such because they are depressed and dejected. When someone's words or actions penetrate our souls and affect us profoundly, we say that this person "touched my heart."

Given the importance of the heart in Islam, many scholars wrote about it from the spiritual context. Imam an-Nawawi discussed *al-'aql fee al-qalb* referring to "heart as the seat of the mind" and Ibn Katheer's *tafseer* (explanation) of the Qur'an interprets the heart as an organ of understanding. Both scholars suggest that the heart overpowers the mind and is more fundamental in shaping our behavior, especially as regards to fulfilling our faith.

One of the earliest writings on the importance of the heart was by Imam Abu Hameed al-Ghazali, who said that it is obligatory on every Muslim to have knowledge of one's heart. In his well-known work *Ihya'Uloom ad-Deen*, in the section on the "Marvels of the Heart" he writes that the word "heart" has two meanings. The first is that it is a physical organ on the left side of the breast and has within it a hollow cavity. In that cavity, there is black blood, which is the source and origin of the spirit (*rooh*). The second is that it is a spiritual organ, which is subtle and divine and is the essence of humanity. It perceives, knows, is aware, is spoken to, and is responsible for its actions. It is connected with the physical heart, but most people have struggled to understand the exact nature of this connection.

Imam al-Ghazali explains further that the spiritual heart represents the entire human personality. He writes, "It enables man to attain knowledge of Allah (SWT), draw near Him, work for Him, and labor toward Him. It is the heart which rejoices in closeness to Him, prospers when it is purified, and is miserable when corrupted." He also wrote that each heart has a sound and natural disposition (*fitra saliha*) to know the truth because it is from a noble and divine command and therefore different from any other worldly creation.

Imam Ibn Taymiyya wrote in his well-known book, *Diseases of the Heart* that the heart has special importance in Islam because it is considered the leader of the body and it is only through the purification of the leader that the organs become pure. If the heart is corrupted, they also become corrupted.

These concepts of the human heart in Islam are centuries old. Early Muslim scholars studied all phenomena from an integrated perspective, combining the physical and spiritual aspects of human existence. This integrated learning among Muslims stopped for centuries due to various reasons, one of them being that as a community, Muslims abandoned the habit of thinking and probing into the mysteries of the universe and uncovering the treasures of the powers hidden in nature. As a result, lethargy and inaction took over them.

Research and scholarship in the West continued, mostly in the physical realm, due to the separation of science and religion. There is serious interest, however, in the scientific community about the functions of the heart as an organ that does more than pump blood. Dr. Andrew Armor from Canada writes that until the 1960s, the heart was only considered a pump because we did not have the ability to see the heart in any other form. From his own studies, he discovered a knot in the heart, medically known as cardiac ganglia, which is now described in science as the "heart-brain." The heart-brain is considered the intrinsic cardiac nervous system with an intricate network of complex ganglia, neurotransmitters, protein, and support cells that are the same as those found in the human brain.

We know already that during the embryonic development process, the heart is created long before the brain is, and each cell of the heart is believed to have a memory by which it transports information to the brain with the blood it pumps throughout the body. After intensive research for more than twenty-five years, researchers at the HeartMath Institute Research Center have concluded, "The heart is an access point to wisdom and intelligence that we can call upon to live our lives with more balance, greater creativity, and enhanced intuitive capacities." The Qur'an said this more than 1400 years ago!

The Qur'anic references about how the heart has cognitive abilities are further reinforced by the multiple case studies of heart transplant recipients who received memories, feelings, fears, food preferences, and even musical affinities of their donors. Other case studies showed that patients experiencing transplants experienced changes in their personality, suggesting that the heart retains the memories of the donor's personality that are also transplanted through its memory to the receiver.

When we take a closer look at the importance given to the heart in Islam along with recent scientific findings, it is amazing that the thing that the Qur'an urges Muslims to do—to reflect upon the signs of God— is something that others are doing without knowing the Qur'an!

Brothers and sisters! The desire to exploit and dominate others; the excessive love of wealth, power, and status; the diseases of hypocrisy, jealousy; the tendencies to meddle in people's lives, gossip, spread rumors, backbite; these are manifestations of diseases found nowhere but in the heart. Every criminal, every miser, every abuser, every boastful, arrogant, and hateful person does what he does because of a diseased heart. In the Qur`an, one of the descriptions of the Day of Judgment is,

يَوْمَ لَا يَنْفَعُ مَالٌ وَلَا بَنُونَ ○ إِلَّا مَنْ أَتَى اللَّهَ بِقَلْبٍ سَلِيمٍ ○

*The day when neither wealth nor children will benefit anyone; except for someone who comes to Allah with a sound heart. (ash-Shu'ara`, 26:88-89)*

The sound heart is understood to be free from diseases of the heart. This sound heart is actually the spiritual heart and not necessarily the physical organ, although in Islamic tradition the spiritual heart is centered in the physical. We understand from this that the heart—and not the brain—is the true center of the intellect, human consciousness, and conscience.

Indeed, those who possess a sound heart are the best people in this world. It was narrated that 'Abdullah ibn 'Amr ibn al-'Aas (RAA) said, "It was once asked to the Messenger of Allah (SAS) 'Which of the people is best?' He said, 'Everyone who is pure of heart and sincere in speech.' They said, 'Sincere in speech-- we know what this is, but what is pure of heart?' He said, 'It is (the heart) that is pious and pure, with no sin, injustice, rancor, or envy in it.'"

Brothers and sisters! It is crucially important to be aware of the spiritual diseases of the heart. This understanding is at the essence of Islamic teachings. The Qur`an defines three types of people The first is the believers, *al-mu`minoon*. The second type is the disbelievers, *al-kafiroon* and the third group is the hypocrites, *al-munafiqoon*.

The believers are described as people whose hearts are alive and full of light, while the disbelievers are in darkness. Allah says in the Qur`an,

أَوَمَنْ كَانَ مَيْتًا فَأَحْيَيْنَاهُ وَجَعَلْنَا لَهُ نُورًا يَمْشِي بِهِ فِي النَّاسِ كَمَنْ مَثَلُهُ فِي الظُّلُمَاتِ لَيْسَ بِخَارِجٍ مِنْهَا كَذَلِكَ زُيِّنَ لِلْكَافِرِينَ مَا كَانُوا يَعْمَلُونَ ○

*Can he who was dead, to whom We gave life, and a light whereby he could walk among people be like him who is in utter darkness from which he can never emerge? Thus the deeds of those who deny the truth have been made fair seeming to them. (al-An'am, 6:122)*

According to the commentators of the Qur`an, "the one who was dead" refers to someone who had a spiritually dead heart which Allah revived with the light of guidance. Also, the Prophet Muhammad (SAS) said, "The difference between the one who remembers Allah and one who does not is like the difference between the living and the dead." In essence, the believer is someone whose heart is alive, while the disbeliever is someone whose heart is spiritually dead. The hypocrite, however, is somebody whose heart is diseased.

Our beloved Prophet (SAS) spoke of the heart as a repository of knowledge and a vessel sensitive to the deeds of the body. He said, for example, that wrongdoing irritates the heart. So the heart actually perceives wrong action. The Prophet (SAS) said, "Sin is that which causes discomfort within your heart and you do not like people to know it." A peaceful heart, however, is one that is enlightened with faith (*iman*) and always sides with truth, justice, righteousness, and virtue.

The problems we see in our society come down to covering up or suppressing the symptoms of the restless or troubled heart. The agents used to do this include alcohol, drugs, sexual experimentation, power grabs, wealth, arrogance, pursuit of fame, and the like. These enable people to submerge themselves into a state of heedlessness concerning their essential nature. Heedlessness starves the heart and robs it of its spiritual nourishment. One enters into a state of unawareness of God and of humanity's ultimate destination: the infinite world of the hereafter.

When people are completely immersed in the material world, believing that the world is all that matters and all that exists and that they are not accountable for their actions, they bring about a spiritual death of their hearts. However, before the heart dies, it shows symptoms of affliction. These afflictions are the spiritual diseases of the hearts. From this perspective, Islam places great emphasis on the health of hearts and calls for cleansing them from sins for it is the heart at which Allah (SWT) will look on the Day of Judgment. In the Qur'an, Allah tells us that the believers pray to Him about the state of their hearts.

رَبَّنَا لَا تُزِغْ قُلُوبَنَا بَعْدَ إِذْ هَدَيْتَنَا وَهَبْ لَنَا مِنْ لَدُنْكَ رَحْمَةً إِنَّكَ أَنْتَ الْوَهَّابُ ◯

*Our Lord! Do not let our hearts deviate after you have guided us. Grant us Your mercy.*
*You are indeed the Giver of all bounties. (Aal 'Imran, 3:8)*

رَبَّنَا اغْفِرْ لَنَا وَلِإِخْوَانِنَا الَّذِينَ سَبَقُونَا بِالْإِيمَانِ وَلَا تَجْعَلْ فِي قُلُوبِنَا غِلًّا لِلَّذِينَ آمَنُوا رَبَّنَا إِنَّكَ رَءُوفٌ رَحِيمٌ ◯

*Our Lord, forgive us and our brothers who preceded us in faith, and leave no malice in*
*our hearts toward those who believe. Our Lord, You are indeed full of kindness, most*
*merciful. (al-Hashr, 59:10)*

# • 41 •

# HYPOCRISY *(NIFAQ)*

Brothers and sisters! In today's *khutbah*, I want to talk to you about a serious disease that believers should be reminded of all the time. It is the disease of hypocrisy or *nifaq*, as it is called in Arabic. What is *nifaq* and who is a *munafiq*? What are some of the misconceptions surrounding *nifaq*? What are the signs and consequences of *nifaq*? What is the cure to this spiritual disease of the heart? These are some of the points that will be discussed, *insha`Allah*.

The word *nifaq* is derived from the same root letters (*nun-faa-qaaf*) from which we have the word *nafaq*, which means an underground tunnel with openings at its two ends. The word *naafaqa* refers to a desert lizard that Arabs used to hunt for food. It lives in a tunnel using one of the openings of the tunnel to escape whenever it feels its life to be threatened from the other opening of the tunnel. The underlying principle of this phenomenon is that in reality, the hypocrite, or *munafiq*, is a person who wants to play it "safe." He is two-faced. Categorizing such individuals as a distinct group of people, Allah says in the Qur`an,

وَمِنَ النَّاسِ مَن يَقُولُ آمَنَّا بِاللَّهِ وَبِالْيَوْمِ الْآخِرِ وَمَا هُم بِمُؤْمِنِينَ ۝

*Among the people there are some who say, 'We believe in Allah and in the Last Day,' but they are not believers. (al-Baqara, 2:8)*

Allah explains in the Qur`an that this hypocrisy is a disease of the heart.

فِي قُلُوبِهِم مَّرَضٌ ۝

*There is a disease in their hearts. (al-Baqara, 2:10)*

We learn in other places in the Qur`an that the consequences of having this disease are very grim, both in this world and in the next. In one place, referring to the hypocrites who have reached a point of no return in their hypocrisy, Allah (SWT) addresses the Prophet (SAS) in the following words,

اسْتَغْفِرْ لَهُمْ أَوْ لَا تَسْتَغْفِرْ لَهُمْ إِن تَسْتَغْفِرْ لَهُمْ سَبْعِينَ مَرَّةً فَلَن يَغْفِرَ اللَّهُ لَهُمْ ذَلِكَ بِأَنَّهُمْ كَفَرُوا بِاللَّهِ وَرَسُولِهِ
وَاللَّهُ لَا يَهْدِي الْقَوْمَ الْفَاسِقِينَ ۝

*It makes no difference whether you ask forgiveness for them or not: Allah will not forgive them even if you ask seventy times, because they reject Allah and His Messenger. Allah does not guide those who rebel against Him. (at-Tawba, 9:80)*

This is how serious the disease of hypocrisy is. Allah (SWT) would not even accept the *du'a`* of the Prophet (SAS) in their favor! The hypocrites, however, even though they declare themselves to be Muslims, are branded in this *ayah* as "the rebellious ones" (*al-fasiqeen*). There is another *ayah* that should make those who have the germs of hypocrisy in their hearts tremble with fear.

إِنَّ الْمُنَافِقِينَ فِي الدَّرْكِ الْأَسْفَلِ مِنَ النَّارِ وَلَنْ تَجِدَ لَهُمْ نَصِيرًا ◯

*The hypocrites will be in the lowest depths of hell, and you will find no one to help them.*
*(an-Nisa`, 4:145)*

There are certain misconceptions among Muslims regarding *nifaq* that need to be addressed and clarified. The first misconception is that *munafiqeen* existed only at the time of the Prophet (SAS), and that there are no *munafiqeen* among us today. This statement may only be partially true. The *munafiqeen* did exist in the time of the Prophet (SAS), and Allah (SWT) even disclosed their names to him. Yet, it is wrong to think that hypocrisy is not prevalent among Muslims today. *Munafiqeen* exist today and will continue to exist until the end of time. However, while the Prophet (SAS) knew the *munafiqeen* of his time by name, as he was informed about them by Allah (SWT), we are not in a position to say anything or pass any judgment about the degree or state of possible *nifaq* of a Muslim.

The second misconception regarding *nifaq* is that as Muslims we are immune from it. As a matter of fact, the disease of *nifaq* is so dangerous that no one should claim to be immune. This matter is brought to light through a story from the life of the Prophet (SAS). A companion by the name of Hudhayfa ibn al-Yaman (RAA) used to keep a list of the hypocrites which was given to him by the Prophet (SAS) with instructions to keep the names on the list a closely guarded secret. After 'Umar (RAA) became the caliph, he would go to Hudhayfa (RAA) and ask him if his name was on the list. Such was the fear of 'Umar (RAA) regarding the disease of *nifaq* that even he did not consider himself secure from being infected by it. We can now perhaps appreciate that no one should feel himself or herself immune from *nifaq*. We should be alarmed as soon as we see any symptoms of *nifaq* within ourselves and we should take immediate steps to address them.

The third misconception about *nifaq* is that all *munafiqeen* are conscious of their *nifaq*. This is not so. The majority of the Muslims are not even aware of their *nifaq*. We have to take lessons from the story of 'Umar (RAA) and work to become conscious of the disease of *nifaq*. What are some of the common signs of a *munafiq*? The Prophet (SAS) gave us some signs.

Whenever he speaks, he lies.

Whenever he is entrusted, he violates that trust.

Whenever he argues, he behaves in an evil and insulting manner.

Whenever he promises, he does not fulfill it.

The first sign of a *munafiq* is whenever he speaks, he lies. This means that there is some element of falsehood in his speech. Lying becomes part of his speech, whether this lie is to impress others, to get out of trouble, or to make someone happy for unfair reasons or out of fear. People lie for different reasons. A habitual liar, therefore, is a hypocrite. So, one should get rid of the habit of telling lies.

Secondly, whenever he is entrusted with something, he violates that trust. After all, a person is trusted to do his job right. He is trusted to show up on time and leave on time. He is entrusted to take a thirty-minute break from work. He is entrusted to give his employees their checks on time. He is entrusted with things at his work, at his business, within his family, and elsewhere. There is also a trust between a student and a teacher. To be entrusted with something and not to take it seriously is a sign of hypocrisy.

Thirdly, he gets mad and insults anyone who argues with him. It is quite normal to get into disagreements. One can get into disagreements about anything with anyone. But in any discussion or argument, whether it is regarding something trivial or something significant, if it takes very little for someone to get extremely angry, then that is a sign of hypocrisy.

Finally, whenever he makes a promise, he does not fulfill it. This person makes a promise such as "I will visit you," but doesn't visit you. He says, "I will call you," but doesn't call you. He says, "I will show up" but he doesn't show up. This is a sign of hypocrisy. We seek Allah's protection from all these and other symptoms of hypocrisy.

Brothers and sisters! Let me share with you a few signs of the *munafiq* given in the Qur'an. In *Surat an-Nisa'* Allah says,

$$\text{وَإِذَا قَامُوا إِلَى الصَّلَاةِ قَامُوا كُسَالَى يُرَاءُونَ النَّاسَ وَلَا يَذْكُرُونَ اللَّهَ إِلَّا قَلِيلًا ۝}$$

*And when they stand up for prayer, they do so reluctantly and to be seen by others and they hardly remember Allah at all. (an-Nisa', 4:142)*

In the time of the Prophet (SAS), a person could be considered as belonging to the Islamic community unless he prayed his *salah* regularly. In those days, a person's absence from congregational prayers was considered a clear indication of his indifference toward Islam. If he excused himself regularly from congregational prayers, he was no longer held to be a Muslim. In those days, therefore, even the worst hypocrites had to attend the five daily prayers in the mosque. What distinguished a true believer from the hypocrite was that the sound believer came to the mosque with devotion, fervor, and eagerness. Everything about him indicated that his heart was in the prayer. For the hypocrite, however, the call to the prayer seemed like the announcement of a calamity. When such a person set off for the mosque, he did so very reluctantly. His entire demeanor testified that the remembrance of Allah was not really in his heart.

In contemporary times, and in our present environment and circumstances, it may be genuinely difficult to pray all the five prayers in congregation in the mosque, but this is not an excuse for not coming to the mosque at all or for being lazy toward our prayers. Being lazy about prayers is one of the characteristics of the *munafiq*. Another sign of the *munafiq* according to the Qur`an is,

وَلَا يُنْفِقُونَ إِلَّا وَهُمْ كَارِهُونَ ۝

*And they do not spend but reluctantly. (at-Tawba, 9:54)*

This refers to spending for the sake of Allah (SWT). Nothing comes out of their pockets for the sake of Allah except that they think twice about it. When the call is being made to give something for the sake of Allah, the first thing that comes to their mind is, "What about the other things I want to spend money on?" And they hardly ever think twice when they are on a shopping spree spending money on luxuries and unnecessary things. When it comes to giving for the sake of Allah, Shaytan begins to whisper to them, "Listen! You need to think about this! You need this money! You could be doing so much more with it."

الشَّيْطَانُ يَعِدُكُمُ الْفَقْرَ وَيَأْمُرُكُم بِالْفَحْشَاءِ وَاللَّهُ يَعِدُكُم مَّغْفِرَةً مِّنْهُ وَفَضْلًا ۝

*Shaytan promises you with poverty and commands you to do foul deeds. But Allah promises His forgiveness and His bounty. (al-Baqara, 2:268)*

Brothers and sisters! Without being judgmental about the hypocrisy of others, we have to look for the signs of hypocrisy (*nifaq*) within ourselves. The Prophet (SAS) said, "Nobody feels safe from hypocrisy except a hypocrite, and nobody is afraid of hypocrisy except the *mu`min* (the believer)." Some of the ways to cure hypocrisy are to make *du'a`* and beg Allah to protect us from this disease. Live your life and do deeds in such a way that if people knew about it, you would not be ashamed of it. Do not do anything in secret which, if made public, you would be embarrassed. Speak the truth. Keep your promises. Perform *salah* on time. Spend in the way of Allah without the desire to show off. Seek knowledge. Be mindful of Allah. Reflect on the punishment of the hereafter for the hypocrites. Purify your heart by seeking repentance from Allah (SWT). The Prophet (SAS) taught us to pray,

اللَّهُمَّ إِنِّي أَعُوذُ بِكَ مِنَ الشِّقَاقِ وَالنِّفَاقِ وَسُوءِ الْأَخْلَاقِ ۝

*O Allah! I seek refuge in You from opposing the truth, hypocrisy, and bad manners.*

# 42

# *IMAN* AND ITS IMPLICATIONS

In today's *khutbah*, I wish to share some thoughts with you on the topic of *iman*. What is meant by *iman* and what are its implications? In order to understand the real meaning of *iman*, it is necessary to realize that any individual who has attained maturity of intelligence should begin to ponder over questions such as:"Who am I?""Where did I come from?""Where do I go after I die?" "What is the nature of the universe?""Was it always there or was it created in time?" Without an answer to these questions, a human being is in the dark about himself, about the purpose of his life, about his own beginning and end, and about the beginning and end of the universe. It is evident that these questions cannot be answered merely by our physical senses. The question of whether or not we had any existence before our creation in this world, and whether after death there will be any continuity of our existence or not, cannot be answered by our senses. Living in this world, we can neither see into the world of existence prior to our birth nor can we see beyond after our physical death.

Despite these natural limitations, a number of people throughout history have claimed that they had a special source of knowledge which they called "revelation" or *way* in Arabic. Through the authority of revelation, they knew for certain that this universe did not always exist, and that it will not remain in existence forever. It has been brought into existence by a Creator who is unique in His essence and attributes. He has always existed and will continue to exist forever. It is He Who has created us, and it is He Who causes us to die. It is He who will again bring us back to life after death—to a life that will be everlasting.

*Iman* means to believe in Allah (SWT) as He is in His names and attributes, and to accept His commands as mentioned in the primary sources of Islam, the Qur'an and the Sunnah. This is the generalized form of *iman* which is called *al-iman al-mujmal*. Then there is the detailed form of *iman* which is called *al-iman al-mufassal* which is described in a well-known hadeeth commonly called the Hadeeth of Jibreel. This includes the individual parts of *iman* or what we also call the "six pillars of *iman*" of belief in Allah, His Angels, His Books, His Messengers, in the Last Day, and in divine destiny or *qadr*.

The Prophet (SAS) said, "*Iman* is knowledge in the heart, voicing with the tongue, and activity with the limbs." The heart is the specific faculty or spiritual organ that separates human beings from animals. Thus, a human being without a functioning spiritual heart is an animal, or worse. Allah has an example in the Qur'an of such people when He says,

أَمْ تَحْسَبُ أَنَّ أَكْثَرَهُمْ يَسْمَعُونَ أَوْ يَعْقِلُونَ إِنْ هُمْ إِلَّا كَالْأَنْعَامِ بَلْ هُمْ أَضَلُّ سَبِيلاً ◯

*Do you think most of them can hear or understand? They are like cattle. Indeed, they are even more astray. (al-Furqan, 25:44)*

The nature of a healthy heart is to understand the nature of things. Unfortunately there are many hearts that are diseased, rusted, or locked. Allah (SWT) describes such hearts in the Qur`an.

فِي قُلُوبِهِم مَّرَضٌ فَزَادَهُمُ اللَّهُ مَرَضًا ◯

*In their hearts is a disease, which Allah has increased. (al-Baqara, 2:10)*

كَلَّا بَلْ رَانَ عَلَى قُلُوبِهِم مَّا كَانُوا يَكْسِبُونَ ◯

*No. In fact what they have been doing has rusted their hearts. (al-Mutaffifeen, 83:14)*

When someone asked the Prophet (SAS), "What could cleanse the hearts again," he replied, "Frequent remembrance of death and recitation of the Qur`an." Allah also says in the Qur`an,

أَفَلَا يَتَدَبَّرُونَ الْقُرْآنَ أَمْ عَلَى قُلُوبٍ أَقْفَالُهَآ ◯

*Will they not, then, ponder over this Qur`an? Or are there locks upon their hearts?*
*(Muhammad, 47:24)*

The condition of the spiritual heart must always be kept in mind. Nothing shall benefit man on the Day of Judgment except if he comes to Allah (SWT) with a sound heart.

يَوْمَ لَا يَنْفَعُ مَالٌ وَلَا بَنُونَ ◯ إِلَّا مَنْ أَتَى اللَّهَ بِقَلْبٍ سَلِيمٍ ◯

*The day when neither wealth nor children will benefit anyone; except for someone who comes to Allah with a sound heart. (ash-Shu'ara`, 26:88-89)*

When people are completely immersed in the material world, believing that the world is all that exists and all that matters and that they are not accountable for their actions, they bring about a spiritual death of their hearts. May Allah save us from this situation.

The tongue is the tool of expressing what you have in your heart and mind. When the heart recognizes the truth, there should be a way to express it. It is the capacity to speak that allows us to communicate with our Creator through our prayers, supplications, repentance, and constant remembrance of Him.

*Iman* must be manifested through one's actions. The Qur`an frequently mentions *iman* and good deeds together. Good deeds are an index of true *iman*. Allah says,

إِنَّ الَّذِينَ آمَنُوا وَعَمِلُوا الصَّالِحَاتِ إِنَّا لَا نُضِيعُ أَجْرَ مَنْ أَحْسَنَ عَمَلًا ◯

*As for those who believe and do good deeds, We do not let the reward of anyone who does*

*a good deed go to waste. (al-Kahf, 18:30)*

So long as *iman* is confined to the stage of verbal confession and is limited to utterance of words only, actions could be different to what is confessed, as commonly found in our society.

كَبُرَ مَقْتاً عِندَ اللَّهِ أَن تَقُولُوا مَا لاَ تَفْعَلُونَ ◯

*It is very hateful to Allah that you should say what you do not do. (as-Saff, 61:3)*

Describing *iman*, Imam Hasan al-Basri (RA) said, "*Iman* is neither appearance nor mere wishes. It is what you have in your heart which is confirmed by your deeds." This means that what is actually desirable is true faith and not mere verbal affirmation of faith. But when *iman* reaches a state of certainty in our heart, then our actions will necessarily be changed because the actions of a man are based on what he believes in firmly.

For example, we know that fire can burn us, so we would never put even a finger in it. If a person believes with utmost certainty that Allah exists and that He is All-Seeing, All-Hearing, and All-Knowing; if he knows that every movement, every word which he utters, and every intention of his heart is known to Allah; and if he knows that after death he shall have to present himself before Allah and give full account of his entire life; and if he knows that there will be no chance of escaping from Allah's punishment, nor any hope of deliverance through ransom or intercession; then that person would never dare to intentionally lead a sinful life.

The Prophet (SAS) described this phenomenon when he said, "No fornicator commits fornication while he has *iman*. No thief commits a theft while he has *iman*. And no wine drinker drinks wine while he has *iman*." This means that these sins only committed when the real faith or *iman* of a person has vanished from their heart. The *iman* which the Qur`an regards as true faith has been explained in numerous verses of the Qur`an.

إِنَّمَا الْمُؤْمِنُونَ الَّذِينَ آمَنُوا بِاللَّهِ وَرَسُولِهِ ثُمَّ لَمْ يَرْتَابُوا ◯

*True believers are those who believe in Allah and His Messenger, then entertain no doubt. (al-Hujurat, 49:15)*

إِنَّمَا الْمُؤْمِنُونَ الَّذِينَ إِذَا ذُكِرَ اللَّهُ وَجِلَتْ قُلُوبُهُمْ ◯

*True believers are those whose hearts tremble with awe, whenever Allah is mentioned to them. (al-Anfal, 8:2)*

وَالَّذِينَ آمَنُوا أَشَدُّ حُبًّا لِلَّهِ ◯

*Those who have iman, love Allah most. (al-Baqara, 2:165)*

A companion by the name of Abi ʿAmrah Sufyan ibn ʿAbdullah (RAA) said to the Prophet (SAS), "O Messenger of Allah, tell me something of Islam which I can ask of no one but you." The Prophet (SAS) replied, "Say 'I believe in Allah', and then be steadfast." The Prophet (SAS) also said, "Indeed, the one who is pleased with Allah as his Lord (*rabb*), Islam as his religion (*deen*), and Muhammad (SAS) as his Messenger has tasted the sweetness of *iman*." May Allah (SWT) make us among them. *Ameen!*

My dear brothers and sisters! It is important that we keep assessing our level of *iman* in the light of these and other such Qurʾanic verses and Prophetic traditions.

My dear brothers and sisters! *Iman* leads to two results. The first is that a believer's internal anxiety will disappear, and he achieves inner peace and tranquility. This tranquility is called *amn* in Arabic. *Iman* and *amn* are derived from the same root letters *hamza-meem-noon*. One who possesses *iman* attains *amn* and becomes a friend of Allah (*wali Allah*).

أَلَا إِنَّ أَوْلِيَاءَ اللَّهِ لَا خَوْفٌ عَلَيْهِمْ وَلَا هُمْ يَحْزَنُونَ ۝

*Behold! The friends of Allah will feel no fear nor will they grieve. (Yunus, 10:62)*

The second result is a reform of one's actions and lifestyle. A true righteous believer should be adorned with high morals and virtuous deeds, and should be free from degrading actions. The Prophet (SAS) said, "*Iman* wears out in the heart of any one of you just as clothes wears out, so ask Allah to renew the *iman* in your hearts." The Prophet (SAS) taught us to pray,

اللَّهُمَّ حَبِّبْ إِلَيْنَا الْإِيمَانَ وَزَيِّنْهُ فِي قُلُوبِنَا، وَكَرِّهْ إِلَيْنَا الْكُفْرَ وَالْفُسُوقَ وَالْعِصْيَانَ، وَاجْعَلْنَا مِنَ الرَّاشِدِينَ ۝

*O Allah! Make iman beloved to us and beautify it in our hearts, and make disbelief, sinfulness, and disobedience hateful to us, and make us from among the rightly guided ones.*

It is crucial for all of us to keep a regular check on our *iman*. If we feel it is diminishing in any way, then we should take measures to restore it. It is our responsibility to know those things that decrease our *iman* and how to avoid them, and those that increase our *iman* and how to embrace them.

May Allah (SWT) make us among the people of true *iman*. *Ameen.*

# 43

# IMPORTANCE OF *SALAH*

My *khutbah* today is on the importance of *salah*. This is just to serve as a reminder to me and you.

$$\text{وَذَكِّرْ فَإِنَّ الذِّكْرَىٰ تَنفَعُ الْمُؤْمِنِينَ} \bigcirc$$

*And keep reminding, because reminding benefits the believers.* (adh-Dhariyat, 51:55)

I have chosen to talk on this topic because, despite the importance of *salah* in our *deen*, it is a sad fact that many Muslims either do not pray or do not fulfill the conditions of the prayer. The purpose of *salah* is to put ourselves in touch with Allah (SWT), to strengthen our relationship with Him, to be grateful for all His blessings, and to remind ourselves of His greatness. Just as the body has physical needs such as food and water, the soul has spiritual needs that are provided through acts of worship, the most important of which is *salah*.

In the Prophet's (SAS) mission on earth, every instruction and every commandment from Allah (SWT) was sent down through the Angel Jibreel (AS). But there was one commandment that was not. It was such an important commandment that instead of sending Jibreel (AS) down, it was given to the Prophet (SAS) in the seventh heaven during *al-Isra` wa al-Mi'raj*. That commandment was *salah*, the five daily prayers. When the Prophet (SAS) was first given the instruction to pray, it was initially to pray fifty times per day. After asking Allah (SWT) to make it easier, the number was eventually reduced to five times a day, with the reward of the original fifty prayers.

Imagine, for a moment, praying fifty times a day! Would we be able to do anything else but pray? No! And that's the point. It is to illustrate that our life's true purpose and priority is to worship and obey Allah (SWT). This means that our lives should revolve around *salah*. Something is seriously wrong when we put aside our *salah* in order to watch a TV series, or postpone our *salah* to attend to other worldly activities. And that is for those who pray. There are those who have abandoned their *salah* completely.

The Prophet (SAS) said, "Between disbelief and faith, is abandoning the *salah*." Through *salah*, we are able to connect with our Lord. The Arabic word *salah* is actually derived from the word meaning "connection." *Salah* also conveys the meaning of *du'a`* or supplication. The Prophet (SAS) also said, "The nearest a servant comes to his Lord is when he is prostrating himself, so make supplication often."

As one of the pillars of Islam, *salah* is the most regular compulsory action in a

Muslim's life. Obligatory fasting is just for one month. Obligatory charity (*zakat*) is paid on one's savings calculated at the end of one year. Pilgrimage to Mecca is only once in a lifetime. However, prayer is the one act that must be fulfilled at least five times a day, regardless of the situation. In fact, Allah (SWT) did not even exempt the Muslims from praying even during the battle! Allah says in the Qur`an,

حَافِظُوا عَلَى الصَّلَوَاتِ وَالصَّلَاةِ الْوُسْطَىٰ وَقُومُوا لِلَّهِ قَانِتِينَ فَإِنْ خِفْتُمْ فَرِجَالًا أَوْ رُكْبَانًا فَإِذَا أَمِنتُمْ فَاذْكُرُوا اللَّهَ كَمَا عَلَّمَكُم مَّا لَمْ تَكُونُوا تَعْلَمُونَ ◯

*Guard the prayers, and the middle prayer, and stand before Allah in total devotion. If you are in danger, then pray on foot or while riding, but when you are safe again, remember Allah, as He has taught you what you did not know. (al-Baqara, 2:238-239)*

Man was created weak and without help from Allah, it will be impossible to refrain from evil. Allah tells us in the Qur`an,

إِنَّ الصَّلَاةَ تَنْهَىٰ عَنِ الْفَحْشَاءِ وَالْمُنكَرِ ◯

*Surely salah keeps one away from indecency and evil. (al-'Ankabut, 29:45)*

There is no doubt that the one who stands in front of Allah willingly will be different from the one who doesn't. How can one continue to commit the same sins if one is standing before Allah five times a day? By realizing Allah's greatness and dependence on Him, a believer gets rid of his false pride and arrogance. He humbles himself in *salah* and places his head—the source of his honor and intellect—to the ground and says,

سُبْحَانَ رَبِّيَ الْأَعْلَى ◯

*How perfect is my Lord, The Most High.*

Humbleness is one of the qualities which Allah has associated with success. Allah says,

قَدْ أَفْلَحَ الْمُؤْمِنُونَ الَّذِينَ هُمْ فِي صَلَاتِهِمْ خَاشِعُونَ ◯

*Successful indeed are the believers; those who humble themselves in their prayers. (al-Mu`minoon,23:1-2)*

Of course, this can only be achieved when we understand what we are reciting and concentrate with humility. We should try our best to learn what we recite in our *salah*. Knowingly or unknowingly, intentionally or unintentionally, people commit sins. However, Allah has provided, in *salah* a way to wipe out those sins.

وَأَقِمِ الصَّلَاةَ طَرَفَيِ النَّهَارِ وَزُلَفًا مِّنَ اللَّيْلِ إِنَّ الْحَسَنَاتِ يُذْهِبْنَ السَّيِّئَاتِ ذَٰلِكَ ذِكْرَىٰ لِلذَّاكِرِينَ ◯

*Establish salah at each end of the day and in the first part of the night. Surely, good*

*deeds wipe out evil deeds. This is a reminder for the mindful. (Hud, 11:114)*

The Prophet (SAS) gave a beautiful example when he said to his companions, "Consider if one of you had a river by his door in which he bathed five times a day. Would any filth remain on him?" They said, "No." Then the Prophet (SAS) replied, "Likewise, Allah wipes away sins with the five daily prayers."

Man is surrounded by numerous trials and problems. Once we focus on strengthening our relationship with our Lord who is All-Powerful, He will fix our problems.

$$ يَا أَيُّهَا الَّذِينَ آمَنُوا اسْتَعِينُوا بِالصَّبْرِ وَالصَّلَاةِ إِنَّ اللَّهَ مَعَ الصَّابِرِينَ ۝ $$

*O you who believe, seek help through patience and salah; surely, Allah is with the patient ones. (al-Baqara, 2:153)*

When the prayer is performed in congregation, it cultivates brotherhood, equality, and humility between Muslims. The worshippers stand in rows, shoulder to shoulder, without any distinction of race, nationality, color, wealth, family, or status, and pray altogether as one body. This act of unity helps demolish the barriers which stand between people. The Prophet (SAS) said, "Prayer in congregation is better than praying alone by twenty-seven degrees." We not only have to perform *salah*, but have to "establish" it, which means that the system of prayer should be organized on a collective basis. One of the prayers that the Prophet Ibraheem (AS) made while building the Ka'ba was,

$$ رَبِّ اجْعَلْنِي مُقِيمَ الصَّلَاةِ وَمِن ذُرِّيَّتِي رَبَّنَا وَتَقَبَّلْ دُعَاءِ ۝ $$

*My Lord! Make me and my descendants people who establish salah. Our Lord, accept my prayer. (Ibraheem, 14:40)*

If there is a person in a locality who prays individually but no arrangements are made for congregational prayer, it cannot be claimed that prayer is established in that locality. The whole purpose of our existence is to worship Allah. Yet those who do not perform or establish *salah* as prescribed are disobeying their Creator every day. The Qur`an tells us that the people in hell will be asked,

$$ مَا سَلَكَكُمْ فِي سَقَرَ ۝ قَالُوا لَمْ نَكُ مِنَ الْمُصَلِّينَ ۝ $$

*What has caused you to enter hell? They will say: We were not of those who used to pray. (al-Muddaththir, 74:42-43)*

How many of us will be among those who say, "We were not of those who prayed," or "We were not of those who prayed on time," or "We were not of those who made prayer a priority in our lives." Why is it that if we are in class or at work or fast asleep at the time of *fajr* and we need to use the restroom, we make time for that? In fact, the question almost sounds absurd. We don't even consider it an option not to do so. The truth is that we put the needs of our body above the needs of our soul. We feed our bodies because if we didn't, we would die. When we starve our souls by not praying, we cause our souls to die. Ironically, the body that we tend to is only temporary, while the soul that we neglect is eternal. Prayer satisfies our spiritual need to be in contact with our Creator. This gives the soul peace and contentment. Allah reminds us in the Qur`an,

$$أَلَا بِذِكْرِ اللَّهِ تَطْمَئِنُّ الْقُلُوبُ ۝$$

*Truly it is in the remembrance of Allah that hearts find peace. (ar-Ra'd, 13:28)*

Allah (SWT) commanded the Prophet Musa (AS) to establish *salah*.

$$وَأَقِمِ الصَّلَاةَ لِذِكْرِي ۝$$

*And establish salah to remember Me. (Ta Ha, 20:14)*

The person who does not pray regularly, who does not remember Allah (SWT) constantly, and who has no connection with Allah (SWT) becomes a person who helplessly seeks alternatives to look for calmness and happiness. He does so in vain and wanders aimlessly. Allah (SWT) says,

$$وَمَنْ أَعْرَضَ عَن ذِكْرِي فَإِنَّ لَهُ مَعِيشَةً ضَنكًا وَنَحْشُرُهُ يَوْمَ الْقِيَامَةِ أَعْمَىٰ ۝$$

*And whoever turns away from My remembrance; indeed for him is a life of hardship. And on the Day of Resurrection, We shall raise him blind. (Ta Ha, 20:124)*

What excuses will be given on the Day of Judgment by a person who does not pray at all, or who does not pray regularly? May Allah (SWT) give us the *tawfeeq* to establish *salah*, and to remember Him.

Brothers and sisters! Refusing the invitation of our Creator to establish this close relationship with Him through *salah* is the ultimate ingratitude. Allah tells us,

$$قُلْ هُوَ الَّذِي أَنشَأَكُمْ وَجَعَلَ لَكُمُ السَّمْعَ وَالْأَبْصَارَ وَالْأَفْئِدَةَ قَلِيلًا مَّا تَشْكُرُونَ ۝$$

*Say, It is He who created you, and made for you hearing, eyesight, and hearts. Little do you thank. (al-Mulk, 67:23)*

The Prophet's (SAS) feet would sometimes get swollen because he would stand in prayer for lengthy periods, and when asked about why he did this, he would reply, "Should I not be a grateful servant (of Allah)?"

We learn from studying the life of the Prophet (SAS) that when something serious troubled him, he took refuge in *salah*. Explaining the benefits of *salah*, Ibn al-Qayyim al-Jawziyya says in his well-known book *The Prophetic Medicine*, "Prayer can bring about one's provision (*rizq*). It preserves health, wards off harm, repels diseases, strengthens the heart, brightens the face, gladdens the soul, removes laziness, invigorates the limbs, reinforces the faculties, expands the breast, nourishes the spirit, lights up the heart, preserves well-being, protects against affliction, attracts blessings, keeps Satan at a distance, and brings one closer to the Merciful Lord...Prayer has a wonderful effect in warding off the evils of this life, especially when it is given its due and is properly performed, outwardly and inwardly."

On a final note, let us remind ourselves that we have to hold firmly to the *salah* till we die, for Allah says,

$$\text{فَسَبِّحْ بِحَمْدِ رَبِّكَ وَكُنْ مِنَ السَّاجِدِينَ ۝ وَاعْبُدْ رَبَّكَ حَتَّى يَأْتِيَكَ الْيَقِينُ ۝}$$

*So glorify the praise of your Lord and be among the ones who prostrate themselves.*
*And worship your Lord until what is certain comes to you. (al-Hijr, 15:98-99)*

Brothers and sisters! *Salah* was the first act of worship of Allah (SWT) to be legislated, and the last ritual worship that the Prophet (SAS) advised his *ummah* to guard. This shows the importance and centrality of *salah* in a believer's life.

May Allah make us understand the importance of *salah* and may He grant us the *tawfeeq* to pray as we are required to pray. *Ameen.*

• 44 •

# IMPORTANCE OF STUDYING THE *SEERAH*

In my *khutbah* today, I intend to share some thoughts with you on the importance of studying the *seerah* of the noblest and the greatest of all souls ever to be born, and the most influential human being to set foot on earth till the end of times: our beloved Prophet Muhammad (SAS). We are passing through the month of Rabi' al-Awwal. It is the third month of the Islamic lunar calendar. Both the birth and the death of Muhammad (SAS) are said to have taken place during this month, and both are said to fall on the 12th of Rabi' al-Awwal.

What is *seerah*? It refers to the study of the life of the Prophet Muhammad (SAS) and all that is related to him. This includes knowledge of the events that preceded his birth. It includes details of his interactions and dealings with his companions, his family, and the people around him including the believers, the disbelievers, the hypocrites, and the People of the Book. *Seerah* also covers events that occurred in the years immediately following his death.

Why is studying the *seerah* important? There are several good reasons why we should study the *seerah*. The first and foremost is to understand the Qur`an. We know that Allah Himself has preserved and protected the Qur`an for all times to come for He says,

$$ إِنَّا نَحْنُ نَزَّلْنَا الذِّكْرَ وَإِنَّا لَهُ لَحَافِظُونَ ◯ $$

*It is We Who have sent down the Reminder and We Who will preserve it. (al-Hijr, 15:9)*

Preservation of the Qur`an is not only restricted to protecting its words from change. If that was the case, its meanings could be manipulated according to human desires while its words remained intact. However, Allah (SWT) also protected the essential meanings of the Qur`an from change by entrusting the explanation and the interpretation of the meanings of the Qur`an to the Prophet (SAS). In this respect, Allah (SWT) says,

$$ وَأَنْزَلْنَا إِلَيْكَ الذِّكْرَ لِتُبَيِّنَ لِلنَّاسِ مَا نُزِّلَ إِلَيْهِمْ وَلَعَلَّهُمْ يَتَفَكَّرُونَ ◯ $$

*And We have sent down the Reminder to you so that you can make clear to mankind what has been sent down to them so that hopefully they will reflect. (an-Nahl, 16:44)*

To understand the meanings of rulings and commandments in the Qur`an, we have to consider what the Prophet (SAS) said or did regarding them. For example, in the Qur`an, Allah commands the believers to offer salah, to pay zakat, to fast, and to perform hajj. However, in order to obey these instructions correctly, one must study the methodology of the Prophet (SAS) in this regard. Among his many clarifications concerning salah, Allah's Messenger instructed his followers by saying, "And pray as you have seen me praying." Likewise, he gave specific instructions regarding zakat, fasting, the rites and rituals of hajj, and many other rulings pertaining to the daily lives of the believers. Therefore, the Prophet's sayings and actions recorded in the collections of hadeeth were primarily based on revelation from Allah (SWT) and are considered a fundamental source of guidance in Islam. Concerning this aspect of Prophet (SAS), Allah (SWT) says in Surat an-Najm,

$$ وَمَا يَنْطِقُ عَنِ الْهَوَى إِنْ هُوَ إِلاَّ وَحْيٌ يُوحَى ◯ $$

*He does not speak from his own desire. It is nothing but Revelation revealed. (an-Najm, 53:3-4)*

And the Prophet (SAS) reiterated this point when he said, "Indeed, I was given the Qur`an and something similar to it along with it." He was referring to his divinely guided sayings and actions.

Another reason for studying the *seerah* is that it helps us to follow the example of the Prophet's exemplary character. Because the Prophet (SAS) was guided by revelation in his personal life, his character and social interactions became prime examples of moral conduct for Muslims until the Last Day. Exhorting believers to follow the Prophet's example, Allah says in *Surat al-Ahzab*,

لَقَدْ كَانَ لَكُمْ فِي رَسُولِ اللَّهِ أُسْوَةٌ حَسَنَةٌ لِمَنْ كَانَ يَرْجُو اللَّهَ وَالْيَوْمَ الآخِرَ وَذَكَرَ اللَّهَ كَثِيرًا ◯

*The Messenger of Allah is an excellent model for those of you who put your hope in Allah and the Last Day and remember Allah very often. (al-Ahzab, 33:21)*

The daily life of the Prophet (SAS) represents the ideal code of good conduct. In fact, when the Prophet's wife 'A`isha (RAA) was asked about his conduct, she replied, "His character was the Qur`an."He followed the Qur`an very meticulously and lived the Qur`an at every moment, in every detail of his life. His life was the reflection of Allah's words. He became the Qur`an in person, the embodiment of the Qur`an. Addressing His beloved Prophet, Allah says in *Surat al-Qalam*,

وَإِنَّكَ لَعَلى خُلُقٍ عَظِيمٍ ◯

*And you are surely on an exalted standard of character. (al-Qalam, 68:4)*

The uniqueness of the Prophet Muhammad (SAS) is that he was not only a great person in his own time, but he is great for all times, for all people of any race, color, nationality, or geographical location. His example was good for the seventh century Arabs and his example continues to be followed today in the twenty-first century. He is an excellent example for rich and poor, for young and old, for rulers and ruled, for the most intelligent as well as the most common of people. Allah sent him as His Prophet for all humanity.

Study of the *seerah* also helps to develop the love of Prophet (SAS) in our hearts. Loving the Prophet (SAS) is *'ibada*(an act of worship), a part of *iman*(faith). In a well-known hadeeth, the Prophet (SAS) said, "*None of you will attain true faith until you love me more than your parents, your children, and the whole world.*"What does that mean? It means that you are willing to give up your desires to follow the way of the Prophet (SAS), which means preferring him over everyone and everything else. In fact, in *Surat Aal 'Imran* Allah (SWT) makes following the Prophet (SAS) a condition for loving Allah (SWT) when He says,

قُلْ إِنْ كُنْتُمْ تُحِبُّونَ اللَّهَ فَاتَّبِعُونِي يُحْبِبْكُمُ اللَّهُ وَيَغْفِرْ لَكُمْ ذُنُوبَكُمْ وَاللَّهُ غَفُورٌ رَحِيمٌ ◯

*Say: If you love God, follow me, and God will love you and forgive you your sins; God is*

*most forgiving, most merciful. (Aal 'Imran, 3:31)*

Everybody loved, cherished, and respected the Prophet (SAS) because his demanding personality enabled him to transcend his ego and to give of himself. He carried a universal message, both in the experience of love present throughout his life and in his reminders to people of the need to adhere to a universal ethics that transcends divisions, affiliations, and rigid identities. He was the beloved of God and is an example among humans.

Another good reason to study the *seerah* is that it helps us to appreciate the sacrifices the Prophet (SAS) made for his *ummah*. Whenever we go through tough times, we find comfort and consolation in the *seerah* because the Prophet (SAS) went through the hardest of times yet stood firm and maintained his calm and composure. He spread the message of Islam in Arabia at a time when human rights had no meaning, when might was right, and when the society was entrenched in paganism. In this environment, Prophet Muhammad (SAS) taught a message of justice, peace, human rights, animal rights, and even environmental rights as ordained by God, the One True Creator of all that is in the universe.

Allah has shown us in the character of Prophet Muhammad (SAS) the model of a compassionate person. He treated everyone—friends and foe, man and woman, young and old—with kindness and respect. Even when some of the pagan Arabs reacted to his message with extreme hatred, he showed love and kindness. Showing mercy and forgiving others can only be the attributes of the strong. Referring to the Prophet's universal all-embracing mercy, Allah (SWT) says in *Surat al-Anbiya`*,

$$\text{وَمَا أَرْسَلْنَاكَ إِلَّا رَحْمَةً لِلْعَالَمِينَ}$$

*And We have not sent you except as a mercy to the worlds. (al-Anbiya`, 21:107)*

Finally, study of the *seerah* also helps in developing a Muslim identity. We see all around that Muslims are suffering from an identity crisis. Many of us know the names of celebrities or players in their favorite soccer teams, yet do not know the names of the prominent companions of the Prophet (SAS). One way to overcome this identity crisis is to study the history of Islam which chiefly is the life history of the Prophet (SAS), his companions, and the righteous predecessors.

I strongly recommend that you study the noble *seerah* of the Prophet (SAS). There is a huge collection of works on *seerah* ranging from the earliest classical works of the first century of the *hijra* to ones written in present times. May Allah (SWT) give us the *tawfeeq* to study the *seerah* and make us motivated to follow the example of our beloved Prophet (SAS). *Ameen!*

# • 45 •

# IS ISLAM EASY AND SIMPLE OR
# DIFFICULT AND COMPLICATED?

Very often we find that there are different interpretations of Islamic rulings followed
by different sects, groups, movements, and schools of thought within Islam. Even
though these differences are usually on minor issues , they sometimes give rise to
confusion in the minds of many Muslims. Some Muslims developed an idea that Islam
itself is difficult and complicated. The topic of my *khutbah* today is: "Is Islam Easy and
Simple or Difficult and Complicated?"

If we look back to the times of the Prophet Muhammad (SAS), we see the
simplicity and beauty of Islam as preached and practiced by the noble Messenger and
his followers. There is a story in the *seerah* of the Prophet (SAS) that once a Bedouin
Arab came to him while he was in the company of his companions. The Bedouin asked
the Prophet (SAS) three questions: "Who raised the heaven?" "Who spread out the
earth?" and "Who erected the mountains?" To each of these questions, the Prophet
(SAS) replied, "Allah." Then the Bedouin said, "I ask you by the Creator of the heaven,
the earth, and the mountains. Did Allah send you as a Messenger to us?" The Prophet
(SAS) replied, "Yes." Then the Bedouin asked four more questions in succession: "Did
your Lord order us to pray five times a day?""Did your Lord order us to fast in the
month of Ramadan?""Did your Lord order us to pay *zakat* from our wealth?""Did your
Lord order us to perform hajj once in a lifetime for whoever has the means to do so?"
To each of these questions, the Prophet (SAS) replied, "Yes." Then the Bedouin said, "I
bear witness that there is no God but Allah, and I bear witness that Muhammad is the
Messenger of Allah." Then he turned away to leave and said to the Prophet (SAS), "By
He Who has sent you with the truth, I will not add anything to these things and I will
not decrease anything from them." The Prophet (SAS) turning to his companions said,
"If he has spoken truthfully, he will certainly enter paradise."

The above story reflects the simplicity of Islam. No discussion was raised in this
entire conversation about the intricacies and subtleties of religion. Oftentimes, without
focusing on the essence and spirit of the basic and simple teachings of Islam, Muslims
immerse themselves in discussions about secondary issues of *fiqh* and local cultural
practices. More often than not, these topics become fertile ground for unnecessary
disputes among Muslims.

There is a misunderstanding among many people that Islam is difficult and a burden to follow. Such people either have an incorrect understanding of Islam or do not realize how easy the rules of Islam are to follow. The general principle regarding things of this world is that everything is permissible unless proven otherwise. So, the burden of proof actually falls on those who say that anything is prohibited. Allah reassures us in the Qur`an,

يُرِيدُ اللَّهُ بِكُمُ الْيُسْرَ وَلَا يُرِيدُ بِكُمُ الْعُسْرَ ◯

*Allah wishes to make things easy for you, and not to make things difficult for you. (al-Baqara, 2:185)*

وَمَا جَعَلَ عَلَيْكُمْ فِي الدِّينِ مِنْ حَرَجٍ ◯

*He has not imposed hardships on you in religion. (al-Hajj, 22:78)*

Imam al-Bukhari has a chapter in his *Saheeh* book of hadeeths called "The Chapter of the Religion Being Easy" and ample proof for this point can be found in that chapter. The Prophet (SAS) said, "Religion is very easy and whoever overburdens himself in his religion will not be able to continue in that way. So you should not be extremists but aim to be near to perfection and receive the good tidings that you will be rewarded, and gain strength by worshipping in the mornings and the nights."

When the Prophet (SAS) appointed Mua'dh ibn Jabal as a governor in Yemen, he advised him to invite the People of the Book there toward Islam step by step, starting from *tawheed*, then progressing to *salah*, *zakat*, and so on. The Prophet (SAS) never gave extensive instructions to his companions when sending them as his envoys to convey the message of Islam to others. We also learn from this story that Islam teaches gradualism instead of radicalism. This principle is well-established by a hadeeth found in the *Saheeh* of Bukhari. 'A`isha, the wife of the Prophet (SAS), said that the first verses of the Qur`an were related mostly to heaven and hell. Then, after a long time, when the people's hearts had softened, the specific commands to abstain from adultery and drinking were revealed in the Qur`an. This is a clear proof that for social change, Islam advocates the "evolutionary" method, rather than the "revolutionary" method. The Qur`an is the basis and fountain head of the Islamic faith. All universal Islamic principles are found in it. Allah (SWT) says in the Qur`an,

مَا فَرَّطْنَا فِي الْكِتَابِ مِنْ شَيْءٍ ◯

*We have not omitted anything from the Book. (al-An'am, 6:38)*

The universal message of beliefs, morals, and ethics, and the pure, simple teachings of Islam found in the Qur`an are same as those contained in the earlier scriptures. Allah tells us,

شَرَعَ لَكُمْ مِنَ الدِّينِ مَا وَصَّى بِهِ نُوحًا وَالَّذِي أَوْحَيْنَا إِلَيْكَ وَمَا وَصَّيْنَا بِهِ إِبْرَاهِيمَ وَمُوسَى وَعِيسَى أَنْ أَقِيمُوا الدِّينَ وَلَا تَتَفَرَّقُوا فِيهِ ○

*He (Allah) has ordained for you the same religion which He enjoined on Noah, and which We have revealed to you, and which We enjoined upon Abraham and Moses and Jesus, so that you should remain steadfast in religion and not become divided in it.*
(ash-Shura, 42:13)

Islam stands as the most rational and precise religion. Maybe other religions don't encourage believers to think, but Islam is a religion rooted in thinking. When the *ummah* stops thinking, then the next generation is only Muslim because their parents are Muslim. We should ask questions until our hearts are satisfied. Also, Islam is a natural religion as it appeals to the inborn human nature (*fitra*). Allah says in *Surat ar-Rum*,

فَأَقِمْ وَجْهَكَ لِلدِّينِ حَنِيفًا فِطْرَةَ اللَّهِ الَّتِي فَطَرَ النَّاسَ عَلَيْهَا ○

*Devote yourself single-mindedly to the true faith; and adhere to the true nature on which Allah has created human beings. (ar-Rum, 30:30)*

Islam is easy to understand and follow for anyone who wants to do so. It fulfills man's basic needs without asking him to do anything unnatural. We cannot find even one ruling in the Qur`an and Sunnah that goes against human nature. Islam does not ask us to do anything that we are incapable of doing. We are not required to give up our personalities, social lives, or money. We are not required to pray all night or fast every day, in fact such things are prohibited. Islam emphasizes that we live a balanced life fulfilling our obligations to Allah (SWT) as well as our obligations toward people and even our own selves.

The simplicity of Islamic teachings must also be manifested in a Muslim's entire life. The Prophet (SAS) said, "The believer is kind and gracious for there is no goodness in one who is neither kind nor gracious. The best of people are those who are most beneficial to people." He also said, "Among the Muslims the most perfect, as regards his faith, is the one whose character is excellent, and the best among you are those who treat their wives well." This is the way of living and presenting Islam to others. The believer is also soft-hearted. He is pleasant and easily approachable. The Prophet (SAS) demonstrated this in his behavior toward his companions and others. The Qur`an alludes to this when addressing the Prophet (SAS).

فَبِمَا رَحْمَةٍ مِنَ اللَّهِ لِنْتَ لَهُمْ وَلَوْ كُنْتَ فَظًّا غَلِيظَ الْقَلْبِ لَانْفَضُّوا مِنْ حَوْلِكَ ○

*It is out of Allah's mercy that you have been lenient with them. Had you been cruel or hard-hearted, they would have certainly abandoned you. (Aal'Imran, 3:159)*

The Prophet (SAS) said, "Shall I not tell you for whom the hellfire is forbidden? It is forbidden for every person who is accessible, polite, and mild." This means that the person is accessible to people, against harshness, easygoing in his character, and generous in his personality.

While instilling the qualities of kindness and graciousness, Islam teaches us to control our anger. Because almost everyone struggles with anger at some time or another in their lives, this comprehensive and far-reaching advice should be applied to everyone. Describing the righteous believers in the Qur`an, Allah says,

الَّذِينَ يُنْفِقُونَ فِي السَّرَّاءِ وَالضَّرَّاءِ وَالْكَاظِمِينَ الْغَيْظَ وَالْعَافِينَ عَنِ النَّاسِ وَاللَّهُ يُحِبُّ الْمُحْسِنِينَ ○

*The ones who spend in prosperity and adversity, and who repress anger, and who pardon the people; Allah loves the good doers. (Aal'Imran, 3:134)*

Islam also teaches us to forgive others. We are responsible for our actions, but we also make mistakes and we are constantly in need of forgiveness. Islam speaks about two elements of forgiveness: Allah's forgiveness and human forgiveness. We need both because we do wrong in our relationship with Allah (SWT) as well as in our relationships with one another. Allah (SWT) is ever-forgiving (*al-Ghafoor*) and most merciful (*ar-Raheem*). Allah (SWT) keeps forgiving us. We too have to learn to forgive each other.

Brothers and sisters! One of the reasons why people with generous hearts are always happy is because they forgive and forget the mistakes of others, especially those closest to them, their relatives, neighbors, and friends. This is a great act of virtue. Allah (SWT) praises people who forgive.

وَلَمَنْ صَبَرَ وَغَفَرَ إِنَّ ذَلِكَ لَمِنْ عَزْمِ الْأُمُورِ ○

*And for he who is patient and forgives, then surely that is an indication of strength.*
(ash-Shura, 42:43)

Islam teaches us to be truthful. In Islam, truthfulness is the conformity of the outer with the inner, the action with the intention, the speech with the belief, and the practice with the preaching. Islam also teaches us not to be extravagant.

وَلَا تُسْرِفُوا إِنَّهُ لَا يُحِبُّ الْمُسْرِفِينَ ○

*And do not act extravagantly; surely He does not love the extravagant. (al-An'am, 6:141)*

Yet many times we complicate our own lives with extravagance, such as when we celebrate marriages or host social functions and parties.

*Al-hamduli-llah!* Life is simple and enjoyable when we smile. The Prophet (SAS) even informed us that every good deed is an act of charity, such that even smiling at your brother is act of charity.

One of the principles of success that Islam teaches us is to begin from the possible. This principle is well-explained in another saying of 'A`isha (RAA). She said, "Whenever the Prophet had to choose between two options, he always opted for the easier choice."Choosing the easiest option means beginning from what is possible, and one who begins from the possible will surely reach his goal.

In the early days of Mecca, there were many problems and difficulties. At that time, a guiding verse in the Qur`an was revealed.

إِنَّ مَعَ الْعُسْرِ يُسْرًا ◯

*With every hardship, there is ease. (al-Inshirah, 94:6)*

This means that if there are some problems, there are also opportunities at the same time. And the way to success is to ignore the problems and avail the opportunities. This is like seeing advantage in disadvantage.

The basic teachings of Islam are simple to understand and practical to implement, making Islam a simple and universal religion that can be practiced by anyone regardless of his or her intellectual or physical capabilities. It is this pure simplicity of Islam that makes it so universally appealing and applicable for all times and places.

However, it should be clear that presenting Islam as a simple, easy, and universal religion does not mean that Muslims do not take it seriously and make it a reason for gradually losing their faith. The divinely mandated laws, principles, and guidance in Islam have to be followed in letter and spirit by the believers. Allah cautions us in the Qur`an,

يَا أَيُّهَا الَّذِينَ آمَنُوا ادْخُلُوا فِي السِّلْمِ كَافَّةً وَلَا تَتَّبِعُوا خُطُوَاتِ الشَّيْطَانِ إِنَّهُ لَكُمْ عَدُوٌّ مُبِينٌ ◯

*O believers! Enter into Islam wholeheartedly and do not follow Satan's footsteps. He is clearly your enemy. (al-Baqara, 2:208)*

Heedlessness of the divinely guided code of conduct invites serious consequences both in this life and in the hereafter. May Allah bless each one of us in understanding the Islamic way of life that He has ordained for us. *Allahumma ameen.*

# ISLAMIC CULTURE

In today's *khutbah*, I intend to talk to you about our Islamic culture. My *khutbah* will address questions such as: What is culture? Does Islam have a distinct culture? What are some of the core features of the Islamic culture? Is the Islamic culture monolithic or is it diverse? Are there some elements in the Islamic culture that change and some other elements that do not change? We should know that one of the many beauties of Islam is its culture.

What is culture? People generally think culture refers to art, music, and some social habits. The word culture, however, is more comprehensive in meaning. Culture is the total range of activities and ideas of a people with shared traditions, which are transmitted and reinforced by members of the group. There are over 1.6 billion Muslims throughout the world, and though they speak hundreds of different languages and live in numerous different countries, they still share a common Islamic culture. This culture is embedded in certain common beliefs, modes of worship, rules of behavior, styles of dressing, ways of producing and cooking food, political and economic systems, and so on.

Islam has a distinct culture, but it has varieties and a rich diversity. It is not monolithic. There are elements of Islamic culture that integral to the Islamic way of life. They do not change and are universally accepted by all Muslims. There are also elements in Islamic culture that are different from place to place and from people to people. The universals are based on the Qur`an and the Sunnah while the variables are based on local customs of various people. Thus, there is an Arab Islamic culture, an Indo-Pakistani-Bangladeshi Islamic culture, an African Islamic culture, a Chinese Islamic culture, an American, European or Western Islamic culture, an Indonesian Islamic culture, a Malaysian Islamic culture, and many other Islamic cultures.

Wherever we happen to live, we have to develop our distinct Islamic culture while cooperating and interacting with people of other diverse cultures. Our culture is based on the Qur`an and the Sunnah as well as on legacy of human experience and learning. We have benefited from the knowledge of all people and we should be open to all beneficial knowledge in order to keep our culture strong and dynamic. However, wherever we live, we should always keep in mind the basic features and characteristics of our Islamic culture. We should not forget these prominent features. These features are constant, and no Islamic culture can be without them.

What are some characteristics of Islamic culture? First, our culture is God-centered. Islam is founded on the belief that there is only one God without associates or partners. He is the universal Creator, Sustainer, and Cherisher of all. We believe in divine guidance that came to us through God's many prophets and messengers and finally through the Last Prophet Muhammad (SAS). According to the Qur'an, a Muslim must believe in all the prophets of God and must accept them and respect them. They all represent one brotherhood of faith. They were all "Muslims" in the broad sense of the word. They all submitted themselves to God, and they all conveyed the same universal message. We also believe in life after death and the Day of Judgment. We prioritize our worship: *salah* (prayers), *siyam* (fasting), *zakat* (obligatory charity), and hajj (pilgrimage to Mecca). We also understand that God has permitted certain things and forbidden certain things and we uphold these rules accordingly.

Secondly, Islamic culture emphasizes that all people are equal. Islam does not discriminate between people on the basis of their color, race, ethnicity, nationality, or the language they speak. We believe in the worth and value of all human beings and all creations of God. We believe in the freedom of religion. There is no compulsion in matters of religion. Islam accepts plurality in human societies. Pluralism means living peacefully with those who hold different beliefs and convictions. Addressing the entire human race, Allah (SWT) says in the Qur'an,

يَا أَيُّهَا النَّاسُ إِنَّا خَلَقْنَاكُمْ مِنْ ذَكَرٍ وَأُنْثَى وَجَعَلْنَاكُمْ شُعُوبًا وَقَبَائِلَ لِتَعَارَفُوا إِنَّ أَكْرَمَكُمْ عِنْدَ اللَّهِ أَتْقَاكُمْ إِنَّ اللَّهَ عَلِيمٌ خَبِيرٌ ○

*O humankind! We (Allah) have created you from a single (pair) of a male and a female and have made you into nations and tribes, so that you may come to know one another. Verily, the most honored of you in the sight of Allah is the most righteous of you. Surely, God is All-Knowing, All-Aware. (al-Hujurat, 49:13)*

This sweeping statement in the Qur'an about broad human brotherhood and sisterhood is a profound basis for promoting peace among all. Humanity is like a bouquet of flowers in which each flower is beautiful in its own right. Yet, the combination of all flowers and the rich diversity of their colors is more beautiful. God is One and is impartial toward His creation. He provides for all, including those who deny Him. He cares for the well-being of all and gives them ample opportunity to repent to Him; to end the state of separateness suffered by those who reject Him or are unmindful of Him. This implies that all humans are equal before God in terms of their humanity, irrespective of their particular beliefs. No human should be oppressed or mistreated by other fellow humans because of the theological position he or she holds.

These values lead to an attitude of tolerance and accepting people as they are. Our culture is tolerant to people of all faiths, especially to the People of the Book; that is the Jews and the Christians. The human is a free agent, and as such, each person is individually responsible before God for his or her beliefs and moral choices. A person can be held accountable in this life only if their choice infringes on the rights of individuals or society, such as the commission of crimes or acts of aggression. In other words, no human is entitled to dehumanize or punish another human on the sole ground that the latter is following a different religion or no religion at all. This value implies that peaceful coexistence among followers of all religions and respecting their humanity is not only possible, but mandated.

The Qur`an gives various reasons why each human being must be honored and dignified on account of being human and irrespective of his or her chosen beliefs. Such honor is symbolized by the way the Qur`an describes God's creation of the human as being "in the best of molds." The human being is the crown of God's creation. The Qur`an describes this human as the trustee of God on earth. God created everything on earth and in the heavens for the benefit of human beings. Human life is held sacred. Allah says in the Qur`an,

مَنْ قَتَلَ نَفْسًا بِغَيْرِ نَفْسٍ أَوْ فَسَادٍ فِي الْأَرْضِ فَكَأَنَّمَا قَتَلَ النَّاسَ جَمِيعًا وَمَنْ أَحْيَاهَا فَكَأَنَّمَا أَحْيَا النَّاسَ جَمِيعًا ◯

*If anyone slays a human being, unless it be for murder, or for spreading mischief on earth, it shall be as though he had slain all humankind; whereas, if anyone saves a life, it shall be as though he had saved the lives of all humankind. (al-Ma`ida, 5:32)*

We also believe that all Muslims are brothers and sisters in faith irrespective of their cultural backgrounds. The sense of brotherhood in faith must be very strong among Muslims, regardless of the geographic boundaries or changing political or economic conditions. We must also keep good relations with all human beings, especially our neighbors.

One of the most prominent features of our Islamic culture is that it emphasizes struggle, change, social justice, and removal of evil and oppression. Let us pray to Allah (SWT) to keep us on the right path and help us to promote peace and justice in this world and to try to remove all forms of injustice and oppression.

Another important feature of the Islamic culture is that it stresses truthfulness, honesty, modesty, and cleanliness, both outward and inward. It is against extravagance, showing off, or extremism. It teaches self-confidence and self-reliance. It emphasizes charity and generosity. Our Islamic culture is family-oriented with great emphasis on good spousal relations, good care of children, and love and respect for the elders. The sharing and caring attitude goes beyond one's immediate family to one's extended families and ultimately to the entire human family.

Among other things, our Islamic culture encourages learning and seeking knowledge. It does not differentiate between religious and secular education. We believe that any beneficial knowledge is important. We must emphasize open-mindedness and willingness to accept the wisdom from any source. The Prophet (SAS) said, "Wisdom is the lost property of the believer, so wherever he finds it then he has a right to it."

Our Islamic culture also emphasizes promoting good things with wisdom and patience. Ours is not a dominating or colonizing culture, but it is also not an isolationist culture. We believe in inviting all people to Islam without coercion. Our Islamic culture teaches us to listen and engage in dialogue with others. We believe that human nature is inherently good and if people are given the chance to know and learn Islam as it is, they will find it satisfying and fulfilling.

Islamic culture promotes art, architecture, aesthetics, a healthy environment, and wholesome entertainment. Islamic culture, as such, does not give a detailed list of the entertainments that are allowed. It does, however, give a list of items that are not allowed. In other words, all entertainments are allowed except those that fall in the forbidden category. Islam teaches us to remember that we haven't come into this world primarily to play. However, if we get bored, or feel like doing something different in order to keep our spirits alive, we are permitted to get involved in any entertainment of our choice provided it is within the bounds of the Islamic laws, ethics and values.

There are certain matters of belief and practice that are poles apart from the Islamic culture. For example, the notion of multiple deities or objects of worship is completely ruled out in the Islamic culture. Dealing in *riba* (usurious transactions), eating pork, drinking alcohol, using drugs and other intoxicants, indulging in gambling or any game of chance, and engaging in any intimate spousal relationship outside the institution of marriage are some of the practices that are totally in contrast to the Islamic culture. Please note that wherever we live, at any time, and among any people, we must uphold these constant values of our Islamic culture. We cannot be true Muslims if our culture compromises on any of these principles.

Last but not least, our Islamic culture emphasizes patience and reminds us that we should keep working in a steadfast manner and put our total trust in our Creator, Allah (SWT), the Lord and Sustainer of the worlds. We strongly believe that the truth will prevail, and falsehood will vanish. Every believer must participate in pursuing this goal.

وَقُلْ جَاءَ الْحَقُّ وَزَهَقَ الْبَاطِلُ إِنَّ الْبَاطِلَ كَانَ زَهُوقًا ○

*Say: Truth has come, and falsehood has vanished. Falsehood is always bound to vanish. (al-Isra`, 17:81)*

It is our duty to educate people about these values of our Islamic culture. Needless to say, we must keep trying to improve ourselves, especially in areas where we find ourselves deficient.

---

*Based on the thoughts and writings of Dr. Muzammil H Siddiqi, Director of the Islamic Society of Orange County in Garden Grove, CA.

# ISLAMIC ETIQUETTE OF DEALING WITH PEOPLE

Today's *khutbah* is on the topic: "Islamic Etiquette of Dealing with People." We know that the state of the heart impacts our behavior and dealings with people. Islamic teachings put great emphasis on moral conduct and how we deal with people in our daily lives. The Prophet Muhammad (SAS) said, "Indeed, I was sent to make perfect the moral conduct."

The Qur`an includes the laws revealed by Allah (SWT) that are designed to govern our lives, and it also indicates the code of ethics and etiquette which we are advised to maintain in our dealings with each other. As Muslims, we have to be aware of how each one of us deals with one another. Our good dealings will not only ensure that we are not violating other people's rights, but can also make us accepted, loved, and appreciated by others. Experience shows that life becomes pleasant when we manage our relationships with people well.

The human being, as we know, is made up of the body and the spirit. The essential reality of the human, however, lies in the spirit or *rooh*. The Prophet (SAS) said, "There is in the body a piece of flesh which, if it is sound, then the whole body is sound, and if it is corrupt, then the whole body is corrupt. Indeed, it is the heart." He also told us, "Allah neither looks at your figures, nor at your outward appearance; He looks at your hearts and your deeds." The references in these Prophetic traditions are to the spiritual heart.

Just as there are diseases of the physical heart, there are also diseases of the spiritual heart. It is extremely important for the spiritual heart to be sound. Spiritual health is as important as physical health, if not more. Physical health is important for a meaningful life and success in this world. Spiritual health is essential for success both in this world and in the hereafter.

To feel good and get along with people, we have first to know what diseases of the spiritual heart we suffer from. Some of the diseases of the heart include arrogance, showing off, jealousy, suspicion, backbiting, spying, anger, stinginess, making fun of others, and more. Let me very briefly touch upon them and see how getting rid of them can improve our relationships with people.

Arrogance, or *takabbur*, is the first step to many evils. No one likes an arrogant or boastful person. It is so easy to get carried away by whatever we may possess of wealth and the good things of life. It is so easy to credit ourselves with our achievements and feel proud of them, and then to turn and look down upon others who have not been able to reach what we have achieved. Besides, arrogance is always unjustified, because all of the blessings and bounties that we have are from Allah. Allah reminds us in the Qur`an,

وَمَا بِكُمْ مِنْ نِعْمَةٍ فَمِنَ اللَّهِ ○

*Whatever blessing you have is from Allah. (an-Nahl,16:53)*

The way to avoid arrogance is to remember Allah as much as we can until it becomes a habit to instantly thank Him for any good that comes our way. Thankfulness to Allah creates humility in us and makes us aware that we would not have had all the good things of life if Allah had not willed them for us nor can we retain them if He decides to take them away from us. We have to keep reminding ourselves that we are totally dependent on Him for our very existence.

Showing off or *riya`* is referred to as the "hidden *shirk*." This disease of the heart is so hidden and so dangerous that the one who feels safe from it is usually the one who gets entrapped in it. Even the person who performs the *salah* becomes guilty of showing off if his or her intention is to impress others. Allah says in *Surat al-Ma'un*,

فَوَيْلٌ لِلْمُصَلِّينَ ○ الَّذِينَ هُمْ عَنْ صَلَاتِهِمْ سَاهُونَ ○ الَّذِينَ هُمْ يُرَاءُونَ ○ وَيَمْنَعُونَ الْمَاعُونَ ○

*Woe to those who pray; who are unmindful of their prayers; those who show off; who are uncharitable even over very small things. (al-Ma'un, 107:4-7)*

The best cure for this disease is to check one's intention (*niyya*) before any action. Any action done should only be for the sake of Allah (SWT).

Jealousy or *hasad* is also a disease of the heart. A person who is jealous or envious of another hurts himself with feelings of rage and frustration that consume his heart, and in this process, he loses his peace of mind. One must realize that being jealous of others is actually a form of being displeased with Allah for His bounties upon that person. Allah in His infinite wisdom bestows upon whom He wills what He wills. We have to be able to deal with the situation by being grateful for what He has given us and being patient with what has not been given to us. It is not blameworthy for one to ask Allah to give him what has been given to another person, but it is blameworthy to ask for it to be taken away from that person. We have been asked to seek Allah's refuge from envious people.

قُلْ أَعُوذُ بِرَبِّ الْفَلَقِ ○ مِنْ شَرِّ مَا خَلَقَ ○ وَمِنْ شَرِّ غَاسِقٍ إِذَا وَقَبَ ○ وَمِنْ شَرِّ النَّفَّاثَاتِ فِي الْعُقَدِ ○ وَمِنْ شَرِّ حَاسِدٍ إِذَا حَسَدَ ○

*Say, I seek refuge in the Lord of the daybreak; from the evil of what He has created;*

*from the evil of darkness as it falls; from the evil of those who blow on knots; and from the evil of an envier when he envies. (al-Falaq, 1-5)*

A treatment to get rid of envy is to compete with others in acts of goodness and this should be an incentive to achieve more and do better.

Suspicion (*dhann*) or misgivings (*shakk*) must also be avoided. A suspicious person usually thinks negatively of others. Suspicion may sometimes lead to making wrong decisions. It is good to be cautious and careful, but it is also important to have a positive attitude about others. If we want to be trusted, we must trust others as well. Allah says in the Qur'an,

يَا أَيُّهَا الَّذِينَ آمَنُوا اجْتَنِبُوا كَثِيرًا مِنَ الظَّنِّ إِنَّ بَعْضَ الظَّنِّ إِثْمٌ ◯

*O you who believe! Avoid much suspicion; verily some suspicion is a sin. (al-Hujurat, 49:12)*

It helps to think well of others. Even when we hear something negative about them, we should not get carried away, and instead make discreet inquiries before jumping to conclusions. Attributing positive motives to others' actions helps in understanding them better. Let us also remind ourselves whenever we attempt to judge others that no one is perfect. We, too, have our own shortcomings which we would not like being mentioned or discussed. Fairness requires that we do good to others as we expect them to do good to us.

Backbiting (*gheeba*) is also very common among people. Backbiting means to talk about someone in his or her absence in a manner which he or she may not like. It is one of the major sins in Islam. We should also have the moral courage to stop others from backbiting, for even if we don't contribute to it, we become participants who are also guilty of the sin by being silent listeners. The best means of avoiding participation in backbiting is by changing the topic or saying that we don't really know the whole truth of the matter. We should not be unfair to anyone by talking behind his back, and not giving him a chance to defend or clarify himself.

Spying (*tajassus*) or peeping into other people's lives with the intention of exposing their faults or unveiling their secrets is also a sin. Allah says,

وَلَا تَجَسَّسُوا وَلَا يَغْتَبْ بَعْضُكُمْ بَعْضًا ◯

*And spy not, neither backbite one another. (al-Hujurat, 49:12)*

Anger (*ghadhab*) is a natural human trait, but if it is not properly controlled, it becomes very destructive. In a hadeeth the Prophet (SAS) called it "fire." The Prophet (SAS) is reported to have said that in a state of anger, one should change one's environment, one's position, and drink some water. He also said, "The strong is not the one who overcomes the people by his strength, but the strong is the one who controls himself while in anger."

Stinginess is also a horrible disease. The Prophet (SAS) taught us to seek Allah's refuge from stinginess. It leads to an attitude of not caring for others. It holds people from fulfilling their duties and recognizing the rights of others. Allah says in the Qur`an,

$$\text{وَمَنْ يَبْخَلْ فَإِنَّمَا يَبْخَلُ عَنْ نَفْسِهِ}$$

*And whoever is stingy is only being stingy to himself.* (Muhammad, 47:38)

This is because Allah (SWT) multiplies what we spend in His way and gives it back to us both in this world as well as putting it toward our homes in *jannah*. Thus, the miser is only miserly toward himself or herself.

Mocking others or taking pleasure in making fun of them is also a problem found among people. The ego craves the satisfaction of proving oneself better than others by looking out for their weaknesses and laughing at them. But Allah admonishes us,

$$\text{يَا أَيُّهَا الَّذِينَ آمَنُوا لَا يَسْخَرْ قَوْمٌ مِنْ قَوْمٍ عَسَى أَنْ يَكُونُوا خَيْرًا مِنْهُمْ}$$

*O you who believe! Let not a group scoff at another group, it may be that the latter are better than the former.* (al-Hujurat, 49:11)

Allah tells us that our knowledge is restricted by our limited perception. Since we are not aware of any one's real worth, it is foolish to laugh at those who might actually be better than us.

These are some of the negative aspects of human behavior that should be avoided when dealing with people.

Brothers and sisters! How about some of the positive aspects of human behavior? Let us discuss some of them. We all know, as the Prophet (SAS) taught us, that smiling at others is an act of charity. We know very well what a sincere smile can convey: absence of ill feelings, acceptance, warmth, and the willingness to share our time and space. Let us not be miserly about brightening our face with a cheerful smile. We are drawn to people who smile. We should not let the differences we might have with people keep us away from greeting them with a smile. Smiling helps us to stay positive because when we smile, our body is sending the message that life is good. Indeed, loving and giving are the essence of charity, so start now by meeting your family and friends with a smile. Our beloved Prophet (SAS) was reported to be smiling the most. He would always show a smile to the people. He saw smiling as a gift of joy, an emotional gift, a gift whose substance is received by the heart.

Also, expressing gratitude for favors done and help rendered is not only the basic requirement of good manners and social etiquette, but has far reaching effects. It strengthens our relationship and adds warmth to it. On the other hand, taking others for granted causes disappointment and conveys the impression that we don't know how to value people, that we just know how to use them. Thanks and appreciation expressed sincerely with a smile gives off a bright glow which is felt by the heart.

The whole purpose of our life is to prepare ourselves for the hereafter, and with this long-term goal in mind, we have to overcome pettiness and meanness. Our constant struggle is with two real enemies. One is Satan who keeps making the world more and more alluring for us. The other is our own ego that inflates our importance in our eyes beyond any sensible measure. It is these two things that cause conflicts and misunderstandings.

Brothers and sisters, each and every one of us should know which spiritual diseases have afflicted us and then try our utmost to get rid of them. Spiritual health has to do with curing the diseases of the hearts. Remembrance of Allah is a cure for the hearts. Reflecting upon the Qur'an is a cure for the hearts. Leaving sins and doing righteous deeds is a cure for the hearts. Making sincere repentance to Allah is a cure for the hearts. Leaving bad company and being in the company of good people is a cure for the hearts. Being charitable is a cure for the hearts. And last but not least, remembering that we have one day to leave this world and being prepared for it is a cure for the hearts.

Bad habits picked up over the years in dealing with people can sometimes be difficult to let go. Oftentimes we may not even feel that our habits are that bad. But we need to strive to keep on improving ourselves so that our families, friends, community members, and others can live together in peace and harmony.

May Allah (SWT) bless us all with physical, mental, and spiritual health, and may He grant us pure Islamic *fitra*, and sound hearts. May Allah bless our families, our communities, and humanity at large. *Allahumma ameen.*


· 48 ·

# ISLAMIC VIEW OF RELIGIOUS PLURALISM

The topic of my *khutbah* today is: "Islamic View of Religious Pluralism." Religious pluralism implies the diversity of religious belief systems coexisting in a society.

Pluralism is an attitude or policy that various religious, ethnic, racial, and political groups should be allowed to thrive in a single society. It also means peaceful coexistence with those who hold differing beliefs.

Islam not only accepts but also advocates pluralism in human societies. Talking about the diversity found among humans, Allah says in the Qur`an,

يَا أَيُّهَا النَّاسُ إِنَّا خَلَقْنَاكُم مِّن ذَكَرٍ وَأُنثَى وَجَعَلْنَاكُمْ شُعُوبًا وَقَبَائِلَ لِتَعَارَفُوا إِنَّ أَكْرَمَكُمْ عِندَ اللَّهِ أَتْقَاكُمْ ○

*O Humankind, We created you all from a single man and a single woman and made*
*you into races and tribes so that you should recognize one another. The noblest among*
*you in Allah's sight are those who are most mindful of Him. (al-Hujurat, 49:13)*

This statement in the Qur`an about broad human brotherhood and sisterhood is a profound basis for promoting peace among all. This is a reminder that diversity in unity and unity within diversity are possible. While the notion of pluralism may appear to be a relatively new concept, it is not new to those who are familiar with the Qur`an. Allah informs us quite explicitly in the Qur`an that if He willed, He would have made all mankind one nation or community.

وَلَوْ شَاءَ اللَّهُ لَجَعَلَكُمْ أُمَّةً وَاحِدَةً وَلَكِن لِّيَبْلُوَكُمْ فِي مَا آتَاكُمْ فَاسْتَبِقُوا الْخَيْرَاتِ إِلَى اللَّهِ مَرْجِعُكُمْ جَمِيعًا
فَيُنَبِّئُكُم بِمَا كُنتُمْ فِيهِ تَخْتَلِفُونَ ○

*If Allah had willed, He would have made you one community, but His Will is to test*
*you with what He has given each of you. So compete with one another in doing good.*
*To Allah you will all return. Then He will inform you of the truth regarding your*
*differences. (al-Ma`ida, 5:48)*

Allah further states that differences in beliefs and views should not be suppressed as this will never lead to genuine agreement or true unity.

وَلَوْ شَاءَ رَبُّكَ لَجَعَلَ النَّاسَ أُمَّةً وَاحِدَةً وَلَا يَزَالُونَ مُخْتَلِفِينَ ○

*And had your Lord wished, He could have made all mankind one nation, but they still*
*would continue to disagree. (Hud, 11:118)*

This also implies that no one can be compelled to believe. Forcing people to believe runs against God's decree of free will, which includes the fact that some will not believe in Him. Allah says in the Qur`an,

وَلَوْ شَاءَ رَبُّكَ لَآمَنَ مَن فِي الْأَرْضِ كُلُّهُمْ جَمِيعًا أَفَأَنتَ تُكْرِهُ النَّاسَ حَتَّى يَكُونُوا مُؤْمِنِينَ ○

*Had your Lord willed, everyone on earth would have believed; are you then going to*
*compel the people to become believers? (Yunus, 10:99)*

لَا إِكْرَاهَ فِي الدِّينِ ○

*There is no compulsion in religion. (al-Baqara, 2:256)*

This means that there is no coercion in matters of faith.

فَذَكِّرْ إِنَّمَا أَنْتَ مُذَكِّرٌ ⭘ لَسْتَ عَلَيْهِمْ بِمُسَيْطِرٍ ⭘

*So remind them, for you are but a reminder, and not a taskmaster over them. (al-Ghashiya, 88:21-22)*

The Qur`an does not prescribe any worldly punishment for rejecting the invitation to accept Islam. The ultimate reward or punishment for accepting or rejecting belief in God is deferred until the Day of Judgment. This value inculcates the attitude of being non-judgmental and accepting people as they are. Acceptance of pluralism does not mean accepting the plurality of ultimate truths, nor does it prevent sharing one's faith with others or even inviting them to it. Pluralism is the belief that people of different social classes, religions, races, and ethnicities in a society should live together in peace and harmony.

The blessed life of the Prophet Muhammad (SAS) is full of incidents that illustrate his tolerant, merciful, and pluralistic attitude toward people of other faiths. These include his early encounters with Christian monks to whom he looked with respect. They played an important role in his life on a number of occasions, including immediately after the first Qur`anic revelation. He also sent his early followers to Abyssinia to seek refuge with a Christian king, Najashi, who extended them protection from the Quraysh.

When the Prophet (SAS) migrated from Mecca to Medina, he found himself in a pluralistic society where there was religious as well as tribal diversity. He not only accepted this diversity but legitimized it by drafting an agreement between the different religious and tribal groups that recognized the rights of each group. The charter became known as the Medina Constitution. This document was particularly significant for the time and place as it laid the foundation for a new vision of society that was based not on tribal or religious affiliations, but on the concept of a unified single community where every member was guaranteed their rights and freedom of religious practice. The companions of the Prophet (SAS) continued this pluralistic attitude and behavior.

During the centuries of Muslim rule in lands with both minority and majority populations of different faiths, Muslims generally practiced a level of pluralism that was unique for that time. This pluralism is still in evident today with the centuries-old churches and synagogues found throughout the Middle East that continue to function freely under Muslim rule. These are just a few of the precedents of Muslims from the pre-modern period when the concept of pluralism, tolerance, and equal rights was little known or valued.

All humans are equal before God in terms of their humanity, irrespective of their beliefs. In *Surat al-Baqara*, Allah tells us that people of other faiths who do good are also assured of their reward from God.

إِنَّ الَّذِينَ آمَنُوا وَالَّذِينَ هَادُوا وَالنَّصَارَى وَالصَّابِئِينَ مَنْ آمَنَ بِاللَّهِ وَالْيَوْمِ الْآخِرِ وَعَمِلَ صَالِحًا فَلَهُمْ أَجْرُهُمْ عِنْدَ رَبِّهِمْ وَلَا خَوْفٌ عَلَيْهِمْ وَلَا هُمْ يَحْزَنُونَ ◯

*Indeed, the believers, the Jews, the Christians, and the Sabians all those who believe in God and the Last Day and do good deeds will be rewarded by their Lord; they shall have no fear, nor shall they grieve. (al-Baqara, 2:62)*

The judgment of each person on the Day of Judgment lies only with Allah, and each person will be judged individually by Allah.

وَكُلُّهُمْ آتِيهِ يَوْمَ الْقِيَامَةِ فَرْدًا ◯

*Each of them will come to Him on the Day of Judgment all alone. (Maryam, 19:95)*

إِنَّ إِلَيْنَا إِيَابَهُمْ ◯ ثُمَّ إِنَّ عَلَيْنَا حِسَابَهُمْ ◯

*Surely to Us is their return, and then it is for Us to call them to account. (al-Ghashiya, 88:25-26)*

Allah clearly says that everyone has to return to Him, and their eternal fate is in His hands because of what they have been doing on earth. This is a lesson for all of us, so we embrace this fact and avoid committing the sin of judging others as if we know everything about them. Allah knows about the inner thoughts and beliefs of a person better than us. How can we possibly judge someone as "good" or "bad" just because of their conduct or appearance, without knowing about what they have gone through in their past, what they are doing now, and what they can do in the future? 'Umar ibn al-Khattab (RAA) used to be the leading person in hatred of the Prophet (SAS), but after embracing Islam, he became the second caliph of the Muslims.

Al-hamduli-llah, we are Muslims, but what if we weren't born in a Muslim family? Would we still be Muslims? Generally, a person becomes a Jew, Christian, Muslim, Hindu, Sikh, Buddhist, or follower of any other religion or creed because of his parents who brought him into this world and raised him. Are we Muslims by chance or by choice? Think about it.

Sharing or propagating faith is not the same as compulsion in religion. In fact, the Qur'an makes communicating the message of Islam an obligation.

وَكَذَلِكَ جَعَلْنَاكُمْ أُمَّةً وَسَطًا لِتَكُونُوا شُهَدَاءَ عَلَى النَّاسِ وَيَكُونَ الرَّسُولُ عَلَيْكُمْ شَهِيدًا ◯

*Thus We have made you a moderate nation, so that you may act as witnesses for mankind, and the Messenger may be a witness for you. (al-Baqara, 2:143)*

"Being witnesses for Allah" includes both witnessing through righteous deeds and sharing what one believes as the truth. The Qur'anic term for such sharing is *da'wa*, which literally means "invitation." The term itself means that the invitee has every right to accept or reject that invitation. Compulsion, threats, bribery, deception, manipulation, and exploitation of the invitee's vulnerability are inconsistent with the notion of invitation. The Qur'an gives guidance on how to invite others to Islam. Invitation should be with wisdom and in the most gracious way.

ادْعُ إِلَى سَبِيلِ رَبِّكَ بِالْحِكْمَةِ وَالْمَوْعِظَةِ الْحَسَنَةِ وَجَادِلْهُمْ بِالَّتِي هِيَ أَحْسَنُ إِنَّ رَبَّكَ هُوَ أَعْلَمُ بِمَنْ ضَلَّ عَنْ سَبِيلِهِ وَهُوَ أَعْلَمُ بِالْمُهْتَدِينَ ◯

*Invite to the Way of your Lord with wisdom and kind advice, and only debate with them in the best manner. Surely your Lord alone knows best who has strayed from His Way and who is rightly guided. (an-Nahl, 16:125)*

May Allah bless each one of us and grant us a deep understanding of the *deen*.

Brothers and sisters! The Qur'an gives various reasons why each human being must be honored and dignified on account of being human and irrespective of his or her chosen beliefs. Such honor is symbolized by the way the Qur'an describes Allah's creation of the human in the best of molds. Humans are the crown of Allah's creation. The Qur'an describes the human as Allah's trustee on earth. Allah created everything on earth and in the heavens for the benefit of the human race. Human life is held sacred.

However, the human is a free agent, and as such, each person is individually responsible before Allah for his or her beliefs and moral choices. A person can be held accountable in this life only if such a moral choice infringes on the rights of individuals or society, such as the commission of crimes or acts of aggression. In other words, no human is entitled to dehumanize or punish another human just because the latter is following a different religion or no religion at all. This value implies that peaceful coexistence among followers of all religions and respecting their humanity is not only possible, but also mandated in the Qur'an. Addressing the Prophet (SAS), Allah says,

وَمَا أَرْسَلْنَاكَ إِلَّا رَحْمَةً لِّلْعَالَمِينَ ◯

*We have not sent you, but as mercy to all the worlds. (al-Anbiya', 21:107)*

To remove any particularization of this mercy, the Prophet Muhammad (SAS) explained that mercy is not just being merciful to one's companions but merciful to all. He also explained, "He who is not merciful to others, will not be treated mercifully." It is obvious that Muslims are not the only inhabitants of the earth. Hence the command to be merciful applies to all. In fact, mercy also applies to animals and other creatures of Allah. A logical fruit of this attitude of mercy is to love humankind as fellow honored creatures of Allah, while dissociating oneself from their erroneous beliefs or rejection of Allah. This love finds its greatest form when we love good and guidance for fellow humans. This does not mean we love their wrongdoing or their rejection of faith in Allah. It means we love for them to find guidance and well being in this life and in the life to come.

It may be concluded that the basic rule governing the relationship between Muslims and non-Muslims is that of peaceful coexistence, justice, and compassion. This is the Islamic view of religious pluralism.

•   49   •

# ISLAMOPHOBIA

In today's *khutbah*, I intend to share some thoughts with you on the much talked about topic of Islamophobia. As Muslims living in the West, how should we respond to it? How should we go about confronting it with tolerance and understanding?

The term "Islamophobia" was first introduced as a concept in 1991 and defined as "unfounded hostility toward Muslims, and therefore fear or dislike of all or most Muslims." The term was coined in the context of Muslims in the United Kingdom in particular and Europe in general. It was devised on the xenophobia framework. Xenophobia means the hatred or fear of foreigners or of their politics or culture.

As far back as 2004, Kofi Annan, the then Secretary General of the United Nations, had said that the consequences of recent developments had left many Muslims around the world feeling aggrieved and misunderstood, concerned about the erosion of their rights, and even fearing for their physical safety. He felt, and rightly so, that coining a term that took account of increasingly widespread bigotry was a sad and troubling development.

Brothers and sisters! Such is the case with Islamophobia. It basically reflects a social anxiety toward Islam and Muslim cultures. The pressures of living together with people of different cultures and different beliefs are real, especially in a world of intense economic competition, and with sudden waves of migrants crossing borders. But that cannot justify demonization or the deliberate use of fear for political purposes.

It is interesting to know that most of the people who are Islamophobic have no true knowledge of Islam and have probably never met a Muslim. If you were to ask people, especially those living in the West, to write down with honesty all the words that come to their mind when they think of the words "Islam" or "Muslims," you will likely get words or expressions like jihad, terrorist, extremist, fanatic, retrogressive, fundamentalist, and so on. And most likely they will associate names like Saddam Hussein, Osama bin Laden, Taliban, Al-Qaeda, ISIS, and so on with Islam and Muslims.

Some of the prevailing notions or attitudes among those who harbor Islamophobic attitudes are, (1) Islam is monolithic and cannot adapt to new realities, (2) Islam does not share common values with other major faiths, (3) Islam as a religion is archaic, barbaric, and irrational, (4) Islam is a religion of violence and supports terrorism, and (5) Islam is a violent political ideology.

You may be surprised to know that Islamophobia is not new. Dante, a major Italian poet of the Middle Ages in his book *The Divine Comedy*, written in the third quarter of the fourteenth century, depicts the Prophet Muhammad (SAS) in the lowest depths of hell. Based on this book, an Italian silent film called *L'Inferno* was released in the year 1911. We have the more recent cases of the Danish cartoons, *The Satanic Verses*, the releasing of the film *Fitnah* and the much-publicized burning of the Qur`an incident. A well-known American Christian Evangelist and missionary said, "We're not attacking Islam, but Islam has attacked us. The God of Islam is not the same God of the Christians or Judeo-Christian faith. It's a different God. And I believe that Islam is a very evil and wicked religion."

If you happen to search Islamophobia on the Internet, you will find blogs like *Jihad Watch*. Its author is the co-founder of an anti-Muslim organization called *Stop the Islamization of America*. There are others like this author who are accused of being racists. Their views are dangerous because they open the door to persecution of Muslims. You have a website run by Evangelical Christians called *Answering Islam*. There is another one called *The Clarion Project* that focuses on the alleged "threats" of Islamic extremism and radical Islam.

In a post-9/11 world, many Americans merge the mainstream Muslim majority with the beliefs and actions of an extremist minority. Typically, stereotypes depict Muslims as opposed to the West. But what do the world's Muslims think about the West, or about democracy, or about extremism itself? A book called *Who Speaks for Islam: What a Billion Muslims Really Think*, authored by John Esposito and Dalia Mogahed, is the product of a six-year study (2001 to 2007) in which the survey conducted by the Gallup Organization gives the views of 90 percent of the Muslim world. Contrary to the stereotype, most of the Muslims polled did not indicate that they hate the Western way of life or its freedoms. On the contrary, they admire the freedom of the press, freedom of speech, rule of law, and technological advances of the West. This does not mean, however, that they want to copy the West in all aspects, particularly in the areas of family values and attitudes toward sex. Many Muslims voiced concern about the West's moral decay and the breakdown of traditional values. Interestingly enough, non-Muslim Americans voiced similar concerns.

Brothers and sisters! You know as much as I do that people get carried away by propaganda. This is not to say that Muslims, Christians, and Jews, as well as followers of other belief systems, do not have their black sheep. Groups of extremists and terrorists who claim to be following a particular religion do not represent the core teachings of their religion. This is as true for Muslim extremists and terrorists as much as it is true for Christian and Jewish extremists and terrorists or followers of any faith for that matter. Thus, the violent extremist fringe groups such as ISIS and the Ku Klux Klan are not true representatives of the faiths they claim.

Writing in the *Time* magazine, the well-known British author Karen Armstrong rightly suggests that regarding Osama bin Laden as an authentic representative of Islam would be akin to considering James Kopp, the alleged killer of an abortion provider in Buffalo, N.Y., as a representative Christian, or seeing Baruch Goldstein, who shot 29 worshippers in the Hebron mosque in 1994, as a representative of Jews.

A couple of weeks back, the Imam's Council of the Michigan Muslim Community Council (MMCC) issued a press release stating that the executions, the ethnic cleansing of religious minorities, and the desecration of places of worship by the self-proclaimed Islamic State of Iraq and Syria (or "ISIS") are fundamentally against the teachings of Islam. The press release also condemned the atrocities taking place in Gaza. The blatant Zionist attacks against innocent men, women, and children are in total contradiction of the teachings of the Jewish faith. Similarly, the Christian militia that continues to brutally massacre Muslims in Central African Republic, and the Buddhist regime that is bent upon eliminating Muslims in Myanmar are also doing just the opposite of what Christianity and Buddhism teach them to do.

May Allah (SWT) give us the wisdom and the *tawfeeq* to see and understand situations in their proper perspectives.

Brothers and sisters! Islamophobia, as stated earlier, is not a new phenomenon. During the lifetime of the Prophet Muhammad (SAS), when the adversaries of Islam began to see that their own family and friends had started to enter into the fold of Islam, they launched a malicious campaign to distort Islam and its teachings. Through misinformation, they attempted to portray the Prophet of Islam as a poet, a sorcerer, and a soothsayer in order to build up a public opinion against him. They called him *majnoon*, meaning an insane person. They brought false accusations against him claiming that the Qur`an was taught to him and dictated to him by some human being. Allah explains in the Qur`an,

وَقَالُوا أَسَاطِيرُ الْأَوَّلِينَ اكْتَتَبَهَا فَهِيَ تُمْلَىٰ عَلَيْهِ بُكْرَةً وَأَصِيلًا ○

*And they said, it is just fables of the ancients, which he has had written down. They are dictated to him morning and evening. (al-Furqan, 25:5)*

وَقَالُوا مَا هَذَا إِلَّا إِفْكٌ مُفْتَرًى وَقَالَ الَّذِينَ كَفَرُوا لِلْحَقِّ لَمَّا جَاءَهُمْ إِنْ هَذَا إِلَّا سِحْرٌ مُبِينٌ ◯

*And they said, this is nothing but an invented lie; and the unbelievers say of the truth
when it comes to them, this is nothing but plain magic. (Saba`, 34:43)*

These "haters" managed to create conditions conducive to the masses believing anything said about the Prophet (SAS) and the Qur`an without independent judgment. All this was done to discredit him and his teachings. But how did the Prophet (SAS) face up to this campaign of distortions? Although he was on the receiving end, he took everything that was thrown at him and kept his spirits high. He did not react angrily, or trade insults with the opposite side, as do those people who are easily agitated. He was calm and collected in all his exchanges with the adversaries of Islam. That is because he did not view it as a personal matter. It was a matter of the message he was sent to spread. It was, therefore, inevitable that dialogue was conducted in a way which was guided by Islam's straight path, its ideology, and its tolerance. Doesn't Allah say in the Qur`an,

فِي الدِّينِ لَا إِكْرَاهَ ◯

*There is no compulsion in religion.... (al-Baqara, 2:256)*

And doesn't Allah also say,

لَكُمْ دِينُكُمْ وَلِيَ دِينِ ◯

*For you is your deen (way of life), and for me is my deen. (al-Kafiroon, 109:6)*

We should know that there are many sincere people in our society among atheists, agnostics, humanists, and followers of other religions and belief systems who are in search of truth. The negative stereotypes and vicious propaganda against Islam and Muslims have dramatically brought Islam into limelight. People have become curious about Islam. They want to learn about Islam. And what is the outcome? A multitude of ordinary people along with numerous people from among the elites are in search of truth. Clerics, judges, scientists, doctors, scholars, politicians, academicians, journalists, professionals, technocrats, artists, athletes, and celebrities have embraced Islam, and are continuing to do so. You just have to read their stories to know how they were captivated by the truth of Islam. There are hundreds and thousands of such stories published in print and electronic media. To relate just one story, in 2013, a Dutch politician by the name of Arnoud Van Doorn, a harsh critic of Islam who had helped to produce the highly controversial anti-Islam film called *Fitnah* that depicted Islam as evil and extreme, converted to Islam and performed hajj. So, the bottom-line, my brothers and sisters, is that Islamophobia is proving to be a blessing in disguise.

This is not to say that we should not make an effort to remove Islamophobia and remove misconceptions about Islam. Until today, many Americans think that Allah is a "moon god!" The use of a lunar calendar and the popularity of crescent moon imagery in Islam is claimed as "proof" for this concept. Many Americans believe that Muslims are required to kill non-Muslims. Such misconceptions must be corrected through proper education. Any strategy to combat Islamophobia must depend heavily on education, not just about Islam, but about all religions and traditions, so that myths and lies can be seen for what they are.

Interfaith dialogue is also useful. But problems are not caused by the similarities among religions that are typically celebrated in such dialogue. They are caused by other similarities between humans, chiefly, the inclination of human beings to favor their own groups, beliefs, and cultures at the expense of others. Interfaith activities could take a more practical direction by building on the examples of those communities in which different peoples come together regularly such as professional associations, on the sports field, or in other social settings. Such day-to-day contacts can be especially useful in demystifying the "other." Let us pray to Allah (SWT) to increase us in knowledge and to guide us to that which is right. A Prophetic tradition teaches us to say,

اللَّهُمَّ ○ انْفَعْنِي بِمَا عَلَّمْتَنِي وَ عَلِّمْنِي مَا يَنْفَعُنِي وَ زِدْنِي عِلْمًا

*O Allah, benefit me from that which You taught me, and teach me that which will benefit me, and increase me in knowledge.*

• 50 •

# LAWFUL AND UNLAWFUL IN ISLAM

In his book *The Lawful and the Prohibited in Islam*, Shaykh Yusuf al-Qaradawi defines the *halal* (lawful) as that which is permitted, concerning to which no restriction exists, and the doing of which the Law-Giver has allowed. The *haram*, or unlawful, is that which the Law Giver has prohibited absolutely, and anyone who engages in it is liable to incur Allah's punishment in the hereafter, as well as legal punishment in this world. The *makrooh*, or detested, actions are those that are disapproved by Allah (SWT). These actions are lesser in degree than the *haram*. However, one must refrain from them because committing them leads one to committing the *haram*. To begin with, there are two general rules to understanding the concept of *halal* and *haram*.

First: The general rule is that everything is lawful except what has been declared to be unlawful. This is in contrast to the trend of thinking that everything is unlawful except what has been declared to be lawful. Such a distorted idea can only discourage and depress a person, rather than encourage and motivate him or her.

Second: Only Allah (SWT) can determine what is *halal* and what is *haram*. The Prophet (SAS)was given the privilege to enact laws subject to Allah's laws, and this way, he exercised the right of legislation under divine supervision and approval. When it came to divine revelation or a divinely revealed law, he never spoke of his own.

وَمَا يَنْطِقُ عَنِ الْهَوَى ۝ إِنْ هُوَ إِلاَّ وَحْيٌ يُوحَى ۝

*He (the Prophet) does not speak from his own desire. It (the Qur`an) is but a revelation revealed. (an-Najm, 53:3-4)*

There are issues not addressed directly in the Qur`an. For example, Prophetic rulings forbidding men to wear silk or adorn themselves with gold and silver are not to be found in the Qur`an. There is no choice for Muslims in matters which Allah (SWT) or His messenger has decreed.

Prohibiting the allowed and allowing the prohibited are acts of transgressing the limits of Allah (SWT). The Qur`an severely chides the Jews and the Christians for empowering their rabbis and monks to decree what is lawful and unlawful on their own.

اتَّخَذُوا أَحْبَارَهُمْ وَرُهْبَانَهُمْ أَرْبَابًا مِنْ دُونِ اللَّهِ ۝

*They have taken their learned men and their monks for their lords besides God. (at-Tawba, 9:31)*

It is reported that when the Messenger of Allah (SAS) recited this *ayah*, 'Adi ibn Hatim (RAA), who had converted to Islam from Christianity commented, "They did not worship them." The Prophet (SAS) said, "Yes they did. They (the rabbis and monks) prohibited the allowed and allowed the prohibited for them, and they (the "People of the Book") obeyed them. This is how they worshipped them."

The divine injunction prohibiting anything is due to its impurity and harmfulness. It is Allah (SWT) alone who knows through His infinite wisdom what is ultimately good for us and what is not.

Whatever leads to *haram* is also *haram*. Islam employs the principle of *sadd adh-dhara'i* which means blocking the means to unlawful ends. For example, to prevent the unlawful practice of sex outside marriage, all doors that may lead to it have been closed. Obscene literature, vulgar songs, display of nudity, putting on sexually appealing or scanty clothing, private and casual mixing between men and women, and all actions that may lead to the evil of adultery or fornication have been prohibited. It is also important to realize that the sin of the *haram* isn't only limited to the perpetrator of the sin. It extends to all those who have contributed to or have been a party to that sinful act.

Good intentions do not make the *haram* acceptable. Any ill-gotten wealth, for example, cannot be used toward investing in a good cause, however noble it may be. Islam does not consent to using *haram* means to achieve praise-worthy ends. Such a practice does not fall into the maxim of "the end justifies the means." The intention, the means employed, and the end should all be honorable. The Prophet (SAS) said, "Allah is pure and accepts nothing but what is pure."

Allah (SWT) has made it very clear what is *halal* and what is *haram*. However, there is a gray area between the clearly *halal* and the clearly *haram*. This is the area of what is doubtful. Some people may not be able to decide whether a particular matter is permissible or forbidden. In such matters, Islam considers it an act of piety for the Muslim to avoid doing what is doubtful in order to stay clear of doing something *haram*.

"Necessity allows exception" is one of the legal maxims formulated by the Muslim jurists. Islam takes awareness of the demands of life and to human weakness and their capacity to face them. For example, it permits the Muslim, under the compulsion of necessity to eat prohibited food in quantities sufficient to remove the necessity and save himself from death. May Allah (SWT) bless us with a proper understanding of His *deen, ameen*.

Brothers and sisters! As discussed, the lawful and the unlawful are clear without any shadow of doubt. However, between these two positions there are matters which are ambiguous and which most people don't know about, whether they are permissible or impermissible. These are matters about which there are differences of opinion among the scholars of Islam.

In this regard, the Prophet (SAS) gave some practical solutions that are known through prophetic traditions. When we encounter a doubtful matter, the teachings of the Prophet (SAS) guide us to follow the instincts of our heart rather than blindly rely on the *fatwas* of *muftis*. There is a beautiful advice given through a hadeeth reported by Hassan ibn 'Ali ibn Abi Talib (RAA), the grandson of the Prophet (SAS) who said, "I memorized from the Messenger of Allah, 'Leave that which makes you doubt for that which does not make you doubt.'" A God-fearing and God-conscious person follows such recommendations without any hesitation. It becomes difficult for a person who engages in doubtful matters to prevent himself from falling into sin. On the other hand, by staying away from doubtful matters, he protects himself from falling into sin. Therefore, staying at the center of the sphere of the permissible is the safest way to remain happy and content.

Many people who are not conversant with the spirit of the *shari'a* insist on using these boundaries to the limits, and a point is reached where only a hair's breadth separates obedience from disobedience. Consequently, many people fall prey to disobedience, even to absolute error and wrongdoing. Once a man arrives at this point, he is seldom capable of distinguishing between right and wrong and maintaining the absolute self-control needed to keep within the lawful limits. Well-known and qualified scholars may be asked for clarifications and rulings when confronted with doubtful matters. After all, they carry the *amana* (trust) of guiding the believers to the straight path. A person should never regret having to abandon the doubtful in order to please Allah (SWT). Allah (SWT) will bless such a person in ways he cannot imagine.

وَمَنْ يَتَّقِ اللَّهَ يَجْعَلْ لَهُ مَخْرَجًا ◯ وَيَرْزُقْهُ مِنْ حَيْثُ لَا يَحْتَسِبُ ◯

*Whoever has taqwa of Allah—He will find a way out for him and provide for him from where he does not expect. (at-Talaq, 65:2-3)*

Despite the issuance of any *fatwa*, it is the heart that should be engaged in the decision-making process. The heart is the seat of intellect, logic, and reasoning. Moreover, it is also the abode of *taqwa*. After making one's heart the last resort for arriving at a decision, if one is still fumbling to choose between options, then one should exercise the use of the *istikhara* prayer. *Istikhara* means to ask Allah (SWT) to guide one to the right thing concerning any affair in one's life, especially when one has to choose between two or more alternatives.

This is the attitude toward decision making that a God-fearing and God-conscious person possessing a sound heart has. One who follows Allah's instructions given in the Qur`an and follows the Prophet's teachings through his Sunnah is the one who has a spiritually healthy heart. The one who does not do so has a spiritually sick heart. The former is the one who holds on to the lawful, and the latter is the one who gets stuck to the unlawful.

Indeed, Allah (SWT) chose Islam as the complete and perfect *deen* for us, showered His favors upon us, and blessed us with the best of humanity—our beloved Prophet Muhammad (SAS), who taught us our *deen*. May Allah (SWT) make us live with what is lawful and keep us far away from what is unlawful. *Ameen.*

# LEAVE THAT WHICH DOES NOT CONCERN YOU

My *khutbah* today is based on a hadeeth, in which the Prophet (SAS) says, "Part of someone's being a good Muslim is his leaving alone that which does not concern him." It is a sound hadeeth transmitted by Tirmidhi and others. This hadeeth explains an essential but often overlooked aspect of completing and perfecting our practice of Islam. Actually, the excellence of a person's Islam is its perfection, such that one remains steadfast in the submission to the commands and prohibitions of Allah, and leaves that which is not important or befitting of him; whether in thought, speech, or action.

This simple yet powerful principle was mentioned by Prophet Muhammad (SAS) over fourteen hundred years ago. The Prophet was describing a quality that helps people not only improve their faith but also their way of life. How much more energy, focus, and time would we enjoy as a result of applying this principle in our lives?

Islam consists of acting as well as abstaining. The only way a person abandons all that does not concern him is by busying himself with that which does concern him, in matters of faith, and in competing with one another to do as many good deeds as possible.

$$وَلِكُلٍّ وِجْهَةٌ هُوَ مُوَلِّيهَا فَاسْتَبِقُوا الْخَيْرَاتِ ۝$$

*Everyone has a direction toward which he turns. So compete with one another in good deeds. (al-Baqara, 2:148)*

However, there is no way of recognizing what concerns us and what doesn't concern us—except through knowledge, which helps us to recognize and sift out any action, characteristic, or mannerism that is condemned in the Qur`an and the Sunnah. How well these things are accomplished determines the position of the believer with Allah (SWT).

This hadeeth tells us that we should not concern ourselves with matters that are none of our business. A good Muslim avoids doing something or saying something that does not concern him. He does and says only that which concerns him, meaning he has something to do with it. Refraining from that which does not concern him also has to do with guarding one's tongue against idle talk.

'Umar ibn 'Abd al-'Azeez (RA) is reported to have said that the one who regards his words as being among his deeds speaks little except about that which concerns him. Many people do not regard their words as being among their deeds, so they are careless and do not watch what they say.

There is a story that once a man noticed the wise sage Luqman surrounded by his followers, and asked him, "Weren't you the slave of so and so? Weren't you the shepherd of so and so? How did you get to such a respectful position among people?" Hakeem Luqman replied, "Truthful speech, and long silence upon what does not concern me." In a hadeeth, the Prophet (SAS) said, "Whoever believes in Allah and the Last Day let him say what is good or remain silent."

The challenge of leading a life that engages with things that only concern us is that we need to define what does and what doesn't concern us in life. Which means that we have to think about our purpose in life, our goals, and our vision and mission. However, that's hard, and it takes time; and so we just dive into what does not concern us. Unfortunately, this comes with a price: stress, wasted energy, and wasted time.

Brothers and sisters! The reality of time allotted to each one of us is that each heartbeat taken draws us nearer to our graves. Imam al-Hasan al-Basri used to say, "O Man, your life comprises of a few breaths that can be counted. With every breath that you draw, a part of your existence has diminished!" He also said that one of the signs that Allah (SWT) has turned away from a servant is that the servant finds himself continuously preoccupied and engaged in matters which are none of his concern.

How many of our interactions are worthwhile, and how many are useless? We need to stay focused on the priorities that concern us. We have to understand our different priorities of work, family, social activities, and so on. These priorities compete for our energy, focus, and time—all finite resources. It is crucial that every person recognizes and grasps his or her priorities within these resources. Imam al-Ghazali said, "Disregarding the prioritization of good deeds in itself is a bad deed." It is not simply a matter of identifying what concerns us and what does not, but also the degrees of relevance and priority. In the face of the information explosion, social interactions, and distractions around us, an understanding of priorities can help us make choices and stay focused on what actually concerns us.

Let us imagine a scenario. When we switch on our TV and watch the 24/7 news cycle for a couple of hours, more often than not, we will see scenes of disasters, death, and destruction from around the world. We switch off the TV, but often our emotions run high or even worse, we gradually become desensitized and do not feel anything. If we only engage with the news that concerns us and has an impact on our wellbeing and daily life, how much would this extra time help us think of broader, more critical issues in life? The same goes for spending time on social media networks on topics and issues that do not concern us. By being selective, we can save hours of our time for a more productive pursuit. Think about how you spend time.

Brothers and sisters! Keeping away from needless talk and meaningless activity is a vital requirement of good faith and an adornment of personality which lends beauty to the faith of the person concerned. One of the attributes of the true righteous believers mentioned in *Surat al-Mu`minoon* is:

وَالَّذِينَ هُمْ عَنِ اللَّغْوِ مُعْرِضُونَ ⊙

*Those who turn away from laghw. (al-Mu`minoon, 23:3)*

*Laghw* is anything nonsensical, meaningless, vain, which is in no way conducive to achieving one's goal and purpose in life. The believers pay no heed to such useless things, and they show no inclination or interest for them. If by chance, they happen to come across such things, they keep away and avoid them or treat them with the utmost indifference. This attitude has been described by Allah in *Surat al-Furqan*.

وَإِذَا مَرُّوا بِاللَّغْوِ مَرُّوا كِرَامًا ⊙

*If they have to pass by what is useless, they pass by like dignified people. (al-Furqan, 25:72)*

Such is one of the outstanding characteristics of the believer. He is a person who feels the burden of responsibility at all times. He regards the world as a place of test, and life as the limited time allowed for the test. This feeling makes him behave seriously and responsibly throughout life, just like the student who is taking an exam with his whole mind, body and soul absorbed in it. Just as the student knows and feels that each moment of the limited time at his disposal is important and decisive for his future life, and is not inclined to waste it, so the believer also spends each moment of his life on works which are useful and productive in their ultimate results. May Allah (SWT) bless us with a deep understanding of His *deen*. Ameen.

Brothers and sisters! Some of the lessons we get from this hadeeth is that a believer should avoid things that are of no concern to him or they are of no benefit to him in this life or in the hereafter, in terms of belief, speech, or actions. The Prophet (SAS) recommended through this hadeeth a way to avoid societal problems. Islam protects society as a whole from any kind of harm. Much of the harm inflicted on the society are due to people indulging in unnecessary matters like meddling into the affairs of others when one has no right or responsibility for the particular issue.

يَا أَيُّهَا الَّذِينَ آمَنُوا اجْتَنِبُوا كَثِيرًا مِّنَ الظَّنِّ إِنَّ بَعْضَ الظَّنِّ إِثْمٌ وَلَا تَجَسَّسُوا وَلَا يَغْتَب بَّعْضُكُم بَعْضًا ⊙

*O believers! Avoid many suspicions, for indeed, some suspicions are sinful. And do not spy, nor backbite one another. (al-Hujurat, 49:12)*

These types of practices usually lead to great evil in society. A true believer trains himself to be involved in beneficial matters so that this in itself becomes his attitude.

He does not waste time, money, and effort in things that are of no benefit in this life or in the hereafter.

Muslims have enough matters of concern to the extent that one may not have enough time to deal with all of them. We need to be involved with matters that are of concern to us. One of the things that are of concern is to fulfill the obligations, to perform as much as we can of the recommended acts, to avoid the forbidden, and to avoid as much as we can those acts that are disliked. Individual obligations are matters of concern to every one of us. Examples are matters like worship and supplication. Collective obligations must also not be neglected and should be matters of concern to us. An example is to work for the betterment of the community. Everyone with their profession and expertise has a role in contributing toward the community.

Other matters of concern to true righteous believers are to enjoin good and discourage evil, and to compete with one another in doing good works.

$$\text{يُؤْمِنُونَ بِاللَّهِ وَالْيَوْمِ الْآخِرِ وَيَأْمُرُونَ بِالْمَعْرُوفِ وَيَنْهَوْنَ عَنِ الْمُنكَرِ وَيُسَارِعُونَ فِي الْخَيْرَاتِ وَأُوْلَئِكَ مِنَ الصَّالِحِينَ ○}$$

*They believe in Allah and the Last Day and enjoin the doing of what is right and forbid the doing of what is wrong, and compete with one another in doing good works. They are among the righteous. (Aal 'Imran, 3:144)*

Another matter of concern to all Muslims and that which is widely lacking among us is to think about the affairs of the *ummah* or the whole Muslim community. We need to think of how to improve our situation further and not just be content with the current situation. We need to create awareness among each other in facing the issues and challenges of the *ummah*. May Allah (SWT) bless us with the *tawfeeq* to do so. *Ameen.*

• 52 •

# LESSONS FROM *SURAT AL-KAHF*

It is a weekly routine for many of us to recite *Surat al-Kahf* every Friday. Several prophetic traditions speak about the benefits of reciting this *surah*. It is mentioned that this *surah* brings comfort and peace to the heart. It gives its readers the light that will shine for them in this life and in the eternal life. It is also mentioned that those who recite this *surah* will be saved from the trials of the Dajjal. Many Muslims recite this *surah* every Friday. We must understand the context, the general meaning, and the lessons to be derived from this *surah* so that we benefit from the guidance it provides. The blessed *surah* begins with the following words:

الْحَمْدُ لِلَّهِ الَّذِي أَنْزَلَ عَلَى عَبْدِهِ الْكِتَابَ وَلَمْ يَجْعَلْ لَهُ عِوَجَا ۝ قَيِّمًا لِيُنْذِرَ بَأْسًا شَدِيدًا مِنْ لَدُنْهُ وَيُبَشِّرَ الْمُؤْمِنِينَ الَّذِينَ يَعْمَلُونَ الصَّالِحَاتِ أَنَّ لَهُمْ أَجْرًا حَسَنًا ۝ مَاكِثِينَ فِيهِ أَبَدًا ۝

*Praise be to Allah Who sent down the Scripture to His servant and placed no crookedness in it. (He made it) straight, giving warning of severe punishment from Him and giving good news to the believers who do good deeds that theirs will be an excellent reward where they shall abide forever. (al-Kahf, 18:1-3)*

What is the historical background of the revelation of this *surah*? It was revealed to Prophet Muhammad (SAS) toward the middle period of his preaching in Mecca. During this period, the Quraysh had increased their opposition to the Prophet. It is reported that this *surah* was revealed around this period in response to some questions posed by the Meccan polytheists (*mushrikoon*). After consulting with the People of the Book, they put these questions to the Prophet (SAS): (1) Who were the companions of the cave? (2) What is the true nature of the story of the encounter of Musa (AS) with al-Khidr? and (3) What is the story of Dhul-Qarnayn?

All these stories pertained to Jewish and Christian history and the people in the Arabian Peninsula did not know much about them. The People of the Book selected these stories carefully to test whether or not any extraordinary source of knowledge was available to Prophet Muhammad (SAS). Allah (SWT) revealed these stories to the Prophet (SAS), not only to give answers to the questions raised but also to build the morale of Muslims and help them get some lessons for their particular situation.

When we reflect on this *surah*, we see that it mentions four main stories in detail. In the middle of these stories, it also refers to the story of Iblees (the Devil) who refused to obey Allah's command to honor Adam (AS) and instead became the enemy of all human beings. The four main stories of this *surah* are: (1) the story of the companions of the cave, (2) the story of the owner of two gardens, (3) the story of Musa (AS) and his encounter with a mysterious teacher, and (4) the story of the king, Dhu al-Qarnayn. The theme of all these stories is one and the same: They all tell us about the trials of life. People are tested by different trials, and the Devil is there to mislead them and make difficult their path of success and salvation.

The story of the companions of the cave tells about the trials of faith. It tells us how the people of faith are tested and tried in different ways, but those who persevere and remain firm are protected by Allah (SWT). What does the Qur`an omit about this story? The Qur`an deliberately leaves out almost everything that a historian would be interested to know. The Qur`an does not tell us the dates and the time period when this happened, the geographical location of the cave, the names of the companions of the cave, the race or religion of the companions of the cave, their exact number, and so on.

It is, however, interesting to note that while the Qur`an has not given us some of the specifics of this story, it has remarkably told us all its essential elements. The Qur`an has told us that the companions of the cave were young people. They were together and were supporting each other. They had deep faith in the One God and were under threat to be killed for their faith. They were at a loss that their fellow countrymen could not see the foolishness of their false beliefs. They took refuge in a cave. They were very religious and pious. The Qur`an mentions their sincere prayers to their Lord. They had full trust in their Lord. God helped them in mysterious ways and gave them full protection. The cave received the warmth of the sunlight, but in such a way that they were not discovered or seen from outside. Allah (SWT) made them turn from side to side like a mother keeps turning her little baby in the crib. Their dog was in front of the cave. The scene was frightening for the outsider so that no one could enter the cave. When they woke up, they did not know how long they slept. They sent one of them to buy some food for them, but they did not want to be discovered because they were afraid that their countrymen would kill them and force them to abandon their religion.

Allah (SWT) made them wake up at a particular time so that people may learn some lessons: Firstly that Allah's promise is true and secondly that the resurrection will take place. People did not learn the lesson but kept arguing about what kind of monument to build in their honor. One of the things we learn is that instead of arguing about the unnecessary details of this story, we should learn its basic message.

It seems that the Qur`an has universalized this story for all people and for all times. The story could be of people of any time or place. Some of the messages it conveys are:

1. There is only one God—Allah (SWT).

2. Do not give up your faith under hardship or trials.

3. Allah (SWT) has unique ways to help those who are sincere and faithful.

4. Time and history are all in the power of Allah (SWT), He has total control over them.

5. Material power is not permanent; it is the spiritual that will abide.

6. People of truth are found in all places and times—truth is not the exclusive property of any one group or nation.

7. Allah (SWT) tests people. Those who suffer are not necessarily bad people, and those who prosper are not necessarily good people.

8. The truth will ultimately succeed.

9. Allah's promise of help and support is true; and final.

10. The resurrection will definitely take place.

The story of the owner of the two gardens is basically about the trials of wealth. It tells us that wealth and riches could be very tempting and deceiving and often take people away from the right path, so much so that the person even dares to doubt Allah's message regarding the afterlife.

The story of Musa (AS) and al-Khidr tells us about the trials of knowledge. We may think that we know everything, but no one—not even Allah's prophets—can grasp all the mysteries of the events in this world. Knowledge requires a lot of patience and humility, and ultimate knowledge of the seen and unseen belongs to Allah (SWT) alone.

The story of Dhu al-Qarnayn tells us about a great king who was powerful, intelligent, and resourceful. He was also humble and devout. He did not charge his subjects excessive taxes for any projects that he performed. The power and authority did not corrupt him. This is the story of the trials of power and position.

Allah (SWT) narrates to us four different stories relating to four different trials that we encounter during our earthly existence. May Allah (SWT) make us successful in each one of these trials.

The meaning of the translation of the end of *Surat al-Kahf* (verses 103-110) is as follows:

> Say, 'Shall we tell you who the biggest losers are according to their actions? It is those whose efforts are lost in this world and they think that they are doing well.' They disbelieve in their Lord's message and deny that they will meet Him. Their deeds come to nothing on the Day of Resurrection; We shall give them no weight. Their recompense will be hell because they disbelieved and made fun of My message and My messengers. But those who believe and do good deeds shall have as a gift the Gardens of paradise. They shall remain there forever, never wishing to leave. Say, 'If the ocean were ink for (writing) the words of my Lord, it would run dry before those words were exhausted'— even if We were to add another ocean to it. Say, 'I am only a human being, like you, to whom it has been revealed that your God is One. Anyone who hopes to meet his Lord should do good deeds and let him associate no one else in the worship of his Lord. (al-Kahf, 103-110)

Some of the other important lessons and guidance that we get from *Surat al-Kahf* are:
Never say of anything, "I will do that tomorrow, without (adding) if God wills"

وَلَا تَقُولَنَّ لِشَيْءٍ إِنِّي فَاعِلٌ ذَلِكَ غَدًا ○ إِلَّا أَنْ يَشَاءَ اللَّهُ ○

*Never say of anything, "I will do that tomorrow, without (adding) if God wills..." (al-Kahf, 18:23-24)*

Musa (AS) said to Khidr,

قَالَ سَتَجِدُنِي إِن شَاءَ اللَّهُ صَابِرًا وَلَا أَعْصِي لَكَ أَمْرًا ○

*He (Musa) said, God willing, you will find me patient. I will not disobey you in any way. (al-Kahf, 18:69)*

This also goes to show the humility of Musa (AS) when interacting with his teacher. So should we be humble to our teachers and elders.

The truth about the life of this world or what is the likeness of worldly life.

$$\text{وَاضْرِبْ لَهُمْ مَثَلَ الْحَيَاةِ الدُّنْيَا كَمَاءٍ أَنْزَلْنَاهُ مِنَ السَّمَاءِ فَاخْتَلَطَ بِهِ نَبَاتُ الْأَرْضِ فَأَصْبَحَ هَشِيمًا تَذْرُوهُ الرِّيَاحُ وَكَانَ اللَّهُ عَلَى كُلِّ شَيْءٍ مُقْتَدِرًا}$$

*Tell them, what the life of this world is like: We send water down from the skies and the earth's vegetation absorbs it, but soon the plants turn to dry stubble scattered about by the wind: Allah has power over everything. (al-Kahf, 18:45)*

It is Allah (SWT) who gives life and also death. He causes the rise and the downfall of civilizations. It is by His command that situations change. If you are enjoying prosperity today, you should be under no delusion that this condition will remain forever. God, by whose command these things have been bestowed upon you, has the power to snatch away all this by another command.

It is your good deeds that will benefit you in the hereafter.

$$\text{الْمَالُ وَالْبَنُونَ زِينَةُ الْحَيَاةِ الدُّنْيَا وَالْبَاقِيَاتُ الصَّالِحَاتُ خَيْرٌ عِنْدَ رَبِّكَ ثَوَابًا وَخَيْرٌ أَمَلًا}$$

*Wealth and children are the adornment of this worldly life, but the everlasting good deeds are far better with your Lord in reward and in hope. (al-Kahf, 18:46)*

Always be in the company of good people who are God-conscious and who constantly remember their Lord.

$$\text{وَاصْبِرْ نَفْسَكَ مَعَ الَّذِينَ يَدْعُونَ رَبَّهُمْ بِالْغَدَاةِ وَالْعَشِيِّ يُرِيدُونَ وَجْهَهُ وَلَا تَعْدُ عَيْنَاكَ عَنْهُمْ تُرِيدُ زِينَةَ الْحَيَاةِ الدُّنْيَا وَلَا تُطِعْ مَنْ أَغْفَلْنَا قَلْبَهُ عَنْ ذِكْرِنَا وَاتَّبَعَ هَوَاهُ وَكَانَ أَمْرُهُ فُرُطًا}$$

*Keep yourself attached to those who call on their Lord, morning and evening, seeking His pleasure; and do not let your eyes turn away from them, desiring the attraction of worldly life; and do not obey one whose heart We have made heedless of Our remembrance, and follows only his own desires, abandoning all that is good and true. (al-Kahf, 18:28)*

Though these words have been addressed to the Prophet (SAS), they are really meant for the chiefs of the Quraysh who considered it below their dignity to sit with such people as Bilal, Suhayb, 'Ammar, Khabbab, Ibn Mas'ud and others like them who were usually in the Prophet's company. The leaders of the disbelievers used to tell the Prophet (SAS) that they would only be willing to attend his meetings in order to learn about his message if he sent away these certain poor individuals from his companions.

This verse is meant to warn the chiefs of the Quraysh that their wealth, pomp, and show of which they were so proud had no value at all in the sight of Allah (SWT) and His Messenger (SAS). Those poor people were really more worthy in their sight, for they were sincere and always remembered Allah.

So, hopefully, keeping these points in perspective when we recite this *surah* will make us better understand and appreciate its benefits *in sha` Allah*.

# • 53 •

# LIFE OF THIS WORLD AND THE HEREAFTER

The topic of today's *khutbah* is, "Life of this World and the Hereafter." The purpose of my *khutbah* is to remind myself and everyone here to not be diverted by the commotion of our daily lives to the extent that we forget our ultimate destination and our ultimate objective, which is to seek the pleasure of Allah (SWT) and become successful in absolute terms.

My *khutbah* will address questions like: How does this life compare with the hereafter? What is the value that we tend to give to this life? What is the price we pay for living without the consciousness of the life to come? What do we do to give this life its due share? And finally, how can we strike the right balance? To have a firm belief in the hereafter (*akhira*) is one of the six tenets of a Muslim's faith, the others being the belief in Allah, His angels, His revealed books, His prophets and messengers, and His divine decree.

How does this life compare with the hereafter? Our time in this life is limited. We have at best a few more years, and then we will move on to a world about which the Qur`an provides numerous references. Allah (SWT) has repeatedly reminded us in the Qur`an that the value of this life compared to the hereafter is insignificant.

أَرَضِيتُم بِالْحَيَاةِ الدُّنْيَا مِنَ الْآخِرَةِ فَمَا مَتَاعُ الْحَيَاةِ الدُّنْيَا فِي الْآخِرَةِ إِلَّا قَلِيلٌ ○

*Do you prefer the life of the world over the hereafter? Yet the enjoyment of this world is very small compared to that of the hereafter. (at-Tawba, 9:38)*

وَفَرِحُوا بِالْحَيَاةِ الدُّنْيَا وَمَا الْحَيَاةُ الدُّنْيَا فِي الْآخِرَةِ إِلَّا مَتَاعٌ ⟡

*They rejoice in the life of this world but compared with the hereafter the life of this world is but a fleeting enjoyment. (ar-Ra'd, 13:26)*

So, by likening this life to a passing enjoyment, amusement, and a deception, Allah the All Knowing has clearly put the matter regarding the hereafter in perspective for us to reflect upon. He cautions us not to get carried away by the charms of this life, because in comparison with the hereafter, this life has a very limited span. As we go through life's challenges and attractions, we have to ensure that we do not deviate from the straight path. Sometimes the diversions are from temptations, sometimes from problems and sufferings. We should always be careful not to fall prey to man-made philosophies, rather, we should adhere to the straight path ordained by Allah (SWT).

Our beloved Prophet Muhammad (SAS) also clarified the value of this life concerning the hereafter. He said, "The life of this world compared to the hereafter is as if one were to put one's finger in the ocean and take it out again; compare the water that remains on one's finger to the water that remains in the ocean."

What is the value that we tend to give to this life? Knowing the limited time that we have in this life, giving it anything more than its due proportion, therefore, wouldn't be prudent. Nevertheless, we also know that Allah (SWT) has made this life a test and adorned it with enough temptations and attractions to make the weak among us get diverted and deceived. Allah (SWT) warns in the Qur'an in the following words:

فَلَا تَغُرَّنَّكُمُ الْحَيَاةُ الدُّنْيَا وَلَا يَغُرَّنَّكُم بِاللَّهِ الْغَرُورُ ⟡

*Do not let the life of the world deceive you and do not let the Deceiver (Shaytan) deceive you about Allah. (Fatir, 35:5)*

However, the reality is that the attractions of this life do blind us from seeing the big picture that includes our impending departure from this life and then our resurrection in the next eternal life. Fearing that our means of sustenance in this life are something we cannot do without, we make the mistake of turning means into goals. We run after wealth, believing it will buy and secure our present and the future. Thus we become obsessed with gaining benefits, pleasures and comforts, and in doing so we pursue to acquire more and more, be it wealth, name, fame, status, power, or authority. We compete with others in pursuit of these and lose sight of the hereafter. The Qur'an alludes to this situation when it says,

أَلْهَاكُمُ التَّكَاثُرُ ⟡ حَتَّى زُرْتُمُ الْمَقَابِرَ ⟡

*Striving for more distracts you until you go into your graves. (at-Takathur, 102:1-2)*

What is the price we pay for living without consciousness of the life to come? Focusing on the present life with lack of consideration for the hereafter can push us to a state where we feel rightfully entitled to have our wishes and desires fulfilled, and entitled to enjoy all that life can offer. Confronted with the reality of limited time in this life, and to acquire and enjoy this life's resources, we plant the seeds of greed and dissatisfaction within us. That often leads to injustice, deprivation of the rights of people, misuse of power and authority, and so on. The Prophet (SAS) expressed his concern for our *iman* when he said, "By Allah, it is not poverty that I fear for you, but I fear that this world will be spread out in front of you as it was spread out in front of those before you, and then you will compete for it as they competed for it, and it will destroy you as it destroyed them."

The price that we pay for going overboard in our quest for the best that this world can offer is that we become part of a cutthroat culture where material success is the measure of a person's worth, and failure in worldly acquisitions is regarded as a matter of shame and humiliation. Enamored by this life, people become heedless of Allah, the hereafter, the moral bounds and responsibilities, the rights of others, and their own obligations to fulfill those rights. They strive to acquire more at any cost and become forgetful about their end. About such people Allah (SWT) says,

أُولَٰئِكَ الَّذِينَ اشْتَرَوُا الْحَيَاةَ الدُّنْيَا بِالْآخِرَةِ فَلَا يُخَفَّفُ عَنْهُمُ الْعَذَابُ وَلَا هُمْ يُنْصَرُونَ ◯

*They are the ones who bought the life of this world for the hereafter; so their punishment shall not be lightened, nor will they be helped. (al-Baqara, 2:86).*

But then Allah, the Most Benevolent, gives people what they yearn for and whatever they work for as He also says,

مَنْ كَانَ يُرِيدُ الْحَيَاةَ الدُّنْيَا وَزِينَتَهَا نُوَفِّ إِلَيْهِمْ أَعْمَالَهُمْ فِيهَا وَهُمْ فِيهَا لَا يُبْخَسُونَ ◯

*As for those who desire the life of the world and its adornments, We will give them full payment in it for their actions. They will not be deprived here of their due. (Hud, 11:15)*

Allah (SWT), therefore, lets those who are eager to lose themselves in this world remain content with it. However, He also warns that they're buying these pleasures at the price of the hereafter. A man came to the Prophet (SAS) and said, "Oh Messenger of Allah! Guide me to such an action, that when I do it, Allah will love me, and the people will love me." He replied, "Be detached from this world and then Allah will love you and do not be attracted to what people have and then the people will love you".

This hadeeth shows that Allah (SWT) loves those who live simply in this life. It has been said that if having love for Allah is the best state to be in, then living simply is the best condition to be in. May Allah (SWT) guide us to that which pleases Him.

What do we do to give this life its due share? Of course, we *do* have to live this life and give this life its due share. We cannot escape from it, nor can we ignore the real challenges it poses. Moreover, Islam does not expect us to withdraw ourselves from the world. Allah (SWT) tells us in the Qur`an,

وَابْتَغِ فِيمَا آتَاكَ اللَّهُ الدَّارَ الْآخِرَةَ وَلَا تَنْسَ نَصِيبَكَ مِنَ الدُّنْيَا وَأَحْسِنْ كَمَا أَحْسَنَ اللَّهُ إِلَيْكَ وَلَا تَبْغِ الْفَسَادَ فِي الْأَرْضِ إِنَّ اللَّهَ لَا يُحِبُّ الْمُفْسِدِينَ ◯

*Seek the abode of the Next World with what Allah has given you, without forgetting your portion of this world. And do good as Allah has been good to you. And do not seek to cause corruption in the earth. Allah does not like the corrupters. (al-Qasas, 28:77)*

We see from the life of the Prophet (SAS) that he was an active and successful merchant before being chosen as a prophet. During his life of prophethood, he had family and dealt with worldly affairs like any fully engaged human being. He is an excellent example for the rich and poor, for young and old, for rulers and ruled, and for the most intelligent as well as the most ordinary people. He was exemplary as a teacher, preacher, imam, leader, statesman, judge, and commander of the armies as well as a husband, a father, a grandfather, a businessman, a neighbor, and a friend. We, too, are supposed to lead life, utilizing all the resources Allah Most Gracious has bestowed on us. Accordingly, we need to educate ourselves in worldly matters and use that knowledge to lead a good life and also to help prevent injustices and exploitation of humanity at large.

The life and example of the Prophet (SAS) should make clear how we are to engage ourselves in the activities of this life. No one should withdraw from life and forget his responsibilities. The Prophet (SAS) said, "The upper hand is better than the lower hand, (meaning he who gives charity is better than him who takes it.) And whoever abstains from asking others for some financial help, Allah will give him and save him from asking others, Allah will make him self-sufficient."

How can we strike the right balance? The obligation to live this life while providing for ourselves and our families effectively and by ensuring that we are not violating others' rights may create conflicts that must be managed accordingly. We ought to adopt attitudes where our actions strike the right balance between any competing and conflicting situations. We need to remind ourselves that by respecting the tenets of *halal* (the lawful) and *haram* (the unlawful) as laid out by Allah (SWT), we can lead a life where we can make the most of this life. At the same time, our hearts are always conscious of, and devoted to, Allah (SWT) and the hereafter.

Let us remember that when we live our lives according to what Islam teaches us, we not only lead fulfilling lives, we also please Allah (SWT). However, while living this life, nothing should divert us from our real purpose of life which is to attain the favor of Allah (SWT). Allah (SWT) says in the Qur`an,

بَلْ تُؤْثِرُونَ الْحَيَاةَ الدُّنْيَا ◯ وَالْآخِرَةُ خَيْرٌ وَأَبْقَى ◯ إِنَّ هَذَا لَفِي الصُّحُفِ الْأُولَى ◯ صُحُفِ إِبْرَاهِيمَ

وَمُوسَى ○

*But you prefer the worldly life, even though the hereafter is better and more lasting; All this is in the earlier scriptures; the Scriptures of Ibraheem and Musa. (al-A'la, 87:16-19).*

Let us supplicate to Allah (SWT) as we have been taught to supplicate for good in this life and in the hereafter.

رَبَّنَا آتِنَا فِي الدُّنْيَا حَسَنَةً وَفِي الْآخِرَةِ حَسَنَةً وَقِنَا عَذَابَ النَّارِ ○

*Our Lord, give us good in this world, and good in the Next World, and safeguard us from the punishment of the Fire. (al-Baqara, 2:201)*

• 54 •

# LIVING IN THIS WORLD WITHOUT BEING ATTACHED TO IT

How do we live in this world without our hearts being attached to it? How do we struggle against materialism and hedonism? How does the Qur`an describe the reality of this life? How does the life of this world compare with the life of the hereafter? These are some of the questions that I'll address in my *khutbah* today.

What is the reality of this world? As real as it may appear, it is no more than an illusion. We are told in *Surat Aal 'Imran*,

وَمَا الْحَيَاةُ الدُّنْيَا إِلاَّ مَتَاعُ الْغُرُورِ ○

*The life of this world is only a deceptive pleasure. (Aal 'Imran, 3:185)*

And we are told in *ayah* 64 of *Surat al-'Ankabut*,

وَمَا هَذِهِ الْحَيَاةُ الدُّنْيَا إِلاَّ لَهْوٌ وَلَعِبٌ وَإِنَّ الدَّارَ الآخِرَةَ لَهِيَ الْحَيَوَانُ لَوْ كَانُوا يَعْلَمُونَ ○

*The life of this world is nothing but amusement and play, but the home of the hereafter is indeed life, if they only knew. (al-'Ankabut, 29:64)*

Referring to the impermanence of this world, we have in *Surat al-Rahman*:

كُلُّ مَنْ عَلَيْهَا فَانٍ ۝ وَيَبْقَى وَجْهُ رَبِّكَ ذُو الْجَلَالِ وَالْإِكْرَامِ ۝

*All that is on earth will perish: while your Lord's own Self will remain full of majesty and glory. (ar-Rahman, 55: 26-27)*

In *Surat al-Hadeed* Allah (SWT) describes the reality of this life through an analogy.

اعْلَمُوا أَنَّمَا الْحَيَاةُ الدُّنْيَا لَعِبٌ وَلَهْوٌ وَزِينَةٌ وَتَفَاخُرٌ بَيْنَكُمْ وَتَكَاثُرٌ فِي الْأَمْوَالِ وَالْأَوْلَادِ كَمَثَلِ غَيْثٍ أَعْجَبَ الْكُفَّارَ نَبَاتُهُ ثُمَّ يَهِيجُ فَتَرَاهُ مُصْفَرًّا ثُمَّ يَكُونُ حُطَامًا وَفِي الْآخِرَةِ عَذَابٌ شَدِيدٌ وَمَغْفِرَةٌ مِنَ اللَّهِ وَرِضْوَانٌ وَمَا الْحَيَاةُ الدُّنْيَا إِلَّا مَتَاعُ الْغُرُورِ ۝

*Know that the life of this world is only play and amusement, an adornment, a cause of boasting among you, of competition in wealth and children. It is like plants that spring up after the rain. Their growth at first delights the farmers, but then you see them wither away, turn yellow, and become stubble. There is terrible punishment in the next life as well as forgiveness and approval from Allah; the life of this world is only a deceptive pleasure. (al-Hadeed, 57:20)*

When we look at this verse, the order by which Allah (SWT) describes the life of this world is worth noting. To begin with, life is described as play. To a child, all that really matters is playing with toys. If a child is given any other thing, no matter how expensive it is, the child will not care—all a child cares about is toys. This is because all that matters at that point in his *dunya* is playing. Later, as an adolescent, the focus shifts from playing with toys to finding other ways of amusement and entertainment such as hobbies and sports. It is no longer about playing with toys.

As a teenager in high school, the emphasis is mostly on looks. The *dunya* becomes all about the external appearance: the hairstyles, clothing, makeup, fashion, and so on. After high school, when we start applying to different colleges and universities, the focus of our *dunya* changes again. What we wear is not that important and something else becomes more important. Then it's all about showing off the universities one is going to, and mutual boasting about our accomplishments.

Next, one settles down, gets married and has kids. Now what is the *dunya* about? It is no longer relevant what toys one played with during childhood, or the entertainment, or what was worn at high school, or even what university one went to. Now it is about competing in the matters of one's wealth and children. Now the focus is "what my child did" versus "what your child did." "What university is your child in?" versus "what university is my child is in?" And "how much money did I spend on my child?" versus "how much money did you spend on your child?" And "how much did my house and car cost?" versus "how much did your house and car cost?"

In essence, we are all at different stages on this timeline. But after all that, Allah (SWT) gives us a parable—the parable of plants that spring up after a rain. The farmer becomes delighted with their growth. But what happens over time to the vegetation?

It dries up, and you see it turning yellow and crumbling. This is its natural life cycle. Now if we go back to the beginning of this *ayah* and review the things that are listed: the play, the entertainment, the boasting, and the competition, we see that they are all beautiful for a moment at different stages of our life. In the end, they all fade into insignificance. And in the end, all that is left is either Allah's severe punishment or His forgiveness and good pleasure. A part of this verse says,

$$وَمَا الْحَيَاةُ الدُّنْيَا إِلَّا مَتَاعُ الْغُرُورِ ۝$$

*...the life of this world is only a deceptive pleasure. (al-Hadeed, 57:20)*

What is a *mata'a*? When translated, it usually refers to pleasure or enjoyment, but when we look at the root of this word, it is a resource or tool. Now, imagine we are given a box of tools so we can build a house. How many of us will open the box and pick out the hammer, the screwdriver, the nail and then fall in love with these tools, forgetting what we're supposed to do with them?

What we have done in this life is precisely that. Allah (SWT) has given us a box of tools, and the purpose of those tools is to build our home in paradise. But what we do is that we fall in love with the tools and forget the purpose for which they were given. We fall in love with the money, with the people in our lives, with wealth, power, and status—and we forget that all of these things are just tools or means to achieve the end.

It is okay to own money, but there is a problem when the money begins to own you, and your heart gets attached to it. This worldly life, the *dunya*, is just like the ocean. While our hearts are the ships. As long as the ocean's water remains outside the ship, the ship will continue to float and be in control. But what happens as soon as the water creeps into the ship? What happens when the *dunya* enters our hearts? That is when the boat sinks. That is when we drown in the ocean of *dunya*.

There is a wonderful story of Imam Abu Haneefa (RA) that illustrates this. He was a merchant. Once while he was teaching, some people came to him and told him that his ships carrying merchandise had sunk. This is like someone finding out that he had lost a lot of money. Imam Abu Haneefa paused for a moment and said, "*al-hamduli-llah*" and continued teaching. A while later, they went back to him and told him that they were mistaken and that it wasn't his ships that sunk, and his ships were fine. Again, Imam Abu Haneefa paused and said, "*al-hamduli-llah*" and continued teaching. When he was asked about that, he explained that when he was first told that his ships had sunk, he paused to examine his heart. He found it unmoved by the loss, so he said "*al-hamduli-llah*." And then again, when he was told that his ships were fine, he paused and examined his heart. Again, he found it unmoved by the gain, so he said "*al-hamduli-llah*." His "*al-hamduli-llah*" wasn't about the gain or the loss. His "*al-hamduli-llah*" was about the fact that his heart was not attached to the gain or the loss.

My dear brothers and sisters! All the blessings and bounties of life are gifts from Allah (SWT). Allah gives us health, wealth, intellect, well-being, family, and all other bounties. Our problem is that when we receive the gifts, we hold them in our hearts. There is nothing wrong with having the gifts as long as they stay in our hands. As long as the money is in our hands, as long as the status is in our hands, as long as the relationships with the creation are in our hands, we are fine. The problem arises when we begin to love these things more than the One who gave them to us. And when we do that, these things start to control us.

How do we know if we are holding the gift in the heart instead of the hand? There are specific indications by which we can know: What do you think about all day? What occupies your mind most of the day? What is the first thing you think about when you wake up in the morning? And what is the last thing you think about when you sleep? What keeps you awake at night? What makes you cry? What are you most afraid of losing? What makes you most angry? And what causes you the most pain in your life? Upon examination, if the answers to all these questions are related to the usual things of this world—my money, my job, my children, my spouse, or what people think of me, and so on—then this tells us what is really filling our heart.

The truth is that when we love something, we are always thinking about what we love. It is impossible to be in love with something and not think about it. Thus, we have to re-examine our claim of love toward Allah (SWT) and His Messenger (SAS). In *Surat at*-Tawba Allah clearly lays out the criterion.

قُلْ إِنْ كَانَ آبَاؤُكُمْ وَأَبْنَاؤُكُمْ وَإِخْوَانُكُمْ وَأَزْوَاجُكُمْ وَعَشِيرَتُكُمْ وَأَمْوَالٌ اقْتَرَفْتُمُوهَا وَتِجَارَةٌ تَخْشَوْنَ كَسَادَهَا وَمَسَاكِنُ تَرْضَوْنَهَا أَحَبَّ إِلَيْكُمْ مِنَ اللَّهِ وَرَسُولِهِ وَجِهَادٍ فِي سَبِيلِهِ فَتَرَبَّصُوا حَتَّى يَأْتِيَ اللَّهُ بِأَمْرِهِ وَاللَّهُ لَا يَهْدِي ◯ الْقَوْمَ الْفَاسِقِينَ ◯

*Say, if your fathers and your sons and your brothers and your spouses and your family ties, and the worldly goods which you have acquired, and the commerce which you fear will decline, and the homes you love are dearer to you than Allah and His Messenger and the struggle for His cause, then wait until Allah fulfills His decree. Allah does not guide the disobedient people. (at-Tawba, 9:24)*

This is a frightful concept because the punishment is not specific, and the decree is to be fulfilled here, in this life before the next life. And the very thing that we love more than Allah (SWT) and His Messenger and striving in His cause will be the cause of our greatest pain. And yet, it is the passing and fleeting life of this world that the multitude of humanity prefers over the real and permanent life of the hereafter.

بَلْ تُؤْثِرُونَ الْحَيَاةَ الدُّنْيَا ◯ وَالْآخِرَةُ خَيْرٌ وَأَبْقَى ◯

*But you prefer the life of this world, although the hereafter is better and more lasting.*
*(al-A'la, 87:16-17)*

What is it about this life that hurts us? First, it is not perfect, and it can never be perfect. Second, it does not last—no matter what we do or what heights we achieve, we have to leave everything behind us. No wonder our beloved Prophet Muhammad (SAS) said in a hadeeth, "Be in the world as if you are a stranger or a traveler." So how can we prefer this life when the hereafter is better and everlasting? Live in this *dunya* but keep your hearts attached to the hereafter. It is perfect. It lasts forever, and it doesn't end. There, we don't have to worry about getting sick, getting old, or dying.

Therefore, we need to start focusing and seeing the real thing, and when we do that, it becomes easier to let our hearts not get attached to this world. It will be easier to give up the *haram*. It will be easier to perform the ritual prayers and other modes of worship. In other words, it will be easier to hold on to the straight path. This way, we will become more conscious of our ultimate destination, and will *in sha` Allah* qualify for Allah's mercy and forgiveness.

• 55 •

# LOVE FOR ALLAH (SWT)

Praise be to Allah (SWT) who breathed into us of His Spirit and placed the light of His guidance in our innermost being. Praise be to Allah (SWT) who blessed us with the guidance of His prophets and messengers. Praise be to Allah (SWT) whose Mercy encompasses everything. Praise be to Allah (SWT) who knows our needs and answers our calls and brings peace to our hearts.

Brothers and sisters! My *khutbah* today is based on some thoughts regarding increasing our love for Allah (SWT). One of the words for love in the Arabic language is *mahabba*, derived from the three root letters *ha-ba-ba*. The word *habba*, which means a grain or seed, is also derived from the same three letters. In the Arabic language, there is always a relationship between the multiple derived forms of a word. Hence, there is a relationship between a seed, (a *habba*), and the love (the *mahabba*) of Allah (SWT). The *habba* of *mahabba* or "the seed of love" for Allah (SWT) has been planted in the heart of every human being.

In our primordial state, before our earthly existence, Allah (SWT) planted that seed of His love when He gathered all the human souls and took a covenant from them by asking them, "Am I not your Lord?" to which they all replied, "We testify that indeed

You are!" And they got two things at that moment: Firstly, they got the *baraka* (blessing) of knowledge as they understood what Allah (SWT) asked of them, and secondly, they got the seed of *mahabba* that was planted in the heart of every human being.

*Mahabba* or love is part of human nature. The *qalb* or the spiritual heart contains the seed of love. Every human being falls in love. Every human being has love for something or someone. Every human being feels attracted toward something. It is human to love. Allah (SWT) designed us that way so that we would use this human attribute of love to love Allah. There is *khayr* (goodness) and *noor* (light) in loving Allah, and there is *dhulm* (injustice) and *dhulma* (darkness) in loving objects of worship other than Allah (SWT). Just as there is no room except that it either has light or darkness in it, similarly there is no heart except that it either has the *noor* of the love of Allah (SWT) in it or the darkness of loving objects of worship other than Allah.

When we realize that human beings were made to love and that our hearts must love, then why not use our hearts to love Allah (SWT), our Creator? If you love the creation, then know that one day you will be separated from what you love. If you love Allah, then know that you shall meet Him and be united with Him in the hereafter. Allah (SWT) is that Supreme Being whose association with us is real and eternal. Therefore the love that we have for that Being is real and eternal.

We see that in this life, it is love that drives everything. If a person has love for this world, then everything he does will be based on that love and on the desire for this *dunya*. Similarly, if a person has love for Allah (SWT) in his heart, then all his thoughts would be for Allah. All his actions, statements, feelings, and emotions will emanate from that love for Allah (SWT). Because the *deen* of Islam teaches us that we must make Allah (SWT) dominant in our lives, so it only makes sense that we should make Allah our true beloved. The more and more one nourishes and nurtures the love of Allah, the more and more one has *iman* (faith) in Allah. Those who have strong *iman* love Allah (SWT) most.

$$\text{وَالَّذِينَ آمَنُوا أَشَدُّ حُبًّا لِّلَّهِ}$$

*Those who believe love Allah most. (al-Baqara, 2:165)*

Without the love for Allah, our *iman* is going to remain weak. Just like Allah (SWT) gives life to the soil by sending rain and thus allowing the plant to grow, He waters the seed of *mahabba* all the time through His continuous blessings.

Our reality is like a radio with little or no battery power to receive the signals which are being broadcast all the time. Allah's mercy and blessings are being broadcast to the hearts of the true righteous believers twenty-four hours a day. However the problem is that we are people who have either turned the receiver off, or we are not able to tune the receiver. And we have placed interference in the signal due to our sins. Our sins block the mercy and blessings of Allah (SWT) that are showered on us all the time.

A person who leaves sin and become a person of *taqwa* also becomes a lover of Allah. Allah (SWT) befriends him and takes him out of darkness to light.

اللَّهُ وَلِيُّ الَّذِينَ آمَنُوا يُخْرِجُهُم مِّنَ الظُّلُمَاتِ إِلَى النُّورِ ◯

*Allah is the friend of those who believe and leads them out of darkness into light. (al-Baqara, 2:257)*

The truth is that when we love something, we are always thinking about what we love. It is impossible to be in love with something and not think about it. A reliable test of how true our love is for Allah (SWT) is to see how much we are able to serve others and to give of ourselves generously and openly for Allah's sake. The quality of our faith is reflected in our intentions, attitudes, and behavior.

Brothers and sisters! What does a person get if he or she takes this plunge into this ocean of the love of Allah? According to *hadeeth qudsi*, the Prophet (SAS) tells us that Allah (SWT) says, "I am as My servant expects me to be. I am with him when he makes mention of Me. If he makes mention of Me to himself, I make mention of him to Myself. If he makes mention of Me in an assembly, I make mention of him in an assembly better than it. And if he draws near to Me an arm's length, I draw near to him a fathom's length. And if he comes to Me walking, I go to him running." And Allah (SWT) says in the Qur'an,

أَلَا إِنَّ أَوْلِيَاءَ اللَّهِ لَا خَوْفٌ عَلَيْهِمْ وَلَا هُمْ يَحْزَنُونَ ◯

*Look, the friends of Allah shall have no fear, nor shall they grieve. (Yunus, 10:62)*

Brothers and sisters! How does one increase one's love for Allah (SWT)? Do we feel this deep love for Allah (SWT) in our hearts? Do we yearn for Him? Most probably, an honest reply would be that we don't. If we can examine ourselves honestly and know what we love, then we have taken a major step forward. If we find that what we love is Allah (SWT), then we are blessed with a great gift for which all praise is due to Allah. But if what we love is other than Allah, then at least we know, and we have the opportunity to seek to change what is in our hearts.

Those who have only tasted the pleasures of this world don't know about the taste of the love for Allah (SWT). If anyone derives pleasure from committing sins, then the only thing that can take him or her out of that situation is to taste the pleasure of intimacy with Allah (SWT). Without that, the person will most likely continue to sin even after praying, even after fasting for a whole month in Ramadan, and even after performing hajj. It is difficult to give up the pleasures of this world until one gets a greater pleasure, and that is the pleasure of feeling close and intimate with Allah (SWT). He has given us the gift of His companionship, for He says,

هُوَ مَعَكُمْ أَيْنَ مَا كُنتُمْ ◯

*He is with you wherever you are. (al-Hadeed, 57:4)*

Allah (SWT) is with you wherever you may be—in a *masjid*, home, workplace, or anywhere else—whether you remember Him or not, whether you are mindful of Him or not, whether you worship Him or not. He is with you even when you are sinning against Him, just waiting for you to turn to Him in repentance.

وَإِذَا سَأَلَكَ عِبَادِي عَنِّي فَإِنِّي قَرِيبٌ أُجِيبُ دَعْوَةَ الدَّاعِ إِذَا دَعَانِ ◯

*And when My servants ask you about Me, say that I am near. I respond to the call of one who calls, whenever he calls Me. (al-Baqara, 2:186)*

And Allah (SWT) says,

فَاذْكُرُونِي أَذْكُرْكُمْ ◯

*So remember Me and I will remember you. (al-Baqara, 2:152)*

Our remembrance of Allah (SWT) is His remembrance of us. Our call to Him is His answer to us. Remembrance is the way of intimacy with Allah. And we still don't desire to be close to Him. We still don't wish to love Him. We still disobey Him. We still distance ourselves from Him. Brothers and sisters! Allah (SWT) did not create us to send us to hell. He created us to be eternally happy and to live in *jannah*. And how close is Allah (SWT) to us—closer than we can imagine for He says,

وَنَحْنُ أَقْرَبُ إِلَيْهِ مِنْ حَبْلِ الْوَرِيدِ ◯

*We are nearer to him than his jugular vein. (Qaf, 50:16)*

This means that Allah (SWT) is closer to us than our own selves. The relationship of love between us and Allah (SWT), between us and others, and between us and all of creation is essential to reaching our full potential as human beings. When we nourish our hearts with love, when we manifest Allah's love in our lives with our families, with our friends, in our work, in our prayers, and in everything that we do, the entire meaning of life changes for us and our own experience of our humanness is transformed. Of course, love of Allah (SWT) requires us to love what Allah (SWT) loves and to dislike what displeases Him.

Brothers and sisters! Allah's grace multiplies with our sincere efforts and honest intentions to come closer to Him. Whatever we give to Him comes back manifold to us. In this way, little by little, our love for Allah (SWT) grows and develops, and it transforms us into loving, noble human beings.

Let me conclude by sharing with you one of the *du'a`s* that the Prophet (SAS) used to make to express his love, awe, and longing for Allah (SWT). He used to say,

اللَّهُمَّ إِنِّي أَسْأَلُكَ حُبَّكَ وَحُبَّ مَنْ يُحِبُّكَ وَالْعَمَلَ الَّذِي يُبَلِّغُنِي حُبَّكَ ◯

*"O Allah, I ask for Your love, and the love of those who love You and love of actions that bring me closer to Your love."*

May Allah (SWT) bless us with His love, and the love of those who love Him. May Allah (SWT) fill our hearts with love. *Ameen!*

## • 56 •

# MAKING BEST USE OF TIME

Are we making the best use of time in this life? Are we fulfilling both our religious and worldly responsibilities? Are we even conscious about how we are using our time? These are some of the questions we should be asking ourselves to make best use of our time and to get most from our lives. This is crucial because we have, at best, only a few years to live. Considering where we are in the various phases of our lives individually, the available time may be even shorter.

Will we do things differently if we knew how much time is remaining for us in this life? What if our remaining time is very little? Each heartbeat draws a person nearer to his or her grave. This is the reality of time allotted to each one of us. Imam al-Hasan al-Basri used to say, "O Man, your life comprises of a few breaths that can be counted. With every breath that you draw, a part of your existence has diminished!"

In my *khutbah* today, I want to share some thoughts with you about making the best use of time. We ought to know that time is one of the most valuable assets that we have. Wise people make use of this asset carefully and sensibly. *Surat al-'Asr* begins with Allah (SWT) swearing by time. The first verse says *"wa al-'Asr"* which has been variously translated as "by Time," "by the flight of time," "by the passage of time," "by the time through the ages," and so on. All these expressions show "time" to be something that is fleeting and running out. *'Asr* refers to time that passes swiftly.

In a beautiful hadeeth, our beloved Prophet Muhammad (SAS) advised us to take advantage of five things before five, before time takes them away from us. He says, "Seize the opportunity of five before five: your youth before your old age, your health before your sickness, your wealth before your poverty, your free time before your preoccupation, and your life before your death."

Those who have run out of time because of age or illness will tell us its value and importance. Ask the terminally ill who have been given only a few months to live. They will tell us how productive they would be if they were to have more time. The reality is that our lives are too busy and our daily routines too engaging. Nevertheless, we must pause to assess what we are earning or what opportunities we are missing, as the time allotted to each one of us keeps shrinking.

One of the ways to ensure that we use our remaining time in this life effectively is to be mindful of our purpose in this life. As Muslims, we believe that Allah (SWT) not only created mankind but clarified our purpose for being here in this world. Questions related to the goal and meaning of life have engaged philosophers for centuries. The foundation of our Islamic beliefs does away with the need to get entangled in the philosophical implications of this topic. Islamic principles make it clear that Allah (SWT) created life. Allah (SWT) created this universe and the rules that govern it. And the purpose of life is to worship, obey, and submit to Him without associating anyone or anything with Him. Among the many verses in the Qur`an that refer to this, let us consider just two of them. In *Surat adh-Dhariyat*, Allah (SWT) says,

$$وَمَا خَلَقْتُ الْجِنَّ وَالْإِنْسَ إِلَّا لِيَعْبُدُونِ ۝$$

*And I did not create the jinn and mankind except that they should worship and obey Me. (adh-Dhariyat, 51:56)*

And *in Surat al-Mu`minoon*, Allah (SWT) says,

$$أَفَحَسِبْتُمْ أَنَّمَا خَلَقْنَاكُمْ عَبَثًا وَأَنَّكُمْ إِلَيْنَا لَا تُرْجَعُونَ ۝$$

*Do you think that We created you without any purpose and that you would not be brought back to Us? (al-Mu`minoon 23:115)*

Needless to say, a sense of purpose can help in reconciling the many complex questions and issues that aren't always that easy for us to comprehend. It helps to instill the energy that we need to keep moving despite whatever challenges we face, while adhering to a system of living that we believe was designed by the Creator for His creation.

Secondly, we should become more action oriented. Declaring faith without translating it into good actions is meaningless. Admonishing the believers in *Surat as-Saff* to put their words into practice, Allah (SWT) says,

$$يَا أَيُّهَا الَّذِينَ آمَنُوا لِمَ تَقُولُونَ مَا لَا تَفْعَلُونَ ۝ كَبُرَ مَقْتًا عِنْدَ اللَّهِ أَنْ تَقُولُوا مَا لَا تَفْعَلُونَ ۝$$

*O you who believe, why do you say what you do not do. It is most hateful to Allah that you say what you do not do. (as-Saff, 61: 2-3)*

There are numerous verses in the Qur`an where the mention of faith is coupled with the need to do righteous deeds. We will be judged on what we do. Our faith is incomplete without us following it up with good actions. What is it that prevents us from taking action or from failing to accomplish enough? We should ask ourselves if we could have accomplished more by this time in our lives. As it turns out, many of us fall victim to procrastination. We wish to do something, so we make plans, but very often we lack the discipline or the courage to act. The result is that time passes without us accomplishing much, or we accomplish much less than we could have achieved. Refocusing to become more action-oriented will help us accomplish more, thus making our lives more fulfilling.

Thirdly, we should not concern ourselves with unnecessary matters. The Prophet (SAS) tells us, "From the perfection of a person's Islam is that he leaves alone that which does not concern him."

Today, we find ourselves exposed to a wide range of information outlets waiting to distract us from our key priorities. Sunk in the satellite TV, the internet, smart phones, and various other forms of social media networks, we can end up wasting valuable time by soaking our minds with information that we usually do not need. While a lot of such information may satisfy our curiosities and habits of gossip, they take up valuable time and drain our energies. Indeed, we are be lucky if, after wasting time on the various media channels, we manage to come out without having committed any sins by watching lewd and obscene images or listening to vulgar music or both. We must become selective in using modern techniques and equipment of science and technology based on what benefits us. The Prophet (SAS) used to make a *du'a`*,

$$ اللَّهُمَّ انْفَعْنِى بِمَا عَلَّمْتَنِى وَ عَلِّمْنِى مَا يَنْفَعُنِى وَ ارْزُقْنِى عِلْماً يَنْفَعُنِى ۝ $$

*O Allah! Benefit me with what you taught me and teach me what will benefit me and*
*provide me with knowledge that will benefit me.*

Brothers and sisters! Don't forget the remembrance of Allah(SWT). Many of us make the mistake of thinking about the remembrance of Allah (SWT) as merely a spiritual matter and seeing no connection with the real world. Instead, we should remind ourselves that our success in this life related to our work, our earnings, our family, our health, and all other aspects of life is tied to the remembrance of Allah (SWT)—both in our prayers as well as at other times during the day. Consider what Allah (SWT) tells us in *Surat al-Jumu'ah*,

$$ وَابْتَغُوا مِنْ فَضْلِ اللَّهِ وَاذْكُرُوا اللَّهَ كَثِيرًا لَعَلَّكُمْ تُفْلِحُونَ ۝ $$

*And seek the bounty of Allah, and remember Allah much, that you may be successful.*
(al-Jumu'ah, 62:10)

And listen to what Allah (SWT) tells us in *Surat al-Munafiqoon*,

$$ يَا أَيُّهَا الَّذِينَ آمَنُوا لَا تُلْهِكُمْ أَمْوَالُكُمْ وَلَا أَوْلَادُكُمْ عَنْ ذِكْرِ اللَّهِ وَمَنْ يَفْعَلْ ذَلِكَ فَأُولَئِكَ هُمُ الْخَاسِرُونَ ۝ $$

*O you who believe! Do not let your wealth or your children distract you from remembrance of Allah. Those who do so will be the losers. (al-Munafiqoon, 63:9)*

In a hadeeth, the Prophet (SAS) said, "Should I not inform you of the best of deeds, and the most sanctifying of deeds before your Lord, which does more to raise your positions (with Him), and is better for you than the disbursement of gold and money, or battle with the enemy?" The companions said, "Indeed inform us." He (SAS) then said, "Remembrance of Allah."

Taking the time to pause and reassess how we use our time can help us refocus, reprioritize, and reenergize. It can also prevent us from going to extremes, where we focus on certain priorities of life more than others. It is thus time to reflect on these principles in our actions and accomplishments. Brothers and sisters! I am not preaching. I am only inviting myself and you to reflect individually and collectively as to how to make the best use of the precious gift of time given to us. We have got to strive to change ourselves for the better. Allah (SWT) tells us in the Qur`an,

$$ إِنَّ اللَّهَ لَا يُغَيِّرُ مَا بِقَوْمٍ حَتَّىٰ يُغَيِّرُوا مَا بِأَنْفُسِهِمْ $$

*Allah does not change the condition of a people unless they change what is in themselves. (ar-Ra'd, 13:11)*

May Allah (SWT) give us the *tawfeeq* to make the best use of the precious gift of time given to each one of us. *Allahumma ameen.*

•   57   •

# MERCY OF ALLAH

My *khutbah* today is on a topic that is very dear to us; it is about the mercy of Allah (SWT). All the things we have learned about Islam—the beliefs, the laws, the ethics, the code of conduct and behavior, and the obligations we have to carry out, are essential. These are things that we are supposed to learn and practice. But at times, we become careless and negligent in doing what we are asked to do. When it comes to our relationship with Allah (SWT), does He punish us or take us to task for every mistake we make and every sin we commit? No!

Knowing that we are imperfect and commit mistakes throughout life, He makes it clear that people who make mistakes, but then return to Him in sincerity and ask for His forgiveness, will be forgiven. As long as people are sincerely sorry for the wrong they have done, they must never lose hope in Allah's mercy regardless of the magnitude of their sins. This truth is emphasized in the following verse from the Qur`an:

قُلْ يَا عِبَادِيَ الَّذِينَ أَسْرَفُوا عَلَى أَنْفُسِهِمْ لا تَقْنَطُوا مِنْ رَحْمَةِ اللَّهِ إِنَّ اللَّهَ يَغْفِرُ الذُّنُوبَ جَمِيعًا إِنَّهُ هُوَ الْغَفُورُ الرَّحِيمُ ○

*Say 'O My servants who have committed excesses against their own souls, do not despair of the mercy of Allah. Indeed Allah will forgive all sins. Indeed He is the All-forgiving, the All-Merciful. (az-Zumar, 39:53)*

It has been narrated in a hadeeth that the Prophet (SAS) said, "Had human beings not committed any sin, Allah would have replaced this species with another species that would commit sin so that He could forgive them." So Allah (SWT) wants to forgive us and He wants us to feel His mercy in this life and in the hereafter. One should not misunderstand this hadeeth as a blanket sanction for committing sins. The emphasis of this hadeeth is the imperfection of human beings and its connection with Allah's forgiveness and mercy. Unfortunately, much of the message that we are receiving and delivering to others is not the mercy, love, and compassion of Allah (SWT). More often, we are talking about the power and wrath of Allah and how we should fear Him. The Prophet (SAS) was told to convey to all people the good news that Allah keeps forgiving and is most merciful.

نَبِّئْ عِبَادِي أَنِّي أَنَا الْغَفُورُ الرَّحِيمُ ○

*Tell My servants that I am indeed the Oft-Forgiving, Most Merciful. (al-Hijr, 15:49)*

So that we develop some appreciation of our relationship with Allah (SWT), listen to what Allah (SWT) tells us in the Qur`an:

وَرَحْمَتِي وَسِعَتْ كُلَّ شَيْءٍ ○

*My mercy extends to all things. (al-A'raf, 7:156)*

And we learn through a *hadeeth qudsi* in which the Prophet (SAS) tells us that Allah (SWT) says, "When Allah decreed the creation, he wrote in his Book with him on his Throne: My mercy prevails over my wrath."

Let us understand this phenomenon through an example. Just like the parental relationship with children, there are things children are supposed to do. There are ways the children are expected to behave. There are family rules, traditions, and norms. But, after all, when it comes to parental relationship, it is mostly based on mercy, love, and affection that often override other things.

It is a fact of life that the perception we develop about someone affects our behavior and relationship. If we are afraid of our parents, we may develop one type of relationship. If we develop a relationship based on love and affection, it would be totally different. We have seen that our perception and knowledge of Allah (SWT), especially the way we understand and the way we are presented information and ideas about Him, is primarily how powerful He is in His knowledge and in His ability to affect our lives here and in the hereafter. But is that the only way Allah wants us to know or perceive Him?

In the Qur`an, Allah (SWT) has been identified in many different ways. We all know that there are at least ninety-nine attributes of Allah collected from the Qur`an and the Sunnah. But Allah specifically chose only two of these by which we should remember Him every time we begin something or every time we take the first step toward something. He does not want us to begin something by remembering Him as *al-Qahhar* (the One besides Whose Might all creation is powerless) or *al-Jabbar* (the One Who forces His will on others, and nothing can happen in His domain except whatever He pleases) or by any other name.

There are only two attributes by which Allah (SWT) wants us to remember Him every time we take a step in our life. What are those attributes? They are, as we all know, contained in "bismillah ar-Rahman ar-Raheem." According to Ibn al-Qayyim (RA), the name ar-Rahman implies the quality of abounding grace inherent in, and inseparable from, the concept of Allah's Being, while ar-Raheem expresses the manifestation of that grace, and its effect upon, His creation—in other words, an aspect of His activity.

So out of all the attributes of Allah (SWT) that we might know or be familiar with, He wants us to remember Him by these two attributes. These attributes, therefore, are central to proper perception of Allah. The Prophet (SAS) is reported to have said that no man's good deeds are enough to get him admitted into paradise, but it is only by the mercy of Allah that people will enter paradise. Our deeds are only the tools, the means to get close to Allah so that we can be hopeful of His mercy. Therefore, let us do our good deeds, let us have our correct faith, and let us perform our obligations as best as we can, but then leave the rest to Allah's mercy, the same mercy that brings and binds us together as human beings.

Now, how do we develop an appreciation of the mercy or rahma of Allah (SWT)? Allah has used certain examples for us to understand that. In this life, no one shows more unconditional love and affection than a mother. Nobody else! All other relationships are perhaps somewhat mixed and conditional. When it comes to a mother's love, it reaches the closest to understanding the rahma of Allah. This is the understanding we get from Prophet Muhammad (SAS).

In one hadeeth, it is reported that during one of the gatherings of the companions of the Prophet (SAS), a woman prisoner was running anxiously back and forth in search of her missing child. When she found the child, she took it up in her lap, drew it close to her, and suckled it. The Prophet (SAS) asked his companions what they thought of that woman. He asked, "Do you think this mother could ever throw her child into the fire?" The companions replied, "O Messenger of Allah, how can that be, possible?" The Prophet (SAS) then said that if this is so, then do know that Allah loves His servants much more than this mother loves her child.

Let us do our good deeds. But with all our imperfections, we have hope because Allah (SWT) is much more merciful than we perceive and appreciate. It is crucial to understand that Allah (SWT) has not created us as perfect creatures so that we won't make mistakes. Human beings are prone to make mistakes. The very first human being and his mate are perfect examples of our imperfection.

Therefore, Allah (SWT) does not want perfection from us. Instead, He expects that from time to time, if we falter or make mistakes, we should not follow the path of Shaytan and be arrogant and persistent in our mistakes. Instead, we should follow the footsteps of our first parents Adam (AS) and Hawwa (AS), which is that we admit and recognize our mistakes, seek forgiveness and make a determined effort not to repeat the mistake again.

My dear brothers and sisters! The closest we can think about how Allah (SWT) feels toward us is, once again, the mother. It is essential to be aware that the word "rahma" is the root of Allah's two supreme attributes: ar-Rahman and ar-Raheem. The Arabic word for the womb is rahm. Allah (SWT) has brought us to this world through the same reproductive system, which in Arabic is named "rahm" derived from the same root from which the two supreme attributes of Allah: ar-Rahman and ar-Raheem are derived. It then makes sense when Allah (SWT) says, "My mercy extends to all things." Allah Himself wants us to perceive and remember Him with His attributes of mercy.

So let our hearts be filled with mercy so that our family bonds can be better and stronger. So that when we hug our children or kiss them, when we embrace or hold them, when we pass our hands over their heads, it is nothing less than the manifestation of Allah's mercy flowing through us. In our da'wa and message, we also have to deliver this message of love and mercy. Proper understanding of this attribute of Allah (SWT) has deeper implications for us as individuals and as communities.

Once touched by the mercy of Allah (SWT), our personality is transformed. We begin to have positive effects on our relationship at the family level. It would also be reflected in society's political and economic dimensions. Our relationship with neighbors, Muslims or non-Muslims, individuals or nations, would also be positively transformed. From domestic violence to political leadership, from social responsibility to economic development, from conflict resolution to interfaith relations, the implication of assimilating the message of mercy in our life is so pervasive.

The mercy and love that Allah (SWT) has for us should prevent us from disobeying

Him and should motivate us to obey Him. Despite our best sincere efforts, if we falter, however badly, we always have hope for His mercy, forgiveness, and love as long as we are humble, submit to Him, and repent to Him. It is His rahma that is going to save us, not anything else, even though we do have to have the right beliefs and adequate good deeds. But Allah's rahma is ultimately what we need.

Let us supplicate to the All-Merciful, the Ever-Merciful. Ya Allah! Ya arham ar-rahimeen! ("O most merciful of those who show mercy!") Have mercy on us above the earth. Have mercy on us below the earth. And have mercy on us on the day when our deeds will be shown to us. And cause us to be merciful to one another. O Allah! We ask You for those things that lead to Your mercy and forgiveness. We ask You for safety from every vice, for achieving all that is good and righteous, for gaining entry into paradise, and for being saved from the hellfire. Allahumma ameen.

• 58 •

# MODERN-DAY IDOLATRY

We are about to enter the month of *Dhu al-Hijja*. This blessed month calls for asserting the message of the oneness of Allah (SWT), which the Prophet Ibraheem (AS) preached and practiced throughout his life. *In sha` Allah*, today's *khutbah* will focus on the relevance of Ibraheem's message of *tawheed* in our contemporary times. It will also mention some forms of modern-day idolatry, and the need to beware of them and the need to keep away from them.

Allah (SWT) mentions the origins of the hajj in Surat al-Hajj. Some 4,500 years ago, He ordered Ibraheem (AS) to proclaim the hajj to mankind.

وَأَذِّنْ فِي النَّاسِ بِالْحَجِّ يَأْتُوكَ رِجَالًا وَعَلَى كُلِّ ضَامِرٍ يَأْتِينَ مِنْ كُلِّ فَجٍّ عَمِيقٍ ۝

*Proclaim the hajj to mankind; they will respond, coming to the Sacred House on foot, riding every possible conveyance; coming from every distant path. (al-Hajj, 22:27)*

When the Ka'ba was built, the hajj was performed in accordance with the rites prescribed by Ibraheem (AS), but after he passed away, and gradually with the passage of time, both the form and the spirit of hajj were changed drastically.

As idolatry spread throughout Arabia, the Ka'ba lost its purity, and eventually over

360 idols came to be placed around it. During the hajj season, the atmosphere around the sacred area of the Ka'ba began to look like a show. Men and women would go round the Ka'ba naked, arguing that they should present themselves before Allah (SWT) in the same condition as they were born. Their prayers became devoid of all sincere remembrance of Allah (SWT) and was instead reduced to a series of hand-clapping, whistling and the blowing of horns. Singing, drinking, and other acts of immorality were widespread among the pilgrims. Poetry competition became a major hajj event in which poetries were sung to praise the bravery and splendor of one's own tribe and criticize the cowardice and miserliness of other tribes. The chief of each tribe would feed the pilgrims, just to become well-known for his generosity.

The house that Ibraheem (AS) had made pure for the worship of Allah (SWT) alone had been totally desecrated by the pagans, and the rites which he had established were completely distorted by them. This sad state of affairs continued for nearly two and a half thousand years. But then after this long period, the time came for the supplication of Ibraheem (AS) to be answered, and the supplication was:

رَبَّنَا وَابْعَثْ فِيهِمْ رَسُولًا مِنْهُمْ يَتْلُو عَلَيْهِمْ آيَاتِكَ وَيُعَلِّمُهُمُ الْكِتَابَ وَالْحِكْمَةَ وَيُزَكِّيهِمْ إِنَّكَ أَنْتَ الْعَزِيزُ الْحَكِيمُ ○

*Our Lord, raise up among them a Messenger from them to recite Your Signs to them and teach them the Book and Wisdom and purify them. You are the Almighty, the All-Wise. (al-Baqara, 2:129)*

Prophet Muhammad (SAS) was born in the very city in which Ibraheem (AS) had made this supplication centuries earlier. For twenty-three years, the Prophet Muhammad (SAS) spread the message of *tawheed*—the same message that Ibraheem (AS) and all other prophets came with—and established the law of Allah (SWT) upon the land. He made every effort toward making the word of Allah supreme. Truth prevailed over falsehood.

The Ka'ba was purified of all the idols in and around it, and once again it became the universal center for the worshippers of the one True God. Not only did Prophet (SAS) rid the Ka'ba of all its impurities, but he also reinstated the rites of hajj which were established by Allah's permission, in the time of Ibraheem (AS). Specific injunctions in the Qur'an were revealed in order to eliminate all the false rites which had become rampant in the pre-Islamic period. All indecent and shameful acts were banned. The Qur'an declared:

فَلَا رَفَثَ وَلَا فُسُوقَ وَلَا جِدَالَ فِي الْحَجِّ ○

*There should be no vulgarity, bad behavior, or quarrel during the hajj. (al-Baqara, 2:197)*

Muslims around the globe answer Allah's call to make hajj, at least once in their lifetime. In choosing Ibraheem (AS) to make the initial awesome call to hajj, Allah (SWT) honored him with one of the most profound descriptions ever given to a human being. Praising him, Allah (SWT) says,

إِنَّ إِبْرَاهِيمَ كَانَ أُمَّةً قَانِتًا لِّلَّهِ حَنِيفًا وَلَمْ يَكُ مِنَ الْمُشْرِكِينَ ۝

*Truly Ibraheem was a nation, devoutly obedient to Allah, a man of pure natural belief.*
*He was not one of the idolaters. (an-Nahl, 16:120)*

Allah (SWT) describes Ibraheem (AS) as a nation. One interpretation is that he was a repository of all good human traits and virtues. During his long and distinguished life, Ibraheem (AS) demonstrated characteristics such as sacrifice, patience, hospitality, graciousness, and most importantly, an uncompromising commitment to upholding the Oneness of Allah (SWT). We, as Muslims, should exert our utmost to embody these and other prophetic virtues. Furthermore, we should realize that it is our duty to call humanity to these virtues. Allah (SWT) orders us in *Surat Aal 'Imran*,

وَلْتَكُنْ مِنْكُمْ أُمَّةٌ يَدْعُونَ إِلَى الْخَيْرِ وَيَأْمُرُونَ بِالْمَعْرُوفِ وَيَنْهَوْنَ عَنِ الْمُنْكَرِ وَأُولَئِكَ هُمُ الْمُفْلِحُونَ ۝

*Let there be a community among you who call to the good, and enjoin the right, and*
*forbid the wrong. And it is these who are successful (Aal 'Imran, 3:104)*

Naturally, Ibraheem (AS) was a strict monotheist. The magnitude of this characteristic is brought home to us when we realize that Ibraheem (AS) was all alone in a world of idolatry. Despite that, he was prepared to sacrifice his life to defend and uphold the standard of the Oneness of Allah (SWT). In his days, the idols that people worshipped were idols of wood and stone.

Today, the idols people worship have changed. The modern and postmodern conditions have handed down to humanity a variety of idols, which are worshipped besides the One Supreme God. The term "idol" has come to be used in a broader connotation and need not necessarily imply an image or symbol; it can also mean a cause or idea.

Nationalism, for example, is a form of modern-day idolatry. Humanism is another example of idolatry. Under the banner of humanism, man becomes the measure of all things. When man is no longer directed by God and His commandments, man replaces God with an idol of his own making. In the modern hall of idols, art also has its place. People speak with awe of music, painting, poetry, regarding their creators as some sort of divine intermediaries.

Celebrity worship is also idolatry. More and more people want to look like their favorite celebrity on TV. People's minds are absolutely saturated with celebrities. Everything, from the clothes they wear to the cars they drive, is affected by the film industry. But perhaps the greatest idol arising from our condition is the individual's worship of himself. A contemporary American historian and sociologist describes the present modern culture of the West as a culture of narcissism or self-centeredness in which there is an excessive love and admiration for oneself. In the light of this observation, it is easy to appreciate the penetrating question asked by Allah (SWT) in the Qur'an:

$$أَفَرَأَيْتَ مَنِ اتَّخَذَ إِلَهَهُ هَوَاهُ ○$$

*Have you seen him who takes his whims and desires to be his God? (al-Jathiya, 45:23)*

Many of the problems facing humanity, such as grinding poverty, growing disparities between the rich and the poor, the continued and accelerating destruction of the environment, and our enhanced ability to kill each other with increasingly sophisticated weapons are all facilitated by an international environment shaped by dominant corporations and institutions. Devout people fear that corporations, and virtually all giant organizations, have become "idols." The corporation has become a false god that promises the moon but brings sorrow and grief.

While acknowledging and benefiting from the many positive advancements given to humanity by Western civilization, we should have the vision and courage to work to minimize the damage caused by its negative and darker innovations. May Allah (SWT) give us the *tawfeeq* to do so.

Brothers and sisters! Gratefulness and thankfulness to Allah (SWT) should have a high place in the life of every Muslim. As Muslims living in Western lands, we have more to thank Allah for than any other group of Muslims on earth. We have experienced the fullness of the meaning conveyed by the following verse of *Surat Luqman*:

$$وَأَسْبَغَ عَلَيْكُمْ نِعَمَهُ ظَاهِرَةً وَبَاطِنَةً ○$$

*He has completed His Blessings upon you, in open and hidden ways. (Luqman, 31:20)*

Among the open blessings we could mention are food, drink, clean water, sanitation, health, wealth, shelter, clothing, security, education, and despite certain well-publicized abuses, the overwhelming majority of us live under the protection of the law. Among the hidden blessings, we could mention understanding, discernment, psychological stability, and faith—the greatest blessing of all.

All of these blessings, and countless others that could be mentioned, are subordinate to two other blessings, which are frequently completely taken for granted—the blessing of our existence and the blessing of sustenance. No matter what heights of arrogance and ingratitude a human being may reach, there is no one who will go so far as to claim that he has brought himself into existence, or that he sustains his own life. Regarding our existence, we are reminded in *Surat al-Insan*:

$$\text{هَلْ أَتَى عَلَى الْإِنْسَانِ حِينٌ مِنَ الدَّهْرِ لَمْ يَكُنْ شَيْئًا مَذْكُورًا} \, \bigcirc$$

*Was there not a period of time when man was nothing to speak of? (al-Insan, 76:1)*

It is certain that the physical world existed long before man was ever heard of or mentioned, as geological records prove. And regarding our sustenance, we are told in *Surat Hud*,

$$\text{وَمَا مِنْ دَابَّةٍ فِي الْأَرْضِ إِلَّا عَلَى اللَّهِ رِزْقُهَا} \, \bigcirc$$

*There is no creature on the earth which is not dependent upon Allah for its sustenance.*
(Hud, 11:6)

Therefore, we should passionately and wholeheartedly express our gratitude to our Lord through pure, unadulterated worship and devotion. We should rededicate ourselves to the worship of the only One God. This is what Ibraheem (AS) stood for.

Let us also remember that Allah (SWT) does nothing in vain. Our being Muslim at this critical juncture in history is not without purpose. Our existence here is part of a divine plan, and the deeper our understanding of that plan, the more profound our realization of the tremendous responsibility we shoulder. Our situation presents us with overwhelming challenges. However, if we take up those challenges with even a fraction of the courage, determination, vision, and patience that Ibraheem (AS) and Muhammad (SAS) displayed throughout their lives, we may be blessed to change the course of history.

We have the divine guidance—the Qur`an—with us. We have the *milla* (the way) of Ibraheem (AS) with us. We have the Sunnah and the *uswa* (the example) of Prophet Muhammad (SAS) with us. We just need to be sincere, work in earnest, and have full faith and trust in Allah (SWT).

May Allah (SWT) make it easy for those Muslims who have not yet performed hajj to fulfill their obligation of performing hajj, and may he accept the hajj of those who have done it. And for those who are going this year from our community, may Allah (SWT) ease their journey. And may He accompany them in this journey and guard over their household that they have left behind. May their hajj be accepted by Allah (SWT). We humbly request them to keep us, our community, our *masjid*, and all believing men and women, and all fellow humans in their prayers.

May Allah (SWT) protect us from idolatry, both in its manifest as well as in its hidden forms. May He give us the *tawfeeq* to work sincerely and seriously to enable us to contribute toward the betterment of the society at large. *Allahumma ameen.*

---

*This *khutbah* transcript has been excerpted, adapted and paraphrased from an article titled, "The Significance of Abraham in Our World Today Needs to Be Asserted" by Imam Zaid Shakir

# MODESTY *(HAYA')*

My dear brothers and sisters! We learn through a hadeeth that the Prophet (SAS) said, "Every religion has a chief characteristic, and the chief characteristic of this religion (i.e., Islam) is modesty." This hadeeth in which the Prophet (SAS) informs us that modesty, or haya` in Arabic, is a prominent feature of Islam. The Prophet (SAS) also said, "Modesty is a branch of faith."

*In sha` Allah*, in today's *khutbah*, I'll share some thoughts with you on the concept of modesty or *haya`* from the Islamic Perspective. The word *haya`* has different shades of meaning. Some of its meanings are modesty, self-respect, shame, shyness, bashfulness, honor, and humility. Islam encourages and treasures *haya`*. It is one of the most important traits that each and every Muslim should acquire and possess. *Haya`* is a quality that keeps a person from committing a sinful act. It is the feeling of rejection for every disgraceful matter. It prevents man from doing anything disgraceful no matter how minor it is. It is an attribute that pushes one to avoid anything detestable or distasteful. If a person has no modesty, he or she will do almost anything. Muslims should possess both an inner as well as an outer modesty. This is reflected in behavior, speech, and appearance, and includes being mindful of Allah (SWT) at all times.

Allah (SWT) created human beings with *fitra*, which is a natural disposition that is inclined toward right action and submission to Allah. Our inborn *fitra* can direct us toward *haya`* and good morals. Our *fitra* is programmed to feel uneasiness when codes of morality are violated. The believer is most in touch with his or her *fitra* and is keen to act in accordance with this natural disposition. *Haya`* is a quality that, for some people, comes naturally, and some may need to struggle to instill it in some aspects of their life. It is possible to revive and kindle this great quality of *haya`*, just as it is possible to ruin it by consistently neglecting it. Nurturing *haya`* in our hearts is part of the process of our spiritual development and building our relationship with Allah (SWT).

We often find that shyness, humility, and bashfulness are frowned upon by our society as a weakness or a lack of confidence when, in fact, these are quality of dignified upright human beings, who are conscious of their actions and their responsibilities in life.

We are living in a time where we are constantly exposed to nakedness and shamelessness to the extent that we get desensitized to it. When someone sees something lewd and vulgar for the first time, he gets disturbed because his sense of shame is still intact. But if he sees it over and over again, he no longer considers it a big deal. He becomes desensitized. The more he becomes desensitized to shamelessness, the more spiritually bankrupt he becomes. He begins to question: Why are people making such a big deal about it? Why is it that it's such an evil? When the heart is not disturbed by sin anymore, when the heart is not troubled by evil anymore and you don't find a problem with it anymore, that is a deep spiritual problem. And if we have that problem, then we will not be able to concentrate in our prayers. We will not be able to humble ourselves before Allah (SWT). We will not be able to cry before Him. Those things will disappear from our life because we allowed shamelessness to take over us; to take over our life.

Modesty is referred to in the Qur`an in *Surat an-Noor.*

قُل لِّلْمُؤْمِنِينَ يَغُضُّوا مِنْ أَبْصَارِهِمْ وَيَحْفَظُوا فُرُوجَهُمْ ذَٰلِكَ أَزْكَىٰ لَهُمْ إِنَّ اللَّهَ خَبِيرٌ بِمَا يَصْنَعُونَ ۝

*Say to the believing men that they should lower their gaze and guard their modesty: that will make for greater purity for them: And Allah is well acquainted with all that they do. (an-Noor, 24:30)*

وَقُل لِّلْمُؤْمِنَاتِ يَغْضُضْنَ مِنْ أَبْصَارِهِنَّ وَيَحْفَظْنَ فُرُوجَهُنَّ وَلَا يُبْدِينَ زِينَتَهُنَّ إِلَّا مَا ظَهَرَ مِنْهَا وَلْيَضْرِبْنَ بِخُمُرِهِنَّ عَلَىٰ جُيُوبِهِنَّ وَلَا يُبْدِينَ زِينَتَهُنَّ ۝

*And say to the believing women that they should lower their gaze and guard their modesty; that they should not display their beauty and ornaments except what (must ordinarily) appear thereof; that they should draw their veils over their bosoms and not display their beauty. (an-Noor, 24:31)*

Addressing the entire humanity, Allah (SWT) says in *Surat al-A'raf,*

يَا بَنِي آدَمَ قَدْ أَنزَلْنَا عَلَيْكُمْ لِبَاسًا يُوَارِي سَوْآتِكُمْ وَرِيشًا وَلِبَاسُ التَّقْوَىٰ ذَٰلِكَ خَيْرٌ ذَٰلِكَ مِنْ آيَاتِ اللَّهِ لَعَلَّهُمْ يَذَّكَّرُونَ ۝

*O children of Adam, We have bestowed upon you clothing to conceal your private parts and as adornment. But the clothing of righteousness – that is best. That is from the signs of Allah that perhaps they will remember. (al-A'raf, 7:26)*

It is reported that the Messenger of Allah (SAS) said, "Among the things that people have found from the words of the previous prophets was: 'If you feel no shame, then do as you wish.'" This hadeeth can be understood in several ways because there are different explanations given by scholars. It is interesting that all these explanations are correct and are possible simultaneously. One way to understand it is as a threat: Do whatever you want, but be prepared to face the consequences. This mode of expression is well known in the Arabic language, and it is used for threatening someone. This mode is used by the Qur`an in *Surat Fussilat,* which says,

$$\text{اعْمَلُوا مَا شِئْتُمْ إِنَّهُ بِمَا تَعْمَلُونَ بَصِيرٌ} \; \bigcirc$$

*Do what you like. He sees whatever you do. (Fussilat, 41:40)*

A second interpretation is that if you engage in an act and it is such that there is no reason to be ashamed of doing it before Allah (SWT) or the people, then you may do that act. The command here is in the form of permission. A third interpretation is that the hadeeth is not a command but a statement of fact, meaning that if a person does not have any modesty, then there is nothing to prevent him or her from doing anything. This problem can manifest on two levels: on an individual level where someone is openly indecent and sinful, and on a community level where society as a whole embraces immorality. There are many Prophetic traditions related to modesty. A few of these are: "*Haya*' and *iman* are two that go together. If one is lifted, the other is also lifted." "*Haya*' will not bring anything but good." "*Iman* consists of more than sixty branches, and *haya*' is a part of *iman*."

There are many manifestations of *haya*'. One of them is to have *haya*' toward Allah (SWT). A Muslim should feel ashamed to have Allah (SWT) see him doing something or hear him saying something undesirable, and that may displease Allah (SWT). There is *haya*' toward the angels, as they are noble and dignified creatures who witness the acts performed by humans. Then there is *haya*' toward other humans, an essential characteristic that keeps people from harming one another and from performing indecent acts. There is also *haya*' toward the person himself, such that he should be ashamed of his shameful acts. Basically, the sense of *haya*' should affect a Muslim's conduct before Allah (SWT); before others, and even when one is alone.

The Islamic concept of *haya*' should be promoted through all possible means and at all levels and by everyone: educators, teachers, preachers, lecturers, and parents. While modern-day technology, when used wisely, is of utmost benefit, at the same time when it is abused, it brings nothing but harm and destruction. Evildoers leave no stone unturned to promote anything that distorts and corrupts *haya*'. Entertainment is taking new destructive directions. Chances of committing crimes become higher in a society where nudity, adultery, violence, drug addiction, lewd music, and distasteful acts are all looked as a means of entertainment. When *haya*' is distorted, *iman* gets distorted too.

It was narrated on the authority of Ibn 'Umar that he called on the Prophet (SAS) and found him crying. He asked him, "Why are you crying, O Messenger of Allah?" The Prophet said, "I was told by Jibreel that Allah feels shy to punish a slave whose hair turned white while in Islam; so shouldn't this (person) feel shy to sin after his hair turned white while in Islam?"

Unfortunately, this hadeeth applies to many of those who may not have much time left. Yet they are still heedless. They still look forward to this life and collecting as much money as they can. They still do not pray, do not give their *zakat*, do not perform hajj, or even remember Allah (SWT). Moreover, they do not try to avoid sinning. How disgraceful, arrogant, and heedless can they be? May Allah protect us and bless us with the right sense of modesty.

My dear brothers and sisters! What course of action should a person take if he or she happens to do something evil, immoral, or shameful? Let me share with you the advice given in the Qur`an in this regard. In *Surat Aal 'Imran* Allah says,

وَالَّذِينَ إِذَا فَعَلُوا فَاحِشَةً أَوْ ظَلَمُوا أَنفُسَهُمْ ذَكَرُوا اللَّهَ فَاسْتَغْفَرُوا لِذُنُوبِهِمْ وَمَن يَغْفِرُ الذُّنُوبَ إِلَّا اللَّهُ وَلَمْ يُصِرُّوا عَلَىٰ مَا فَعَلُوا وَهُمْ يَعْلَمُونَ ⬤

*And those who, when they have committed fahisha (shameless acts) or wronged themselves with evil, remember Allah and ask forgiveness for their sins; – and none can forgive sins but Allah – and do not persist in what (wrong) they have done, while they know. (Aal 'Imran, 3:135)*

This *ayah* is telling us about persons who, when they have committed a shameless act, such as they looked at something they shouldn't have looked at, they went somewhere where they shouldn't have gone, they were with someone that they shouldn't have been with, or they did something they shouldn't have done; but then, upon realizing their mistake, they turn to Allah (SWT) in repentance. So, if we want to save ourselves from becoming shameless, and if we do fall into any act of shamelessness, then the remedy for protecting ourselves is to immediately remember Allah (SWT), and to immediately ask Allah (SWT) to forgive our sins. Who else is going to forgive our sins other than Allah (SWT)?

Brothers and sisters! When we do something shameless, we feel really bad about ourselves. When we feel bad about ourselves, *Shaytan* comes and says, "How are you going to talk to Allah now? What face are you going to show Him? First, you do this, and now you think you're going to pray to Allah?" And so we say, "Yes, I shouldn't talk to Allah." And we become distanced from Allah (SWT). And *Shaytan* succeeds. When we do something evil, especially an act of shamelessness, something that's humiliating, we should immediately ask Allah (SWT) to forgive us. But we should not persist in doing that act again. To have the attitude of persisting in a shameless act means that we are not sorry before Allah (SWT). So, this is a Qur`anic advice for getting out of the cycle of shamelessness.

There is *haya`* in the way we dress, in what we watch, in what we listen to, and in what we say. There is *haya`* in the way we conduct ourselves, in how we treat others, in the friends we choose, in the places we go, and in what we do.

May Allah (SWT) make us people adorned with the garment of *haya`* and God-consciousness (*taqwa*). May Allah (SWT) allow us to have the gift of good company and keep us away from brazen and shameless activities. May Allah (SWT) protect us from all kinds of shamelessness, and may He protect our *iman* and make us live and die on Islam. *Allahumma ameen.*

# • 60 •

# MORALS AND MANNERS IN ISLAM

My *khutbah* today is on the teachings of morals and manners in Islam. Out of all the problems that surround man, be they moral, social, economic, political, or any other, the greatest of them is the moral problem. All other problems are only aspects of this major problem. Be it on the individual or collective level, every crime—murder, theft, adultery, fornication, injustice, oppression, dishonesty, abuse of resources, unjustified greed, arrogance, hypocrisy, bigotry, racism, hatred, or any other evil—is rooted in the moral or ethical problems of man.

Islam gives this problem the importance it deserves. Islam is built on the basis of values which are not only for the group which adheres to them, but for the whole of humankind. It provides guidance in all spheres of life and covers the moral, ethical, social, economic, and political aspects of human life. Islam provides a perfectly balanced approach to address the core issues of society. During the twenty-three years that the Prophet Muhammad (SAS) spread his message, he offered the world truth, clarity, and a sense of purpose. It was a message that was exemplified by the character of Prophet (SAS).

The early generation of Muslims had understood and internalized Islam. That's why their lives reflected Islam in action. As for Muslims today, a vast majority of them have neither understood nor internalized Islam in letter and spirit; hence the deep crisis in which they find themselves despite being about one-fourth of the total world population.

The true application of an Islamic system is not visible anywhere, not even in the Muslim majority countries. There is little wonder, therefore, that when non-Muslims are invited to see the simplicity, universality, and practicality of Islam, eyebrows are raised. Where in contemporary times, do we have a successful Islamic system that can be presented to the world as a successful system based on the Islamic model?

Islamic teachings lay great emphasis on moral conduct and how we should deal with people in our daily lives. The question for Muslims today is whether they are living that message. In the Arabic language, the word *khalq* means creation, and the word *khuluq* means character, manners, or morals. While *khalq* mainly refers to the physical appearance, *khuluq* refers to the deep inner self of a person. The Qur'an and the Prophetic traditions have commended those who possess a good character. Praising his Messenger (SAS) Allah (SWT) says,

وَإِنَّكَ لَعَلَى خُلُقٍ عَظِيمٍ ⬤

*And you are surely on an exalted standard of character. (al-Qalam, 68:4)*

Because the Prophet (SAS) was guided by revelation in his personal life, his character and social interactions became prime examples of moral conduct for Muslims until the Last Day. Exhorting believers to follow the Prophet's example, Allah (SWT) says in *Surat al-Ahzab,*

لَقَدْ كَانَ لَكُمْ فِي رَسُولِ اللَّهِ أُسْوَةٌ حَسَنَةٌ لِمَنْ كَانَ يَرْجُو اللَّهَ وَالْيَوْمَ الآخِرَ وَذَكَرَ اللَّهَ كَثِيرًا ⬤

*The Messenger of Allah is an excellent model for those of you who put your hope in Allah and the Last Day and remember Allah very often. (al-Ahzab, 33:21)*

The daily life of the Prophet (SAS), as recorded in hadeeth, represents an ideal code of good conduct. In fact, when the Prophet's wife 'A`isha (RAA) was asked about his conduct, she replied, "His character was the Qur`an." The Prophet (SAS) followed the Qur`an very meticulously and lived the Qur`an at every moment, in every detail of his life. His life was the reflection of Allah's words. He became the embodiment of the Qur`an.

The Prophet (SAS) himself urged his followers to possess and practice good manners and abstain from the bad ones. The Prophet promoted making peace among the people, assisting one to ride an animal or to load his luggage on, speaking mild words, advising people to offer compulsory and optional prayers, maintaining family ties, spreading greeting of peace among the people, feeding the hungry, treating the poor and orphans with compassion, and taking care of the affairs of the Muslims and those under their protection. He had also promoted being moderate in eating and drinking, dressing, spending in Allah's cause, showing kindness to one's spouse, being good to neighbors, guarding secrets, having politeness in speech, and honoring the guests. These are only some of the many forms of good manners that the Prophet (SAS) encouraged people to cultivate. In a hadeeth, Prophet Muhammad (SAS) said, "Verily, I was sent for no other reason, except to perfect the noble traits of character."

One of the Prophet's (SAS) goals, or his primary mission, was to demonstrate a lifestyle that directed one to perfect one's character. He provided warnings, encouragement, and practical advice for the improvement of manners, behavior, and character. He had much to offer in the way of guidance in this respect. His general advice to those who inquired was, "Say, 'I believe in Allah,' and then be upright." This concise answer shows that faith alone, or the claim of faith, is insufficient and that words must be proven by actions. A Muslim is required to be upright in all his dealings, and especially toward his Creator through careful obedience and sincere worship. Then, he must be honest, ethical, and considerate with respect to all people, creatures, and creations.

The virtues of good manners are seen in various sayings of Prophet Muhammad (SAS) such as, "The most beloved of Allah's servants to Allah are those with the best manners." "Nothing is weightier on the Scale of Deeds than one's good manners." 'Abdullah ibn 'Amr said, "The Prophet of Allah was never obscene or coarse. Rather, he used to tell us that the best among us were those with the best manners." Jabir ibn 'Abdullah reported, "The Messenger of Allah said, 'Verily, the most beloved and nearest to my gathering on the Day of Resurrection are those of you with the best character. Verily, the most reprehensible of you to me and the furthest from my gathering on the Day of Resurrection will be the pompous, the extravagant, and the pretentious.' They said, 'O Messenger of Allah, we know the pompous and the extravagant, but who are the pretentious?' The Prophet said, 'The arrogant.'"

One positive aspect of a believer's character is satisfaction with whatever Allah (SWT) has provided and decreed; an appreciation of his Lord's blessings and not being overly concerned with worldly pleasures and comforts. He can then turn more of his attention to things that will benefit him in the eternal life to come. The Prophet (SAS) stated, "Wealth is not in an abundance of goods, but it is in contentment of the soul." "Eat, drink, give charity, and dress without extravagance or pride." "Look to him (whose condition is) below you and do not look to him above you, for that is more likely that you will not underestimate Allah's favor upon you." "Whoever would like to be saved from the fire and enter paradise should meet death believing in Allah and the Last Day, and should do to people as he would like done to him. None of you truly believes until he likes for his brother what he likes for himself." "Do not consider anything good as insignificant, even meeting your brother with a pleasant face." "Allah is generous and loves generosity, and He loves high morality and hates base morality."

The Prophet (SAS) directed people to recognize within themselves the signs of righteousness and wrongdoing, saying, "Righteousness is good morals, and wrongdoing is that which causes discomfort (or pinches) within your soul and which you dislike that people should come to know of it." This goes to show that the human being is created with an internal mechanism to sense which acts are sinful, and that the soul is uneasy when it performs sinful acts. The Prophet (SAS) taught through his own example, but his instructions and advice provide additional emphasis. He said, "Whoever of you sees a wrong, let him change it by his hand; and if he is not able, then with his tongue; and if he is not able, then with his heart, and that is the weakest of faith."

When speaking in public or addressing a group of people, the Prophet (SAS) reminded not to whisper, while leaving out another person. 'Abdullah ibn Mas'ud (RAA) reported that the Prophet (SAS) said, "If they are three, two of them should not carry on a conversation from which the third is excluded, for surely that will be distressing to him." Causing suspicion when speaking to others is also frowned upon in Islam, especially in today's age where technology causes the world to lose its borders can sometimes lead to spying on each other or competing and despising one another without realizing it. The Prophet (SAS) said, "Be careful of suspicion, for it is the most mistaken of all speech. Do not spy on others, compete among yourselves, envy one another, or despise one another. Rather, be servants of Allah and brothers!"

There are among Muslims those who lie, backbite, criticize, use vulgar language, falsely accuse others, flatter, exaggerate, brag, mimic, and make fun of people. This kind of irresponsible speech sometimes has far-reaching consequences in the lives of people and can cause great harm and pain. Just as we will be held accountable for all our actions, big or small, so too, we will be held accountable for each and every word that comes out of our mouths. There is a stern warning in the Qur`an regarding this:

مَا يَلْفِظُ مِنْ قَوْلٍ إِلاَّ لَدَيْهِ رَقِيبٌ عَتِيدٌ ۝

*Not a single word is uttered by anyone except that there is an observer near him, ready to record. (Qaf, 50:18)*

Indeed this is a frightening prospect. During the course of the day, we say so many things without realizing how harmful they are. We pass remarks about people's looks and about people's negative traits. So-and-so is ugly, fat, stupid, lazy, worthless, and so on. We use abusive language. Worse still are the biting remarks some of us make without knowledge about Islam, about the Qur`an, about the prophets, and sometimes even about Allah (SWT), never stopping to think that it's all being recorded and will be presented to us on the Day of Resurrection. Sometimes, mindless chatter leads to gossip, which could lead to intentional or unintentional defamation, backbiting, or other irresponsible speech. There are many Prophetic traditions on the issue of guarding and controlling one's tongue. The Prophet (SAS) said, "Whosoever gives me a guarantee to safeguard what is between his jaws (meaning the tongue), and what is between his legs (meaning the private parts), I shall guarantee him paradise." We have to remember that on the Day of Judgment, our physical organs will stand as witnesses against us if we use them in the wrong way. As Allah (SWT) says in *Surat an-Nur*,

يَوْمَ تَشْهَدُ عَلَيْهِمْ أَلْسِنَتُهُمْ وَأَيْدِيهِمْ وَأَرْجُلُهُم بِمَا كَانُوا يَعْمَلُونَ ۝

*On the Day when their own tongues, hands and feet shall bear witness against them about what they did. (an-Nur, 24:24)*

According to a hadeeth, the Prophet (SAS) said, "Whoever believes in Allah and the last day, let him either speak good or keep silent." He also said, "The Muslim is the one from whose tongue and hand the Muslims are safe, and the *muhajir* (emigrant) is the one who abandons what Allah has forbidden." On one occasion, he also said, "Most of the sins of the children of Adam are on their tongues."

In a twist on good manners, the Prophet (SAS) did encourage gifts for one another. Giving gifts is yet another way to foster relations based on kindness for each other. He (SAS) advised, "Give gifts to one another and you will love one another."

Allah (SWT) has shown us in the character of Prophet Muhammad (SAS) the model of a companionate person. According to a hadeeth the Prophet (SAS) said, "He who does not show mercy to the young and show esteem for our elders is not one of us." The Prophet (SAS) treated everyone, friends and foe, man and woman, young and old, with kindness and respect. Even when some of the pagan Arabs reacted to his message with extreme hatred, he showed love and kindness. Showing mercy and forgiving others can only be the attributes of the strong. Referring to the Prophet's universal, all-embracing mercy, Allah (SWT) says in *Surat al-Anbiya`*,

وَمَا أَرْسَلْنَاكَ إِلَّا رَحْمَةً لِّلْعَالَمِينَ ۝

*And We have not sent you except as a mercy to the worlds. (al-Anbiya`, 21:107)*

As Muslims, we should follow Prophet Muhammad (SAS) in order to become among the best of Muslims with the best possible manners as a stepping stone to grow closer to Allah (SWT) and to have a permanent resting abode in paradise.

• 61 •

# MOTHERHOOD FROM THE ISLAMIC PERSPECTIVE

*In sha` Allah* in today's *khutbah*, I'll be sharing some thoughts on the concept of motherhood from the Islamic perspective. Here in the United States, a special day called Mother's Day is celebrated annually on the second Sunday of May. It is a day to appreciate and honor mothers by giving them gifts, cards, flowers, or other treats. The tradition of Mother's Day in the United States was established around the late 19th or early 20th century.

Whether Muslims should celebrate Mother's Day or not is a controversial issue among contemporary Muslim scholars. A group of them considers it as impermissible since it's a kind of blind imitation of the Western non-Islamic habits, which have no benefit for Muslims. While another group sees it as permissible on the condition that showing gratitude and dutifulness to parents is not confined to a specific time. It is an obligation that should be observed every time.

Since there is generally a negative stereotype of how Islam views women, many people may not know that parents in general and mothers in particular, are held in very high esteem in Islam. There is an observable pattern found in the Qur`an that the command to fulfill the rights of Allah (SWT) is usually followed by the command to fulfill the rights of one's parents.

وَإِذْ أَخَذْنَا مِيثَاقَ بَنِي إِسْرَائِيلَ لَا تَعْبُدُونَ إِلَّا اللَّهَ وَبِالْوَالِدَيْنِ إِحْسَانًا ◯

*Remember when We made a covenant with the Children of Israel, Worship none but Allah and be good to your parents. (al-Baqara, 2:83)*

وَاعْبُدُوا اللَّهَ وَلَا تُشْرِكُوا بِهِ شَيْئًا وَبِالْوَالِدَيْنِ إِحْسَانًا ◯

*Worship Allah and do not associate anything with Him. Be good to your parents. (an-Nisa`, 4:36)*

قُلْ تَعَالَوْا أَتْلُ مَا حَرَّمَ رَبُّكُمْ عَلَيْكُمْ أَلَّا تُشْرِكُوا بِهِ شَيْئًا وَبِالْوَالِدَيْنِ إِحْسَانًا ◯

*Say, Come! I will tell you what your Lord has really forbidden you. Do not ascribe anything as a partner to Him; be good to your parents. (al-An'am, 6:151)*

Allah (SWT) enjoins man regarding his parents. Our parents have rights over us, for the simple reason that they are the root of our existence. They brought us up, reared us, fed us, and invested in us. Among the rights due to people (*huqooq al-'ibad*), parents deserve the highest level of respect, regard, obedience, and gratefulness from their children. Children are responsible for the support and maintenance of their parents. The rights of parents do not end with their death but remain in force even after they are deceased. This is made clear through a hadeeth in which the Prophet (SAS) tells us that some of the rights of parents continue even after their death. They are: to pray for them, to supplicate for their forgiveness, to fulfill their promises after their death, to maintain the ties of kinship which cannot be maintained except through them, and to honor their friends.

On one occasion, the Prophet (SAS) said, "Let him be humbled, let him be humbled." It was said, "Allah's Messenger, who is he?" He said. "He who finds his parents in old age, either one or both of them, and does not enter paradise." While good treatment of parents is regarded as one of the most virtuous acts, mistreating them is one of the major sins in Islam. Making our mothers and fathers angry with us is making Allah (SWT) angry at us. We learn through a hadeeth that the Prophet (SAS) said, "The major sins are: associating others with Allah (*shirk*), disobeying one's parents, killing a soul (murder), and speaking falsely." Allah (SWT) teaches us to make *du'a`* for our parents.

رَّبِّ ارْحَمْهُمَا كَمَا رَبَّيَانِي صَغِيرًا ⃝

*My Lord, have mercy upon them as they have raised me when I was small. (al-Isra`, 17:24)*

There is another Qur`anic *du'a`* that teaches us to say:

رَبَّنَا اغْفِرْ لِي وَلِوَالِدَيَّ وَلِلْمُؤْمِنِينَ يَوْمَ يَقُومُ الْحِسَابُ ⃝

*Our Lord, forgive me, my parents, and the believers on the Day of Reckoning. (Ibraheem, 14:41)*

وَوَصَّيْنَا الْإِنسَانَ بِوَالِدَيْهِ إِحْسَانًا حَمَلَتْهُ أُمُّهُ كُرْهًا وَوَضَعَتْهُ كُرْهًا وَحَمْلُهُ وَفِصَالُهُ ثَلَاثُونَ شَهْرًا ⃝

*We have instructed man to be kind to his parents. His mother carried him with difficulty and gave birth to him with difficulty. His bearing and weaning period is thirty months. (al-Ahqaf, 46:15)*

While both parents deserve our best treatment, our mothers enjoy a still higher status, as is evident from Prophetic traditions. We can appreciate this when we realize the difficulties of pregnancy, labor, breastfeeding, and other sacrifices the mother has to make while bearing and rearing her children. As pregnancy proceeds, the mother begins to experience weakness because the embryo feeds on her blood. Her energy gets sapped and sucked out from within by the embryo, which is developing in her womb. After her child's birth, she nurtures it.

It is reported that a man came to the Prophet (SAS) and said, "O Messenger of God! Who among the people is the most worthy of my good companionship?" The Prophet said, "Your mother." The man said, "Then who?" The Prophet said, "Then your mother." The man further asked, "Then who?" The Prophet said, "Then your mother." The man asked again, "Then who?" The Prophet said, "Then your father." A man once consulted the Prophet (SAS) about taking part in a military campaign. The Prophet (SAS) asked the man if his mother was still living. When told that she was alive, the Prophet (SAS) said, "Then stay with her, for paradise is at her feet." On another occasion, the Prophet (SAS) said, "Allah has forbidden for you to be undutiful to your mothers."

In the first hadeeth, the Prophet highlights the importance of the mother over the father by repeating "your mother" three times and then saying "your father" once in response to the man's question. The second hadeeth illustrates the significance of the mother by placing caring for her over going to war to defend Islam. In other words, caring for his mother is also a way for a man to serve Allah (SWT). By saying that entrance into paradise is linked to caring for and respecting a mother, the Prophet (SAS) accords them a great honor. In the last hadeeth, the Prophet (SAS) asserts that disobedience toward mothers is a sin. Thus we see that the verses of the Qur`an and the Prophetic traditions demonstrate the status and importance of mothers in Islam.

They also show that the mother is given higher honor than even the father for the responsibilities she has toward her child.

Out of the many beautiful names and attributes of Allah (SWT) that we are familiar with, He wants us to remember Him by two attributes every time we take a step in our life. They are contained in "*bismillah ar-Rahman ar-Raheem*," meaning, "In the name of Allah, Most Gracious (*ar-Rahman*), Most Merciful(*ar-Raheem*)". These attributes, therefore, are central to proper perception about Allah (SWT). How do we develop an appreciation of the mercy or *rahma* of Allah (SWT)? The closest we can think about how Allah (SWT) feels toward us is, once again, the mother. The Arabic word for the womb is "*rahm*". Allah (SWT) has brought us to this world through the same reproductive system, which in Arabic is named *rahm* derived from the same root word as the two supreme attributes of Allah: *ar-Rahman* and *ar-Raheem*. In this life, no one shows more unconditional love and affection than a mother. Nobody else! All other relationships are perhaps somewhat mixed and conditional.

Brothers and sisters, a mother's love is an expression of Allah's mercy. A mother's love is unmatched. Whether young or old, healthy or handicapped, troublesome or obedient; the child is still beloved to the mother. This love may be displayed in various forms. Sometimes children misinterpret her scolding them to be a sign of lack of love. It is crucial to assure the child that he is always loved, even when his behavior warrants disciplinary measures. Such a child becomes confident and happy and will never seek solace elsewhere. The love of the mother becomes a source of happiness and peace at home. Children feel attached to the home because of the mother.

When children are born, they are wired to want their mother, be fed by her, and be nurtured by her simply because that's part of a woman's instinct. Allah (SWT) has made her that way and prepared her for this job. For a woman to feel a strong attachment toward her baby is in her genes. This is the understanding we get from Prophet Muhammad (SAS). 'Umar ibn Al-Khattab reported, "Some prisoners of war were brought in front of the Prophet, and a woman among them was breastfeeding. Whenever she found a child among the prisoners, she would take it to her chest and nurse it. The Prophet said to us, "Do you think this woman could throw her child in the fire?" We said, "No, not if she is able to stop it." The Prophet said, "Allah is more merciful to His servants than a mother is to her child."

We can't put any numerical figure on Allah's mercy. Yet, to make us understand, there is a hadeeth in which the Prophet (SAS) says, "Allah has one hundred mercies, out of which He has sent down only one for jinn, mankind, animals, and insects, through which they love one another and have compassion for one another, and through which wild animals care for their young. Allah has retained ninety-nine mercies to deal kindly with His slaves on the Day of Resurrection."

Brothers and sisters! There are differences in the genes of men and women. Allah

(SWT) made women biologically and psychologically very much suited to concentrate on the home and family and all that is required to operate and develop this institution and its associated areas. According to a hadeeth, "A woman is the shepherd of her husband's house and is responsible for her flock." This is a tremendous responsibility. And no one else can either take it away from her or adequately attend to it. The function of child-bearing remains incomplete without its more crucial part of child-rearing and upbringing, their education, orientation, character-building, and general initiation into religion and culture. It is because of this aspect that family care becomes a full-time job. No other institution or even several institutions can take care of this function. Men have different natural abilities and predispositions. They are traditionally hunters, doers and bread-winners, while women are usually homemakers.

Addressing women, the Prophet (SAS) said, "Take care of your home for that is your jihad." Declaring home-making as jihad for women is giving it the highest possible status in an Islamic society. The home will always remain a woman's most valuable work. It requires sacrifice; but this sacrifice, in reality, is an investment that reaps rich dividends. Islam confers different roles of man and woman. As such, women and men do not compete with each other, rather they complement each other.

Islam lays great emphasis on women's education. In a well-known hadeeth the Prophet (SAS) says, "Seeking knowledge is an obligation upon every Muslim." Muslim here is inclusive of both males and females. More or less, half the world's population consists of women. An educated mother is a blessing for her children. A newborn baby is totally unaware of the outside world. The mother plays a crucial role in introducing the child to the world. The outlook that the child will form toward life will always have a lasting impression on its mind. This depends a lot on the mother. Her habits, behavior, lifestyle, and whatever a child observes from her will have an impact. As is well known, "mother's lap is the first school." Sometimes it becomes difficult for the mothers. However, it is not perfection that Islam demands from Muslim mothers, but a willingness to accept the responsibility of teaching in their children Islamic values, morals, manners, and behavior.

On Mother's Day, you may make your mother feel overwhelmed with love by sending her Mother's Day quotes to express your love, appreciation, and understanding of all that she did for you over the years. But in Islam, every day is Mother's Day.

# • 62 •

# *MUHARRAM*

We bid farewell to another year of the hijra. After the passing of the blessed month of *Dhu al-Hijja*, we are now in the sacred month of *Muharram* of the new Hijri year—1441.

Do we realize that the year contains many days and nights, which are what makes up our lifespan? When a day passes, then a part of us has passed. We are but a body and spirit existing in a limited period. When that period comes to an end, our worldly life comes to an end. We move on to the realm of the life to come. There, we will be judged on how we spent our time in this world. We will be judged on our intentions and actions and rewarded or punished accordingly. It is only those of sound heart and intellect who realize the true value of these days and nights that pass.

We hope that, *in sha` Allah*, all of us tried to round off the last year with acts based on good intentions, as according to a well-known hadeeth, the Prophet (SAS) said, "Actions are but by intentions and every man shall have only that which he intended."

We welcome this new Hijri year and pray that Allah (SWT), in His infinite grace and mercy, blesses us and keeps us busy with deeds that will draw us close to Him, in this new year, and beyond. I want to share some thoughts with you in today's *khutbah* on the historical aspect, the significance, and the virtues of this blessed month.

The Islamic calendar was first introduced during the era of 'Umar ibn al-Khattab (RAA). He asked the people as to which year they think should mark the beginning of the Islamic calendar. Some held that it should start from the birth of the Prophet (SAS). Others suggested that it should begin from the year he passed away. Still, others said that it should commence from the very first day the Prophet (SAS) began his mission. A fourth group believed that the calendar should start with the Hijra. 'Umar (RAA) chose the last suggestion, perhaps because the Hijra marked the point in history when Allah (SWT) differentiated between truth and falsehood. The Hijra was not only a historical event, but one that changed the course of history.

The month of *Muharram* derives its sacredness from the two primary sources of Islamic guidance, the Qur`an and the Sunnah. Allah (SWT) says,

إِنَّ عِدَّةَ الشُّهُورِ عِنْدَ اللَّهِ اثْنَا عَشَرَ شَهْرًا فِي كِتَابِ اللَّهِ يَوْمَ خَلَقَ السَّمَاوَاتِ وَالْأَرْضَ مِنْهَا أَرْبَعَةٌ حُرُمٌ ۝

*Indeed, the number of months with Allah is twelve months in Allah's Book, the day when He created the heavens and the earth. Of these, four are sacred. (at-Tawba, 9:26)*

In a hadeeth, Prophet Muhammad (SAS) identified these four sacred months to be *Dhu al-Qa'da, Dhu al-Hijja, Muharram*, and *Rajab*. In fact, these four months were regarded as sacred by the Arabs, even before the arrival of Islam. All fighting was deemed wrong, and warfare was considered improper and irreligious during these months.

The month of *Muharram* features important events in the lives of earlier Prophets and Messengers of Allah (AS). The most significant of these is the one related by Ibn 'Abbas (RAA). He reports that when the Prophet (SAS) first arrived in Medina, he found the Jews fasting on the day of *'Ashura`* (the 10th of *Muharram*). They used to say, "This is a great day on which Allah saved Musa (AS) and the *Bani Israel* from the tyranny and persecution of Fir'awn. Musa (AS) used to fast on this day, as a sign of gratitude to Allah." The Prophet (SAS) replied, "We have more right to Musa than you." So he observed the fast on that day and commanded the Muslims to do so. This was one of the first forms of fasting that the early Muslims engaged in before the fasting of Ramadan.

Based on evidences, scholars of Islam have recommended three equally valid formats of fasting that can be observed during *Muharram*: (1) fasting for the three consecutive days of the 9th, 10th and 11th of *Muharram*, (2) fasting two days; either the 9th and 10th, or 10th and 11th of *Muharram*, or (3) fasting only on the 10th of *Muharram*. Fasting on the day of *'Ashura`* was a gradual step in the process of introducing the obligatory fasting during the month of Ramadan. It is reported from Ibn Mas'ud (RAA) that when the fasting in the month of Ramadan was made compulsory, it was no longer obligatory to fast on *'Ashura`*, but it is still *mustahabb* or desirable. And is one of the ways through which Muslims uphold the sacredness of the month of *Muharram*. In a hadeeth, the Prophet (SAS) said, "For fasting the day of *'Ashura`*, I hope that Allah (SWT) will accept it as expiation for the year that went before." According to Imam an-Nawawi (RA) this expiation is for all minor sins.

*Muharram* is the beginning of a new Hijri year. So, it is a good time for all of us to take stock of our lives and to make new year resolutions that will lead to self-improvements in our lives. These resolutions should be balanced and should include spiritual, as well as physical, intellectual, and social goals. For example, it is commendable to make resolutions of increasing our voluntary acts of worship such as prayers and fasting. However, we should not limit ourselves to these noble and worthy goals only. But also make some modest resolutions concerning our physical health and well-being, improving our interpersonal relations with members of our family and friends, and advancing our knowledge.

May Allah (SWT) grant us peace, security, health, and happiness. May this be the year of mutual love, respect, understanding, reconciliation, and compassion.

Brothers and sisters! The tenth of *Muharram* also marks a significant day in the Muslim calendar for a tragic event that took place in the 61st year of the Hijra, the martyrdom of Imam Husayn (RAA), the beloved grandson of the Prophet at Karbala in Iraq. Imam Husayn challenged the authority of Yazeed, the Umayyad ruler, and established the principle that sometimes the goals of life become more important than life itself. Imam Husayn stood for the Qur`anic principle of justice and fairness. He spoke for those who were marginalized by a class of rulers—those who were laying the foundation of dynastic rules in Islam. Imam Husayn refused to surrender to the forces of oppression, knowing well that he could perish in the process.

*Muharram* is a month of serious reflections for the Muslim world. Unfortunately, in many parts of the world, this month has become a point of conflict between the Shi'as and the Sunnis. Thus, Imam Husayn and his legacy were seen as a sectarian event. We should remember that Imam Husayn was the grandson of the Prophet (SAS), who lived his life the way he watched his grandfather live it. He embodied the qualities of the Prophet (SAS) in his character, and he remained deeply committed to the Qur`anic values of justice and equality. His struggle was for fairness and Islamic values for common men and women.

When the power was usurped by the Umayyad rulers and the people's right to elect their Caliph was turned into a dynastic rule with little regard for human life, human dignity, freedom, and justice. Imam Husayn mobilized first his family then his supporters to challenge the brutal might of a well-organized, well-equipped, and well-trained army. The outcome was known from the beginning. Imam Husayn was aware of the imbalance in power. He had the choice to make a tactical withdrawal. He had the option of accepting the rule of the Umayyads and give legitimacy to their claim. Yet he chose to stand his ground knowing well that he and his followers may not survive at the end of the conflict. He did not run away. He knew why he was there and why he had challenged the authority. He fought bravely and left the world with violent wounds as a testimony of his belief that sometimes, in the life of nations, come moments when liberty and justice become more important than life itself.

Imam Husayn's martyrdom at Karbala provides evidence of the moral victory of right over wrong, of virtue over vice, of principle over compromise, and of the oppressed over the oppressor. It represents the ultimate victory of blood over sword. It was a sacrifice given in support of human rights and human dignity. It is this sacrifice that has inspired millions throughout history to challenge injustice and inhumanity on the part of political powers. Imam Husayn is a living legacy of Muslims. This legacy should not be split into Sunni or Shi'a conflict.

Shi'as and Sunnis both need to work together to uphold the legacy and sacrifice that the grandson of Prophet Muhammad (SAS), Imam Husayn (RAA), gave. Shi'as need to look at this observance beyond the passion plays, and Sunnis should recognize this historical tragedy beyond a sectarian and political divide. All Muslims need to remember Imam Husayn for his commitment to justice as taught by the Qur`an.

وَأْمُرْ بِالْمَعْرُوفِ وَانْهَ عَنِ الْمُنْكَرِ وَاصْبِرْ عَلَى مَا أَصَابَكَ إِنَّ ذَلِكَ مِنْ عَزْمِ الْأُمُورِ ۝

*Command what is right and forbid what is wrong and be steadfast in the face of all that happens to you. Surely, this is something which requires firm resolve. (Luqman, 31:17)*

We ask Allah (SWT) to make us live on Islam and to make us die on *iman*. May He help us to do that what pleases Him. We ask Him to help us to remember Him and to be thankful to Him, to obey Him and to worship Him. May He accept our good deeds and forgive us for our misdeeds. May He make us of those who are mindful of Him. *Ameen.*

## • 63 •

# ON BEING POSITIVE

We all know that in any situation, and as a matter of principle, being positive is always better than being negative. But isn't it true that many a time we become very negative in our attitudes and behavior? If we want happiness in our lives, our homes, and our community, we have to learn to be positive. In today's *khutbah*, I'll share a few thoughts on being positive.

With all the news of war, violence, crimes, injustices, bigotry, along with financial crisis, job loss, death in the family, sickness—and the list goes on—it can be easy to take out all the stress and negativity on the people around us. But this way, life would get more miserable, and we will not be happy. It is our choice of how we observe and handle every situation. Do we want to see the glass half empty or half full?

Negativity and pessimism engulf many of us today. It's almost like the air we breathe. Reconnecting with our noble *deen* can help us to instill hope and positivity in us in many ways. Any adversity has to be taken as an opportunity to get closer to Allah (SWT). He is the only one who can turn things around for the better.

أَلَا بِذِكْرِ اللَّهِ تَطْمَئِنُّ الْقُلُوبُ ۝

*Only in the remembrance of Allah can the heart find peace. (ar-Ra'd, 13:28)*

Positivity is what our religion teaches. Positivity is what our *deen* emphasizes. On the Day of Judgment, Allah (SWT) will find a speck of good in a person and then use it as an excuse to forgive that person. This is Allah (SWT) picking the positive. We want Allah (SWT) to pardon our sins and bless our good deeds—our positives, however minimal or limited they may be. It is only through Allah's mercy and His overlooking our negatives that we can be admitted into the abode of eternal bliss. Remember the well-known hadeeth about the woman who took water from a well to quench the thirst of a dog. She was an unchaste woman, but just based on this one good deed, Allah (SWT) forgave her and rewarded her.

There is a story of a student who was seeking religious knowledge from a scholar. One day the student came to the scholar and said, "I find many deficiencies in myself. I don't study much. I don't always pray in time, I hardly read the Qur'an, I hardly pray the Sunnah prayers..." and he kept on talking about a number of his shortcomings. The scholar patiently listened and made sure that the student had said everything he wanted to say. He then replied, "When the general of an army gets sick, the whole army gets very concerned, but when a soldier gets sick it's not such a big deal." This means that by becoming a student of religion, you are training yourself to be a general. Since you will be a leader in the community, Allah (SWT) will soon cure you and make you strong in *deen*, because other people will be dependent on you to seek knowledge. The scholar basically just took the one positive thing of his student, amidst all his negatives and focused on that single positive—that he was a student seeking religious knowledge.

Overlooking the negative and picking the positive is very significant. What is the secret to a happy married life? It is to accept the deficiency of a human being and to find something positive within him or her. If we overlook mistakes, find the positive, and learn to magnify them, then the negatives will most likely be dispelled. The same applies to every relationship; a little bit of positive attitude and behavior goes a very long way to put matters right. Even in the painful situation of a divorce, amidst the negativity of a strained relationship, Allah (SWT) provides words of comfort to the parties involved and brings out the positive. Allah (SWT) says in *Surat at-Talaq*,

$$\ldots\text{وَمَن يَتَّقِ اللَّهَ يَجْعَل لَّهُ مَخْرَجًا} \bigcirc \text{وَيَرْزُقْهُ مِنْ حَيْثُ لَا يَحْتَسِبُ وَمَن يَتَوَكَّلْ عَلَى اللَّهِ فَهُوَ حَسْبُهُ إِنَّ اللَّهَ}$$
$$\text{بَالِغُ أَمْرِهِ قَدْ جَعَلَ اللَّهُ لِكُلِّ شَيْءٍ قَدْرًا} \bigcirc$$

*Whoever has the taqwa of Allah, He will make a way out for him. And will provide for him from where he does not expect. And whoever relies upon Allah—then He is sufficient for him. (at-Talaq, 65:2-3)*

The Prophet (SAS) was a master of positivity. In all his actions, the Prophet (SAS) would radiate a positivity that transformed those around him. His ever-beaming smile would display optimism. He had a manner of treating people so well that all around him felt as if they were the most special persons, and most liked by the Prophet (SAS). His words, whether of warning or good news, inspired positive action. He advised us to be hopeful and to be optimistic and not to lose hope and become a pessimist. His sayings focus on positive attitude, behavior, and action; and help us to be productive in all circumstances. He used to say, "Give glad tidings, and do not scare people away. Make things easy, and do not make things difficult."

He advised that at time of death, hope should prevail over fear. Once, he went to a young man who was on his death bed and asked him, "How do you feel?" The young man said, "I have much hope from Allah, but I also fear for my sins." The Prophet (SAS) said, "The believer who has these two thoughts simultaneously at such time, Allah fulfills his hopes and grants him security from fear."

Focusing on the positive aspect of all affairs of a believer, the Prophet (SAS) said, "How wonderful is the affair of the believer for there is good for him in every matter and this is not the case with anyone except the believer. If he is happy, then he thanks Allah (SWT) and thus there is good for him. If he is harmed, then he shows patience and thus there is good for him." Just three days before his death, the Prophet (SAS) said, "None of you should die but hoping only good from Allah, the Exalted and Glorious."

Even in times of struggle, we have to keep expressing gratitude for the positive things happening in our lives and around us. We have to remind ourselves of all the blessings we have and talk about them with our loved ones and with those who are close to us. This will calm us down. Expressing gratitude isn't about ignoring our current problems. Instead it is about accepting life's trials and becoming more humble, knowing that it is, Allah (SWT) who brings both hardship and ease, but patience has been advised in times of difficulties. Such times are seen as testing times from Allah (SWT) and can be the means to being rewarded. Allah (SWT) says in the Qur`an,

$$وَلَنَبْلُوَنَّكُم بِشَيْءٍ مِّنَ الْخَوْفِ وَالْجُوعِ وَنَقْصٍ مِّنَ الْأَمْوَالِ وَالْأَنفُسِ وَالثَّمَرَاتِ وَبَشِّرِ الصَّابِرِينَ ۝$$

*And We will test you with some fear and hunger, and a shortage in money and lives and fruits. And give good news to those who are patient. (al-Baqara, 2:155)*

Those who show ingratitude and displeasure with Allah's decree end up in a situation where not only will they have to go through their hardship but will also suffer the consequences of being discontent with Allah's decree.

When the Prophet (SAS) received good news, he would say, *al-hamduli-llahi alladhi bi-ni'matihi tatimmu as-saalihaat* which means "all praise is for Allah by whose favor good works are accomplished." When he received disturbing news, he would say, *al-hamduli-llahi 'ala kulli haal* meaning "all praise is for Allah in all circumstances." May Allah (SWT) grant us positivity in our attitudes, actions, and behavior. *Ameen.*

Brothers and sisters! Having a positive support group and good friends and companions is very important. Surrounding ourselves with positive people will not only help in troubling times but also inspire us to have an optimistic approach to life. Nobody likes a negative person. It is good to avoid friendship with highly negative people; otherwise, we may start getting influenced by their negative approach to everything. However, we should act in good faith without being judgmental about others and without being overly suspicious about them.

يَا أَيُّهَا الَّذِينَ آمَنُوا اجْتَنِبُوا كَثِيرًا مِنَ الظَّنِّ إِنَّ بَعْضَ الظَّنِّ ⏺

*O you who believe! Avoid much suspicion. Indeed some suspicion is sin. (al-Hujurat, 49:12)*

Suspicion by itself is not forbidden. One may have a good assumption about someone. It is sinful, however, to entertain suspicion about someone without any ground, or to entertain suspicion about people whose apparent conditions show that they are good and noble. We also have to avoid all sorts of negative behavior such as mocking or ridiculing someone.

يَا أَيُّهَا الَّذِينَ آمَنُوا لَا يَسْخَرْ قَوْمٌ مِنْ قَوْمٍ عَسَى أَنْ يَكُونُوا خَيْرًا مِنْهُمْ وَلَا نِسَاءٌ مِنْ نِسَاءٍ عَسَى أَنْ يَكُنَّ خَيْرًا مِنْهُنَّ وَلَا تَلْمِزُوا أَنْفُسَكُمْ وَلَا تَنَابَزُوا بِالْأَلْقَابِ ⏺

*O you who believe! Let not a group of you mock another. Perhaps they are better than you. Let not women mock each other; perhaps one is better than the other. And do not find fault with one another or insult each other with derogatory nicknames. (al-Hujurat, 49:11)*

Helping others is one of the best ways to bring positivity into our lives. Volunteering in a local center, taking out time for community service, helping those in need, visiting the sick, and other such righteous and humanitarian deeds can bring a smile that will go a far way to wipe off the despair and negativity we face during our difficult times. There is always light at the end of the tunnel.

فَإِنَّ مَعَ الْعُسْرِ يُسْرًا ⏺

*So, surely with every hardship there is ease. (al-Inshirah, 94:5)*

One has to put one's trust in Allah.

وَعَلَى اللَّهِ فَلْيَتَوَكَّلِ الْمُؤْمِنُونَ ⏺

*Let the believers put their trust in Allah. (Aal 'Imran, 3:122)*

Regardless of how easy or difficult our situation is today; it won't last long. Through the grand depictions of paradise and hellfire, Allah (SWT) encourages us to have a futuristic vision so that our focus is on the bigger picture. We have to positively transform our lives so that after having lived for a defined and limited time in this world, we achieve salvation in the hereafter—our ultimate destination.

Let me conclude by saying that if we are positive in our attitude and behavior, people will love to be around us. Employers, co-workers, neighbors, family members, friends, and volunteers will be attracted to our optimism. People are naturally attracted to those who offer hope and practical advice. A result-driven, positive attitude is the mark of an achiever in this life and the hereafter.

•   64   •

# OUR OBLIGATIONS TO THE QUR'AN

*In sha` Allah*, in my *khutbah* today, I shall try to discuss the obligations we, as Muslims, owe to the Qur`an. What are these obligations? How do we go about fulfilling these obligations? What does the Qur`an demand from us? Indeed, it is impossible to comprehend the greatness and majesty of the Qur`an fully. There is a verse in the Qur`an, which suggests an analogy that might help us to understand the magnificence of the Qur`an. Allah (SWT) says in *Surat al-Hashr*,

لَوْ أَنْزَلْنَا هَذَا الْقُرْآنَ عَلَى جَبَلٍ لَرَأَيْتَهُ خَاشِعًا مُتَصَدِّعًا مِنْ خَشْيَةِ اللَّهِ وَتِلْكَ الْأَمْثَالُ نَضْرِبُهَا لِلنَّاسِ لَعَلَّهُمْ يَتَفَكَّرُونَ ◯

*Had We had sent this Qur`an down on a mountain, you would have seen it humbled and split apart out of fear of Allah. We offer these examples to people so that they may reflect. (al-Hashr, 59:21)*

It is sad but true that by and large, Muslims have abandoned the Qur`an. Had it not been so, the Muslim *ummah* would not be in the crisis, in which it finds itself today. To rectify our condition, we must understand our responsibilities toward the Qur`an and try our best to fulfill them. The Qur`an demands of every Muslim five obligations. A Muslim is required to (1) believe in the Qur`an, (2) read the Qur`an regularly, (3) seek to understand the Qur`an, (4) act upon its teachings, and (5) convey its message to others.

Our first obligation is to have faith in the divine origin of the Qur`an. *Iman* (faith) has two phases: (1) verbal profession (*iqrar bi l-lisan*); and (2) heart-felt conviction (*tasdeeq bi l-qalb*). To believe in the Qur`an means to verbally profess that the Qur`an is the word of Allah (SWT), as revealed by Him through the angel Jibreel (AS) to the last of His Messengers—Prophet Muhammad (SAS). But verbal attestation is not enough. We also need to develop conviction that the Qur`an is truly from Allah (SWT) and that it has been sent as the ultimate source of guidance for all of humanity. Only then our hearts and minds would come under the guiding light of the Qur`an. The conviction of the companions of the Prophet (SAS) that the Qur`an is the word of Allah (SWT) created in them a love and devotion for it. They accepted it as absolute truth.

Since our faith is weak, we do not turn to the Qur`an for guidance. We need to check ourselves to see if our belief in the Qur`an is a mere dogma that has nothing to do with practical life, or we truly believe in the Qur`an as the ultimate source of guidance for all of humanity. If the Qur`an is studied and its meanings pondered upon in a quest for truth, all the veils of darkness shall be lifted from one's heart, and the light of true faith will illuminate the soul. Faith is not something that can be planted in us from the outside. It is a conscious realization of fundamental truths that already exist deep inside our souls. To be able to do justice to the other four obligations we have to the Qur`an, we need to fulfill the first obligation first.

The second obligation is to read the Qur`an. To be able to recite the Qur`an properly, we should learn the basic rules of *tajweed*. We should also try to beautify our voice during recitation. We should begin our recitation by seeking Allah's refuge from the accursed Satan by saying, "*a'oodhu bi l-llahi min ash-shaytani ar-rajeem*". We should also recite with *tarteel*, meaning with a slow, measured rhythmic tone. Finally, we should memorize as much of the Qur`an as we can. To be able to fulfill this obligation, we need to establish a daily recitation schedule and recite as much as we can daily. Just as our bodies are in constant need of food for sustenance, our spirits are also in perpetual need of proper nourishment. Just as the food for our bodies is derived from the earth, the nourishment for our spirits is obtained from the word of Allah (SWT)—the Qur`an.

The third obligation of the Qur`an is to understand it. If we read it without understanding, how can we put it into practice? For those of us who have not yet learned Arabic, we should start by reading translations and explanation (*tafseer*) in the languages we know best. We should, however, strive to learn Arabic because translations will never do justice to the Qur`an. Once we have a basic knowledge of Arabic, we can proceed to the first stage of understanding, which is *tadhakkur*. *Tadhakkur* in the Qur`an means to understand its meaning as provided on the surface, and this is not difficult. In this sense, the Qur`an is an easy book to follow. Allah (SWT) tells us four times in *Surat al-Qamar*:

$$\text{وَلَقَدْ يَسَّرْنَا الْقُرْآنَ لِلذِّكْرِ فَهَلْ مِنْ مُدَّكِرٍ}$$

*And We made the Qur`an easy to learn. Do any of you wish to learn? (al-Qamar, 54:17)*

*Tadhakkur* has the same root as the word *dhikr*, which means remembrance. By reading the Qur`an regularly, we will constantly be reminded of the message. Deep inside, all of us know what is right and what is wrong. It is just that we are humans, and we forget easily. That is why *tadhakkur* is so important. The second stage of understanding the Qur`an is *tadabbur* or deep pondering over the Qur`an. This stage is much more challenging. *Tadabbur* in the Qur`an is to dive deep into the Qur`an to discover the hidden treasure of knowledge and wisdom from the Qur`an. In this sense, it is the most difficult book because it is unfathomable. No one can claim to have found all the treasures of the Qur`an, even after devoting his whole life to its study. We should, however, try our best to gain at least its basic understanding. After all, we are responsible for the amount of effort we put in into understanding the word of Allah (SWT). To sum up, the first three obligations of the Qur`an are to believe in it, to read it, and to understand it. May Allah (SWT) give us the *tawfeeq* to do so.

Brothers and sisters! The fourth obligation we owe to the Qur`an is to follow its teachings, not partially but fully. This is crucial. We can't pick and choose and only follow the commands that are easy or appealing to our *nafs*. Allah (SWT) warns the people who do this:

أَفَتُؤْمِنُونَ بِبَعْضِ الْكِتَابِ وَتَكْفُرُونَ بِبَعْضٍ فَمَا جَزَاءُ مَنْ يَفْعَلُ ذَلِكَ مِنْكُمْ إِلَّا خِزْيٌ فِي الْحَيَاةِ الدُّنْيَا وَيَوْمَ الْقِيَامَةِ يُرَدُّونَ إِلَى أَشَدِّ الْعَذَابِ وَمَا اللَّهُ بِغَافِلٍ عَمَّا تَعْمَلُونَ ◯

*Do you believe in one part of the Book and reject the other? What repayment will there be for any of you who do that except disgrace in this world and a severe punishment on the Day of Resurrection. Allah is never unaware of what you do. (al-Baqara, 2:85)*

We need to be determined to follow everything in the Qur`an and modify our character accordingly. Otherwise, if we read from the Qur`an but do not follow it, then we will be inflicting harm upon ourselves. For example, if we read the first verse of *Surat al-Mutaffifeen* which says, "Woe to those who give less in measure and weight", or we read the first verse of *Surat al-Humaza* which says, "Woe to every slanderer and backbiter" while we are guilty of these sins, then we become the target of these warnings! We need to be very careful. We don't want the wrath of Allah (SWT) upon us! To avoid it, we need to strive to follow the teachings of the Qur`an. That will cause our character to be transformed. Our best example is that of our Prophet Muhammad (SAS) about whom the mother of the believers, 'A`isha (RAA) said, "His character was the Qur`an."

The commands of the Qur`an can be divided into two categories: individual and collective. Individually, Muslims must mold their life according to the teachings of the Qur`an. The Prophet (SAS) said, "None of you can become a true believer until his desires become subordinate to what I have brought (meaning the Qur`an)." The best way to benefit from studying the Qur`an is to change our lifestyles and mend our ways following its teachings. At the collective level of the community, we do not have a society that is fully governed by the principles of our noble *deen*. So what should we do? We should strive to create such a society—a society based on a system of social justice—as mentioned in the Qur`an.

The fifth and final obligation that we owe to the Qur`an is to convey its message to others. This task was first assigned to our Prophet Muhammad (SAS). This is mentioned many times in the Qur`an. One example is in *Surat al-Ma`ida*, where Allah (SWT) says,

يَا أَيُّهَا الرَّسُولُ بَلِّغْ مَا أُنْزِلَ إِلَيْكَ مِنْ رَبِّكَ وَإِنْ لَمْ تَفْعَلْ فَمَا بَلَّغْتَ رِسَالَتَهُ ۞

*O Messenger, deliver whatever has been sent down to you by your Lord. If you do not do so, you will not have conveyed His message. (al-Ma`ida, 5:67)*

After the demise of the Prophet (SAS), this responsibility of conveying the message falls upon the shoulders of his *ummah*. In his farewell sermon, the Prophet (SAS) said, "Those who are present should convey (Allah's message) to those who are not." He also said, "Convey from me even though it be a single verse."

Let me conclude by summarizing what I said. We need first to understand and accept these five obligations that we have toward the Qur`an. We need to firmly believe that the Qur`an is the Book of Allah and the source of guidance for all of humanity. We need to read it regularly with proper etiquette. We need to understand what we read. We need to follow its teachings, and then finally, we need to convey the message to others. And we have the authentic hadeeth in which the Prophet (SAS) says, "The best among you are those who learn the Qur`an and teach it."

May Allah (SWT) have mercy upon us by means of the Qur`an; and may He make it a source of light, guidance, and mercy for us. May He remind us from the Qur`an that which we have been made to forget and teach us from it regarding which we are ignorant. May He bless us with its recitation, and may He make it a proof for us and not against us on the Day of Judgment. *Allahumma ameen.*

---

*The *khutbah* transcript is excerpted from the audio recordings of Late Dr. Israr Ahmad (RA) and duly modified and paraphrased for clarity.

•   65   •

# PATIENCE DURING TRIALS AND TRIBULATIONS

We often engage ourselves in debates and discussions as to why Muslims alone among all people have to face trials and tribulations day in and day out, and what is to be done to overcome this situation?

Some of us may think that we are being punished for our disobedience to Allah (SWT) as a consequence of our not following Islam in letter and spirit. Some others may blame the rulers of the Muslim world for the current situation. Some may attribute this crisis to centuries of Western domination and colonialism over Muslim lands. Others may argue that the primary reason for our problems is the lack of initiative and effort to acquire religious knowledge. Yet others may point toward sectarianism and narrow-mindedness prevalent among Muslims.

Some relate the problems to the disunity among Muslims. Then there are those who say that the tests and trials come due to general erosion of moral and ethical values. Others think that we are not progressive enough in our thoughts and actions. Some other reasons that are attributed are said to be our dependence on the West—politically and economically.

Thus, there are many reasons—historical, social, economic, political, moral, and more—that are put forward as reasons for the trials and tribulations we face, and these are manifested in many ways. I will hasten to add that Muslims, too, are part of the problem because the Qur`an unequivocally says,

$$ \text{إِنَّ اللَّهَ لَا يُغَيِّرُ مَا بِقَوْمٍ حَتَّى يُغَيِّرُوا مَا بِأَنْفُسِهِمْ} $$

*Allah will not change the condition of a people until they change what is in themselves.*
(ar-Ra'd, 13:11)

This means that we as an *ummah* are primarily responsible to bring about a positive change in ourselves and our present condition.

Having said this, how should we know whether any trial that we are confronted with is a punishment from Allah (SWT), a wakeup call from Him, or simply a test of our patience so that we may show patience and get closer to Him? In reality, the condition of the heart is what determines if you are undergoing a test or a punishment with every trial. If you are grateful to the Creator, and at peace with life regardless of how bad things are; if you keep saying *al-hamduli-llah* ("all praise and thanks are for Allah"), then know that you are getting closer to Allah (SWT) with every test that you endure patiently.

$$ \text{وَلَنَبْلُوَنَّكُمْ بِشَيْءٍ مِنَ الْخَوْفِ وَالْجُوعِ وَنَقْصٍ مِنَ الْأَمْوَالِ وَالْأَنْفُسِ وَالثَّمَرَاتِ وَبَشِّرِ الصَّابِرِينَ} $$

*And certainly, We shall test you with something of fear, hunger, loss of wealth, lives and fruits, but give glad tidings to the patient ones. (al-Baqara, 2:155)*

Basically, my *khutbah* today is about showing patience or *sabr* in times of trials and tribulations. *Sabr* provides light in moments of darkness as the Prophet (SAS) said, "Patience is light." *Sabr* comes from an Arabic root which means to restrain oneself.

In the spiritual sense, it means to stop oneself from losing hope and panicking, and to stop one's tongue from complaining. It means that we act wisely and restrain ourselves from doing things that will cause more harm. Islam emphasizes patience and perseverance in adversity or calamity.

وَاصْبِرُوا إِنَّ اللَّهَ مَعَ الصَّابِرِينَ ◯

*And be steadfast. Allah is with the steadfast. (al-Anfal, 8:46)*

Throughout history, all believers have been put to tests and tribulations whether they were prophets and messengers of Allah or ordinary believers like us, living as individuals, as families, as communities, and as an *ummah*. Allah (SWT) says,

أَحَسِبَ النَّاسُ أَن يُتْرَكُوا أَن يَقُولُوا آمَنَّا وَهُمْ لَا يُفْتَنُونَ ◯

*Do people think that once they say, we believe, they will be left alone and will not be tested? (al-'Ankabut, 29:2)*

And He says,

وَلَقَدْ فَتَنَّا الَّذِينَ مِن قَبْلِهِمْ فَلَيَعْلَمَنَّ اللَّهُ الَّذِينَ صَدَقُوا وَلَيَعْلَمَنَّ الْكَاذِبِينَ ◯

*We tested those before them so that Allah would know the truthful and would know the liars. (al-'Ankabut, 29:3)*

Allah (SWT) gives striking examples of patience in the lives of the prophets because they showed patience in situations that we cannot even imagine. Yusuf (AS) was thrown in a well by his brothers. Yunus (AS) had to remain in the belly of a whale for three days. Ayyub (AS) was tested with loss of health, wealth and family. We have the stories of the *ulu al-'azm*, the five who were most strong-willed and persevering: Nuh, Ibraheem, Musa, and Isa (peace be upon them all) and Muhammad (SAS). They never deviated from their devotion to Allah (SWT) and remained resolute in the face of adversities. In fact, Allah (SWT) tests most those whom He loves most. Thus, the prophets whom He loved the most were tested the most.

Today as we are confronted with bigotry, rejection, hatred, and even physical abuse, we should remain steadfast. Musa (AS) said to his people,

اسْتَعِينُوا بِاللَّهِ وَاصْبِرُوا ◯

*Seek help through Allah and be patient. (al-A'raf, 7:128)*

Patience has been divided into three categories: (1) patience in obeying Allah (SWT), (2) patience in refraining from the forbidden, and (3) patience in the face of adversity. Islam provides powerful psychological leverage in the form of patience to deal with adversities. Patience, therefore, has to be adopted by the believers as a way of life. It is a great blessing and virtue and gives allows us to connect and bond deeply with Allah (SWT).

Patience leads to intelligence in thought and action. One of the major factors preventing people from acting intelligently is their impulsive thinking and behavior brought about by impatience. Sudden anger or desire shuts down the mind and pushes people to act without thinking. It is perhaps for this reason, that when the Prophet (SAS) was asked for advice by one of his companions, he replied, "Don't get angry." The companion kept on asking for more advice, and each time, the messenger of Allah (SAS) responded, "Don't get angry."

Every single time we practice patience, Allah (SWT) removes our sins from us. A hadeeth tells us, "No fatigue, disease, sorrow, sadness, hurt, or distress befalls a Muslim, even if it were the prick of a thorn, except that Allah expiates some of his sins for that." May Allah (SWT) give us the *tawfeeq* to understand situations in their proper perspective.

Brothers and sisters! How do we acquire the patience that is required of us in times of trials and tribulations? One of the best ways is to engage in *dhikr* or the remembrance of Allah (SWT).

$$ أَلاَ بِذِكْرِ اللّهِ تَطْمَئِنُّ الْقُلُوبُ ۝ $$

*Verily in the remembrance of Allah do hearts find rest. (ar-Ra'd, 13:28)*

One of the six articles of the Islamic faith is to have *iman* in *qadr* which means faith in divine destiny. If we are firm in our belief that only Allah (SWT) possesses knowledge of the past, present, and future, we will be able to put our trust in Him. Allah (SWT) has wisdom beyond the reach of our rational capacities. His way of operating the world is beyond our comprehension. We don't always know why? Allah (SWT) does what he does to unfold that we do not know. So having faith in *qadr* instills patience in us.

Unfortunately, Islamophobic remarks have intensified recently, especially in the presidential debates. Muslims were here in America long before Christopher Columbus set foot on these shores! When Columbus made his journey to the United States, it is said he took with him a book written by Portuguese Muslims who had navigated their way to the New World in the 12th century.

Another way of acquiring patience is to take lessons from the life of the Prophet (SAS). During his lifetime, when the adversaries of Islam began to see that their own family and tribal members had started to enter into the fold of Islam, they launched a malicious campaign to distort Islam and its teachings. They managed to create conditions that were conducive to people's accepting anything negative said about the Prophet (SAS) and the Qur`an without independent judgment.

All this was done to discredit the Prophet (SAS) and his teachings. But how did he face this campaign of distortions? Although he was on the receiving end, he took everything that was thrown at him and kept his spirits high. He did not react angrily, as do those Muslims who are easily agitated when they are provoked and start trading insults with the opposite side. He was calm and collected in all his exchanges with the adversaries of Islam. From his perseverance and endurance, the number of Muslims grew to over a billion and a half. Brothers and sisters! Be reminded of this amazing hadeeth in which the Prophet (SAS) says, "This message (of Islam) will reach to wherever the night and day have reached. Allah shall not leave any home built by clay or stones or by animal skin (tent) except that Allah will make this religion to enter it."

Brothers and sisters! We may not always be able to control what happens to us, but we can always control our attitude toward what happens to us. A pessimist sees the difficulty in every opportunity; an optimist sees opportunity in every difficulty. I will leave you with a beautiful verse from *Surat Aal 'Imran* that says,

وَلَا تَهِنُوا وَلَا تَحْزَنُوا وَأَنتُمُ الْأَعْلَوْنَ إِن كُنتُم مُّؤْمِنِينَ ⃝

*Do not be weak, and do not grieve, for you will have the upper hand, if you are believers.*
(Aal 'Imran, 3:139)

## • 66 •

# PERFECTION OF ACTION *(ITQAN)*

I intend to discuss in today's *khutbah* the Islamic concept of itqan. The Arabic word itqan is used to indicate the highest level of quality work and the correct and complete performance of duties. It has to do with arranging and doing things in a way that yields perfect results. Itqan or perfection of action is a part of our trust (amana). Being thorough in doing something is an obligation upon Muslims.

In Islam, quality work has a special spiritual flavor because of its association with Allah (SWT). The *itqan* or perfection with which Allah creates everything is mentioned in numerous verses of the Qur`an. For example, in *Surat an-Naml* Allah (SWT) tells us,

صُنْعَ اللَّهِ الَّذِي أَتْقَنَ كُلَّ شَيْءٍ ⃝

*This is the handiwork of God who has perfected all things.* (an-Naml, 27:88)

In *Surat as-Sajda* we read that Allah (SWT) perfected everything which He created.

$$الَّذِي أَحْسَنَ كُلَّ شَيْءٍ خَلَقَهُ ۝$$

*Who perfected everything which He created and began the creation of man from clay.*
(as-Sajda, 32:7)

*Surat at-Teen* says that Allah (SWT) created man in the best of forms.

$$لَقَدْ خَلَقْنَا الْإِنْسَانَ فِي أَحْسَنِ تَقْوِيمٍ ۝$$

*We have certainly created man in the best of stature. (at-Teen, 95:4)*

We also get a glimpse of the perfection of Allah's creation in *Surat al-Mulk.*

$$الَّذِي خَلَقَ سَبْعَ سَمَاوَاتٍ طِبَاقًا مَّا تَرَى فِي خَلْقِ الرَّحْمَنِ مِن تَفَاوُتٍ فَارْجِعِ الْبَصَرَ هَلْ تَرَى مِن فُطُورٍ ۝ ثُمَّ ارْجِعِ الْبَصَرَ كَرَّتَيْنِ يَنقَلِبْ إِلَيْكَ الْبَصَرُ خَاسِئًا وَهُوَ حَسِيرٌ ۝$$

*He who created the seven heavens, one above the other; you will not see any flaw in
what the Lord of Mercy creates. Look again! Can you see any flaw? Look again! And
again! Your sight will turn back to you, weak and defeated. (al-Mulk, 67:3-4)*

*Itqan* means to strive for perfection, without sacrificing the quality of the work one
is doing. *Itqan* is a criterion for achievement and excellence, which comes through
working hard and not giving up. Indeed this is what has been shown by our beloved
Prophet (SAS). He did not give up while spreading the message of Islam to his people
despite the obstacles that came in his way. Through hard work, patience, persistence,
and perseverance, he not only changed a pagan community into a civilized society,
but was supremely successful on both the religious and secular levels. All his actions
were done at the highest level of *itqan.* His companions followed him in his footsteps
and with enormous effort, and *itqan* managed to spread the message and blessings
of Islam to a large part of the globe including Asia, Africa, and Europe in less than a
hundred years.

The Prophet (SAS) always called upon people to perfect their work. On the
authority of 'A`isha (RAA), when he saw a little gap between bricks in a grave, the
Prophet (SAS) immediately ordered his companions to fill it, saying, "Allah loves that
whenever any of you does something, you should perfect it." In other words, Allah
(SWT) is pleased with the one who, when performing a deed, does so with excellence.
This matter concerned only a gap that caused neither harm nor benefit to the dead.
Yet the Prophet (SAS) did not permit it to remain in that condition, and so ordered that
it also should get its share of perfection. *Itqan,* in this hadeeth, refers to the attitude
of being careful, meticulous, diligent, and excellent in carrying out responsibilities
and tasks. If a person is willfully negligent, wastes his or her time, then of course, this
person will incur the displeasure of Allah (SWT). We read in *Surat at-Tawba,*

$$وَقُلِ اعْمَلُوا فَسَيَرَى اللَّهُ عَمَلَكُمْ وَرَسُولُهُ وَالْمُؤْمِنُونَ وَسَتُرَدُّونَ إِلَى عَالِمِ الْغَيْبِ وَالشَّهَادَةِ فَيُنَبِّئُكُم بِمَا كُنتُمْ$$

تَعْمَلُونَ ◯

*Do deeds! Allah will see your deeds, and (so will) His Messenger and the believers. And you will be brought back to the All-Knower of the unseen and the seen. Then He will inform you of what you used to do. (at-Tawba, 9:105)*

This verse tells us that our deeds will be shown to us on the Day of Judgment. Indeed, we have to be very careful and very watchful of whatever we do.

*Iman* or faith should propel a person to work in as perfect a manner as possible, be it for the welfare of this world or for the afterlife. When doing anything at the level of *itqan*, our attitude always remains positive. We do not become complacent, and we do not become selfish. Therefore, we do not have to doubt the quality of the work we produce. A society having *itqan* in its work ethics is more proactive, more responsible, and more sensitive toward others. Doing something without *itqan* leads to an attitude of mediocrity or taking things for granted. This attitude prevents a person from achieving any kind of success. We need to educate ourselves, our families, and our children to avoid this mediocre attitude. Success does not come by doing things half-heartedly.

People with negative attitudes always utter words of discouragement to themselves and those around them. Rather than achieving excellence in what they do, they continue to criticize, condemn, complain, and make excuses. They always complain about not having enough time, enough resources, and enough opportunities. They usually have very low self-esteem themselves and lack confidence in themselves. And what they love to do is to give up halfway and let go of responsibilities. They also love blaming others for their shortcomings and weaknesses.

Let me share with you a very positive cultural practice of the Japanese people. It is the culture of the Japanese people to strive for total professionalism in whatever they do. Any task is taken seriously and is done with utmost dedication. In Japanese organizations, employees at all levels are expected to seek perfection in their respective professions. This is true even for low-grade workers. The general attitude is that the only way to do a job is to do it perfectly. The Japanese are known to practice a simple philosophy called *kaizen*, which means "to become good through change." It is a philosophy of continuous improvement, restructuring and organizing every aspect of a system to ensure that it remains at peak efficiency. *Itqan* is doing all this and much more. It is a value that has been emphasized by our beloved Prophet Muhammad (SAS).

I invite myself and you to strive to improve. Let today be better than yesterday, and let tomorrow be better than today. Let us keep improving ourselves in our daily duties and dealings with family members, friends, and all others, at all times and all places.

Brothers and sisters! Islam demands that whatever we undertake to do, we do it really well. There are no half-hearted measures in Islam. No sloppy, shoddy work.

If you are a Muslim and you do something, you have to do it well. But unfortunately this is something many of us have forgotten. This is one of those important lessons of our culture and history that we need to re-learn. When we do something, whatever it may be, those looking at our work should be able to say, "Ah, a Muslim must have done it!" That is how our predecessors in faith used to be, and that is what we need to become. Excellence and superior performance need to stop at us. Our dedication and commitment to our work will not only let us progress further in work, but will earn for us the blessings and mercy from Allah (SWT). The Prophet (SAS) said in a hadeeth, "O people, Allah is good, and He therefore accepts only that which is good."

This hadeeth encourages us to work carefully and responsibly to earn the pleasure of Allah (SWT). Regardless of the nature of the job, be it a ritual, a mode of worship, maintaining good relationships with our fellow human beings, or any other type of work, we are called upon to have *itqan*. If we perform our prayers merely to fulfill a responsibility, then our prayers may not have the desired effect on us. In our professional lives, if we do our jobs and perform our duties just for the sake of earning a livelihood, we may remain mediocre all our lives. As students, if we study just to pass the exams and our feelings are devoid of the quest to learn more in-depth into what we study, then we will end up being ordinary students and not outstanding ones.

As a community, we must always look for ways to improve our situation. We must discard any poor image of ourselves and our work ethics. Do we make appointments and not stick to them? Do we make promises and not fulfill them? Do we undertake a job and settle for poor performance by not working hard enough? We have to strive to change this general image of Muslims. Good practices and work attitudes of other communities should be good examples for us. Of course, we are fortunate to have the best guide, and the best model is our beloved Prophet (SAS). We can change and improve when we truly desire to do so, and when we make sufficient effort to do so. In the Qur`an, Allah (SWT) tells us that our situation will not change for the better if we do not put in any effort to change it ourselves.

إِنَّ اللَّهَ لَا يُغَيِّرُ مَا بِقَوْمٍ حَتَّىٰ يُغَيِّرُوا مَا بِأَنفُسِهِمْ ○

*God does not change the condition of a people unless they change what is in themselves.*
(ar-Ra'd, 13:11)

May Allah (SWT) give us the *tawfeeq* and guidance to improve for the better, and to have *itqan* in all that we do. *Ameen.*

# POVERTY OF THE SOUL

I intend to speak today on a topic that has to do with poverty of the soul. Poverty of the soul describes the unmoved soul; the soul that has been created but has still failed to realize its purpose. It is the soul that lives a purposeless life. There is only one thing that makes the soul poor, and that is to deprive it of its only true need: to be near to its Creator—Allah (SWT).

Spiritual deprivation is true poverty. It means standing poor on the Day of Judgment. Despite this reality, many people live this life feeding their bodies, but starving their souls. The paradox of this situation is that this body to which all our focus is directed, is only temporary, while the soul we neglect is eternal. Death of the body is not true death. It's only the movement from one realm to another realm. There are people whose bodies are well-nourished and alive but whose souls are blind, weak, sick, and almost dead. In the language of the Qur'an it is not only the eyes that get blind; the hearts also become blind.

فَإِنَّهَا لَا تَعْمَى الْأَبْصَارُ وَلَكِنْ تَعْمَى الْقُلُوبُ الَّتِي فِي الصُّدُورِ ⏾

*It is not their eyes which are blind but the hearts in their breasts which are blind. (al-Hajj, 22:46)*

Imam al-Ghazali says that every organ of our body has a function, and when it fails to do its function, it means it is not well. The function of the soul or the spiritual heart is to know its Creator, to love Him, and to seek closeness to Him. If the heart fails in this function, then we must know that it is sick. When the heart gets sick, it loses its desire and ability to do right and good deeds. This affects one's morals, manners, and general behavior. This means that when we fail to use any created thing for the purpose for which it was created, it breaks; it starves, and it suffers the most painful poverty.

The human heart is like a boat in the ocean of the world. The boat keeps sailing and drowns only if it allows the ocean's water to enter into it. Similarly, the heart that allows this world to enter into it becomes owned by this life, by our jobs, our gadgets, our social networking services, and many other distractions, such as the fashion trends, the marketing tools, the money, the power, the status, and the list goes on.

The heart that is owned by this life is a prisoner of the worst kind. The heart that is owned by any other master, than the Master of masters, is the weakest of all slaves.

That is true oppression, true poverty, and true death. As human beings, we enslave ourselves to different things and love them as we should love Allah (SWT). If asked, "Who do you love most?" most of us will say we love Allah (SWT) most. We say this with our tongues. We say this in our minds. But our hearts and our actions say otherwise. How do we know? Let us ask ourselves. When we are sad, depressed, and in low spirits, where do we seek refuge? When we need something who do we ask? Who do we think about most? Who defines success for us? Who defines poverty for us? Who defines richness for us?

What type of poverty are we most afraid of? The truth is we are most afraid of the loss of things we love most. When we love money most, that's what we are afraid to lose. We are afraid to lose the person whom we love most. We leave the orbit of the Creator and enter the orbit of the creation. In the orbit of the creation, we rise and fall with the wave of the creation; the wave of praise and criticism. Our standards for success and failure come from the creation, from society. The standards for richness and poverty come from society. But the standard given to us by Allah's messenger (SAS) is different. Prophet Muhammad (SAS) told us, "Richness is not the quantity of possessions that one has; rather true richness is the richness of one's self (or contentment)." And we know that contentment is something directly related to the heart or soul.

But how do we avoid true poverty of the soul? No one likes to fall. And no one likes to drown. But in struggling through the ocean of this life, it's very difficult not to let the world get inside us. Sometimes the ocean does get inside us. The *dunya* does seep into our hearts. And like the water that breaks the boat, when *dunya* enters, it shatters our heart. It shatters the boat, and we sink to the depth of the sea and are surrounded by darkness.

The good news is that this dark place is not the end. We should remember that the light of dawn follows the darkness of night. Sometimes, the ocean floor is only a stop in the journey. And it is when we are at this lowest point, that we are faced with a choice. We can stay there at the bottom until we drown. Or we can gather pearls and swim up to the surface, stronger, and richer.

If we seek Allah (SWT), He will raise us up, and replace the darkness of the ocean, with the light of His Guidance. He can transform what was once our greatest weakness into our greatest strength, and a means of growth, purification, and salvation. It should be known that transformation sometimes begins with a fall. We have to rise and begin to see our nothingness and His greatness; we have to become more humble and more aware of our need for Him. Fortunate are those who see this reality, and the one who is truly deceived is the one who sees his own self—but not Him.

Deprived is the one who has never witnessed his own desperate need for Allah (SWT). Relying heavily on his own means, he forgets that his means, his very soul, and everything else in existence is Allah's creation. We have to seek Allah (SWT) to lift us from our fall, for when He does that, He will rebuild our ship. The heart that we thought was forever damaged will be mended. What was shattered will be whole again. Since it is only Allah (SWT) who can do this, let us seek Him. And when He saves us, we should beg forgiveness for the fall, feel guilty and shameful over it—but not despair. Allah (SWT) reminds us in the Qur`an never to lose hope.

قُلْ يَا عِبَادِيَ الَّذِينَ أَسْرَفُوا عَلَى أَنْفُسِهِمْ لَا تَقْنَطُوا مِنْ رَحْمَةِ اللَّهِ إِنَّ اللَّهَ يَغْفِرُ الذُّنُوبَ جَمِيعًا إِنَّهُ هُوَ الْغَفُورُ الرَّحِيمُ ◯

*Say: 'O my Servants who have transgressed against their souls! Despair not of the Mercy of Allah. For Allah forgives all sins: for He is Oft-Forgiving, Most Merciful.' (az-Zumar, 39:53)*

We ask Allah (SWT) to turn our hearts to His *deen* and His obedience.

يَا مُقَلِّبَ الْقُلُوبِ ثَبِّتْ قُلُوبَنَا عَلَى دِينِكَ ◯

*O, Turner of the hearts, keep our hearts firm on your deen (religion).*

اللَّهُمَّ مُصَرِّفَ الْقُلُوبِ صَرِّفْ قُلُوبَنَا عَلَى طَاعَتِكَ ◯

*O Allah, the Turner of the hearts, turn our hearts to your obedience.*

My dear brothers and sisters! There is a powerful and amazing thing about *tawba* (repentance) and turning back to Allah (SWT). We are told that it is a polish for the heart. What is amazing about a polish is that it does not just clean. It makes the object that it polishes even brighter than before it got dirty. If we come back to Allah (SWT), seek His forgiveness, and are mindful of Him, our hearts *in sha`Allah* will begin to shine. Sometimes falling and rising again gives us wisdom and humility that we may never have had otherwise.

But how do we fill our hearts with the true richness? How do we escape the constant bombardment from every direction commanding us to worship other things and commanding us to love them as we should only love Allah? How do we escape the true poverty of the heart? To escape the true poverty, we must be overflowing in our love for Allah (SWT).

وَمِنَ النَّاسِ مَنْ يَتَّخِذُ مِنْ دُونِ اللَّهِ أَنْدَادًا يُحِبُّونَهُمْ كَحُبِّ اللَّهِ وَالَّذِينَ آمَنُوا أَشَدُّ حُبًّا لِلَّهِ ◯

*Some people set up equals to Allah, loving them as they should love Allah. But those who have iman have greater love for Allah. (al-Baqara, 2:165)*

Our strongest love should be for Allah (SWT). But we can't love someone we don't know. We need to know Him. We don't know someone we never speak to. We have to speak to Him. We have to ask of Him.

$$\text{وَقَالَ رَبُّكُمُ ادْعُونِي أَسْتَجِبْ لَكُمْ} \bigcirc$$

*Your Lord says: Call on Me and I will answer you. (Ghafir, 40:60)*

We can't love someone we don't remember. We have to remember Him; remember Him often. Allah (SWT) says,

$$\text{فَاذْكُرُونِي أَذْكُرْكُمْ} \bigcirc$$

*So remember Me; I will remember you. (al-Baqara, 2:152)*

We don't love someone if we are ungrateful to him. Allah (SWT) says,

$$\text{وَاشْكُرُوا لِي وَلَا تَكْفُرُونِ} \bigcirc$$

*Be thankful to Me and do not be ungrateful. (al-Baqara, 2:152)*

Brothers and sisters, no one has to confess his or her sins to anyone except Allah (SWT). Anyone who has entered the ocean of *dunya*, who sunk into its depths and become trapped by its crushing waves must rise to the real world; to our freedom, and back to life, leaving the death of our souls behind us. The polish of *tawba* remakes the heart even more beautiful than it was before it got soiled.

Some of us may foolishly think that we can live our lives the way we like, and then at the time of death, we will just say, *la ilaha illa Allah.* But at the time of death, the tongue cannot speak, except what the heart commands. Whatever is in the heart will come out. The bankrupt heart will have nothing but love of *dunya* to speak of on that day. If our heart is empty of Allah (SWT) during our life, how can it be full of Allah (SWT) during our death? If our heart is full of love of this life, love of status, love of wealth, love of the creation over the Creator, it is that which will come on our tongue when we die.

Let me conclude by saying that if our hearts truly throbs with *la ilaha illa Allah* and we live with the firm belief that in reality, there is no refuge, no shelter, no deity worthy of worship but Allah (SWT). Then and only then will the tongue be given permission at the time of our departure to say *la ilaha illa Allah, Muhammadun rasul Allah.* May Allah (SWT) make us among those good souls.

---

*Based on the thoughts of Yasmin Mogahed, http://www.yasminmogahed.com/2012/10/02/poverty-of-the-soul-united-for-change-conference/

# • 68 •

# THE PROBLEM OF STRESS

In today's *khutbah*, I intend to speak on a topic that has to do with the problem of stress and how to go about tackling it spiritually. What is stress? It is a condition that causes physical, mental, or emotional strain. There are many kinds of health problems caused by stress involving both the body and the mind. Stress seems to increase the risk of conditions like obesity, heart disease, Alzheimer's disease, diabetes, anxiety, depression, gastrointestinal problems, and asthma. Studies have shown that stress does not only make us feel awful emotionally, but can also intensify just about any health condition we can think of. Hardly anyone can be said to be completely free from stress but some deal with it better than others.

If we feel depressed, we are not alone. It has been estimated that 75 to 90 percent of all visits to primary care physicians in America are for stress-related problems. This is why it is wise to consult a doctor if you are having physical symptoms of stress. However, some tips can help us from an Islamic perspective. Let us first try to understand some of the factors that contribute toward increasing our stress. These include:

Fear of the unknown and trying to see through, and control destiny.

Losses in our lives of people and things dear to us and our inability to recover from those losses.

The inner conflict of the heart and mind; between the truth and our failure to accept that truth.

Let us examine the guidance we get from the Qur`an and the Sunnah to deal with such situations. As for our destiny, it is predetermined. We do not have control on that part. What we can control is a limited free will related to our actions and the choices we make—our choices to do good or bad. But we have no control over events not associated with our actions or the choices we make. Worrying over such things is of no use. Although we know that only Allah (SWT) is in control and that He has decreed all things, we are responsible for making the right choices and doing the right things in all situations of our lives.

We should think, plan, and make sound choices, and then put our trust in Allah (SWT). If things happen as we want, we should praise and thank Him. If things do not happen as we wish, we should still praise and thank Him, recognizing that He knows best what is good in the overall scheme of things.

As for mourning over losses in our lives of those that are dear to us and our inability to recover from those losses, an inner conflict takes place between our heart and mind, between what is known to be the truth and our failure to accept it as truth. Acceptance of truth may require changing our habits and way of life. Let us examine how the Qur`an deals with such situations. Allah (SWT) says,

وَلَنَبْلُوَنَّكُمْ بِشَيْءٍ مِنَ الْخَوْفِ وَالْجُوعِ وَنَقْصٍ مِنَ الْأَمْوَالِ وَالْأَنْفُسِ وَالثَّمَرَاتِ وَبَشِّرِ الصَّابِرِينَ ◯ الَّذِينَ إِذَا أَصَابَتْهُمْ مُصِيبَةٌ قَالُوا إِنَّا لِلَّهِ وَإِنَّا إِلَيْهِ رَاجِعُونَ ◯ أُولَئِكَ عَلَيْهِمْ صَلَوَاتٌ مِنْ رَبِّهِمْ وَرَحْمَةٌ وَأُولَئِكَ هُمُ الْمُهْتَدُونَ ◯

*We will certainly test you with some fear and hunger and loss of wealth and life and fruits. But give good news to those who are patient; who, when disaster strikes them, say `We belong to Allah and to Him we shall return.` Those are the people who will have blessings and mercy from their Lord; they are the ones who are guided.* (al-Baqara, 2:155-157)

It is reported that a person asked ʿAli ibn Abi Talib (RAA) as to how one would know whether a hardship that befalls a person is a test from Allah (SWT) or punishment from Him. ʿAli (RAA) replied, "If the hardship takes one closer to Allah, then it's a test, and if it takes one further away from Allah, then it's a punishment." Look how profound and clear this statement is. As we move forward in life, this is a message that is worthy of being imprinted in our beings.

In Islam, we do not have the concept of absolute ownership of goods and life. Man owns nothing. Whatever we possess, is an *amana*—a trust given to us by Allah (SWT). Everything belongs to Allah (SWT) and returns to him. So if we don't own anything, why keep on mourning its loss, and increasing our stress? In situations of panic and despair, believers should behave differently than non-believers. Non-believers have no one to return to, no one to ask for mercy and forgiveness. Their life is this life, which they cannot control, and thus they get more depressed and more diseased. Rejection of faith is like a disease. After denial of truth, which is basically due to arrogance, one sets up an inner conflict between heart and mind.

We should turn each anxiety, each fear, and each concern into a *du'a*—a supplication. Allah (SWT) listens and already knows what is in our hearts, but He wants us to ask Him for what we want. The Prophet (SAS) said, "Allah is angry with those who do not ask Him for anything." Allah says in the Qur`an,

ادْعُوا رَبَّكُمْ تَضَرُّعًا وَخُفْيَةً ◯

*Call on your Lord humbly and secretly.* (al-Aʿraf, 7:55)

Also, we should turn each *du'a* into an action plan. If we are worried about the state of the world, are we part of any peace movement? Is our *masjid* part of the peace movement? Are we part of an interfaith group with an agenda of peace and justice?

Are we working with a group fighting discrimination and injustice? If our answer is no, it is time that we sit down to plan our share of time and money in finding solutions to the problems we face.

$$\text{إِنَّ اللَّهَ لَا يُغَيِّرُ مَا بِقَوْمٍ حَتَّىٰ يُغَيِّرُوا مَا بِأَنْفُسِهِمْ}$$

*Allah never changes a people's state until they change what is in themselves. (ar-Ra'd, 13:11)*

While we need to carry out our duty to the best of our abilities, always remember that you don't control the outcome of events. Even the Prophets did not control the outcome of their efforts. Some were successful, and others were not. Once you have done your duty, leave the results to Allah (SWT). Regardless of the results of your efforts, you will be rewarded for the part you have played. However, never underestimate your abilities. If you are sincerely exerting yourselves, Allah (SWT) will bless the work you do. It will be full of *baraka*.

My dear brothers and sisters! In difficult times, we should also seek Allah's help through *sabr* and *salah*—patience and prayers.

$$\text{وَاسْتَعِينُوا بِالصَّبْرِ وَالصَّلَاةِ وَإِنَّهَا لَكَبِيرَةٌ إِلَّا عَلَى الْخَاشِعِينَ}$$

*And seek help with patience and prayer: It is indeed hard, but not to the humble. (al-Baqara, 2:45)*

This instruction from Allah (SWT) provides us with two critical tools that can ease our worries and pain. *Sabr* and *salah* are two oft-neglected stress busters. *Sabr* is often translated as patience, but it is not just that. It includes self-control, perseverance, endurance, and a focused struggle to achieve one's goal. Unlike patience, which implies resignation, the concept of *sabr* includes a duty to remain steadfast to achieve your goals despite all odds. Use the five daily prayers as a means to become more hereafter-oriented and less attached to this temporary world. Start distancing yourself as soon as you hear the call to prayer. When you stand ready to pray, mentally prepare yourself to leave this world and all of its worries and stresses behind you.

By reminding ourselves that Allah (SWT) is the Provider, we will remember that getting a job or providing for our family in these economically and politically challenging times is in Allah's Hands, not ours. We read this beautiful *ayah* in *Surat Hud*, in which Allah says,

$$\text{وَمَا مِنْ دَابَّةٍ فِي الْأَرْضِ إِلَّا عَلَى اللَّهِ رِزْقُهَا وَيَعْلَمُ مُسْتَقَرَّهَا وَمُسْتَوْدَعَهَا كُلٌّ فِي كِتَابٍ مُبِينٍ}$$

*There is no creature on the earth which is not dependent upon Allah for its provision. He knows where it lives and where it dies. All this is recorded in a clear book. (Hud, 11:6)*

It is also important to keep reminding ourselves that we don't control all the variables in the world. Allah (SWT) does. He is the Wise, the All-Knowing. Sometimes our limited human faculties are not able to comprehend His wisdom behind what happens to us and to others. But knowing that He is in control, as human beings, we should submit to His will. This enriches our humanity and enhances our obedience toward him. We should strive to have *taqwa*, the consciousness of Allah (SWT) as much as we can.

$$\text{فَاتَّقُوا اللَّهَ مَا اسْتَطَعْتُمْ} \bigcirc$$

*Be conscious of Allah as much as you can. (at-Taghabun, 64:16)*

We should hasten to seek Allah's forgiveness.

$$\bigcirc \text{اسْتَغْفِرُوا رَبَّكُمْ إِنَّهُ كَانَ غَفَّارًا}$$

*Ask forgiveness of your Lord: He is ever forgiving. (Nuh, 71:10)*

We should keep Allah's remembrance alive in our hearts.

$$\text{أَلَا بِذِكْرِ اللَّهِ تَطْمَئِنُّ الْقُلُوبُ} \bigcirc$$

*Truly, it is in the remembrance of Allah that hearts find peace. (ar-Ra'd, 13:28)*

To conclude, it may be said that stress results from a lack of inner peace due to conflicts within us and leads to external disturbances in our behavior and health. Inner peace is achieved by believing in Allah, the Almighty, and remembering Him frequently and asking for His help and forgiveness in times of difficulties.

## • 69 •

# THE PROBLEM OF SUFFERING

In today's *khutbah*, I intend to talk about something that we all experience in our lives. It is the phenomenon of suffering. Every human being, without exception, at some time or other, has to endure hardship, pain, and suffering. One may well ask, "Why do pain and suffering exist in the world?" We see people commit crimes and nations wage wars. We witness storms, earthquakes, floods, and famine. There are evils caused by human beings, and there are natural disasters. There is suffering for individuals and suffering for entire peoples and nations. Some argue that if Allah (SWT) is All-Merciful, then why do people suffer? Why do innocent men, women, and children have to endure unspeakable hardships?

On the other hand, we see beauty, health, prosperity, wisdom, and progress. We also see virtue, piety, faith, sincerity, charity, love, and the spirit of sacrifice among people. Moreover, it is a fact that the element of good exists more in the creation than the element of evil. We all see more people who are healthy than those who are sick. There are more that eat well than those who starve. There are many more who lead a decent life than those who commit crimes. Goodness is the rule, and evil is the exception. But the question remains, "Why does Allah (SWT) allow this exception to the rule?"

Being finite, human beings cannot comprehend the infinite. They cannot fully grasp Allah's infinite Will and Wisdom. He runs His universe the way He deems fit. In the Qur`an Allah tells us,

$$وَأَنَّ اللَّهَ لَيْسَ بِظَلَّامٍ لِّلْعَبِيدِ ۞$$

*God is never unjust to His servants. (Aal 'Imran, 3:182)*

As far as the problem of human suffering is concerned, there are several points that we should keep in mind to understand this issue. First of all, Allah (SWT) has not made this world a permanent place to live. This is a temporary abode, and everything here has a limited time. Everything fades away and dies down at the appointed time.

We are here for a short time, and we are being tested. Those who see suffering as a "problem" are saying that they believe they have a right to a life of uninterrupted happiness, with no discomfort, no pain, and no grief. But that's not what this earthly life is all about! Eternal bliss has been promised to us only in the hereafter and not in this world. We're not there yet! We still have to strive to qualify for Allah's mercy to enter paradise.

Secondly, Allah (SWT) has placed certain physical and moral laws in this universe. These laws are based on cause and effect. He allows suffering to occur when one of these laws is broken. Sickness occurs if one does not take care of one's health or is exposed to infections. Car accidents usually take place because of negligent drivers, faulty vehicles, bad road conditions, and violation of traffic rules. Poverty, hunger, and deprivation of the basic needs of people occur because of social, economic, and political injustice. Moral decadence in society becomes widespread when the divine guidance of moral and ethical behavior is either ignored or replaced by man-made rules. The study of cause and effect is very important to facilitate safeguards.

The ways we transgress the measures set by Allah (SWT) and the audacity with which we violate His laws of cause and effect are incredible. Strictly speaking, the question should not be why does Allah (SWT) allow suffering, but how much Allah

(SWT) saves us and protects us despite our negligence and irresponsible behavior. Allah says in the Qur`an,

وَلَوْ يُؤَاخِذُ اللَّهُ النَّاسَ بِمَا كَسَبُوا مَا تَرَكَ عَلَىٰ ظَهْرِهَا مِن دَابَّةٍ وَلَٰكِن يُؤَخِّرُهُمْ إِلَىٰ أَجَلٍ مُّسَمًّى ⃝

*If God were to punish people according to what they deserve, He would not leave a single living creature on the surface of the earth; but He grants them respite until an appointed time. (Fatir, 35:45)*

But sometimes Allah (SWT) does punish people because they violate His laws, whether they are physical or moral. In the Qur`an Allah tells us that many nations and communities were destroyed because of their sinful lifestyles.

فَكَأَيِّن مِّن قَرْيَةٍ أَهْلَكْنَاهَا وَهِيَ ظَالِمَةٌ ⃝

*How many a town We destroyed which was given to wrongdoing. (al-Hajj, 22:45)*

Suffering can also be a test and trial for some people. We need to understand that part of being in this world is that we will be tested.

لَتُبْلَوُنَّ فِي أَمْوَالِكُمْ وَأَنْفُسِكُمْ ⃝

*You will surely be tried and tested in your possessions and in your personal selves. (Aal 'Imran 3:186)*

The most important tools that have to be used in times of suffering are patience, perseverance, and prayers. There are several verses in the Qur`an that refer to the value of applying these tools.

يَا أَيُّهَا الَّذِينَ آمَنُوا اسْتَعِينُوا بِالصَّبْرِ وَالصَّلَاةِ إِنَّ اللَّهَ مَعَ الصَّابِرِينَ ⃝

*O you, who believe, seek help through patience and prayer. Surely, Allah is with those who are patient. (al-Baqara, 2:153)*

Good people sometimes suffer, but their sufferings heal others and bring goodness to their communities. People learn lessons from their good examples. Allah (SWT) sometimes allows some people to suffer to test others and to see how they react. Every person who is sick, poor, and needy is a test for all those who are in good health and well-off financially. Every deaf, mute, and blind person is a test for those who can hear, talk, and see. Allah (SWT) is there with that suffering person to test your charity, your sense of gratitude, and your faith.

We are informed in *Surat al-Baqara* that when believers are afflicted with a calamity, they say,

إِنَّا لِلَّهِ وَإِنَّا إِلَيْهِ رَاجِعُونَ ⃝

*We belong to God and to Him we shall return. (al-Baqara, 2:156)*

But are we conscious of the fact that peace and prosperity are also a test for us: a test of our gratitude to Allah (SWT), a test to see our sharing and caring attitude toward other fellow humans. Allah's help is always near! It's much closer than we think! Allah (SWT) wants us to really feel and experience our desperate need for Him. He wants us to be patient. He wants us to repose our complete trust in His mercy so that we can set ourselves apart from those who disbelieve, those who stand against faith. Blessed are the people who believe in God, who have absolute certainty of meeting Him in the hereafter.

And miserable, confused, and lonely are those who live without faith, hope, and longing for life after death, and who live fearing the unknown. When nonbelievers suffer, their lack of faith leads them to endless despair. Let us thank Allah (SWT) for illuminating our hearts with the light of His guidance.

In times of trials, tribulations, and suffering, our weak faith can sometimes drive us to question the justification of all that is happening to us and of all that is going against us. In this context, we should remind ourselves that believing in *al-qadr* or the divine decree is one of the pillars of Islamic faith. Allah (SWT) says in the Qur'an,

$$\text{مَا أَصَابَ مِنْ مُصِيبَةٍ فِي الْأَرْضِ وَلَا فِي أَنْفُسِكُمْ إِلَّا فِي كِتَابٍ مِنْ قَبْلِ أَنْ نَبْرَأَهَا ۝}$$

*No misfortune happens, either in the earth or in yourselves, that is not set down in writing before We bring it into existence. (al-Hadeed, 57:22)*

As part of this belief, we should recognize that Allah (SWT) does what He wills for reasons that are only known to Him. Any attempt to comprehend with our limited minds His wisdom, or to understand how our current situation fits in His overall plan can only lead us to erroneous conclusions. True believers know that their suffering ultimately holds something good for them. The Prophet (SAS) said in a hadeeth, "There is nothing that befalls a believer, not even a thorn that pricks him, but Allah (SWT) will record a *hasana* (a good deed) for him thereby, or erase from him a sin."

The mystical poet, Jalal ad-Deen Rumi said, "Suffering is a gift. In it is a hidden mercy." Suffering teaches *sabr* or patience, and it also teaches us *ridha* or the serene acceptance of whatever Allah (SWT) has decreed. It teaches us to persevere and to work hard to seek Allah's good pleasure. It teaches us humility, and it teaches compassion for those less fortunate than ourselves.

Our beloved Prophet Muhammad (SAS) said, "Strange are the ways of a believer for there is good in every affair of his, and this is not the case with anyone else except in the case of a believer: For if he has an occasion to feel delight, he thanks (Allah), thus there is good for him in it, and if he gets into trouble and shows resignation (enduring it patiently), there is good for him in it."

Believers are truly blessed, regardless of the circumstances of their lives. Disbelievers consider themselves fortunate only if they are healthy, wealthy, happy, and more. But believers are lucky all the time. This is because they are accruing rewards for *jannah* whether they are healthy, or sick, prosperous, or needy. This is indeed a unique favor of Allah (SWT) to his pious servants.

There is really no "problem" of suffering. The problem is human ignorance. If we don't know Allah (SWT), we won't be able to accept His decree. We won't know our place in the vast cosmic scheme of things. We won't know who we really are, why we are here, where we have come from, and where we are going to after our death. According to a wise saying, "He who knows himself knows his Lord." There is a hadeeth narrated by Tirmidhi and others, in which the Prophet (SAS) says, "Be mindful of Allah, and you'll find Him before you."

So to summarize, we can say that sufferings occur to teach us that we must adhere to Allah's natural and moral laws. It is sometimes to punish those who violate Allah's natural or moral laws. It is also to test our faith in Allah (SWT) and to test our commitment to human values and charity. Whenever we encounter suffering, we should ask ourselves, "Have we broken any law of Allah?" Let us study the cause of the problem and use the corrective methods. "Could it be a punishment?" Let us repent and ask forgiveness and reform our ways. "Could it be a test and trial for us?" Let us work hard to pass this test. Believers face sufferings with prayers, repentance, and good deeds.

We pray to Allah (SWT) to give us the strength and courage to bear the trials and suffering of this world with patience and perseverance. To forgive our shortcomings, to not place on us a burden greater than we can bear, and to be merciful on us on the Day of Judgment when every soul shall be summoned in front of him individually to give an account of its earthly existence. May Allah (SWT) keep us on the right path. *Ameen!*

# • 70 •

# THE PROPHET (SAS) AS A COUNSELOR *(MURABBI)*

Today is the last day of *Rabi' al-Awwal*—the third month of the Islamic lunar calendar. Both the birth and death of our beloved Prophet Muhammad (SAS) are said to have taken place during this month. *In sha` Allah*, in my *khutbah* today, I intend to share some thoughts on an important aspect of the blessed life of the Prophet (SAS), and that is his role as a *murabbi*. *Murabbi* means a counselor, a teacher, a guide, an educator, or a mentor.

The Prophet Muhammad (SAS), the universal *murabbi*, brought the comprehensive universal message of Allah (SWT) that suits all classes and professions. For the wheels of life keep moving; the world needs the leaders and the led, the poor and the rich, the professionals and the laypeople. It is also a fact that the life of man consists of a wide range of moods and inclinations governing his actions in different situations and circumstances. We stand and sit, we walk and talk, we eat and sleep, we laugh and weep, we give and take; in short, we act in different ways on different occasions. Sometimes we are praying to God. At others, we are engaged in our business. Sometimes we are guests and sometimes we are hosts. And for all these occasions we need an example, or a standard to know the correct way of behavior suited for that occasion.

Besides actions involving physical exertions, there are also those which relate to the mind and heart of man, which we call sentiments. Our sentiments are ever-changing. Often we are pleased, and at times, we get angry. We experience feelings of hope and dejection, of pleasure and pain, and of success and failure. These are different states of mind that take hold of us and influence our actions. Moderation in these emotions holds the key to the best and correct behavior in all circumstances. Therefore, we require a practical model to discipline our emotions and feelings. We need a practical example to regulate our behavior in each of these varied conditions. But where are we to look for them except in the Prophet (SAS). He is a model that can serve as a standard for every class of people acting under different circumstances and states of human emotions.

Islam stands as the most rational and precise religion that Allah (SWT) has given to mankind. It gives importance to education, which is the process of teaching and acquiring knowledge, which includes beliefs, values, attitudes, manners, and skills. In fact, Allah (SWT) sent the Prophet Muhammad (SAS) not only as His final messenger and the seal of the prophets but also as the greatest *murabbi* or teacher to mankind.

We learn in a hadeeth that the Prophet (SAS) stressed that he was sent as a teacher. There is an incident related to this statement. Once, the Prophet (SAS) entered the mosque before it was time for prayers. He found two groups in the mosque. The people in one group were busy with their acts of worship. Some were reading the Qur`an while others were making *du'a`*. Another group was in a corner. The group were learning to read and write and discussing Islamic teachings, and its application to their daily lives. Looking at both, the Prophet (SAS) said, "They are both engaged in useful pursuits. But I am a teacher. I shall join the group assembled to learn." So he sat with the group of students.

To understand the Prophet's role as a *murabbi*, let me share with you some of the principles deduced from the teachings of the Prophet (SAS) which a *murabbi* should adopt during the process of educating people. To gain a following, most leaders and educators make tempting promises to their followers. They promise things like power, wealth, position, or a bright future. However, the Prophet (SAS) made no such promises to his students and followers. He conquered their minds and hearts and promised them Allah's good pleasure and paradise, and to gain that, his followers sacrificed themselves in his way willingly. He always sought to prepare them for the eternal peace and permanent bliss while himself setting for them a good example of that peace and bliss.

The Prophet (SAS) practiced what he preached and guided people in every aspect of life. He practiced with utmost sincerity and honesty what he communicated to others. History has witnessed many leading persons who, since they did not practice what they preached or propagated, did not have a large, devoted following. Their ideas did not have an enduring effect on people, and the systems they established did not last long. However, the Prophet (SAS) endured all kinds of hardships and persecutions for no reason other than conveying Allah's message to people. The hardships endured by the Prophet (SAS) included things such as sleeping on the hard earth, suffering hunger for several consecutive days, being expelled from his homeland, becoming subject to mockeries and insults, and so on.

A *murabbi* must possess high moral conduct. Addressing His beloved Prophet, Allah (SWT) says in *Surat al-Qalam*,

$$\text{وَإِنَّكَ لَعَلى خُلُقٍ عَظِيمٍ} \bigcirc$$

*And you are surely on an exalted standard of character. (al-Qalam, 68:4)*

The Prophet (SAS) appeared in the heart of a desert, which was one of the most uncivilized parts of the inhabited world and where people were immersed in the worst kinds of immorality. Who do you think brought him up as the most virtuous human being with the highest morality and best conduct? His teacher was God, as the Prophet (SAS) himself said, "My Lord educated me and taught me good manners, and how well he educated me and how beautifully He taught me good manners!" On another occasion he said, "Indeed I was sent to make perfect the moral conduct."

A *murabbi* must know his people very well to educate them and urge them to the realization of a cause. The Prophet (SAS) knew everyone to whom he would convey his message. He knew the person's character, abilities, shortcomings, feelings, bent of mind, and level of understanding. Besides, he also knew very well how to act in certain conditions and gave the best decision in times of crisis. He succeeded in bringing the most refined, well-mannered, and civilized society out of an extremely backward, uncivilized, and rough people of the seventh century Arabian Peninsula.

He made them teachers and masters, especially, to the civilized nations. He conquered their minds, spirits, hearts, and souls, and became the beloved of hearts, the teacher of minds, the trainer of souls, and the ruler of spirits. Through his limitless love, compassion, forgiveness, and tolerance, he made ruthless, warmongering people into the best community in human history. May Allah (SWT) give us the *tawfeeq* to follow in the footsteps of our beloved Prophet Muhammad (SAS).

When correcting people's mistakes, there is another cardinal rule, and that is to remain calm when dealing with their mistakes, especially when being too harsh could make matters worse and do more harm than good. Let me narrate to you two stories from the *seerah*.

Anas ibn Malik, said, "While we were in the mosque with the Messenger of Allah, a Bedouin came and stood urinating in the mosque. The companions of the Messenger of Allah said, 'Stop it! Stop it!' But the Messenger of Allah said, 'Do not interrupt him. Leave him alone.' So they left him until he had finished urinating, then the Messenger of Allah called him and explained to him that in mosques, it was not right to do anything like urinating or defecating, and that mosques are only for remembering Allah, praying, reading the Qur'an, and so on. Then he commanded a man who was there to bring a bucket of water and the place was cleaned." The principle which the Prophet (SAS) followed in dealing with this mistake was to treat the man gently, and not to be harsh with him.

In another story, Imam Ahmad recorded Abu Ummah saying that a young man came to the Prophet (SAS) and said, "O Messenger of Allah! Give me permission to commit *zina* (unlawful sex)." The people surrounded him and rebuked him, saying, "Stop! Stop!" But the Prophet said, "Come close." The young man came to him, and he said, "Sit down." So he sat down. The Prophet said, "Would you like it (meaning the act of *zina*) for your mother?" He said, "No, by Allah, may I be ransomed for you." The Prophet said, "Neither do the people like it for their mothers!" The Prophet said, "Would you like it for your daughter?" He said, "No, by Allah, may I be ransomed for you." The Prophet said, "Neither do the people like it for their daughters!" The Prophet said, "Would you like it for your sister?" He said, "No, by Allah, may I be ransomed for you." The Prophet said, "Neither do the people like it for their sisters!" The Prophet said, "Would you like it for your paternal aunt?" He said, "No, by Allah, O Allah's Messenger! May I be ransomed for you." The Prophet said, "Neither do the people like it for their paternal aunts!" The Prophet said, "Would you like it for your maternal aunt?" He said, "No, by Allah, O Allah's Messenger! May I be ransomed for you." The Prophet said, "Neither do the people like it for their maternal aunts!" Then the Prophet (SAS) put his hand on him and said, "O Allah, forgive his sin, purify his heart and guard his chastity." After that, the young man never paid attention to anything of that nature.

In the process of teaching and guiding, Muhammad (SAS) explained the truth to the people. Convincing people of the truth of what we teach to them and making it approved by them wholeheartedly is of vital importance in good education. This is what the Prophet (SAS) did. Allah (SWT) says in the Qur`an:

$$لَقَدْ كَانَ لَكُمْ فِي رَسُولِ اللَّهِ أُسْوَةٌ حَسَنَةٌ لِمَنْ كَانَ يَرْجُو اللَّهَ وَالْيَوْمَ الآخِرَ وَذَكَرَ اللَّهَ كَثِيرًا ۞$$

*You have an excellent model in the Messenger of Allah, for all who put their hope in Allah and the Last Day and remember Allah much. (al-Ahzab, 33:21)*

Understanding the Prophet's methodology in guiding human beings is of great importance for every *murabbi*, because the Prophet (SAS) was guided by his Lord, and his words and deeds were supported by revelation. His methods are wiser and more effective, and using his approach is the best way to get people to respond positively.

• 71 •

# PROTECTING OURSELVES FROM ATHEISM

The topic of my *khutbah* today may seem a little strange because it's rarely discussed in our mosques. However, the topic is both relevant and crucial to our times and calls for serious thinking and discussion. My *khutbah* today is on the topic of "Protecting Ourselves from Atheism." Atheism is the doctrine or belief that there is no God. You may be wondering what atheism has got to do with us. *Al-hamduli-llah*, we are all Muslims, and we all believe in Allah (SWT).

Studies conducted by the Pew Research Center show that Islam is the fastest growing religion in the world. But at the same time, according to the Center's 2012 global study of 230 countries and territories, 16% of the world's population is not affiliated with any religion. Some studies indicate that atheism as an ideology, has been spreading at a very fast rate.

Shockingly and regretfully, atheism has struck the Muslim community as well. Some ex-Muslims have lost faith in God altogether and don't believe any longer. In a statement, the "Council of Ex-Muslims of Britain" has claimed that thousands of ex-Muslims in Britain are living in fear of violent revenge for abandoning the Islamic faith. In contrast, others are afraid to admit they no longer believe. So the topic needs to be addressed.

Generally, while addressing this topic, it's always directed toward atheists. Believers often argue with atheists and try to explain to them the existence of God from a philosophical, rational, or scientific perspective. But that's not the topic I want to discuss today. Today's discussion is not for atheists. It is for my fellow Muslim brothers and sisters. I'm going to talk about what we can do as Muslims to protect our hearts from the onslaught of atheism. Belief and disbelief are matters of the heart. Whether we realize it or not, atheism is a huge problem. It's a problem that will take a Muslim away from Allah (SWT), from his *deen*, and direct him toward hellfire We seek refuge in Allah (SWT) from that situation.

Initially, there are four points that I want to highlight. Firstly, why is atheism spreading? Secondly, why is it important to choose Islam as a way of life, and not to be just Muslims by chance? Thirdly, why is it important to seek authentic knowledge? And fourthly, why is it important to have a close connection with our Creator—Allah (SWT)? The first point is the problem, and the remaining three points are the solutions to the problem.

Doubt about the existence of God is a disease of the heart. It's the result of a heart that is disconnected from Allah (SWT), a heart that is spiritually dead or almost dead. Why is atheism spreading when the bulk of humans history have always believed in God? They may have been followers of any religion, but they have believed in God. Why is it in the 20th century, and more so in the 21st century, that we see entire countries and systems of government that are atheistic?

Communism is an atheistic concept. Its entire system revolves around atheism. China has the most atheists in the entire world. For the first time ever, Norway now has more people who do not believe in God than those who do. In the US, a nation whose dollar bill states, "In God We Trust," belief in the Christian deity is also at an all-time low. Research found that compared to 1980, nearly twice as many Americans in 2014 said they did not believe in God. Why does this happen? This is because people have lost faith in their religion. People find numerous contradictions in the Bible. Except for the Qur`an, none of the other scriptures is available in their original forms. People also lose faith when they see religious leaders advocating and doing things that go against the teachings of their scriptures.

Having nowhere to turn to, people get inclined to atheism. And this is why when you read stories of brothers and sisters who have converted to Islam, atheism was usually a part of their journey because they had lost faith in their religion. Either they had not heard about Islam, or they had heard only negative stereotypes about it as being a religion of hate and violence. There are many stories of people being in a particular religion, then losing their faith in that religion, then becoming atheists, and then converting to Islam. So, one of the primary reasons why atheism is spreading is that people have lost faith in their religion. And this is happening in the Muslim community as well.

While teaching recitation of the Qur`an, when some of the teachers beat children to discipline them, some of the children end up either being disillusioned by Islam or getting alienated from it when they grow up. The action of beating children while teaching them has nothing to do with Islam or Islamic practice. There is not a single Prophetic narration that supports this action. On the contrary, those who teach and preach the message of truth must be soft-hearted. What does Allah (SWT) say in the Qur`an about the Prophet's behavior toward his companions?

فَبِمَا رَحْمَةٍ مِنَ اللَّهِ لِنْتَ لَهُمْ وَلَوْ كُنْتَ فَظًّا غَلِيظَ الْقَلْبِ لَانْفَضُّوا مِنْ حَوْلِكَ ◯

*It is a mercy from Allah that you deal with them gently. Had you been harsh and cruel-hearted, they would have scattered from around you. (Aal 'Imran, 3:159)*

The noble companions of the Prophet would have run away from Islam if the one presenting Islam to them had been hard and harsh upon them. What did Allah (SWT) say to Musa (AS) and Haroon (AS) when sending them to Fir'awn—one of the most tyrant and cruel of human beings ever to live?

اذْهَبَا إِلَى فِرْعَوْنَ إِنَّهُ طَغَى ◯ فَقُولَا لَهُ قَوْلًا لَيِّنًا لَعَلَّهُ يَتَذَكَّرُ أَوْ يَخْشَى ◯

*Go, both of you to Pharaoh, for he has transgressed all bounds. But speak gently to him; perhaps he may take heed or even feel afraid. (Ta Ha, 20:43-44)*

So, we should understand that harshness when dealing with people, especially when conveying to them the message of Islam, chases them away from religion and may well drive them toward atheism.

Another reason why atheism is spreading in the modern world is that people find religion coming in the way of fulfillment of their desires—their *nafs*. They choose their *nafs* over their *deen*. Muslims, for example, are prohibited from fornicating, eating pork, drinking alcohol, gambling, dealing in usury, or engaging in any immoral or unlawful activity. Those with weak *iman* and with no or little knowledge of the Qur`an and Sunnah sometimes begin to question the justification of these prohibitions and prefer to abandon the religion because it stops them from following their desires. And this attitude comes from our lifestyle, living in secular Western societies. But we now see that this is becoming a global phenomenon. The media around us is all about fulfilling our desires. When the fulfillment of desires becomes the object of worship, that is when people start going astray.

أَفَرَأَيْتَ مَنِ اتَّخَذَ إِلَهَهُ هَوَاهُ وَأَضَلَّهُ اللَّهُ عَلَى عِلْمٍ وَخَتَمَ عَلَى سَمْعِهِ وَقَلْبِهِ وَجَعَلَ عَلَى بَصَرِهِ غِشَاوَةً ◯

*Have you seen someone who has taken his desires as his God? God knowingly lets him go astray and seals off his hearing and his heart and places a covering over his eyesight. (al-Jathiya, 45:23)*

This is enough about the problem. Now, let's go into the solution in the second part of the *khutbah*. May Allah (SWT) save us from the *fitna* of atheism.

Brothers and Sisters! Are we Muslims by chance or by choice? If someone asks you, "Are you a Muslim?" The immediate answer will be, "Yes, I am." But what if someone asks you, "Why are you a Muslim"? This will make you pause and start to think. For most of us, the answer might be, "It's because I was born and raised in a Muslim family." But is that the correct answer? What if we weren't born in a Muslim family? What if we were born in a Jewish, Christian, Hindu, or any other non-Muslim family? Would we still be Muslims?

Why many Muslims are unable to take Islam seriously, unable to practice Islam, and unable to love Allah (SWT) is because they haven't chosen Islam yet. They have only adopted Islam as a culture. So, the first step to solving our problem is to stop equating Islam with culture and to embrace Islam completely and whole-heartedly as a way of life.

$$يَا أَيُّهَا الَّذِينَ آمَنُوا ادْخُلُوا فِي السِّلْمِ كَافَّةً وَلَا تَتَّبِعُوا خُطُوَاتِ الشَّيْطَانِ إِنَّهُ لَكُمْ عَدُوٌّ مُبِينٌ ○$$

*O you who believe, enter Islam completely (whole-heartedly), and do not follow the footsteps of Satan. Surely, he is an open enemy for you. (al-Baqara, 2:208)*

One of the reasons why a Muslim woman may choose to distance herself from Islam and become a radical feminist is because she might have become a victim of domestic violence. She might have been forced to marry someone whom she didn't want to marry. She might have been stopped from going to the *masjid*. But there are some Muslims who do these things in the name of Islam. The Qur`an promotes good treatment of one's wife: she is to be honored and treated kindly, even when one no longer feels love in one's heart toward her. Allah (SWT) says,

$$وَعَاشِرُوهُنَّ بِالْمَعْرُوفِ فَإِنْ كَرِهْتُمُوهُنَّ فَعَسَى أَنْ تَكْرَهُوا شَيْئًا وَيَجْعَلَ اللَّهُ فِيهِ خَيْرًا كَثِيرًا ○$$

*And live with them honorably. If you dislike them, it may be that you dislike a thing and Allah brings through it a great deal of good. (an-Nisa`, 4:19)*

The Prophet (SAS) is reported to have invalidated a marriage in which the father had forced his daughter to marry someone she did not want to marry. He is also reported to have told men not to stop women from going to the *masjid*. People doing such actions without clear knowledge erroneously think that all this is part of Islam, while it is not. Instead, such and similar actions go a long way in alienating Muslim women from Islam.

Also, there are Muslims living in countries and communities across the globe who believe in all types of superstitions about things that bring good luck and bad luck. When people do not know what Islam teaches and are unaware of the un-Islamic cultural practices taken from here and there are, they begin to mistake culture for religion.

And this brings me to the second solution to the problem of atheism, and that is the importance of seeking authentic knowledge—knowledge that helps us to separate wrong cultural practices that have nothing to do with Islam from real Islam. Each one of us has an obligation to seek that knowledge and to teach it to our family members. What are some of the ways to acquire authentic knowledge? The first is to learn the Qur'an and to fulfill its obligations. The Qur'an demands of every Muslim five obligations. A Muslim is required (1) to believe in the Qur'an, (2) to read it, (3) to understand it, (4) to act upon its teachings, and (5) to convey its message to others.

We also need to learn and follow the Prophetic teachings through the Prophet's divinely guided lifestyle called the Sunnah. After all, his character was the true reflection of the Qur'an.

This brings me to the final point. If we want to protect our hearts from doubt and disbelief, we have to develop a strong relationship with our Creator. One of the ways to do this is to do quality *'ibada* (worship). And one of the ways to do that is through *salah*. We should try our best to offer our *salah* with concentration and understanding. We should try to wake up before *Fajr* and offer at least two *rak'as* of *tahajjud*. We should cry to Allah (SWT) and make *du'a*' to Him from the bottom of our hearts and not just mechanically without humbling ourselves. Needless to add, it is incumbent upon us to do all other acts of *'ibada* or modes of worship in the best possible manner.

When our *'ibada* has quality, we will then *in sha' Allah* experience a closeness to Allah (SWT) and taste the sweetness of *iman*. We'll experience the happiness that comes when a *du'a*' is answered. A person going through such experiences will never doubt the existence of a Supreme Being. True belief comes from practicing the *deen*.

May Allah (SWT) protect our hearts from any tinge of atheism and disbelief and doubts about our noble *deen*. *Ameen*.

اللَّهُمَّ حَبِّبْ إِلَيْنَا الْإِيمَانَ وَزَيِّنْهُ فِي قُلُوبِنَا، وَكَرِّهْ إِلَيْنَا الْكُفْرَ وَالْفُسُوقَ وَالْعِصْيَانَ، وَاجْعَلْنَا مِنَ الرَّاشِدِينَ ⃝

*O Allah! Make iman beloved to us and beautify it in our hearts, and make disbelief, sinfulness and disobedience hateful to us, and make us from among the rightly-guided ones.*

# PURIFICATION OF THE SOUL
## (TAZKIYAT AN-NAFS)

In today's *khutbah*, I want to share with you some thoughts on the concept of *tazkiyat an-nafs* or purification of the soul, which is the basis for the development and improvement of the personality. *Tazkiyat an-nafs* is a long, pro-active, and uphill task. It is not a quick-fix formula. It is not something that can be achieved overnight. It can be a difficult process, especially at the start.

Literally, the term *tazkiya* encompasses two meanings: one is to purify while the other is to improve and develop toward the height of perfection. Technically, it conveys the sense of checking oneself from erroneous tendencies and beliefs and turning them to the path of virtue and piety.

Misunderstanding of the concept of *tazkiya* becomes evident when people look for quick methods of becoming more spiritual. *Tazkiya* is not accidental. It must be based on the good and sincere intention to please Allah (SWT) and draw near to Him. The process of *tazkiya* can't be sustained if done for any other reason.

One of the most important tasks for which our beloved Prophet Muhammad (SAS) was sent was to purify the souls of people. Speaking of this mission, Allah (SWT) says,

هُوَ الَّذِي بَعَثَ فِي الْأُمِّيِّينَ رَسُولًا مِنْهُمْ يَتْلُو عَلَيْهِمْ آيَاتِهِ وَيُزَكِّيهِمْ وَيُعَلِّمُهُمُ الْكِتَابَ وَالْحِكْمَةَ وَإِنْ كَانُوا مِنْ قَبْلُ لَفِي ضَلَالٍ مُبِينٍ ۝

*It is He who has raised among the unlettered people a messenger from among themselves who recites His revelations to them, and purifies them, and teaches them the Book and wisdom, for they had formerly been clearly misguided. (al-Jumuah, 62:2)*

Indeed, the success of a person has been linked with the purity of his soul.

قَدْ أَفْلَحَ مَنْ زَكَّاهَا ۝ وَقَدْ خَابَ مَنْ دَسَّاهَا ۝

*He who purifies it (i.e., the soul) will indeed be successful. And he who corrupts it is sure to fail. (ash-Shams, 91:9-10)*

This illustrates that Allah (SWT) created the human soul with both evil and good inclinations and gave man with the ability to distinguish between the two. *Falah* or eternal success is achieved by choosing good instead of evil and striving to make it prevail. The person undertaking *tazkiya* must be true to himself, to others, and to Allah

(SWT). All human effort at *tazkiya* should always be accompanied by supplication for Allah's intervention without which human effort will bear no fruit. Allah (SWT) says,

أَلَمْ تَرَ إِلَى الَّذِينَ يُزَكُّونَ أَنْفُسَهُمْ بَلِ اللَّهُ يُزَكِّي مَنْ يَشَاءُ وَلَا يُظْلَمُونَ فَتِيلًا ◯

*Have you not seen those who consider themselves pure? It is indeed Allah who purifies whoever He pleases, and none shall be wronged by as much as a hair's breadth. (an-Nisa`, 4:49)*

On the other hand, it is wrong for a human to make no effort and passively expect Allah (SWT) to intervene. Humans must play their roles before expecting Allah's help. The human can do a lot to refine the soul.

Useful knowledge is one of the primary means to purify the soul. Any knowledge that brings man closer to Allah (SWT), increases man's consciousness of Allah (SWT), and guides man to do good deeds is useful knowledge. The Prophet (SAS) used to make a *du'a`* saying,

اللَّهُمَّ إِنِّي أَعُوذُ بِكَ مِنْ عِلْمٍ لاَ يَنْفَعُ وَمِنْ قَلْبٍ لاَ يَخْشَعُ وَمِنْ نَفْسٍ لاَ تَشْبَعُ وَمِنْ دَعْوَةٍ لاَ يُسْتَجَابُ لَهَا ◯

*"O Allah! I seek your refuge from knowledge that is not useful, from a heart that does not humble, from a soul that is not satisfied and from a supplication that is not granted."*

Ibn Rajab al-Hanbali said, "A sign of the people of knowledge is that they are humble, they hate reverence and people's high remarks of them, they do not look down on people, they are always seeking the hereafter taking from this world only what they need, and they are constantly worshipping Allah. The more knowledge they have, the more fearful, the more humble, and the more submissive to Allah they become." We read in *Surat Fatir*:

إِنَّمَا يَخْشَى اللَّهَ مِنْ عِبَادِهِ الْعُلَمَاءُ ◯

*Only those of His servants who possess knowledge fear Allah. (Fatir, 35:28)*

Some of the effects of useful knowledge in purifying the soul are: (1) correct and firm belief, the fulfillment of acts of worship, (2) avoiding the forbidden, (3) being conscious of the Creator, and (4) constant meditation about the creation. So we should all help one another to acquire useful knowledge through learning and teaching. This way, *tazkiya* or soul purification is collective and continuous until we meet Allah (SWT).

Purification of the soul is based upon two principles: (1) *iman* (faith), and (2) righteous actions. Corruption in *iman* and corruption in righteous actions corrupts the soul. *Iman* is, in general related to things of the unseen. The unseen that we believe in is something that the mind cannot perceive. For example, we can't perceive the nature of angels, and we can't perceive the qualities of how paradise and hell are. We can't see Allah (SWT), and the mind can't perceive the nature of Allah (SWT). The only way we know something about Allah (SWT) is through the Qur`an and authentic Sunnah. Likewise, righteous actions, which Allah (SWT) loves and rewards us for, and evil actions that Allah (SWT) dislikes and may punish us for, can only be known by knowing what Allah (SWT) and the Prophet (SAS) have commanded and what they have prohibited. Therefore purification of the soul is to be undertaken within this Prophetic paradigm of *iman* and righteous action. Islam is a practical religion. Good actions help in the achievement of *tazkiya* because they wipe out sins. Allah says in the Qur`an,

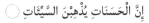

*Good actions drive away bad actions.* (Hud, 11:114)

May Allah (SWT) make us among those who strive to purify our souls through *iman* and righteous actions. As to the conceptualization of the human soul, there are, according to Imam al-Ghazali, four aspects of a man that signify his spiritual identity. These are the *nafs*, the *'aql*, the *rooh*, and the *qalb*. All of these are intertwined and influence man in his behavior.

The *nafs* is like the ego that gives rise to reactions to the environment. The *nafs* is developed through the lifespan. It may be reflective of an animalistic side of the individual at its lowest untrained level. The *nafs* has been likened to an animal that, if untrained, may not be very pleasant. However, if one were to train an animal, it can be of service to its master. From the Islamic perspective, the *nafs* is not intrinsically bad. If it learns good habits, then it will be of service to the individual. If it learns bad ones, it can be a barrier to one's growth. The three types of *nafs* are: (1) the *nafs al-ammara* (the unruly animal self that dictates evil), the *nafs al-lawwama* (the self-reproaching soul), and the *nafs al-mutma`inna* (the satisfied soul).

The *'aql* is the rational faculty of man. It is home to logic, reason, and acquired intellectual beliefs. The *rooh* is the spirit of man that, if kept healthy, allows one to live a meaningful and wholesome life. Finally, the *qalb* is the heart, also called the soul. The heart is where the effects of the other three elements manifest. The heart may also be home to spiritual diseases such as arrogance, jealousy, greed, and stinginess, which are results of the evil inclinations of the *nafs*. To remove these sicknesses of the heart, one must work toward modifying the inclinations of the *nafs* toward good, restructuring and acquiring positive thoughts in the *'aql*, and feeding the spirit through remembrance of Allah (SWT).

The person who strives toward *ihsan* begins with the challenge of freeing himself from the influence of *Shaytan* and the *nafs al-ammara*, which commands one to sensual pleasures and lusts and pulls the heart (*qalb*) in a downward direction. It is the resting place of evil and the source of blameworthy morals and bad actions. In its primitive stage, the *nafs* incites us to commit evil. In the Qur`an, Allah (SWT) informs us about Yusuf (AS) saying,

$$وَمَا أُبَرِّئُ نَفْسِي إِنَّ النَّفْسَ لَأَمَّارَةٌ بِالسُّوءِ إِلَّا مَا رَحِمَ رَبِّي ○$$

*I do not pretend to be blameless, for man's very soul incites him to evil unless my Lord shows mercy: He is most forgiving, most merciful. (Yusuf, 12:53)*

The sense of the word *lawwama* is that of resisting wrongdoing and asking for Allah's forgiveness after we become conscious of wrongdoing. The original reference to this state is found in *Surat al-Qiyama*.

$$وَلَا أُقْسِمُ بِالنَّفْسِ اللَّوَّامَةِ ○$$

*And I swear by the self-reproaching soul. (al-Qiyama, 75:2)*

At this stage, we begin to understand the negative effects of our habitual self-centered approach to the world, even though we cannot yet change. Our misdeeds now begin to become hateful to us. We enter a cycle of going wrong, regretting our mistakes, going wrong again, and seeking Allah's forgiveness for our lapses. In the Qur`an Allah (SWT) explains how one can achieve the state of the *nafs al-mutma`inna* or the satisfied soul in *Surat ar-Ra'd*:

$$الَّذِينَ آمَنُوا وَتَطْمَئِنُّ قُلُوبُهُم بِذِكْرِ اللَّهِ أَلَا بِذِكْرِ اللَّهِ تَطْمَئِنُّ الْقُلُوبُ ○$$

*Those who have iman and whose hearts find peace in the remembrance of Allah. Only in the remembrance of Allah can the heart find peace. (ar-Ra'd, 13:28)*

*Tazkiya* and moral development aim to attain *falah* or success, thus realizing the *nafs al-mutma`inna*. On this level, one is firm in one's faith and leaves bad manners behind. The soul becomes at peace. It remains pleased with Allah (SWT) and satisfied with His decrees. In *Surat al-Fajr*, Allah (SWT) addresses the peaceful soul in the following words:

$$يَا أَيَّتُهَا النَّفْسُ الْمُطْمَئِنَّةُ ○ ارْجِعِي إِلَى رَبِّكِ رَاضِيَةً مَّرْضِيَّةً ○ فَادْخُلِي فِي عِبَادِي ○ وَادْخُلِي جَنَّتِي ○$$

*O soul at peace, return to your Lord well pleased and pleasing (to Him); join My servants; and enter My paradise. (al-Fajr, 89: 27-30)*

If man travels the path of purification, Allah (SWT) will aid and guide him. As Allah maintains in *Surat al-'Ankabut*,

$$وَالَّذِينَ جَاهَدُوا فِينَا لَنَهْدِيَنَّهُمْ سُبُلَنَا وَإِنَّ اللَّهَ لَمَعَ الْمُحْسِنِينَ ○$$

*We will surely guide in Our ways those who strive hard for Our cause, Truly, Allah is with the righteous. (al-'Ankabut, 29:69)*

May Allah (SWT) make us among such people who strive to purify themselves, both outwardly and inwardly, physically and spiritually. *Allahumma ameen.*

## • 73 •

## QUALITIES OF THE SLAVES OF THE MOST COMPASSIONATE

Today's *khutbah* is on the topic of sifaat *'ibaad ar-Rahman* translated in English as "qualities of the slaves of the Most Compassionate." It is to be remembered that man's voluntary obedience and worship of Allah (SWT) based on his free will is far superior to the submission of other creatures to the laws of nature ordained for them by their Creator. The latter has no choice but to obey. Hence, Allah (SWT) designating individuals as His slaves is an act of conferring them with the highest of honors. We, too, should aspire to earn this title. Prophet Muhammad (SAS) said: "Do not exaggerate in praising me as the Christians praised the son of Mary, for I am only a slave. So, call me the slave of Allah and His messenger."

While the characteristics of *'ibad ar-Rahman* are mentioned in numerous verses of the Qur'an, they are especially highlighted in verses 63 to 74 of *Surat al-Furqan*. A reflection upon these verses provides us with an opportunity to adorn ourselves with the qualities of such believers whom Allah (SWT) has praised and honored. Allah (SWT) says,

وَعِبَادُ الرَّحْمَنِ الَّذِينَ يَمْشُونَ عَلَى الْأَرْضِ هَوْنًا وَإِذَا خَاطَبَهُمُ الْجَاهِلُونَ قَالُوا سَلَامًا ۝

*The slaves of the Most Compassionate are those who walk on the earth humbly, and when the foolish address them improperly, they only respond with peace. (al-Furqan, 25:63)*

The first characteristic of the true servants of Allah (SWT) to which attention has been drawn here is their gait or the way they walk. This is because the gait indicates the character of an individual. If a man walks in a humble and dignified way, as opposed to an arrogant, vain, and proud manner, it shows that he is a humble, modest, and gentle person. More often than not, arrogant people are seen to walk in a very boastful manner. To walk humbly is a Qur`anic injunction.

Moreover, the 'ibaad ar-Rahman do not believe in vengeance, even though they may have to deal with the ignorant people who behave rudely and insolently toward them. If they happen to come across such people, they wish them peace and turn away. Describing them further, Allah says,

$$وَالَّذِينَ يَبِيتُونَ لِرَبِّهِمْ سُجَّدًا وَقِيَامًا ○$$

*Those who pass the night prostrating and standing before their Lord. (al-Furqan, 25:64)*

That is, they neither spend their nights in fun and merry-making nor in gossips and telling tales, nor in doing wicked deeds, for these are the ways of the ignorant people. The 'ibad ar-Rahman pass their nights in worshipping and remembering Allah (SWT) as much as they can.

$$وَالَّذِينَ يَقُولُونَ رَبَّنَا اصْرِفْ عَنَّا عَذَابَ جَهَنَّمَ إِنَّ عَذَابَهَا كَانَ غَرَامًا ○ إِنَّهَا سَاءَتْ مُسْتَقَرًّا وَمُقَامًا ○$$

*Those who say, 'Our Lord, avert from us the punishment of hell; its punishment is inescapable pain. It is an evil home and a foul resting place. (al-Furqan, 25:65-66)*

That is, their worship has not made them so vain and proud to presume that they are the beloved ones of Allah (SWT) and that the fire of hell will not touch them. Meanwhile, despite their worship and good deeds, they are filled with fear of hell. They pray to Allah (SWT) for safety, as they don't depend upon their work for success in the hereafter but upon Allah's mercy.

$$وَالَّذِينَ إِذَا أَنْفَقُوا لَمْ يُسْرِفُوا وَلَمْ يَقْتُرُوا وَكَانَ بَيْنَ ذَلِكَ قَوَامًا ○$$

*They are those who are neither wasteful nor niggardly when they spend but keep to a just balance. (al-Furqan, 25:67)*

That is, they adopt the golden mean between the two extremes in spending their money. They neither go beyond necessity in expenditure nor live in wretched circumstances to save and hoard money. The way taught by Islam is the golden mean between the two extremes. They are prudent. The Prophet (SAS) has said that it is a sign of wisdom to adopt the golden mean in one's living.

$$وَالَّذِينَ لَا يَدْعُونَ مَعَ اللَّهِ إِلَهًا آخَرَ وَلَا يَقْتُلُونَ النَّفْسَ الَّتِي حَرَّمَ اللَّهُ إِلَّا بِالْحَقِّ وَلَا يَزْنُونَ وَمَنْ يَفْعَلْ ذَلِكَ يَلْقَ أَثَامًا ○$$

*Those who never invoke any other deity besides Allah, nor take a life which Allah has made sacred, except with the right to do so, nor commit adultery. Anyone who does that will receive a severe punishment. (al-Furqan, 25:68)*

They keep themselves far away from the three major sins mentioned in this verse. These are: associating partners with Allah (SWT) (*shirk*), murder, and fornication or adultery. The first of these major sins is *shirk*. It is the worst sin that one could commit. Allah (SWT) is willing to pardon any person for any sin except the sin of *shirk*.

إِنَّ اللَّهَ لَا يَغْفِرُ أَنْ يُشْرَكَ بِهِ وَيَغْفِرُ مَا دُونَ ذَلِكَ لِمَنْ يَشَاءُ وَمَنْ يُشْرِكْ بِاللَّهِ فَقَدْ ضَلَّ ضَلَالًا بَعِيدًا ۝

*Surely, Allah will not forgive the ascribing of partners to Him. He forgives whoever He will for anything other than that. Whoever ascribes partners to Allah has strayed far indeed. (an-Nisa`, 4:116)*

The *'ibaad ar-Rahman* call on their Lord in all aspects pertaining to their lives. For every matter, they seek the help of Allah (SWT) and no one else. They understand that Allah (SWT) created them and that only Allah (SWT) has the sole supreme power to help them when they are stricken with any calamity or adversity. If they lose the means of their livelihood, they cry out to Allah (SWT), who is the best of the providers. The Qur`an is full of verses that ask people to invoke Allah (SWT) alone as He listens and responds to the one who calls Him.

The *'ibaad ar-Rahman* do not take a life which Allah (SWT) has made sacred except for a just cause. This echoes the commandment that appears in *Surat al-Isra`*.

وَلَا تَقْتُلُوا النَّفْسَ الَّتِي حَرَّمَ اللَّهُ إِلَّا بِالْحَقِّ ۝

*Do not take life, which Allah has made sacred, except with the right to do so. (al-Isra`, 17:33)*

What does this commandment imply? A person's life may be taken only in a few very exceptional cases. If Muslims go to war to defend their religion (*deen*), their country, their property, and their honor against the enemy, they are allowed to kill the combatants who committed aggression against them. Another occasion to take life would be in the case of a murderer convicted in court after due process of law. The murderer, unless proven to be insane, faces the death penalty under Islamic law. The death penalty for committing murder is found in many countries, including the USA. Punishment by death for taking someone's life without a just cause is also found in the Mosaic Law.

The *'ibaad ar-Rahman* also do not commit fornication or adultery. This act is an act of immorality (*fahsha`*), and a sin against God in all the three Abrahamic faiths (Judaism, Christianity, and Islam). The *'ibaad ar-Rahman* abide by the Qur`anic injunction which says,

وَلَا تَقْرَبُوا الزِّنَا إِنَّهُ كَانَ فَاحِشَةً وَسَاءَ سَبِيلًا ۝

*And do not go near to zina. It is an indecent act and an evil way.* (al-Isra`, 17:32)

They are modest, righteous, and pious. They do not renounce the world but lead a balanced and healthy life. They do not suppress their sexual urge by not marrying. Rather, they lawfully satisfy their sexual urge through marriage. In verse sixty-nine of *Surat al-Furqan* Allah tells us,

يُضَاعَفْ لَهُ الْعَذَابُ يَوْمَ الْقِيَامَةِ وَيَخْلُدْ فِيهِ مُهَانًا ۝

*Multiplied for him shall be the torment on the Day of Resurrection, and he shall therein abide disgraced.* (al-Furqan, 25:69)

That is his punishment will never come to an end, but it will continue being inflicted, and he will be accountable for each of his major and minor sins none of which will be pardoned.

إِلاَّ مَنْ تَابَ وَآمَنَ وَعَمِلَ عَمَلًا صَالِحًا فَأُولَئِكَ يُبَدِّلُ اللَّهُ سَيِّئَاتِهِمْ حَسَنَاتٍ وَكَانَ اللَّهُ غَفُورًا رَحِيمًا ۝

*Except for those who repent and believe and do good deeds. Allah will change the evil deeds of such people into good ones: He is most forgiving and most merciful.* (al-Furqan, 25:70)

This is good news for those people who sincerely repent and reform themselves, for they will have the benefit of the general amnesty. This amnesty not only redeems them but fills them with hope.

وَمَنْ تَابَ وَعَمِلَ صَالِحًا فَإِنَّهُ يَتُوبُ إِلَى اللَّهِ مَتَابًا ۝

*He who repents and does good deeds has truly turned to Allah.* (al-Furqan, 25:71)

The exception to this severe punishment is only for those who sincerely repent, believe, and mend their ways by doing righteous deeds. May Allah (SWT) bless each one of us and keep each one of us on the right path.

Brothers and sisters! The other great qualities of the *'ibaad ar-Rahman* are mentioned in verses 72 to 74 of *Surat al-Furqan*.

وَالَّذِينَ لَا يَشْهَدُونَ الزُّورَ وَإِذَا مَرُّوا بِاللَّغْوِ مَرُّوا كِرَامًا -وَالَّذِينَ إِذَا ذُكِّرُوا بِآيَاتِ رَبِّهِمْ لَمْ يَخِرُّوا عَلَيْهَا صُمًّا وَعُمْيَانًا ۝ -وَالَّذِينَ يَقُولُونَ رَبَّنَا هَبْ لَنَا مِنْ أَزْوَاجِنَا وَذُرِّيَّاتِنَا قُرَّةَ أَعْيُنٍ وَاجْعَلْنَا لِلْمُتَّقِينَ إِمَامًا

*And those who do not bear false witness, and who, when they pass by some idle talk, pass by with dignity; and when they are reminded of the revelations of their Lord, do not fall at them deaf and blind; and who are prone to pray: Our Lord! Grant us that our spouses and our offspring be a joy to our eyes, and do make us the leaders of the God-fearing.* (al-Furqan, 25:72-74)

Falsehood includes *kufr, shirk*, lies, and all acts of sin. The *'ibaad ar-Rahman* do not give evidence concerning a false thing to prove it right, when in fact, it is a falsehood. They have no intention to witness anything false, evil, or wicked as spectators. They pass by all that is vain, useless, and meaningless in a dignified manner as if it were a heap of filth. They do not stay there to enjoy the filth of moral impurity, obscenity, or foul language, nor do they intentionally go anywhere to hear or see or take part in any sort of filth.

They do not ignore the revelations of Allah (SWT), when they are recited to them for their caution. They do not turn a deaf ear to their teachings and message and do not deliberately close their eyes to the signs that they are asked to observe, but are deeply moved by them. They follow and practice what they are enjoined and refrain from what is forbidden.

They are concerned about the faith of their beloved ones. Therefore, while praying to Allah (SWT) asking for salvation, they pray for the salvation of their wives and children so that they become a source of comfort for them. Furthermore, they want to excel in piety, righteousness, and good works, so that they may lead the pious people in the propagation of virtue and piety in the world. This characteristics of the ʿibaad ar-Rahman are in great contrast to that of the disbelievers, who compete with one another for superiority only in worldly power and wealth.

May Allah (SWT) make us among the true righteous believers and among the ʿibaad ar-Rahman. Ameen.

## • 74 •

# *RAMADAN:* A BLESSED MONTH

All praises and thanks are due to Allah (SWT), who made us reach the month of Ramadan. Let us take a moment to ponder over the fact that some of our families, friends, and acquaintances are no longer here to celebrate Ramadan with us this year. They have left this world and returned to their Lord.

إِنَّا لِلَّهِ وَإِنَّا إِلَيْهِ رَاجِعُونَ ۝

*We belong to Allah, and to Him is our return. (al-Baqara, 2:156)*

Perhaps there may be some among us who may not live to witness another Ramadan.

Death is inevitable. Its time is decreed. And indeed, time is fleeting. It is running out. So, let us seize the opportunity to make the most out of this Ramadan. The Prophet (SAS), starting a whole two months before Ramadan, used to make a *du'a`* in these words:

اللَّهُمَّ بَارِكْ لَنَا فِي رَجَبٍ وَ شَعْبَانَ وَ بَلِّغْنَا رَمَضَانَ ○

*"O Allah, bless us in the months of Rajab and Sha`ban and make us reach Ramadan."*

*Al-hamduli-llah*, by the grace of Allah (SWT), we have reached Ramadan. Ramadan Mubarak to all of you. May Allah (SWT) bless you and your families and bless the Muslim *ummah* in this most special and precious month of Ramadan.

What makes this month so special? It is a month of infinite blessings from Allah (SWT). It is a month of patience. It is a month of generosity. It is a month of charity. Most importantly, it is a month of opportunities, which are not available throughout the year. It was in this month that the Qur`an was revealed. We learn through a hadeeth that the earlier scriptures—the scrolls (*suhuf*) of Ibraheem (AS), the *Tawrat* given to Musa (AS), the *Zaboor* given to Dawood (AS), and the *Injeel* given to 'Isa (AS)—were also revealed in the month of Ramadan. The Qur`an was revealed in two stages. The entire Qur`an, which is part of the *Umm al-Kitab* that contains other divine scriptures in the *Lawh al-Mahfoodh* (The Preserved Book), was sent down to the first earthly heaven on the Night of Power (*Laylat al-Qadr*), which falls in Ramadan.

إِنَّا أَنْزَلْنَاهُ فِي لَيْلَةِ الْقَدْرِ ○

*Truly We sent it down on the Night of Power. (al-Qadr, 97:1)*

Thereafter, under Allah's (SWT) command, the Qur`an was revealed gradually by Jibreel (AS) to Muhammad (SAS) over twenty-three years of his prophethood. Hence this is the month to rediscover the Qur`an, which is the guidance to mankind.

هُدًى لِلنَّاسِ وَبَيِّنَاتٍ مِنَ الْهُدَى وَالْفُرْقَانِ ○

*Guidance for mankind with clear proofs of guidance and the criterion. (al-Baqara, 2:185)*

This guidance distinguishes between right and wrong, between good and evil, and between truth (*haqq*) and falsehood (*batil*). It should be well understood that the Qur`an is the verbatim word of Allah (SWT). The Orientalists and other scholars have subjected the Qur`an to rigorous historical criticism to prove that it has undergone a process of revision and editing and hence cannot be authentic. All their efforts, however, have been futile. The human intervention, manipulation, and fabrication that other scriptures have gone through do not apply to the Qur`an. This last revelation and divine guidance for the entire humanity is preserved and protected from any change.

This protection has been undertaken by Allah (SWT) Himself, as stated in the Qur`an.

إِنَّا نَحْنُ نَزَّلْنَا الذِّكْرَ وَإِنَّا لَهُ لَحَافِظُونَ ◯

*It is We Who have sent down the Reminder and it is We Who will preserve it. (al-Hijr,*
*15:9)*

The purpose and timing of the revelation regarding fasting must be understood in the backdrop of the difficult situations the companions of the Prophet (SAS) had to encounter at Mecca before they emigrated to Medina. These, among others, included oppression, persecution, starvation, social and economic boycott, and living in a climate of fear. After the *hijra*, the believers had to be made ready for further challenges. They had to be organized into a group that could bravely and successfully engage with the polytheists of Mecca, who had evicted them from their houses and deprived them of their homes and belongings.

There was no general practice among the pagan Arabs to fast. While there were remnants of some rituals of hajj, *'umrah*, and *tawaf* remaining with them from the days of Ibraheem (AS), fasting was absent from their lives. However, they knew what fasting implied as they used to make their horses fast in the scorching heat of the desert. This enabled and trained the horses to endure long hours without eating and drinking during battles.

Initially, fasting was introduced as a voluntary act. It was not mandatory. It is narrated that the Prophet (SAS) found the Jews in Medina to be fasting on the 10th of *Muharram* ('Ashura') to commemorate the day of their freedom from the bondage of Fir'awn, and to thank Allah (SWT) for that. Henceforth, the Prophet (SAS) commanded the Muslims to fast on that day and another day preceding or following that day. Up to this time, fasting was a *sunnah* and not a *fard* or an obligatory act.

After the emigration to Medina, the *ayah* about obligatory fasting in the month of Ramadan was revealed in *Surat al-Baqara*.

فَمَنْ شَهِدَ مِنْكُمُ الشَّهْرَ فَلْيَصُمْهُ ◯

*Therefore, whoever of you is present in that month, should fast. (al-Baqara, 2:185)*

As-siyam literally means to restrain oneself and to abstain from something. As a term in the *shari'a*, *siyam* means to abstain from food, drink, and spousal relations with the purest of intentions just for the sake of Allah (SWT). But the meaning of fasting is not restricted to this literal sense. The spiritual aspects of fasting include an added emphasis on refraining from gossip, lies, backbiting, obscenity, and in general, any sinful act.

Fasting is one of the pillars of Islam and a very special mode of worship. Why is it special? If you look at any other worship, Allah (SWT) orders you to do something.

In fasting, you are ordered not to do something for a specified time, something which you used to do outside Ramadan. Fasting has been ordained upon every sane, mature, and adult Muslim who is able to fast. What is the objective of fasting? As the *ayah* of *Surat al-Baqara* suggests, it is to attain self-restraint, piety, and God-consciousness or *taqwa*.

يَا أَيُّهَا الَّذِينَ آمَنُوا كُتِبَ عَلَيْكُمُ الصِّيَامُ كَمَا كُتِبَ عَلَى الَّذِينَ مِنْ قَبْلِكُمْ لَعَلَّكُمْ تَتَّقُونَ ۝

*O you who believe, fasting is prescribed for you, as it was prescribed for those before you, so that you may be conscious of God. (al-Baqara, 2:183)*

What is *taqwa*? The word *taqwa* is derived from the Arabic root "*waqa*" which among other meanings means "to be protected from the harmful." So, *taqwa* is to save and protect yourself from things that harm you. We read this *du'a`* in the Qur`an:

رَبَّنَا آتِنَا فِي الدُّنْيَا حَسَنَةً وَفِي الْآخِرَةِ حَسَنَةً وَقِنَا عَذَابَ النَّارِ ۝

*Our Lord, give us good in this world and in the hereafter, and protect us from the punishment of the Fire. (al-Baqara, 2:201)*

So *siyam* and *taqwa* have a direct relationship. *Siyam* provides an opportunity for every believer to draw closer to Allah (SWT) and to protect himself from the punishment of the hellfire.

By the grace of Allah (SWT), fasting too, is a source for the forgiveness of sins. The Prophet (SAS) said, "Whoever fasts the month of Ramadan with faith (iman) and hoping for its reward shall have all of his previous sins forgiven for him." The Prophet (SAS) also said, "Fasting is a shield" because fasting guards us and protects us from sins and hellfire. Further, our fasting and the Qur`an will intercede for us on the Day of Judgment. The Prophet (SAS) said, "The fast and the Qur`an shall come as intercessors on the Day of Resurrection. The fast shall say, 'O Lord, I prevented him from his food and drink during the day, so let me intercede for him.' The Qur`an will say, 'I kept him from sleep during the night, so let me intercede for him.' Then they will be allowed to intercede."

Brothers and sisters! Man is a combination of body and spirit. During fasting, when our physical body gets weak, our spirit is elevated. The *dhikr* or remembrance of Allah (SWT) is the spiritual nourishment for the soul, and the best and greatest of *dhikr* is the Qur`an. We are all aware that we are often unjust to ourselves in the sense that we often subject our bodies and souls to excesses. Fasting in Ramadan is an excellent opportunity to attain physical and spiritual healing. According to a *hadeeth qudsi*, the Prophet (SAS) informs us that Allah (SWT) says, "Every good deed of Adam's son is for him except fasting; it is for Me. and I shall reward for it."

According to another *hadeeth qudsi*, the Prophet (SAS) tells us that Allah (SWT) says, "For every good deed that the son of Adam does, he will have (the reward of) ten times as much, except for fasting. It is for Me, and I shall reward for it."

The virtues and greatness of the month of Ramadan should never be underestimated. It is not only the month of fasting but also the month of the Qur'an, the month of mercy, piety, patience, charity, forgiveness, and thankfulness to Allah (SWT). As we fast, we should not forget the poor and the less fortunate ones. We should not forget our relatives who are in need. We should give them the provisions that Allah (SWT) has blessed us with. We should also donate to the organizations that are worthy of our charity. When we remember a past sin, we should not forget to ask for forgiveness. We should not let this month pass away without doing our utmost to please Allah (SWT) and having our sins forgiven.

May Allah (SWT) make us among those who can take advantage of the opportunities provided to us in this blessed month. May He make us among the people of *taqwa*. May He forgive us and keep us safe from the hellfire and make us all enter into *jannah* (paradise). May Allah (SWT) bless all the Muslims in this month, and inspire them to do righteous deeds while accepting such deeds with a beautiful acceptance. We also pray for the *ummah*, particularly for our brothers and sisters in Yemen, Iraq, Syria, Egypt, Kashmir, Burma, and throughout the Muslim world and beyond. We pray for justice and peace for all.

•  75  •

# RELIGION IS *NASEEHA*

My *khutbah* today is on the topic: *ad-deen an-naseeha*, which means that the *deen*, or the religion or the way of life, is *naseeha*. The mode of expression here is similar to when the Prophet (SAS) said, "*al-hajju 'Arafa*," (the hajj is 'Arafa), signifying that among other rituals and actions of hajj, the predominant one is that of the standing at 'Arafa. Similarly, when he said. "*ad-deen an-naseeha*" ("the religion is *naseeha*"), this is a very profound statement which implies that the essence of religion can be found within this concept. The latter part of the hadeeth says that the people asked, "To whom?" The Prophet (SAS) replied, "To Allah and to His book and to His Messenger and to the leaders of the Muslims and to the common folk of Muslims."

The Prophet (SAS) has equated the entire religion to giving *naseeha*, but what exactly is *naseeha*? It is an Arabic word that translates to mean sincerity or sincere advice but embodies every type of virtue. So if you are giving *naseeha* to someone, you wish the best to the person with your intention and actions.

What does making *naseeha* to Allah mean? Allah (SWT) is Self-Sufficient and does not need any of His creation. When the believer makes *naseeha* to Allah (SWT), he is drawing himself closer to Allah (SWT) and purifying himself. The one who benefits from this *naseeha* is the believer and not Allah (SWT).

*Naseeha* to Allah (SWT) implies believing in Him and His attributes. It is to deny that there any partners with Him, and to have the correct intention in one's heart to fulfill the rights of Allah (SWT). This requires fulfilling our obligatory duties to Him in the best possible manner. This should be the goal of every Muslim. We should strive to draw nearer to Allah (SWT) through what He has made obligatory upon us, and by performing voluntary good deeds, as well as avoiding what is forbidden or disliked by Him. We should love whatever He loves and hate whatever He hates, be they objects, persons, sayings, or deeds. This is the *naseeha* to Allah (SWT) referred to in this hadeeth. May Allah (SWT) assist us in remembering Him as He should be remembered, thanking Him as He should be thanked, and worshipping Him as He should be worshipped.

*Naseeha* to the book of Allah requires that we believe in all the revealed books. We should believe that the Qur`an is the speech of Allah (SWT). The Qur`an demands of every Muslim certain obligations. A Muslim is required to believe in the Qur`an, to read it correctly, to understand it, to act upon its teachings, and to convey its message to others. What place does the Qur`an hold in our daily lives? Do we turn to it as our first source of guidance? Do we know the lessons that it teaches us? Are we striving to recite it in the best possible way? And are we conveying its message to others? Teaching and explaining the Qur`an to others are part of giving *naseeha* to Allah's book.

*Naseeha* to Allah's Messenger (SAS), is to know him, to understand his life, and the struggles he went through and to relate his struggles to our daily life. It includes believing in the message that he brought and believing it to be divinely inspired. It also includes accepting the Prophet (SAS) as a true leader and the best example for the believers. Allah (SWT) asks us to follow his model.

لَقَدْ كَانَ لَكُمْ فِي رَسُولِ اللَّهِ أُسْوَةٌ حَسَنَةٌ لِمَنْ كَانَ يَرْجُو اللَّهَ وَالْيَوْمَ الآخِرَ وَذَكَرَ اللَّهَ كَثِيرًا ۝

*The Messenger of Allah is an excellent model for those of you who put your hope in Allah and the Last Day and remember Allah very often. (al-Ahzab, 33:21)*

Obeying him, honoring him, and reviving his Sunnah are all important aspects of giving *naseeha* to the Prophet (SAS). *Naseeha* to Allah's Messenger (SAS) also includes loving him more than anybody else, including our own selves, and also loving those who follow, defend, and strive to revive his Sunnah.

*Naseeha* to Allah (SWT), His book, and His Messenger, in fact, implies giving *naseeha* to ourselves in respect of purifying our relationship with Allah (SWT), His Book, and His Messenger. The Prophet (SAS) explains that naseeha should also be given to others, including the leaders of the Muslims, as well as the common folk in the wider society. This statement of the Prophet (SAS) shows us that no one is above receiving or accepting naseeha, no matter how high-ranking a person may be. Concerning our submission to Allah (SWT) and our need to follow His law and guidance, we are all equal, and everyone needs naseeha.

As for leaders, they deserve our respect because of the responsibility they undertake. Indeed, if they are sincere, they will change their views if they are shown to be wrong and are given sincere advice. There are two kinds of leaders among Muslims, and both are referred to in the wording of this hadeeth. The first are the religious leaders or scholars, and the second are the worldly leaders or rulers. Giving naseeha to the scholars implies to take the knowledge that they pass on and apply the same to our daily lives, to accept their rulings if they provide sound proofs for their decisions, and to have good thoughts about them.

Naseeha to the worldly leaders of the Muslims includes helping them when they are following the truth, obeying them in what is right, reminding them if they make an error or forget, being patient with them when they do things that people do not like, and praying for their guidance and piety. It is the right of the Muslim subject who has knowledge and understanding to advise the rulers to what is best and to forbid them from evil. Because the actions of those in power affect so many people, making naseeha to them is of even more importance. If at all possible, naseeha should be given face-to-face. If that is not possible, it can be done through those who are in contact with them or by writing to them directly. This is from sincerity toward the people in authority. Many scholars state that it is preferable to advise leaders in private and not in public.

What has generally become of Muslim rulers of today? Where can we see any example of rulers who are truly living and implementing Islam, and who are willing to listen to the naseeha of their subjects? Abu Bakr (RAA) asked of the believers when he was entrusted with leadership, "As long as I command you to do what Allah and His Messenger commanded you to do, then you should obey me, but if I don't then you should set me straight."

Giving naseeha or sincere advice to the common Muslims includes guiding them to what is best for them in this life and the hereafter. Teaching them about their religion and other things that they may be ignorant about. Helping them in times of need, providing what is beneficial for them, encouraging them to do good and forbidding them from evil with kindness and sincerity, and showing mercy toward them. The Prophet (SAS) said, "He is not one of us who does not show mercy to our young ones and respect to our elderly."

We should not hold any hatred for Muslims in our hearts. It's unfortunate to imagine, but there is a lot of enmity in the hearts of Muslims toward fellow Muslims. Communities become polarized through following different scholars, and even within like-minded communities, there are differences and quarreling.

May Allah (SWT) guide us to what is best and grant unity to the Muslim *ummah*. May Allah (SWT) bless each one of us with a desire to love for our brothers and sisters in faith and humanity, what we love for ourselves.

Brothers and sisters! There is a difference between giving *naseeha* and unnecessarily exposing or embarrassing another person. Mentioning a Muslim's faults or sins simply to blame, ridicule, or shame him is forbidden. However, if there is some overriding benefit in mentioning such faults, then it becomes either recommended or obligatory to do so. This was the case when hadeeth scholars had to speak out against the reliability of some narrators of hadeeth. This action was part of their naseeha to the Muslim community as a whole, so that they could accurately preserve the hadeeth of the Prophet (SAS). This type of naseeha also becomes obligatory when refuting a misinterpretation of the Qur'an or the Sunnah that people may try to spread throughout the Muslim community. It is obligatory to refute this type of act even if it is done in public, as long as the goal is not to ridicule them, but rather to correct their mistakes.

Are we willing to listen if someone wants to advise us on what is best concerning our conduct, our speech, or how we conduct ourselves? Pride gets in the way. We don't want to be told what to do, even if what we are being advised to is best for us in terms of our religion. We should reflect not only on giving naseeha to others, but also on how to accept it, and to change our conduct for the sake of Allah (SWT). Naseeha, therefore, plays an important role for the Muslim community as a whole. It is one of the key aspects to protect society from the spread of evil.

The one who gives *naseeha* should be free of hypocrisy. His outward and inward should be the same regarding sincerity and truthfulness. Exposing someone's evil and propagating it under the pretense of advising, while only aiming to condemn and cause harm, is nothing but hypocrisy. The one giving *naseeha* should be free of all kinds of deceit and deceptiveness. The Prophet (SAS) said, "Whoever deceives us is not from us." He should be free of every blameworthy characteristic, and he should adorn himself with all the noble and virtuous manners and characteristics.

*Ad-deen an-naseeha* ("the religion is *naseeha*") is a very profound hadeeth that covers almost every single act we do concerning ourselves and those around us. The Prophet (SAS) summed up the religion of Islam in just one word—*naseeha*. Being engaged in *naseeha* to Allah (SWT), to His book, to His Messenger, to the leaders of the Muslims and to the common folk of the Muslims impacts every aspect of our lives. If we were to be effectively engaged in these types of *naseeha*, we would purify both ourselves and our societies.

May Allah (SWT) help us give proper *naseeha* and forgive us if we fall short in our duties toward our souls and people around us. *Allahumma ameen.*

• 76 •

# REMEMBERING DEATH

In today's *khutbah*, I want to bring to your mind a topic that people often avoid talking about, and that is remembering death. Surprising as it may seem, remembering death can motivate us to live a purposeful and useful life. Among the reasons why death is an important topic is because everyone will experience it. Almost every day, we hear of the death of someone. Yet, most people ignore the fact that they have to die one day. The knowledge of the reality of death can help us understand it and prepare ourselves for its coming. Death is certain and unavoidable. Allah says in the Qur`an,

كُلُّ نَفْسٍ ذَائِقَةُ الْمَوْتِ وَإِنَّمَا تُوَفَّوْنَ أُجُورَكُمْ يَوْمَ الْقِيَامَةِ ۞

*Every human being is bound to taste death: and you shall receive your rewards in full on the Day of Resurrection. (Aal 'Imran, 3:185)*

أَيْنَمَا تَكُونُوا يُدْرِككُّمُ الْمَوْتُ وَلَوْ كُنتُمْ فِي بُرُوجٍ مُشَيَّدَةٍ ۞

*Wherever you may be, death will overtake you, even if you be in strongly built towers.*
(an-Nisa`, 4:78)

This being the case, do we ever think about the day we will die? Are we ready and prepared for our departure from this earth? Are we scared of death? There is no denying that fear of death is something natural. It hangs around with each one of us. The celebration of every birthday is a year closer to death. Every day that passes by brings us closer to death. Every breath we take takes away a portion of our lives and brings us closer to death. No sooner than the appointed time comes, we belong among the dead. Then it becomes clear that life is like a flower that blooms; then withers, or like a lamp that illuminates; then dies down. Reference to drawing the last breath or the trance or the stupor of death is found in the Qur`an.

وَجَاءَتْ سَكْرَةُ الْمَوْتِ بِالْحَقِّ ذَٰلِكَ مَا كُنتَ مِنْهُ تَحِيدُ ⬡

*The trance of death will come revealing the truth: that is what you were trying to escape.* (Qaf, 50:19)

These are the moments when the dying person bids this vanishing world goodbye and casts a last look at it. Life will pass before his eyes like a flash, and he will realize how short it really was, how he wasted it, how he did not perform the purpose behind his very creation: to worship the Almighty—his Lord and the Lord of all creation.

لَقَدْ كُنتَ فِي غَفْلَةٍ مِّنْ هَٰذَا فَكَشَفْنَا عَنكَ غِطَاءَكَ فَبَصَرُكَ الْيَوْمَ حَدِيدٌ ⬡

*You were heedless of this, but now We have removed your veil, so your sight today is sharp.* (Qaf, 50:22)

Indeed, the sight of the dying person during the stupors of death will be quite sharp. He will, for the first time, be able to see angels, who are created of light, and the jinn who are created of smokeless fire. He will be able to see and hear his family, relatives, friends, and strangers who are around him at the time of death and who will soon bear his casket to the cemetery. But he will not be able to show any reaction because he has lost control over his temporal body, and his soul now takes over.

As believers, if we trust in Allah (SWT), think positively of Allah (SWT), humble our hearts before Allah (SWT), and try our best to have the *taqwa* of Allah (SWT), then we should know that death is a return to the most generous and merciful Lord. We are told by the Prophet (SAS), "None of you should die except hoping good from Allah."

We should never ever despair of Allah's mercy. Allah tells us very clearly,

قُلْ يَا عِبَادِيَ الَّذِينَ أَسْرَفُوا عَلَىٰ أَنفُسِهِمْ لَا تَقْنَطُوا مِنْ رَحْمَةِ اللَّهِ إِنَّ اللَّهَ يَغْفِرُ الذُّنُوبَ جَمِيعًا إِنَّهُ هُوَ الْغَفُورُ

الرَّحِيمُ ⬡

*Say: 'O My servants who transgressed against themselves, do not despair of Allah's mercy. For Allah forgives all sins. He is the Forgiver, the Merciful.'* (az-Zumar, 39:53)

Brothers and sisters! Remembering death softens the heart. It is an inspiration to leave bad habits, to do more and more good deeds, to help people in need, and to be good to our families and societies. It is said that whoever frequently remembers death is honored with three things: (1) quick repentance, (2) contentment, and (3) energy for acts of worship. And whoever forgets death is punished with three things: (1) delayed repentance, (2) lack of contentment, and (3) laziness in acts of worship. Now let us look at ourselves: are we often delaying our repentance and remaining unhappy with what we have? Do we feel too lazy to pray? All of these are signs that we don't remember death productively. Remember that life and death are part of a divinely mandated plan. They are a test to see who among us would strive to be the best in deeds. As Allah

(SWT) says in *Surat al-Mulk*,

الَّذِي خَلَقَ الْمَوْتَ وَالْحَيَاةَ لِيَبْلُوَكُمْ أَيُّكُمْ أَحْسَنُ عَمَلًا ◯

*He who created death and life to test which of you is best in action. (al-Mulk, 67:2)*

There is no one on the face of this earth who is not undergoing a test. Sometimes we are tested in prosperity and other times in adversity, sometimes we are tested in ease and comfort, and other times we are tested in difficulties and hardships. Through the journey of life, we are tested as to how best we conduct ourselves in different circumstances.

What is the reality of death? When it occurs, the spirit leaves the body. We learn through prophetic traditions that a good soul comes out of the body with ease, while an evil soul, which resists leaving the body, is taken out harshly by the angel of death. During a wicked person's dying moments, he wishes that death was delayed so that if he were a non-believer, he would become a believer; or if he were a disobedient believer, he would repent from his sins. Allah (SWT) says,

حَتَّى إِذَا جَاءَ أَحَدَهُمُ الْمَوْتُ قَالَ رَبِّ ارْجِعُونِ ◯ لَعَلِّي أَعْمَلُ صَالِحًا فِيمَا تَرَكْتُ ◯

*When death comes to any of them, he says: My Lord, send me back; that I may act righteously in what I have left behind. (al-Mu`minoon, 23:99-100)*

The two types of souls—the good and the evil are honored or dishonored in their respective journeys to their heavenly abodes. *Sijjeen* is the record where deeds of the evil souls are preserved, while *'Iliyyeen* is the record in which the deeds of the righteous souls are preserved.

كَلَّا إِنَّ كِتَابَ الْفُجَّارِ لَفِي سِجِّينٍ ◯

*Indeed! The record of the wicked is in the Sijjeen. (al-Mutaffifeen, 83:7)*

كَلَّا إِنَّ كِتَابَ الْأَبْرَارِ لَفِي عِلِّيِّينَ ◯

*Indeed, the record of the righteous is in the 'Iliyyeen. (al-Mutaffifeen, 83:18)*

Man takes nothing with him in his grave. We learn through a hadeeth in which the Prophet (SAS) says, "When a man dies, his deeds come to an end except for three things: ongoing charity(*sadaqa jariya*), beneficial knowledge that he leaves behind, or a virtuous descendant who prays for him." Such admonitions remind us that we should hasten in doing good deeds lest our time is up and our book of deeds gets closed forever. We should not be among those hypocrites who will cry to Allah (SWT) to give them more time to spend in His way and to be one of the righteous.

وَأَنفِقُوا مِن مَّا رَزَقْنَاكُم مِّن قَبْلِ أَن يَأْتِيَ أَحَدَكُمُ الْمَوْتُ فَيَقُولَ رَبِّ لَوْلَا أَخَّرْتَنِي إِلَى أَجَلٍ قَرِيبٍ فَأَصَّدَّقَ وَأَكُن

مِّنَ الصَّالِحِينَ ⬤

*Give from what We have provided for you before death comes to one of you and he says:*
*My Lord, if only you would give me a little more time so that I can give sadaqa and be*
*one of the righteous! (al-Munafiqoon, 63:10)*

Pursuing lawful means of livelihood is fine, but we should not get entangled in the
*dunya* to the extent that we cannot extricate ourselves from it to invest some of our
time, energy, money, and capabilities in the way of Allah (SWT).Allah (SWT) has
undertaken upon Himself to provide for all His creatures.

وَمَا مِن دَابَّةٍ فِي الْأَرْضِ إِلَّا عَلَى اللَّهِ رِزْقُهَا ⬤

*There is no creature on earth except that its provision is from Allah. (Hud, 11:6)*

One of the basic differences between this world and the hereafter is that in this life
there is death, while in the hereafter there is no death. The inhabitants of paradise
will live forever. Those who are in the hellfire will also live forever. This takes us to
the question: what are we doing in this life to prepare for a death that will lead us to
eternal blissful life? Our children will inherit the good and bad that we leave behind.
What kind of example are we going to leave behind for them? Brothers and sisters! Our
ultimate goal should be to reach a level that, when we die, we know that we couldn't
have done better.

Brothers and sisters! If we ponder over reality, we learn that the world deceives
the one who craves for it. One who keeps death in front of his eyes not only performs
his routine tasks sincerely but constantly strives to do more and more good deeds
to seek the pleasure of his Lord—Allah (SWT). He is aware that death can overtake
him at any moment, and he does not have time on his side. The Prophet (SAS) said,
"Surely the heart rusts like iron." People asked, "How can it be polished?' He replied,
"By remembering death and with the recitation of the Qur`an." What is the best way to
prepare oneself for death? Always be mindful of Allah (SWT), do what He commanded
us to do, and don't do what has been prohibited to us. Having faith and doing good
deeds is how we prepare for a good life and a good death. Allah (SWT) says,

مَنْ عَمِلَ صَالِحًا مِنْ ذَكَرٍ أَوْ أُنْثَى وَهُوَ مُؤْمِنٌ فَلَنُحْيِيَنَّهُ حَيَاةً طَيِّبَةً وَلَنَجْزِيَنَّهُمْ أَجْرَهُمْ بِأَحْسَنِ مَا كَانُوا
يَعْمَلُونَ ⬤

*Whoever does good deeds, male or female, and has faith, We shall give a good life and*
*reward them according to the best of their actions. (an-Nahl, 16:97)*

This means that such a person will have peace, contentment, and lawful provision in
this life, and paradise in the hereafter. Death being the most certain reality, a conscious
believer prepares himself here in this world for the eternal and perpetual blissful life of

the hereafter. We must learn from death, for the secret of life is hidden in the message it has to teach us. Death shows us that we are not our masters; that our stay on earth is only temporary; that the world is no place for the realization of our dreams. Death teaches us how to live; it shows us the way to real success. The Prophet (SAS), in one of his sayings, said, "Clever is the one who controls his passions and prepares for life after death." May Allah (SWT) give us the *tawfeeq* to remember death and grant us that the *kalima: La ilaha illa Allah* will be on our lips at the time of our death.

# • 77 •

# REPENTANCE *(TAWBA)*

The topic of today's *khutbah* is *tawba*. *Tawba* signifies the act of being repentant for one's misdeeds, atoning for them, and having a strong determination to abandon them completely. From *tawba* we have the word *tawwab*. *Tawwab*, when applied to man, means one who repents a lot and returns from disobedience to obedience of Allah (SWT). And *tawwab*, when applied to Allah (SWT), means the One who returns much to forgiveness toward His servants who turn to Him. We read in *Surat al-Baqara*,

إِنَّ اللَّهَ يُحِبُّ التَّوَّابِينَ وَيُحِبُّ الْمُتَطَهِّرِينَ ۞

*Allah loves those who turn to Him in repentance and He loves those who keep themselves pure and clean. (al-Baqara, 2:222)*

And we read in *Surat at-Tawba*,

أَلَمْ يَعْلَمُوا أَنَّ اللَّهَ هُوَ يَقْبَلُ التَّوْبَةَ عَنْ عِبَادِهِ وَيَأْخُذُ الصَّدَقَاتِ وَأَنَّ اللَّهَ هُوَ التَّوَّابُ الرَّحِيمُ ۞

*Do they not know that it is Allah Himself who accepts repentance from His servants and receives what is given freely for His sake? He is always ready to accept repentance, most merciful. (at-Tawba, 9:104)*

It is reported that the Prophet (SAS) said, "*an-nadamu tawbatun*" meaning "regret is repentance." This means that a repenting person has to regret and turn to Allah (SWT) with a guilt-torn heart full of shame and remorse and a stubborn resolve not to commit the same sin again that he or she may have committed. And what is sin? The Prophet (SAS) defined sin as follows, "Sin is what causes discomfort within your soul

333

and which you dislike that people should come to know of it."

The human being is created with an internal mechanism to sense which acts are sinful, and the soul is uneasy when it performs sinful acts. Sin breeds more sin until it dominates a person, and he cannot escape from it. It gradually strengthens his will to commit sin and weakens his will to repent until there is no will in his heart to repent at all. Even if he seeks forgiveness and expresses repentance, it is merely words on the lips, like the repentance of the liars whose hearts remain determined to sin and persist in it. He becomes desensitized and no longer finds sins hateful; so it becomes his habit, and he is not bothered if people see him committing the sin or talk about him.

The Prophet (SAS) also informs us, "The one who repents from sin is like one who did not sin." This means that if a person commits a sin, then repents sincerely from it, gives it up, regrets having done it, prays for forgiveness, and does not go back to it, Allah (SWT) will accept his repentance and treat him like one who did not sin.

A Muslim should not look at how small or great the sin is, instead he should look at the greatness and might of the One Whom he is disobeying. Minor sins can easily lead someone to commit a major sin. Furthermore, habitual sinning causes a Muslim to lose faith and disregard the commandments of Allah (SWT). The sin stands in the way of obedience to Allah (SWT). Insistence and firmness on sins blacken and harden the heart, which may at times even lead to disbelief. *Tawba* or repentance is one of the acts of the heart. Sincere *tawba* purifies the heart from the filth of sins. Repentance from all sins is obligatory on every adult Muslim. This is emphasized by Allah (SWT) when He says,

$$وَتُوبُوا إِلَى اللَّهِ جَمِيعًا أَيُّهَ الْمُؤْمِنُونَ لَعَلَّكُمْ تُفْلِحُونَ ۝$$

*And repent to Allah, all of you believers that you may succeed. (an-Nur, 24:31)*

Indeed, Allah (SWT) is very happy when any of His slaves repents. If he repents, he will have a peaceful life in this world and blissful life in the hereafter. If however, he does not repent, then he makes himself liable to be punished for his sins.

*Tawba* is returning from disobedience to obedience, from sins to good deeds, and from the path of Satan to the path of Allah (SWT). A repenting person must change his ways, change the company he or she keeps, and change the place where he or she hangs around. Sincere repentance according to the scholars has certain conditions: (1) to stop doing the sinful act, (2) to regret for the sin done, and (3) to determine never to go back to that sin again. If any of these conditions is not met, then the repentance will not be perfect. It is only the pure, sincere repentance that is acceptable to Allah (SWT).

$$يَا أَيُّهَا الَّذِينَ آمَنُوا تُوبُوا إِلَى اللَّهِ تَوْبَةً نَصُوحًا ۝$$

*O you who believe; turn to Allah in sincere repentance. (at-Tahreem, 66:8)*

The one who repents should feel that his sin is repulsive and harmful. He should not derive any pleasure when he remembers his past sins. He should not wish to repeat those sins in the future. Ibn al-Qayyim (RA) mentions many of the harmful effects of sin. Some of these are: (1) loss of knowledge, (2) difficulty in one's affairs, (3) loss of desire to obey Allah (SWT), (4) absence of blessing, (5) unhappiness, (6) disgrace in the sight of Allah (SWT), (7) disgrace in the sight of people, (8) sealing of the heart, (9) not having *du'a`* answered, (10) falling into the clutches of *Shaytan*, and (11) an unhappy end and punishment in the hereafter.

Some Muslims have indulged in so many sinful activities that they start believing that their sins are too much to be forgiven. They get into a state of desperation and lose all hope in Allah's mercy. So they never repent. But Allah (SWT) says,

قُلْ يَا عِبَادِيَ الَّذِينَ أَسْرَفُوا عَلَى أَنْفُسِهِمْ لَا تَقْنَطُوا مِنْ رَحْمَةِ اللَّهِ إِنَّ اللَّهَ يَغْفِرُ الذُّنُوبَ جَمِيعًا إِنَّهُ هُوَ الْغَفُورُ الرَّحِيمُ ○

*Say: O My servants who transgressed against themselves, do not despair of Allah's mercy. For Allah forgives all sins. He is the Forgiver, the Merciful. (az-Zumar, 39:53)*

One of Allah's names is al-Ghaffar (one who forgives a lot). We read in *Surah Ta Ha*,

وَإِنِّي لَغَفَّارٌ لِمَنْ تَابَ وَآمَنَ وَعَمِلَ صَالِحًا ثُمَّ اهْتَدَى ○

*And I am most forgiving to those who repent, believe, do righteous deeds and then stick to the true guidance. (Ta Ha, 20:82)*

It is Allah's mercy upon His slaves that He has left the door of repentance open. It is narrated that the Prophet (SAS) said, "Allah holds out His Hand during the night to receive the repentance of the one who has committed wrong during the day and holds outs His Hand during the day to receive the repentance of the one who has committed wrong during the night." This is because of His limitless mercy toward His creatures. Speaking about the mercy of Allah (SWT), says in the Qur`an,

كَتَبَ عَلَى نَفْسِهِ الرَّحْمَةَ ○

*He has made mercy incumbent upon Himself. (al-An'am, 6:12)*

A man once went to Rabi'a bint Isma'eel al-'Adawiyya, who was known by the title, "Mother of Goodness," and said to her, "Indeed, I have committed a great number of sins. If I repent, do you think that Allah will accept my repentance?" She said, "Woe unto you! Do you not see that Allah invites those who turn away from Him? Why wouldn't He accept the repentance of those who turn toward Him?" May Allah (SWT) give us the *tawfeeq* to turn toward Him in repentance every single day of our life.

Brothers and sisters, the Prophet (SAS) said in a hadeeth that Allah (SWT) accepts the repentance of a person as long as he or she is not on the point of death. Therefore, we should hasten to repent. We should be aware and conscious that death can come to us suddenly. Some people are indeed denied repentance by their not being prepared for death, and some who are lucky enough to repent sincerely before death. Hence they are admitted among the righteous people. It is also narrated that the Prophet (SAS) told us that Allah (SWT) is more pleased with the repentance of His servant than a person who finds his lost camel in a waterless desert. And we learn through a hadeeth in which the Prophet (SAS) informs us that Allah (SWT) says, "When Allah decreed the creation, he wrote in his book with him on his Throne: My mercy prevails over My wrath."

The Prophet (SAS) also said, "If you were not to commit sins, Allah would have swept you out of existence and would have replaced you by another people who have committed sin, and then asked forgiveness from Allah." Addressing His beloved Messenger, Allah (SWT) says in the Qur`an,

إِنَّا فَتَحْنَا لَكَ فَتْحًا مُبِينًا لِيَغْفِرَ لَكَ اللَّهُ مَا تَقَدَّمَ مِنْ ذَنْبِكَ وَمَا تَأَخَّرَ ◯

*Surely, We have given you a clear victory, so that Allah may forgive your past and future sins. (al-Fath, 48:2)*

And yet the Prophet (SAS) said, "I ask for forgiveness from Allah and turn to Him in repentance one hundred times a day," and in another tradition, "seventy times a day." Repentance is an act of worship done by all prophets, messengers, and pious believers.

Brothers and sisters! We are on a path of continual improvement. People do make mistakes, but believers analyze their mistakes and take positive actions to correct them. Some Muslims intentionally commit wrongful acts with the intention to repent afterward. But who knows? One may die before one repents or even during the act of committing the sin. A person with a pure heart and pure intention may falter and slip, but he always repents to Allah (SWT), and that is all that Allah (SWT) asks for: sincere effort and sincere repentance that comes from a pure heart.

Let me conclude by saying that human beings are commanded by Allah (SWT) to repent. Who is it, or who believes or who thinks that he or she is faultless and can commit no sin? Look at the hadeeth in which the Prophet (SAS) says, "Every son of Adam commits sin, and the best of those who commit sin are those who repent."

We all have defaulted with Allah (SWT) and His rights upon us. And that is one reason why we should always be ready to repent. Remember that Allah (SWT) gets pleased and delighted when one of His servants repents. Allah (SWT) loves to see the believer repent more than He hates to see him sin. So, let us sincerely repent to Allah (SWT) for our sins—major and minor, intentional or unintentional, open or secret. Indeed He accepts sincere repentance. He is the Most Forgiving and the Most Merciful.

# 78

# SEEKING THE PROTECTION
# OF ALLAH (SWT)

There is a hadeeth in which the Prophet (SAS) conveys a piece of very important advice and a general ruling in Islam on seeking protection of Allah (SWT). The Prophet (SAS) said, "Be mindful of Allah, you shall find Him in front of you. Get to know Allah in prosperity, and He will know you in adversity. Know that whatever passed you by could never have happened, and what happened could never have been avoided. Know that victory comes with patience, relief comes with affliction, and ease comes with hardship." *In sha`Allah*, in today's *khutbah*, we will try to understand this hadeeth in a little more detail.

This hadeeth reveals some of the core truths about the nature of our relationship with Allah (SWT). If you take care of your relationship with Him, He will take care of you. Whatever you need or desire, in the end, it can only come from Him. This is not to say that we can never ask people for help, but we should understand that ultimately Allah (SWT) is the source of all help that comes our way. The companions used to ask Allah (SWT) for help in everything, large or small.

We sometimes get bogged down with the side issues in our *deen*: with definitions, *fiqh* issues, and the differences between us, while forgetting the essence of our relationship with the Creator. The Prophet (SAS) captured this essence for us and taught us that as long as we turn to Allah (SWT), we will be all right. To understand this truth, we must try it out. It is one thing to read about it and another to experience finding Allah (SWT) at our side in moments of hardship.

The phrase "be mindful of Allah" also means to observe Allah's obligations and to avoid His prohibitions. If we are mindful of Allah (SWT), He will be close to us by giving us guidance, help, and victory. He will also protect us.

Allah (SWT) will protect His servants' *deen* and *iman*. He will protect us from being misled or influenced by misconception and by the evil around us. He will help us and guide us so that we are protected from negative influences. For example, there may be a situation where Allah (SWT) prevents us from doing something which we want to do. This is actually a protection from Allah (SWT). He protects us by not allowing us to perform a particular deed, which in effect, saves us from a disaster or from committing a sin. Allah (SWT) also protects us from *Shaytan's* attempt to lead us astray at the last moments of our life. This will ensure that we will leave this world having the *iman* of a true believer.

Allah (SWT) will also protect His servants in their worldly affairs. We enjoy the mercy and bounty of Allah (SWT) in our faculties of sight, hearing, and speech. Even as we grow old, Allah (SWT) still allows us to enjoy these senses as well as our intellect and mental faculties. Allah (SWT) also protects our family, property, and wealth. If one is mindful of Allah (SWT) during his youth, Allah (SWT) will protect him during his adulthood.

The other narration of this hadeeth mentions that if we are mindful of Allah (SWT) during times of ease, He will help us during our times of hardship. Therefore, when we are blessed with comfort and prosperity, we should use that blessing to obtain the pleasure of Allah (SWT). Then He will look after us during our times of hardship, weakness, and sickness. Even if we are no longer able to do something good that we used to do during our times of ease, Allah (SWT) will continue to reward us for that act.

Gaining Allah's protection does not come automatically. We have to strive to maintain *taqwa* and do actions being mindful of Him. Some of the things we have to do to gain Allah's protection include the following:

(1) Performing the daily *salah* on time and in the best way we can. (2) Protecting our hearts from being involved in sins, especially major sins. (3) Guarding our senses—we should ensure that whatever we see, hear, or say is pleasing to Allah (SWT). We should fear Allah (SWT) and not use these senses in a wrongful manner. (4) Maintaining cleanliness and purity. (5) Always being truthful. (6) Fulfilling our oaths and promises. (7) Ensuring that the food and drink we consume are always *halal*. (8) Observing that our dealings and transactions are *halal*.

Allah (SWT) has already written down in *al-Lawh al-Mahfoodh* (The Preserved Tablet) what is to take place. These are events and occurrences that we have no control over, e.g., falling sick, the untimely death of a loved one, falling into unexpected hardship, and so on. Appropriately facing these events necessitates contentment or *ridha*, which is the highest level for us to attain by accepting and being content with whatever Allah (SWT) has chosen for us. The second highest level is patience or *sabr*, where we need to be tolerant, patient, and calm. When we are in a difficult circumstance, we need to exercise restraint without saying or doing anything that may displease Allah (SWT).

There are several verses in the Qur'an emphasizing the same meaning that the hadeeth under discussion conveys.

$$\text{مَا أَصَابَ مِن مُّصِيبَةٍ فِي الْأَرْضِ وَلَا فِي أَنفُسِكُمْ إِلَّا فِي كِتَابٍ مِّن قَبْلِ أَن نَّبْرَأَهَا إِنَّ ذَٰلِكَ عَلَى اللَّهِ يَسِيرٌ ۝}$$

*Nothing occurs, either in the earth or in yourselves, without its being in a Book before*
*We make it happen. That is something easy for Allah. (al-Hadeed, 57:22)*

وَإِن يَمْسَسْكَ اللَّهُ بِضُرٍّ فَلَا كَاشِفَ لَهُ إِلَّا هُوَ وَإِن يُرِدْكَ بِخَيْرٍ فَلَا رَادَّ لِفَضْلِهِ يُصِيبُ بِهِ مَن يَشَاءُ مِنْ عِبَادِهِ وَهُوَ الْغَفُورُ الرَّحِيمُ ◯

*If Allah inflicts harm on you, no one can remove it but He, and if He intends good for you, no one can withhold His bounty; He grants His bounty to any of His servants whom He wills. He is the Most Forgiving, and the Most Merciful. (Yunus, 10:107)*

In a hadeeth in Sahih Muslim, the Prophet (SAS) informs us that Allah (SWT) recorded *qadr* or divine destiny of all creation fifty thousand years before He created the heavens and the earth. Belief in *qadr* is one of Islam's six articles of faith, along with belief in the oneness of Allah (SWT), the revealed books, the prophets, the Day of Resurrection, and the angels.

*Qadr* regarding occurrences can be broadly categorized into two categories: (1) occurrences not under our control wherein we have to surrender to the will of Allah (SWT), and (2) occurrences under our control and these may be either negative or positive. Negative events can happen as a result of our recklessness, laziness, or carelessness, such as engaging in erratic driving or speeding that leads to an accident. Positive events, meanwhile, occur through our diligence, carefulness, and hard work, such as a student who studies well and then does well in his exam.

Generally speaking, we are responsible for whatever we do. Thus, we should act in a careful manner and to the best of our ability. We are also reminded of the importance of *ihsan* in our actions which, generally leads to good results. We should always try to improve ourselves and constantly tell ourselves that we can do better. At the same time, we should not focus too much on future occurrences about which we have no knowledge of or what is beyond our control. We should do the best we can and leave the rest to Allah (SWT).

Part of the proper understanding and belief of *qadr* is to stay away from things that are potentially harmful to us. Things like not wearing a seatbelt while driving or eating a diet very high in cholesterol may cause harm to us. We should be mindful to avoid things that are harmful to us, and not blame it on *qadr* if it happens out of our recklessness or negligence. Seeking treatment for an illness does not contradict *qadr*. If we are faced with a problem, we should make every effort to solve it or to minimize it.

Many people tend to view *qadr* negatively because of their lack of insight and a correct understanding of this topic. *Qadr* needs to be understood positively. The Prophet (SAS) commanded us to be proactive with regards to *qadr* by being diligent in doing good deeds, and not blaming *qadr* for our inactivity in doing good. Furthermore, we need to differentiate between things that we have control over versus things that we do not have control over. Instead of merely accepting whatever has occurred as *qadr*, we should accept responsibility for all that we do and the choices that we make. We should analyze the reasons for why things have occurred in our life. We should make the effort to improve the situation and think of how we can avoid pitfalls.

We should also remember that nothing occurs or exists except that it reflects Allah's infinite wisdom, for He is *al-Hakeem* (The All-Wise). There is always the big picture, a larger context that we are unable to perceive with our shortsightedness. Allah (SWT) is fully aware of how things unfold in the long run, and we must place our trust in Him, fully realizing that there is wisdom in His decisions. In this regard, our Prophet (SAS) advised us to maintain a good opinion of our Lord, for the Prophet (SAS) informs us that Allah (SWT) says in a *hadeeth qudsi*, "I am in the opinion of My servant" or "I am as My servant thinks I am." If we are convinced that Allah (SWT) is looking out for our best interests when He decrees painful situations and that He will replace what is lost with something much better for us in both this life and the next, then that is exactly how we will find Him, without a doubt.

Brothers and sisters! What transformation will take place when we internalize the guidance in this hadeeth? There is tremendous freedom from the hindrances of fear and loneliness when we rely only on Allah (SWT). Great acts of courage, patience, and independence become possible because a person senses the company of Allah (SWT) by his or her side. This hadeeth teaches us the importance of complete reliance and awareness of Allah (SWT). Those who are mindful of Allah (SWT), find Him as their Protector and Helper.

$$وَاللَّهُ وَلِيُّ الْمُتَّقِينَ ○$$

*Allah is the Protector of all who are mindful of Him. (al-Jathiya, 45:19)*

$$وَمَنْ يَتَّقِ اللَّهَ يَجْعَلْ لَهُ مِنْ أَمْرِهِ يُسْرًا ○$$

*Allah makes things easy for those who are mindful of Him. (at-Talaq, 65:4)*

Part of the proper mindfulness of Allah (SWT) is to have *ridha* and *sabr* in *qadr*. In addition to this realization, we still need to understand *qadr* positively. We need to be proactive and take responsibility for all our actions. We also should take proper precautions so that a negative result does not occur because of our negligence.

Applying this hadeeth will lead us to a life in which we are content and stress-free. In this way, we will be mindful of Allah (SWT), fulfill His obligations, and fully trust and accept whatever He wills for us.

# 79

# SIGNIFICANCE OF THE *HIJRA*

We bid farewell to another year of the Hijra. After the passing of the blessed month of *Dhu al-Hijja*, we are now in the sacred month of *Muharram* of the new Hijri year—1440. It is reported that the companions of Prophet Muhammad (SAS) would say the following *du'a`* for when the new month or new year would begin:

اللهم أَدْخِلْهُ عَلينا بِالأَمْنِ وَالإيمانِ وَالسَّلامَةِ وَالإِسْلام وَرِضْوانٍ مِّنَ الرَّحْمن وِجوارٍ مِّنَ الشَّيْطان ۝

*O Allah, bring this upon us with security, iman, safety, Islam, pleasure from the most merciful, and protection from Shaytan.*

My *khutbah* today is on the topic: "Significance of the Hijra." The Hijra refers to the migration of Prophet Muhammad (SAS) from Mecca to Medina in the year 622. The Islamic calendar was introduced during the era of 'Umar ibn al-Khattab (RAA) and began on a day corresponding with the first day of the month of Muharram.

The Hijra was not only a historical event, but an event that changed the course of history. Every Islamic New Year is reminiscent of this very significant occasion in the history of Islam, which brought in its wake an end to tyranny, persecution, discrimination, pain, and grief of the believers in Mecca and ushered in a new era of freedom, fraternity, equality, and justice in Medina. The Hijra was the beginning of a new phase in the life of Prophet Muhammad (SAS) and his companions.

The first phase of the Prophetic mission, known as the Meccan period, lasted for thirteen years (610-622). The second phase, which began with the Hijra is called the Medinan period and lasted for ten years (622-632). This Hijra from Mecca to Medina was executed by the Prophet (SAS) and his companions under a divine command and was mandatory, unlike the optional migration of a few companions to Abyssinia in the early days of the Prophet's mission. This mission had begun with the first revelation to the Prophet (SAS) in the cave of *Hira`* situated at the peak of *Jabal an-Nur*.

It was a simple command to "read" (*iqra`*) and thus began the journey, which along its way, transformed his companions into beacons, illuminated with the light of faith (*iman*), and led to the establishment of Islam as a concrete historical reality. This was the fruit of the *iman* that was instilled in the believers' minds and hearts during the Meccan period. Their training (*tarbiya*) and their purification(*tazkiya*) by the Prophet (SAS), the adversities they endured in the path of Allah (SWT), and their life-experiences during the Prophetic era had made the metaphysical concepts of the unseen, the life hereafter, and the reckoning on the Day of Judgment as not only comprehensible for them, but also *real*. They could not help but cry out,

رَبَّنَا إِنَّنَا سَمِعْنَا مُنَادِيًا يُنَادِي لِلْإِيمَانِ أَنْ آمِنُوا بِرَبِّكُمْ فَآمَنَّا رَبَّنَا فَاغْفِرْ لَنَا ذُنُوبَنَا وَكَفِّرْ عَنَّا سَيِّئَاتِنَا وَتَوَفَّنَا مَعَ الْأَبْرَارِ ◯ رَبَّنَا وَآتِنَا مَا وَعَدْتَنَا عَلَى رُسُلِكَ وَلَا تُخْزِنَا يَوْمَ الْقِيَامَةِ إِنَّكَ لَا تُخْلِفُ الْمِيعَادَ ◯

*Our Lord! We have heard someone calling us to faith; believe in your Lord, and we have believed. Our Lord! Forgive us our sins, wipe out our bad deeds, and grant that we join the righteous when we die. Our Lord! Bestow upon us all that You have promised us through Your messengers. Do not humiliate us on the Day of Resurrection. You never break Your promise. (Aal 'Imran, 3:193-194)*

The believers' intense and deep-rooted *iman* made them withstand all forms of persecution, hardship, and torture done by the arch-enemies of Islam, including Abu Jahl and the Prophet's own uncle Abu Lahab. They vented their wrath against them just for proclaiming the true testimony of faith and living by it. Bilal, 'Ammar, Yasir, Sumayya, among other companions of the Prophet (SAS) were brutally tortured, and some of them were actually killed.

The noble Prophet (SAS) himself was subjected to verbal abuse and constant harassment, and many intrigues and murderous plots were hatched against him. His agony reached a climax when he was chased out from the city of Ta`if near Mecca, where he had gone to convey Allah's message to its inhabitants, and stones were pelted at him. But the Prophet's mercy, kindness, and magnanimity knew no bounds. The angel of mountains asked if he may cause the mountains surrounding Ta`if to move in and destroy its inhabitants because they had tortured and abused Allah's messenger. The Prophet responded that they should be left safe as their progeny and future generations perhaps would heed to the message brought by him and worship the one and only true God.

Allah (SWT) in His infinite mercy responded to the cry of the believers who were being tormented day in and day out during the Meccan period at the hands of the Pagan Quraysh and others, and ordered them to migrate to Medina, a city about 200 miles north of Mecca.

During the Meccan period of thirteen years, the Prophet's mission was focused on inculcating three basic doctrinal beliefs in the hearts of the believers: (1) faith in Allah (SWT), (2) faith in Prophethood, and (3) faith in the hereafter. These three cardinal articles of faith revolve around two-thirds of the Qur`anic text revealed during the Meccan period.

The implicit faith in the Creator that the Prophet (SAS) and his companions possessed and the intense desire to please Him caused them to march to Medina to establish a community where Allah's rule would reign supreme. On his way to Medina, the Prophet (SAS) established the first *masjid* at Quba, where the Muslims could freely worship Allah (SWT) alone without fear of any persecution. The first thing that happened upon the Prophet's arrival at Medina was that the hostility between the two feuding tribes of *Aws* and *Khazraj* came to an end. Allah (SWT) fostered brotherhood between them. They came to be known as the Ansar or helpers. Allah (SWT) mentions this phenomenon in the following verse of the Qur'an:

وَاذْكُرُوا نِعْمَةَ اللَّهِ عَلَيْكُمْ إِذْ كُنْتُمْ أَعْدَاءً فَأَلَّفَ بَيْنَ قُلُوبِكُمْ فَأَصْبَحْتُمْ بِنِعْمَتِهِ إِخْوَانًا وَكُنْتُمْ عَلَى شَفَا حُفْرَةٍ مِنَ النَّارِ فَأَنْقَذَكُمْ مِنْهَا كَذَلِكَ يُبَيِّنُ اللَّهُ لَكُمْ آيَاتِهِ لَعَلَّكُمْ تَهْتَدُونَ ◯

*Remember Allah's favor to you: you were enemies and then He brought your hearts together and you became brothers by His grace; you were about to fall into a pit of fire and He saved you from it- in this way Allah makes His revelations clear to you so that you may be rightly guided. (Aal 'Imran, 3:103)*

Upon his arrival at Medina, Prophet (SAS) laid the foundation of the first Islamic center, the Prophet's mosque—a *masjid* cum school that catered to both the worshipping and learning needs of the believers. Many great companions were graduates of this school. Second, the Prophet engendered a strong feeling of fraternity between the *ansar* (helpers) and the *muhajiroon* (emigrants), which went a long way to unite and strengthen the Muslim community of Medina. The *ansar* demonstrated a unique self-sacrificing spirit when they welcomed their Meccan brothers with open arms and cheerfully shared their wealth and possessions with them just for the sake of Allah (SWT). Third, the Prophet (SAS) made alliance pacts with different tribes and communities, including the Jews. This ensured the safety and security of Medina against foreign aggression as all parties to the alliance, whether Muslim or non-Muslim, whether hostile or friendly to each other, were legally and morally bound to stand against their common enemy.

The Prophet (SAS) was constrained to engage in defensive wars when the aggressive Quraysh, along with their allies, invaded Medina. With the help of Allah (SWT), within a few years, the Prophet (SAS) and his companions emerged successful, and this success culminated when he along with his companions marched toward Mecca and restored the sanctity of the sacred Ka'ba by cleansing it from idols and other objects of worship. This victory of Mecca was achieved without spilling blood. The Prophet (SAS), in keeping with his usual benevolence declared a general amnesty, even for those disbelievers who had crossed limits in their persecution and opposition of the believers. May we derive useful lessons from the noble life and teachings of the Prophet (SAS).

Brothers and sisters! Just two months before his passing, in 632, the Prophet (SAS) performed the hajj during which he delivered his famous farewell sermon. Among many advices, he admonished the believers to be good to one another, to be kind to women, to avoid usury, to eliminate prejudices of ethnicity and tribalism, and to be alert of the accursed Satan. On this occasion, Allah (SWT) signaled His pleasure to the Prophet (SAS) and to the community of believers by revealing what is believed to be the last revealed verse of the Qur'an.

الْيَوْمَ أَكْمَلْتُ لَكُمْ دِينَكُمْ وَأَتْمَمْتُ عَلَيْكُمْ نِعْمَتِي وَرَضِيتُ لَكُمُ الْإِسْلَامَ دِينًا ○

*Today I have perfected for you your faith, and have completed My favor upon you, and
am well-pleased with Islam as your deen. (al-Ma`ida, 5:3)*

Medina became the capital of the newborn Islamic state. The trials and tribulations of the believers in the Meccan period and their sincere commitment to struggle in the path of Allah (SWT) eventually resulted in the creation of a social order based on fairness and justice. This social order and stability were not restricted to Mecca and Medina; rather, it spread throughout the Arabian Peninsula and beyond.

Many of us are immigrants (*muhajiroon*) to the USA. We should create the same bond of brotherhood and sisterhood with the native *ansar* population of this land, such as the Muslim Caucasian, Latino, and African-American brothers and sisters, among others. We have to be united and not divided. We have to turn our mosques into centers of learning, as the Prophet (SAS) had done. Such centers of learning will unify, energize, and rejuvenate their students to struggle in the path of Allah (SWT) and to practice and convey Islam. We also need to engage the community and work with whoever likes to work with us toward providing social and humanitarian services. We have to come to terms with our opponents and repel evil with good. Allah (SWT) says,

وَلَا تَسْتَوِي الْحَسَنَةُ وَلَا السَّيِّئَةُ ادْفَعْ بِالَّتِي هِيَ أَحْسَنُ فَإِذَا الَّذِي بَيْنَكَ وَبَيْنَهُ عَدَاوَةٌ كَأَنَّهُ وَلِيٌّ حَمِيمٌ ○

*Good and evil cannot be equal. Repel evil with what is better, and your enemy will
become as close as an old and valued friend. (Fussilat, 41:34)*

There is also another type or dimension of Hijra that takes place in the heart of a believer. It is mentioned in a hadeeth in which the Prophet (SAS) says, "A Muslim is the one from whose tongue and hands the Muslims are safe and, an emigrant (*muhajir*) is the one who migrates from what Allah has forbidden."

This means that Hijra is not just physically moving to a new place, but also spiritually and ethically moving away from what Allah (SWT) has forbidden and struggling to stay on the right path. This implies being knowledgeable and mindful of God's commands and prohibitions, being strong enough to control one's urges, being aware of the world around us, and seeking to rise in rank in Allah's sight by constantly working to be a better person and a better Muslim. And this is best done by following the Prophet's model, for Allah (SWT) Himself attests to this.

لَقَدْ كَانَ لَكُمْ فِي رَسُولِ اللَّهِ أُسْوَةٌ حَسَنَةٌ لِمَنْ كَانَ يَرْجُو اللَّهَ وَالْيَوْمَ الْآخِرَ وَذَكَرَ اللَّهَ كَثِيرًا ○

*The Messenger of Allah is an excellent model for those of you who put your hope in
Allah and the Last Day and remember Allah often. (al-Ahzab, 33:21)*

# • 80 •

# SINCERITY *(IKHLAS)*

In today's *khutbah*, I intend to share some thoughts with you on the concept of *ikhlas*, or sincerity, which is an essential part of Islam. What is *ikhlas*? It is the intention to please Allah in whatever we do. The opposite of *ikhlas* is *nifaq* (hypocrisy) or *riya`* (showing off), both of which destroy faith and spoil good deeds. A believer must be a sincere person in every aspect of his or her life. Allah has commanded us to be sincere in our *deen* which means in our entire life.

قُلْ إِنَّ صَلَاتِي وَنُسُكِي وَمَحْيَايَ وَمَمَاتِي لِلَّهِ رَبِّ الْعَالَمِينَ ۝

*Say, My prayer, my sacrifice, my life, and my death are all for Allah, the Lord of the worlds. (al-An'am, 6:120)*

The Prophet (SAS) told a story about a scholar, a martyr, and a charitable man being judged by Allah on the Day of Judgment. As would be expected, they would be residents of paradise because of their highly virtuous and meritorious deeds. Instead, they were thrown into the hellfire, because their deeds were done with the intention of seeking praise from the people and not with the intention of pleasing Allah.

On the other hand, there is the story of the unchaste woman who was rewarded with paradise for giving water to a thirsty dog. What truly got her into paradise? Was it just her simple act? It could not have been because the acts of the scholar, martyr, and charitable man were far greater in terms of the sacrifices they made. However, they were punished because they wanted praise from the people, which they received as a worldly reward. They were insincere in their relationship with Allah. But the woman who had helped the dog did so for Allah's sake only.

Look how the sincerity of intention elevates a person's deeds. This is why the scholars have said that *ikhlas* is the most important act of worship of the heart. The driving force of one's acts should always be to seek the pleasure of Allah only.

Allah tells us that Iblees promised to lead all the human beings astray except those who were sincere and purified.

قَالَ فَبِعِزَّتِكَ لَأُغْوِيَنَّهُمْ أَجْمَعِينَ ۝ إِلَّا عِبَادَكَ مِنْهُمُ الْمُخْلَصِينَ ۝

*(Iblees) said, "By Your Honor, I will lead all of them astray, except for those among them who are Your sincere worshippers." (Saad, 38:82-83)*

And we are told in the story of Yusuf (AS) that he was saved from falling into the trap of

'Azeez's wife, who tried to seduce him, because he was sincere and purified.

$$\text{وَلَقَدْ هَمَّتْ بِهِ وَهَمَّ بِهَا لَوْلَا أَن رَّأَىٰ بُرْهَانَ رَبِّهِ كَذَٰلِكَ لِنَصْرِفَ عَنْهُ السُّوءَ وَالْفَحْشَاءَ إِنَّهُ مِنْ عِبَادِنَا الْمُخْلَصِينَ} \ \bigcirc$$

*And she desired him, and he would have desired her, had it not been that he saw the proof of his Lord. Thus We warded off evil and indecency from him, for he was one of our servants; sincere and purified. (Yusuf, 12:24)*

The Qur`an also tells us about the story of the mother of Maryam having a beautiful private conversation with Allah. Expecting that she would give birth to a male child, she told Allah that she would pledge the child in her womb to His service. For the sincerity of her intention, Allah accepted that female child to fulfill her mother's pledge. And we know that Maryam (AS), mother of 'Isa (AS) is among the best women described in the Qur`an.

We learn from the stories of the *sahaba* that Khalid ibn al-Waleed (RAA) was removed from his post as commander of the Muslim army by 'Umar ibn al-Khattab (RAA). This was not done to humiliate Khalid ibn al-Waleed in any way. This was done to let the Muslims realize that it was not because of Khalid's bravery and military leadership that they won every battle under his command, but it was solely because of Allah's favor upon them. After being demoted, instead of being offended and refusing to fight, Khalid ibn al-Waleed fought with even more vigor. When he was asked the reason for this, he said, "I fight for Allah and not for 'Umar."

Even a small deed done with *ikhlas* is extremely valuable. Once Mu'adh ibn Jabal (RAA) asked the Prophet (SAS) for an advice, and the Prophet (SAS) said to him, "Be sincere in your *deen*; even a small deed will be enough for you."

Only Allah knows the sincerity of a person. Some scholars say *ikhlas* is a secret between the human being and Allah. Even the Angels don't write it down because they don't know it. Reflective of this is the story of the martyr, the scholar, and the charitable man that was mentioned above. The Angels had written down their good acts, but it was Allah who exposed their intention behind those acts. Do we ever ask ourselves how sincere we are in our devotion to Allah (SWT)? We have the command in *Surat az-Zumar*,

$$\bigcirc \ \text{قُلْ إِنِّي أُمِرْتُ أَنْ أَعْبُدَ اللَّهَ مُخْلِصًا لَّهُ الدِّينَ}$$

*Say, "I have been commanded to worship Allah, with sincere devotion." (az-Zumar, 39:11)*

What does "sincere devotion" mean, and how can we determine our level of sincerity toward Allah? As travelers moving spiritually toward our ultimate destination, we should always be assessing our level of sincerity. How can we measure and boost our sincerity? There are several ways of measuring *ikhlas*. One is to look within, examining our emotions and contemplating our sense of closeness to Allah. Are we performing our actions only for Allah? How indifferent are we to what others think of us? Are our hearts and minds actively engaged in what we do?

Yet as valuable as these questions are, there is a danger in only turning inward, as all spheres of life are ultimately interconnected in Islam. The interior is fundamentally inseparable from the exterior. In *Surat al-Ma'oon*, for example, Allah links the oppressor of orphans with the man who does not urge others to feed the poor and who shows off in prayer.

أَرَأَيْتَ الَّذِي يُكَذِّبُ بِالدِّينِ ۞ فَذَلِكَ الَّذِي يَدُعُّ الْيَتِيمَ ۞ وَلَا يَحُضُّ عَلَى طَعَامِ الْمِسْكِينِ ۞ فَوَيْلٌ لِلْمُصَلِّينَ ۞ الَّذِينَ هُمْ عَنْ صَلَاتِهِمْ سَاهُونَ ۞ الَّذِينَ هُمْ يُرَاءُونَ ۞ وَيَمْنَعُونَ الْمَاعُونَ ۞

*Have you seen him who denies the deen? Who turns away the orphan, and who does not urge the feeding of the poor; so woe to those who pray; but whose hearts are not in their prayer; those who show off, and deny help to others. (al-Ma'oon, 107:1-7)*

The common feature of such people is their lack of sincerity toward Allah (SWT). For this reason, it is our actions and social relations that we must turn to if we wish to assess our level of sincerity or *ikhlas*. May Allah give us the *tawfeeq* to do so.

Brothers and sisters! Consider the following scenarios, all of which should raise a question:

A Muslim says, "I love Allah" but does not pray.

A Muslim says, "I love the Prophet (SAS)" but is reluctant to follow the Sunnah or the Prophet's way.

A Muslim says, "O Allah, I repent" but then defiantly persists in his disobedience.

A Muslim tells his spouse, "I love you" but then neglects her emotionally or abuses her physically.

In all of these situations there is no connection between the intention and the action. A beautiful advice from our beloved Prophet Muhammad (SAS) was, "Have *taqwa* of Allah wherever you are."

*Taqwa*, besides its meanings of righteousness, piety, and saving oneself from harm, also means to be conscious and mindful of Allah. When we are truly conscious of Allah, we will avoid actions that are displeasing to Him. Had the individuals mentioned in *Surat al-Ma'oon* been truly conscious of Allah, would they have done what they did? One of the great scholars by the name of Isma'eel ibn al-Husayn al-Jurjani provided an excellent benchmark for *ikhlas* when he said, "*Ikhlas* is when you don't ask anyone to witness your work except Allah." We should all try to meet this standard. Thus, when we perform any good deed or engage in an act of worship, let us ask ourselves: "Are we truly focused on our worship?" "Are we doing this for Allah only?" "Are we indifferent to what others might think, whether it be positive or negative?"

Once we know our level of *ikhlas*, we can pursue a variety of paths in order to boost it even higher. We should remember that perfection belongs only to Allah (SWT). As humans we make mistakes, but we shouldn't let this discourage us. Allah tells us through a *hadeeth qudsi*, "If you take one step toward Me, I take ten toward you." We should strive to be consistent in all our actions. We should equip ourselves with self-knowledge of both our shortcomings and our deficiencies. If we don't know our own faults how can we improve them? We should endeavor to be as trustworthy as we can with our fellow human beings by fulfilling all of our obligations at work, home, and in the community. When we build trust with our fellow human beings, we build trust with Allah (SWT). We should examine our current relationships and search for ways to improve upon them.

Have we deceived someone in the past? Is there someone we need to apologize to? No matter how much time has passed it is never too late to improve a relationship. There may be other paths, as well, to boosting our sincerity. Sincerity requires right intention and right action whether the action is done in private or in public.

However, we must also keep in mind that not everything done with right intention is acceptable in Islam. It must be based on right actions as well. Only lawful, truthful, and moral actions are good when done with the sincerity of heart.

May Allah (SWT) make us among those people who strive to be among the sincere ones. *Allahumma ameen.*

<br>

• 81 •

# SOURCES OF BLESSING *(BARAKA)*

In today's *khutbah*, I want to share some thoughts with you on the topic of *baraka*, or divine blessing. What is *baraka*? It is the attachment of divine goodness to something. It also means an increase in the amount of good in something. *Baraka* cannot be quantified. For example, having more *baraka* in one's wealth does not mean the dollar amount increases; rather it means that the benefit emerging from that amount increases. In terms of our everyday life activities it means that if you have *baraka*, a little suffices and you are happy and satisfied without any problem. If we get a raise, but most of it ends up being spent on extravagance and unforeseen expenses which do not add value to our lives, then that raise or increment we got lacked *baraka*. Similarly, if we have spent our lives toiling hard to educate our children in the best schools only to find them to be lacking in the values we expect from them, then our efforts were without *baraka*.

Muhammed Faris of the "Productive Muslim" website writes, "If we were to look for an Islamic definition of productivity it can probably be summarized in the word *baraka*. Being able to achieve more with few resources, doing much in little time, and generating a lot with little effort is surely a blessing from Allah." Another important aspect of *baraka* is that the end result should be productive, not only in this world, but also in the hereafter. Therefore, short term gains that result in disasters in the hereafter, even if they appear profitable in this world, definitely lack *baraka*.

*Baraka* seems to be missing from our lives. Often, we hear people complaining that there's no *baraka* in their money, no *baraka* in their time, no *baraka* in their life, and so on. Actually, *baraka* is right in front of them, but it is handed over only to those who work for it. What are some of the means of bringing *baraka* into every aspect of our lives? Some of the things that we can do to have *baraka* in our lives are:

1. To have good intentions. If we want something to have *baraka* attached to it, we must have purity of intention, which means that whatever we do should be for the sake of Allah (SWT). If the intention is not pure, then what we do will not have divine goodness attached to it, and therefore, there will be no *baraka*. The Prophet (SAS) said in a hadeeth, "Actions are judged by intentions and every man shall have only that which he intended."

2. To earn a lawful and wholesome income. We should ensure that our line of work does not contravene the Sacred Law and that our wealth is *halal* (lawful). Our work should be moral and ethical. The Prophet (SAS) said, "O people, Allah is good and He, therefore, accepts only that which is good." It is said the limbs of one who eats *haram* will disobey Allah whether he likes it or not, and that the limbs of one who eats *halal* and seeks *halal* income will do good and will be given permission to seek goodness.

3. To work with excellence, loyalty, and honesty. The Prophet (SAS) said in a hadeeth, "Allah loves that if one does a job, he perfects it." In other words, Allah (SWT) is pleased with the person who when he performs a deed, he executes it with excellence. *Itqan*, or perfection of action, is a part of our *amana*. Being thorough in doing something is an obligation upon Muslims. We have to be loyal and honest at work. We should not squander the time and resources at our disposal. Lying, cheating, and deceiving others removes *baraka* from our lives. Allah warns in the Qur`an,

وَيْلٌ لِلْمُطَفِّفِينَ

*Woe to those who defraud. (al-Mutaffifeen, 83:1)*

4. To have the *taqwa* of Allah (SWT), which means to be conscious and mindful of Allah (SWT). Allah (SWT) says in *Surat at-Talaq*,

$$وَمَنْ يَتَّقِ اللَّهَ يَجْعَلْ لَهُ مَخْرَجًا وَيَرْزُقْهُ مِنْ حَيْثُ لَا يَحْتَسِبُ ◯$$

*Allah will find a way out for those who are conscious of Him and will provide for them from sources they could never imagine. (at-Talaq, 65:2-3)*

Further, Allah also says,

$$وَمَنْ يَتَّقِ اللَّهَ يَجْعَلْ لَهُ مِنْ أَمْرِهِ يُسْرا ◯$$

*Allah makes things easy for those who are mindful of Him. (at-Talaq, 65:4)*

Thus we know that the people of *taqwa*, the people who are righteous and pious, are blessed.

5. To give thanks to Allah in abundance. We should thank Allah with our tongue, with our heart, and through our actions by using His blessings for good purposes, and by worshipping and obeying Him. Allah says in the Qur'an,

$$لَئِنْ شَكَرْتُمْ لَأَزِيدَنَّكُمْ ◯$$

*If you are thankful, I will give you more. (Ibraheem, 14:7)*

So Allah is promising the person who thanks Him an increase in blessings. He also says,

$$إِنَّ اللَّهَ لَا يُخْلِفُ الْمِيعَادَ ◯$$

*Allah never breaks His promise. (Aal 'Imran, 3:9)*

6. To repent for one's sins and ask Allah for forgiveness. Sins strip away *baraka* from our lives, while repentance restores the *baraka*. We learn from the stories of our pious predecessors that once a person came to Imam Hasan al-Basri (RA) and complained of a drought in his community. The imam told him to repent. Another came to see him complaining of poverty, and again, he was told to repent. Another came to see him complaining of not having children, and again, he was told to repent. He was asked why his advice remained the same whatever the issue he was confronted with. The imam replied that this was not his own advice; it was the advice of Nuh (AS) to his people as mentioned in the Qur'an,

$$فَقُلْتُ اسْتَغْفِرُوا رَبَّكُمْ إِنَّهُ كَانَ غَفَّارًا ◯ يُرْسِلِ السَّمَاءَ عَلَيْكُمْ مِدْرَارًا ◯ وَيُمْدِدْكُمْ بِأَمْوَالٍ وَبَنِينَ وَيَجْعَلْ لَكُمْ جَنَّاتٍ وَيَجْعَلْ لَكُمْ أَنْهَارًا ◯$$

*I said, pray to your Lord for forgiveness. Indeed, He is All-forgiving; He will send rain to you in abundance. He will give you wealth and sons; He will provide you with gardens and rivers. (Nuh, 71:10-12)*

7. To say *bismillah*. How many times do we actually forget to mention Allah when we start doing something? According to the Productive Muslim, "When we say *bismillah* before anything we do we're invoking the name of Allah (SWT) on that activity. Not only will that activity be blessed, but Shaytan cannot take part in it! So we should always say *bismillah* before anything we do!" The habit of pronouncing the name of Allah is bound to make one think before committing an evil act and to consider how such an act can be reconciled with the uttering of Allah's name.

8. To wake up early. We should try to work in mornings, and try to become productive after *Fajr* by not sleeping through the early part of the day. The Prophet (SAS) prayed, "Oh Allah, give *baraka* to my *ummah* in their early morning work." Waking up early is an important step to being blessed and feeling good throughout the day.

9. To read the Qur`an. This is the fountain of *baraka*! But *subhan Allah*, we rarely drink from it. Allah (SWT) says in *Surat al-An'am*,

$$\text{وَهَٰذَا كِتَابٌ أَنزَلْنَاهُ مُبَارَكٌ}$$

*This is a blessed Book We have sent down.* (al-An'am, 6:92)

It is reported that the Prophet (SAS) said, "Indeed, the house in which the Qur`an is recited—the goodness in it increases..." and in another version, "things are made easier for its family." So we should read the Qur`an and observe the blessings and *baraka* of Allah enter our lives. The further we are from this book of guidance the less *baraka* we will have in our lives.

10. To make du'a` for baraka. The Prophet (SAS) always used to make du'a` for baraka. Some of his du'a`s include:"O Allah I ask You for the good of this day, for its victory and its help, for its light and its baraka, and its guidance." Before eating, he used to say, "O Allah, give baraka in it for us and give us more of it." For the host he would pray, "O Allah, give them baraka in that which you have provided them, forgive them, and have mercy on them." To a newly wedded couple he would say, "May Allah bless you and shower his blessings upon you and keep you together in goodness."

Other areas of life where we should ask for *baraka* are in our time and wealth. Nowadays, despite the fact that technology and other material possessions exist to make our lives easier and save us time, we still feel dissatisfied and struggle to find time to fulfill our responsibilities. This is a symptom of our lives being devoid of *baraka* and is certainly something to ponder upon. *Baraka* in our wealth gives us contentment and satisfaction, and we feel that we are receiving value for our money.

11. To give in charity. However illogical it may sound, giving in charity does not decrease one's wealth. This is confirmed both by the Qur`an and the sayings of

our beloved Prophet Muhammad (SAS). The Prophet (SAS) said, "Charity does not reduce wealth." The physical amount appears to decrease outwardly, but the remaining amount attracts *baraka* so that the actual benefit from it is not less. We have to try to fight the urge to be stingy. Allah says in *Surat al-Hashr*,

وَمَن يُوقَ شُحَّ نَفْسِهِ فَأُولَٰئِكَ هُمُ الْمُفْلِحُونَ ۝

*And those who are saved from the stinginess of their own souls are truly successful.*
(al-Hashr, 59:9)

12. To maintain ties of kinship. The Prophet (SAS) said that by maintaining good relations with relatives one's life is prolonged, sustenance and provisions are blessed and increased, happiness and prosperity become the natural consequence, and one protects oneself from the evil ends. Most of all be obedient, dutiful, and respectful to your parents.

13. To eat together. It is said that some of the companions of the Prophet (SAS) complained that they ate but did not feel satisfied. The Prophet (SAS) said, "Perhaps you eat separately." They said, "Yes." He said, "If you gather together and mention Allah's name, you will be blessed in it." He is also reported to have said, "Eat together and do not eat separately, for the blessing (*baraka*) is with the company."

14. To follow the Sunnah of the Prophet (SAS). The most productive man in the history of mankind is none other than our beloved Prophet Muhammad (SAS). Therefore, by following his lifestyle we obtain a great source of *baraka*. Following the example of the life of the most blessed man on earth is surely a source of blessing.

My dear brothers and sisters! These are a few of the numerous ways to fill one's life with *baraka*. However, the general rule of thumb to attract *baraka* is always the same. When we attach our hearts to Allah (SWT), submit to Him completely, and make Him our sole goal and purpose, then the *baraka* will enter our lives from all sides without us having to worry about it. May Allah (SWT) increase the *baraka* in our lives, in our time, in our knowledge, in our health, in our wealth, in our families, and in our communities and societies. May He give each one of us a deep understanding of our noble *deen* and bless each one of us to be successful in both the worlds. *Ameen.*

---

*This *khutbah* is based on and summarized from "The Productive Muslim, *18 Sources of Barakah*." https://productivemuslim.com/18-sources-of-barakah/

# 82

# SPENDING IN THE WAY OF ALLAH

*Al-hamduli-llah*, we are passing through the blessed month of Ramadan. It is not only the month of fasting but also the month of Qur`an. It is the month of compassion. It is the month of piety, patience, forgiveness, and thankfulness to Allah (SWT). It is also the month of spending in charitable causes to attain the pleasure of Allah. My *khutbah* today is on the topic of spending in charitable causes, especially during the holy month of Ramadan. It is well known that our beloved Prophet Muhammad (SAS) was charitable throughout his life, but one finds him still more charitable during the month of Ramadan. The rewards of acts of charity during Ramadan are multiplied many times over.

We learn from the Qur`an that man by his very nature loves wealth and other material possessions intensely.

وَتُحِبُّونَ الْمَالَ حُبًّا جَمًّا ۝

*And you love wealth with a passion. (al-Fajr, 89:20)*

زُيِّنَ لِلنَّاسِ حُبُّ الشَّهَوَاتِ ۝

*Appealing to man is the enjoyment of worldly desires. (Aal 'Imran, 3:14)*

Despite the inherent attachment to material things the attitude of Muslims toward wealth is not the same as other people. This is because Muslims have the true divine guidance with them while others do not. People generally do not understand the Islamic concept of wealth, which boils down to the fact that man owns nothing. The real owner of everything is Allah (SWT). Whatever we have is only a sacred trust, an *amana*, from Him. Muslims understand that what they possess is not their earnings, but the favor, blessing, and *fadl* (bounty) of Allah. In *Surat al-Jumu'ah* Allah makes this notion very clear.

فَإِذَا قُضِيَتِ الصَّلَاةُ فَانتَشِرُوا فِي الْأَرْضِ وَابْتَغُوا مِن فَضْلِ اللَّهِ وَاذْكُرُوا اللَّهَ كَثِيرًا لَّعَلَّكُمْ تُفْلِحُونَ ۝

*Then when the prayer has ended, disperse in the land and seek out Allah's fadl (bounty).*
*Remember Allah often so that you may prosper. (al-Jumu'ah, 62:10)*

Believers are told to spend from whatever Allah (SWT) has given them:

وَآتُوهُم مِّن مَّالِ اللَّهِ الَّذِي آتَاكُمْ ۝

*And give them some of the wealth Allah has given you.* (an-Nur, 24:33)

The *muttaqeen*, those who are mindful of Allah (SWT), spend from what Allah (SWT) has given them. Describing them, Allah (SWT) says,

الَّذِينَ يُؤْمِنُونَ بِالْغَيْبِ وَيُقِيمُونَ الصَّلَاةَ وَمِمَّا رَزَقْنَاهُمْ يُنْفِقُونَ ◯

*(They are) those who believe in the unseen, and are steadfast in prayer, and spend out of what We have provided them with.* (al-Baqara, 2:3)

While people tend to think that being the owners of their wealth, they can dispose of it the way they like, Muslims understand that their wealth has been provided by Allah (SWT) only to satisfy and fulfill their needs. Any surplus has to be spent in the way of Allah (SWT).

وَيَسْأَلُونَكَ مَاذَا يُنْفِقُونَ قُلِ الْعَفْوَ ◯

*They ask you what they should give: Say: "Give what you can spare."* (al-Baqara, 2:219)

This has been explained in verse 215 of *Surat al-Baqara.*

يَسْأَلُونَكَ مَاذَا يُنْفِقُونَ قُلْ مَا أَنْفَقْتُم مِّنْ خَيْرٍ فَلِلْوَالِدَيْنِ وَالْأَقْرَبِينَ وَالْيَتَامَىٰ وَالْمَسَاكِينِ وَابْنِ السَّبِيلِ وَمَا تَفْعَلُوا مِنْ خَيْرٍ فَإِنَّ اللَّهَ بِهِ عَلِيمٌ ◯

*They ask you what they should give. Say: "Whatever you give should be for parents, close relatives, orphans, the needy, and travelers." Allah is well aware of whatever good you do.* (al-Baqara, 2:215)

Muslims understand that the poor and the needy have a known right in their wealth.

وَالَّذِينَ فِي أَمْوَالِهِمْ حَقٌّ مَّعْلُومٌ ◯

*And in whose wealth there is a known right.* (al-Ma'arij, 70:24)

The attributes of piety, of real virtue, and of spending in the way of Allah (SWT) are all linked with each other. Virtue and piety have to do with *iman* and a host of other good deeds including spending in the path of Allah. Spending in the path of Allah is such a meritorious act that Allah calls it a trade that will never decline.

إِنَّ الَّذِينَ يَتْلُونَ كِتَابَ اللَّهِ وَأَقَامُوا الصَّلَاةَ وَأَنْفَقُوا مِمَّا رَزَقْنَاهُمْ سِرًّا وَعَلَانِيَةً يَرْجُونَ تِجَارَةً لَّن تَبُورَ ◯

*Those who recite Allah's Book, keep up the prayer, give secretly and openly from what We have provided for them, may hope for a trade that will never decline.* (Fatir, 35:29)

To encourage others to give one may spend openly also, as long as this is done with the sincerest of intentions, and without a trace of *al riya`*, or showing off. Showing off is so dangerous that the Prophet (SAS) called it the minor *shirk*. He said, "Indeed the thing I fear for you the most is the minor *shirk*." The companions of the Prophet (SAS) asked him, "What is minor *shirk*, O Messenger of Allah?" He said, "*ar-riya.*" Muslims give because they know that Allah (SWT) is has guided them, and that He compensates by giving back many times over.

إِن تُقْرِضُوا اللَّهَ قَرْضًا حَسَنًا يُضَاعِفْهُ لَكُمْ وَيَغْفِرْ لَكُمْ وَاللَّهُ شَكُورٌ حَلِيمٌ ◯

*If you make a good loan to Allah, He will multiply it for you and forgive you. Allah is all-appreciative and forbearing. (at-Taghabun, 64:17)*

In another place we are reminded,

وَمَا تُنفِقُوا مِنْ خَيْرٍ فَلِأَنفُسِكُمْ وَمَا تُنفِقُونَ إِلَّا ابْتِغَاءَ وَجْهِ اللَّهِ وَمَا تُنفِقُوا مِنْ خَيْرٍ يُوَفَّ إِلَيْكُمْ وَأَنتُمْ لَا تُظْلَمُونَ ◯

*Whatever charity you give benefits your own soul, provided you do it for the sake of Allah. Whatever you give will be repaid to you in full, and you will not be wronged.*
*(al-Baqara, 2:272)*

May Allah (SWT) grant us understanding and goodness.

My dear brothers and sisters! Allah (SWT) gives an example of those who spend in His way:

مَّثَلُ الَّذِينَ يُنفِقُونَ أَمْوَالَهُمْ فِي سَبِيلِ اللَّهِ كَمَثَلِ حَبَّةٍ أَنبَتَتْ سَبْعَ سَنَابِلَ فِي كُلِّ سُنبُلَةٍ مِّائَةُ حَبَّةٍ وَاللَّهُ يُضَاعِفُ لِمَن يَشَاءُ وَاللَّهُ وَاسِعٌ عَلِيمٌ ◯

*Those who spend their wealth in Allah's cause are like grains of corn that produce seven ears, each bearing a hundred grains. Allah gives multiple increase to whoever He wishes: He is limitless and all knowing. (al-Baqara, 2:261)*

The recipients of such grace of Allah (SWT) are those who do not follow their spending with reminders or hurtful words hurled upon those whom they given support or a gift.

الَّذِينَ يُنفِقُونَ أَمْوَالَهُمْ فِي سَبِيلِ اللَّهِ ثُمَّ لَا يُتْبِعُونَ مَا أَنفَقُوا مَنًّا وَلَا أَذًى لَّهُمْ أَجْرُهُمْ عِندَ رَبِّهِمْ وَلَا خَوْفٌ عَلَيْهِمْ وَلَا هُمْ يَحْزَنُونَ ◯

*Those who spend their wealth in Allah's cause, and do not follow their spending with reminders of their benevolence or hurtful words, will have their rewards with their Lord: no fear for them, nor will they grieve. (al-Baqara, 2:262)*

At the same time we should never be harsh upon or repel those who ask us for something.

فَأَمَّا الْيَتِيمَ فَلَا تَقْهَرْ وَأَمَّا السَّائِلَ فَلَا تَنْهَرْ ◯

*So do not be harsh with the orphan, and as for the beggar, do not scold him. (ad-Duha, 93:9-10)*

However illogical it may sound, giving in charity does not decrease one's wealth. On the contrary, it increases it, and becomes a source of inner peace and contentment. The companions of the Prophet (SAS) used to be afraid that the day they stopped giving, Allah (SWT) would stop providing for them. The Prophet (SAS) said, "Charity does not decrease wealth. No one forgives except that Allah increases his honor, and no one humbles himself for Allah except that Allah raises his status."

My dear brothers and sisters! Man takes nothing with him in his grave. The Prophet (SAS) said, "When a man dies, his deeds come to an end except for three things: (1) ongoing charity (*sadaqa jariya*), (2) beneficial knowledge that he leaves behind, and (3) a virtuous descendant who prays for him." Such admonitions remind us that we should hasten in doing good deeds before our time is up and our book of deeds gets closed forever. We should not be among those who will cry to Allah (SWT) to give them more time to spend in His way and to be one of the righteous.

وَأَنفِقُوا مِن مَّا رَزَقْنَاكُم مِّن قَبْلِ أَن يَأْتِيَ أَحَدَكُمُ الْمَوْتُ فَيَقُولَ رَبِّ لَوْلَا أَخَّرْتَنِي إِلَىٰ أَجَلٍ قَرِيبٍ فَأَصَّدَّقَ وَأَكُن مِّنَ الصَّالِحِينَ ⬡

*Give from what We have provided for you before death comes to one of you and he says: "My Lord, if only you would give me a little more time so that I can give sadaqa and be one of the righteous!" (al-Munafiqoon, 63:10)*

The blessed month of Ramadan provides us a chance to attain multiplied rewards. Indeed, the month of Ramadan is the month of giving and receiving charity. Righteous believers are steadfast in seeking the favor of their Lord. They pray regularly and spend secretly and openly out of what they have been provided with. They ward off evil with good. While they do all this on a regular basis, they do so more consciously during the month of Ramadan. And in return, they are promised the eternal abode of paradise.

وَالَّذِينَ صَبَرُوا ابْتِغَاءَ وَجْهِ رَبِّهِمْ وَأَقَامُوا الصَّلَاةَ وَأَنفَقُوا مِمَّا رَزَقْنَاهُمْ سِرًّا وَعَلَانِيَةً وَيَدْرَءُونَ بِالْحَسَنَةِ السَّيِّئَةَ أُولَٰئِكَ لَهُمْ عُقْبَى الدَّارِ ⬡

*And those who exercise patience to gain the pleasure of Allah, who are steadfast in prayer, who spend for the cause of Allah privately and in public, and who keep away evil with good will have the eternal abode. (ar-Ra'd, 13:22)*

May Allah (SWT) make us among those who are able to give generously for every good cause. May Allah (SWT) make us of the dwellers of paradise and save us from the fire of hell. *Allahumma ameen.*

# 83

# STAGES OF PURIFICATION
# BEFORE ENTERING *JANNAH*

Regarding paradise, there is a *hadeeth qudsi* in which the Prophet (SAS) tells us that Allah (SWT) said, "I have prepared for my righteous servants what no eye has seen, no ear has heard, and the mind of no man has conceived…" And a verse in the Qur`an Allah tells us,

فَلَا تَعْلَمُ نَفْسٌ مَّا أُخْفِيَ لَهُم مِّن قُرَّةِ أَعْيُنٍ جَزَاءً بِمَا كَانُوا يَعْمَلُونَ ۝

*No soul can imagine what delights are kept in store for them as a reward for what they used to do. (as-Sajda. 32:17)*

In another verse we read,

وَسِيقَ الَّذِينَ اتَّقَوْا رَبَّهُمْ إِلَى الْجَنَّةِ زُمَرًا حَتَّى إِذَا جَاءُوهَا وَفُتِحَتْ أَبْوَابُهَا وَقَالَ لَهُمْ خَزَنَتُهَا سَلَامٌ عَلَيْكُمْ طِبْتُمْ فَادْخُلُوهَا خَالِدِينَ ۝

*And those who were mindful of their Lord will be driven to paradise in crowds. When they reach it, its gates will open, and its custodians will say, "Peace be upon you; you have done well, so enter it to reside there eternally." (az-Zumar, 39:73)*

Based on Prophetic traditions, scholars have said that it is essential for those who will be admitted to *jannah* to be washed and purified of all their sins before they enter it. The cleansing of sins will take place in this world or in the hereafter or both. There are twelve stages of purification from sins for a believer who testifies to the oneness of Allah (SWT) before he or she is admitted into paradise: four are in this life, three after death, and five on the Day of Judgment after resurrection takes place. The first stage of purification is that any sin committed is followed with good deeds.

إِنَّ الْحَسَنَاتِ يُذْهِبْنَ السَّيِّئَاتِ ۝ وَأَقِمِ الصَّلَاةَ طَرَفَيِ النَّهَارِ وَزُلَفًا مِّنَ اللَّيْلِ ۝

*And establish prayer at the beginning and end of the day, as well as during parts of the night. Surely, good deeds drive away evil deeds. (Hud, 11:114)*

One of the best ways of purification is to establish prayers (*salah*). It reminds a person of Allah over and over again and produces those good characteristics in him that help him fight against evil. We should be smart enough to do as many good deeds as possible on a daily basis. While good deeds eradicate our evil deeds, they also accumulate for us in the records that are maintained for each one of us in the hereafter. Allah out of His mercy rewards a good deed at least ten times over, while a bad deed is repaid only with its equivalent.

مَنْ جَاءَ بِالْحَسَنَةِ فَلَهُ عَشْرُ أَمْثَالِهَا وَمَنْ جَاءَ بِالسَّيِّئَةِ فَلَا يُجْزَى إِلَّا مِثْلَهَا وَهُمْ لَا يُظْلَمُونَ ⬤

*Whoever comes with a good deed will be rewarded tenfold. But whoever comes with a bad deed will only be repaid with its equivalent. They will not be treated unjustly.*
(al-An'am, 6:160)

The second stage of purification is to actively and constantly seek Allah's forgiveness (*istighfar*). Istighfar is the process of admitting one's sin and being painfully sorry for it. We should have some moments of privacy with Allah, and beg Him to purify us by forgiving our misdeeds. We are not born in sin, but we are born in weakness. Allah (SWT) says,

يُرِيدُ اللَّهُ أَن يُخَفِّفَ عَنكُمْ وَخُلِقَ الْإِنسَانُ ضَعِيفًا ⬤

*Allah wants to lighten your burden as human beings were created weak.* (an-Nisa`, 4:28)

We are prone to fall prey to the many temptations that are part of our test in this life. Allah (SWT) says,

وَاسْتَغْفِرُوا اللَّهَ إِنَّ اللَّهَ غَفُورٌ رَحِيمٌ ⬤

*And ask Allah for His forgiveness. Truly, Allah is oft-forgiving, most merciful.* (al-Baqara, 2:199)

The third stage of purification is *tawba* (repentance). It means to move away from past sinful and evil activities and to firmly resolve to abstain from them in future. Both the Qur`an and the hadeeth incorporate the word *tawba* to refer to the act of leaving what Allah (SWT) has prohibited and returning to what He has commanded. One of the most beautiful things about *tawba* is that Allah not only wipes the sins off but also replaces them with good deeds.

مَن تَابَ وَآمَنَ وَعَمِلَ عَمَلًا صَالِحًا فَأُولَٰئِكَ يُبَدِّلُ اللَّهُ سَيِّئَاتِهِمْ حَسَنَاتٍ وَكَانَ اللَّهُ غَفُورًا رَحِيمًا ⬤

*Those who repent, believe, and do good deeds, Allah will change the evil deeds of such people into good ones. He is most forgiving, most merciful.* (al-Furqan, 25:70)

The fourth stage of purification comes through natural disasters, calamities, and adversities that we often encounter in our lives. We have to recognize that trials and tribulations are woven into our lives. Allah says,

وَلَنَبْلُوَنَّكُم بِشَيْءٍ مِنَ الْخَوْفِ وَالْجُوعِ وَنَقْصٍ مِنَ الْأَمْوَالِ وَالْأَنفُسِ وَالثَّمَرَاتِ وَبَشِّرِ الصَّابِرِينَ ◯

*We will test you with a certain amount of fear and hunger and loss of wealth and life
and fruits. But give good news to those who are patient. (al-Baqara, 2:155)*

The Prophet (SAS) said, "No fatigue, disease, sorrow, sadness, hurt, or distress befalls
a Muslim, even if it was the prick he receives from a thorn, but that Allah expiates
some of his sins for that."

For those believers who have not been purified of all their sins while living there
are three stages of purification when they die. One of them is the supplication or
*du'a'* of the believers for the deceased, such as their offering the funeral prayer for
him. This prayer is one of the means of the deceased person being forgiven, and the
more people pray on the body of the deceased, the more sins will be forgiven for that
deceased person. Therefore, our relationship with other Muslims and other human
beings should be cordial so that when we die more people come to perform the *salat
al-janaza* over us.

When the son of Adam dies and his soul departs, and he is placed in his grave, the
angels who are charged with questioning come and ask him what he used to believe
in this world: who was his Lord, what was his religion, and who was his Prophet? If he
gives a good answer all is well, but if he does not answer them they inflict a severe and
painful beating on him. This is the *fitna*, or tribulation, that he suffers and one of the
stages that expiates his sins.

Good deeds done on behalf of those who have passed away are also a source of
forgiveness and purification for them. The scholars are agreed that the benefits of
*du'a'*, praying for forgiveness, giving charity, and hajj reach the deceased. We should
make *du'a'* for the living and the dead. That is how one of the *du'a'*s begins in funeral
prayer,

اللهُمَّ اغْفِرْ لِحَيِّنَا وَمَيِّتِنَا ◯

*"O Allah! Forgive our living and our dead."*

With regard to our parents, whether living or dead, one of the best ways of benefiting
them is to make a lot of *du'a'* for them, for Allah says,

وَقُل رَّبِّ ارْحَمْهُمَا كَمَا رَبَّيَانِي صَغِيرًا ◯

*And say: "O Lord, have mercy on them as they did in looking after me when I was
small." (al-Isra', 17:24)*

With regard to charity, it was narrated from 'A'isha (RAA) that a man said to the
Prophet (SAS), "My mother died suddenly and she did not leave a will, but I think that
if she could have spoken she would have given in charity. Will she have a reward if
I give in charity on her behalf?" The Prophet (SAS) said, "Yes." With regard to hajj,

the Prophet (SAS) said to one who asked him about hajj, "Don't you think that if your mother had a debt, you would pay it off for her?" The person said, "Yes." The Prophet (SAS) said, "A debt owed to Allah (SWT) is more deserving of being paid off." And it was narrated that the Messenger of Allah (SAS) said, "When a man dies all his good deeds come to an end except three: ongoing charity, beneficial knowledge, and a righteous child who will pray for him."

Brothers and sisters! There are five stages of purification on the Day of Judgment after resurrection takes place for those who still need to be purified of their evil deeds before they are admitted into *jannah.*

The first of these stages of purification takes place in the difficulties, hardships, and pain that people will have to undergo while experiencing the horrors of the Day of Judgment in varying degrees based on their faith, deeds, and how they conducted themselves here on this earth.

The second stage of purification will take place at the time when all people will have to stand before Allah (SWT) to give an account of their deeds during their stay on earth. Even those whose good deeds are found to exceed their evil deeds will still have no idea how they will fare in the phases that were still to come.

The third stage of purification will be the great intercession of the Prophet Muhammad (SAS) and others such as angels, martyrs, and those whom Allah will give permission to intercede for sinners. In one of the Prophetic traditions, the Prophet (SAS) said, "My intercession will be for those among my *ummah* who committed major sins, and I was given the choice between admitting half of my *ummah* to *jannah* and intercession, and I chose intercession because it is more general and greater. Do you think it will be only for the pious? No, it will be for the sinners who contaminated themselves with sins."

The fourth stage of purification will be at the time of crossing the *sirat,* the bridge over hell. The Prophet (SAS) informed us that people will go through different experiences when crossing the *sirat.* Some will cross it safely, others will be wounded and have their limbs maimed by the hooks found on the *sirat* that will be ordered to wound them then release them, and another group of people will be cast into hell and the Prophet (SAS) will be standing on the *sirat* invoking Allah the Almighty for their salvation. This will continue until the last person is found unable to cross the *sirat* except by crawling.

After passing the phase of the *sirat,* there will be another *sirat* for settling grievances as mentioned in a hadeeth where the Prophet (SAS) informs us that when believers are saved from hell they will be prevented from entering *jannah* and ordered to stand at the edge of the *sirat* close to paradise. There they will settle the scores between them for any wrongs that they did to one another in this world, and when they have been cleansed and purified, and completely purged of guilt, they will be given permission to enter paradise. Then they will say,

الْحَمْدُ لِلَّهِ الَّذِي صَدَقَنَا وَعْدَهُ وَأَوْرَثَنَا الْأَرْضَ نَتَبَوَّأُ مِنَ الْجَنَّةِ حَيْثُ نَشَاءُ فَنِعْمَ أَجْرُ الْعَامِلِينَ ⬤

*"Praise be to Allah who has kept His promise to us and given us this land as our own. Now we may live wherever we please in the Garden. How excellent is the reward of those who labor!" (az-Zumar, 39:74)*

The fifth and ultimate stage of purification for success and salvation will be the all-embracing mercy of the All Merciful bestowed on His slaves. After passing through these stages, if the Muslims who believed in Allah (SWT) alone are still not completely purified for some reason, then they will enter hell so that they may be purified completely therein. But they will not live therein forever, rather they will be brought forth by the intercession of those who intercede and even without intercession on anyone's part by the mercy of the Most Merciful, Allah (SWT). Then there will be no one left in hell except those whom the Qur`an rules will abide therein forever, namely the disbelievers.

Considering all this, it is apparent how serious the Day of Judgment will be. It will be a horrific situation for all people, and none will feel safe until they are admitted into *jannah*. May Allah the Almighty make us among those whose final destination is *jannah*, without having to undergo the difficult stages of purification, especially in the hereafter.

رَبَّنَا آتِنَا فِي الدُّنْيَا حَسَنَةً وَفِي الْآخِرَةِ حَسَنَةً وَقِنَا عَذَابَ النَّارِ ⬤

*Our Lord! Grant us the good of this world and the hereafter, and protect us from the torment of the Fire. (al-Baqara, 2:201)*

## • 84 •

# *SUNNAH* OF GOOD COMMUNICATION

The ability to communicate with one another is a priceless gift that Allah has given to humans.

الرَّحْمَنُ ⬤ عَلَّمَ الْقُرْآنَ ⬤ خَلَقَ الْإِنْسَانَ ⬤ عَلَّمَهُ الْبَيَانَ ⬤

*The Most Compassionate; He taught the Qur`an; He created man; and He taught him to communicate. (ar-Rahman, 55:1-4)*

We communicate with people on a daily basis. It's important to know some of the etiquettes that could improve our communication. In today's *khutbah*, I want to share some of the etiquettes that the Prophet (SAS) taught us to use while communicating with people. Allah (SWT) tells us to follow the Prophet's model in whatever we do.

لَقَدْ كَانَ لَكُمْ فِي رَسُولِ اللَّهِ أُسْوَةٌ حَسَنَةٌ لِمَنْ كَانَ يَرْجُو اللَّهَ وَالْيَوْمَ الآخِرَ وَذَكَرَ اللَّهَ كَثِيرًا ○

*The Messenger of Allah is an excellent model for those of you who put your hope in Allah and the Last Day and remember Allah very often. (al-Ahzab, 33:21)*

One of the fundamental rules of good communication has to do with listening skills. Most of us talk more and listen less. But the Prophet (SAS) was known to be a patient listener. We have in *Surat at-Tawba*,

وَمِنْهُمُ الَّذِينَ يُؤْذُونَ النَّبِيَّ وَيَقُولُونَ هُوَ أُذُنٌ قُلْ أُذُنُ خَيْرٍ لَكُمْ ○

*Among them are some who insult the Prophet by saying, "He will listen to anything." Say, "He listens for your own good." (at-Tawba, 9:61)*

One example of his patient listening is that he was once walking with 'Adi ibn Hatim when a girl approached him and took the Prophet's hand, saying that her mother wanted to talk to him. The three of them went to see her mother who had some family issues. The family took a long time complaining and talking, and the Prophet (SAS) had to lean against something as he was standing there for a long time listening to them. He did not stop them and kept listening. 'Adi ibn Hatim was struck by the Prophet's example of his patience, his listening ability, and the respect he had for every person in the society.

Another element of communication is listening with respect and without contempt, as we saw in the story just narrated. If we follow the Prophet's example of listening patiently, listening with respect, and listening with mercy and kindness, we too can be good communicators. Allah (SWT) says in *Surat al-Isra`*,

وَلَقَدْ كَرَّمْنَا بَنِي آدَمَ وَحَمَلْنَاهُمْ فِي الْبَرِّ وَالْبَحْرِ وَرَزَقْنَاهُمْ مِنَ الطَّيِّبَاتِ وَفَضَّلْنَاهُمْ عَلَى كَثِيرٍ مِمَّنْ خَلَقْنَا تَفْضِيلًا ○

*We have honored the children of Adam and carried them by land and sea. We have provided good sustenance for them and favored them specially above many of those We have created. (al-Isra`, 17:70)*

The children of Adam include all human beings: the men, the women, the rich, the poor, the young, the old, the strong, the weak, the healthy, the sick, the believer, and the nonbeliever, regardless of who they are. When Allah (SWT) has honored them who are we to look down upon them. If any time we feel otherwise, we should remind ourselves of this *ayah*.

The Prophet (SAS) actively communicated with the people around him; he treated those who came to visit him kindly and he visited those who were not able to visit him. He practiced and recommended his followers to be hospitable to guests, to maintain relationships, to visit the sick, and to attend funerals.

Psychologists say that the way you speak is actually more important than what you say. According to research, the words spoken contribute seven percent of the effect, the tone of voice thirty-eight percent, and the gestures and body language have fifty-five percent of the effect in communication between people.

The Prophet (SAS) was the most effective orator of all times. He knew how to address the hearts of his followers, and thus he became the beloved one of their hearts. He first made himself loved, and then sought the ways to educate people. He used a style in his speeches that affected people and made them think, so he achieved permanent behavior change in people by means of the best educational methods.

The Prophet (SAS) said, "If you love a fellow Muslim, let them know." One day he took hold of Mu'adh ibn Jabal's hand and said, "O Mu'adh, I swear to Allah that I truly love you." Then he said, "O Mu'adh, do not neglect to say at the end of every prayer,

اللَّهُمَّ أَعِنِّي عَلَى ذِكْرِكَ وَشُكْرِكَ وَحُسْنِ عِبَادَتِكَ ⟡

*"O Allah! Help me to remember You, to thank You, and to worship You in the best of manners."*

One of the important principles of communication presented by the Prophet (SAS) was addressing the minds and emotions of those around him when communicating with them. For example, some of the companions told him, "O Allah's Prophet! The wealthy have taken the blessings and gone. They pray like us, they fast like us, but they give more to charity than we can." The Prophet replied, "Do you think that Allah has given you nothing to donate? Every time you praise Allah, every time you say *al-hamduli-llah*, every time you say *la ilaha illa Allah* whenever you command good or forbid evil, these are donations to be blessed."

The Prophet (SAS) would give gifts to those around him and receive gifts from others to strengthen friendship, consolidate love, to win hearts, to direct them toward Islam, to prevent possible evil, or as a reward. Once he bought a camel from a young companion, and after paying the money for the camel, he presented it to the young man.

The Prophet (SAS) was careful about individual differences when conversing with people. For example, he had a conversation with a Bedouin, whose wife had given birth to a black child; the Bedouin denied that the child was his. The Bedouin said, "My wife gave birth to a black child. I want to reject this child." The Prophet (SAS) asked, "Do you have camels?" "Yes." "What color are those camels?" The Bedouin answered, "Red." The Prophet (SAS) then asked him, "Are there any white, black, or grey camels among these?" and the Bedouin replied, "Yes, of course. There are grey camels among them." So the Prophet probed further and asked him, "Well, where do you think these grey camels came from?" The Bedouin replied, "O Prophet, that is in their blood; they take after the ancestors. Perhaps this boy has taken after someone in his ancestry." Taking care to use an example that is related to the Bedouin's life, the Prophet (SAS) was able to solve a problem in a convincing manner by having the Bedouin come up with the solution himself.

The Prophet (SAS) paid attention to the ability of the human mind to process and perceive information, and as necessitated by the prophetic mission, he presented the divine message gradually, starting first with what was simple and easy. The Prophet Muhammad (SAS) sent Mu'adh to Yemen and made the following recommendation to him: "You are going to a tribe from the People of the Book. Invite them to testify that there is no god but Allah and that I am His Messenger. If they accept this, inform them that Allah has commanded them to pray to Him five times a day, every day. If they accept this, inform them that Allah has commanded a *zakat* (charitable alms) to be paid by the wealthy to the poor. If they accept this, do not take the most valuable goods (for this). Be wary of the curses of the oppressed, because there is no veil between the curses of the oppressed and Allah."

The Prophet (SAS) gave the people around him the responsibility to spread the message of Islam. In his farewell sermon, he said, "You who are here take my words to those who are not here. Perhaps those who are here will bring my words to ones who have better comprehension of my words and who will protect my words better." In this way, the Prophet Muhammad (SAS) ensured that the message would be passed on. He also gave responsibility to those around him to protect the authenticity of his words when spreading the message.

The Prophet (SAS) listened to women in his society, who often experienced denial of their rights and ill treatment. He guided them to express themselves and claim real freedom of heart and conscience. The Prophet (SAS) loved the innocence and gentleness of children. He kissed them, carried them on his shoulders, and played with them, reaching toward their innocence.

When Fatima (RAA) used to visit her father, the Prophet (SAS), he would get up, kiss her forehead, have her sit in his place, and sit with her. This is how he showed the world his respect for his daughter. He would shorten *salah* if a child was crying out of consideration for the mother of the child. He cared about the feelings of people. These are examples of his respect and care for all.

We should take care not to hurt the feelings of people when communicating with them. This is one of the essential elements of good communication. Mercy, kindness, and sincerity toward others are important parts of the teachings of our religion. May Allah bless each one of us and give us a deep understanding of the *deen*. *Ameen*.

Brothers and sisters! When talking about communication, a hadeeth comes to mind where the Prophet (SAS) said, "Your smiling in the face of your brother is charity." This is a gesture to start any conversation positively and goes a long way to remove any past ill feelings that could be present. Smiling brings joy, both to the giver and the receiver.

Starting a conversation with the Islamic greetings of peace, *as-salaamu 'alaykum* (peace be upon you), is recommended. This goes toward repelling hate and creating love between parties. We also have to pay attention to the tone and volume of our voice. Our tone determines whether we will make our relationship or break it. Any undesirable loudness in our voice could put people off and make any further attempts to communicate futile.

We should inquire about people and ask them how they are doing and inquire about their health and wellbeing and that of their family and friends. They will feel loved and cared for. We should use every chance to enjoin the good and forbid the evil. If there is ever a need for us to say something corrective in nature, we should do so gently keeping in mind the age, status, and temperament of the person we are talking to. We should use simple, concise words, and speak with clarity to make people understand easily. These are just a few of the basic etiquettes from the Sunnah on communicating effectively with people.

Good communications with our family, our relatives, our friends, our coworkers, our fellow citizens, and every human being is so important in our lives. The Messenger of Allah (SAS) left us such a good example by how he interacted with everyone.

May Allah (SWT) enable us to follow the example of our beloved Prophet (SAS). May Allah bless each one of us and the *ummah* at large. May He create affection in our hearts for each other. May He guide each one of us to the right path. May He help our suffering fellow Muslims and the humanity at large. *Allahumma ameen*.

# SUPPLICATIONS (DU'A')

The topic of my *khutbah* today is: "*Du'a*`." Generally, people seem to have forgotten the power of *du'a*` or supplication. Overwhelmed by the advances made in science and technology, people have begun to believe that they are masters of their own destinies and start to feel independent of their Creator, Allah (SWT).

Once, the Prophet Muhammad (SAS) passed by a community that was going through a stressful situation. He advised, "Why don't they make *du'a*` to Allah for assistance?" With all the suffering and disasters Muslims are facing in various parts of the world, this question can be directed to all of us today.

It is not that we have forgotten *du'a*` completely, but our attitude and practices regarding *du'a*` have become somewhat distorted. The problem is that *du'a*` for many people has become a ritual and a final option after all other options and means have been exhausted. In the proper scheme of things, *du'a*` should be the first and last course of the believer, with all his plans and actions coming in between. In *Surat al-Ghafir* Allah (SWT) tells us,

$$\text{وَقَالَ رَبُّكُمُ ادْعُونِي أَسْتَجِبْ لَكُمْ} \bigcirc$$

*And your Lord said: Call on me. I will respond to you.* (al-Ghafir, 40:60)

*Du'a*` is an act of worship. The Prophet (SAS) said, "Indeed *du'a*` is worship." In another hadeeth he said, "*Du'a*` is the essence of worship."

While there are certain opportune times, places, and circumstances when *du'a*` is accepted, there are hardly any restrictions or specifications on the act of *du'a*`. It can be made at any time, in any place, in any language, and in any state; even in the state of *janaba* or ritual impurity.

*Du'a*` is a conversation with Allah (SWT). This fact itself is of great significance. It is the most uplifting, liberating, and transforming conversation a person can ever have. We turn to Allah (SWT) because we know that He alone can lift our sufferings and solve our problems. We feel relieved after describing our difficulties to our Creator. We sense His mercy all around us after talking to the Most Merciful.

As human beings, our life in this world is characterized by fluctuating conditions making us happy and sad. Our conditions of health and sickness, our affluence and poverty, our joys and sorrows, our apparent successes and failures, our gains and losses; all of them are just a test. Life by its very nature is a test.

$$\text{وَنَبْلُوكُم بِالشَّرِّ وَالْخَيْرِ فِتْنَةً وَإِلَيْنَا تُرْجَعُونَ ۝}$$

*We test you all through the bad and the good, and to us you will all return. (al-Anbiya`, 21:35)*

In this worldly life, people are constantly put to all types of tests. As believers, we ought to believe that every condition is a manifestation of the will of Allah (SWT). What has passed us was not meant to befall us, and what has befallen us was not meant to pass us. Our faith and belief are tested when we undergo difficulties. These difficulties may be physical, emotional, financial, psychological, or otherwise. This is shown in the following verses:

$$\text{وَلَنَبْلُوَنَّكُم بِشَيْءٍ مِنَ الْخَوْفِ وَالْجُوعِ وَنَقْصٍ مِنَ الْأَمْوَالِ وَالْأَنفُسِ وَالثَّمَرَاتِ وَبَشِّرِ الصَّابِرِينَ ۝}$$

*We shall certainly test you with fear and hunger, and loss of property, lives, and crops. But give good news to those who are patient. (al-Baqara, 2:155)*

$$\text{الَّذِي خَلَقَ الْمَوْتَ وَالْحَيَاةَ لِيَبْلُوَكُمْ أَيُّكُمْ أَحْسَنُ عَمَلًا ۝}$$

*It is He who created death and life to test which of you is best in action. (al-Mulk, 67:2)*

Pleasant and favorable conditions demand that we be grateful and humble. Adverse conditions require us to be patient and to seek Allah's help. Our ultimate success or failure in the hereafter will depend on how we acted in the different circumstances that Allah (SWT) chose for us.

*Du'a`* can change our life, our outlook, and even our fate. It is the most potent weapon of a believer. The Qur`an and hadeeth literature tell us about the extraordinary importance of praying to Allah (SWT) for all our needs.

$$\text{وَإِذَا سَأَلَكَ عِبَادِي عَنِّي فَإِنِّي قَرِيبٌ أُجِيبُ دَعْوَةَ الدَّاعِ إِذَا دَعَانِ فَلْيَسْتَجِيبُوا لِي وَلْيُؤْمِنُوا بِي لَعَلَّهُمْ يَرْشُدُونَ ۝}$$

*When My servants ask you about Me, say that I am near. I respond to the call of one who calls, whenever he calls to Me: let them, then, respond to Me, and believe in Me, so that they may be rightly guided. (al-Baqara, 2:186)*

We learn from a hadeeth that the Prophet (SAS) said, "Any one of you for whom the door to *du'a`* has been opened, the door to mercy has been opened for him. And the thing that Allah (SWT) likes most to be asked for is 'afiya, which means health, security, protection, and wellbeing. In another hadeeth the Prophet (SAS) tells us that Allah (SWT) is angry with those who do not make supplications to Him. The Prophet (SAS) also said, "*Du'a`* is beneficial regarding calamities that have fallen and calamities that have not fallen. So, servants of Allah, devote yourselves to *du'a`*." This means that *du'a`* can prevent a disaster that was going to happen as well as lift the one that has already happened. Also, the Prophet (SAS) said, "Ask Allah for everything, even the lace of your shoes." So, my dear brothers and sisters! Make *du'a* for everything you want, no matter how big or small.

Man is prone to haste and ignorance, and at times he may think something is good for him, but if the thing is given it may prove disastrous and evil for him in the life of this world or the life of the hereafter. Allah (SWT) is the All Knowing, All Wise, and He knows perfectly well the condition of each and every one of His slaves. Allah (SWT) knows and we do not know.

The Prophet (SAS) said, "Nothing is dearer to Allah than one's supplication to Him." He also said, "Your Lord, the Blessed and the Exalted One, is modest and generous, and He is shy to turn away His servant empty handed when he raises his hands to Him in supplication."

Our attitude to *du'a* should be in line with what is taught to us in the Qur'an and various Prophetic traditions.

ادْعُوا رَبَّكُمْ تَضَرُّعًا وَخُفْيَةً إِنَّهُ لَا يُحِبُّ الْمُعْتَدِينَ ⦿

*Call on your Lord humbly and secretly. Surely He does not love those who exceed the limits. (al-A'raf, 7:55)*

We should make *du'a* with great hope and conviction. The Prophet (SAS) said, "Pray to Allah with the conviction that you will be answered, and know that Allah does not answer a supplication that comes from a careless and inattentive heart."

In another hadeeth the Prophet (SAS) tells us, "Any Muslim who makes a *du'a*, provided the *du'a* contains nothing which is sinful or which involves breaking family ties, Allah will give one of three things: He will quickly grant him what he asked for, or save the reward for him for the hereafter, or turn away from him a similar hardship." This means that the hardship would have hit him in the absence of that *du'a*.

So we must make *du'a* to Allah (SWT), then be patient, have faith in his unquestionable decision, and trust His absolute wisdom. Never have the impression that Allah (SWT) Almighty has opened the door of making *du'a* but has closed the door of answering it. Sometimes, Allah (SWT) delays answering the *du'a* to give a better reward and a better blessing than that which was asked for. May Allah (SWT) help us remember Him, thank Him, and worship Him in the best of manners. *Ameen.*

Brothers and sisters! Please note that response to a *du'a* is unlikely for the one who eats, drinks, and wears haram things, for we learn through a hadeeth that the Prophet (SAS) mentioned a man who undertakes a lengthy journey and while he is disheveled and covered with dust, and he spreads out his hands to the sky saying, "O Lord! O Lord!" but his food is haram, his drink is haram, his clothing is haram, and he has been nourished with haram. How can his supplication be answered?

Many times, there is some sin that we commit which acts as a roadblock in having our *du'a`* accepted. So, we need to examine ourselves and see if there are any sins that we're persistently committing and resolve to abandon them lest our *du'a`* is not accepted. Allah (SWT) is ready to respond to our *du'a`*. He is waiting for us to ask Him so that He can fulfill our *du'a`*. But, we should ask ourselves, "Are we worthy of His response while we continue to lead disobedient and sinful lives?"

Also, for our *du'a`* to be accepted, we have to engage ourselves in enjoining good and forbidding evil. The Prophet (SAS) said, "I swear by Him in whose Hands is my soul: enjoin good and forbid evil, or else Allah will certainly soon send His punishment to you. Then you will make supplication and it will not be accepted."

The Prophet (SAS) said, "Whoever likes Allah to answer his *du'a`* in hard times and periods of worry, he should abundantly make *du'a`* in good times." We need *du'a`* in all circumstances and at all times. But in troubling times, we need them even more.

While we should make *du'a`* for ourselves and others, we should also request others to pray for us. 'Umar ibn al-Khattab (RAA) narrates, "I asked the Prophet (SAS) for permission to perform *'umrah* and he gave me permission saying, 'Dear brother, include us in your *du'a`* and do not forget us.' This expression ('dear brother') that he said, I would not be willing to exchange it for the world."

Brothers and sisters! Do we seek Allah's help when we need His help, or are we too arrogant to ask? Do we show gratitude for His blessings, or are we too proud of our own achievements? We should pray to Allah (SWT) because He alone can give. Allah (SWT) gave us life and everything that we possess.

وَمَا بِكُم مِّن نِّعْمَةٍ فَمِنَ اللَّهِ ۞

*Whatever blessing you have is from Allah. (an-Nahl, 16:53)*

We cannot even count His favors and blessings upon us, for Allah tells us in the Qur`an,

وَإِن تَعُدُّوا نِعْمَةَ اللَّهِ لَا تُحْصُوهَا إِنَّ اللَّهَ لَغَفُورٌ رَّحِيمٌ ۞

*If you tried to count Allah's blessings, you would never be able to count them. Surely, Allah is ever forgiving and most merciful. (an-Nahl, 16:18)*

Allah (SWT) is not answerable to any authority, and everyone is answerable to Him. He has power over everything, and none can overpower Him. His knowledge is infinite, while ours is insignificant compared to His. He is the Lord. We are His slaves.

يَا أَيُّهَا النَّاسُ أَنتُمُ الْفُقَرَاءُ إِلَى اللَّهِ وَاللَّهُ هُوَ الْغَنِيُّ الْحَمِيدُ ۞

*O mankind! It is you who stand in need of Allah. Allah is self-sufficient, and praiseworthy. (Fatir, 35:15)*

I will conclude with a *hadeeth qudsi* in order to get a glimpse of the vast treasures of the One whom we should ask, for the Prophet (SAS) said that Allah (SWT) said, "O my servants, were the first of you and the last of you, the human of you and the jinn of you, to rise up in one place and make a request of me, and were I to give everyone what he requested, that would not decrease what I have any more than a needle would decrease the ocean if put into it."

• 86 •

# *SURAT AD-DUHA:* A REMEDY FOR SADNESS AND GRIEF

There are times in every person's life when he or she feels sad and sorrowful for some reason or the other. There is a *surah* in the Qur`an that was especially revealed to comfort and cheer up our beloved Prophet Muhammad (SAS) at a time when he was feeling sorrowful, because the revelation was suspended for a period of time. There are various narrations that say this period lasted anywhere from twelve days to forty days. In any case, the period was so long that it made the Prophet (SAS) sad. His opponents found this as an opportunity to taunt him, and they said that his Lord had "abandoned" him. The pause in the revelation from Allah seriously distressed the Prophet (SAS) and he began to think that Allah was displeased with him, and that He had forgotten him.

Does this situation sound familiar to us? Do we also sometimes feel sad and lost? Sometimes we may feel as though Allah hates us or that He is angry with us. We feel like our prayers are not being answered, that our *salah* is not having a positive impact on our hearts, and that Allah doesn't love us or doesn't care about us.

*Surat ad-Duha* was revealed to the Prophet (SAS) to relieve him of these negative feelings and to give him hope and the assurance that Allah was with him. When we go through similar states of depression, sadness, and hopelessness, we too can find peace, hope, and a renewed faith in Allah (SWT) through this *surah*. So what does this *surah* say? The first verse reads,

وَالضُّحَى ◯

*By the morning brightness. (ad-Duha, 93:1)*

This is the first thing we need to hear when we are depressed. We need to be reminded that everything in life is not doom and gloom. There is sunshine, there is light, there is beauty. In other words, look up! Look at the bright side of things. The second verse reads,

وَاللَّيْلِ إِذَا سَجَى ○

*And by the night when it covers with darkness. (ad-Duha, 93:2)*

Allah (SWT) reminds the Prophet (SAS) and us that the brightening of the day and the spreading of the darkness and stillness of night do not mean that Allah is pleased with the people during the day and displeased with them during the night. Instead, both states are based on supreme wisdom. Likewise, the sending down of revelation to the Prophet (SAS) followed by a pause in it is also based on wisdom, not a sign of Allah's displeasure or abandonment. On the contrary, it is a mercy from Allah. Do we not notice that if man is constantly exposed to the light of day it tires him? Therefore, it is necessary that night should fall after the day has remained bright for a certain period so that man may have rest and peace in it.

Likewise, if you were constantly exposed to the light of revelation, your nerves could not stand it. Therefore, a break or gap in the revelation has also been provided by Allah so that the strain of bearing the revelation passes and complete peace is restored to the Prophet (SAS). Allah clarifies this in the next verse when He says,

مَا وَدَّعَكَ رَبُّكَ وَمَا قَلَى ○

*Your Lord has neither abandoned you, nor is He displeased with you. (ad-Duha, 93:3)*

Swearing an oath by the light of the day and the peacefulness of the night, the Prophet (SAS) is told clearly that his Lord has forsaken him, nor is He displeased with him.

وَلَلْآخِرَةُ خَيْرٌ لَكَ مِنَ الْأُولَى ○

*And the next life is certainly better for you than the present life. (ad-Duha, 93:4)*

This good news was given by Allah to the Prophet (SAS) in a state when he had only a handful of Muslims with him, the entire community was hostile, and there was not even a remote chance of success. The candle of Islam was flickering only in Mecca and storms were brewing all around to blow it out. At this juncture Allah said to His Prophet (SAS): Do not grieve at the hardships of the initial stage, your future will be better for you than the former period. Your power, glory, honor, and prestige will grow, and your influence will spread. This promise is not only confined to the world, but it also includes the promise that his rank and position in the hereafter will be far higher and nobler than the rank and position he attains in the world.

Often when we are depressed, we think, "Is this all my life going to be? Is it never going to get better?" This verse serves as a perfect answer to those questions, reminding us that life in this world is temporary and that the hereafter is certainly a better, more permanent place for us than this world could ever be. This makes us look forward to attaining our place in *jannah* and helps us look at any problems in our lives as temporary tests of our faith from Allah. Allah continues to reassure the Prophet (SAS),

$$\text{وَلَسَوْفَ يُعْطِيكَ رَبُّكَ فَتَرْضَى} \bigcirc$$

*Soon your Lord will give you that with which you will be pleased. (ad-Duha, 93:5)*

Allah lets the Prophet (SAS) know that although it will take some time, very soon your Lord will bless you with so much that you will be pleased and happy. This promise was fulfilled during the lifetime of the Prophet (SAS) such that all of Arabia came under his control, from the southern coasts of Yemen to the Syrian frontiers of the Byzantine empire and the Iraqi frontiers of the Persian empire in the north; and from the Arabian Gulf in the east to the Red Sea in the west. For the first time in the history of Arabia this land became subject to one law and rule. The people not only bowed their heads in obedience, their hearts were also conquered. Their beliefs, morals, and behavior were revolutionized. It is unprecedented in human history that a nation sunk in paganism completely changed in only twenty-three years. Thereafter, the movement started by the Prophet (SAS) gathered such power that it spread over a larger part of Asia, Africa, and Europe and its influence reached every corner of the world. This is what Allah gave His Messenger (SAS) in the world. The glory and extent of what He will give him in the hereafter cannot be imagined.

Isn't this the best thing to hear when we are depressed and fed up with this worldly life and the problems we are facing? Very soon Allah will replace our sorrow with good! He promises us that we will be satisfied with what He gives us! And the promise of Allah is true! Next, Allah reminds the Prophet (SAS),

$$\text{أَلَمْ يَجِدْكَ يَتِيمًا فَآوَى} \bigcirc$$

*Did He not find you an orphan, and shelter you? (ad-Duha, 93:6)*

That is, there can be no question of abandoning you and being displeased with you! We have, in fact, been good to you ever since the time you were born as an orphan. The Prophet's father passed away three months before his birth, and therefore he was considered an orphan at birth. (Arabian culture considers a child an "orphan" if they have lost one of their parents.) But Allah did not leave him without support even for a day. His mother and wet-nurse and extended family nourished and looked after him. After the death of his mother, his grandfather took him and brought him up with great love. When his grandfather died, the Prophet's (SAS) uncle, Abu Talib, became his guardian and treated him with such rare love that no father could treat his son better. After the entire nation turned hostile to the Prophet (SAS), Abu Talib alone stood firm as his chief supporter for as long as ten years.

Now many of us may think: How would this verse about orphans relate to most of us? Think about it. Weren't there many times in our lives when we were sick or lonely and felt like nobody cared about us? Who was the only one by our side at that time? It was Allah who took care of us and guided us out of that stage in life.

$$وَوَجَدَكَ ضَالًّا فَهَدَى ۝$$

*And He found you wandering and guided you. (ad-Duha, 93:7)*

Before prophethood the Prophet (SAS) was certainly a believer in the existence of Allah and His unity, and his life was free from sin and reflected excellent morals. Yet he was unaware of the principles and injunctions of true faith. This verse may also mean that the Prophet (SAS) found himself lonely in a society that was lost in ignorance. It may also imply that the extraordinary qualities that Allah had blessed him with were going waste in this unfavorable environment of ignorance. How many of us, despite being born Muslims, have found ourselves misguided and straying away from Islam in the past? It was Allah who gave us guidance and brought us back to the straight path and to Him.

Allah says in the next verse of this blessed *surah,*

$$وَوَجَدَكَ عَائِلًا فَأَغْنَى ۝$$

*And found you in want and made you free from want. (ad-Duha, 93:8)*

Most of us have gone through periods in our lives when we have been short of money and wealth. Now, when we look back, we realize that it was only Allah who gave us that provision (*rizq*) and got us through those tough financial times. When a person is depressed, giving him or her examples of how Allah has helped them in the past will strengthen their conviction and belief in the promises Allah makes in this *surah* for their future.

In the next part of this *surah,* Allah gives some instructions.

$$فَأَمَّا الْيَتِيمَ فَلَا تَقْهَرْ ۝$$

*So as for the orphan, do not oppress him. (ad-Duha, 93:9)*

This verse is the ultimate antidote to feelings of depression! When we are feeling sad and down, we are mostly consumed with our own situation and feel that nobody could possibly be in a worse situation. This verse reminds us to look at people who are in far worse situations than ourselves. Look at the orphans, who have no family or loved ones, and nobody to care for them. Yet we can have families and parents who love us, a roof over our heads, and food on the table, and we can still think we're in a bad situation.

Allah continues by telling us,

وَأَمَّا السَّائِلَ فَلَا تَنْهَرْ ○

*And as for one, who begs, do not scold him. (ad-Duha, 93:10)*

He gives us the example of the beggar in order to once again remind us of the many material blessings such as food, clothing, and shelter that Allah has given us and that we take for granted. How many of us have ever gone to sleep hungry? How many of us don't have clothes to wear? Or don't have a home to go to? These examples of the orphan and the beggar should constantly remind us to be grateful to Allah for the countless blessings He has given us. This will greatly help us in getting over our sadness and will help us to feel more connected to Allah and His help.

Finally, Allah commands,

وَأَمَّا بِنِعْمَةِ رَبِّكَ فَحَدِّثْ ○

*And as for your Lord's blessing, proclaim it. (ad-Duha, 93:11)*

This final verse is about maintaining that renewed faith and bond with Allah by pondering, glorifying, and talking about the blessings of Allah. This could be through discussions with family and friends, doing *dhikr*, participating in *da'wa* work, reading the Qur`an, participating in *halaqas*, listening to lectures, and so on. Remember that Allah says in *Surat ar-Ra'd*,

أَلَا بِذِكْرِ اللَّهِ تَطْمَئِنُّ الْقُلُوبُ ○

*Truly, hearts find peace only in the remembrance of God. (ar-Ra'd, 13:28)*

The remembrance of Allah is the ultimate deed that will reduce our feelings of sorrow and despair.

So the next time we feel disconnected, disheartened, or depressed with our level of *iman* and our connection with Allah, we should read *Suratad-Duha* and ponder over its meanings. It will restore our faith and increase our belief in the greatness and power of Allah.

We praise and thank Allah (SWT) in every situation: *Al-hamduli-llahi 'ala kulli haal!*

# TAKE ADVANTAGE OF FIVE BEFORE FIVE

My *khutbah* today is based on a hadeeth, the message of which is to take advantage of five situations before the happening of five other situations. The purpose of my *khutbah* is to remind myself and you to pay heed to the noble sayings of our beloved Prophet Muhammad (SAS). In this hadeeth, the Prophet (SAS) said, "Seize the opportunity of five before five: your youth before your old age, your health before your sickness, your wealth before your poverty, your free time before your preoccupation, and your life before your death."

The Prophet (SAS) is pointing out that these five matters are very easy to get hold of because they are treasures that everyone possesses but very few appreciate. What are these five things?

One of the things that most people take for granted is their youth. Youth is a time when a person is most energetic; when he lays out the foundations for his future, and when he plans his life. So one has to take advantage of this time before the time comes when that enthusiasm is either lost or greatly reduced. It is very seldom that the enthusiasm and energy that we are blessed with in our youth will ever again be given to us after that age. Therefore, the Prophet (SAS) is advising the youth to seize this moment and take advantage of it. The youth should utilize this energy for the sake of Allah (SWT) by seeking knowledge, obtaining *halal* means of sustenance, and worshipping Allah (SWT) through acts that he or she might not be able to do later on in life. When people lose their youth, they find it harder to do these deeds which were easier to do at a younger age. "Youth" here does not mean the concept of youth where youthfulness finishes after the age of eighteen or nineteen. In Islamic scholarship, the concept of "youth" actually refers to one's life up until the age of forty.

Secondly, we are advised to take advantage of our good health before we are overcome with illness or disability. What we often don't realize is that our health is a blessing from Allah (SWT). When we are in good health, we take it for granted and don't always appreciate what we have. It is only when we fall sick that we realize what a great blessing we had and how we lost it by not doing as much as we could have done. Everyone falls sick, so there will certainly come a time when we also fall sick. Sometimes the sickness may be severe. So the Prophet (SAS) is reminding us that we do not know how long we will enjoy the full possession of our faculties of physical strength and mental capacities. Therefore, we should take advantage of our good health before that time comes when we may be deprived of it.

The Prophet (SAS) said, "The majority of mankind does not appreciate two blessings: health and free time." *Al-hamduli-llah*, we have been blessed with sound minds in sound bodies. Look at someone who Allah (SWT) has tested with blindness. It is a very severe test. We have been blessed not just with eyesight, but also with hearing, limbs, energy, vitality, and countless other blessings. Should we not appreciate these blessings from Allah (SWT)? Do we not realize how enormous the blessing of health is? Allah reminds us in the Qur`an in *Surat an-Nahl*,

وَمَا بِكُمْ مِنْ نِعْمَةٍ فَمِنَ اللَّهِ ثُمَّ إِذَا مَسَّكُمُ الضُّرُّ فَإِلَيْهِ تَجْأَرُونَ ◯

*Any blessing you have is from Allah. Then when harm touches you, it is to Him alone*
*you cry for help. (an-Nahl, 16:53)*

The least we can do, brothers and sisters, is to perform the *fard* (mandatory) actions, such as the five daily prayers, fasting in Ramadan, and going for hajj. All these modes of worship require physical exertion. That is the least that we can do, or the bare minimum. Of course, the more one exerts, the better it is for him. So this is the second of the five matters: "Take advantage of your health before you fall sick."

The third is to take advantage of your wealth before you experience poverty. One day we might have much more than we need, and the next day, we might not have anything. One day, a person might have the best of jobs or the best of businesses; yet, the next day something happens, and he does not have the job or the business and loses all his sources of income. The wise person uses his wealth before he loses it. He invests for his future.

As far as making investments for worldly benefits is concerned, the *kafir* (disbeliever), and the Muslim are the same; they both do that. Of course, we have to ensure that we have enough money for our family, our children, and ourselves so that we don't have to beg. But while investing in the *dunya*, let us not forget that we also need to invest in the hereafter, where we need the benefits of our investments much more than we need in this world. We need to invest for our real future, our eternal life in the hereafter.

The Prophet (SAS) once asked his companions, "Who among you loves his inheritors' money more than his own money?" The companions said, "O Messenger of Allah! All of us love our own money more than we love the money of our inheritors. We guard it and protect it more than the money of our inheritors." Then the Prophet (SAS) said, "Indeed, the money that you spend in charity is your money, and the money that you leave behind is the money of your inheritors." So this is the third of the five matters: "Take advantage of your wealth before your poverty."

The fourth blessing is the free time that we have. In fact, it is a great treasure that all of us have to some degree or the other. We must make use of our free time before we become too busy. How much free time do we have and what do we waste it on? Think about it. Think about the free time all of us have been blessed with. Let us not waste our free time. Perhaps the greatest wasters of time are the television and the internet. I am not referring to the time which is utilized productively, getting something useful and beneficial from these devices. What I mean to say is that very often we gain no benefit for this world or the next from being glued to the TV or internet for hours on end. Furthermore, we will be lucky if after wasting time we come out without committing any sin of watching lewd and obscene images, listening to vulgar music, or both.

When we have some free time, we should take advantage of it. The greatest thing that we can do in this free time is to engage in the remembrance and worship of Allah (SWT). Also, one of the greatest acts of worship is to seek knowledge. We should do whatever we can to increase our knowledge, meaning, any knowledge that benefits. The Prophet (SAS) used to make a *du'a`*,

اللَّهُمَّ انْفَعْنِى بِمَا عَلَّمْتَنِى وَ عَلِّمْنِى مَا يَنْفَعُنِى وَ ارْزُقْنِى عِلْماً يَنْفَعُنِى ◯

*"O Allah! Benefit me with what you taught me, teach me what will benefit me, and provide me with knowledge that will benefit me."*

Spending free time wisely does not necessarily mean engaging in religious activities only. One way to spend time is to visit one another, and particularly to visit the sick for the sake of Allah (SWT). Time could also be invested in learning a trade or skill that can benefit us and others in this world. In fact, all acts done for the sake of Allah (SWT) and to seek the pleasure of Allah (SWT) are transformed into acts of worship. Of course, there are religious deeds that need to be done. Besides the obligatory ritual prayers, we should pray some extra prayers as well; a few *sunnah* prayers or *nafl* prayers (exceptional prayers beyond the *sunnah*). Each one of us should recite the Qur`an every day even if it's only for five or ten minutes. It is very important to have a relationship with the Qur`an. There are many acts that can be rewarded if our *niyya*, or intention, is to do them for the sake of Allah (SWT). This is the fourth of the five matters: "Take advantage of your free time before you become busy."

Brothers and sisters! The last thing that we have been advised to take advantage of is our life before our death. This point summarizes all the others. Every one of us has a life; that is why we are here right now. And every one of us has to die. Every night when we go to sleep, we enter a state where a part of our soul leaves us. When we wake up, it is only because Allah (SWT) has blessed us by returning our souls to us, thereby granting us the opportunity to worship Him, to seek His forgiveness, and to do some more good deeds before it is our last day on earth. Upon waking up in the morning, the Prophet (SAS) used to say,

أَلْحَمْدُ لِلَّه الَّذِى أَحْيَانَا بَعْدَ مَا أَمَاتَنَا وَ إِلَيْهِ النُّشُوْر ◯

*"Praise be to Allah who gave me life after death, and to Him is the final return."*

Often we do not fully appreciate how great a blessing it is to be given another chance. We become relaxed about death, and we don't fully comprehend or appreciate that at some point– and only Allah (SWT) knows when– our life will be taken away from us for good, leaving no second chance, no opportunity to make up for the wrongs we have done, and there will be no turning back. We must not forget what a blessing and mercy life is. We should value every moment of life and use it to our best advantage. This means that we should struggle to qualify for Allah's mercy and get rewarded with peace of heart in this world, and with the abode of peace (*dar as-salaam*) or *jannah* in the next world.

Good things don't just come to us. We have to strive for them, day in and day out. Whether we are at school, at work, or raising a family, we have to excel in whatever we do. We know that we have to work hard, and the harder we work, the better the reward. *Jannah* is no exception to this. If we strive hard enough, Allah (SWT) will reward us with the ultimate prize of paradise *in sha` Allah*. Allah says in *Surat an-Najm*,

لَيْسَ لِلْإِنْسَانِ إِلَّا مَا سَعَى ۝

*Man receives only what he strives for. (an-Najm, 53:39)*

Brothers and sisters! The wise person is the one who strives to achieve the pleasure of Allah, places his trust in Allah, and then expects the best from Allah. The foolish person is the one who blindly follows his desires and then presumes that Allah (SWT) will reward him. May Allah (SWT) make us among those who are successful in both worlds. *Ameen*.

• 88 •

# TAKING ACCOUNT OF ONESELF

My *khutbah* today is on the topic of *muhasaba*, which means taking account of oneself or subjecting oneself to self-assessment. Do we take out some time in our busy lives to do this? Ideally, we should be engaged in self-assessment every day; assessing our actions, our emotions, and our thoughts. This will prepare us for our return to Allah (SWT). Are we conscious of the day when we shall be made to return to Allah (SWT)? The Qur`an warns us,

وَاتَّقُوا يَوْمًا تُرْجَعُونَ فِيهِ إِلَى اللَّهِ ○

*Be conscious of the day when you shall be made to return to Allah. (al-Baqara, 2:281)*

Are we conscious of the day when Allah (SWT) will bring us to account for our intentions and our deeds? The Qur`an reminds us,

وَإِن تُبْدُوا مَا فِي أَنفُسِكُمْ أَوْ تُخْفُوهُ يُحَاسِبْكُم بِهِ اللَّهُ ○

*Whether you make known what is in your souls or hide it, Allah will bring you to account for it. (al-Baqara, 2: 284)*

Generally, we avoid thinking that we are on a journey toward our ultimate destination. It's almost impossible to imagine that so many years have passed since our childhood. Every moment someone from the vast multitude of humanity stands on the threshold of completing his or her life's journey. We are all moving gradually, almost unnoticeably from this world to the next.

According to a hadeeth narrated by Shaddad ibn `Aws (RAA) and transmitted by Imam at-Tirmidhi, the Prophet (SAS) said, "A wise person is one who keeps a watch over his bodily desires and passions, and checks himself from that which is harmful and strives for that which will benefit him after death; and a foolish person is one who subordinates himself to his cravings and desires and expects from Allah the fulfillment of his futile desires."

Imam at-Tirmidhi indicates that the expression "who keeps a watch over his bodily desires and passions" refers to "a person who calls his carnal self to account before it is called to account in the hereafter." He reports 'Umar ibn al-Khattab (RAA) as saying, "Call yourself to account before you are called to account."

Imam al-Hasan al-Basri explaining *muhasaba* said, "A believer keeps watch over himself. He assesses and judges himself for the sake of Allah. The final judgment may end up mild for some simply because they were quick to judge themselves in this life, or it may end up to be a tough ordeal for some who were unconcerned about what they did in this life, thinking they would not be called to account."

Regulating one's actions in consideration of their repercussions in the hereafter is the attitude of the wise. Allah (SWT) cautions us by saying,

وَلْتَنظُرْ نَفْسٌ مَّا قَدَّمَتْ لِغَدٍ ○

*And let every soul consider carefully what it sends ahead for tomorrow. (al-Hashr, 59:18)*

Honest self-criticism is an important way to purify our souls. Purification of the soul leads to success. Alluding to this, Allah (SWT) also says,

قَدْ أَفْلَحَ مَن زَكَّاهَا وَقَدْ خَابَ مَن دَسَّاهَا ○

*Truly he has succeeded who purifies it. And truly, he has failed who corrupts it. (ash-Shams, 91:9-10)*

Self-criticism is achieved by being honest with oneself. This is not easy, for it requires admission of one's wrongdoings. It means acknowledgement within ourselves that we have committed a sin, whether against our own souls or others, against our Creator or against anyone or anything in creation. For most of us, such a confession is a very tough thing to do. Pride prevents some of us from owning our faults, especially in front of other people.

According to Imam al-Ghazali, a businessman formulates a business plan, seeks out business partners, records his gains and losses, balances his books, and seeks out advice when in need of improvement. As Muslims, our success in the hereafter is of far greater importance than the finances of any businessman.

We can begin by setting up a "business plan" of our own with the goal of success in the hereafter. There is a partnership that we enter into with our spouses, families, community members, and friends so that we may work together and support one another. Imam al-Ghazali recommends that we elevate this concept to a spiritual level by forging a partnership within ourselves as well—between our minds, hearts, and physical needs—for if they are in conflict, we become like an ineffective business led by disputing partners.

When we speak, let us use our minds to monitor our speech and avoid speaking foul words. When we eat, let us listen to our stomach so that we can stop when we are full. When we pray, let us throw our heart into prayer. When our minds, hearts, and physical needs work together, then we are guided to desire only that which is good and to dislike that which is harmful. Without their mutual cooperation we may incline only toward our lower desires and the whispering of Shaytan.

We must not deceive ourselves by ignoring the losses accumulated from things like not praying or deliberately committing sins because on the Day of Judgment we may find our gains outweighed by our losses. These losses are accrued because of our mistreatment of parents, spouses, children, neighbors, and other fellow human beings. On the Day of Judgment, all mistreated persons will testify against their oppressors and will be recompensed.

One can subject oneself to accounting by addressing questions such as: "Was I grateful for Allah's favor upon me? What did I do that I should not have done? What did I fail to do, or what is it that I did poorly? Did I commit any major sin? Did I violate the rights of others? Did I use my faculties of sight, hearing, and intellect in unlawful ways? Did I fail to use something lawful in the best possible way?"

Brothers and sisters! As we question ourselves, we should be aware of potential pitfalls. One pitfall, highlighted by a scholar named Imam Qatada, is a type of procrastination in which we put off important actions by performing acts of lower priority first. This is like a businessman who closes his shop during business hours to restock the shelves. We could thus deceive ourselves into thinking that we are using our time wisely when in fact we are not. If we find ourselves in such a state, we should ask: "Why do we delay doing what we should do now?" and "What are our real priorities?"

One method for identifying our faults and shortcomings is to employ the Qur`an as our advisor and use its criteria to critique ourselves. The Qur`an tells us clearly that our books of deeds are like preserved records of all that we have ever said and done. We should question our actions, past and present. Our sins should be a source of worry for us.

Once we have identified our shortcomings, what should we do? Mere guilt and regret are not enough. We should not let ourselves be comforted by just confessing our failures because that does not diminish their weight in the sight of Allah (SWT), nor does it prevent us from doing them again. In fact, the Prophet (SAS) encouraged us to conceal our sins and to repent for them privately. We must strive to determine their cause and to develop a plan to prevent them from happening in the future. If we missed a prayer due to a distracting television program, for example, we can ask ourselves, "Why was I so caught up in this program, and how can I prevent it from happening again?" It is important that we reach the most important stage, which is implementation. Allah (SWT tells us in the Qur`an,

$$إِنَّ اللَّهَ لَا يُغَيِّرُ مَا بِقَوْمٍ حَتَّىٰ يُغَيِّرُوا مَا بِأَنْفُسِهِمْ ۗ$$

*Allah does not change the condition of a people unless they change what is in themselves. (ar-Ra'd, 13:11)*

If, *in sha` Allah*, we are successful in changing ourselves for the better, let us thank Allah (SWT) for enabling us to improve, and then we must seek to remain constant in our performance. If we are not successful in changing ourselves for the better, let us repent and redouble our efforts for the future. Brothers and sisters! Every one of us is the author of his own book of deeds that will be presented to him on the Day of Accounting. Although the things of this world may be necessary for our sustenance and our comfort, we must not let them distract us from the approaching Day of Judgment. On that Day, nothing but our good deeds can benefit us. Allah tells us in *Surat al-Inshiqaq,*

$$فَأَمَّا مَنْ أُوتِيَ كِتَابَهُ بِيَمِينِهِ ۗ فَسَوْفَ يُحَاسَبُ حِسَابًا يَسِيرًا ۗ وَيَنْقَلِبُ إِلَىٰ أَهْلِهِ مَسْرُورًا ۗ$$

*As for him who is given his Book in his right hand, he will be called to account in an easy manner, and return to his family joyfully. (al-Inshiqaq, 84:7-9)*

May Allah (SWT) accept our actions and make us among those who receive their books in their right hands. *Allahumma ameen.*

# THE NIGHT JOURNEY AND THE ASCENSION *(AL-ISRA` WA AL-MI'RAJ)*

We are passing through the month of Rajab. In today's *khutbah*, I wish to share some thoughts with you on the great event of *isra`* and *mi'raj*. Most of the scholars of the *seerah* or biography of the Prophet (SAS), say that the *isra`* and *mi'raj* took place a year prior to the *hijra* on the 27th night of the month of *Rajab*. The incident of *al-isra` wa al-mi'raj* refers to an amazing journey undertaken by the best of creation—our beloved Prophet Muhammad (SAS).

The first leg of this journey called *isra`* refers to the night journey from *al-Masjid al-Haram* in Mecca to *al-Masjid al-Aqsa* in Jerusalem. We find this mentioned in the first verse of *Surat al-Isra`*.

سُبْحَانَ الَّذِي أَسْرَى بِعَبْدِهِ لَيْلًا مِنَ الْمَسْجِدِ الْحَرَامِ إِلَى الْمَسْجِدِ الْأَقْصَى ○

*Glory be to Him who took His slave on a journey by night from al-Masjid al-Haram to al-Masjid al-Aqsa. (al-Isra`, 17:1)*

We know about *al-Masjid al-Haram*. It is the location of the Ka'ba at Mecca. This we know from the Qur`an because Allah says,

إِنَّ أَوَّلَ بَيْتٍ وُضِعَ لِلنَّاسِ لَلَّذِي بِبَكَّةَ مُبَارَكًا وَهُدًى لِلْعَالَمِينَ ○

*The first house established for mankind was that at Mecca, a place of blessing and guidance for all beings. (Aal 'Imran, 3:96)*

But what is the origin of *al-Masjid al-Aqsa*? Ibraheem (AS) had built the Ka'ba in Mecca with his firstborn son Isma'eel (AS). He had also established a place of worship in Jerusalem. This place would later be known as Bethel, which in the Hebrew language means "the house of Allah." Forty years after the construction of Ka'ba, Ibraheem (AS) expanded the Bethel and called it *al-Masjid al-Aqsa* which means "the farthest *masjid*" because of its far distance from *al-Masjid al-Haram* in Mecca. Both these mosques are considered holy, blessed, and interlinked with one another, making it incumbent upon the Muslims to protect their sacredness from any intervention, invasion, destruction, or occupation. This is an *amana*, or a trust. entrusted to the Muslim *ummah*.

The reference to the second leg of the journey called *mi'raj*, or the ascension, is made in *Surat an-Najm*,

وَلَقَدْ رَآهُ نَزْلَةً أُخْرَى ۝ عِنْدَ سِدْرَةِ الْمُنْتَهَى ۝ عِنْدَهَا جَنَّةُ الْمَأْوَى ۝ إِذْ يَغْشَى السِّدْرَةَ مَا يَغْشَى ۝ مَا زَاغَ الْبَصَرُ وَمَا طَغَى ۝ لَقَدْ رَأَى مِنْ آيَاتِ رَبِّهِ الْكُبْرَى ۝

*And, indeed, he (Muhammad) saw him (Jibril) a second time; by the lote tree of the farthest limit, near which is the Garden of Abode, when the lote tree was covered in mystic splendor. His (Muhammad) eye did not waver nor did he look away. He saw some of the greatest signs of his Lord. (an-Najm, 13-18)*

Some people claim that all the events of the *isra`* and *mi'raj* took place in a state of dream, but this is not the case. The Prophet (SAS) experienced them with both his body and soul. Had this been merely something the Prophet (SAS) experienced in his dream, the disbelievers of Quraysh would not have had difficulty accepting it. They would not have asked, "How could you have travelled to Jerusalem last night and be with us in Mecca this morning?"

What is the background of *al-isra` wa al-mi'raj*? During the ten long years of preaching in Mecca, the Prophet (SAS), his companions, and the small community of believers were subjected to all kinds of humiliation, abuse, economic sanctions, and boycott by the larger community of Mecca. As if this was not enough, following the deaths of his uncle Abu Talib and his beloved wife, Khadija (RAA)—both supportive of him to the utmost—plots were hatched to eliminate the Prophet (SAS).

Prior to the occurrence of *al-isra` wa al-mi'raj*, the Prophet (SAS) had displayed great patience in the face of hardship. One of Allah's wisdoms is that He bestows His gifts accompanied with hardships. Allah (SWT) says in the Qur`an,

مَسَّتْهُمُ الْبَأْسَاءُ وَالضَّرَّاءُ وَزُلْزِلُوا حَتَّى يَقُولُ الرَّسُولُ وَالَّذِينَ آمَنُوا مَعَهُ مَتَى نَصْرُ اللَّهِ أَلَا إِنَّ نَصْرَ اللَّهِ قَرِيبٌ ۝

*They encountered suffering and adversity and were shaken such that the Messenger and those of faith who were with him said: "When will Allah's assistance come?" Truly Allah's assistance is always near. (al-Baqara, 2:214)*

At the end of his life, the Messenger of Allah (SAS) said that the worst treatment that he received from the disbelievers was his violent rejection at the hands of the people of Ta`if. The cruel inhabitants of Ta`if not only rejected the Prophet's call but also drove him out, throwing stones at him to the point that he left Ta`if with his feet bleeding and his heart broken. This was one of the most difficult periods he had faced in his missionary work. Disappointed and saddened, and with no one to turn to for help, he turned to his Lord for help and support.

A most powerful and touching prayer emerged from the lips of the Prophet (SAS) expressing his weakness and helplessness before his Lord. He cried out, "O Allah! To You I complain of my weakness, of my helplessness, and of my lowliness before people. O Most Merciful of the Merciful. You are the Most Merciful of the Merciful. You are the

Lord of the weak and You are my Lord. Under whose care have You placed me? Under an enemy who oppresses me or under some far-off stranger who has been empowered over me? If You are not displeased with me, then I care not. However, Your ease is better for me. I seek refuge with the glory of Your light, which the heavens and earth are lit from, that Your anger does not befall on me, nor Your displeasure descends on me. To You is the supplication until You are pleased, and there is no control or power except by You."

To comfort the Prophet (SAS), Allah (SWT) responded to this *du'a*` in an exceptional way. He called him to His divine presence. This, brothers and sisters, is the background to the occurrence of the night journey followed by the Prophet's ascension to the divine presence of the Lord of the Worlds.

It was one year prior to the *hijra*. One night, the angel Jibreel asked the Prophet Muhammad (SAS) to mount a white, winged, horse-like creature named Buraq. Buraq took him to *al-Masjid al-Aqsa* in Jerusalem, where all the prophets from Adam (AS) to 'Isa ibn Maryam (AS) were gathered together. The Prophet Muhammad (SAS) led them all in prayer, as confirmation of being the seal of all prophets and messengers of Allah (SWT).

From *al-Masjid al-Aqsa*, The Prophet (SAS) and Jibreel (AS) began the final leg of their journey, up to the heavens. This is known as the *mi'raj* or ascension of the Prophet (SAS). While travelling upward toward his destination in heaven, the Prophet (SAS) met Adam, Yahya, 'Isa ibn Maryam, Yusuf, Idrees, Haroon, Musa, and Ibraheem (peace be upon them all) at each of the seven heavenly stations as they affirmed and expressed faith in his Prophethood.

At the highest heavenly station, the Prophet (SAS) witnessed the "much frequented house" (*al-Bayt al-Ma'moor*), a replica of the Holy *Ka'ba*. Angels perform *tawaf* (revolutions) around *al-Bayt al-Ma'moor*. Engulfed in the glory and light of the divine presence, Muhammad (SAS) experienced an indescribable ecstasy and an inexpressible joy, bliss, and delight. He fell into prostration before the Lord of the Worlds. Allah (SWT) then ordered him to raise his head and the Prophet (SAS) said,

التَّحِيَّاتُ للهِ وَالصَّلَوَاتُ والطَّيِّبَات ○

*"Greetings, blessings and the best of prayers to Allah."*

Allah (SWT) responded,

السَّلامُ عَلَيْكَ أَيُّهَا النَّبِيُّ وَرَحْمَةُ اللهِ وَبَرَكاتُه ○

*"Peace be upon you, O Prophet, and the mercy and blessings of Allah."*

At this point, the Prophet (SAS) wished to remember the righteous members of his *ummah* and of the previous nations. He said,

السَّلَامُ عَلَيْنَا وَعَلَى عِبَادِ اللهِ الصَّالِحِين ⬤

*"Peace be upon us and upon Allah's righteous slaves."*

At that point, every angel of the heavens cried out,

أَشْهَدُ أَنْ لا إِلـهَ إِلاَّ الله ، وَأَشْهَدُ أَنَّ مُحَمَّداً عَبْدُهُ وَرَسولُه ⬤

*"I testify that there is no deity other than Allah and that Muhammad is His slave and messenger."*

This is the *tashahhud* prayer that we recite in our *salah*. The Prophet (SAS) and his followers were given the gift of fifty daily prayers, which were later reduced to five, but the reward of the reduced number of five prayers was kept equivalent to that of fifty prayers.

In a hadeeth in the *musnad* of Imam Ahmad, the Prophet (SAS) said, "When I went up on the journey of *al-isra` wa al-mi'raj*, Allah gave me three things: (1) He commanded me to pray five times a day, (2) He gave me the last two verses of *Surat al-Baqara*, and (3) He promised me that anybody from my *ummah* who didn't do any major sin would be forgiven and go to paradise."

This does not mean that no believers will enter hell. It means that any sin can be forgiven and that a believer will not stay in hell forever even if he is a sinner. The believers who have more rewards than sins will go to paradise directly after going through the various stages of purification of sins both in this world and the hereafter, but those who have more sins than rewards will remain in hell for a certain period so that they too are purified of their sins, and then they will go to paradise.

*Al-isra` wa al-mi'raj* not only signifies the end of the period of persecution and passive resistance through migration to Medina, but also signifies the role of leadership of the Muslim *ummah* over Mecca and Jerusalem. The leadership role of the *ummah* of Musa (AS) was transferred to the *ummah* of Muhammad (SAS). This happened about two years after the *hijra* when the Prophet (SAS) and his followers were ordered to change their *qibla* from *al-Masjid al-Aqsa* in Jerusalem to *al-Masjid al-Haram* in Mecca.

This shift in leadership is very significant to the Muslims because after the Prophet Muhammad (SAS), it is the Muslims who assume the role of conveying the message of truth. Allah's *sunnah* of preferring one *ummah* over another is based on how it conducts itself. There was a time when the Children of Israel was given preference over all other nations.

يَا بَنِي إِسْرَائِيلَ اذْكُرُوا نِعْمَتِيَ الَّتِي أَنْعَمْتُ عَلَيْكُمْ وَأَنِّي فَضَّلْتُكُمْ عَلَى الْعَالَمِينَ ⬤

*O Children of Israel, remember how I blessed you and favored you over other people.*
(al-Baqara, 2:47)

This was followed by a time when the Children of Israel fell into disgrace for rejecting the signs of Allah (SWT), for killing the prophets of Allah (SWT), and for their constant disobedience and transgressions. Praising the newly installed Muslim *ummah*, Allah (SWT) says,

$$كُنْتُمْ خَيْرَ أُمَّةٍ أُخْرِجَتْ لِلنَّاسِ تَأْمُرُونَ بِالْمَعْرُوفِ وَتَنْهَوْنَ عَنِ الْمُنْكَرِ وَتُؤْمِنُونَ بِاللَّهِ ○$$

*You are the best nation ever to be produced before mankind. You enjoin the right, forbid the wrong and have iman in Allah. (Aal 'Imran, 3:110)*

The significance of the whole episode of *al-isra` wa al-mi'raj* can hardly be exaggerated. The incidents that took place during this journey show the significance of the occasion while providing useful lessons at the same time. I will conclude by repeating some of the blessed words that emerged from the lips of the Prophet (SAS) when he invoked Allah (SWT) at Ta`if. He said, "O Most Merciful of the Merciful. You are the Most Merciful of the Merciful. You are the Lord of the weak and You are my Lord."

If we recognize our lowliness, Allah (SWT) will actualize His Majesty and Lordship in our lives. But if on the other hand we boastfully claim independence for ourselves, we will be left alone until we finally realize that it is He who is in charge.

May Allah (SWT) make us live and die in complete submission to Him, as He says in the Qur`an,

$$وَاعْبُدْ رَبَّكَ حَتَّى يَأْتِيَكَ الْيَقِينُ ○$$

*And worship your Lord until what is certain (death) comes to you. (al-Hijr, 15:99)*

• 90 •

# TRUST *(AMANA)*

In my *khutbah* today, I intend to speak on the concept of *amana* in Islam. Though the word *amana* is quite common, its concept and meaning are very profound, and Muslims need to keep reminding each other of its importance.

*Amana* literally means trust, trustworthiness, loyalty, faithfulness, integrity, and honesty. Both *amana* and *iman* originate from the same three letter root verb, *amina*, which means to be in a state of peace, safety, and security.

The Qur`an mentions the *amana*, or trust, given to mankind. This is a trust which the heavens, the earth, and mountains refused to accept because they were afraid of its heavy burden. This trust requires the establishment of justice in society. We are told in *Surat al-Ahzab*:

إِنَّا عَرَضْنَا الْأَمَانَةَ عَلَى السَّمَاوَاتِ وَالْأَرْضِ وَالْجِبَالِ فَأَبَيْنَ أَنْ يَحْمِلْنَهَا وَأَشْفَقْنَ مِنْهَا وَحَمَلَهَا الْإِنْسَانُ إِنَّهُ كَانَ ظَلُومًا جَهُولًا ◯

*Surely We offered the trust to the heavens and the earth and the mountains, but they refused to undertake it and feared from it, but man undertook it; surely he is unjust, ignorant. (al-Ahzab, 33:72)*

Human beings are a special creation of Allah (SWT). He has created man as His vicegerent or *khaleefa* and has created everything else in the universe for the service of man. Everything in creation is an *amana*, or trust, from Allah to man, and as *khaleefa* of Allah on earth, man has been assigned to establish a just social order, a peaceful society, and civilization on earth.

This understanding of man's role as Allah's vicegerent on earth, and the use of its resources by him as Allah's *amana* to him, gives a much deeper meaning to the concept of ownership is Islam. It implies that ownership in an Islamic society, whether private or public, is not absolute. Resources are only an *amana* whose actual owner is Allah (SWT). Whatever one owns is actually what one holds in trust and therefore it must be used to achieve just ends. From this goal-oriented utilization of resources emerges a whole dynamic of business ethics with social responsibility, respect for private property, dignity of labor, and its fair share in production, and a duty to earn one's living with honesty.

Accountability, honesty, transparency, and perfection of action are all parts of *amana*. The concept of *amana* makes human life more meaningful because man is squarely charged with creating a moral social order. Thus, it provides him the opportunity to demonstrate his ability to be Allah's vicegerent on earth.

The term *amana* is used in the Qur`an and the Sunnah to indicate a very broad and deep meaning. It defines man's rights and responsibilities in relation to all the other humans, his environment, and the rest of Allah's creation. Everything given to us by Allah (SWT) is a kind of *amana* that should be managed appropriately according to the laws and rules revealed by Allah (SWT). Every task or responsibility assigned to us is considered an *amana*.

The first *amana*we were entrusted with was to be the vicegerent of Allah (SWT). This means we are to live in this world obeying Allah's laws and commands. We have been given two abilities to help us fulfill this trust. First, we have been given the mental faculty and the rational power by which we can distinguish between what is good and what is bad and what is right and what is wrong. Second, we have been given the free will or choice with which we can decide to do good or bad, to worship Allah (SWT) and submit to His will, or to worship others and submit to them.

Our bodies, our souls, our eyes, our ears, our intellect, our provisions, our clothing, our homes, and all other blessings and bounties of Allah (SWT) have been given to us as *amana*. When something is given in trust, it must be either returned back to the owner or used according to his instructions. That is why we will be questioned about whether we used these bounties and managed them properly or not. Allah tells us in the Qur`an,

$$\text{ثُمَّ لَتُسْأَلُنَّ يَوْمَئِذٍ عَنِ النَّعِيمِ} \bigcirc$$

*Then on that day you shall most certainly be questioned about the bounties.* (at-Takathur, 102:8)

The Prophet (SAS) said, "Before the end of the Day of Judgment everyone will be questioned about the following: In what did he spend his life? What did he do with his knowledge? From where did he get his wealth and on what did he spend it? How did he use his physical and mental faculties?"

In *Surat al-Isra`* Allah tells us,

$$\text{إِنَّ السَّمْعَ وَالْبَصَرَ وَالْفُؤَادَ كُلُّ أُولَئِكَ كَانَ عَنْهُ مَسْئُولا} \bigcirc$$

*The hearing, sight, and hearts will all be questioned.* (al-Isra`, 17:36)

Referring to the moral fiber of believers, Allah (SWT) declares,

$$\text{وَالَّذِينَ هُمْ لِأَمَانَاتِهِمْ وَعَهْدِهِمْ رَاعُونَ} \bigcirc$$

*And those who honor their trusts and their contracts.* (al-Mu`minoon, 23:8)

This prepares the believers intellectually and morally to be serious and accountable for their own lives, and to their families and societies. The Qur`an further says,

$$\text{يَا أَيُّهَا الَّذِينَ آمَنُوا لَا تَخُونُوا اللَّهَ وَالرَّسُولَ وَتَخُونُوا أَمَانَاتِكُمْ وَأَنْتُمْ تَعْلَمُونَ} \bigcirc$$

*O you who believe, do not betray God and His Messenger, and do not knowingly violate your trusts.* (al-Anfal, 8:27)

*Amana* is considered by the Prophet (SAS) as a sign of faith, while breaching it is a sign of hypocrisy. He (SAS) used to keep reminding his companions about this. Anas Ibn Malik (RAA) reported, "Whenever the Prophet (SAS) preached to his companions, he used to say, 'The person who does not keep trust has no faith and the person who does not respect his covenant (and promise) has no religion.'"

If one is entrusted with keeping any deposits, it would be the duty of such person to keep them properly and return them safely whenever they are wanted by their owner. We have been told in *Surat an-Nisa`*,

إِنَّ اللَّهَ يَأْمُرُكُمْ أَنْ تُؤَدُّوا الْأَمَانَاتِ إِلَى أَهْلِهَا ○

*Surely Allah commands you to render back trusts to their owners. (an-Nisa`, 4: 58)*

All the prophets of Allah (SWT) were the most trustworthy people even before their prophethood. The Prophet Muhammad (SAS) was called *al-Ameen* (the trustworthy). When the daughter of Shu'ayb described Prophet Musa (AS) to her father, she described him as one who is strong and trustworthy.

يَا أَبَتِ اسْتَأْجِرْهُ إِنَّ خَيْرَ مَنِ اسْتَأْجَرْتَ الْقَوِيُّ الْأَمِينُ ○

*O my father, hire him, for the best to be hired is one who is strong and trustworthy.*
*(al-Qasas, 28:26)*

What are the trusts that Allah (SWT) has left for each and every individual? One of the most important trusts between us and Allah (SWT) is holding on to our religion (*deen*).

يَا أَيُّهَا الَّذِينَ آمَنُوا اتَّقُوا اللَّهَ حَقَّ تُقَاتِهِ وَلَا تَمُوتُنَّ إِلَّا وَأَنْتُمْ مُسْلِمُونَ ○

*O you who believe! Fear Allah as He should be feared, and die not except in a state of Islam."* (Aal 'Imran, 3:102)

وَاعْبُدْ رَبَّكَ حَتَّى يَأْتِيَكَ الْيَقِينُ ○

*And worship your Lord until what is certain [death] comes to you. (al-Hijr, 15:99)*

In Islam, *amana* is a contract between an individual and his society, the animal world, the plant world, and with the overall environment. The Prophet (SAS) has explained this responsibility in a hadeeth saying, "Every one of you is a custodian, and everyone will be asked about his subjects. The leader is a custodian, and he will be asked about his subjects. A man is the custodian of the persons in his household, and he will be answerable about them. A woman is the custodian of her husband's house, and she will be asked about her responsibility. An employee is the custodian of the property of his employer, and he is answerable about his responsibility."

*Amana* demands that if a person is appointed to a certain public position, he should not use it for self-promotion or for the benefit of his relatives. The use of public funds for personal purposes is a crime. Allah (SWT) says in the Qur`an,

وَمَنْ يَغْلُلْ يَأْتِ بِمَا غَلَّ يَوْمَ الْقِيَامَةِ ○

*And he who misappropriates shall come on the Day of Judgment with what he misappropriated. (Aal 'Imran, 3:161)*

The fulfillment of Allah's trust or *amana* is a responsibility of the community. Since no person can survive alone, the personal needs of an individual necessitate human cooperation in society. Community as a whole becomes responsible for the accomplishment of the trust.

May Allah (SWT) bless us with the *tawfeeq* to understand the concept of *amana*, and may He enable us to fulfill the same, both in our individual and collective capacities. *Ameen.*

• 91 •

# TRUST IN ALLAH *(TAWAKKUL)*

In today's *khutbah*, I want to share some thoughts with you on the subject of *tawakkul*, a virtue that the Qur`an seeks to inculcate in believers. *Tawakkul* means to have trust in Allah.

وَعَلَى اللهِ فَلْيَتَوَكَّلِ الْمُؤْمِنُونَ ۝

*Let the believers put their trust in Allah. (Aal 'Imran, 3:122)*

One of the names of Allah (SWT) is *al-Wakeel*. It means the one who can be trusted—the Trustee. *Al-Wakeel* also means the Guardian, the Protector, the Defender, and the Disposer of affairs.

وَتَوَكَّلْ عَلَى اللَّهِ وَكَفَى بِاللَّهِ وَكِيلًا ۝

*And put your trust in Allah. Allah is sufficient as a Trustee. (an-Nisa`, 4:81)*

We should trust in Allah (SWT) because everything belongs to Him.

لَهُ مَا فِي السَّمَاوَاتِ وَمَا فِي الْأَرْضِ وَكَفَىٰ بِاللَّهِ وَكِيلًا ۝

*Everything in the heavens and earth belongs to Him and Allah is sufficient as a Trustee. (an-Nisa`, 4:171)*

We should trust in Allah (SWT) because He is the Lord of the east and the west and there is none other worthy of worship but Him.

رَّبُّ الْمَشْرِقِ وَالْمَغْرِبِ لَا إِلَهَ إِلَّا هُوَ فَاتَّخِذْهُ وَكِيلًا ۝

*Lord of the east and the west; there is no god but Him so take Him as your Trustee. (al-Muzzammil, 73:9)*

We should trust in Allah (SWT) because He alone is Ever Living and does not die.

وَتَوَكَّلْ عَلَى الْحَيِّ الَّذِي لَا يَمُوتُ ۝

*And put your trust in the Ever Living, the One Who does not die. (al-Furqan, 25:58)*

We should trust in Allah (SWT) because He is the Mighty, the Wise.

وَمَنْ يَتَوَكَّلْ عَلَى اللَّهِ فَإِنَّ اللَّهَ عَزِيزٌ حَكِيمٌ ۝

*And whoever trusts in Allah, then surely Allah is the Mighty, the Wise. (al-Anfal, 8:49)*

We should trust in Allah (SWT) because He is the Mighty, the Merciful.

وَتَوَكَّلْ عَلَى الْعَزِيزِ الرَّحِيمِ ۝

*And put your trust in the Mighty, the Merciful. (ash-Shu'ara`, 26:217)*

We should trust in Allah (SWT) because He alone has the knowledge of the unseen in the heavens and the earth, and all affairs will return to Him for decision.

وَلِلَّهِ غَيْبُ السَّمَاوَاتِ وَالْأَرْضِ وَإِلَيْهِ يُرْجَعُ الْأَمْرُ كُلُّهُ فَاعْبُدْهُ وَتَوَكَّلْ عَلَيْهِ ۝

*To Allah belongs the unseen of the heavens and the earth, and all affairs will return to Him. Hence worship Him and put your trust in Him. (Hud, 11:123)*

We should trust in Allah (SWT) because He alone provides the right guidance. The prophets and messengers of Allah (SWT) used to say,

وَمَا لَنَا أَلَّا نَتَوَكَّلَ عَلَى اللَّهِ وَقَدْ هَدَانَا سُبُلَنَا ۝

*How should we not put our trust in Allah when He has guided us in our ways? (Ibraheem, 14:12)*

Putting one's trust in Allah (SWT) is not only advantageous for the above reasons, but it is also one of the demands of faith.

وَعَلَى اللَّهِ فَتَوَكَّلُوا إِنْ كُنْتُمْ مُؤْمِنِينَ ۝

*So put your trust in Allah if you are believers." (al-Ma`ida, 5:23)*

One of the blessed names of the Prophet Muhammad (SAS) is *al-Mutawakkil*, meaning "one who puts his trust in Allah." Remember what the Prophet (SAS) said to Abu Bakr (RAA) when they were in a cave during their *hijra* to Mecca and some of their enemies had reached the very mouth of the cave,

إِذْ هُمَا فِي الْغَارِ إِذْ يَقُولُ لِصَاحِبِهِ لَا تَحْزَنْ إِنَّ اللَّهَ مَعَنَا ۝

*When they were both in the cave, he [Muhammad] told his companion, "Do not worry; for Allah is with us." (at-Tawba, 9:40)*

How often are we depressed and worried about our future and about the future of our children? Allah (SWT) tells us to put our trust in Him because He will manage our affairs in the way that is best for us.

$$وَمَن يَتَوَكَّلْ عَلَى اللَّهِ فَهُوَ حَسْبُهُ ○$$

*Whoever puts his trust in Allah — He will be sufficient for him. (at-Talaq, 65:3)*

The Prophet (SAS) told us whoever when leaving his house says,

$$بِسْمِ اللهِ ، تَوَكَّلْتُ عَلَى اللهِ وَلَا حَوْلَ وَلَا قُوَّةَ إِلَّا بِاللهِ$$

*"In the name of Allah, I put my trust in Allah and there is no power and no strength except with Allah," it will be said to him, "You are taken care of and you are protected and guided, and the devils will move away from him..."*

The Prophet (SAS) also tells us that whoever says the following *du'a* seven times in the morning after *Fajr*, and seven times after *'Asr*, Allah (SWT) will take care of whatever worries him of the matters of this world and the hereafter. We are instructed by Allah to say:

$$حَسْبِيَ اللهُ لَاَ إِلَهَ إِلَّا هُوَ عَلَيْهِ تَوَكَّلْتُ وَهُوَ رَبُّ الْعَرْشِ الْعَظِيمِ ○$$

*Allah is sufficient for me. There is none worthy of worship, but Him. I have placed my trust in Him, and He is the Lord of the Majestic Throne. (at-Tawba, 9:129)*

Allah (SWT) ordered Musa (AS) to take the Children of Israel from the darkness of oppression to the light of freedom by rescuing them from the clutches of the Pharaoh. As they escaped, running for their lives, he followed them with his army. The Children of Israel were stuck right in front of the Red Sea. Some of them lost hope, some of them cursed Musa (AS) for only bringing them more trouble, and some of them just kept looking back at the approaching army. Musa (AS) remained calm. He trusted in Allah and said,

$$إِنَّ مَعِيَ رَبِّي سَيَهْدِينِ ○$$

*Most certainly, my Lord is with me and He will guide me. (ash-Shu'ara', 26:62)*

Allah (SWT) ordered Musa (AS) to strike the sea with his staff, and the sea split. Musa (AS) trusted in Allah (SWT), and Allah (SWT) split the sea for him.

It is important to understand, however, that *tawakkul* does not mean to sit back and think that one's problems will be solved just by believing that Allah (SWT) will take care of everything. Putting one's complete trust in Allah (SWT) is not equivalent to fatalism or the doctrine that all events are inevitable or subject to fate. One has to place trust in Allah (SWT) only after doing all that is in their power in regard to that matter. Ya'qoob (AS) placed his trust in Allah (SWT) and he was praised for that. And yet, before sending his sons to Egypt in search of Yusuf (AS), he asked them to take the necessary precautions.

Here we can see that *tawakkul* is regarded as being complimentary, and not antithetical or opposed to planning and using one's judgment. The same lesson is taught when Allah (SWT) tells the Prophet Muhammad (SAS),

وَشَاوِرْهُمْ فِي الْأَمْرِ فَإِذَا عَزَمْتَ فَتَوَكَّلْ عَلَى اللَّهِ إِنَّ اللَّهَ يُحِبُّ الْمُتَوَكِّلِينَ ۝

*And consult with them upon the conduct of affairs; and when you have decided, then place your trust in Allah; surely Allah loves those who trust. (Aal 'Imran, 3:159)*

Just as *iman* is the combination of faith and acting upon that faith, the same goes for *tawakkul*. Don't give up on your own efforts. Rather strive and work with the attitude that Allah (SWT) will take care of your affairs and will help you get through your trials. This proactive attitude is, in fact, part of you having *tawakkul*. It is reported that one day Prophet Muhammad (SAS) noticed a Bedouin leaving his camel without tying it. He asked the Bedouin, "Why don't you tie down your camel?" The Bedouin answered, "I put my trust in Allah." The Prophet (SAS) then said, "Tie your camel first, then put your trust in Allah." Taking advantage of available means is not only consistent with *tawakkul*, but an intrinsic aspect of expressing it.

May Allah (SWT) make us of the *mutawakkiloon*; those who gracefully rely on Him. May He guide us to work in this world to our full potential. May He protect us and make us entrust our souls to Him, both in times of ease and in times of hardship. *Ameen!*

Brothers and sisters! Every human being comes to this earth by the decree of Allah (SWT) with a preordained plan that balances the nature of his temporary abode with good and evil, with ease and difficulties, and with death and life. As Muslims, we should believe that Allah (SWT) may decide out of His wisdom, for reasons that only He knows, to let our plans not work out the way we desire. The fruit of *tawakkul* is the acceptance of Allah's decree. Whoever leaves his affairs to Allah (SWT) and then accepts what he is given has truly relied on Allah (SWT). Believing in *qadr*, or Allah's divine decree, is one of the articles of our faith. In every matter there is good for a believer.

Yusuf (AS) was thrown into a well. This was wrong. He was picked up and sold into slavery. This was outrageous. His master's wife tried to seduce him, and when he refused, he was put into prison! This was blatant injustice. And yet, all of this was good for him! And that is why later when Yusuf (AS) became the Ruler of Egypt, he remarked that Allah (SWT) was *lateef* toward Him. *Al-Lateef* is the One who is subtle. He is the One who brings benefit to His servant in a way that the servant can never perceive.

Brothers and sisters! *Tawakkul* requires training. We are humans, and every now and then, we face situations of discomfort and uncertainty. We begin to wonder whether or not our plans will work out. These are moments when we should remind ourselves to trust Allah (SWT). If we truly rely on Allah (SWT), then this reliance gives us peace of mind and tranquility of heart knowing that Allah (SWT) is always doing the best for us.

One of the ways of achieving *tawakkul* is to perform the *istikhara* prayer whenever a need arises. *Istikhara* is the prayer of decision making. In this prayer you ask Allah (SWT) that if the matter is good for you to make it easy for you, and if not, to take it away from you. Then you ask Allah (SWT) to make you content with His decree. We should make it a habit to practice this *sunnah* in our daily life. The Prophet (SAS) used to teach his companions to make *istikhara* just as he used to teach them the Qur`an.

Brothers and sisters! *Tawakkul* is to entrust our affairs to Allah (SWT) and be content knowing that He will take care of us. *Tawakkul* is to know that all will be well, even if things look impossible. *Tawakkul* is to understand and appreciate that when Allah (SWT) takes something away from us, He is actually redirecting us to something better. *Tawakkul* is to know and believe that there is light at the end of the tunnel, even if we don't see it.

Let us remind ourselves that Allah (SWT) is *al-Wakeel*, the ultimate and the best Trustee. Let us give ourselves and our affairs over to Him with a sense of full comfort and certainty in our hearts. Everything He decrees for us is good for us. He is the best disposer of affairs. He always opens a pathway for success when we have firm faith in Him. He is sufficient for all of us.

May Allah (SWT) give us the wisdom to use all His blessings in the best way we can while trusting in Him and depending on Him. *Allahumma ameen*.

•    92    •

# TRUTHFULNESS

The topic of my *khutbah* today is "Truthfulness." I will try to share some thoughts with you on the meaning of truthfulness as a moral virtue in Islam. It is well known that truthfulness and honesty have always been regarded as great virtues, and falsehood and deceit have always been considered great vices. Hence, Islam commands truthfulness and forbids falsehood and deception. The Qur`an commands believers to speak the truth and to be with those who are truthful.

يَا أَيُّهَا الَّذِينَ آمَنُوا اتَّقُوا اللَّهَ وَقُولُوا قَوْلًا سَدِيدًا ⃝

*O you who believe, be conscious of Allah and speak the truth. (al-Ahzab, 33:70)*

يَا أَيُّهَا الَّذِينَ آمَنُوا اتَّقُوا اللَّهَ وَكُونُوا مَعَ الصَّادِقِينَ ⃝

*O you who believe, fear Allah, and be with the truthful. (at-Tawba, 9:119)*

Generally, people understand truthfulness to be restricted to truthful speech. Islam, however, teaches that truthfulness is far more than having an honest tongue. In Islam, truthfulness is the conformity of the outer with the inner, the action with the intention, the speech with the belief, and the practice with the preaching. As such, truthfulness is the very cornerstone of the upright Muslim's character and the springboard for his virtuous deeds. Among the various attributes of sincere believers, one is that they are truthful. Allah (SWT) says in *Surat al-Hujurat*,

إِنَّمَا الْمُؤْمِنُونَ الَّذِينَ آمَنُوا بِاللَّهِ وَرَسُولِهِ ثُمَّ لَمْ يَرْتَابُوا وَجَاهَدُوا بِأَمْوَالِهِمْ وَأَنفُسِهِمْ فِي سَبِيلِ اللَّهِ أُولَئِكَ هُمُ الصَّادِقُونَ ⃝

*The believers are those who believe in Allah and His messenger, leave all doubt behind, and strive with their wealth and their persons for Allah's cause. Such are the truthful ones. (al-Hujurat, 49:15)*

One of the repeated descriptions of the prophets in the Qur`an is that they were truthful.

وَاذْكُرْ فِي الْكِتَابِ إِبْرَاهِيمَ إِنَّهُ كَانَ صِدِّيقًا نَّبِيًّا ⃝

*Mention Ibraheem in the Book. He was a man of truth and a prophet. (Maryam, 19:41)*

وَاذْكُرْ فِي الْكِتَابِ إِدْرِيسَ إِنَّهُ كَانَ صِدِّيقًا نَّبِيًّا ⃝

*Mention Idrees in the Book. He was a man of truth and a prophet. (Maryam, 19:56)*

وَاذْكُرْ فِي الْكِتَابِ إِسْمَاعِيلَ إِنَّهُ كَانَ صَادِقَ الْوَعْدِ وَكَانَ رَسُولًا نَّبِيًّا ⃝

*Mention Isma'eel in the Book. He was true to his promise, and he was a messenger and a prophet. (Maryam, 19:54)*

People called the Prophet Muhammad (SAS) *al-Ameen* meaning the truthful or trustworthy, even before he became a prophet. Even his enemies, such as Abu Sufyan, before he became a Muslim, acknowledged the Prophet's trustworthiness. When asked by Heraclius, the Byzantine Roman Emperor what Muhammad (SAS) taught them, Abu Sufyan answered that he taught them to worship Allah (SWT), to pray, to be truthful, to be chaste and to be kind to relatives. In a well-known hadeeth, the Prophet

(SAS) said, "Truthfulness leads to righteousness, and righteousness leads to paradise. A man will keep speaking the truth and striving to speak the truth until he will be recorded with Allah as a *siddeeq*, or truthful person. Lying leads to immorality, and immorality leads to hellfire. A man will keep telling lies and striving to tell lies until he is recorded with Allah as a liar."

This hadeeth indicates that truthfulness leads to righteousness. Righteousness is an all-embracing concept that includes all kinds of goodness and different kinds of righteous deeds. Immorality is basically an inclination toward deviation from the truth, and the immoral person is one who is inclined to turn away from the path of guidance. Hence, immorality and righteousness are diametrically opposed to each other. Therefore, truthfulness is a characteristic which is to be cultivated until it becomes implanted in a person's soul and disposition and is reflected in his or her character.

We learn through a hadeeth that the Prophet (SAS) said, "Guarantee for me six things and I will guarantee paradise for you: (1) tell the truth when you speak, (2) fulfill your promises, (3) be faithful when you are trusted, (4) safeguard your private parts, (5) lower your gaze, and (6) withhold your hands (from harming others)."

As for the next life, through Allah's grace and mercy, the obedient ones and practitioners of truthfulness will reach a station in paradise alongside those most fortunate of souls that are mentioned in *Surat an-Nisa`*.

وَمَنْ يُطِعِ اللَّهَ وَالرَّسُولَ فَأُولَئِكَ مَعَ الَّذِينَ أَنْعَمَ اللَّهُ عَلَيْهِمْ مِنَ النَّبِيِّينَ وَالصِّدِّيقِينَ وَالشُّهَدَاءِ وَالصَّالِحِينَ وَحَسُنَ أُولَئِكَ رَفِيقًا ◯

*And he who obeys Allah and the Messenger, they shall be with those whom Allah has favored, the prophets, those steadfast in truthfulness, the martyrs, and the righteous. How excellent will they be for companions? (an-Nisa`, 4:69)*

The *siddeeq*, or the one who is steadfast in truthfulness, is someone who is utterly honest, whose devotion to truth has reached a very high point. Such a person is always upright and straightforward in his dealings. He supports nothing but right and justice and does so with sincerity. He opposes whatever is contrary to truth and does not waver in his opposition to falsehood. His life is so unblemished and selfless that even his enemies, let alone his friends, expect nothing of him except goodness and justice.

In contrast to truthfulness, deception and lying are mentioned in the Qur`an and the hadeeth as the worst of sins. A man came to the Prophet (SAS) and asked, "Which action makes the highest number of people the inmates of hell?" The Prophet (SAS) replied, "Lying. When a believer speaks a lie, he becomes prone to commit every other sin, and when this happens, he commits *kufr* (disbelief) which then makes him enter hell."

Indeed, lying is a grave sin. Some false words lead to war between two tribes or two sections of the society. Some lies damage the honor of thousands of people, endanger their lives, or lead to economic disasters. Often due to lying, innocent people are sentenced to death and their families destroyed.

We must be very careful and cautious when coming across the fake news that has become so rampant. Fake news is a type of hoax or deliberate spread of misinformation with the intent to mislead in order to gain financially or politically. It is carried out via the traditional print or broadcasting news media or via Internet based social media. Another expression called "alternative truth" or "alternative fact" has found its way recently into the political discourse. It is nothing but a misstatement of the truth, a lie. A Qur`anic verse from which we can draw a close parallel in our social media saturated life is the verse:

يَا أَيُّهَا الَّذِينَ آمَنُوا إِن جَاءَكُمْ فَاسِقٌ بِنَبَإٍ فَتَبَيَّنُوا أَن تُصِيبُوا قَوْمًا بِجَهَالَةٍ فَتُصْبِحُوا عَلَىٰ مَا فَعَلْتُمْ نَادِمِينَ ◯

*O you who believe! If a known wicked person brings you news, investigate to avoid harming people out of ignorance and later regret what you have done. (al-Hujurat, 49:6)*

This verse advises us to verify any news before we take action. Today it is more important than ever to follow this advice. Viruses developed to infect computers can damage them. Fake news, alternative facts, or just plain lies also act like viruses that can damage the human mind and can corrupt our societies in a far more diabolical way. And what does Allah (SWT) say about the liars?

إِنَّ اللَّهَ لَا يَهْدِي مَنْ هُوَ مُسْرِفٌ كَذَّابٌ ◯

*Allah does not guide one who transgresses and lies. (Ghafir, 40:28)*

إِنَّ اللَّهَ لَا يَهْدِي مَنْ هُوَ كَاذِبٌ كَفَّارٌ ◯

*Allah does not guide one who is a liar and ungrateful. (az-Zumar, 39:3)*

In one hadeeth, the Prophet (SAS) said, "The worst betrayal is to tell a lie to a brother of yours while he trusts you and believes in you." He also said, "Three are the signs of a hypocrite: When he speaks, he lies; when he makes a promise, he breaks it; and when he is trusted, he betrays his trust." This hadeeth should make us think that we should not be like hypocrites who say something that they don't really mean. The most dangerous and highly condemned act of lying according to the Qur`an and Sunnah is to lie about Allah (SWT) and to attribute things to Allah (SWT) that He did not reveal.

وَمَنْ أَظْلَمُ مِمَّنِ افْتَرَىٰ عَلَى اللَّهِ كَذِبًا ◯

*Who could be more wicked than someone who invents a lie against Allah. (al-An'am, 6:93).*

Also, any fabricator of a hadeeth has been warned by the Prophet (SAS) who said, "Whoever lies about me deliberately, let him take his seat in the hellfire."

This factor contributed to the introduction of critical review in the science of hadeeth in order to determine the value and worth of the people through whom traditions of the Prophet (SAS) reached the later generations. The Muslim jurists also established this principle while considering the "law of evidence." The evidence of a corrupt person, or a person of questionable character, would be unacceptable.

There is a famous *du'a`* which says,

اللهمَّ أَرِنا الْحَقَّ حقّاً وارْزُقْنا اتِّبَاعَه وأَرِنا الْباطِلَ باطِلاً وارْزُقنا اجْتِنابَه ◯

*This du'a` means, "O Allah! Show us the truth as true, and inspire us to follow it. Show us falsehood as falsehood, and inspire us to abstain from it."*

Brothers and sisters! What are the implications of truthfulness or the lack of it on a social and political level? The basic rule is that telling or spreading a lie is worse when it harms a greater number of people, which is why the Prophet (SAS) said that a person who lies and his lies reach far and wide will be severely punished on the Day of Judgment. This, for example, applies to demagogues, dishonest politicians, or people who spread falsehood through the media and other devices. If people who are able to reach large numbers of people spread falsehood, then the harm would be great, and as such, the punishment of such liars will be great.

Concerning economic life, the Prophet (SAS) said that if people who buy and sell are truthful, Allah (SWT) will bless their sale. He also said that it is not lawful for a believer to sell an item while knowing that it has a defect without telling buyers about it. Even lying to children is not permitted. The Prophet (SAS) said, "If a person calls his child over in order to give him something and doesn't, it will be written against him as a lie." Psychologically and morally, it is very important to be truthful with children. The basic rule with regard to lying is that it is not permitted, but there are certain circumstances in which Islam permits lying to serve a greater purpose or to prevent harm. Asma` bint Yazeed said, "The Messenger of Allah (SAS) said, 'Lying is not permitted except in three cases: (1) a man's speaking to his wife to make her happy, (2) lying at times of war, and (3) lying in order to reconcile between people.'" Needless to say, even while lying on these three occasions, Allah (SWT) knows our intention and will judge us accordingly.

Truthfulness has been mentioned in the Qur`an as related to *iman*, or faith, in Allah (SWT). It is an attribute which enhances the moral character of the believer. May Allah (SWT) make us among the truthful ones. *Allahumma ameen.*

# • 93 •

# VOLUNTEERING FOR THE
# SAKE OF ALLAH

My *khutbah* today is on the topic of "Volunteering for the Sake of Allah," which means being involved in any activity, project, or cause that is initiated with the sole purpose of gaining Allah's pleasure. Allah (SWT) has enabled and created each one of us uniquely. Our sole purpose in this life is to gain His pleasure and use all the means He has blessed us with to do so. Allah (SWT) has chosen Muslims to be role models for the whole of humanity. There is an *ayah* in the Qur`an that sums up the role and position Allah (SWT) expects every Muslim to live up to:

كُنتُمْ خَيْرَ أُمَّةٍ أُخْرِجَتْ لِلنَّاسِ تَأْمُرُونَ بِالْمَعْرُوفِ وَتَنْهَوْنَ عَنِ الْمُنكَرِ وَتُؤْمِنُونَ بِاللَّهِ ۞

*You are the best community brought forth for the good of mankind. You enjoin what is right and forbid what is wrong, and believe in Allah. (Aal 'Imran, 3:110)*

Our beloved Prophet Muhammad (SAS) also said, "Convey from me, even if it be an *ayah*." Allah (SWT) has blessed us with the beautiful gift of Islam. He has also blessed us with a lot of free time. If we are really honest with ourselves, and analyze how we spend our time every day and how we could have spent it better, we'll be amazed to find out how much free time we actually have every day and how much of it we have been wasting.

When we decide to work for Allah's sake, full time or part time, we should be constantly asking ourselves, "Is what I am doing for His sake and to gain His pleasure?" There are some useful guidelines that we may follow when we embark upon the journey of working for the sake of Allah (SWT).

First of all, it is important that we purify our intentions. We are well aware of the famous hadeeth, "Verily actions are by intentions, and for every person is what he intended." We should be very cautious and careful not to fall into *riya`*, or showing off. You may be remembering that the Prophet (SAS) told us how Allah (SWT) throws a martyr, a scholar, and a wealthy generous person into hellfire because of their insincere intentions and because of their desire to show off their deeds. So sincerity is the key. It is ok if what we do is shown to the community around us in order to encourage and motivate others, but we should make sure that we do good deeds in private as well.

We should start simple and remain consistent. It is good to be among those who work behind the scenes, those without whom the event, the project or the program wouldn't have happened the way it did. No one talks about them except perhaps a few. They talk less and work more. They fear showing off, and they fear hypocrisy. We should keep reminding ourselves about the beautiful *du'a* taught to us in the Qur`an:

قُلْ إِنَّ صَلَاتِي وَنُسُكِي وَمَحْيَايَ وَمَمَاتِي لِلَّهِ رَبِّ الْعَالَمِينَ ۝

*Say, "My prayer and my sacrifice and my life and my death are all for Allah, the Lord of the worlds." (al-An'am, 6:162)*

This will help us to remain focused in what we do.

We also have to discover our potential. There are innumerable ways to work for Allah's sake, and numerous opportunities to reach out to the world with our talents, skills, and abilities. We have to find out what we are made of and contribute accordingly. Each one of us has something special about us. Each one of us is specially created with some means to serve Allah (SWT). We should constantly make *du'a* to Allah (SWT) to guide us to our maximum potential so as to be able to serve His cause. Allah (SWT) says,

وَلِكُلٍّ وِجْهَةٌ هُوَ مُوَلِّيهَا فَاسْتَبِقُوا الْخَيْرَاتِ ۝

*And everyone has a direction to which he turns to; so compete with one another in doing good deeds. (al-Baqara, 2:148)*

Once we've planned to volunteer for a cause in addition to our normal day-to-day routine work, we should start organizing our life and be clear about our priorities. We should not take on more tasks than we can handle. Every responsibility we take on is a trust that we must fulfill, so we should take on only as much as we can deliver with excellence. Before signing up for a volunteering position we should ask ourselves, "What am I going to learn from this?" Through every volunteering opportunity, there is learning. We have to keep on learning and enriching ourselves while we plan to give to others. No matter how religious we may think we are, Shaytan traps us in different ways, mainly through doubts and desires. We have to keep seeking refuge in Allah from Shaytan. Volunteering for the sake of Allah (SWT) is not about achieving the desired results. It is about contributing toward making a positive change. The effort is in your hand, but the result is with Allah (SWT). And the only goal is to gain His pleasure.

Brothers and sisters! How can we reap maximum benefit and reward while working as a volunteer? To begin with, we have to be passionate in whatever we do. As mentioned before, each one of us is uniquely created to serve Allah's *deen* in our own ways. Every single thing He created serves a unique purpose. If our presence in this world didn't have any significant purpose, we wouldn't have been created. Our spirituality is driven by understanding and living our purpose. Living our purpose is what drives our closeness to Allah (SWT) in the form of making a worthwhile contribution in whatever way we can.

In addition to discovering our potential, we should find out what the need of the hour is by identifying the problems faced by the community around us and what we can do about them based on our skills and resources. If we need people with certain expertise that we don't have, then we should form a team of passionate people with potential to do the job. If there are projects and organizations already doing that job, then we should try to be a part of them in whichever way we can.

It is also very important that whatever we do for the sake of Allah (SWT), we do it very seriously, to the best of our capability, and to the point of perfection. The Prophet (SAS) said, "Indeed Allah loves one who when he does a work, he does it with *itqan*." In other words, Allah (SWT) is pleased with the person who performs his deeds with perfection. *Itqan* refers to the attitude of being careful, meticulous, diligent, and excellent in carrying out responsibilities and tasks. Islam demands that whatever we undertake to do, we do it really well. There are no halfhearted measures in Islam. No sloppy, shoddy work. If you are a Muslim and you do something, you have to do it well. Unfortunately, this is something many of us have forgotten.

This is one of those important lessons of our culture and history that we need to relearn. When we do something, whatever it may be, those looking at our work should be able to say, "Ah! A Muslim must have done it!" That is how our predecessors used to be, and that is what we need to become. Our dedication and commitment to our work will not only let us progress further in work, but will earn for us blessings and mercy from Allah (SWT). The Prophet (SAS) said in a hadeeth, "Allah is good and accepts only that which is good." This hadeeth encourages us to work carefully and responsibly to earn the pleasure of Allah (SWT). As a community, we must always look for ways to improve our situation. We must discard any poor image of ourselves and our work ethic. Allah tells us in the Qur`an that our situation will not change for the better if we do not put in any effort to change it ourselves.

إِنَّ اللَّهَ لَا يُغَيِّرُ مَا بِقَوْمٍ حَتَّى يُغَيِّرُوا مَا بِأَنْفُسِهِمْ ○

*Allah does not change the condition of a people unless they change what is in themselves. (ar-Ra'd, 13:11)*

We should make *du'a`* seeking refuge from laziness and helplessness. A Prophetic *du'a`* teaches us to say,

اللَّهُمَّ إِنِّي أَعُوذُ بِكَ مِنَ الهَمِّ وَ الْحُزْنِ، والْعَجْزِ والكَسَلِ والبُخْلِ والجُبْنِ، و أَعْوذُ بِكَ مِن غَلَبَةِ الدَّيْنِ وَقَهْرِ الرِّجَالِ ○

*"O Allah! I take refuge in You from anxiety and sorrow, weakness and laziness, miserliness and cowardice, and I seek refuge in You from the burden of debts and from*

*being overpowered by men."*

We are also taught to say,

اللَّهُمَّ أَعِنِّي عَلَى ذِكْرِكَ وَشُكْرِكَ وَحُسْنِ عِبَادَتِكَ ◯

*"O Allah! Help me to remember You, to thank You, and to worship You in the best of manners."*

May Allah (SWT) bless us all and give us all a deep understanding of the *deen* that He has ordained for us. *Ameen!*

Brothers and sisters! Respecting differences of opinion is a trait every volunteer should have to avoid becoming self-righteous and arrogant. Another important point to note is that we should conduct *shura*, or consultation, when working in a team. Allah (SWT) says,

وَالَّذِينَ اسْتَجَابُوا لِرَبِّهِمْ وَأَقَامُوا الصَّلَاةَ وَأَمْرُهُمْ شُورَى بَيْنَهُمْ وَمِمَّا رَزَقْنَاهُمْ يُنْفِقُونَ ◯

*And those who respond to their Lord, pray regularly, conduct their affairs by mutual consultation, and give of what We have provided for them. (ash-Shura, 42:38)*

*Shura* is to take sincere opinions into consideration seriously. In other words, you are open to other ideas and haven't yet made up your mind. It also involves exchanging ideas with the knowledge that maybe what you had in mind isn't the best, and what others offer may be better, or a combination of the two can be worked out.

Doing voluntary work for the sake of Allah (SWT) is a highly dignified and honorable deed. We don't want to demoralize it with unacceptable behavior. We have to exhibit good character. The Prophet (SAS) said, "Nothing is placed on the Scale that is heavier than good character. Indeed the person with good character will have attained the rank of the person of fasting and prayer." Therefore, we must keep purifying our spiritual hearts with the remembrance of Allah (SWT). Let me conclude by saying that any Islamic project can only be successful if it is run according to Islamic guidelines. Volunteering allows us to follow our passion while contributing to a cause that is important to us. We're all in this together. It is a great way to meet and get to know others in our community. Always remind yourself of what an honor you are carrying on your shoulders by working for the sake of Allah (SWT). May Allah (SWT) give us the wisdom to do voluntary work for His sake and may He accept it from us.

# 94

# WE BELONG TO ALLAH AND TO HIM WE SHALL RETURN

The topic of today's *khutbah* is "We belong to Allah and to Him we shall return." A couple of hours back, I got the news of my beloved mother's passing away in India.

My mother's passing away reminded me of my own approaching death. Generally, people consider it inauspicious to speak about death and avoid remembering their own future death. Surprising as it may seem, remembering death can actually motivate us to live a purposeful and useful life. This is so central to a Muslim's life that even during the auspicious occasion of a Muslim's wedding, we recite the third verse of *Surat Aal 'Imran* in the *khutbah* of *nikah* (the marriage contract) to remind the young couple and those witnessing the *nikah* to have *taqwa* of Allah (SWT) and not to die except as Muslims.

يَا أَيُّهَا الَّذِينَ آمَنُواْ اتَّقُواْ اللَّهَ حَقَّ تُقَاتِهِ وَلاَ تَمُوتُنَّ إِلاَّ وَأَنتُم مُّسْلِمُونَ ۝

*O you who believe, be conscious of Allah with all the consciousness that is due to Him, and do not die except as Muslims. (Aal 'Imran, 3:102)*

It is important to remind ourselves that we belong to Allah (SWT) and to Him we shall return because each and every one of us has to experience death. Almost every day we hear of the death of someone. Yet, most people ignore the fact that they have to die one day. The knowledge of the reality of death can help us understand it and prepare ourselves for its coming. Death is certain and unavoidable, as Allah reminds us in the Qur`an,

كُلُّ نَفْسٍ ذَائِقَةُ الْمَوْتِ وَإِنَّمَا تُوَفَّوْنَ أُجُورَكُمْ يَوْمَ الْقِيَامَةِ ۝

*Every human being is bound to taste death: and you shall receive your rewards in full on the Day of Resurrection. (Aal 'Imran, 3:185)*

أَيْنَمَا تَكُونُوا يُدْرِككُّمُ الْمَوْتُ وَلَوْ كُنتُمْ فِي بُرُوجٍ مُّشَيَّدَةٍ ۝

*Wherever you may be, death will overtake you, even if you be in strongly built towers. (an-Nisa`, 4:78)*

This being the case, do we ever think about the day we will die? Are we ready and prepared for our departure from this earth and our return to Allah (SWT)? Are we scared of death? There is no denying that fear of death is something natural. It hangs over each one of us. Every day that passes brings us closer to death. Every breath we take reduces a portion of our life and brings us nearer to death. As soon as the appointed time comes, we belong among the dead. Then it becomes clear that life is like a flower that blooms and then withers, or like an oil lamp that illuminates and then dies down. Let us not be among those who at their dying moments will realize how they wasted their lives and how they did not fulfill the purpose of their creation, which is to worship their Lord. Allah (SWT) says in the Qur`an,

$$وَمَا خَلَقْتُ الْجِنَّ وَالْإِنْسَ إِلَّا لِيَعْبُدُونِ ○$$

*I did not create jinn and humans except to worship Me. (adh-Dhariyat, 51:56)*

References to drawing the last breath, or the trance and stupor of death are found in the Qur`an.

$$وَجَاءَتْ سَكْرَةُ الْمَوْتِ بِالْحَقِّ ذَٰلِكَ مَا كُنتَ مِنْهُ تَحِيدُ ○$$

*The trance of death will come revealing the truth: that is what you were trying to escape. (Qaf, 50:19)*

$$لَّقَدْ كُنتَ فِي غَفْلَةٍ مِّنْ هَٰذَا فَكَشَفْنَا عَنكَ غِطَاءَكَ فَبَصَرُكَ الْيَوْمَ حَدِيدٌ ○$$

*You were heedless of this, but now We have removed your veil, so your sight today is sharp. (Qaf, 50:22)*

These are the moments when the dying person bids this vanishing world goodbye and casts a last look at it. Life will pass before his eyes like a flash, and he will realize how short it really was. What is the reality of death? When it occurs, the spirit leaves the body. We learn through prophetic traditions that a good soul comes out of the body with ease while an evil soul, which resists leaving the body, is taken out harshly by the angel of death. During a wicked person's dying moments, he wishes that death were delayed so that if he were a nonbeliever, he would become a believer, or if he were a disobedient believer he would repent from his sins.

$$حَتَّىٰ إِذَا جَاءَ أَحَدَهُمُ الْمَوْتُ قَالَ رَبِّ ارْجِعُونِ ○ لَعَلِّي أَعْمَلُ صَالِحًا فِيمَا تَرَكْتُ ○$$

*When death comes to any of them, he says: My Lord, send me back; that I may act righteously in what I have left behind. (al-Mu`minoon, 23:99-100)*

There are two types of souls: the good and the evil. They are honored or dishonored in their respective journeys to their heavenly abodes. *Sijjeen* is the record in which the deeds of the evil souls are preserved, while *'Iliyyeen* is the record in which the deeds of the righteous souls are preserved. Allah tells us in the Qur`an,

كَلَّا إِنَّ كِتَابَ الْفُجَّارِ لَفِي سِجِّينٍ ⭕

*Indeed! The record of the wicked is in the Sijjeen. (al-Mutaffifeen, 83:7)*

كَلَّا إِنَّ كِتَابَ الْأَبْرَارِ لَفِي عِلِّيِّينَ ⭕

*Indeed, the record of the righteous is in the 'Iliyyeen. (al-Mutaffifeen, 83:18)*

Man takes nothing with him in his grave. The Prophet (SAS) told us, "When a man dies, his deeds come to an end except for three things: ongoing charity(*sadaqa jariya*), beneficial knowledge that he leaves behind, or a virtuous descendant who prays for him." Such admonitions remind us that we should hasten in doing good deeds lest our time is up, and our book of deeds gets closed forever. We should not be among those who will cry to Allah (SWT) to give them more time to spend in His way and to be one of the righteous.

وَأَنفِقُوا مِن مَّا رَزَقْنَاكُم مِّن قَبْلِ أَن يَأْتِيَ أَحَدَكُمُ الْمَوْتُ فَيَقُولَ رَبِّ لَوْلَا أَخَّرْتَنِي إِلَىٰ أَجَلٍ قَرِيبٍ فَأَصَّدَّقَ وَأَكُن مِّنَ الصَّالِحِينَ ⭕

*Give from what We have provided for you before death comes to one of you and he says: My Lord, if only you would give me a little more time so that I can give sadaqa and be one of the righteous! (al-Munafiqoon, 63:10)*

Pursuing lawful means of livelihood is fine but we should not get entangled in the *dunya* to the extent that we cannot extricate ourselves from it to invest some of our time, energy, money, and capabilities in the way of Allah (SWT).Allah (SWT) has undertaken upon Himself to provide for all His creatures.

وَمَا مِن دَابَّةٍ فِي الْأَرْضِ إِلَّا عَلَى اللَّهِ رِزْقُهَا ⭕

*There is no creature on earth except that its provision is from Allah. (Hud, 11:6)*

As believers, if we trust in Allah (SWT), think positively of Allah (SWT), humble our hearts before Allah (SWT), and try our best to have *taqwa* of Allah (SWT), then we should know that death is a return to the most generous and merciful Lord. The Prophet (SAS) said, "None of you should die except hoping good from Allah."

We should never ever despair of Allah's mercy, as Allah said,

قُلْ يَا عِبَادِيَ الَّذِينَ أَسْرَفُوا عَلَى أَنفُسِهِمْ لَا تَقْنَطُوا مِنْ رَحْمَةِ اللَّهِ إِنَّ اللَّهَ يَغْفِرُ الذُّنُوبَ جَمِيعًا إِنَّهُ هُوَ الْغَفُورُ الرَّحِيمُ ⭕

*Say, O My servants who transgressed against themselves, do not despair of Allah's mercy. For Allah forgives all sins. He is the Forgiver, the Merciful.(az-Zumar, 39:53)*

Brothers and sisters! Remembering death softens the heart. It is an inspiration to leave bad habits, to do more and more good deeds, to help people in need, and to be good to our families and societies. It is wisely said that whoever frequently remembers death is honored with three things: quick repentance, contentment, and energy for acts of worship. Also, whoever forgets death is punished with three things: delayed repentance, lack of contentment, and laziness in acts of worship.

Now let us look at ourselves. Are we often delaying our repentance and remaining unhappy with what we have? Do we feel too lazy to pray? All of these are signs that we don't remember death in a productive way.

Remember that life and death are part of a divinely mandated plan. They are a test to see who among us would strive to be the best in deeds.

الَّذِي خَلَقَ الْمَوْتَ وَالْحَيَاةَ لِيَبْلُوَكُمْ أَيُّكُمْ أَحْسَنُ عَمَلًا ◯

*He who created death and life to test which of you is best in action. (al-Mulk, 67:2)*

There is no one on the face of this earth who is not undergoing a test. Sometimes we are tested in prosperity and other times in adversity; sometimes we are tested in ease and comfort, and other times in difficulties and hardships. Through the journey of life, we are tested as to how best we conduct ourselves in different circumstances.

One of the basic differences between this world and the hereafter is that in this life there is death, while in the hereafter there is no death. The inhabitants of paradise will live forever. Those who are in the hellfire will also live forever. This takes us to the question: What are we doing in this life to prepare for a death that will lead us to an eternal blissful life? Our children will inherit the good and bad that we leave behind, so we should also ask the question: What kind of example are we going to leave behind for them?

Brothers and sisters! Our ultimate goal should be to reach a level that when we die, we know that we couldn't have done better.

Brothers and sisters! If we think deeply about reality, we learn that the world deceives the one who craves it. One who keeps death in front of his eyes not only performs his routine tasks sincerely but constantly strives to do more and more good deeds to seek the pleasure of his Lord—Allah (SWT). He is aware that death can overtake him at any moment, and he does not have time on his side. The Prophet (SAS) said, "Surely the heart rusts like iron." People asked, "How can it be polished?" He replied, "By remembering death and with the recitation of the Qur'an." What is the best way to prepare oneself for death? Being mindful of Allah (SWT) all the time, doing that which he has commanded us to do, and not doing that which He has prohibited us to do, is how we prepare for death. Having faith and doing good deeds is how we prepare for a good life and a good death. Allah (SWT) says,

مَنْ عَمِلَ صَالِحًا مِنْ ذَكَرٍ أَوْ أُنْثَى وَهُوَ مُؤْمِنٌ فَلَنُحْيِيَنَّهُ حَيَاةً طَيِّبَةً وَلَنَجْزِيَنَّهُمْ أَجْرَهُمْ بِأَحْسَنِ مَا كَانُوا

يَعْمَلُونَ ◯

*Whoever does good, whether male or female, and is a believer, We will surely bless them with a good life, and We will certainly reward them according to the best of their deeds. (an-Nahl, 16:97)*

This means that such persons will have peace, contentment, and lawful provision in this life and paradise in the hereafter. Death being the most certain reality, a conscious believer prepares himself or herself here in this world for the eternal and perpetual blissful life of the hereafter. We must learn from death, for the secret of life is hidden in the message it has to teach us. Death shows us that we are not our own masters, that our stay on earth is only temporary, and that the world is no place for the realization of our dreams. Death teaches us how to live; it shows us the way to real success. The Prophet (SAS) in one of his sayings said, "Clever is the one who controls his passions and prepares for life after death."

May Allah (SWT) give us the wisdom to remember death, and may He grant us the statement of faith ,*La ilaha illa Allah Muhammadun Rasool Allah,* in our inner most being and on our lips while we are living in this world, and also while we are leaving this world to return to Him.

O Allah! Forgive our living and our dead, those who are with us and those who are absent, our young and our old, our men and our women. O Allah! To whomever you give life from among us, give them life in Islam; and from whomever you take away from us, take them away in faith."

O Allah, surely Safia Haque bint Sayyid Zamiruddin Ahmed is under Your protection, and in the embrace of Your security, so save her from the trial of the grave and from the punishment of the fire. You fulfill promises and grant rights, so forgive her and have mercy on her. Surely, You are Most Forgiving, Most Merciful. O Allah, forgive her, raise her rank among the rightly guided, safeguard the family she left behind, and forgive us and her. O Lord of the worlds! Widen her grave and illuminate it for her. O Allah, forgive her. O Allah, strengthen her. O Allah, ease upon her all matters and make light for her whatever comes hereafter. Honor her with Your meeting and make that which she has gone to better than that which she came out from.

إِنَّ لِلَّهِ مَا أَخَذَ، وَلَهُ مَا أَعْطَى، وَكُلُّ شَيْءٍ عِنْدَهُ بِأَجَلٍ مُسَمًّى، فَلْتَصْبِرْ وَلْتَحْتَسِبْ ◯

*"Surely, to Allah belongs that which He takes and that which He gives, and everything has an appointed time with Him. So one should be patient and seek reward from Him."*

# 95

# WEALTH: THE ISLAMIC VIEW

We praise, thank, and exalt Allah (SWT) for the blessings of faith, health, and wealth He has bestowed upon us. The topic of my *khutbah* is about the Islamic view of wealth. We learn from the Qur`an that man by his very nature loves wealth and other material possessions intensely.

وَتُحِبُّونَ الْمَالَ حُبًّا جَمًّا ○

*And you love wealth with a passion. (al-Fajr, 89:20)*

وَإِنَّهُ لِحُبِّ الْخَيْرِ لَشَدِيدٌ ○

*And he is truly excessive in his love of wealth. (al-'Adiyat, 100:8)*

زُيِّنَ لِلنَّاسِ حُبُّ الشَّهَوَاتِ ○

*Appealing to man is the enjoyment of worldly desires. (Aal 'Imran, 3:14)*

Despite our inherent attachment to material things, the attitude of believers toward wealth should not be the same as disbelievers. Generally, people do not understand the Islamic concept of the blessing of wealth. The fact is that man owns nothing. The real owner of everything is Allah (SWT). Whatever we have is only a sacred trust—an *amana* from Him. True righteous believers understand that the things they possess are not from their earnings but the favor, blessing, and bounty of Allah (SWT). In the tenth verse of *Surat al-Jumu'ah* the notion of the bounty of Allah (SWT) is made very clear.

فَإِذَا قُضِيَتِ الصَّلَاةُ فَانْتَشِرُوا فِي الْأَرْضِ وَابْتَغُوا مِنْ فَضْلِ اللَّهِ وَاذْكُرُوا اللَّهَ كَثِيرًا لَعَلَّكُمْ تُفْلِحُونَ ○

*Then when the prayer has ended, disperse in the land and seek out Allah's fadl (bounty).*
*Remember Allah often so that you may prosper. (al-Jumu'ah, 62:10)*

Wealth is one of the greatest blessings from Allah (SWT) that we cannot do without. Indeed, it is the backbone of life and plays a major role in the building of civilizations. Allah (SWT) asks us to acquire wealth and enjoy the good permissible things.

قُلْ مَنْ حَرَّمَ زِينَةَ اللَّهِ الَّتِي أَخْرَجَ لِعِبَادِهِ وَالطَّيِّبَاتِ مِنَ الرِّزْقِ ○

*Say, who has forbidden the adornment of Allah, which He has brought forth for His*

*servants and good things, clean and pure, which Allah has provided for His servants?*
(*al-A'raf*, 7:32)

On the same matter, the Prophet (SAS) said, "Those whom Allah has favored with a bounty, then Allah likes to see the effect of His bounty on His creation." Each person is entitled to enough provision sufficient to meet one's basic needs. One may enjoy, according to one's social status, the basic needs of shelter, food, clothing, transportation, and similar things. However, all wasteful expenditure has to be avoided. Allah (SWT) does not like the extravagant.

وَلَا تُسْرِفُوا إِنَّهُ لَا يُحِبُّ الْمُسْرِفِينَ

*Do not waste anything. He does not love the wasteful.* (*al-An'am*, 6:141)

Others also have a legitimate right over our wealth and property.

وَالَّذِينَ فِي أَمْوَالِهِمْ حَقٌّ مَعْلُومٌ ۝ لِلسَّائِلِ وَالْمَحْرُومِ ۝

*And in whose wealth there is a known right for the beggars and the deprived.* (*al-Ma'arij*, 70:24-25)

We are also told to spend from whatever Allah (SWT) has given us.

وَآتُوهُم مِّن مَّالِ اللَّهِ الَّذِي آتَاكُمْ ۝

*And give them some of the wealth Allah has given you.* (*an-Nur*, 24:33)

Wealth is a test from Allah (SWT). It is Allah (SWT), the All Wise who gives whatever He wills to whomever He wills.

اللَّهُ يَبْسُطُ الرِّزْقَ لِمَن يَشَاءُ وَيَقْدِرُ ۝

*Allah gives abundantly to whoever He wills, and sparingly to whoever He wills.* (*ar-Ra'd*, 13:26)

It is Allah's wisdom that He has made his servants unequal in terms of their wealth.

وَاللَّهُ فَضَّلَ بَعْضَكُمْ عَلَىٰ بَعْضٍ فِي الرِّزْقِ ۝

*Allah has favored some of you above others with provisions.* (*an-Nahl*, 16:71)

Allah (SWT) says in *Surat az-Zukhruf*,

أَهُمْ يَقْسِمُونَ رَحْمَةَ رَبِّكَ نَحْنُ قَسَمْنَا بَيْنَهُم مَّعِيشَتَهُمْ فِي الْحَيَاةِ الدُّنْيَا وَرَفَعْنَا بَعْضَهُمْ فَوْقَ بَعْضٍ دَرَجَاتٍ لِيَتَّخِذَ بَعْضُهُم بَعْضًا سُخْرِيًّا وَرَحْمَةُ رَبِّكَ خَيْرٌ مِّمَّا يَجْمَعُونَ ۝

*Is it they who distribute your Lord's blessing? It is We who distribute among them their livelihood in the life of this world, and raise some of them above others in rank, so that they may take one another into service. (az-Zukhruf, 43:32)*

This means that having little wealth or no wealth is not considered to be a sign that Allah (SWT) is displeased with His servant, nor is having abundant wealth a sign that Allah is pleased with His servant. The poor and the rich are both undergoing tests, the poor for striving hard to improve their lot while being patient and content with what they have, and the rich to spend for the sake of Allah from any wealth that is over and above their needs. Regardless of how much material wealth one has, one is under constant test from his Lord.

وَاعْلَمُوا أَنَّمَا أَمْوَالُكُمْ وَأَوْلَادُكُمْ فِتْنَةٌ ۞

*And know that your wealth and your children are only a test. (al-Anfal, 8:28)*

We are responsible for whatever we have, and we will surely be held accountable on the Day of Judgment for the worldly favors and pleasures bestowed upon us by Allah (SWT).

ثُمَّ لَتُسْأَلُنَّ يَوْمَئِذٍ عَنِ النَّعِيمِ ۞

*And on that day, you will surely be asked about the pleasures you enjoyed. (at-Takathur, 102:8)*

Describing the people of *taqwa*, Allah says,

الَّذِينَ يُؤْمِنُونَ بِالْغَيْبِ وَيُقِيمُونَ الصَّلَاةَ وَمِمَّا رَزَقْنَاهُمْ يُنْفِقُونَ ۞

*(They are) those who believe in the unseen, and are steadfast in prayer, and spend out of what We have provided them with. (al-Baqara, 2:3)*

While people tend to think that, being the owners of their wealth, they can dispose of it the way they like, true righteous believers understand that their wealth has been provided by Allah only to satisfy and fulfill their needs. Any surplus has to be spent in the way of Allah.

وَيَسْأَلُونَكَ مَاذَا يُنْفِقُونَ قُلِ الْعَفْوَ ۞

*They ask you what they should give. Say, "Give what you can spare." (al-Baqara, 2:219)*

This has been explained later in *ayah* 215 of *Surat al-Baqara*.

يَسْأَلُونَكَ مَاذَا يُنْفِقُونَ قُلْ مَا أَنْفَقْتُمْ مِّنْ خَيْرٍ فَلِلْوَالِدَيْنِ وَالْأَقْرَبِينَ وَالْيَتَامَىٰ وَالْمَسَاكِينِ وَابْنِ السَّبِيلِ وَمَا تَفْعَلُوا مِنْ خَيْرٍ فَإِنَّ اللَّهَ بِهِ عَلِيمٌ ۞

*They ask you what they should give. Say, "Whatever you give should be for parents, close relatives, orphans, the needy, and travelers. Allah is well aware of whatever good you do." (al-Baqara, 2:21)*

The attributes of piety, real virtue, and spending in the way of Allah (SWT) are all linked with each other. Virtue and piety have to do with *iman* and a host of other good deeds including spending in the path of Allah (SWT). It is such a meritorious act that Allah (SWT) calls it a trade that will never decline.

إِنَّ الَّذِينَ يَتْلُونَ كِتَابَ اللَّهِ وَأَقَامُوا الصَّلَاةَ وَأَنفَقُوا مِمَّا رَزَقْنَاهُمْ سِرًّا وَعَلَانِيَةً يَرْجُونَ تِجَارَةً لَّن تَبُورَ ⦿

*Those who recite Allah's Book, keep up the prayer, give secretly and openly from what We have provided for them, may hope for a trade that will never decline. (Fatir, 35:29)*

Allah (SWT) compensates them by giving back many times over.

إِن تُقْرِضُوا اللَّهَ قَرْضًا حَسَنًا يُضَاعِفْهُ لَكُمْ وَيَغْفِرْ لَكُمْ وَاللَّهُ شَكُورٌ حَلِيمٌ ⦿

*If you make a good loan to Allah, He will multiply it for you and forgive you. Allah is all appreciative and forbearing. (at-Taghabun, 64:17)*

In another verse we are reminded,

وَمَا تُنفِقُوا مِنْ خَيْرٍ فَلِأَنْفُسِكُمْ وَمَا تُنفِقُونَ إِلَّا ابْتِغَاءَ وَجْهِ اللَّهِ وَمَا تُنفِقُوا مِنْ خَيْرٍ يُوَفَّ إِلَيْكُمْ وَأَنتُمْ لَا تُظْلَمُونَ ⦿

*Whatever charity you give benefits your own soul, provided you do it for the sake of Allah. Whatever you give will be repaid to you in full, and you will not be wronged.*
*(al-Baqara, 2:272)*

To make our wealth full of blessing (baraka), we should ensure that our wealth is lawful and that our work does not fall into the realm of haram. Our work and the means of our livelihood should also be moral and ethical. The Prophet (SAS) said, "O people, Allah is good and He, therefore, accepts only that which is good." He also said, "Wealth is not having vast riches. It is in contentment." Baraka in our wealth gives us contentment and satisfaction. May Allah (SWT) bless each one of us and grant us understanding and goodness.

My dear brothers and sisters! Allah (SWT) gives an example of those who spend their wealth in His way.

مَّثَلُ الَّذِينَ يُنفِقُونَ أَمْوَالَهُمْ فِي سَبِيلِ اللَّهِ كَمَثَلِ حَبَّةٍ أَنبَتَتْ سَبْعَ سَنَابِلَ فِي كُلِّ سُنبُلَةٍ مِّائَةُ حَبَّةٍ وَاللَّهُ يُضَاعِفُ لِمَن يَشَاءُ وَاللَّهُ وَاسِعٌ عَلِيمٌ ⦿

*Those who spend their wealth in Allah's cause are like grains of corn that produce seven ears, each bearing a hundred grains. Allah gives multiple increase to whoever He wishes. He is limitless and all knowing. (al-Baqara, 2:261)*

And there is good news for those who do not follow their spending with reminders or hurtful words hurled upon those to whom they give. Allah says,

الَّذِينَ يُنفِقُونَ أَمْوَالَهُمْ فِي سَبِيلِ اللَّهِ ثُمَّ لَا يُتْبِعُونَ مَا أَنفَقُوا مَنًّا وَلَا أَذًى لَهُمْ أَجْرُهُمْ عِندَ رَبِّهِمْ وَلَا خَوْفٌ عَلَيْهِمْ وَلَا هُمْ يَحْزَنُونَ ۝

*Those who spend their wealth in Allah's cause, and do not follow their spending with reminders of their benevolence or hurtful words, will have their rewards with their Lord: no fear for them, nor will they grieve. (al-Baqara, 2:262)*

At the same time we are told not to be harsh toward or repel those who ask us for something.

فَأَمَّا الْيَتِيمَ فَلَا تَقْهَرْ وَأَمَّا السَّائِلَ فَلَا تَنْهَرْ ۝

*So do not be harsh with the orphan, and as for the beggar, do not scold him. (ad-Duha, 93:9-10)*

However illogical it may sound, giving in charity does not decrease one's wealth. On the contrary, it increases it, and becomes a source of inner peace and contentment. This is confirmed both by the Qur`an and the sayings of our beloved Prophet Muhammad (SAS). The physical amount appears to decrease outwardly, but the remaining amount attracts *baraka* so that the actual benefit from it is increased. We have to try to fight the urge to be stingy.

وَمَن يُوقَ شُحَّ نَفْسِهِ فَأُولَٰئِكَ هُمُ الْمُفْلِحُونَ ۝

*And those who are saved from the stinginess of their own souls are truly successful.*
*(al-Hashr, 59:9)*

In the hereafter, we should not be among those who will cry out to Allah (SWT) to give them more time to spend in His way and to be among the righteous.

وَأَنفِقُوا مِن مَّا رَزَقْنَاكُم مِّن قَبْلِ أَن يَأْتِيَ أَحَدَكُمُ الْمَوْتُ فَيَقُولَ رَبِّ لَوْلَا أَخَّرْتَنِي إِلَىٰ أَجَلٍ قَرِيبٍ فَأَصَّدَّقَ وَأَكُن مِّنَ الصَّالِحِينَ ۝

*Give from what We have provided for you before death comes to one of you and he says, "My Lord, if only you would give me a little more time so that I can give sadaqa and be one of the righteous!" (al-Munafiqoon, 63:10)*

I'll leave you with a beautiful reminder of at least one way we can increase wealth and at the same time come nearer to Allah (SWT). It's what Nuh (AS) told to his people.

فَقُلْتُ اسْتَغْفِرُوا رَبَّكُمْ إِنَّهُ كَانَ غَفَّارًا ۝ يُرْسِلِ السَّمَاءَ عَلَيْكُم مِّدْرَارًا ۝ وَيُمْدِدْكُم بِأَمْوَالٍ وَبَنِينَ وَيَجْعَل لَّكُمْ جَنَّاتٍ وَيَجْعَل لَّكُمْ أَنْهَارًا ۝

*Ask forgiveness of your Lord. He is ever forgiving. He will send down abundant rain from the sky for you and will provide you with wealth and children and He will give you gardens and rivers. (Nuh, 71:10-12)*

May Allah (SWT) make us among those who are able to give generously for good causes from whatever we possess from His blessings. May He bless our faith, health, and wealth. *Allahumma ameen.*

• 96 •

# WHO ARE THE SUCCESSFUL ONES?

The topic of my *khutbah* is "Who are the Successful Ones?" True success is not confined to transitory worldly and material prosperity, but it comprises both success in this life and in the life of the hereafter. It is attained by sincere faith and righteous deeds. This is a fundamental principle which cannot be falsified either by the worldly success of the evildoers or by the temporary failure of the righteous people. Where could we find a more accurate explanation or description of an attribute of a successful person other than in the book of Allah? Describing the successful ones, Allah (SWT) tells us in the Qur`an at the beginning of *Surat al-Mu`minoon,*

قَدْ أَفْلَحَ الْمُؤْمِنُونَ ◯

*It is the believers who are successful. (al-Mu`minoon, 23:1)*

The first and most important attribute which is fundamental and basic to everything else is that a person should be a true believer. This assertion is followed by six attributes that these true believers possess.

الَّذِينَ هُمْ فِي صَلَاتِهِمْ خَاشِعُونَ ◯

*Those who are humble in their prayers. (al-Mu`minoon, 23:2)*

The word *khashi'oon* in the text is from *khushu',* which is a condition of the heart as well as of the body. *Khushu'* of the heart is to stand in fear and awe of someone powerful, and *khushu'* of the body is to bow one's head and lower one's gaze and voice in his presence. In *salah*, one is required to show *khushu'* both of the heart and the body, and this is the essence of the prayer. The *shari'a* has enjoined certain rules of etiquette which, on one hand, help produce *khushu'* in the heart, and on the other, help sustain the physical act of the prayer in spite of the fluctuating condition of the heart. According to this etiquette, one should neither turn to the right or left, nor raise his head to look up. As far as possible, one must fix the gaze on the place where the forehead would rest in prostration. The expectation is that each aspect of the prayer should be performed in peace and tranquility, and unless one aspect has been completely performed, the next should not be begun. Along with this etiquette of the body, it is also important that one should avoid thinking irrelevant things during the prayer. If thoughts come to the mind unintentionally, this is a natural human weakness. But overall, one should try their utmost to ensure that the mind and heart are wholly turned toward Allah (SWT) and the mind is in full harmony with the tongue. As soon as one becomes conscious of irrelevant thoughts, one should immediately return their attention to the prayer.

وَالَّذِينَ هُمْ عَنِ اللَّغْوِ مُعْرِضُونَ

*Those who turn away from useless talk. (al-Mu`minoon, 23:3)*

The believers avoid *laghw* or whatever is vain and frivolous. *Laghw* is anything nonsensical, meaningless, and vain, which is not conducive to achieving one's goal and purpose in life. The believers pay no heed to such useless things and they show no inclination or interest for them. If by chance they happen to come across such things, they keep away and avoid them or treat them with utmost indifference. Allah (SWT) has described this attitude in *Surat al-Furqan*, which says,

وَإِذَا مَرُّوا بِاللَّغْوِ مَرُّوا كِرَامًا

*If they have to pass by what is useless, they pass by like dignified people. (al-Furqan, 25:72)*

This is one of the outstanding characteristics of the believer. He is a person who feels the burden of responsibility at all times. He regards the world as a place of test and life as the limited time allowed for the test. This feeling makes him behave seriously and responsibly throughout life just like the student who is taking an exam with his whole mind, body, and soul absorbed in it. Just as the student knows and feels that each moment of the limited time at his disposal is important and decisive for his future life and is not inclined to waste it, so the believer also spends each moment of his life on works which are useful and productive in their ultimate results. So much so that even in matters of recreation and sport, he makes a choice of only those things which prepare him for higher ends in life and do not result in mere wastage of time. For him time is not something to be killed but used profitably and productively.

وَالَّذِينَ هُمْ لِلزَّكَاةِ فَاعِلُونَ

*And those who pay zakat. (al-Mu`minoon, 23:4)*

The believers pay their *zakat*. The word *zakat* literally means purification and development, to help something grow up smoothly and develop without obstruction. As an Islamic term, it implies both the portion of wealth taken out for the purpose of purifying the rest of the wealth and the act of purification itself. The words of the original text mean that the believer constantly practices purification. Thus the meaning is not confined to the paying of *zakat* only, but it is extended to self-purification, which includes purification of morals as well as wealth, property, and life in general. This concept of purification has also been stated at other places in the Qur`an, for instance,

قَدْ أَفْلَحَ مَنْ تَزَكَّى ○ وَذَكَرَ اسْمَ رَبِّهِ فَصَلَّى ○

*Successful is he who purifies himself and invokes the Name of his Lord and prays. (al-A'la, 87:14-15)*

قَدْ أَفْلَحَ مَنْ زَكَّاهَا ○ وَقَدْ خَابَ مَنْ دَسَّاهَا ○

*Successful is he who purifies himself and doomed is he who corrupts himself. (ash-Shams, 91:9-10)*

Other attributes of believers given in *Surat al-Mu`minoon* are:

وَالَّذِينَ هُمْ لِفُرُوجِهِمْ حَافِظُونَ ○ إِلاَّ عَلَى أَزْوَاجِهِمْ أَوْ مَا مَلَكَتْ أَيْمَانُهُمْ فَإِنَّهُمْ غَيْرُ مَلُومِينَ ○ فَمَنِ ابْتَغَى وَرَاءَ ذَلِكَ فَأُولَئِكَ هُمُ الْعَادُونَ ○

*Those who guard their private parts, except with their wives, and what their right hands possess, for then they are free from blame, but whoever seeks beyond that are the transgressors. (al-Mu`minoon, 23:5-7)*

The believers also guard their private parts. They are modest in every sense of the word. They are free from sex abuse and sex perversion. Those who do not transgress the divine laws of modesty are free from blame. This exception is meant to remove the common misunderstanding that sexual desire is an evil thing in itself and satisfying it even in lawful ways is not desirable, particularly for the righteous and godly people. This misunderstanding would have been strengthened had it been only said that the believers guard their private parts, because it would have implied that they live unmarried lives, away from the world, like monks and hermits. Therefore it is made clear that there is nothing wrong in satisfying sexual desire in lawful ways. What is evil is that one should transgress the prescribed limits for satisfying sexual desire.

وَالَّذِينَ هُمْ لِأَمَانَاتِهِمْ وَعَهْدِهِمْ رَاعُونَ ○

*Those who honor their trusts and promises. (al-Mu`minoon, 23:8)*

The believers fulfill the terms of the trusts which are placed in their charge. In this connection it should be noted that the Arabic word *amana*(trust) used in this verse is very comprehensive and includes all those trusts which are placed in their charge by Allah (SWT) or society or individuals. Likewise, the word *'ahd* (promises) used here includes all those pledges and promises which are made between Allah and man, as well as those made between men. The Prophet (SAS) himself used to stress the importance of the fulfillment of pledges in his addresses. He said, "The one, who does not fulfill the terms of his trust has no faith, and the one who does not keep promises and pledges has no Islam." The Prophet (SAS) said, "Four characteristics are such that if a person has all four in him, he is beyond any doubt a hypocrite, and the one who has one of these is a hypocrite to that extent until he gives it up: When something is placed in his trust, he commits breach of the trust; when he speaks, he tells a lie; when he makes a promise, he breaks it; and when he has a quarrel with somebody, he exceeds all limits of decency and morality."

وَالَّذِينَ هُمْ عَلَى صَلَوَاتِهِمْ يُحَافِظُونَ ○

*Those who safeguard their prayers. (al-Mu`minoon, 23:9)*

Notice how Allah (SWT) comes back to *salah*. In an earlier verse, the word *salah* was used in the singular because the emphasis was on *khushu'*, or humbleness, which is the essence of all prayers whether obligatory or voluntary. Here the word *salah* is used in the plural, *salawat*. Here, to safeguard one's prayers means to offer the obligatory prayers regularly at their appointed times, with due regard for their prerequisites, conditions, and articles, and with clean body, dress, and necessary ablutions. They do not recite mechanically but try to understand what they recite and are conscious that they are supplicating to their Lord like humble servants. May Allah (SWT) make us among such believers. *Ameen.*

Brothers and sisters! A careful study of the above attributes would show that they encompass all the duties which man owes to Allah (SWT) and to fellow human beings. A person who possesses these attributes and adheres to them is a *mu`min* or true believer and deserving of success (*falah*) in this world and in the hereafter. It will also be noted that these attributes begin, and also end, with a reference to prayers which suggests that if prayers are offered in the prescribed manner with all their requirements, the other attributes will appear automatically.

To sum up, let me reinforce the attributes of the believers about whom *Surat al-Mu`minoon* says they are successful:

Those who offer their *salah* with *khushu'*; that is, with complete focus, concentration and humbleness.

Those who avoid *laghw*, meaning anything that does not add any value to their lives in this world or the next, such as gossip, backbiting, lewd and indecent conversation, etc.

Those who pay their *zakat* proactively.

Those who protect their private parts and do not commit fornication, adultery, or engage in any activity that may lead to these major sins.

Those who keep their promises and trusts.

Those who safeguard their five obligatory prayers.

The blessed *surah* goes on to say,

أُولَئِكَ هُمُ الْوَارِثُونَ ○ الَّذِينَ يَرِثُونَ الْفِرْدَوْسَ هُمْ فِيهَا خَالِدُونَ ○

*Those are the heirs who will inherit paradise and live in it forever. (al-Mu`minoon, 23:10-11)*

The good Muslims who possess the attributes described above have been declared in this verse to be the heirs to the garden of paradise. There is a suggestion here that just as the assets of a deceased person must devolve on his heirs, similarly the possessors of these attributes will, without doubt, enter paradise.

What a beautiful reward? *Al-hamduli-llah!* We must note down the above six qualities and ask ourselves in which areas do we need further improvements. Let's start working in earnest to improve in those areas for our own success and eternal happiness.

بَارَكَ الله لِيْ وَلَكُمْ فِي الْقُرْآنِ الْكَرِيْمِ، وَنَفَعَنِيْ وَإِيَّاكُمْ بِمَا فِيْهِ مِنَ الْآيَاتِ وَالذِّكْرِ الْحَكِيْمِ.

*May Allah (SWT) bless you and I through the guidance of this noble Qur`an, and benefit you and I from its signs and its wise reminders.*

• 97 •

# WISDOM *(HIKMA)*

In today's *khutbah* I intend to share some thoughts with you toward understanding the concept of *hikma*, or wisdom, in Islam. Many times, people confuse wisdom with knowledge and knowledge with information. Muslim scholars, philosophers, and thinkers have defined and explained *hikma* in a variety of ways such as (a) "profound truths or subtle realities," (b) "the art of understanding properly," (c) "coming to know the essence of things as they really are," (d) "the ability to make correct judgments and decisions,"(e) "making the best use of available knowledge," (f) "reaching the truth with knowledge and action," (g) "thinking what is best and doing what is best in any given situation," (h) "insight that guides one to that which is correct and accurate in his movements and actions," and so on.

It was one of the missions of the prophets and messengers of Allah (SWT) to impart wisdom to their people. When Ibraheem (AS) prayed for the fulfillment of the mission of prophets, he invoked Allah in these words,

$$ رَبَّنَا وَابْعَثْ فِيهِمْ رَسُولًا مِّنْهُمْ يَتْلُو عَلَيْهِمْ آيَاتِكَ وَيُعَلِّمُهُمُ الْكِتَابَ وَالْحِكْمَةَ وَيُزَكِّيهِمْ إِنَّكَ أَنتَ الْعَزِيزُ الْحَكِيمُ ◯ $$

*Our Lord, raise up among them a Messenger from them to recite Your ayat to them and teach them the book and wisdom and purify them. You are the Almighty, the All Wise.*
(al-Baqara, 2:129)

The commentators from among the companions and their immediate successors have advanced different connotations of the word *hikma*. Some say that it refers to the commentary and *tafseer* of the Qur`an. Others believe that it means the proper understanding of the *deen*, the injunctions of the *shari'a*, or such commandments of Allah (SWT) which have been received through the word of the Prophet (SAS). But the truth of the matter is that despite the variety of expressions used, the substance of all these statements is the same, namely, the way or Sunnah of the Prophet (SAS) and the hadeeth. This is the interpretation reported from Qatada by Ibn Katheer and Ibn Jareer.

The word *hikma* is used repeatedly in the Qur`an as a characteristic of the righteous, and as a quality of those who truly understand. Referring to the favors bestowed upon Dawood (AS), Allah (SWT) says,

$$ وَآتَاهُ اللَّهُ الْمُلْكَ وَالْحِكْمَةَ وَعَلَّمَهُ مِمَّا يَشَاءُ ◯ $$

*And Allah gave him kingship and wisdom and taught him whatever He willed. (al-Baqara, 2:251)*

Referring to the favors bestowed upon the descendants of *Ibraheem* (AS), Allah (SWT) says,

$$ فَقَدْ آتَيْنَا آلَ إِبْرَاهِيمَ الْكِتَابَ وَالْحِكْمَةَ وَآتَيْنَاهُم مُّلْكًا عَظِيمًا ◯ $$

*We gave the family of Ibraheem the book and wisdom, and We gave them a great kingdom. (an-Nisa`, 4:54)*

Asking 'Isa (AS) to remember the favors bestowed upon him and his mother, Allah (SWT) says,

وَإِذْ عَلَّمْتُكَ الْكِتَابَ وَالْحِكْمَةَ وَالتَّوْرَاةَ وَالْإِنجِيلَ ⟡

*And when I taught you the book and wisdom, and the Torah and the Injeel. (al-Ma`ida, 5:110)*

"Wisdom" in these verses is referred to as an integral component of the message and guidance provided by divine revelation. To possess *hikma* is to have one of the greatest blessings of Allah (SWT), for Allah (SWT) says,

يُؤْتِي الْحِكْمَةَ مَن يَشَاءُ وَمَن يُؤْتَ الْحِكْمَةَ فَقَدْ أُوتِيَ خَيْرًا كَثِيرًا وَمَا يَذَّكَّرُ إِلَّا أُولُو الْأَلْبَابِ ⟡

*He grants wisdom to whom He wills; and whoever is granted wisdom has indeed been granted abundant good. But only insightful people bear this in mind. (al-Baqara, 2:269)*

When we convey the message of Islam, it should be done with *hikma*, for Allah (SWT) says,

ادْعُ إِلَى سَبِيلِ رَبِّكَ بِالْحِكْمَةِ وَالْمَوْعِظَةِ الْحَسَنَةِ ⟡

*Call to the way of your Lord with wisdom and good advice. (an-Nahl, 16:125)*

In this verse, "wisdom" implies that one should use discretion in the work of conveying the message of Islam and should not do this blindly like foolish people. Wisdom demands that one should keep in view the intelligence, capability, and circumstances of the audience, and convey the message in accordance with the requirements of the occasion. Moreover, one should refrain from applying one and the same method to each and every person or group but instead should first diagnose the real disease of the audience and then cure it by appealing to their head and heart. In *Surat Luqman* Allah says,

وَلَقَدْ آتَيْنَا لُقْمَانَ الْحِكْمَةَ أَنِ اشْكُرْ لِلَّهِ وَمَن يَشْكُرْ فَإِنَّمَا يَشْكُرُ لِنَفْسِهِ وَمَن كَفَرَ فَإِنَّ اللَّهَ غَنِيٌّ حَمِيدٌ ⟡

*And certainly, We gave Luqman wisdom, saying, be thankful to Allah: he who is thankful, is thankful only for the good of his own soul. But if anyone is unthankful, then surely Allah is self-sufficient and praiseworthy. (Luqman, 31:12)*

The relationship between wisdom and thankfulness is something that should be pondered very deeply. *Shukr* is the faculty of being thankful to someone who has done some good. With the ongoing evolution of human reasoning, it is now well-known and understood that the forces of nature like the sun, the moon, the oceans, the winds, the rains, the mountains, the fire, and so on to which people used to show reverence as a gesture of thankfulness are nothing but humble servants in a grand cosmic order that has been made subservient to man. They have no will or determination of their own. They submit to the natural laws created by Allah (SWT).

People practicing primitive religions are known for their worship of nature. Reason and logic dictate that Allah (SWT) alone is worthy of our worship, praise, glory, and thankfulness. Thus, it is the faculty of understanding that makes one reach from thankfulness to *tawheed*. Thus, to thank Allah (SWT) is to have reached the threshold of wisdom. 'Abdullah ibn Mas'ud (RAA) would say during his sermons, "The best provision is *taqwa* (mindfulness of Allah), and the peak of wisdom is the fear of Allah the Exalted."

One of the noble and exclusive attributes of Allah (SWT) is that He alone is *al-Hakeem* or the Most Wise! Whatever is associated with Him is based on His *hikma*, be it His creation, His laws, His books, His messengers, His commands, His guidance, or His judgment. Whatever and whoever is not associated with Him is bound to be devoid of wisdom. *Al-Hakeem* carries out His divine will with His perfect wisdom: He judges, decrees, inflicts, and relieves in the most rightful way, place, and time. He is All Wise in His creating and perfecting, in His commands, and in His sayings and actions.

Wisdom, when it concerns man, is to strive to use his faculties of intelligence and power of reasoning, and recognize *al-Hakeem* and submit to Him. Everything one does in alignment with *al-Hakeem's* guidance will be based on *hikma*; and anything one does which is not aligned to His guidance will be devoid of *hikma*. The Prophet (SAS) said, "A wise person is one who keeps a watch over his bodily desires and passions, checks himself from that which is harmful, and strives for that which will benefit him after death. And a foolish person is one who subordinates himself to his cravings and desires and expects from Allah (SWT) the fulfillment of his futile desires."

Allah's name *al-Hakeem* is often paired with *al-'Aleem* (The All Knowing).

وَاللَّهُ عَلِيمٌ حَكِيمٌ ○

*And Allah is All Knowing, All Wise. (al-Mumtahina, 60:10)*

*Al-Hakeem* is also often paired with *al-'Azeez* (The Most Powerful).

هُوَ الَّذِي يُصَوِّرُكُمْ فِي الْأَرْحَامِ كَيْفَ يَشَاءُ لَا إِلَهَ إِلَّا هُوَ الْعَزِيزُ الْحَكِيمُ ○

*It is He who shapes you in the womb how He wills. There is no god but He, the Almighty, the All Wise. (Aal 'Imran, 3:6)*

This shows us that Allah (SWT) uses both His knowledge and His power in the wisest way to guide us through the life of this world, testing us with tailor-made trials, challenges, and opportunities for us to give proof of our faith in *al-Hakeem*.

Knowing that Allah (SWT) is *al-Hakeem*, how can we live by this name? We can live by this name by putting our trust in His *hikma* and in His wisdom at all times, no matter how hard it may seem! If *al-Hakeem* decides that we should lose or gain something, there is wisdom behind it. If something happens that displeases us, it would be unwise to be unhappy with *al-Hakeem*. How many times in life have we looked back and seen the wisdom behind things that happened to us? May we lead our lives to seek the pleasure of *al-Hakeem*.

Brothers and sisters! The law and guidance of *al-Hakeem* are intended to reform the creation and not to cause hardship in life. In other words, His laws are best for us. If we don't understand His laws, we should not blame the laws but our own understanding. We should keep reflecting on the perfection of *al-Hakeem's* work, and keep reminding ourselves of His wisdom reflected in His creation. The Qur`an is referred to as the Wise Qur`an, and a book of wisdom.

الر تِلْكَ آيَاتُ الْكِتَابِ الْحَكِيمِ ○

*Alif Lam Ra. These are the verses of the book of wisdom. (Yunus, 10:1)*

يس ○ وَالْقُرْآنِ الْحَكِيمِ ○ إِنَّكَ لَمِنَ الْمُرْسَلِينَ ○

*Ya Seen. By the Wise Qur`an. You are indeed one of the messengers.*
*(Ya Seen, 36:1-3)*

An oath has been taken by the Qur`an, and the word 'wise' has been used as a description of the Qur`an. Allah (SWT) is telling the Prophet Muhammad (SAS) that this Qur`an, which is full of wisdom, testifies that the person who is presenting such wise revelations is most surely a messenger of Allah. The more we follow the commands of the All Wise, the wiser we will become. So let us make the Qur`an our close companion by believing in it, reciting it, understanding it, acting upon it, and conveying it to others.

The Prophet (SAS) said, "There is no envy except in two cases: (1) A man whom Allah has given wealth and he spends it righteously, and (2) A man whom Allah has given wisdom and he acts according to it and teaches it to others." In another hadeeth the Prophet (SAS) said, "Wisdom is the lost property of the believer; let him take it wherever he finds it." Let us use our blessings with wisdom by using them to gain the pleasure of *al-Hakeem*. How many of us have wealth but do not utilize it properly? How many of us have health and take it for granted?

Being wise is using our intelligence, wealth, health, time, and skills to please *al-Hakeem*. Those who submit their free will to the will of their Creator with their Allah-gifted intelligence and power of reasoning, will be the "wise" in His sight, deserving His mercy, forgiveness, and grace. The ones who do not submit their free will to the will of their Creator will be the ignorant and arrogant in His sight, deserving His wrath and anger.

The truth is that wisdom prevents man from committing wrong actions and guides him to take the right way. It gives him a broad perspective on everything in life. It deepens his understanding and increases his awareness of the surrounding circumstances so that he may reach the right words and actions.

May Allah (SWT) grant us wisdom in dealing with ourselves and others and in spreading His message to humanity. *Ameen.*

•   98   •

# WORLDVIEW OF ISLAM

In today's *khutbah* I want to share some thoughts with you on a very profound and philosophical topic, and that is the worldview of Islam, or the Islamic worldview. What is a worldview? It is the way in which a person perceives and understands the world and his place in it. Throughout the history of mankind, there have been different ways of perceiving the world. The worldview a person holds shapes his or her attitude and affects the way he or she thinks, acts, and behaves.

A person's worldview is largely shaped in accordance with his or her responses to the fundamental questions about man, life, and creation. Some of these basic questions are: "Who am I?" "Where have I come from?" "What is the purpose of my life?" "Where do I go after I die?" "Has this world been created or it has been existing since eternity?"

People always demand answers to the ultimate and final questions pertaining to God, life, universe, and the unseen world. Throughout history, different answers based on speculations have been given to such metaphysical questions. With the onslaught of atheism, agnosticism, secular humanism, and an increasing bombardment of ideologies that are diametrically opposed to the ideology of Islam, it is important that we as Muslims make ourselves conversant with the worldview of Islam.

The worldview of Islam is based on the primary sources of Islam, the Qur`an and the Sunnah, which give us the exact and accurate answers to these questions. To the question "Who am I?" one may say, "I am a human being." But the reality and origin of the human being can only be a matter of theoretical speculation. Divine revelation is the only source of knowing about the origin of the human being.

We learn from the Qur`an that Allah (SWT) shared with the angels His plan to bring about the creation of man even before actually creating him.

وَإِذْ قَالَ رَبُّكَ لِلْمَلَائِكَةِ إِنِّي خَالِقٌ بَشَرًا مِّن صَلْصَالٍ مِّنْ حَمَإٍ مَّسْنُونٍ ○

*Your Lord said to the angels, "I will create a human being out of dried clay, formed from dark mud." (al-Hijr, 15:28)*

فَإِذَا سَوَّيْتُهُ وَنَفَخْتُ فِيهِ مِن رُّوحِي فَقَعُوا لَهُ سَاجِدِينَ ○

*When I have perfected him in due proportion and breathed My spirit into him, bow down in prostration. (al-Hijr, 15:29)*

The spirit came from up high, from Allah (SWT), and the body came from the crust of the earth. Thus, according to the Qur`an, I am a creation of Allah (SWT), a human being made up of two entities, the spirit and the body. It is this spirit, blown into man, which elevates him and distinguishes him from all other creation.

To the next question, "where have I come from?" the common answer would be, "I have come from my biological parents," which is true. How about them? Where did they come from? The answer would again be, "from their biological parents." This chain continues until we reach the very first human pair and progenitor of all mankind—Adam and Hawwa (*alayhim as-salaam*). And for the question, "Where did the first human come from?" we find that the Allah tells us in the Qur`an that Adam came from dust. Allah explains,

وَمِنْ آيَاتِهِ أَنْ خَلَقَكُم مِّن تُرَابٍ ثُمَّ إِذَا أَنتُم بَشَرٌ تَنتَشِرُونَ ○

*And of His Signs is that He created you from dust and behold, you became human beings, scattered far and wide. (ar-Rum, 30:20)*

Therefore the answer to the second question, "Where have I come from?" would be, "My spirit came from Allah (SWT) and my body came from the earth." Now to the question, "Which came first, the spirit or the body?" the answer is that the spirit came first. There is an *ayah* in *Surat al-A'raf* that answers this question. Allah (SWT) says,

وَإِذْ أَخَذَ رَبُّكَ مِن بَنِي آدَمَ مِن ظُهُورِهِمْ ذُرِّيَّتَهُمْ وَأَشْهَدَهُمْ عَلَى أَنفُسِهِمْ أَلَسْتُ بِرَبِّكُمْ قَالُوا بَلَى شَهِدْنَا أَنْ تَقُولُوا يَوْمَ الْقِيَامَةِ إِنَّا كُنَّا عَنْ هَذَا غَافِلِينَ ○

*When your Lord took out all their descendants from the loins of the children of Adam and made them testify against themselves "Am I not your Lord?" They said: "We testify that indeed You are!" Lest you say on the Day of Rising, "We knew nothing of this." (al-A'raf, 7:172)*

This explains the reality of who we are and where we came from. Indeed, there was a time when we existed in the forms of spirits without even having bodies. While in our spiritual forms before our earthly existence Allah (SWT) took a covenant from all potential human beings after which He put them in a state of pause, which may be conceived of as a state of death. He then created the entire universe. He created man out of clay until we became humans, each spirit being united with every fetus in its embryonic stage.

The implication of this covenant is that as believers, Muslims have no option but to honor that pledge and that covenant. This covenant in reality answers the third question, "What is the purpose of my life?" In simple terms, Allah (SWT) spells out the purpose of our existence by saying,

وَمَا خَلَقْتُ الْجِنَّ وَالْإِنسَ إِلَّا لِيَعْبُدُونِ ○

*I have not created the jinn and human beings except to worship Me. (adh-Dhariyat, 51:56)*

While in our mother's wombs, we go through the embryonic stages of creation and it is during this process that Allah (SWT) gives us the faculties of hearing, sight, and intellect. All these faculties are very important, and Allah (SWT) gives them to man to help him fulfill his purpose on earth, which is to obey and worship Allah (SWT). Through these faculties, we are being tested by Allah (SWT) whether we are grateful or ungrateful to Him, and whether we honor the covenant we made with Him or not. And this is why we are here in this world, to be tested by Allah (SWT).

الَّذِي خَلَقَ الْمَوْتَ وَالْحَيَاةَ لِيَبْلُوَكُمْ أَيُّكُمْ أَحْسَنُ عَمَلًا وَهُوَ الْعَزِيزُ الْغَفُورُ ○

*It is He who created death and life to test which of you is best in action. He is the Almighty, the Forgiving. (al-Mulk, 67:2)*

Coming to the fourth question, "Where do we go after we die?" the Qur`an teaches us to say,

إِنَّا لِلَّهِ وَإِنَّا إِلَيْهِ رَاجِعُونَ ○

*We belong to Allah and to Him is our return. (al-Baqara, 2:156)*

We belong to Allah (SWT). We can now understand what the Prophet Muhammad (SAS) meant when he said in a hadeeth, "Be in this world as though you are a stranger or a traveler on a journey." Indeed, he spoke the truth. We are travelling; this is not our permanent home. In another hadeeth the Prophet (SAS) said, "This *dunya* is a prison for the believers and a paradise for the disbelievers." A believer is bound by certain commandments that Allah (SWT) has set for him, of the permissible and the impermissible and the things he should do and the things he should not do. He is free to move within the parameters set by Allah (SWT). May Allah (SWT) guide us, protect us, make us comply with His divine teachings, and make us live within the limits set by Him.

As Muslims, we believe that our death is a transition to another dimension of life wherein every soul shall be resurrected to give account to its Creator of its transitory stay on this earth and rewarded accordingly with everlasting bliss or eternal doom. The true believers are mindful of Allah (SWT) and conscious of the covenant they made with Him. They work hard to please their Lord and their activities are focused on being successful in the hereafter(al-akhira). Allah declares in the Qur`an,

كُلُّ نَفْسٍ ذَائِقَةُ الْمَوْتِ وَإِنَّمَا تُوَفَّوْنَ أُجُورَكُمْ يَوْمَ الْقِيَامَةِ فَمَنْ زُحْزِحَ عَنِ النَّارِ وَأُدْخِلَ الْجَنَّةَ فَقَدْ فَازَ وَمَا الْحَيَاةُ الدُّنْيَا إِلاَّ مَتَاعُ الْغُرُورِ ۝

*Every soul shall have a taste of death. You will be paid your wages in full on the Day of Resurrection. Anyone who is kept away from the Fire and admitted to the Garden has certainly succeeded. The life of this world is nothing but an illusory enjoyment. (Aal 'Imran, 3:185)*

Studies in anthropology have established that the concept of Allah (SWT) is ingrained in human nature. Belief in Allah (SWT) runs in our blood. By nature, every man and woman are born believers. Especially in times of helplessness and crisis, we realize that there is a Supreme Being. Every human being experiences this sometimes in his or her life. If the concept of Allah (SWT) is present in our flesh and blood, why does one question the existence of Allah (SWT)? And yet there are many who do so. The reason is very simple. People want to know whether there is a rational basis to their inner belief and whether there is some scientific proof in favor of their inner feelings.

Science tells us that the universe came into existence after the Big Bang which took place some fourteen billion years ago. Scientists have found evidence to believe that in the beginning there was what they call a cosmic ball. All the particles now present in the universe were tightly bound to each other in this cosmic ball in a highly compressed state. According to known physical laws, only an inner journey was possible for these particles. Physically, there was no possibility of their outward journey to space.

Then, according to astronomical studies, this cosmic ball suddenly exploded. The compact particles scattered outward and the present universe came into existence. What external source intervened so that the compact particles scattered outwardly? It was Almighty Allah (SWT) who intervened.

أَوَلَمْ يَرَ الَّذِينَ كَفَرُوا أَنَّ السَّمَاوَاتِ وَالْأَرْضَ كَانَتَا رَتْقًا فَفَتَقْنَاهُمَا ۝

*Do not those who deny the truth see that the heavens and the earth were joined together and that We then split them asunder? (al-Anbiya`, 21:30)*

This miraculous phenomenon is enough to make us believe that the Big Bang explosion was certainly preplanned. And when it is proven that it was preplanned, it is automatically proven that behind this preplanning there was a planner, and it is this super planner who is Allah (SWT) Almighty. When we reflect deeply about our world, we find that all over the universe, there are clear signs of planning, design, and intelligent control. These signs lead us to believe that there is a creator of creation, a designer of designs, and a mover of movements.

It is Allah (SWT) who created the heavens and the earth and all that is between them and beyond them. The entire creation submits to the will of Allah (SWT). After being given the guidance, man has also been given free choice to use his rational mind and choose between right and wrong. There is no discrepancy between reason and revelation in Islam. May Allah (SWT) guide us on the right path, .

<br>

# • 99 •

# WORSHIP ('IBADA)

In today's *khutbah* I intend to share some thoughts with you on the concept of *'ibada*. Generally, people understand *'ibada* to mean performance of ritual acts of worship such as prayers, fasting, charity, and hajj. However, this limited perception of *'ibada* conveys only one aspect of its meaning. In fact, all activities are considered acts of worship if done in compliance with the divine law and guidance. *'Ibada* in Islam is a very profound term. It is derived from the Arabic root letters *'ayn-baa-daal* from which we have the word *'abd*, which means a slave. The duty of a slave is to obey his master. The slave has to do what his master asks him to do. We learn from the Qur`an that the children of Israel were the slaves of Fir'awn, the Egyptian Pharaoh. What did Fir'awn and his followers say to Musa (AS) and Haroon (AS) on being invited by them to the path of Allah?

فَقَالُوا أَنُؤْمِنُ لِبَشَرَيْنِ مِثْلِنَا وَقَوْمُهُمَا لَنَا عَابِدُونَ ○

*They said: "Are we to believe in two human beings like ourselves, while their people are our slaves?" (al-Mu`minoon, 23:47)*

In this verse, the word *'abidoon* which means "serving in humility and obedience" has been used exclusively for slavery and does not have any notion of worship in it. The Children of Israel never worshipped Fir'awn. They only served him. It is important to note that a slave of someone else does not obey his master out of love.

However, a slave of Allah worships, obeys, and serves Allah out of intense love, gratitude, and devotion. By doing the *'ibada* of Allah, man is fulfilling the purpose of his creation and existence, for Allah says,

وَمَا خَلَقْتُ الْجِنَّ وَالْإِنسَ إِلَّا لِيَعْبُدُونِ ۝

*I only created jinn and man to do my 'ibada. (adh-Dhariyat, 51:56)*

'Ibada of Allah includes (1) worship and admiration, (2) obedience and submission, and (3) service and subjection.

Such an attitude of willing self-abasement cannot justly be adopted toward anyone except Allah (SWT). It is important to realize that this 'ibada—this state of worship, obedience, and service—does not entail loss of freedom, for freedom is actually the ability to act as one's true nature demands, that is, as one's *fitra* demands.

*Fitra* is an Arabic word. It is the inborn natural disposition which is inclined toward submission to One God. It is the pure and original state upon which Allah (SWT) creates all human beings and which is inclined toward that which is morally and spiritually pure, upright, and wholesome. The concept of *fitra* comes from the Qur`an, which states,

فَأَقِمْ وَجْهَكَ لِلدِّينِ حَنِيفًا فِطْرَةَ اللَّهِ الَّتِي فَطَرَ النَّاسَ عَلَيْهَا لَا تَبْدِيلَ لِخَلْقِ اللَّهِ ذَلِكَ الدِّينُ الْقَيِّمُ وَلَكِنَّ أَكْثَرَ النَّاسِ لَا يَعْلَمُونَ ۝

*Devote yourself single mindedly to the true faith; and adhere to the true nature on which Allah has created human beings. There is no altering in the creation of Allah. That is the true straight faith, although most people do not know. (ar-Rum, 30:30)*

While reciting *Surat al-Fatiha*, when we say *iyyaka na'budu* we are telling Allah (SWT) that it is "You alone we worship." In other words, our worship and total devotion, our unreserved obedience, and our absolute servitude are only for Allah (SWT) and no one else. It is equally natural and logical to turn for help in everything to Him alone. Hence the following expression "it is from You alone that we seek help." Therefore, we should not love or fear or depend upon anyone else as we love or fear or depend upon Allah (SWT), nor should we show complete self-abasement and total humility to anyone as we are required to do before Allah (SWT) through acts such as bowing and prostrating.

Many classical scholars of Islam have explained the term 'ibada. Imam Ibn Taymiyya (RA) said, "'Ibada is obedience to Allah by following that which He ordered upon the tongues of His Messengers." He also said, "'Ibada is a comprehensive term covering everything that Allah loves and is pleased with, whether sayings, or actions, outward and inward."

Imam al-Qurtubi (RA) said, "The root of 'ibada is humility and submissiveness. The various duties that have been prescribed upon the people are called 'ibadaat (the plural of 'ibada) since what is required is that these acts of worship must be done with humility and submissiveness to Allah (SWT)."

Imam Ibn Katheer (RA) said, "And *'ibada* is obedience to Allah by acting upon what He commands and abandoning what He forbids. This is the reality and essence of Islam. And the meaning of Islam is submission and surrender to Allah (SWT), along with the utmost compliance, humility, and submissiveness to Him."

Imam al-Ghazali (RA) in his book *The Forty Principles of the Religion* has enumerated ten forms which *'ibada* can take: 1) prayers, (2) prescribed alms-giving, (3) fasting, (4) hajj or pilgrimage to Mecca, (5) reciting the Holy Qur`an, (6) remembrance of Allah in all possible situations, (7) earning one's livelihood in accordance with the regulations of the *shari'a*, (8) fulfilling one's obligations toward one's companions and neighbors, (9) persuading people to act righteously and dissuading them from what is blameworthy and forbidden, and (10) following the Sunnah, or the practice of the Holy Prophet (SAS).

This holistic concept of *'ibada* appears to have disappeared during centuries of decline and decay of the Muslim *ummah*. While we worshipped Allah (SWT) through prayers, fasting, alms giving, and hajj, we did not always remain obedient to Him. Rather we were obedient to our colonial masters: the British, the French, the Italians, the Dutch, and the Portuguese.

*Al-hamduli-llah*, with the revival of the spirit of *deen* observable in the Islamic world, the concept of *'ibada* has once again started to be understood as total obedience to Allah (SWT) in all aspects of human life including individual, collective, social, economic, and political. However, obedience to Allah should not be merely mechanical or for worldly or political ends. It should be with full love for Allah. Obedience is only the body of *'ibada* while love of Allah is the spirit, or *rooh*, of *'ibada*. It is reported that the Prophet (SAS) used to recite the following supplication after every *salah*:

اَللَّهُمَّ اَعِنِّى عَلى ذِكْرِكَ وَشُكْرِكَ وحُسْنِ عِبادَتِك ○

"O Allah, help me remember You, to be grateful to You, and to do your 'ibada in an excellent manner."

It is to be understood that there are two aspects of *tawheed*—the theoretical, or philosophical, and the practical. The theoretical *tawheed* has to do with one's *'aqeeda*, or dogma of belief, and the practical *tawheed* has to do with one's *'ibada*.

It is a fact of life that we do obey others other than Allah (SWT). For example, we obey our parents, our elders, and our teachers, and we obey the call of our *nafs* by fulfilling its permissible rights. The point to note is that obedience to anyone or anything should not entail disobedience to Allah. The Prophet (SAS) said, "There is no obedience to any created thing if it entails disobedience to the Creator."

Allah explains this phenomenon in the Qur`an when He says,

أَفَرَأَيْتَ مَنِ اتَّخَذَ إِلَهَهُ هَوَاهُ ○

*Have you seen him who takes his whims and desires to be his God? (al-Jathiya, 45:23)*

This means that if one were to follow lust and the base desires of one's *nafs* that go against Islamic law and morals, one would be making one's *nafs* the object of *'ibada* or worship. For example, a person deliberately earning through unlawful or *haram* means against all dictates of the *shari'a* would be said to be the slave of his *nafs* and not of Allah (SWT). That is why in a hadeeth related by Bukhari, the Prophet (SAS) said, "Accursed is the slave of the dinar and the slave of the dirham." This means that such people have become slaves of wealth rather than slaves of Allah.

Every prophet or messenger of Allah called people to do the *'ibada* of Allah (SWT).

$$\text{يَا قَوْمِ اعْبُدُوا اللَّهَ مَا لَكُم مِّنْ إِلَٰهٍ غَيْرُهُ}$$

*O my people. Do the 'ibada of Allah; you have no other God but Him. (al-A'raf, 7:85)*

Being the representative of Allah (SWT) on earth, every prophet or messenger of Allah told his people,

$$\text{اعْبُدُوا اللَّهَ وَاتَّقُوهُ وَأَطِيعُونِ}$$

*Do the 'ibada of Allah, have taqwa of Him and obey me. (Nuh, 71:3)*

And obeying the Messenger of Allah means obeying Allah, for Allah says,

$$\text{مَّن يُطِعِ الرَّسُولَ فَقَدْ أَطَاعَ اللَّهَ}$$

*Whoever obeys the Messenger obeys Allah. (an-Nisa`, 4:80)*

Mankind was ordered only to do the *'ibada* of Allah.

$$\text{أَمَرَ أَلَّا تَعْبُدُوا إِلَّا إِيَّاهُ}$$

*And He orders you not to do the 'ibada (of anyone) but Him. (Yusuf, 12:40)*

The generic meaning of *'ibada* of Allah (SWT) means to worship, obey, and serve Him and to be His humble and obedient slave. The philosopher-poet Muhammad Iqbal remarked in one of his lectures on the meaning of prayers that during *salah*, the finite ego of the slave comes face to face with the infinite ego of Allah. In *Surat Ta Ha*, Allah says when conversing with Musa (AS),

$$\text{إِنَّنِي أَنَا اللَّهُ لَا إِلَٰهَ إِلَّا أَنَا فَاعْبُدْنِي وَأَقِمِ الصَّلَاةَ لِذِكْرِي}$$

*I am Allah, there is no God but Me. So worship Me(i.e. do my 'ibada) and keep up the prayer so that you remember Me. (Ta Ha, 20:14)*

Mankind was told to call on Allah alone without associating partners with Him.

$$\text{فَلَا تَدْعُوا مَعَ اللَّهِ أَحَدًا}$$

*Do not call on anyone else besides Allah. (al-Jinn, 72:18)*

There is *shirk* committed when one begs someone other than Allah (SWT) for their needs. And we know that *shirk* is an unforgivable sin, unless one repents to Allah and comes back to the *'ibada* of the One, and only One—Allah.

$$\text{إِنِ الْحُكْمُ إِلَّا لِلَّهِ} \bigcirc$$

*Sovereignty belongs to Allah alone. (Yusuf, 12:40)*

There is no one who is partner with Him in His kingdom.

$$\text{وَقُلِ الْحَمْدُ لِلَّهِ الَّذِي لَمْ يَتَّخِذْ وَلَدًا وَلَمْ يَكُن لَّهُ شَرِيكٌ فِي الْمُلْكِ} \bigcirc$$

*And say: "Praise be to Allah Who has no son and Who has no partner in His Kingdom."*
*(al-Isra`, 17:111)*

The biggest manifestation of *shirk* today is the concept of human sovereignty or sovereignty of the people. This is in stark contravention to the divine injunction,

$$\bigcirc \text{وَلَا يُشْرِكُ فِي حُكْمِهِ أَحَدًا}$$

*And He does not share His authority with anyone. (al-Kahf, 18:26)*

Through their disobedience and flagrant violation of divine laws people have become oblivious of the fact that supreme greatness is only for Allah (SWT). We are reminded in *Surat al-Hashr*,

$$\text{هُوَ اللَّهُ الَّذِي لَا إِلَهَ إِلَّا هُوَ الْمَلِكُ الْقُدُّوسُ السَّلَامُ الْمُؤْمِنُ الْمُهَيْمِنُ الْعَزِيزُ الْجَبَّارُ الْمُتَكَبِّرُ} \bigcirc$$

*He is Allah, there is no God but Him. He is the King, the Most Pure, the Perfect Peace, the Trustworthy, the Granter of security, the Almighty, the Supreme Authority, the Supremely Great. (al-Hashr, 59:23)*

May Allah (SWT) give us the wisdom to be His humble and obedient *'ibad* by doing *'ibada* through worshipping Him, obeying Him, and serving Him with utmost humility.

# *ZAKAT:* ITS MEANING AND SIGNIFICANCE

My *khutbah* today is on the topic of *zakat*. This *khutbah* is to serve as a reminder to you and me. Allah says in the Qur`an,

وَذَكِّرْ فَإِنَّ الذِّكْرَىٰ تَنفَعُ الْمُؤْمِنِينَ ○

*And keep reminding, because reminding benefits the believers. (adh-Dhariyat, 51:55)*

Despite the importance of *salah* and *zakat* in our *deen*, it is a sad fact that just as many Muslims do not offer their *salah* or do not fulfill the conditions of *salah*, many Muslims also do not understand the importance of fulfilling the obligation of *zakat*.

*Zakat* is one of the five pillars of Islam. It was made compulsory in the second year after the *hijra*. Prior to that period, it was not an obligatory mode of worship. During the Meccan era, Muslims used to make contributions from their wealth, but only by way of optional charity, or *sadaqa*. The proof for *zakat* is found in the Qur`an, in the Sunnah, and in the consensus of the scholars. Allah tells us in *Surat an-Nur,*

وَأَقِيمُوا الصَّلَاةَ وَآتُوا الزَّكَاةَ وَأَطِيعُوا الرَّسُولَ لَعَلَّكُمْ تُرْحَمُونَ ○

*Establish salah and pay zakat and obey the Messenger so that hopefully mercy will be shown to you. (an-Nur, 24:56)*

This is just one of the many places in the Qur`an where Allah (SWT) gives the command to paying *zakat*, which is usually found coupled with *salah* as an obligatory act of worship.

The word *zakat* means to grow, to increase, and to purify. When said about a person, it means to improve or to become better. Consequently *zakat* means blessing, growth, purification, and betterment. In the *shari'a*, the word *zakat* refers to the determined share of wealth prescribed by Allah (SWT) to be distributed among the deserving categories of those entitled to receive it. *Zakat* is not a "tax." It is a mode of worship or *'ibada*. Allah (SWT) tells the Prophet (SAS),

خُذْ مِنْ أَمْوَالِهِمْ صَدَقَةً تُطَهِّرُهُمْ وَتُزَكِّيهِم بِهَا ○

*Take zakat from their wealth to purify and cleanse them. (at-Tawba, 9:103)*

The Qur`an describes the objective of taking *zakat* out of wealth as purification and cleansing. *Zakat* is not only a means to purify one's wealth, but it is also a spiritual purification which serves as a means to bring an individual closer to Allah (SWT).

As a mode of worship, *zakat* is not exclusive to the *ummah* of Muhammad (SAS). It has been a religious obligation for the previous nations as well. This is evident from many verses of the Qur'an.

وَاذْكُرْ فِي الْكِتَابِ إِسْمَاعِيلَ إِنَّهُ كَانَ صَادِقَ الْوَعْدِ وَكَانَ رَسُولًا نَبِيًّا ۞ وَكَانَ يَأْمُرُ أَهْلَهُ بِالصَّلَاةِ وَالزَّكَاةِ وَكَانَ عِنْدَ رَبِّهِ مَرْضِيًّا ۞

*And mention Isma'eel in the Book. He was true to his promise and was a Messenger and a Prophet. He used to command his people to perform salah and give zakat and his Lord was pleased with him. (Maryam, 19:54-55)*

Addressing the Children of Israel, an *ayah* in *Surat al-Baqara* says,

وَأَقِيمُوا الصَّلَاةَ وَآتُوا الزَّكَاةَ وَارْكَعُوا مَعَ الرَّاكِعِينَ ۞

*Establish salah and pay zakat and bow with those who bow. (al-Baqara, 2:43)*

In *Surat Maryam*, 'Isa (AS) says to his people,

إِنِّي عَبْدُ اللَّهِ آتَانِيَ الْكِتَابَ وَجَعَلَنِي نَبِيًّا ۞ وَجَعَلَنِي مُبَارَكًا أَيْنَ مَا كُنْتُ وَأَوْصَانِي بِالصَّلَاةِ وَالزَّكَاةِ مَا دُمْتُ حَيًّا ۞

*I am the slave of Allah. He has given me the Book and made me a Prophet. He has made me blessed wherever I am and directed me to perform salah and give zakat as long as I live. (Maryam, 19:30-31)*

Thus, we see that the prophets of Allah (SWT) conveyed to their people the twin obligations of establishing *salah* and paying *zakat*. Willfully rejecting either of them brings a Muslim to the threshold of disbelief or *kufr*. So we should fear Allah and not be careless in obeying the divine injunctions pertaining to both *salah* and *zakat*. Describing the true righteous believers in *Surat al-Mu'minoon*, Allah says:

وَالَّذِينَ هُمْ لِلزَّكَاةِ فَاعِلُونَ ۞

*(They are) those who pay the zakat. (al-Mu'minoon, 23:4)*

In *Surat at-Tawba*, Allah (SWT) describes eight categories of people or groups who qualify to be the beneficiaries of *zakat*:

The *fuqara'*, or those who own property in excess of basic necessities but below the value of *nisab* (see explanation below).

The *masakeen*, or those who are in extreme poverty and possess no wealth whatsoever.

The *'amileen*, or those who are the *zakat* collectors. It is not necessary that they be needy persons.

The *mu`allafat al-quloob*, or those poor and needy persons who are given *zakat* with the intention of strengthening their hearts because they may be recently converted to Islam or because helping them may bring them closer to Islam.

*Ar-riqab*, or those slaves whose masters have agreed to set them free on a payment of money; *zakat* may be used to purchase their freedom.

*Al-gharimeen*, or those persons whose debts exceed their assets, and their net assets are below the *nisab* limit.

*Fee sabeel Allah*, which refers either giving *zakat* to those persons who are away from home in the path of Allah (SWT) or to give in Allah's cause.

*Ibn as-sabeel*, or a traveler, who even though wealthy at his residence is stranded and in need of financial assistance.

*Zakat* is obligatory upon every adult, mentally stable, and free Muslim who possesses a certain minimum amount of wealth, called the *nisab*, for a complete lunar year (*hawl*). It is not obligatory if the amount owned is less than this *nisab*. If "*zakatable*" assets decrease below the value of *nisab*, then the one-year cycle starts from the day wealth again reaches the value of *nisab*. The *nisab* is equivalent to the market value of 87.4 grams of gold or 613.3 grams of silver. The amount to be paid toward *zakat* is 2.5% of the market value of one's savings. The savings are calculated after meeting the expenses of necessities such as food, clothing, shelter, furniture, utensils, vehicles, and other family and day-to-day expenses within a one-year cycle. Deductible items also include money owed to others. For calculating *zakat*, the value of all debt-free *zakatable* assets can be converted to a cash figure, and if the total value is more than the value of *nisab* throughout the year, then *zakat* should be given.

*Zakat* is calculated on cash, gold and silver. There is difference of opinion among jurists whether or not *zakat* is payable on gold and silver jewelry worn by women. The majority of Malikis, Shafi'is, and Hanbalis are of the view that it is not obligatory to do so. The Hanafis are of the view that it is obligatory to pay *zakat* on such jewelry, as there are traditions which speak of the Prophet (SAS) asking women whether or not they had paid *zakat* on the jewelry worn by them and warning them of punishment in the hereafter if they had not done so. Hence, to be on the safe side, it is better to pay. There is no *zakat* on precious stones unless they are for trade. *Zakat* is payable on stocks and shares as well as dividends accrued on them. It is also payable on properties one has for investment purposes and the income generated from such properties. To find out in detail about the kinds of wealth that are included in the calculation of *zakat* such as livestock, agricultural produce, minerals, etc., and other rulings pertaining to *zakat*, one may consult the books of *fiqh* on this subject or ask scholars. There are many Islamic organizations that offer help to people to calculate their *zakat* and answer their *zakat* related questions.

The most in need of *zakat* are the poor and needy people in one's immediate family. *Zakat* can be given to one's brother, sister, nephew, niece, paternal or maternal uncle, paternal or maternal aunt, father-in-law, mother-in-law, step-grandfather, or step-grandmother provided they do not have *nisab*. They should be helped through *zakat* and *sadaqa* before one goes out to help others. As an obligation toward Allah (SWT), *zakat* should be given to those among our relatives even if we do not like them for some reason. It is important to be sensitive to people's feelings and emotions. People, especially one's relatives, should not be made to feel humiliated by telling them that they are being paid out of *zakat*.

*Zakat* is only given by Muslims to Muslims. It cannot be paid to apostates, unbelievers, or atheists. Parents, children, and those in their ascending and descending lineage are not entitled to receive *zakat*, because parents have the responsibility to take care of their children and sons have the responsibility to take care of their parents. The wife is also not entitled to receive *zakat* from her husband since any expense incurred by her is the responsibility of her husband. However, a wife may give *zakat* to her poor husband, as she is not legally responsible for him.

It is not necessary to reveal to the needy person that what is being given to him or her is *zakat*. It is very important to make certain that the recipient of *zakat* is deserving of it. If *zakat* is given without inquiry and subsequently it is discovered that the recipient was not deserving of it, then the *zakat* is not valid and should be given again.

*Zakat* should be given as soon as possible after it becomes due. If it so happens that death occurs before one is able to fulfill their obligations, *zakat* should be taken from the estate of the deceased. The payment of *zakat* must never be stopped or postponed and, like any other *'ibada* or mode of worship, should be done with utmost sincerity of intention, and only for the sake of Allah (SWT). May Allah (SWT) bless each one of us and grant us understanding and goodness.

Brothers and sisters! *Zakat* helps achieve reform, both financially and spiritually. It eliminates miserliness and greed from hearts. When a Muslim pays *zakat*, Allah (SWT) increases his sustenance. Although at a human level it may seem that giving of wealth means reduction of wealth, in reality it is not. The Prophet (SAS) said, "When a slave of Allah pays *zakat*, the angels of Allah pray for him in these words: 'O Allah! Grant abundance to him who spends in Your cause and destroy him who does not spend and restricts to himself his wealth.'" Allah (SWT) has strongly warned those people who are negligent in paying their *zakat*. It is a Divine injunction. It is not a personal matter or a voluntary contribution; rather, it is an obligation for which one will be called to account before Allah (SWT).

Let me conclude with a true story: An example from history which demonstrates how implementation of justice in the collection and distribution of *zakat* can benefit all of society. During the caliphate of 'Umar ibn 'Abd al-'Azeez, which amazingly lasted only two years and five months, he made great efforts to organize the government and ensure justice. His society enjoyed such a golden period that at the time of the annual *zakat* distribution for the poor, *zakat* distributors couldn't even find a single person in need to accept it. Thus, the money was used for helping neighboring societies, building roads, and the overall well-being of the community at large.

The abundant wealth of Muslims at the time and their devotion to properly giving *zakat*, combined with the justice in its distribution, is an excellent example of how positive social change is possible even in such a short period of time.

May Allah (SWT) make us among those righteous servants who fulfill all their duties and obligations toward His *deen. Allahumma ameen.*

# SELECTED BIBLIOGRAPHY/
# WORKS CONSULTED

Ahmed, Israr. Selected audio recordings.

Alkhairo, Wael. *Speaking for Change: A Guide to Making Effective Sermons.* Beltsville, MD: Amana Publications, 1998.

Al-Jaziri, Abd al-Rahman. *Al-Fiqh ʿala al-Madhahib al-Arbaʾa* (4 volumes) [*Fiqh according to the Four School*]. Dar al-Hadith. Cairo. 2004.

Al-Zuhayli, Wahba. *Mawsooʿa al-Fiqh al-Islamiwa al-Qadaya al-Muʾasira* (14 volumes) [The Encyclopedia of Islamic *Fiqh* and Contemporary Issues]. Dar al-Fikr. Damascus. 2013

Hashem, Mazen. *The Muslim Friday Khutba: Veiled and Unveiled Themes.* Washington, DC: Institute for Social Policy and Understanding, October 2009.

Khattab, Abdelmoneim Mahmoud. *Islam: The Sermons of Imam A.M. Khattab.* Imamkhattab.org

Mujahid, Abdul Malik, ed., *Selected Friday Sermons.* Riyadh, Saudi Arabia: Darussalam, 2000.

Sabiq, As-Sayyid. *Fiqh us-Sunnah, Vol. 1, Salatul Jumuʾah (the Friday Prayer).* Oak Brook, IL: American Trust Publications, 1986.

Sakr, Ahmad H. *Khutab from Mehrab.* Lombard, IL: Foundation for Islamic Knowledge, 1998.

Siddiqui, Abdur Rashid. *Lift Up Your Hearts: A Collection of 30 Khutbahs for Friday Prayer* Leicester, United Kingdom: The Islamic Foundation, 2001.

Siddiqui, Abdur Rashid. *Lift Up Your Hearts: A Collection of 25 Khutbahs for Friday Prayer* Leicester, United Kingdom: The Islamic Foundation, 2005.

Zarabozo, Jamal al-Din M. *The Friday Prayer. Vol 1: The Fiqh of the Friday Prayer.* Aurora, CO: IANA, 1994.

"Now What Does Gheebah Mean?" The Khalids, https://thekhalids.org/newsletter-archive/306-now-what-does-gheebah-mean

"Poverty of the Soul," Yasmin Mogahed, http://www.yasminmogahed.com/2012/10/02/poverty-of-the-soul-united-for-change-conference/

"Sin and its Effects on the One Who Commits it," Islam Question & Answer, https://islamqa.info/en/answers/23425/sin-and-its-effects-on-the-one-who-commits-it

"Sources of Blessing (*Baraka*)," Muhammed Faris, "The Productive Muslim, *18 Sources of Barakah.*" *https*://productivemuslim.com/18-sources-of-barakah/

"The Rulings Related to Friday Prayer," Seekersguidance, https://seekersguidance.org/answers/hanafi-fiqh/the-rulings-related-to-friday-prayer/

"The Significance of Abraham in Our World Today Needs to Be Asserted," Imam Zaid Shakir, https://www.newislamicdirections.com/notes/the_significance_of_abraham_in_our_world_today_needs_to_be_asserted/

# APPENDIX 1

## *EXAMPLES OF INTRODUCTORY INVOCATIONS OF THE FIRST KHUTBAH*

اَلْحَمْدُ لِلَّهِ الَّذِيْ أَكْمَلَ لَنَا الدِّيْنَ، وَأَتَمَّ عَلَيْنَا النِّعْمَةَ، وَجَعَلَنَا مِنْ خَيْرِ أُمَّةٍ أُخْرِجَتْ لِلنَّاسِ، أَحْمَدُهُ سُبْحَانَهُ، لَا أُحْصِيْ ثَنَاءً عَلَيْهِ، وَأَشْهَدُ أَن لَّا إِلَهَ إِلَّا اللهُ وَحْدَهُ لَا شَرِيْكَ لَهُ، وَأَشْهَدُ أَنَّ مُحَمَّدًا عَبْدُهُ وَرَسُوْلُهُ، أَرْسَلَهُ بِالدِّيْنِ الْقَيِّمِ وَالْمِلَّةِ الْحَنِيْفِيَّةِ، وَجَعَلَهُ عَلَى شَرِيْعَةٍ مِنَ الْأَمْرِ، صَلَّى اللهُ عَلَيْهِ وَعَلَى آلِهِ وَصَحْبِهِ وَسَلَّم تَسْلِيْمًا كَثِيْرًا مَزِيْدًا إِلَى يَوْمِ الدِّيْنِ

*All praise is due to Allah, who perfected for us our religion, and completed the favor bestowed upon us, and made us of the best nation brought forth for mankind. I praise Him, may He be exalted, yet I am not capable of enumerating His praise. I bear witness that there is no god but Allah, alone and without partner, and I bear witness that Muhammad is His slave and messenger. Allah sent him with the straight and true religion and set him upon the clear way of His command. Allah bless him, his family, and his companions, and grant them peace, in abundance and increase, until the Day of Judgment.*

إِنَّ الْحَمْدَ لِلَّهِ، نَحْمَدُهُ وَنَسْتَغْفِرُهُ وَنَسْتَعِيْنُهُ وَنَسْتَهْدِيْهِ، وَنَعُوْذُ بِاللهِ مِنْ شُرُوْرِ أَنْفُسِنَا وَمِنْ سَيِّئَاتِ أَعْمَالِنَا، مَنْ يَهْدِهِ اللهُ فَلَا مُضِلَّ لَهُ، وَمَنْ يُضْلِلْهُ فَلَا هَادِيَ لَهُ، وَأَشْهَدُ أَن لَّا إِلَهَ إِلَّا اللهُ وَحْدَهُ لَا شَرِيْكَ لَهُ، وَأَشْهَدُ أَنَّ مُحَمَّدًا عَبْدُهُ وَرَسُوْلُهُ، مَنْ بَعَثَهُ اللهُ رَحْمَةً لِلْعَالَمِيْنَ هَادِيًا وَمُبَشِّرًا وَنَذِيْرًا، بَلَّغَ الرِّسَالَةَ وَأَدَّى الْأَمَانَةَ وَنَصَحَ الْأُمَّةَ، فَجَزَاهُ اللهُ خَيْرَ مَا جَزَى نَبِيًّا مِنْ أَنْبِيَائِهِ، صَلَوَاتُ اللهِ وَسَلَامُهُ عَلَيْهِ وَعَلَى كُلِّ رَسُوْلٍ أَرْسَلَهُ

*All praise is due to Allah. We praise Him and seek His forgiveness, His help, and His guidance. We take refuge in Allah from the evil of our very selves and from our evil acts. He whom Allah guides none can lead him astray, and he whom Allah lets go astray, none can guide him. I bear witness that there is no god but Allah, alone and without partner, and I bear witness that Muhammad is his slave and messenger, whom Allah sent as a mercy to all worlds of beings—as a guide, a giver of glad tidings, and a warner. Indeed, he conveyed the message, fulfilled the trust, and attended to the Muslim nation with utter sincerity. Allah reward him the best He has ever rewarded a prophet from among His prophets; may the blessings and peace of Allah be upon him and upon all the messengers Allah sent.*

اَلْحَمْدُ لِلَّهِ الَّذِيْ خَلَقَ كُلَّ شَيْءٍ فَقَدَّرَهُ تَقْدِيْرًا، وَدَبَّرَ عِبَادَهُ عَلَى مَا تَقْتَضِيْهِ حِكْمَتُهُ وَكَانَ بِهِمْ لَطِيْفًا خَبِيْرًا، وَأَشْهَدُ أَنْ لَّا إِلَهَ إِلَّا اللهُ وَحْدَهُ لَا شَرِيْكَ لَهُ، لَهُ الْمُلْكُ وَلَهُ الْحَمْدُ وَكَانَ عَلَى كُلِّ شَيْءٍ قَدِيْرًا، وَأَشْهَدُ أَنَّ مُحَمَّدًا عَبْدُهُ وَرَسُوْلُهُ، أَرْسَلَهُ بَيْنَ يَدَيِ السَّاعَةِ بَشِيْرًا وَنَذِيْرًا، وَدَاعِيًا إِلَى اللهِ بِإِذْنِهِ وَسِرَاجًا مُنِيْرًا، صَلَّى اللهُ عَلَيْهِ وَعَلَى آلِهِ وَأَصْحَابِهِ وَمَنْ تَبِعَهُمْ بِإِحْسَانٍ إِلَى يَوْمِ الدِّيْنِ وَسَلَّمَ تَسْلِيْمًا كَثِيْرًا

*All praise belongs to Allah who created all things and ordered them in due proportion, who planned for His servants in accordance with His wisdom. Indeed, Allah is subtly kind to His servants and well informed of them. I bear witness that there is no god but Allah, alone and without partner, to Him belongs the dominion and all praise, and He has power over all things; and I bear witness that Muhammad is his slave and messenger. Allah sent him before the Final Hour as one who brings glad tidings, as a warner, as one who calls to Allah by His leave, and as a light giving lamp. May Allah bless him, his family, his companions, and all who follow them with excellence till the Day of Judgment, and may He grant them abundant peace.*

اَلْحَمْدُ لِلَّهِ الْمُتَوَحِّدِ بِصِفَاتِ الْعَظَمَةِ وَالْجَلَالِ، الْمُتَفَرِّدِ بِالْكِبْرِيَاءِ وَالْكَمَالِ، الْمُوْلِيْ عَلَى خَلْقِهِ النِّعَمَ السَّابِغَةَ وَجَزِيْلَ النَّوَالِ، وَأَشْهَدُ أَنْ لَّا إِلَهَ إِلَّا اللهُ وَحْدَهُ لَا شَرِيْكَ لَهُ الْكَبِيْرُ الْمُتَعَالِ، وَأَشْهَدُ أَنَّ مُحَمَّدًا عَبْدُهُ وَرَسُوْلُهُ أَفْضَلُ رُسُلِهِ وَأَنْبِيَائِهِ عَظِيْمُ الْأَخْلَاقِ جَلِيْلُ الْخِصَالِ، اللَّهُمَّ صَلِّ وَسَلِّمْ عَلَى سَيِّدِنَا مُحَمَّدٍ، وَعَلَى آلِهِ وَأَصْحَابِهِ خَيْرِ صَحْبٍ وَأَشْرَفِ آلٍ

*All praise is due to Allah, who is unique in His attributes of greatness and majesty, and singular in His exaltedness and perfection, who favors His creation with copious blessings and abundant giving. I bear witness that there is no god but Allah, the Great and High, alone and without partner; and I bear witness that Muhammad is His slave and messenger, the most virtuous of His messengers and prophets, and possessor of great character and tremendous traits. O Allah! Bless and grant peace to our master Muhammad, and his family and companions, the best of companions and the noblest of kin.*

اَلْحَمْدُ لِلَّهِ الَّذِيْ يَقْضِيْ بِالْحَقِّ، وَيَحْكُمُ بِالْعَدْلِ، وَيَهْدِيْ مَنْ يَشَاءُ إِلَى صِرَاطٍ مُسْتَقِيْمٍ، يُقَدِّرُ الْأُمُوْرَ بِحِكْمَةٍ وَهُوَ الْحَكِيْمُ الْعَلِيْمُ، أَرْسَلَ الرُّسُلَ مُبَشِّرِيْنَ وَمُنْذِرِيْنَ، وَأَنْزَلَ مَعَهُمُ الْكِتَابَ لِيَحْكُمَ بَيْنَ النَّاسِ فِيْمَا اخْتَلَفُوْا فِيْهِ وَلِيَقُوْمَ النَّاسُ بِالْقِسْطِ، وَأَشْهَدُ أَنْ لَّا إِلَهَ إِلَّا اللهُ وَحْدَهُ لَا شَرِيْكَ لَهُ، لَهُ الْمُلْكُ وَلَهُ الْحَمْدُ وَهُوَ عَلَى كُلِّ شَيْءٍ قَدِيْرٍ، وَأَشْهَدُ أَنَّ مُحَمَّدًا عَبْدُهُ وَرَسُوْلُهُ، اَلرَّحْمَةُ الْمُهْدَاةُ، وَالنِّعْمَةُ الْمُسْدَاةُ، صَلَّى اللهُ عَلَيْهِ وَعَلَى آلِهِ وَالتَّابِعِيْنَ لَهُمْ بِإِحْسَانٍ إِلَى يَوْمِ الدِّيْنِ وَسَلَّمَ تَسْلِيْمًا

*All praise belongs to Allah, who judges with truth and justice and guides whom he wills to the straight path. He determines matters with wisdom, and He is All Wise and All Knowing. He sent messengers as bearers of good news and as warners and sent down with them the Book to judge between men wherein they differ, and so that men uphold justice. I bear witness that there is no god but Allah, alone and without partner; to Him belongs the dominion and all praise, and he has power over everything. And I bear witness that Muhammad is His slave and messenger, the embodiment of mercy and blessing gifted to creation. Allah bless him, his family, and those who follow them with excellence till the Day of Judgment and grant them abundant peace.*

اَلْحَمْدُ لِلَّهِ رَبِّ الْعَالَمِينَ، الَّذِي أَعَدَّ الْجَنَّةَ بِمُقْتَضَى فَضْلِهِ وَكَرَمِهِ لِعِبَادِهِ الْمُؤْمِنِينَ، وَأَعَدَّ النَّارَ بِمُقْتَضَى عَدْلِهِ وَحِكْمَتِهِ لِعِبَادِهِ الْعَاصِينَ، أَحْمَدُهُ سُبْحَانَهُ، لَا أُحْصِي ثَنَاءً عَلَيْهِ، وَأَسْتَغْفِرُهُ وَأَتُوبُ إِلَيْهِ، وَأَشْهَدُ أَنْ لَّا إِلَهَ إِلَّا اللهُ وَحْدَهُ لَا شَرِيكَ لَهُ، وَأَشْهَدُ أَنَّ سَيِّدَنَا وَنَبِيَّنَا مُحَمَّدًا عَبْدُهُ وَرَسُولُهُ، أُصَلِّي وَأُسَلِّمُ عَلَيْهِ، وَعَلَى آلِهِ وَأَصْحَابِهِ وَأَتْبَاعِهِ، وَكُلِّ مَنْ دَعَا بِدَعْوَتِهِ وَاقْتَفَى أَثَرَهُ، صَلَاةً وَسَلَامًا دَائِمَيْنِ مُتَلَازِمَيْنِ إِلَى يَوْمِ الدِّينِ

*All praise is due Allah, Lord of all the worlds, who prepared for his believing servants paradise in accordance with His beneficence and generosity, and who prepared for his disobedient servants the hellfire in accordance with His justice and wisdom. I praise Him, glorified and exalted, yet I cannot enumerate His praise. And I seek forgiveness of Him and repent unto Him. I bear witness that there is no god but Allah, alone and without partner, and I bear witness that our master and prophet Muhammad is His slave and messenger. I invoke blessings and peace upon him, his family, his companions, and his followers, and all who call with his call and follow in his footsteps; be there blessings and peace perpetually and successively till the Day of Judgment.*

اَلْحَمْدُ لِلَّهِ بَاعِثِ الرُّسُلِ بِآيَاتِهِ، الْمُبِيِّنِ الْحَلَالَ مِنَ الْحَرَامِ، الْمُتَفَضِّلِ عَلَى عِبَادِهِ بِجَزِيلِ الْإِنْعَامِ، الَّذِي أَحَلَّ لَنَا الطَّيِّبَاتِ وَحَرَّمَ الْحَرَامَ، عَلَى أَيْدِي رُسُلِهِ وَأَنْبِيَائِهِ الكِرَامِ، أَحْمَدُهُ سُبْحَانَهُ عَلَى مَا أَنْعَمَ بِهِ عَلَيْنَا مِنَ النِّعَمِ الْجِسَامِ، وَأَشْهَدُ أَنْ لَّا إِلَهَ إِلَّا اللهُ وَحْدَهُ لَا شَرِيكَ لَهُ الْمَلِكُ الْقُدُّوسُ السَّلَامُ، وَأَشْهَدُ أَنَّ مُحَمَّدًا عَبْدُهُ وَرَسُولُهُ أَكْرَمُ مَنْ صَلَّى وَصَامَ، صَلَّى اللهُ عَلَيْهِ وَعَلَى آلِهِ وَأَصْحَابِهِ الْبَرَرَةِ الكِرَامِ، عَدَدَ مَا جَلَّى النَّهَارُ الظَّلَامَ

*All praise belongs to Allah, who sent messengers with His verses that clarified the lawful from the unlawful, who showered upon His servants copious blessings, who permitted us the pure and good and forbade us the unlawful at the hands of His noble messengers and prophets. I praise him, glorified be He, for the tremendous blessings He has bestowed upon us. I bear witness that there is no god but Allah, alone and without partner, the King, the Holy, the Source of Peace, and I bear witness that Muhammad is His slave and messenger, the noblest of any who prayed and fasted. Allah bless him, his folk, and his good and noble companions, the number of times the day brightens the darkness.*

اَلْحَمْدُ لِلَّهِ رَبِّ الْعَالَمِينَ، الَّذِي أَنْقَذَنَا بِنُورِ الْعِلْمِ مِنْ ظُلُمَاتِ الْجَهَالَةِ، وَأَنْقَذَنَا بِنُورِ الْوَحْيِ مِنَ السُّقُوطِ فِي الضَّلَالَةِ، وَأَرْسَلَ رَسُولَهُ بِالْهُدَى بِدِينِ الْحَقِّ إِرْشَادًا لَنَا وَدَلَالَةً، وَأَشْهَدُ أَنْ لَّا إِلَهَ إِلَّا اللهُ وَحْدَهُ لَاشَرِيكَ لَهُ،

وَأَشْهَدُ أَنَّ سَيِّدَنَا مُحَمَّدًا عَبْدُهُ وَرَسُولُهُ، السِّرَاجُ الْمُزْهِرُ الْمُنِيرُ الْأَنْوَرُ، اللّٰهُمَّ صَلِّ وَسَلِّمْ وَبَارِكْ عَلَيْهِ، وَعَلَى آلِهِ الطَّيِّبِينَ الطَّاهِرِينَ، وَأَصْحَابِهِ الغُرِّ الْمَيَامِينَ، وَعَلَى مَنِ اقْتَفَى أَثَرَهُ إِلَى يَوْمِ الدِّينِ

*All praise belongs to Allah, Lord of the worlds, who by the light of knowledge saved us from the darkness of ignorance and by the light of revelation saved us from falling into misguidance. He who sent His messenger with the true religion to guide us. I bear witness that there is no god but Allah, alone and without partner; and I bear witness that our master Muhammad is His slave and messenger, the illuminating and bright lamp. Allah bless him, grant him peace, and increase him in goodness, and likewise his pure family, his blessed companions with radiant brows, and all who follow in his footsteps till the Day of Judgment.*

اَلْحَمْدُ لِلّٰهِ الَّذِي بِنِعْمَتِهِ تَتِمُّ الصَّالِحَاتُ، الْحَمْدُ لِلّٰهِ الَّذِي خَلَقَ الْأَرْضَ وَالسَّمَاوَاتِ، الَّذِي عَلِمَ الْعَثَرَاتِ، فَسَتَرَهَا عَلَى أَهْلِهَا وَأَنْزَلَ الرَّحَمَاتِ، ثُمَّ غَفَرَهَا لَهُمْ وَمَحَا السَّيِّئَاتِ، وَأَشْهَدُ أَنْ لَّا إِلَهَ إِلَّا اللهُ وَحْدَهُ لَا شَرِيكَ لَهُ، وَأَشْهَدُ أَنَّ مُحَمَّدًا عَبْدُهُ وَرَسُولُهُ، سَيِّدُ الْأَوَّلِينَ وَالْآخِرِينَ، وَقَائِدُ الْغُرِّ الْمُحَجَّلِينَ، صَلَّى اللهُ عَلَيْهِ وَعَلَى آلِهِ وَأَصْحَابِهِ، وَمَنْ سَارَ عَلَى نَهْجِهِ وَاسْتَنَّ بِسُنَّتِهِ، وَسَلَّمَ تَسْلِيمًا كَثِيرًا إِلَى يَوْمِ الدِّينِ

*All praise belongs to Allah. By His bounty are good works accomplished. All praise belongs to Allah who created the earth and the heavens, who knows of moral slips, yet conceals those who commit them, continuing to rain down His mercy without pause or stint. Thereafter, He forgives them their slips and effaces their ill deeds. I bear witness that there is no god but Allah, alone and without partner, and I bear witness that Muhammad is His slave and messenger, master of the ancients and the later peoples, and leader of those of radiant brows and limbs. Allah bless him, his family, his companions, and all who tread his path and adopt his way, and grant them peace in abundance till the Day of Judgment.*

إِنَّ الْحَمْدَ للهِ نَحْمَدُهُ وَنَسْتَهْدِيهِ، وَنَسْتَغْفِرُهُ وَنَتُوبُ إِلَيْهِ، وَنَعُوذُ بِاللهِ مِنْ شُرُورِ أَنْفُسِنَا وَمِنْ سَيِّئَاتِ أَعْمَالِنَا، مَنْ يَهْدِ اللهُ فَلَا مُضِلَّ لَهُ، وَمَنْ يُضْلِلْ فَلَا هَادِيَ لَهُ، وَأَشْهَدُ أَنْ لَا إِلَهَ إِلَّا اللهُ وَحْدَهُ لَا شَرِيكَ لَهُ، العَفُوُّ الْمُسْتَغْنِي عَنْ كُلِّ مَا سِوَاهُ، وَالْمُفْتَقِرُ إِلَيْهِ كُلُّ مَا عَدَاهُ، وَأَشْهَدُ أَنَّ سَيِّدَنَا وَحَبِيبَنَا وَقَائِدَنَا وَقُرَّةَ أَعْيُنِنَا مُحَمَّدًا عَبْدُهُ وَرَسُولُهُ، وَصَفِيُّهُ وَحَبِيبُهُ، بَلَّغَ الرِّسَالَةَ، وَأَدَّى الْأَمَانَةَ، وَنَصَحَ الْأُمَّةَ، صَلَّى اللهُ عَلَيْهِ صَلَاةً يَقْضِي بِهَا حَاجَاتِنَا، وَيُفَرِّجُ بِهَا كُرُبَاتِنَا، وَيَكْفِينَا بِهَا شَرَّ أَعْدَائِنَا، وَسَلَّمَ عَلَيْهِ، وَعَلَى صَحْبِهِ الطَّيِّبِينَ الْأَبْرَارِ، وَآلِهِ الْكِرَامِ الْأَطْهَارِ

*All praise is due to Allah. We praise him and seek His guidance. We ask forgiveness of Him and repent unto Him. We take refuge in Allah from the evil of our very selves, and from our evil acts. He whom Allah guides none can lead astray, and he whom Allah lets go astray, none can guide. I bear witness that there is no god but Allah, alone and without partner, the Oft-Forgiving, the one who is free of need of anything besides,* and whom all else is in need of. And I bear witness that our master, our beloved, our leader, and the joy of our eyes Muhammad is His slave and His messenger, His specially chosen friend, and His beloved. Indeed, he conveyed the message, fulfilled the trust, and guided the Muslim community with utter sincerity. Allah bless him with a blessing by which He fulfills our needs, removes our worries, and suffices us against the evil of our enemies. May He grant him peace, and likewise his good and righteous companions and his pure and noble family.

## EXAMPLES OF CONCLUDING INVOCATIONS OF THE FIRST KHUTBAH

بَارَكَ اللهُ لِيْ وَلَكُمْ فِي الْقُرْآنِ الْعَظِيمِ، وَنَفَعَنِي وَإِيَّاكُمْ بِمَا فِيهِ مِنَ الآيَاتِ وَالذِّكْرِ الْحَكِيمِ. أَقُولُ مَا تَسْمَعُونَ، وَأَسْتَغْفِرُ اللهَ لِي وَلَكُمْ وَلِسَائِرِ الْمُسْلِمِينَ مِنْ كُلِّ ذَنْبٍ، فَاسْتَغْفِرُوْهُ، إِنَّهُ هُوَ الغَفُورُ الرَّحِيمُ

May Allah bless you and I through the mighty Qur`an, and benefit you and I by the verses and wise reminder it contains. I say this, and I seek Allah's forgiveness for myself, for you, and for all Muslims from all sin. Seek His forgiveness. Indeed, He alone is the Oft-Forgiving, Most Merciful.

## EXAMPLES OF INTRODUCTORY INVOCATIONS OF THE SECOND KHUTBAH

اَلْحَمْدُ لِلَّهِ الَّذِي أَرْسَلَ رَسُوْلَهُ بِالْهُدَى وَدِيْنِ الْحَقِّ؛ لِيُظْهِرَهُ عَلَى الدِّيْنِ كُلِّهِ وَكَفَى بِاللَّهِ شَهِيْدًا، وَأَشْهَدُ أَنْ لَّا إِلَهَ إِلَّا اللهُ وَحْدَهُ لَا شَرِيْكَ لَهُ إِقْرَارًا بِهِ وَتَوْحِيْدًا، وَأَشْهَدُ أَنَّ مُحَمَّدًا عَبْدُهُ وَرَسُوْلُهُ، صَلَّى اللهُ عَلَيْهِ وَعَلَى آلِهِ وَصَحَابَتِهِ وَسَلَّمَ تَسْلِيْمًا مَزِيْدًا

All praise belongs to Allah who sent His messenger with the guidance and true religion, to make it paramount over all religions; and Allah is sufficient as a witness. By way of affirmation and declaring Allah's oneness, I bear witness that there is no god but Allah, alone and without partner; and I bear witness that Muhammad is His slave and messenger. Allah bless him, his family, and his companions, and grant them all peace, with increase.

اَلْحَمْدُ لِلَّهِ رَافِعِ الْمُؤْمِنِيْنَ دَرَجَاتٍ، وَخَافِضِ الْعَاصِيْنَ دَرَكَاتٍ، وَالصَّلَاةُ وَالسَّلَامُ عَلَى مَنْ خُتِمَتْ بِرِسَالَتِهِ

الرِّسَالَاتِ، نَبِيِّنَا وَقُرَّةِ أَعْيُنِنَا مُحَمَّدِ بْنِ عَبْدِ اللهِ، وَآلِهِ وَصَحْبِهِ ذَوِي الْفَضْلِ وَالْكَمَالَاتِ

*All praise belongs to Allah, the one who raises those who obey whole degrees, and lowers those who disobey whole degrees. Blessings and peace be upon he by whose message all messages were sealed, our prophet and the joy of our eyes, Muhammad ibn 'Abdullah, and also upon his family, and his companions, possessors of virtue and perfections.*

اَلْحَمْدُ لِلّهِ حَمْدًا كَثِيرًا طَيِّبًا مُبَارَكًا فِيهِ كَمَا يُحِبُّ رَبُّنَا وَيَرْضَى، أَحْمَدُهُ سُبْحَانَهُ وَأَشْهَدُ أَنْ لَّا إِلٰهَ إِلَّا هُوَ وَحْدَهُ لَا شَرِيكَ لَهُ، وَأَشْهَدُ أَنَّ مُحَمَّدًا عَبْدُهُ وَرَسُولُهُ، صَلَّى اللهُ عَلَيْهِ وَآلِهِ وَصَحْبِهِ، وَسَلَّمَ تَسْلِيمًا كَثِيرًا

*All praise is due to Allah, with abundance, goodness, and increase therein, in accordance with what our Lord loves and is pleased by. I praise Him, glorified be He, and I bear witness that there is no god but He, alone and without partner. And I bear witness that Muhammad is His slave and messenger. Allah bless him, his family, and his companions, and grant them peace in abundance.*

اَلْحَمْدُ لِلّهِ رَبِّ الْعَالَمِينَ، لَا عِزَّ إِلَّا فِي طَاعَتِهِ، وَلَا سَعَادَةَ إِلَّا فِيْ رِضَاهُ، مَنْ إِذَا أُطِيعَ شَكَرَ، وَإِذَا عُصِيَ تَابَ وَغَفَرَ، وَالَّذِيْ إِذَا دُعِيَ أَجَابَ، وَأَشْهَدُ أَنَّ مُحَمَّدًا عَبْدُ اللهِ وَرَسُولُهُ، صَلَّى اللهُ عَلَيْهِ وَسَلَّمَ تَسْلِيمًا كَثِيرًا

*All praise is due to Allah, Lord of the worlds. There is no glory save in obedience to Him and no bliss save in His good pleasure. It is He who accepts and appreciates when obeyed, and He who relents and forgives when disobeyed, and it is He who answers when called upon. And I bear witness that Muhammad is the slave of Allah and His messenger. Allah bless him and grant him peace abundantly.*

اَلْحَمْدُ لِلّهِ الَّذِيْ خَلَقَ فَسَوَّى، وَقَدَّرَ فَهَدَى، وَأَسْعَدَ وَأَشْقَى، وَمَنَعَ وَأَعْطَى، وَأَشْهَدُ أَنْ لَّا إِلٰهَ إِلَّا اللهُ وَحْدَهُ لَا شَرِيكَ لَهُ الْعَلِيُّ الْأَعْلَى، وَأَشْهَدُ أَنَّ مُحَمَّدًا عَبْدُهُ وَرَسُولُهُ النَّبِيُّ الْمُجْتَبَى، صَلَّى اللهُ عَلَيْهِ وَآلِهِ وَصَحْبِهِ وَمَنِ اهْتَدَى

*All praise belongs to He who created and proportioned well, who ordained and guided to what He willed, who gave bliss and made wretched, and who withheld and bestowed. I bear witness that there is no god but Allah, alone and without partner, the Lofty and Most High, and I bear witness that Muhammad is His slave and messenger, the chosen prophet. Allah bless him, his family, his companions, and those who are guided.*

اَلْحَمْدُ لِلّهِ عَلَى إِحْسَانِهِ، وَالشُّكْرُ لَهُ عَلَى تَوْفِيقِهِ وَامْتِنَانِهِ، وَأَشْهَدُ أَنْ لَّا إِلٰهَ إِلَّا اللهُ وَحْدَهُ لَا شَرِيكَ لَهُ تَعْظِيمًا لِشَأْنِهِ، وَأَشْهَدُ أَنَّ نَبِيَّنَا مُحَمَّدًا رَسُولُهُ الدَّاعِيْ إِلَى رِضْوَانِهِ، صَلَّى اللهُ وَسَلَّمَ عَلَيْهِ وَعَلَى آلِهِ وَأَصْحَابِهِ وَإِخْوَانِهِ

*All praise is due to Allah for His favor, and all thanks are His for success and grace.*

By way of exaltation, I bear witness that there is no god but Allah, alone and without partner. I also bear witness that our prophet Muhammad is His messenger, the one who calls to His good pleasure. Allah bless him and his family, companions, and brothers, and grant them to peace.

اَلْحَمْدُ لِلَّهِ لَا مَانِعَ لِمَا أَعْطَاهُ، وَلَا رَادَّ لِمَا قَضَاهُ، وَأَشْهَدُ أَنْ لَّا إِلَهَ إِلَّا هُوَ وَلَا مَعْبُودَ بِحَقٍّ سِوَاهُ، وَأَشْهَدُ أَنَّ مُحَمَّدًا عَبْدُ اللهِ وَرَسُولُهُ وَمُصْطَفَاهُ، صَلَّى اللهُ وَسَلَّمَ وَبَارَكَ عَلَيْهِ، وَعَلَى آلِهِ وَأَصْحَابِهِ وَمَنْ وَالَاهُ

All praise is due to Allah. What He gives, none withholds, and what He decrees, none overturns. I bear witness that there is no god and no true deity save Him, and I bear witness that Muhammad is the slave of Allah, His messenger, and His chosen one. Allah bless him, grant him peace, and increase him in goodness; and also his family, companions, and those who love and support him.

اَلْحَمْدُ لِلَّهِ الْحَيِّ الَّذِي أَضَاءَ نُورُهُ الآفَاقَ، وَأَشْهَدُ أَنْ لَّا إِلَهَ إِلَّا اللهُ وَحْدَهُ الْمَلِكُ الْخَلَّاقُ، وَأَشْهَدُ أَنَّ مُحَمَّدًا عَبْدُ اللهِ وَرَسُولُهُ أَفْضَلُ خَلْقِهِ عَلَى الْإِطْلَاقِ، صَلَّى اللهُ وَسَلَّمَ عَلَيْهِ وَعَلَى آلِهِ وَأَصْحَابِهِ وَمَنْ تَبِعَهُمْ بِإِحْسَانٍ إِلَى يَوْمِ التَّلَاقِ

All praise belongs to Allah, the Living, whose light illumines the horizons. I bear witness that there is no god but Allah alone, the King, the Creator, and I bear witness that Muhammad is Allah's slave and messenger, the most superior of All His creation without qualification. Allah bless and grant peace to him, his family, companions, and those who follow them with excellence till the day of meeting.

اَلْحَمْدُ لِلَّهِ وَلِيِّ مَنِ اتَّقَاهُ، مَنْ لَاذَ بِهِ وَقَاهُ، وَأَشْهَدُ أَنْ لَّا إِلَهَ إِلَّا اللهُ وَحْدَهُ لَا شَرِيكَ لَهُ، وَأَشْهَدُ أَنَّ مُحَمَّدًا عَبْدُهُ وَرَسُولُهُ وَحَبِيبُهُ وَخَلِيلُهُ وَمُصْطَفَاهُ، صَلَّى اللهُ وَبَارَكَ عَلَيْهِ، وَعَلَى آلِهِ وَصَحْبِهِ، وَمَنِ اهْتَدَى بِهُدَاهُ

All praise belongs to Allah, the protecting friend of those who possess taqwa of Him. Indeed, whoever seeks refuge in Allah, Allah guards and protects. I bear witness that there is no god but Allah, alone and without partner, and I bear witness that Muhammad is His slave and messenger, and His beloved, His intimate friend, His chosen one. Allah bless him and increase him in goodness; and likewise his family, companions, and those who follow his guidance.

اَلْحَمْدُ لِلَّهِ حَمْدًا كَثِيرًا كَمَا أَمَرَ، أَحْمَدُهُ وَأَشْكُرُهُ، لَا أُحْصِي ثَنَاءً عَلَيْهِ؛ هُوَ كَمَا أَثْنَى عَلَى نَفْسِهِ، وَأَشْهَدُ أَنْ لَّا إِلَهَ إِلَّا اللهُ وَحْدَهُ لَا شَرِيكَ لَهُ، وَأَشْهَدُ أَنَّ مُحَمَّدًا عَبْدُهُ وَرَسُولُهُ، صَلَّى اللهُ عَلَيْهِ وَعَلَى آلِهِ وَأَصْحَابِهِ وَسَلَّمَ تَسْلِيمًا كَثِيرًا

All praise belongs to Allah, with abundance, as He has commanded. I praise him and thank him. I cannot enumerate His praise; He is as He has praised Himself. I bear witness that there is no god but Allah, alone and without partner; and I bear witness that Muhammad is His slave and messenger. Allah bless him, his folk, and his companions, and grant them abundant peace.

## EXAMPLES OF CONCLUDING INVOCATIONS OF THE SECOND KHUTBAH

(رَبَّنَا آتِنَا فِي الدُّنْيَا حَسَنَةً وَفِي الْآخِرَةِ حَسَنَةً وَقِنَا عَذَابَ النَّارِ)

(سُبْحَانَ رَبِّكَ رَبِّ الْعِزَّةِ عَمَّا يَصِفُونَ ۞ وَسَلَامٌ عَلَى الْمُرْسَلِينَ ۞ وَالْحَمْدُ لِلَّهِ رَبِّ الْعَالَمِينَ)

قُومُوا إِلَى صَلَاتِكُمْ يَرْحَمْكُمُ اللهُ، (وَلَذِكْرُ اللَّهِ أَكْبَرُ وَاللَّهُ يَعْلَمُ مَا تَصْنَعُونَ) وَأَقِمِ الصَّلَاةَ

*"Our Lord! Grant us great good in this world and in the next, and protect us from the punishment of the hellfire." "Glorious is Your Lord, Lord of glory and might, exalted above that which they ascribe! And peace be upon the messengers. And all praise is due to Allah Lord of the worlds." Rise to perform your ritual prayer, Allah have mercy on you! "And the remembrance of Allah is greater; and Allah knows that which you do." And now make the call to prayer.*

عِبَادَ اللهِ: (إِنَّ اللَّهَ يَأْمُرُ بِالْعَدْلِ وَالْإِحْسَانِ وَإِيتَاءِ ذِي الْقُرْبَى وَيَنْهَى عَنِ الْفَحْشَاءِ وَالْمُنكَرِ وَالْبَغْيِ، يَعِظُكُمْ لَعَلَّكُمْ تَذَكَّرُونَ) . فَاذْكُرُوا اللهَ الْجَلِيلَ يَذْكُرْكُمْ، وَاشْكُرُوهُ عَلَى نِعَمِهِ يَزِدْكُمْ، (وَلَذِكْرُ اللَّهِ أَكْبَرُ وَاللَّهُ يَعْلَمُ مَا تَصْنَعُونَ) . وَأَقِمِ الصَّلَاةَ . وَأَقِمِ الصَّلَاةَ

*O servants of Allah! "Verily Allah commands justice, doing good, and giving to one's relatives; and he forbids indecency, doing wrong, and oppression. He counsels you, so that you may take heed!" So remember Allah the Majestic, He will remember you; and thank Him for His blessings. He shall increase you. "And Allah's remembrance is greater; and Allah knows that which you do." And now make the call to prayer.*

## EXHORTATION TO HAVE TAQWA OF ALLAH IN THE FIRST AND SECOND KHUTBAHS

أَمَّا بَعْدُ: فَأُوصِيكُمْ وَنَفْسِي بِتَقْوَى اللهِ، الَّتِي هِيَ نِعْمَ الْمُدَّخَرُ لِيَوْمِ الْمَعَادِ

*To proceed: I enjoin you and myself to have taqwa of Allah, which is the best thing to store up for the day of returning.*

أَمَّا بَعْدُ: فَأُوصِيكُمْ وَنَفْسِيَ الْمُذْنِبَةَ بِتَقْوَى اللهِ سُبْحَانَهُ. يَقُولُ اللهُ جَلَّتْ قُدْرَتُهُ وَتَعَالَتْ أَسْمَاؤُهُ:

*To proceed: I enjoin you and my sinful self to have taqwa of Allah, glorious and exalted. Allah, great is His power and lofty are His names, says,*

أَمَّا بَعْدُ: فَيَا عِبَادَ اللهِ: اتَّقُوا اللهَ حَقَّ التَّقْوَى، فَقَدْ أَمَرَنَا رَبُّنَا بِذَلِكَ فِي كِتَابِهِ الْكَرِيمِ حَيْثُ قَالَ: (يَا أَيُّهَا الَّذِينَ آمَنُوا اتَّقُوا اللَّهَ حَقَّ تُقَاتِهِ وَلَا تَمُوتُنَّ إِلَّا وَأَنْتُمْ مُسْلِمُونَ)، فَتَقْوَى اللهِ نُورٌ فِي الْقَلْبِ وَذُخْرٌ فِي الْمُنْقَلَبِ

*To proceed: O Servants of Allah! Observe taqwa of Allah as it ought to be observed. Indeed, our Lord has ordered us to do so in His noble book, where he said: "O you who believe! Observe taqwa of Allah as it ought to be observed, and do not die save that you are Muslims." Thus, taqwa of Allah is a light in the heart and a reward stored up in the next world.*

أَمَّا بَعْدُ: عِبَادَ اللهِ: اتَّقُوا اللهَ سُبْحَانَهُ، وَاشْكُرُوهُ عَلَى نِعَمِهِ الَّتِي أَسْدَاهَا إِلَيْكُمْ وَمَنَّ بِهَا عَلَيْكُمْ

*To proceed: Servants of Allah! Have taqwa of Allah, glorious and exalted, and thank Him for the blessings He has bestowed upon you and favored you with.*

أَمَّا بَعْدُ: فَيَا عِبَادَاللهِ: اتَّقُوا اللهَ تَعَالَى حَقَّ تَقْوَاهُ، فَمَا فَازَ إِلَّا الْمُتَّقُونَ

*To proceed: Servants of Allah! Observe taqwa of Allah Most High as it ought to be observed, for none attain salvation save those who possess taqwa.*

أَمَّا بَعْدُ: فَيَا أَيُّهَا الْمُسْلِمُونَ: اتَّقُوا اللهَ حَقَّ التَّقْوَى، وَتَزَوَّدُوا فَإِنَّ خَيْرَ الزَّادِ التَّقْوَى: (وَاتَّقُوا يَوْمًا تُرْجَعُونَ فِيهِ إِلَى اللَّهِ ثُمَّ تُوَفَّى كُلُّ نَفْسٍ مَا كَسَبَتْ وَهُمْ لَا يُظْلَمُونَ)

*To proceed: O Muslims! Observe taqwa of Allah as it ought to be observed, and take provision with you. Indeed, the best of provision is taqwa. "And fear a day in which you shall be returned to Allah. Thereupon, every soul will be given in full measure what it earned, and they shall not be wronged."*

أَمَّا بَعْدُ: فَيَا عِبَادَ اللهِ الْمُؤْمِنُونَ: اتَّقُوا اللهَ تَعَالَى؛ فَإِنَّ مَنِ اتَّقَى اللهَ وَقَاهُ، وَأَرْشَدَهُ إِلَى خَيْرِ أُمُورِ دِينِهِ وَدُنْيَاهُ، وَتَقْوَى اللهِ سُبْحَانَهُ عِزٌّ لِصَاحِبِهَا وَتَمْكِينٌ لَهُ، وَرِفْعَةٌ فِي الدُّنْيَا وَالْآخِرَةِ

*To proceed: Believing servants of Allah! Have taqwa of Allah Most High, for Allah protects one who has taqwa and guides him in his religion and his worldly life to that which is best. Taqwa of Allah, glorious and exalted, is a source of glory and strength for its possessor, and a means of elevation in this world and the next.*

أَمَّا بَعْدُ: فَيَا أَيُّهَا الْمُسْلِمُونَ: اتَّقُوا اللهَ رَبَّكُمْ حَقَّ تُقَاتِهِ، وَاعْمَلُوا بِطَاعَتِهِ وَمَرْضَاتِهِ، وَعَلَيْكُمْ بِسُلُوكِ سَبِيلِ الْمُتَّقِينَ، وَالِاتِّصَافِ بِصِفَاتِ الْمُؤْمِنِينَ الصَّالِحِينَ

To proceed: O Muslims! Observe taqwa of Allah, your Lord, as it should be observed, and act in accordance with His obedience and good pleasure. See well to treading the path of those who possess taqwa and to becoming one who is characterized by the traits of the righteous believers.

أَمَّا بَعْدُ: فَيَا إِخْوَةَ الْإِسْلَامِ: اتَّقُوا اللهَ، وَأَخْلِصُوا لِلَّهِ الْعِبَادَةَ وَالطَّاعَةَ، وَأَحْسِنُوا مَعَ عِبَادِ اللهِ الْمُعَامَلَةَ، وَاتَّصِفُوا بِالصِّدْقِ وَالْأَمَانَةِ، وَابْتَعِدُوا عَنِ الْكَذِبِ وَالْخِيَانَةِ

To proceed: Brothers and sisters in Islam! Have taqwa of Allah and make your worship and obedience sincerely to Him. And do well when dealing with the servants of Allah. Be characterized by truthfulness and trustworthiness, and distance yourselves from lying and treachery.

أَمَّا بَعْدُ: فَيَا إِخْوَةَ الْإِيمَانِ: عَلَيْكُمْ بِتَقْوَى اللهِ، وَاتَّصِفُوا بِصِفَاتِ الْمُتَّقِينَ، فَتَقْوَى اللهِ هِيَ النَّجَاةُ مِنْ جَمِيعِ الشُّرُورِ، وَهِيَ الْحِصْنُ الْمَنِيعُ وَالْمَلَاذُ الْمَتِينُ

To proceed: Brothers and sisters in faith! See well to having taqwa of Allah and be characterized by the traits of those who possess taqwa. Only taqwa is salvation from all evils, and only taqwa is the impenetrable fortress and the strong sanctuary.


## EXAMPLES OF TRANSITIONING TO THE SALAWAT AL-IBRAHIMIYYA PRIOR TO THE CONCLUDING SUPPLICATION


عِبَادَ اللهِ: إِنَّ اللهَ أَمَرَكُمْ بِأَمْرٍ عَظِيمٍ؛ بَدَأَ فِيهِ بِنَفْسِهِ، وَثَنَّى بِمَلَائِكَةِ قُدْسِهِ، وَثَلَّثَ بِكُمْ أَيُّهَا الْمُؤْمِنُونَ، فَقَالَ عَزَّ مِنْ قَائِلٍ جَلَّ فِي عُلَاهُ: (إِنَّ اللهَ وَمَلَائِكَتَهُ يُصَلُّونَ عَلَى النَّبِيِّ يَا أَيُّهَا الَّذِينَ آمَنُوا صَلُّوا عَلَيْهِ وَسَلِّمُوا تَسْلِيمًا)

اللَّهُمَّ صَلِّ عَلَى مُحَمَّدٍ، وَعَلَى آلِ مُحَمَّدٍ، كَمَا صَلَّيْتَ عَلَى إِبْرَاهِيمَ، وَعَلَى آلِ إِبْرَاهِيمَ، إِنَّكَ حَمِيدٌ مَجِيدٌ، وَبَارِكْ عَلَى مُحَمَّدٍ، وَعَلَى آلِ مُحَمَّدٍ، كَمَا بَارَكْتَ عَلَى إِبْرَاهِيمَ، وَعَلَى آلِ إِبْرَاهِيمَ، إِنَّكَ حَمِيدٌ مَجِيدٌ

Servants of Allah! Indeed, Allah has commanded you with a tremendous command, wherein He commenced with Himself, then with the angels who glorify His Holiness, and with you O believers third; for He, how glorious a speaker, majestic in His loftiness, has stated: "Verily Allah and His angels send blessings upon the prophet. O you who believe! Send blessings upon him and abundant peace." O Allah! Bless Muhammad and the family of Muhammad as You blessed Ibraheem and the family of Ibraheem. Indeed, You are Praiseworthy, Most Noble. And increase in good Muhammad and the family of Muhammad as you increased in good Ibraheem and the family of Ibraheem. Indeed, You are Praiseworthy, Most Noble.

هَذَا وَصَلُّوا وَسَلِّمُوا عَلَى مَنْ أَمَرَكُمْ رَبُّكُمْ بِالصَّلَاةِ وَالسَّلَامِ عَلَيْهِ، فَقَالَ عَزَّ مِنْ قَائِلٍ: (إِنَّ اللَّهَ وَمَلَائِكَتَهُ يُصَلُّونَ عَلَى النَّبِيِّ يَا أَيُّهَا الَّذِينَ آمَنُوا صَلُّوا عَلَيْهِ وَسَلِّمُوا تَسْلِيمًا)

اللَّهُمَّ صَلِّ وَسَلِّمْ عَلَى عَبْدِكَ وَنَبِيِّكَ مُحَمَّدٍ، وَارْضَ اللَّهُمَّ عَنِ الْخُلَفَاءِ الرَّاشِدِينَ، الْأَئِمَّةِ الْمَهْدِيِّينَ: أَبِي بَكْرٍ وَعُمَرَ وَعُثْمَانَ وَعَلِيٍّ، وَعَنْ سَائِرِ الْآلِ وَالصَّحَابَةِ، وَالتَّابِعِينَ لَهُمْ بِإِحْسَانٍ إِلَى يَوْمِ الدِّينِ

*I say this, and I ask you to send blessings and peace upon he regarding whom your Lord commanded you to send blessings and peace upon, for Allah, how glorious a speaker, said: "Allah and His angels send blessings upon the prophet. O you who believe! Send blessings upon him and abundant peace." O Allah! Bless and grant peace to Your slave and Your prophet Muhammad, and O Allah! Be pleased with the rightly guided caliphs: Abu Bakr, 'Umar, 'Uthman, and 'Ali, and likewise all the families and companions, and those that followed them in excellence till the Day of Judgment.*

أَلَا وَصَلُّوا عِبَادَ الله عَلَى أَصْدَقِ الصَّادِقِينَ، وَإِمَامِ الْحُنَفَاءِ الْمُخْلِصِينَ، كَمَا أَمَرَكُمْ بِذَلِكَ رَبُّ الْعَالَمِينَ بِقَوْلِهِ: (إِنَّ اللَّهَ وَمَلَائِكَتَهُ يُصَلُّونَ عَلَى النَّبِيِّ يَا أَيُّهَا الَّذِينَ آمَنُوا صَلُّوا عَلَيْهِ وَسَلِّمُوا تَسْلِيمًا)

اللَّهُمَّ صَلِّ وَسَلِّمْ عَلَى عَبْدِكَ وَرَسُولِكَ مُحَمَّدٍ أَزْكَى الْبَرِيَّةِ أَجْمَعِينَ، وَارْضَ اللَّهُمَّ عَنْ خُلَفَائِهِ الرَّاشِدِينَ، الَّذِينَ قَضَوْا بِالْحَقِّ وَبِهِ كَانُوا يَعْمَلُونَ؛ أَبِي بَكْرٍ وَعُمَرَ وَعُثْمَانَ وَعَلِيٍّ، وَعَنْ سَائِرِ الصَّحَابَةِ أَجْمَعِينَ، وَعَنَّا مَعَهُمْ بِعَفْوِكَ وَكَرَمِكَ يَا أَكْرَمَ الْأَكْرَمِينَ

*Pay heed and send blessings O servants of Allah upon the most truthful of the true, the leader of the upright and sincere, as the Lord of the worlds has commanded you to do with His statement: "Verily Allah and His angels send blessings upon the prophet. O you who believe, send blessings upon him and abundant peace." O Allah! Bless and grant peace to Your slave and Your messenger Muhammad, the purest of all creation, and O Allah! Be pleased with the rightly guided caliphs, who judged between people with the truth and themselves acted upon it, namely, Abu Bakr, 'Umar, 'Uthman, and 'Ali, and likewise all the companions, and us too along with them, by Your forgiveness and generosity, O Most Generous of the generous.*

# APPENDIX 2

## *GENERAL SUPPLICATIONS FOR THE MUSLIM COMMUNITY*

اللَّهُمَّ ارْحَمْ مَوْتَانَا وَمَوْتَى الْمُسْلِمِينَ، وَاشْفِ مَرْضَانَا وَمَرْضَى الْمُسْلِمِينَ

*O Allah! Have mercy on our dead, and the dead among all Muslims, and heal our sick,
and the sick among all Muslims.*

اللَّهُمَّ اغْفِرْ لِلْمُسْلِمِينَ وَالْمُسْلِمَاتِ، الأَحْيَاءِ مِنْهُمْ وَالأَمْوَاتِ

*O Allah! Forgive all Muslims, male and female, the living among them, and the dead.*

اللَّهُمَّ أَعِزَّ الإِسْلامَ والمُسْلِمِينَ. اللَّهُمَّ انْصُرِ الإِسْلامَ وَأَعِزَّ الْمُسْلِمِينَ

*O Allah! Elevate Islam and the Muslims in honor and glory. O Allah, aid Islam and
elevate the Muslims in honor and glory.*

اللَّهُمَّ أَدْخِلْ عَلَى قُلُوبِ الْمُؤْمِنِينَ السُّرُورَ، وَأَغْنِ مِنْهُمْ كُلَّ فَقِيرٍ، وَأَشْبِعْ كُلَّ جَائِعٍ، وُرُدَّ كُلَّ غَائِبٍ، وَفُكَّ كُلَّ أَسِيرٍ، وَاشْفِ كُلَّ مَرِيضٍ، وَفَرِّجْ عَنْ كُلِّ مَكْرُوبٍ، وَأَدِّ الدَّيْنَ عَنْ كُلِّ مَدِينٍ

*O Allah! Enter happiness into the hearts of the believers. Provide for the needy among
them, satiate the hungry, return the missing, release the captive, heal the sick, relieve
all that suffer sorrow, and fulfill the debt of the indebted.*

اَللَّهُمَّ آمِنَّا فِي أَوْطَانِنَا، وَوَفِّقْ وُلَاةَ أُمُورِنَا وَوُلَاةَ أُمُورِ الْمُسْلِمِينَ لِمَا فِيهِ صَلَاحُ الدِّينِ وَالدُّنْيَا وَالآخِرَةِ

*O Allah! Grant us peace and security in our lands, and grant the people in charge of
our affairs, and likewise those in charge of affairs of all Muslims, success in bringing
about what is good for the religion, and for life in this world and the next.*

اَللَّهُمَّ أَبْرِمْ لِهَذِهِ الأُمَّةِ أَمْرَ رُشْدٍ، يُعَزُّ فِيهِ أَهْلُ طَاعَتِكَ، وَيُهْدَى فِيهِ أَهْلُ مَعْصِيَتِكَ، وَيُؤْمَرُ فِيهِ بِالْمَعْرُوفِ،
وَيُنْهَى فِيهِ عَنِ الْمُنْكَرِ، يَا سَمِيعَ الدُّعَاءِ

*O Allah! Settle for this nation the matter of guidance, in which those engaged in Your
obedience are honored and those engaged in Your disobedience are guided, and in
which the good is commanded, and the bad forbidden, O He who hears supplication!*

اَللَّهُمَّ ادْفَعْ عَنَّا الْغَلَا وَالْوَبَا وَالرِّبَا وَالزِّنَا، وَالزَّلَازِلَ وَالْمِحَنَ، وَسُوْءَ الْفِتَنِ مَا ظَهَرَ مِنْهَا وَمَا بَطَنَ، عَنْ بِلَادِنَا وَعَنْ سَائِرِالْبِلَادِ يَا رَبَّ الْعَالَمِيْنَ

*O Allah! Repel from us inflation and epidemic, usury and fornication, earthquakes and adversities, and all evil tribulations, outward and inward, from our lands and from all lands, O Lord of the worlds.*

## SUPPLICATION FOR ALL MUSLIMS AFFLICTED WITH ADVERSITY

اللَّهُمَّ أَنْجِ الْمُسْتَضْعَفِيْنَ مِنَ الْمُؤْمِنِيْنَ. اللَّهُمَّ إِنَّهُمْ حُفَاةٌ فَاحْمِلْهُمْ، اللَّهُمَّ إِنَّهُمْ عُرَاةٌ فَاكْسُهُمْ، اللَّهُمَّ إِنَّهُمْ جِيَاعٌ فَأَشْبِعْهُمْ

*O Allah! Save the weak and vulnerable among the believers. O Allah, they are barefoot so carry them. O Allah, they are naked so clothe them. O Allah, they are hungry, so satiate them.*

اللَّهُمَّ ارْحَمْ إِخْوَانَنَا الْمُسْلِمِيْنَ الْمُسْتَضْعَفِيْنَ فِيْ كُلِّ مَكَانٍ، اللَّهُمَّ فَرِّجْ هَمَّهُمْ، وَنَفِّسْ كَرْبَهُمْ، وَأَقِلْ عَثَرَاتِهِمْ، وَتَوَلَّ أُمُوْرَهُمْ، وَارْفَعْ رَايَتَهُمْ، وَوَحِّدْ صَفَّهُمْ، وَاجْمَعْ كَلِمَتَهُمْ، وَرُدَّهُمْ إِلَيْكَ رَدًّا جَمِيْلًا

*O Allah! Have mercy on our weak and vulnerable Muslim brothers in every land. O Allah, relieve their grief, remove their worries, forgive their slips, take charge of their affairs, raise their banner, unify their ranks and voices, and return them to Yourself most beautifully.*

اللَّهُمَّ الْطُفْ بِعِبَادِكَ الْمُسْلِمِيْنَ فِيْ كُلِّ مَكَانٍ يَارَحِيْمُ، اَللَّهُمَّ اجْعَلْ لِإِخْوَانِنَا فِيْ (اسم البلد) فَرَجًا وَمَخْرَجًا، اَللَّهُمَّ احْقِنْ دِمَاءَهُمْ، وَاحْفَظْ أَعْرَاضَهُمْ، اَللَّهُمَّ آمِنْهُمْ فِيْ وَطَنِهِمْ، وَاكْشِفِ الْبَلَاءَ عَنْهُمْ

*O Allah! Show gentle kindness to your Muslim servants in every land, O Most Merciful! O Allah, make an opening of relief and an exit from adversity for our brothers in [mention the country name]. O Allah, keep their blood from being spilled and guard their honor. O Allah, grant them peace and security in their land, and remove from them the tribulation that afflicts them.*

اللَّهُمَّ كُنْ لِأَهْلِ (اسم البلد) يَا ذَا الْقُوَّةِ وَالْمِنَّةِ، اللَّهُمَّ أَنْعِمْ عَلَيْنَا وَعَلَيْهِمْ بِالْأَمَانِ يَا لَطِيْفُ يَامَنَّانُ

*O Allah! Be for the people of [name of the country]! O possessor of power and favor! O Allah, bless us and them with security, O Gently Kind, O Benefactor.*

اللَّهُمَّ انْصُرْ إِخْوَانَنَا فِيْ (اسم البلد)، اللَّهُمَّ دَاوِ جَرْحَاهُمْ، وَفَرِّجْ عَنْ كُرُبَاتِهِمْ، اللَّهُمَّ أَبْدِلْهُمْ بَعْدَ خَوْفِهِمْأَمْنًا، وَبَعْدَ ذُلِّهِمْ عِزًّا وَنَصْرًا، يَاقَوِيُّ يَاعَزِيْزُ، وَحَسْبُنَا اللهُ وَنِعْمَ الْوَكِيْلُ، وَلَا حَوْلَنَا وَلَا قُوَّةَ إِلَّا بِكَ

O Allah! Aid our brothers in [name of the country]! O Allah, treat their injured and remove their worries. O Allah, replace their fear with safety and their abasement with glory and triumph, O All Powerful and All Mighty! Allah is sufficient for us, and the best disposer of affairs; and there is no strength nor power except through You!

## SUPPLICATIONS FROM THE QUR'AN AND SUNNAH

رَبَّنَآ ءَاتِنَا فِي الدُّنْيَا حَسَنَةً وَفِي الْآخِرَةِ حَسَنَةً وَقِنَا عَذَابَ النَّارِ ◯

*Our Lord! Grant us good in this world as well as good in the world to come, and protect us from the punishment of the Fire. (al-Baqara, 2:201)*

رَبَّنَآ أَفْرِغْ عَلَيْنَا صَبْراً وَثَبِّتْ أَقْدَامَنَا وَانصُرْنَا عَلَى الْقَوْمِ الْكَافِرِينَ ◯

*Our Lord! Pour patience on us, make us stand firm, and help us against the disbelievers. (al-Baqara, 2:250)*

رَبَّنَا لَا تُؤَاخِذْنَا إِنْ نَسِينَا أَوْ أَخْطَأْنَا رَبَّنَا وَلَا تَحْمِلْ عَلَيْنَا إِصْرًا كَمَا حَمَلْتَهُ عَلَى الَّذِينَ مِنْ قَبْلِنَا رَبَّنَا وَلَا تُحَمِّلْنَا مَا لَا طَاقَةَ لَنَا بِهِ وَاعْفُ عَنَّا وَاغْفِرْ لَنَا وَارْحَمْنَا أَنْتَ مَوْلَانَا فَانْصُرْنَا عَلَى الْقَوْمِ الْكَافِرِينَ ◯

*Our Lord! Do not take us to task if we forget or make a mistake! Our Lord, do not place on us a load like the one You placed on those before us! Our Lord, do not place on us a load we have not the strength to bear! And pardon us, and forgive us, and have mercy on us. You are our Master, so help us against the disbelieving people. (al-Baqara, 2:286)*

رَبَّنَا لَا تُزِغْ قُلُوبَنَا بَعْدَ إِذْ هَدَيْتَنَا وَهَبْ لَنَا مِنْ لَدُنْكَ رَحْمَةً إِنَّكَ أَنْتَ الْوَهَّابُ ◯

*Our Lord! Do not let our hearts deviate after You have guided us. Grant us Your mercy. You are the Ever Giving. (Aal 'Imran, 3:8)*

رَبَّنَآ إِنَّكَ جَامِعُ النَّاسِ لِيَوْمٍ لاَّ رَيْبَ فِيهِ إِنَّ اللَّهَ لاَ يُخْلِفُ الْمِيعَادَ ◯

*Our Lord! You will gather all people on the Day of which there is no doubt. Allah never breaks His promise. (Aal 'Imran, 3:9)*

رَبَّنَآ إِنَّنَآ ءَامَنَّا فَاغْفِرْ لَنَا ذُنُوبَنَا وَقِنَا عَذَابَ النَّارِ ◯

*Our Lord! We believe in You, forgive us our sins and keep us from the punishment of the fire. (Aal 'Imran, 3:16)*

رَبَّنَآ ءَامَنَّا بِمَآ أَنْزَلْتَ وَاتَّبَعْنَا الرَّسُولَ فَاكْتُبْنَا مَعَ الشَّاهِدِينَ ◯

*Our Lord! We believe in what You have sent down and we follow the messenger, so count us among those who bear witness. (Aal 'Imran, 3:53)*

رَبَّنَا اغْفِرْ لَنَا ذُنُوبَنَا وَإِسْرَافَنَا فِي أَمْرِنَا وَثَبِّتْ أَقْدَامَنَا وَانصُرْنَا عَلَى الْقَوْمِ الْكَافِرِينَ ◯

*Our Lord! Forgive us our sins and our excesses. Make our feet firm, and help us against the disbelievers. (Aal 'Imran, 3:147)*

رَبَّنَا مَا خَلَقْتَ هَٰذَا بَاطِلًا سُبْحَانَكَ فَقِنَا عَذَابَ النَّارِ ◯

*Our Lord! You have not created all this without purpose. Glory be to You! Save us from the torment of the Fire. (Aal 'Imran, 3:191)*

رَبَّنَا إِنَّكَ مَن تُدْخِلِ النَّارَ فَقَدْ أَخْزَيْتَهُ وَمَا لِلظَّالِمِينَ مِنْ أَنصَارٍ ◯

*Our Lord! You humiliate those You condemn to hell. There is no help for the unjust. (Aal 'Imran, 3:192)*

رَبَّنَا إِنَّنَا سَمِعْنَا مُنَادِيًا يُنَادِي لِلْإِيمَانِ أَنْ ءَامِنُوا بِرَبِّكُمْ فَآمَنَّا رَبَّنَا فَاغْفِرْ لَنَا ذُنُوبَنَا وَكَفِّرْ عَنَّا سَيِّئَاتِنَا وَتَوَفَّنَا مَعَ الْأَبْرَارِ ◯

*Our Lord! We have heard a caller calling to the true faith saying, "Believe in your Lord," and we believed. Lord, forgive us our sins, remove from us our bad deeds, and make us die with the virtuous. (Aal 'Imran, 3:193)*

رَبَّنَا وَءَاتِنَا مَا وَعَدتَّنَا عَلَىٰ رُسُلِكَ وَلَا تُخْزِنَا يَوْمَ الْقِيَامَةِ إِنَّكَ لَا تُخْلِفُ الْمِيعَادَ ◯

*Our Lord! Grant us what You have promised to us through Your messengers, and do not humiliate us on the Day of Resurrection. Surely, You never fail to fulfill Your promise. (Aal 'Imran, 3:194)*

رَبَّنَا ءَامَنَّا فَاكْتُبْنَا مَعَ الشَّاهِدِينَ ◯

*Our Lord! We believe, so count us among those who bear witness. (al-Ma`ida, 5:83)*

رَبَّنَا ظَلَمْنَا أَنفُسَنَا وَإِن لَّمْ تَغْفِرْ لَنَا وَتَرْحَمْنَا لَنَكُونَنَّ مِنَ الْخَاسِرِينَ ◯

*Our Lord! We have wronged our souls. If You do not forgive us and have mercy on us, we shall be among the losers. (al-A'raf, 7:23)*

رَبَّنَا لَا تَجْعَلْنَا مَعَ الْقَوْمِ الظَّالِمِينَ ◯

*Our Lord! Do not include us among the wrongdoers. (al-A'raf, 7:47)*

رَبَّنَا أَفْرِغْ عَلَيْنَا صَبْرًا وَتَوَفَّنَا مُسْلِمِينَ ○

*Our Lord! Pour patience upon us, and cause us to die in a state of submission to You.*
*(al-A'raf, 7:126)*

رَبَّنَا لَا تَجْعَلْنَا فِتْنَةً لِّلْقَوْمِ الظَّالِمِينَ - وَنَجِّنَا بِرَحْمَتِكَ مِنَ الْقَوْمِ الْكَافِرِين ○

*Our Lord! Do not make us a test for the wicked people. And save us by Your mercy from*
*the people who deny the truth. (Yunus, 10:85-86)*

رَبَّنَا إِنَّكَ تَعْلَمُ مَا نُخْفِي وَمَا نُعْلِنُ وَمَا يَخْفَىٰ عَلَى اللَّهِ مِن شَيْءٍ فِي الْأَرْضِ وَلَا فِي السَّمَاءِ ○

*Our Lord! You know well what we conceal and what we reveal. Nothing is hidden from*
*Allah, on earth or in heaven. (Ibraheem, 14:38)*

رَبَّنَا اغْفِرْ لِي وَلِوَالِدَيَّ وَلِلْمُؤْمِنِينَ يَوْمَ يَقُومُ الْحِسَابُ ○

*Our Lord! Forgive me, my parents, and the believers on the Day of Reckoning.*
*(Ibraheem, 14:41)*

رَبَّنَا آتِنَا مِن لَّدُنكَ رَحْمَةً وَهَيِّئْ لَنَا مِنْ أَمْرِنَا رَشَدًا ○

*Our Lord! Grant us Your special mercy, and give us right guidance in our affair. (al-*
*Kahf, 18:10)*

رَبَّنَا آمَنَّا فَاغْفِرْ لَنَا وَارْحَمْنَا وَأَنتَ خَيْرُ الرَّاحِمِينَ ○

*Our Lord! We have believed, so forgive us and have mercy on us, for You are the most*
*Merciful. (al-Mu`minoon, 23:109)*

رَبَّنَا اصْرِفْ عَنَّا عَذَابَ جَهَنَّمَ إِنَّ عَذَابَهَا كَانَ غَرَامًا إِنَّهَا سَاءَتْ مُسْتَقَرًّا وَمُقَامًا ○

*Our Lord! Spare us the punishment of hell. Its punishment is dreadful. It is a miserable*
*abode and dwelling place. (al-Furqan, 25:65-66)*

رَبَّنَا هَبْ لَنَا مِنْ أَزْوَاجِنَا وَذُرِّيَّاتِنَا قُرَّةَ أَعْيُنٍ وَاجْعَلْنَا لِلْمُتَّقِينَ إِمَامًا ○

*Our Lord! Grant us joy in our wives and children and make us a model for the righteous.*
*(al-Furqan, 25:74)*

رَبَّنَا اغْفِرْ لَنَا وَلِإِخْوَانِنَا الَّذِينَ سَبَقُونَا بِالْإِيمَانِ وَلَا تَجْعَلْ فِي قُلُوبِنَا غِلًّا لِّلَّذِينَ آمَنُوا رَبَّنَا إِنَّكَ رَءُوفٌ رَّحِيمٌ ○

*Our Lord! Forgive us and our brothers who preceded us in the faith and leave no malice*
*in our hearts toward those who believe. Our Lord! You are indeed most kind and*

*merciful. (al-Hashr, 59:10)*

رَبَّنَا عَلَيْكَ تَوَكَّلْنَا وَإِلَيْكَ أَنَبْنَا وَإِلَيْكَ الْمَصِيرُ ◯

*Our Lord! It is in You that We have put our trust, and it is to You that we turn in utmost sincerity and devotion, and to You is the final return. (al-Mumtahina, 60:4)*

رَبَّنَا لَا تَجْعَلْنَا فِتْنَةً لِّلَّذِينَ كَفَرُوا وَاغْفِرْ لَنَا رَبَّنَا إِنَّكَ أَنتَ الْعَزِيزُ الْحَكِيمُ ◯

*Our Lord! Do not make us a trial for those who disbelieve, and forgive us! Our Lord! You are the Almighty, the all Wise. (al-Mumtahina, 60:5)*

رَبَّنَا أَتْمِمْ لَنَا نُورَنَا وَاغْفِرْ لَنَا إِنَّكَ عَلَىٰ كُلِّ شَيْءٍ قَدِيرٌ ◯

*Our Lord! Perfect our light for us, and forgive us. You have power over all things. (at-Tahreem, 66:8)*

رَبَّنَا تَقَبَّلْ مِنَّا إِنَّكَ أَنتَ السَّمِيعُ الْعَلِيمُ ◯

*Our Lord, accept this from us. You are the All Hearing and the All Knowing. (al-Baqara, 2:127)*

وَتُبْ عَلَيْنَا إِنَّكَ أَنْتَ التَّوَّابُ الرَّحِيمُ ◯

*And accept our repentance. You are the One who accepts repentance, and You are the Most Merciful. (al-Baqara, 2:128)*

اللَّهُمَّ أَنْتَ السَّلَامُ وَمِنْكَ السَّلَامُ، تَبَارَكْتَ يَا ذَا الْجَلَالِ وَالْإِكْرَامِ

*O Allah! You are Peace, and peace comes from You. Blessed You are, O Possessor of Glory and Honor.*

اللَّهُمَّ حَبِّبْ إِلَيْنَا الْإِيمَانَ وَزَيِّنْهُ فِي قُلُوبِنَا، وَكَرِّهْ إِلَيْنَا الْكُفْرَ وَالْفُسُوقَ وَالْعِصْيَانَ، وَاجْعَلْنَا مِنَ الرَّاشِدِينَ

*O Allah! Make iman beloved to us and beautify it in our hearts, and make disbelief, sinfulness,' and disobedience hateful to us, and make us from among the rightly guided ones.*

اللَّهُمَّ اجْعَلني شَكُورًا واجْعَلني صَبُورًا واجْعَلني في عَيْني صَغِيرًا و في أَعْيُنِ النَّاسِ كَبِيرًا

*O Allah! Make me exceedingly thankful, make me exceedingly patient, make me small in my own eyes and great in the eyes of others.*

اللَّهُمَّ أَلْهِمْنِي رُشْدِي، وَأَعِذْنِي مِنْ شَرِّ نَفْسِي

*O Allah! Inspire my heart to guidance and save me from the evil of my soul.*

اللَّهُمَّ إِنِّي أَعُوذُ بِكَ مِنْ شَرِّ مَا عَمِلْتُ وَمِنْ شَرِّ مَا لَمْ أَعْمَلْ

*O Allah! I seek refuge in You from the evil of what I have done and from the evil of what I have not done.*

اللَّهُمَّ إِنِّي أَعُوذُ بِكَ مِنْ جَهْدِ الْبَلَاءِ، وَدَرْكِ الشَّقَاءِ، وَسُوءِ الْقَضَاءِ، وَشَمَاتَةِ الْأَعْدَاءِ

*Oh Allah, I seek refuge in You from the distress of trial, from the lowest level of misery, from the perversity of fate, and from the malicious rejoicing of enemies.*

اللَّهُمَّ إِنِّي أَعُوذُ بِكَ مِنْ مُنْكَرَاتِ الْأَخْلَاقِ، والأعمال، والأهواء

*O Allah! I seek refuge in You from evil character, evil actions, and evil desires.*

اللَّهُمَّ لا تَقْتُلْنَا بِغَضَبِكَ ، وَلَا تُهْلِكْنَا بِعَذَابِكَ ، وَعَافِنَا قَبْلَ ذَلِكَ

*O Allah, don't end our lives with Your wrath, and do not make us perish with Your punishment, and forgive us before that.*

اللَّهُمَّ إِنِّي أَعُوذُ بِكَ مِنْ زَوَالِ نِعْمَتِكَ، وَتَحَوُّلِ عَافِيَتِكَ، وَفُجَاءَةِ نِقْمَتِكَ، وَجَمِيعِ سَخَطِكَ

*O Allah! I seek refuge in you from the withholding of your favor, the decline of the good health You have given, the suddenness of Your vengeance, and from all forms of Your wrath.*

اللَّهُمَّ إِنِّي أَعُوذُ بِكَ مِنَ الهَمِّ وَ الْحُزْنِ، والعَجْزِ والكَسَلِ والبُخْلِ والجُبْنِ، و أَعُوذُ بِكَ مِن غَلَبَةِ الدَّيْنِ وَقَهْرِ الرِّجَالِ

*O Allah! I take refuge in You from anxiety and sorrow, weakness and laziness, miserliness and cowardice, and I seek refuge in You from the burden of debts and from being overpowered by men.*

اللَّهُمَّ إِنِّي أَعُوذُ بِكَ مِنْ عِلْمٍ لاَ يَنْفَعُ وَقَلْبٍ لاَ يَخْشَعُ وَدُعَاءٍ لاَ يُسْمَعُ وَنَفْسٍ لاَ تَشْبَعُ

*O Allah! I seek refuge with You from knowledge that is of no benefit, a heart that is not humble, a supplication that is not heard, and a soul that is not satisfied.*

اَللَّهُمَّ إِنِّي أَعُوذُبِكَ أَنْ أَزِلَّ أَوْ أُزَلَّ أَوْ أَضِلَّ أَوْ أَضَلَّ أَوْ أَظْلِمَ أَوْ أُظْلَمَ اَوْ أَجْهَلَ أَوْ يُجْهَلَ عَلَيَّ

*O Allah! I seek refuge in You lest I stray or be led astray, or slip or made to slip, or cause*

injustice, or suffer injustice, or do wrong, or have wrong done to me.

اللَّهُمَّ إِنِّي أَعُوذُبِكَ مِنَ الْكُفر ، وَالْفَقْر ، وَأَعوذُبِكَ مِنْ عَذابِ القَبْر ، لا إلَهَ إلاّ أَنْتَ

*O Allah! I seek refuge in You from disbelief and poverty. O Allah! I seek refuge in You from punishment in the grave. There is no God but You.*

اللَّهُمَّ إِنِّي أَعُوذُ بِكَ مِنَ الشَّقَاقِ وَالنِّفَاقِ وَسُوءِ الأَخْلاقِ

*O Allah! I seek refuge with You from opposing the truth, from hypocrisy, and from bad manners.*

اللَّهُمَّ إِنِّي أَسْأَلُكَ مِنْ فَضْلِكَ

*O Allah! I ask of You Your grace.*

اللَّهُمَّ إِنِّي أَسْأَلُكَ عِلْماً نافِعاً وَرِزْقاً طَيِّباً ،وَعَمَلاً مُتَقَبَّلاً

*O Allah! I ask You for knowledge which is beneficial, sustenance which is good, and deeds which are acceptable.*

اللَّهُمَّ إِنِّي أَسْأَلُكَ الجَنَّةَ و أَعُوذُ بِكَ مِنَ النَّار

*O Allah! I ask You to grant me paradise, and I take refuge in You from the fire.*

اللَّهُمَّ إِنِّي أَسْأَلُكَ الْجَنَّةَ وَمَا قَرَّبَ إِلَيْها مِنْ قَوْلٍ أَوْ عَمَلٍ وَأَعُوذُ بِكَ مِنَ النَّارِ وَمَا قَرَّبَ إِلَيْها مِنْ قَوْلٍ أَوْ عَمَلٍ

*O Allah, I ask You for paradise and for that which brings one closer to it, in word and deed, and I seek refuge in You from hell and from that which brings one closer to it, in word and deed.*

اَللَّهُمَّ إِنِّي اَسْأَلُكَ الْهُدَى والتُّقَى والْعَفَافَ والْغِنَي

*O Allah! I ask of You for guidance, piety, chastity, and to be free of depending upon anyone.*

اللَّهُمَّ إِنِّي أَسْأَلُكَ حُبَّكَ وَحُبَّ مَنْ يُحِبُّكَ وَالْعَمَلَ الَّذِي يُبَلِّغُنِي حُبَّكَ

*O Allah! I ask You Your love, and the love of whoever loves You and the love of the deed which will draw me in attaining Your love.*

اللَّهُمَّ إِنِّي اَسْأَلُكَ مِنْ خَيْرِ مَا سَأَلَكَ مِنْهُ نَبِيُّكَ مُحَمَّدٌ صَلَّى اللَّهُ عَلَيْهِ وَسَلَّمَ وَنَعُوذُ بِكَ مِنْ شَرِّ مَا اسْتَعَاذَ مِنْهُ نَبِيُّكَ مُحَمَّدٌ صَلَّى اللَّهُ عَلَيْهِ وَسَلَّمَ

*Allah! I ask You for the good that Your Prophet Muhammad has asked You for, and I seek refuge in You from the evil from which Your Prophet Muhammad sought refuge.*

اللَّهُمَّ إِنِّي أَسْأَلُكَ الْعافِيَةَ في الدُّنْيا وَالآخِرَةِ ، اللَّهُمَّ إِنِّي أَسْأَلُكَ الْعَفْوَ وَالعافِيَةَ في ديني وَدُنْيايَ وَأَهْلي وَمالي ، اللَّهُمَّ اسْتُرْ عَوْراتي وَآمِنْ رَوْعاتي ، اللَّهُمَّ احْفَظْني مِن بَيْنِ يَدَيَّ وَمِن خَلْفي وَعَن يَميني وَعَن شِمالي ، وَمِن فَوْقي ، وَأَعوذُ بِعَظَمَتِكَ أَن أُغْتالَ مِن تَحْتي

*O Allah! I ask You for forgiveness and wellbeing in this world and in the hereafter. O Allah, I ask You for forgiveness and wellbeing in my religious and my worldly affairs, my family and my wealth. O Allah, conceal my faults, calm my fears, and protect me from before me and behind me, from my right and my left, and from above me, and I seek refuge in You from being taken unaware from beneath me.*

اللَّهُمَّ إِنَّا نَسْأَلُكَ مِنَ الْخَيْرِ كُلِّهِ، عَاجِلِهِ وَآجِلِهِ، مَا عَلِمْنَا مِنْهُ وَمَا لَمْ نَعْلَمْ، وَنَعُوذُ بِكَ مِنَ الشَّرِّ كُلِّهِ، عَاجِلِهِ وَآجِلِهِ، مَا عَلِمْنَا مِنْهُ وَمَا لَمْ نَعْلَمْ

*O Allah! We ask You for all that is good, in this world and in the hereafter, what we know and what we do not know. And we seek refuge with You from all evil, in this world and in the hereafter, what we know and what we do not know.*

اللَّهُمَّ اغْفِرْ لي، وارْحَمني، واهدِني، وعافِني، وارزُقْني

*O Allah! Grant me pardon, have mercy upon me, direct me to the path of righteousness and provide me sustenance.*

اللَّهُمَّ أَعِنِّي عَلَى ذِكْرِكَ وَشُكْرِكَ وَحُسْنِ عِبَادَتِكَ

*O Allah! Help me to remember You, to thank You, and to worship You in the best of manners.*

اَللَّهُمَّ اَعِنِّي عَلَى غَمَرَاتِ ٱلْمَوْتِ وَ سَكَرَاتِ ٱلْمَوْتِ

*O Allah! Help me over pangs and agony of death.*

اللَّهُمَّ لا سَهْلَ إِلاَّ ما جَعَلْتَهُ سَهْلاً، وأَنْتَ تَجْعَلُ الحَزْنَ إِذا شِئْتَ سَهْلاً

*O Allah! There is no ease except in that which You have made easy, and You make the difficult, if You wish, easy.*

اللَّهُمَّ افْتَحْ لِي أَبْوَابَ رَحْمَتِكَ

*O Allah! Open for me the gates of Your mercy.*

اللَّهُمَّ إِنَّكَ عَفُوٌّ تُحِبُّ الْعَفْوَ فَاعْفُ عَنِّي

*O Allah! You are forgiving and love forgiveness, so forgive me.*

اللَّهُمَّ أَحْسِنْ عَاقِبَتَنَا فِىْ الْأُمُورِ كُلِّهَا وَأَجِرْنَا مِنْ خِزْيِ الدُّنْيَا وَعَذَابِ الْآخِرَةِ

*O Allah! Grant a good end to all our matters, and save us from humiliation in the world and the punishment of the hereafter.*

اللَّهُمَّ عافِنِي في بَدَنِي ، اللَّهُمَّ عافِنِي في سَمْعِي ، اللَّهُمَّ عافِنِي في بَصَرِي ، لا إلَه إِلاَّ أَنْتَ

*O Allah! Grant me health in my body. O Allah! Grant me good hearing. O Allah! Grant me good eyesight. There is no God but You.*

اللَّهُمَّ أتِ نَفْسِيْ تَقْوَاهَا وَ زَكِّهَا أَنْتَ خَيْرُ مَنْ زَكَّاهَا أَنْتَ وَلِيُّهَا وَ مَوْلَاهَا

*O Allah! Make my soul obedient and purify it, for You are the best One to purify it. You are its Guardian and Lord.*

اَللَّهُمَّ اكْفِنِى بِحَلَالِكَ عَنْ حَرَامِكَ وَاَغْنِنِى بِفَضْلِكَ عَمَّنْ سِوَاكَ

*O Allah! Suffice me with Your lawful against Your prohibited, and make me independent of all those besides You.*

اللَّهُمَّ رَحْمَتَكَ أَرْجوفَلا تَكِلني إلى نَفْسِي طَرْفَةَ عَيْن، وَأَصْلِحْ لِي شَأْنِي كُلَّه لَا إِلَهَ إِلَّا أَنْتَ

*O Allah! It is Your mercy that I hope for, so do not leave me in charge of my affairs even for a blink of an eye, and rectify for me all of my affairs. None has the right to be worshipped except You.*

اللَّهُمَّ أَحْيِنِي مَا كَانَتِ الْحَيَاةُ خَيْرُ لِي وَتَوَفَّنِي إِذَا كَانَتِ الْوَفَاةُ خَيْرَاً لِي

*O Allah! Keep me alive as long as there is goodness in life for me, and bring death to me when there is goodness in death for me.*

اللَّهُمَّ رُدَّنَا إِلَيْكَ رَدّاً جَمِيلاً . اللَّهُمَّ رُدَّنَا إِلَيْكَ وَأَنتَ رَاضٍ عَنَّا

*O Allah! Return us to You in a beautiful manner. O Allah! Return us to You in a state wherein You are pleased with us.*

اللَّهُمَّ أَرِنا الْحَقَّ حقّاً وارْزُقْنا اتِّبَاعَه وأرِنا الْباطِلَ باطِلاً وارْزُقنا اجْتِنَابَه

*O Allah! Show us the truth as true, and inspire us to follow it. Show us falsehood as falsehood, and inspire us to abstain from it.*

اللّٰهُمَّ مُصَرِّفَ الْقُلُوْبِ صَرِّفْ قُلُوْبَنَاعَلَى طَاعَتِكَ يَا مُثَبِّتَ الْقُلُوْبِ ثَبِّتْ قُلُوْبَنَا عَلَى دِيْنِكَ

*O Allah! The One who turns the hearts, turn our hearts toward Your obedience. O You Who makes hearts steadfast make our hearts steadfast in adhering to Your religion.*

اللّٰهُمَّ انْفَعْنِى بِمَا عَلَّمْتَنِى وَ عَلِّمْنِى مَا يَنْفَعُنِى وَ ارْزُقْنِى عِلْماً يَنْفَعُنِى

*O Allah! Benefit me with what you taught me, teach me what will benefit me, and provide me with knowledge that will benefit me.*

اللّٰهُمَّ لَا تَدَعْ لِي ذَنْبًا إِلَّا غَفَرْتَهُ وَلَا هَمًّا إِلَّا فَرَّجْتَهُ وَلَا حَاجَةً هِيَ لَكَ رِضًا إِلَّا قَضَيْتَهَا يَا أَرْحَمَ الرَّاحِمِينَ

*O Allah! Do not leave a sin for me without forgiving it or a worry without relieving it or a need that pleases you without granting it. O Most Merciful of those who have mercy.*

اللّٰهُمَّ اغْفِرْ لِي خَطِيئَتِي وَجَهْلِي وَإِسْرَافِي فِي أَمْرِي وَمَا أَنْتَ أَعْلَمُ بِهِ مِنِّي اللّٰهُمَّ اغْفِرْ لِي جِدِّي وَهَزْلِي وَخَطَئِي وَعَمْدِي وَكُلُّ ذَلِكَ عِنْدِي

*O Allah! Forgive me my faults, my ignorance, my immoderation in my concerns. And Thou art better aware (of my affairs) than myself. O Allah, grant me forgiveness (of the faults which I committed) seriously or otherwise (and which I committed inadvertently and deliberately). All these (failings) are in me.*

اللّٰهُمَّ اغْفِرْ لِي مَا قَدَّمْتُ وَمَا أَخَّرْتُ وَمَا أَسْرَرْتُ وَمَا أَعْلَنْتُ وَمَا أَنْتَ أَعْلَمُ بِهِ مِنِّي أَنْتَ الْمُقَدِّمُ وَأَنْتَ الْمُؤَخِّرُ وَأَنْتَ عَلَى كُلِّ شَيْءٍ قَدِيرٌ

*O Allah! Grant me forgiveness from the fault which I did in haste or deferred, which I committed in privacy or in public, and You know them more than myself. You are the First and the Last, and You have power over everything.*

اللّٰهُمَّ اجْعَلْ فِي قَلْبِي نُوْرًا، وَفِي لِسَانِي نُوْرًا، وَاجْعَلْ فِي سَمْعِي نُوْرًا، وَاجْعَلْ فِي بَصَرِي نُوْرًا، وَاجْعَلْ مِنْ خَلْفِي نُوْرًا، وَمِنْ أَمَامِي نُوْرًا، وَاجْعَلْ مِنْ فَوْقِي نُوْرًا، وَمِنْ تَحْتِي نُوْرًا، اللّٰهُمَّ أَعْطِنِي نُوْرًا

*O Allah! Place light in my heart, light in my sight, light in my hearing, light behind me, light in front of me, light above me, light below me. O Allah! Give me light.*

اللّٰهُمَّ أَسْلَمْتُ نَفْسِي إِلَيْكَ، وَفَوَّضْتُ أَمْرِي إِلَيْكَ، وَوَجَّهْتُ وَجْهِي إِلَيْكَ، وَأَلْجَأْتُ ظَهْرِي إِلَيْكَ، رَغْبَةً وَرَهْبَةً إِلَيْكَ، لَا مَلْجَأَ وَلَا مَنْجَا مِنْكَ إِلَّا إِلَيْكَ، آمَنْتُ بِكِتَابِكَ وَنِبِيِّكَ الَّذِي أَرْسَلْتَ

*O Allah! I submit myself to You, entrust my affairs to You, turn my face to You, and lay myself down depending upon You, hoping in You and fearing You. There is no refuge, and no escape, except to You. I believe in Your Book that You revealed and the Prophet*

*whom You sent.*

اللَّهُمَّ أَصْلِحْ لِي دِينِي الَّذِي هُوَ عِصْمَةُ أَمْرِي، وَأَصْلِحْ لِي دُنْيَايَ الَّتِي فِيهَا مَعَاشِي، وَأَصْلِحْ لِي آخِرَتِي الَّتِي فِيهَا مَعَادِي، وَاجْعَلِ الحَيَاةَ زِيَادَةً لِي فِي كُلِّ خَيْرٍ، وَاجْعَلِ المَوْتَ رَاحَةً لِي مِنْ كُلِّ شَرٍّ

*O Allah! Correct for me my faith, which is the guard of my affairs, make better my world where I have my livelihood, set right my hereafter where I have to return ultimately, make my life long, in every type of virtue, and make my death a comfort against all evils.*

اللَّهُمَّ أَنْتَ رَبِّي لَا إِلَهَ إِلَّا أَنْتَ، خَلَقْتَنِي وَأَنَا عَبْدُكَ، وَأَنَا عَلَى عَهْدِكَ وَوَعْدِكَ مَا اسْتَطَعْتَ، أَعُوذُ بِكَ مِنْ شَرِّ مَا صَنَعْتُ، أَبُوءُ لَكَ بِنِعْمَتِكَ عَلَيَّ، وَأَبُوءُ بِذَنْبِي فَاغْفِرْ لِي فَإِنَّهُ لَا يَغْفِرُ الذُّنُوبَ إِلَّا أَنْتَ

*O Allah! You are my Lord. None has the right to be worshipped but You. You created me, and I am Your slave. I am faithful in my covenant and my promise (to You) as much as I can be. I seek refuge in You from all the evil I have done. I acknowledge before You all the blessings You have bestowed upon me, and I confess to You all my sins. So I entreat You to forgive my sins, for nobody can forgive sins except You.*

اللَّهُمَّ إِنَّا نَسْأَلُكَ خَشْيَتَكَ فِي الغَيبِ وَالشَّهَادَةِ، وَنَسْأَلُكَ كَلِمَةَ الحَقِّ فِي الرِّضَا وَالغَضَبِ، وَنَسْأَلُكَ القَصْدَ فِي الفَقْرِ وَالغِنَى، وَنَسْأَلُكَ نَعِيمًا لَا يَنْفَدُ، وَنَسْأَلُكَ قُرَّةَ عَيْنٍ لَا تَنْقَطِعُ، وَنَسْأَلُكَ الرِّضَى بَعْدَ القَضَاءِ، وَنَسْأَلُكَ بَرْدَ العَيْشِ بَعْدَ الْمَوْتِ، وَنَسْأَلُكَ لَذَّةَ النَّظَرِ إِلَى وَجْهِكَ، وَالشَّوْقَ إِلَى لِقَائِكَ، فِي غَيْرِ ضَرَّاءَ مُضِرَّةٍ، وَلَا فِتْنَةٍ مُضِلَّةٍ، اللَّهُمَّ زَيِّنَّا بِزِينَةِ الإِيمَانِ، وَاجْعَلْنَا هُدَاةً مُهْتَدِينَ

*O Allah! We ask You for God-fearingness when people are absent or present, and we ask You for truthful speech when we are pleased or upset. We ask You for balanced conduct in poverty and affluence, and we ask You for blessing that does not perish. We ask You for joy that is not cut off, and we ask You for contentment with Your decree. We ask You for good life after death, and we ask You for the delight of beholding Your face, and for longing to meet You, without the occurrence of hardship that harms one or tribulation that takes one off the path. O Allah! Adorn us with the adornment of faith, and make us guides that are rightly guided.*

# ABOUT THE AUTHOR

Munawar Haque earned his Ph.D. in Islamic Studies with specialization in Islamic Theology and Comparative Religion from the International Islamic University Malaysia (IIUM), where as a Professor, he taught courses on Islamic Worldview, Islamic Jurisprudence, Ethics, and Family Management & Parenting. Presently, he is the Imam at the American Muslim Diversity Association (AMDA) in the city of Sterling Heights, Michigan. He is responsible for leading congregational prayers, delivering sermons, conducting religious discussions, counseling, officiating marriages, leading funeral prayers, participating in interfaith dialogues, and getting involved in community, social, and humanitarian services.

Dr. Haque has also been the editor and staff writer for the Research and Publications Division at the Islamic Organization of North America (IONA) in the city of Warren, Michigan, and an Adjunct Professor at the Ecumenical Theological Seminary (ETS), Detroit, Michigan, where he taught Arabic and Islamic History in the Muslim Chaplaincy Program. He is a member of the Imams Council of Michigan representing Islamic centers in Southeast Michigan, and a certified speaker of the Islamic Speakers Bureau of the Islamic Networks Group (ING). He has also worked as a national and international banker in India and the United Arab Emirates for over two decades.

Dr. Haque has authored, edited, reviewed, and translated a few books and articles on Islam. He is fluent in English, Arabic, Urdu, and Hindi, and enjoys traveling and spending time with his children and grandchildren.

Made in the USA
Monee, IL
23 April 2022

95253398R00267